LEGAL HETERODOXY IN THE GLOBAL SOUTH

This volume challenges the common perception that legal systems in developing countries are outdated or plagued by enforcement issues. Instead, it presents detailed case studies of private law in the Global South, showcasing how countries in the region have embraced legal doctrines that diverge from traditional approaches in the Global North. Chapters cover core areas of private law, including contracts, property, torts, corporations, and legal personality. The case studies range from India's adoption of corporate social responsibility rules to Argentina's protection of hyper-vulnerable consumers. This volume demonstrates how many countries have incorporated social and distributional concerns into their private law regimes. Through these examples, the book presents a set of underappreciated and innovative legal developments in the Global South. This title is also available as Open Access on Cambridge Core.

Kevin E. Davis is a leading scholar of the relationship between law and economic development. His publications include *Between Impunity and Imperialism: The Regulation of Transnational Bribery* (2019) as well as *Governance by Indicators: Global Power through Quantification and Rankings* (2012, with Kingsbury and Merry). He teaches at New York University.

Mariana Pargendler is a leading scholar of corporate law and comparative corporate governance. She is coauthor of *The Anatomy of Corporate Law: A Comparative and Functional Approach* (3rd ed., 2017) and the recipient of writing prizes from the European Corporate Governance Institute and the American Society of Comparative Law. She teaches at Harvard Law School.

Legal Heterodoxy in the Global South

Edited by

KEVIN E. DAVIS

New York University

MARIANA PARGENDLER

Harvard Law School

CAMBRIDGE
UNIVERSITY PRESS

CAMBRIDGE
UNIVERSITY PRESS

Shaftesbury Road, Cambridge CB2 8EA, United Kingdom

One Liberty Plaza, 20th Floor, New York, NY 10006, USA

477 Williamstown Road, Port Melbourne, VIC 3207, Australia

314–321, 3rd Floor, Plot 3, Splendor Forum, Jasola District Centre, New Delhi – 110025, India

103 Penang Road, #05-06/07, Visioncrest Commercial, Singapore 238467

Cambridge University Press is part of Cambridge University Press & Assessment, a department of the University of Cambridge.

We share the University's mission to contribute to society through the pursuit of education, learning and research at the highest international levels of excellence.

www.cambridge.org
Information on this title: www.cambridge.org/9781009539548

DOI: 10.1017/9781009539555

First published 2025

A catalogue record for this publication is available from the British Library

Library of Congress Cataloging-in-Publication Data
NAMES: Davis, Kevin E., editor. | Pargendler, Mariana, editor.
TITLE: Legal heterodoxy in the global South / edited by Kevin E. Davis, New York University; Mariana Pargendler, FGV Law School (São Paulo).
DESCRIPTION: Cambridge, United Kingdom ; New York, NY : Cambridge University Press, 2025. | Includes bibliographical references and index.
IDENTIFIERS: LCCN 2024051056 (print) | LCCN 2024051057 (ebook) | ISBN 9781009539548 (hardback) | ISBN 9781009539531 (paperback) | ISBN 9781009539555 (epub)
SUBJECTS: LCSH: Civil law. | Contracts. | Legal polycentricity. | Conflict of laws.
CLASSIFICATION: LCC K623 .L44 2025 (print) | LCC K623 (ebook) | DDC 346/.124–dc23/eng/20241029
LC record available at https://lccn.loc.gov/2024051056
LC ebook record available at https://lccn.loc.gov/2024051057

ISBN 978-1-009-53954-8 Hardback
ISBN 978-1-009-53953-1 Paperback

Kevin Davis: For GuyLaine, Antoni, and Angélique

Mariana Pargendler: For Carlos, Dora, and Clara

Contents

Tables

Contributors

María Guadalupe Martínez Alles is an assistant professor of law at IE University. She works in the areas of tort theory, comparative private law, consumer law, and punitive damages. She has also served as a professor of law at Universidad de San Andrés and held visiting research positions at Yale Law School, the University of Oxford, and the Max Planck Institute for Comparative and International Private Law. Her forthcoming monograph *Torts and Retribution. The Case for Punitive Damages* (Cambridge University Press, 2025) is the first book that advances a novel retributive framework enabling the analysis of punitive damages across jurisdictions.

Weitseng Chen is an associate professor at the National University of Singapore. He specializes in comparative Asian law with an emphasis on law and development, property law, and financial institutions. He has worked as a Hewlett fellow of the Center on Democracy, Development, and the Rule of Law (CDDRL) at Stanford University and as a corporate lawyer at Davis Polk & Wardwell. His recent publications include *Regime Type and Beyond: The Transformation of Police in Asia* (with H. Fu, Cambridge University Press, 2023), *Authoritarian Legality in Asia: Formation, Development and Transition* (with H. Fu, Cambridge University Press, 2020) and *The Beijing Consensus? How China has Changed the Western Ideas of Law and Economic Development* (Cambridge University Press, 2017).

Kevin E. Davis is Beller Family Professor of Business Law at New York University School of Law. His research and teaching generally concern the relationship between law and economic development, with particular emphasis on anti-corruption law, commercial law, and measurement of the performance of legal systems. His publications include over fifty articles or essays, five edited volumes, and a monograph, *Between Impunity and Imperialism: The Regulation of Transnational Bribery* (Oxford University Press, 2019).

Jorge L. Esquirol is a professor of law at Florida International University, where he teaches commercial law, comparative law, and international trade law. He previously taught at Northeastern University School of Law and was Academic Affairs Director for the Graduate Program at Harvard Law School. He was the Fulbright Distinguished Chair in Law for 2015–16 at the University of Trento; visiting research professor at the Watson Institute Brown University; and is currently Affiliate Professor at Sciences Po – Paris. He is the author of over forty articles and *Ruling the Law: Legitimacy and Failure in Latin American Legal Systems* (Cambridge University Press, 2020).

Eva Wenwa Gao is a litigation associate at Paul, Weiss, Rifkind, Wharton & Garrison LLP. She holds a Bachelor of Laws (LL.B.) degree from Peking University (2015) and a Juris Doctor (J.D.) degree from Columbia Law School (2018). She was previously a postdoctoral research scholar at Columbia Law School.

Carlos Portugal Gouvêa is a professor of commercial law at the University of São Paulo. He has been a visiting researcher at Yale Law School and at the Wharton Business School of the University of Pennsylvania. He is a founding partner of PGLaw, the vice-president of the Commission of Capital Markets and Corporate Governance of OAB-SP, and a member of the board of the Brazilian Fulbright Commission. He was previously a member of the Brazilian Board of Resources of the National Financial System.

Vikramaditya S. Khanna is William W. Cook Professor of Law at the University of Michigan, where he is also the faculty codirector of the Joint Centre for Global Corporate and Financial Law and Policy in partnership with India's Jindal Global Law School. His interests include corporate and securities law, legal issues in India, corporate and white-collar crime, and corporate governance in emerging markets. He was the Bruce W. Nichols visiting professor of law at Harvard Law School, a senior research fellow at Columbia Law School and Yale Law School, as well as a visiting scholar at Stanford Law School.

Benjamin L. Liebman is Robert L. Lieff Professor of Law at Columbia Law School, where he also directs the Hong Yen Chang Center for Chinese Legal Studies and the Parker School of Foreign and Comparative Law. His areas of specialty include international and comparative law, with a focus on Chinese tort law, criminal procedure, and court judgments. He is the author, alongside Curtis J. Milhaupt, of *Regulating the Visible Hand: The Institutional Implications of Chinese State Capitalism* (Oxford University Press, 2015). He practiced law in London and Beijing and served as a law clerk to Justice David Souter and Judge Sandra Lynch.

Daniel Bonilla Maldonado is Full Professor of Law at Universidad de los Andes in Bogotá. He has been a visiting professor or lecturer at multiple institutions, including Yale Law School, Fordham Law School, FGV São Paulo, and Sciences Po. He has received a Fulbright Fellowship and is the author of publications such as *Legal Barbarians: Identity, Modern Comparative Law and the Global South* (Cambridge University Press, 2021) and *Constitutionalism of the Global South* (Cambridge University Press, 2013).

Mariana Pargendler is Beneficial Professor of Law at Harvard Law School. She previously served as Full Professor of Law at FGV Law School in São Paulo, as Global Professor of Law at New York University School of Law (Buenos Aires), and as a visiting professor at Harvard, Yale, Columbia, Stanford, and Penn law schools. Her scholarship focuses on corporate law, corporate governance, and contract law from economic and comparative perspectives. She has published over twenty-five articles in various journals and edited volumes and is a coauthor of *The Anatomy of Corporate Law: A Comparative and Functional Approach* (Oxford University Press, 2017).

Saylon A. Pereira is a doctoral student in the Law and Development program at FGV Law School in São Paulo. He holds degrees in Law (2013) and Social Sciences (2018) from the University of São Paulo (USP/Brazil), where he also completed two years of Mathematics. He earned a master's degree in law from FGV in 2016. His research areas include economic law, constitutional law, and social policies. Since 2018, he has been developing technologies for research and law-related activities. He is also a researcher and assistant coordinator of the Center for Regulation and Democracy at the Instituto de Ensino e Pesquisa (INSPER).

Rachel E. Stern is Professor of Law and Political Science (by courtesy) at Berkeley Law, where she currently holds the Pamela P. Fong and Family Distinguished Chair in China Studies. Her research looks at law in Mainland China especially the relationship between legal institution building, political space, and professionalization. She is the author of *Environmental Litigation in China: A Study in Political Ambivalence* (Cambridge University Press, 2013) as well as numerous articles on legal mobilization and lawyers in contemporary China.

Bianca Tavolari is a professor at FGV Law School in São Paulo, where she focuses on the right to the city, urban social movements, law, and critical theory. She is a researcher of law and democracy at the Brazilian Center of Analysis and Planning (Cebrap) and a principal investigator at Maria Sibylla Merian Centre – Mecila. She previously taught at INSPER and was a researcher of the Right to the City Laboratory at the Architecture and Urbanism school of the University of São Paulo (LabCidade). She has also served as a consultant to the World Bank on the matter of cartel repression in Brazil.

Xiaohan Wu is a PhD candidate in the Department of Political Science at UC San Diego. She holds a master's degree in Electrical Engineering from Columbia University (2018) and a bachelor's degree in Electrical and Electronics Engineering from Tianjin University (2017). She was previously a data science research associate at Columbia Law School.

Preface

This volume marks the culmination of the first stage of a collaborative project designed to showcase legal innovation and adaptation in the Global South. The volume has two main objectives. The first is to introduce the concept of legal heterodoxy to capture legal institutions that diverge from those which have achieved the status of orthodoxy in the Global North. The second objective is to illustrate the variety of forms legal heterodoxy can take in the Global South.

The idea for this project was originally sparked during a dinner conversation at the Annual Meeting of the American Law and Economics Association, held at New York University School of Law in May 2019. Initial drafts of the chapters in this volume were presented and discussed at a special conference convened by NYU and the University of Buenos Aires on April 13–14, 2023 in Buenos Aires. Additionally, a subset of the authors had the opportunity to present and discuss their drafts in a conference held at FGV Law School in São Paulo on May 17, 2023. These sessions were invaluable in helping us to refine the chapters and we are grateful to everyone who participated.

The broader aim of the project is to demonstrate the value of including scholarship on and from the Global South in academic debates about law and legal institutions. We hope that our efforts will encourage other scholars not only to explore other aspects of legal heterodoxy but also to examine other distinctive features of legal systems in the Global South.

Acknowledgments

This volume could not have been completed without input and support from many individuals and institutions. Each of the individual chapters has doubtless benefited from its own set of supporters but we are all grateful for comments we received from participants in the conferences about the volume held at the University of Buenos Aires and FGV Direito SP, namely Marcelo Alegre, Thiago Amparo, Michelle Ratton Sanchez Badin, Paola Bergallo, Guillermo Cabanellas, André Rodrigues Corrêa, Martín Hevia, Nkatha Kabira, Patricio Kenny, Rafael Manóvil, Mario Schapiro, and Pablo Suárez. We are also grateful for the comments on the introductory chapter provided by John Goldberg.

This project has also benefited from the contributions of many research assistants over the years, including Alec Abitbol, Thaís Abreu, Cindy Arrivillaga, Beatriz Brichucka, Imani Jaoko, Maria Eduarda Lessa, Lucas Víspico, Gustavo Schneider, and Bruna Zanini.

New York University School of Law provided invaluable financial support, both for Kevin Davis's research and the project as a whole. FGV São Paulo supported Mariana Pargendler's research in connection with this project.

1

Legal Heterodoxy in the Global South

Adapting Private Laws to Local Contexts

Kevin E. Davis and Mariana Pargendler

1.1 INTRODUCTION

How do legal institutions of the Global South differ from those of the Global North?[1] This question has attracted surprisingly little attention. Comparative law as a discipline has long focused on "legal families" as its central taxonomic division – a framework that views legal systems in the Global South as derivative of, and subordinate to, the "real" legal systems of a handful of wealthy western jurisdictions.[2] A classic comparative law textbook explicitly urges comparativists to "ignore" affiliate legal systems and focus on the "parent" systems.[3] This advice no longer passes unchallenged, but legal systems in the Global South are still often ignored, studied in isolation, or simply measured against benchmarks conceived based on legal institutions from the Global North.[4]

To the extent that scholars have confronted the specificities of legal systems in the Global South, a common perception, which we label the "traditional view," is that

[1] We use the term Global South as a synonym for developing countries. Our approach does not imply a stark dichotomy nor any judgment of superiority or inferiority, but instead suggests a continuum of social, economic, and legal challenges across countries belonging to this traditional classification.

[2] D. B. Maldonado (ed.), *Constitutionalism of the Global South: The Activist Tribunals of India, South Africa, and Colombia* (Cambridge: Cambridge University Press, 2013). See also M. Pargendler, The Rise and Decline of Legal Families (2012) 60 *The American Journal of Comparative Law* 1043–74 (describing a different conception of legal families by Latin American scholars in the nineteenth century, who viewed their systems as belonging to a legal tradition of its own).

[3] K. Zweigert and H. Kötz, *An Introduction to Comparative Law*, 3rd ed. (Oxford: Oxford University Press, 1998).

[4] See, for example, M. Siems, The Power of Comparative Law: What Types of Units Can Comparative Law Compare? (2019) 67 *The American Journal of Comparative Law* 861–88, 865 ("countries may be included within the conventional units of comparative law as far as those countries have adopted a legal system modeled after Western state-based law"). See Section 1.2 for discussion of comparative law scholars who have criticized the discipline's neglect of the Global South.

the legal systems of developing countries are mostly outdated, failed transplants, or plagued by enforcement challenges. This volume offers a different perspective. Rather than viewing the legal systems of developing countries as "failed law" or as a reality of interest only to sociologists or anthropologists,[5] we take them seriously as relevant legal experiences. Rather than measuring them against yardsticks based on the legal systems of the Global North, as in so many academic works and policy indicators,[6] we focus on legal adaptations and innovations in the Global South. We find (i) numerous manifestations of legal doctrines and solutions that deviate from approaches that currently hold the status of orthodoxy in the Global North by (ii) (a) incorporating distinct public policy objectives or (b) reflecting different values and worldviews. We call this phenomenon "legal heterodoxy," and this volume is dedicated to exploring its contours.

This introductory chapter provides the conceptual and theoretical framework for the chapters that follow. Section 1.2 explains the significance of the project. Section 1.3 sets out the traditional view that developing countries will be attracted to legal orthodoxy. Section 1.4 offers countervailing reasons why the appeal of orthodoxy may be limited. In Section 1.5 we define the concept of legal heterodoxy. Section 1.6 summarizes the examples of legal heterodoxy discussed in greater detail in the following chapters. Section 1.7 lays out an agenda for future research and explains how a focus on legal heterodoxy in the Global South leads to new insights about the contours of private law and its future prospects in the Global South and Global North alike. Section 1.8 discusses the relationship between that research agenda and existing literature.

1.2 SIGNIFICANCE OF THE PROJECT

This project marks a departure from the existing literature in terms of its scope, theoretical grounding, and findings. First, we focus on private law institutions in the Global South that have previously received little scholarly attention. Second, we theorize about the forces that drive those institutions to diverge from as well as converge with legal institutions in the Global North. Third, we uncover institutions that diverge in unexpected ways from their counterparts in the Global North.

1.2.1 *Focus on Private Law in the Global South*

This volume examines core areas of *private* law in the Global South: contracts, property, torts, corporations, and the attribution of legal

[5] For a critique of these approaches, see J. L. Esquirol, *The Fictions of Latin American Law and Their Strategic Uses: Legitimacy and Failure in Latin American Legal Systems* (Cambridge: Cambridge University Press, 2019); D. B. Maldonado, *Legal Barbarians: Identity, Modern Comparative Law and the Global South* (Cambridge, Cambridge University Press, 2021).

[6] R. La Porta, F. Lopez-de-Silanes, and A. Shleifer, The Economic Consequences of Legal Origins (2008) 46 *Journal of Economic Literature* 285–332; K. Davis and M. B. Kruse, Taking the Measure of Law: The Case of the Doing Business Project (2007) 32 *Law & Social Inquiry* 1095–119.

personality.[7] This focus reflects two moves: (i) focusing on differences in *legal norms* (including legal rules, principles, doctrines, and caselaw), as opposed to concentrating on enforcement-related issues such as the speed, efficiency or integrity of courts and prosecutors, or the impact of extralegal institutions[8] and (ii) expanding the comparative legal analysis in the Global South beyond public law. While the last decades have seen the emergence of an influential, if still insufficient, body of literature on constitutional law in the Global South,[9] there has been no comparable effort to study distinctive features of private law in the developing world. Emerging scholarship on "critical comparative law"[10] and "decolonial comparative law"[11] is framed in broad terms but applications to specific private law institutions from a comparative perspective remain rare. This is unfortunate, given the key role of private law in providing the legal foundations of global capitalism and in shaping wealth creation and distribution.[12]

By Global South jurisdictions we mean developing countries, that is, countries with low or medium per capita income.[13] We are aware that other works define the

7 For the time being, our focus is limited to domestic laws of countries in the Global South. Although transnational and international norms play an important role in private law, they feature in this volume mainly as points of comparison for domestic laws in the Global South. We leave to future work the task of exploring how countries in the Global South influence transnational and international law.

8 As an example of works arguing that formal laws are not relevant in developing countries, see U. Mattei, Three Patterns of Law: Taxonomy and Change in the World's Legal Systems (1997) 45 *The American Journal of Comparative Law* 5–44 (arguing that "in developing and transition economies of Africa, Latin America, and Eastern Europe … there is no such thing as formal law binding government"); R. Kraakman et al., *The Anatomy of Corporate Law: A Comparative and Functional Approach*, 2nd ed. (Oxford: Oxford University Press, 2009) ("We focus on developed, rather than developing, economies, because where foundational legal institutions, such as functioning courts and the protection of property rights, are absent or compromised, then the way in which corporate law responds to specific problems is less likely to make a difference to the real economy").

9 See, e.g., O. V. Vieira, U. Baxi, and F. Viljoen (eds.), *Transformative Constitutionalism: Comparing the Apex Courts of Brazil, India and South Africa* (Pretoria: Pretoria University Law Press, 2013) (examining how the highest courts in Brazil, Colombia, and South Africa give effect to social rights recognized in their constitutions); Maldonado (ed.), Constitutionalism of the Global South; P. Dann, M. Riegner, and M. Bönnemann, The Southern Turn in Comparative Constitutional Law: An Introduction, in P. Dann, M. Riegner, and M. Bönnemann (eds.), *The Global South and Comparative Constitutional Law* (Oxford: Oxford University Press, 2020), pp. 1–36.

10 See, e.g., G. Frankenberg, Critical Comparisons: Re-thinking Comparative Law (1985) 26 *Harvard International Law Journal* 411–56; P. Legrand, The Impossibility of "Legal Transplants" (1997) 4 *Maastricht Journal of European and Comparative Law* 111–24; G. Frankenberg, *Comparative Law as Critique* (Northampton: Edward Elgar, 2016); R. M. Acuña, Comparación Jurídica desde el Sur Global: Genealogía de un Proyecto Crítico (2018) 73 *Themis Revista de Derecho* 131–45.

11 L. Salaymeh and R. Michaels, Decolonial Comparative Law: A Conceptual Beginning (2022) 86 *Rabel Journal of Comparative and International Private Law* 166–88.

12 K. Pistor, *The Code of Capital: How the Law Creates Wealth and Inequality* (Princeton: Princeton University Press, 2019).

13 The most common definition of the term "Global South" equates it with nation-states in Africa, Asia, and Latin America that are economically underdeveloped. Defined in this way, the term appears to be a successor to and nearly synonymous with the terms "Third World" and "developing countries." The value of this conception of the Global South has been challenged

Global South as "not only, even primarily, a place," but a "specific epistemic, methodological, and institutional sensibility."[14] This broader usage may encompass the "South within the North,"[15] as well as wealthy former colonies that are more peripheral to mainstream comparative law, such as Australia.[16] It also has the advantage of not "othering" the Global South by reifying difference and opposition. While there is much to be said for this broader perspective, this volume concentrates on the laws of developing countries as such because they have been understudied from a comparative standpoint. Our goal is to put them on the map for the comparative study of private law.

The immediate purpose of our project is to test conventional views of the relationship between private law institutions in the North and South, but the value of this exercise goes beyond North–South comparison. To begin, these kinds of studies also facilitate South–South comparisons. The general practice of studying the legal systems of developing countries in isolation – with Global North standards as the sole reference point – is likely to produce an "odd duck syndrome," by which the legal institutions of a given Global South jurisdiction are described as exceptional when in fact they are not. For example, Pargendler's contribution in Chapter 10 reveals surprising commonalities among corporate laws in Global South jurisdictions. Scholars have described India's approach to enterprise liability for environmental harm as "unique" and "revolutionary" from a comparative perspective, while comparable rules exist in Brazil. Similarly, Brazilian commentators often attribute the rise of a welfarist (or social-justice infused) conception of contract law in the country to certain domestic scholarly trends, as well as to new statutory and constitutional provisions, without realizing that similar developments have occurred in other parts of the Global South, as described by Davis and Pargendler in Chapter 2.

Obtaining better information on how legal institutions in the Global South relate to other legal systems, in both the North and South, also makes it possible to re-examine the schemes that scholars and practitioners use to classify legal systems. As noted, the dominant scheme distinguishes legal families defined by relationships to European legal systems and, at a more general level, between common law and civil law systems. That approach, which dates back more than a century, may

on the grounds that it (i) oversimplifies reality by ignoring heterogeneity within both the Global South and the Global North and (ii) reifies domination of the Global South. N. Schneider, Between Promise and Skepticism: The Global South and Our Role as Engaged Intellectuals (2017) 11 *The Global South* 18–38.

14 Dann, Riegner, and Bönnemann, The Southern Turn in Comparative Constitutional Law, p. 3 and 7.

15 C. Levander and W. Mignolo, Introduction: The Global South and World Dis/Order (2011) 5 *The Global South* 1–11, 4.

16 See, e.g., F. Morosini and M. R. S. Badin (eds.), *Reconceptualizing International Investment Law from the Global South* (Cambridge: Cambridge University Press, 2017), including Australia.

warrant reconsideration. Finally, although the analyses in this volume are primarily descriptive, they provide a necessary foundation for research aimed at explaining and evaluating legal institutions in both the North and South.

Having said all that, we should add an important caveat about the scope of this volume: The studies in the following chapters cover a wide range of jurisdictions – Argentina, Bolivia, Brazil, China, Colombia, Ecuador, India, Indonesia, and South Africa – but do not purport to offer a representative sample of Global South experiences. The legal institutions examined include examples from the largest economies in the Global South, which are precisely the places in which we predict that legal innovation and experimentation is more likely due to economies of scale and relative immunity to foreign influence. We do not expect legal heterodoxy to be the norm in Global South jurisdictions more generally and actually would expect it to be less prevalent in countries that are smaller, less affluent, or more dependent on the Global North than the countries covered in this volume. Even in the countries that we do cover, the studies in the chapters that follow are invariably limited to specific areas of law. Accordingly, we do not claim that legal heterodoxy is the norm with respect to all, or most, dimensions of private law in the jurisdictions covered. These limitations reflect the fact that, in preparing this volume, we were constrained by existing literature, our own academic networks, and the range of expertise of our team of contributors. Therefore, the aim is not to offer a definitive account of private law adaptations and innovations in the Global South but to promote a research agenda that encompasses a wider array of jurisdictions, legal issues, and perspectives.

1.2.2 *Theoretical Account of Orthodoxy and Heterodoxy*

In this introductory chapter we offer a theory of the forces that might drive countries in the Global South toward either orthodoxy or heterodoxy. The traditional view that private law in the Global South consists mainly of pale imitations of laws that have achieved the status of orthodoxy in the Global North is widely held, but its theoretical underpinnings are not always fully articulated. Moreover, to the extent that scholars seek to explain divergent private law norms in the Global South, they typically rely on differences in values or worldviews, especially in the Islamic world.[17] We contend that the drivers of legal heterodoxy include but are not limited to differences in values or worldviews.

To be more specific, we maintain that differences in private law rules in the Global South are likely to be explained by one of two broad categories of factors.

[17] On the debate over the influence of religious values on law in the Islamic world, see C. Mallat, Comparative Law and the Islamic (Middle Eastern) Legal Culture, in M. Reimann and R. Zimmermann (eds), *The Oxford Handbook of Comparative Law*, 2nd ed (Oxford: Oxford University Press, 2019).

First, lawmakers or adjudicators may wish to endorse different values or worldviews. We argue that this may explain heterodoxy in private law even outside of the Islamic world. Second, distinctive social, economic, or political features of the local contexts may lead lawmakers or adjudicators in the Global South to make different choices from their counterparts in the Global North.[18] In Section 1.4 we argue that distinctive characteristics of developing countries that are conventionally presumed to attract countries to orthodoxy – namely, a legacy of colonialism, limited fiscal capacity, macro-economic instability, and economic dependence on richer countries – may sometimes encourage heterodoxy.

1.2.3 *Mapping Legal Heterodoxy*

In focusing on legal heterodoxy, we seek to unearth and analyze private law approaches in the Global South that have received insufficient attention. The examples of heterodoxy we document include a greater concern with inequality in contract law adjudication in Brazil, Colombia, and South Africa; a dedicated regime for "hyper vulnerable" consumers in Argentina; pioneering regimes of mandatory corporate social responsibility in India and beyond; the imposition of tort liability in China, irrespective of causation; the erosion of limited liability for the benefit of stakeholders in Brazil and India; the overturning of Brazil's patent extension rule as an unconstitutional violation of the social function of intellectual property and the right to health; legal incentives for Black economic empowerment through greater participation in corporate ownership and governance in South Africa; and the attribution of legal personhood to nature, among others.

Many of the studies in this volume highlight heterodox private law institutions that embrace diverse policy objectives to a greater extent than corresponding institutions in the Global North. In other words, these examples of private law innovations in the Global South offer relatively robust challenges to the "modularity approach" that has dominated law-and-economics thinking and neoliberal policies since the 1970s.[19] The modularity approach posits that each field of law should pursue one narrow efficiency-related objective (e.g., reduction of agency costs in corporate law, reduction of transaction costs in contract law, consumer welfare in antitrust law, and maximization of firm value for the benefit of creditors in insolvency law, to name just a few).[20] Under this modular view, distributive objectives should remain strictly confined to the field of taxation and social transfers.[21]

18 For a defense of such context-specific lawmaking see K. Davis, Legal Universalism: Persistent Objections (2010) 60 *University of Toronto Law Journal* 537–53.

19 M. Pargendler, Controlling Shareholders in the 21st Century: Complicating Corporate Governance beyond Agency Costs (2020) 45 *Journal of Corporation Law* 953–75.

20 Ibid.

21 L. Kaplow and S. Shavell, Why the Legal System Is Less Efficient than the Income Tax in Redistributing Income (1994) 23 *Journal of Legal Studies* 667–81 (arguing that promoting

To be sure, legal institutions in the Global North often do not conform to such a modular approach, which is prescriptive and ideological rather than primarily descriptive.[22] Karl Polanyi's classic work documented how self-regulating markets invariably triggered resistance; in a similar fashion, efforts to implement purely modular regulation have often prompted countervailing reactions.[23] We specifically examine how these social and regulatory reactions take place in the Global South and through private law. In particular, we explore how inequality and crises have led Global South jurisdictions to embrace "antimodularity" in private law in a distinct way from, or to a greater extent than, is currently the norm in the Global North – a possibility that contrasts sharply with the traditional view.[24]

1.3 THE TRADITIONAL VIEW

The traditional view is that the characteristic features of developing countries lead them to adopt simplified versions of legal doctrines designed by either developed countries or international organizations dominated by those countries – "orthodox" doctrines for short. The corollary is that developing countries will not deviate from orthodoxy by adopting "heterodox" or "innovative" laws. We begin by setting out the empirical and theoretical foundations of the traditional view and then summarize its supporting evidence.

1.3.1 *Characteristic Features of Global South Jurisdictions*

It is well documented that developing countries have certain typical characteristics, despite significant heterogeneity in various dimensions. First, almost all developing countries were colonized by European nations in the eighteenth, nineteenth, or early twentieth centuries.[25] Moreover, most of those countries received relatively few European settlers during the colonial period.[26] This implies that the legal

distribution through the tax-and-transfer systems produces fewer behavioral distortions – and thereby increases the size of the pie to be distributed – compared to efforts to effectuate distribution through other areas of law).

[22] See, e.g., M. Pargendler, The Grip of Nationalism on Corporate Law (2020) 95 *Indiana Law Journal* 533–90; Pargendler, Controlling Shareholders in the 21st Century.

[23] K. Polanyi, *The Great Transformation: Economic and Political Origins of Our Time* (New York: Rinehart, 1944).

[24] Our argument also diverges from Polanyi's argument that links institutional diversification in less advanced countries to diversification in advanced countries. Specifically, Polanyi posited that the decline of the international market economy and the gold standard would help countries transcend "the pernicious nineteenth-century dogma of the necessary uniformity of domestic regimes within the orbit of the world economy." Ibid., p. 262.

[25] Exceptions include China, Ethiopia, North Korea, and developing countries located in Europe.

[26] Developing countries with relatively high proportions of Europeans in the population include Argentina, Costa Rica, the Dominican Republic, Dominica, and St. Lucia. See W. Easterly

institutions adopted during the colonial period were designed by Europeans to be applied principally to non-Europeans.

Second, the governments of many present-day developing countries have limited capacity to raise revenue from taxes. There is a strong correlation between the tax/GDP ratio and per capita GDP.[27] Social scientists often equate this lack of fiscal capacity with lack of state capacity, defined as the state's ability to accomplish its intended policy goals.[28]

Third, contemporary developing countries tend to experience greater macroeconomic volatility than countries with higher per capita incomes.[29] In the economics literature, macroeconomic volatility is typically defined as variation in the growth rate of GDP over time.[30] This typically implies volatility in wages and prices and often includes true crises.[31] Consequently, the fact that developing countries experience relatively high levels of economic volatility implies that inhabitants of those countries are systematically exposed to more economic risk than inhabitants of wealthier countries.[32] In addition, states with limited fiscal capacity may struggle to provide insurance that fills the gaps that inevitably will be left by private insurance markets.

Fourth, even after the end of formal colonization, many Global South jurisdictions tend to be dependent on wealthier countries with larger economies. This dependence stems from several factors. Many developing countries are relatively capital-poor. In addition, as noted, their economies tend to be prone to balance-of-payments crises. Their firms also tend to have less access to advanced technology. This means that developing countries generally depend on wealthier countries for access to export markets, advanced technology (which may be tied to foreign direct investment), emergency financing, and foreign aid.[33] These forms of economic dependence often translate into political and military vulnerability.

and R. Levine, The European Origins of Economic Development (2016) 21 *Journal of Economic Growth* 225–57.

27 M. Dincecco, *State Capacity and Economic Development: Present and Past* (Cambridge: Cambridge University Press, 2017), section 1.1, figure 1.

28 Ibid., section 1.1.

29 N. V. Loayza et al., Macroeconomic Volatility and Welfare in Developing Countries: An Introduction (2007) 21 *The World Bank Economic Review* 343–57.

30 Economic analyses use either the standard deviation of the GDP growth rate or the standard deviation divided by the absolute mean growth rate as indicators of economic volatility. See W. Easterly, R. Islam, and J. E. Stiglitz, Shaken and Stirred: Explaining Growth Volatility, in B. Pleskovic and N. Stern (eds.), *Annual World Bank Conference on Development Economics 2000* (Washington: The World Bank, 2001), pp. 191–211; D. Acemoglu et al., Institutional Causes, Macroeconomic Symptoms: Volatility, Crises and Growth (2003) 50 *Journal of Monetary Economics* 49–123.

31 Easterly, Islam, and Stiglitz, Shaken and Stirred.

32 Loayza, Macroeconomic Volatility and Welfare in Developing Countries.

33 For a historical discussion see T. D. Santos, The Structure of Dependence (1970) 60 *American Economic Review* 231–36.

1.3.2 *Theoretical Underpinnings of the Traditional View*

The traditional view rests on a cluster of arguments about the economic and cultural attractions of legal orthodoxy in countries characterized by a colonial heritage, limited fiscal capacity, macro-economic instability, and international economic dependence. One of the most prominent economic arguments is premised on the assumption that developing countries have limited state capacity and, therefore, given the costs of drafting and assessing the effects of new laws, cannot afford to formulate new laws that are likely to improve on those developed in richer countries.[34] A second argument based on the same premise is that developing countries ought to adopt laws that take the form of relatively simple rules in order to conserve scarce local legislative and judicial resources.[35] A third argument is that developing countries should strive to attract foreign direct investment by adopting laws familiar to the greatest possible number of prospective investors, which historically have tended to be the laws of the United States and former European colonial powers.[36] If we assume that policymakers in developing countries are rational actors who try to maximize the net benefits of lawmaking, then all of these arguments support the conventional prediction.

Other arguments focus on the cultural rather than economic attractions of orthodoxy. A variety of actors, including lawmakers and the general public in developing countries, may assign prestige to economically successful countries, including former colonial powers, and associate status with the adoption of those countries' laws.[37] This dynamic might be sustained by disparities in wealth that allow academic institutions and other organizations based in rich countries to dominate the production of information and ideas about the world, including law. Similar dynamics might cause the elites who dominate international financial institutions or donor organizations to make the adoption of orthodoxy a condition for securing emergency or concessional financing. These cultural arguments also support the conventional prediction that developing countries will pursue orthodoxy, but they do not rest on the assumption that orthodoxy is normatively desirable.

Each of these economic and cultural arguments predicts that countries in the Global South will be attracted to laws that originate in the Global North, but not necessarily from the same Global North countries – in other words, they point to different definitions of orthodoxy. For instance, some of the arguments emphasize

[34] R. A. Posner, Creating a Legal Framework for Economic Development (1998) 13 *The World Bank Research Observer* 1–11.

[35] Ibid.; B. Black and R. Kraakman, A Self-Enforcing Model of Corporate Law (1996) 109 *Harvard Law Review* 1911–82.

[36] On the potential benefits of foreign direct investment see L. Alfaro and J. Chauvin, Foreign Direct Investment, Finance and Economic Development, in M. Spatareanu (ed.), *Encyclopedia of International Economics and Global Trade* (Singapore: World Scientific, 2020), vol. I, pp. 231–58.

[37] Esquirol, The Fictions of Latin American Law and Their Strategic Uses.

the attractions of laws of former colonial powers, while others emphasize the attractions of the legal systems of countries that have historically served as large sources of trade and investment and have dominated international organizations. The former set of arguments implicitly identify orthodoxy with the laws of England, France, the Netherlands, Portugal, and Spain, while the latter set point most directly to the United States and the European Union.

For the purposes of this volume, we will define legal orthodoxy to mean laws that are favored in either a former European colonial power, the United States, or the European Union. We define China as belonging to the Global South because, until relatively recently, there has been little doubt that it qualifies as a developing country.[38] We leave to future research the question of China's influence on legal systems in the Global South.

1.3.3 *Evidence Supporting the Traditional View*

There is no question that developing countries sometimes adopt orthodox laws. In many developing countries, important components of the legal system have persisted since colonial times. Many former British colonies still have English or colonial statutes on the books and cite English precedents.[39] In fact, until recently, a fair number of those jurisdictions relied on a predominantly British tribunal, the Privy Council, as their highest appellate court and several continue to employ British judges in their local courts.[40] Meanwhile, developing countries colonized by France, Spain, or Portugal continue to use legislative provisions copied from colonial powers and to cite those powers' decisions and commentaries.[41] There are many examples of developing countries adopting laws inspired by US law, such as Article 9 of the Uniform Commercial Code.[42] More recently, many jurisdictions have adopted data protection laws based on the European Union's General Data

[38] P. Benoit, China Is Developing and Developed at the Same Time, Foreign Policy, May 23, 2023.

[39] H. Spamann, Contemporary Legal Transplants: Legal Families and the Diffusion of (Corporate) Law (2009) 2009 *Brigham Young University Law Review* 1813–77.

[40] A. S. King and P. K. Bookman, Traveling Judges (2022) 116 *American Journal of International Law* 477–533.

[41] M. Siems, *Comparative Law*, 3rd ed. (Cambridge: Cambridge University Press, 2022), pp. 246–252; Esquirol, The Fictions of Latin American Law and Their Strategic Uses, pp. 28–43. But see M. Pargendler, Politics in the Origins: The Making of Corporate Law in Nineteenth-Century Brazil (2012) 60 *The American Journal of Comparative Law* 805–50 (finding greater agency and diverse origins in nineteenth-century corporate lawmaking in Brazil).

[42] F. Fiorentini, Legal Transplants in the Law of Secured Transactions. Current Problems and Comparative Perspectives, in F. Fiorentini and M. Infantino (eds.), *Mentoring Comparative Lawyers: Methods, Times, and Places: Liber Discipulorum Mauro Bussani* (New York: Springer, 2020), pp. 3–23, pp. 10–11 (discussing adoption of OAS Inter-American Model Law on Secured Transactions).

Protection Regulation.[43] Finally, there are notable instances of developing countries that have adopted legal norms proposed by international bodies such as the International Monetary Fund (IMF) and the Organisation for Economic Cooperation and Development (OECD), including in core areas of corporate law.[44]

The fact that developing countries sometimes, or often, adopt orthodox laws does not mean that the traditional view is the only, or the primary, game in town. The key question is whether developing countries also deviate from orthodox solutions in key legal contexts and, if so, why and how.

1.4 LIMITATIONS OF THE TRADITIONAL VIEW

There are several reasons to question the appeal of legal orthodoxy in the Global South. To begin, the sweeping empirical generalizations that underpin the traditional view ignore the remarkable heterogeneity that characterizes the Global South. Moreover, the claims that orthodoxy is economically superior rest upon contestable assumptions about the costs and benefits of adopting laws modeled upon foreign laws. Finally, the arguments premised on the cultural attractions of legal orthodoxy and international pressure neglect the fact that orthodoxy is not necessarily compatible with either the material interests or ideological commitments of people who hold the balance of political power in developing countries.

1.4.1 *Empirical Objections*

Although a legacy of colonialism, limited fiscal capacity, macroeconomic volatility, and international subordination may be general characteristics of countries in the Global South, there is considerable variation both among and within those countries. European colonialism took many different forms in today's developing countries, even within colonial empires, and ended at different points in time. Countries with limited fiscal capacity can deploy scarce tax revenues in very different ways, with very different implications for state capacity. Perhaps most importantly, limited fiscal capacity, economic volatility, and international dependence are negatively correlated with wealth and economic size and so large Global South jurisdictions may exhibit relatively few of the "typical" characteristics of developing countries. For example, Brazil definitely qualifies as a developing country and has struggled to address inequality through fiscal policy and to curb environmental disasters through regulation. At the same time, Brazil's tax/GDP ratio is close to the OECD average and its state apparatus is known for its prowess in international economic matters.[45]

[43] G. Greenleaf, Global Data Privacy Laws 2021: Despite Covid Delays, 145 Laws Show GDPR Dominance (2021) 169 *Privacy Laws & Business International Report*.

[44] M. Pargendler, The Rise of International Corporate Law (2021) 98 *Washington University Law Review* 1765–1820.

[45] OECD, Revenue Statistics in Latin America and the Caribbean – Brazil, 2023; G. Shaffer, *Emerging Powers and the World Trading System: The Past and Future of International Economic Law* (Cambridge: Cambridge University Press, 2021).

There may also be legal variation within countries in the Global South, particularly in large federated states.

1.4.2 *Economic Objections*

To recap, the economic arguments for orthodoxy presume that the costs of using foreign laws as models are low relative to the cost of domestic innovation, and that the benefits, especially in terms of attracting foreign investment, will be significant. Each of these claims is questionable.

The economic implications of adopting foreign laws are complicated by the fact that this strategy will typically entail relying on foreign or foreign-trained legal advisors. On the one hand, harmonization with foreign laws will allow developing countries to tap additional and potentially superior sources of legal advice and legal education. Or, to put it in economic terms, adopting foreign models should increase the supply of legal services, which should, at least in theory, reduce cost and increase quality. On the other hand, the demand side of the market also has to be considered. Foreign law schools and foreign lawyers operate in an international market and the amounts they charge for their services will reflect international demand. The fees charged by local professionals with expertise in foreign law will also be affected by international demand to the extent they can offer their services across international borders, whether in person – which will involve migration – or remotely, as in the case of legal outsourcing. Our point here is that, while harmonization with laws from the Global North may have beneficial effects on the supply of legal services in the Global South, those benefits may be offset to some extent by the effects of increased demand for the legal services required in the South. To further complicate matters, in any given context the net economic effects of legal harmonization will depend not only on market forces but also on factors such as the presence of subsidies and restrictions on cross-border provision of legal services.

The idea that orthodox laws are required to attract foreign direct investment also rests on questionable assumptions. To begin, the evidence is mixed on whether foreign direct investment stimulates economic growth. This calls into question the merits of making attractiveness to foreign investors a central objective of legal reform.[46]

The traditional view also rests on the potentially faulty assumption that developing countries interested in attracting foreign direct investment ought to focus on catering to investors from Western Europe and the United States. This view neglects the growing importance of investment flows from countries outside the Global North, and in particular China. For instance, since 2013, the value of Chinese foreign direct investment flows to Africa has exceeded that of flows from the United States.[47]

46 Alfaro and Chauvin, Foreign Direct Investment, Finance and Economic Development.

47 China Africa Research Initiative, Chinese Investment in Africa, Johns Hopkins School of Advanced International Studies, 2022.

It remains true that adhering to orthodoxy allows developing countries to reap whatever benefits flow from catering to foreign investors from the United States and Western Europe. In many instances, though, it is possible to capture these benefits by permitting foreign actors' affairs to be governed by foreign laws while other actors' transactions are governed by a distinct body of local law. There are many ways to accomplish this kind of "regulatory differentiation."[48] Common techniques include creating separate bodies of "offshore" corporate law and trust law, signing bilateral investment treaties, creating export processing zones, or enforcing arbitration, choice of law, and choice of venue clauses. Admittedly, though, it can be difficult to prevent bodies of law ostensibly designed for foreigners from affecting local actors.

Finally, orthodoxy forgoes the benefits of legal adaptation and innovation. Legal rules that are functional in the Global North may be dysfunctional in other settings – they may be inefficient given realities in the Global South, or even operate to distribute wealth from the Global South to the Global North. The magnitude of the benefits of innovation and adaptation will be context-specific and depends on the extent to which the legal challenges facing the developing country in question are materially different from those of countries whose laws might serve as models. However, there are good reasons to believe that developing countries do face materially different challenges. For instance, the need to conserve scarce judicial resources may prompt innovations that involve more than merely simplifying foreign doctrines.

1.4.3 *Political Drawbacks*

Even if orthodox laws are economically optimal, in the sense that they maximize social welfare within the relevant jurisdiction, there is no guarantee that they will be politically viable in any given Global South jurisdiction.[49] Orthodox laws may not provide material benefits to the groups who hold the balance of political power in the relevant developing country, whether those groups are urban elites or impoverished rural majorities. In the absence of effective progressive tax policy, deviations from orthodoxy may be required to satisfy the economic demands of these influential constituencies.[50] In addition, in many political systems in the Global North and

[48] For a definition of different dual or multiple regulatory strategies, including regulatory competition, regulatory differentiation, and regulatory dualism, see R. J. Gilson, H. Hansmann, and M. Pargendler, Regulatory Dualism as a Development Strategy: Corporate Reform in Brazil, the United States, and the European Union (2011) 63 *Stanford Law Review* 475–537.

[49] M. J. Roe, Backlash (1998) 98 *Columbia Law Review* 217–41; A. L. Chua, The Paradox of Free Market Democracy: Rethinking Development Policy (2000) 41 *Harvard International Law Journal* 287–380.

[50] For example, Chua, The Paradox of Free Market Democracy: Rethinking Development Policy, suggests that, in developing countries that lack effective tax-and-transfer systems, deviations from orthodox policies that favor both free markets and democracy may be required to alleviate tensions resulting from the presence of economically dominant ethnic minorities.

South alike, lawmakers have a bias toward adopting laws that favor the economic interests of nationals ("nationalistic laws") because foreigners operate at a political deficit.[51] This weighs against the conventional prediction that developing countries will adopt private law institutions that cater to foreign actors.

Legal orthodoxy might also lack ideological appeal. In many countries in the Global South, concerns about persistent injustice, often dating back to the colonial era, have inspired legal reforms that make a decisive break with the past and are oriented toward social and economic change. The developments in constitutional law jurisprudence known as transformative constitutionalism are prominent recent examples of this phenomenon.[52] Other examples include steps toward recognition of legal rights for indigenous peoples and people of African descent in Latin America.[53]

1.5 THE CONCEPT OF LEGAL HETERODOXY

In light of its questionable economic and political appeal, it is reasonable to expect at least some countries in the Global South to diverge significantly from orthodoxy in ways that respond to their distinctive social, economic, and political circumstances. We label these kinds of deviations from orthodox approaches "legal heterodoxy." To be more precise, we define legal heterodoxy as the emergence of legal institutions that (i) deviate from orthodox approaches currently prevailing in the Global North by (ii) pursuing distinct and potentially broader public policy objectives or reflecting different values, ideologies, or worldviews.

Our definition of legal heterodoxy acknowledges the existence of variation within the Global North – for example, between the United States and Europe, as well as within Europe – around the policy objectives that are pursued through private law. Recall that our definition of orthodoxy encompasses legal norms adopted in *either* the United States or Europe. We downplay this variation because comparisons focused on legal differences within the Global North – or, more precisely, with respect to a small set of core "parent jurisdictions" in the Wealthy West – have been the object *par excellence* of comparative law scholarship.[54] Our point is that the dominant narrative's focus on intra-North differences has impoverished our understanding of private law institutions around the world. While acknowledging significant variation within the Global North, we aim to capture a portion of the spectrum of legal institutions that is captured by accounts of intra-North variation.

[51] Pargendler, The Grip of Nationalism on Corporate Law.

[52] Vieira, Baxi, and Viljoen (eds.), Transformative Constitutionalism.

[53] R. Sieder, Indigenous Peoples' Rights and the Law in Latin America, in C. R. Garavito (ed.), *Law and Society in Latin America: A New Map* (London: Routledge, 2014), pp. 143–56; T. S. Paschel, *Becoming Black Political Subjects: Movements and Ethno-Racial Rights in Colombia and Brazil* (New Jersey: Princeton University Press, 2016).

[54] Siems, The Power of Comparative Law.

We focus on instances of legal heterodoxy that simultaneously satisfy both components of our definition: rules that (i) differ along North–South lines; and (ii) embody different policies and values. Future works can and should explore each component separately, such as (a) by mapping the incorporation of different public policies and values into private law in the Global North, as well as (b) by examining "ultraorthodoxy" in the Global South (a term coined by Carlos Portugal Gouvêa in Chapter 8), by which we mean pursuing certain orthodox policy objectives even more vigorously than in the Global North.

In the following subsections, we highlight additional features of the concept of legal heterodoxy.

1.5.1 *Anti-modularity*

Our research so far suggests that objectives of heterodox institutions are often strongly "antimodular," i.e., they resist the traditional law-and-economics narrative of functional specialization across different areas of law. That narrative eschews the pursuit of distributional objectives through doctrines of contract, tort, or corporate law and holds that distributional objectives should be pursued exclusively through the fiscal system. We conjecture that there are at least two reasons why lawmakers in the Global South who choose to deviate from the path trodden by their counterparts in the Global North may be drawn to antimodularity.[55] First, lawmakers in countries with limited fiscal capacity but where economic inequality is a serious problem may be drawn to private law doctrines that serve to distribute resources to members of disadvantaged groups, or at least claim to do so. Second, lawmakers in developing countries might favor doctrines that ensure risk-sharing to compensate for the inadequacies of state-sponsored insurance schemes in societies plagued by economic instability.

1.5.2 *Varieties of Heterodoxy*

Our definition clearly implies that heterodoxy can take many different forms. Because there are numerous axes along which lawmakers can diverge from orthodoxy, there can be many varieties of legal heterodoxy. Take, for example, the distinction between *tailored* approaches to distribution through private law rules, on the one hand, and untailored or categorical approaches, on the other. Tailored approaches are based on a granular and context-specific inquiry into markers of vulnerability in each case. For instance, as described by Maria Guadalupe Martínez Alles in Chapter 3, Argentina's consumer protection regime has evolved toward greater tailoring by offering enhanced protection to "hypervulnerable" consumers. By contrast, untailored approaches to distribution determine vulnerability based on

55 Pargendler, Controlling Shareholders in the 21st Century; A. Kovvali, Stakeholderism Silo Busting (2022) 90 *University of Chicago Law Review* 203–60.

less fine-grained analysis. For instance, the broad eviction moratorium discussed by Bianca Tavolari and Saylon A. Pereira in Chapter 6 protected all tenants, despite concerns that it was over-inclusive – both because some tenants were not poor and because some landlords were vulnerable.

Another reason why there are different varieties of heterodoxy is that our definitions of legal orthodoxy and heterodoxy are historically situated and contingent. The content of legal orthodoxy varies depending on the area of law and over time. What is deemed to be part and parcel of orthodoxy in the Global North today – such as workers' compensation schemes and minimum wage laws – was once deemed heterodox.[56] Features of corporatism, as well as some aspects of the era of "social" legal thought,[57] were heterodox before they became part of legal orthodoxy in the Global North, and then fell out of favor. Heterodoxy today may become orthodoxy in the future, and vice versa. Importantly, what we describe as legal heterodoxy from a comparative standpoint – such as the incorporation of social justice objectives into contract law – is often perceived as orthodoxy from the internal perspective of Global South jurisdictions.

1.5.3 *Collapsing the Public/Private Distinction*

While our focus lies on legal heterodoxy in private law, we do not want to reify a public–private law distinction or insist on an artificial decoupling between private and public law developments. In fact, we reject the idea that public and private law are conceptually or causally independent. Our theory of legal heterodoxy suggests that developments in public and private law in the Global South may have common origins and are likely to co-evolve because the distinctive economic, social, political, and legal factors that prompt adaptations and innovations in private law may also call for a distinct vision of the state and its relationship to private actors.

We document multiple instances of the interrelationship of legal heterodoxy and innovative approaches to public law in the Global South. Some of these include "transformative" constitutions in the Global South, which have a symbiotic relationship with heterodox varieties of private law. Examples include explicit constitutional provisions on organizational law; judicial reliance on constitutional principles in reviewing and interpreting corporate law, contract law, and intellectual property; and constitutional justification for strong modes of consumer protection. Brazil's constitution explicitly challenges legal orthodoxy in private law by linking the

[56] M. J. Horwitz, *The Transformation of American Law, 1870–1960, The Crisis of Legal Orthodoxy* (New York: Oxford University Press, 1992) (for a prominent account of the transformation of the United States in moving away from the old legal orthodoxy embodied in classical legal thought).

[57] D. Kennedy, Three Globalizations of Law and Legal Thought: 1850–2000, in D. Trubek and A. Santos (eds.), *The New Law and Economic Development: A Critical Appraisal* (Cambridge: Cambridge University Press, 2006), pp. 19–73.

protection of intellectual property to the "social interest and technological and economic development of the country" – a provision that was included in anticipation of international lawmaking that culminated in the TRIPs agreement.[58]

1.5.4 *Formal versus Functional Divergence*

As we define it, legal heterodoxy encompasses significant divergences from orthodox private law doctrines, but we do not presume that these differences correlate tightly with differences in the outcomes that will be realized in jurisdictions with orthodox and heterodox legal institutions.[59] Legal systems that embrace orthodoxy and heterodoxy may even be functionally equivalent. Such a finding would be consistent with a well-established tradition in comparative law scholarship, which posits that similar economic and social problems necessitate, and produce, similar solutions in different jurisdictions – even if those solutions might be similar in function and outcome, not in form.[60] Yet, even in the face of functional convergence, the existence of heterodoxy might still undermine elements of the traditional view of legal systems in the Global South.

To the extent that heterodoxy simply entails greater acceptance of antimodularity, it definitely need not lead to functional divergence. In various areas of private law, the orthodox view is that conscious policy interventions are more legitimate if they come from legislatures rather than courts.[61] This raises the question whether legal heterodoxy

[58] M. Pargendler, Análise Econômica e Comparada do Art. 40, Parágrafo Único, da Lei de Propriedade Industrial, in A. Frazão, R. R. Monteiro de Castro and S. Campinho (eds.), *Direito Empresarial e suas Interfaces – Homenagem a Fabio Ulhoa Coelho* (São Paulo: Quartier Latin, 2023), vol. II, pp. 65–106. This study reflects an expert opinion on comparative law and law and economics about the constitutionality of the patent extension rule provided in the sole paragraph of art. 40 of the Industrial Property Law. The expert opinion was commissioned by FarmaBrasil, a trade association of Brazilian pharmaceutical manufacturers. Chapter 8, by Carlos Portugal Gouvêa, examines the same controversy.

[59] On the distinction between convergence of form and function, R. J. Gilson, Globalizing Corporate Governance: Convergence of Form or Function (2001) 49 *The American Journal of Comparative Law* 329–57.

[60] For works embracing such a functional approach, see Zweigert and Kötz, An Introduction to Comparative Law; R. Kraakman et al., *The Anatomy of Corporate Law: A Comparative and Functional Approach*, 3rd ed. (Oxford: Oxford University Press, 2017). See also R. Michaels, The Functional Method of Comparative Law, in M. Reimann and R. Zimmermann (eds.), *The Oxford Handbook of Comparative Law* (Oxford: Oxford University Press, 2006), pp. 339–82 (describing different modes and critiques of functionalism, including the dominant approach of "functional equivalence").

[61] See, e.g., K. A. Kordana and D. H. Blankfein-Tabachnick, Rawls and Contract Law (2005) 73 *The George Washington Law Review* 598–632, 623–24 (describing how John Rawls's first principle of justice requires non-constitutional institutions should be designed by a democratically elected legislature). Critical scholars have long resisted this view. See, e.g., D. Kennedy, Distributive and Paternalist Motives in Contract and Tort Law, with Special Reference to Compulsory Terms and Unequal Bargaining Power (1982) 41 *Maryland Law Review* 563–658, 564–65 (questioning the impact of "institutional competence" considerations by challenging the grounds for distinguishing between courts, legislatures and administrative agencies as

in the form of policy-infused judicial decision-making constitutes meaningful divergence from regimes in the Global North that pursue the same policies exclusively through legislation. Heterodox antimodular judicial decisions in the Global South may compensate for failures in the political process in reaching welfare-enhancing outcomes. In other words, judges in the Global South may do more precisely because legislatures do less.[62] This raises the possibility that at least some instances of legal heterodoxy in the Global South may mask functional convergence.

The contributions by Bianca Tavolari and Saylon Alves Pereira (Chapter 6) and by Carlos Portugal Gouvêa (Chapter 8) show how, in functional terms, there might be less to legal heterodoxy than meets the eye. Both chapters describe activist and socially-inspired decisions by Brazil's Supreme Court (imposing a moratorium on fast-track evictions in one case, and ruling a provision of the patent statute unconstitutional, in the other) that only serve to bring Brazilian law approximately into line with norms in the Global North. Nonetheless, the finding that an activist judiciary compensates for legislative failures in a developing country challenges the traditional view that developing countries generally lack judicial capacity.

Even when heterodoxy entails a system-wide commitment to different values or objectives, its direct effects may be mostly symbolic – yielding different optics and rhetoric without necessarily generating different outcomes, at least not directly. Several of the studies in this volume hint at this possibility. Benjamin Liebman et al.'s description of heterodox adjudication of Chinese tort cases in Chapter 5 distinguishes between larger awards, which can operate to create a safety net and compensate for a lack of insurance, and smaller awards, whose effects are mostly symbolic. In describing India's pioneering legal reform mandating spending on corporate social responsibility in Chapter 9, Vikramaditya Khanna highlights the role of optics in buying political legitimacy for market-oriented reforms: it was critical, in his view, that the payments were *seen* as coming from businesses, rather than the state. Neither of these studies rules out the possibility that heterodox institutions whose direct effects are purely symbolic still have important indirect effects.

1.5.5 *Progressive Politics*

The primary aims of this project are descriptive and conceptual: we seek to capture legal phenomena that have been ignored by existing scholarship and offer a framework for

lawmakers"); R. M. Unger, The Critical Legal Studies Movement (1983) 96 *Harvard Law Review* 561–675, 561, 565 (challenging "the belief that lawmaking and law application differ fundamentally").

62 R. Hirschl, *Comparative Matters: The Renaissance of Comparative Constitutional Law* (Oxford: Oxford University Press, 2014) (raising, and questioning, the "common and intuitively plausible claim" that "because the socioeconomic gaps in the global south are often considerably wider than those in the north, and because state capacity is, by and large, lower in the south, constitutional courts in these countries will be more inclined to intervene on behalf of the poor, or to support the constitutional recognition and progressive realization of social and economic rights").

understanding them. The main vision (or politics, if you will[63]) of this comparative law project is to augment the scope of comparative legal analysis in private law, and to reap the associated epistemological gains, with the aim of improving wellbeing and justice in the Global South and beyond. This commitment is, in theory, compatible with a vast array of legal responses and worldviews, but less so with those that are committed to the continued neglect of the particular conditions and values of the South.

This volume aims to document and interpret legal heterodoxies, not to *evaluate* them. It should not be read as glorifying heterodoxy, and disparaging orthodoxy, or vice versa. We leave this critical task – which is not without challenges, as discussed in Section 1.7 – to future work. Indeed, the contributors to this volume may have different views on these matters. Moreover, our theoretical framework suggests that context is key and that legal heterodoxies are unlikely to be uniformly "good" or "bad."

In choosing the orthodoxy/heterodoxy labels as our markers of North–South differences, we sought to use language that lacked a clear ideological or normative connotation, but we acknowledge that the valence of the terms is ambiguous. In our experience, the term heterodoxy functions analogously to a Rorschach test. Those who embrace orthodoxy are often proud of its tenets and ascendance and are disdainful of heterodoxy. Heterodox thinkers, by contrast, proudly view themselves as denouncing mistakes in dominant views. The label orthodoxy – in Greek, "right" (orthos) + "doxa" (opinion) – captures the current (though historically contingent) dominance and power of certain legal ideas and institutions, which critical scholars are, of course, happy to denounce. From this perspective, given past and continued instances of colonialism, present-day legal heterodoxy in the Global South is not "just another type of animal," but a subordinated type of animal.[64] This volume aims to help transform this vision.

In terms of political and ideological leanings, one could argue that modularity tilts right, and antimodularity tilts left. Viewed this way, there is a clear progressive overtone to legal heterodoxy in the Global South. However, that perspective is only valid if one assumes that heterodox policies are adopted in good faith and will be effective in achieving their objectives. A common critique of progressive policies is that their proponents are, wittingly or unwittingly, guilty of "hurting the people one's trying to help."[65]

1.5.6 *Civil Law Approaches*

Some of the distinctive features of legal heterodoxy resemble the features that, according to some scholars, distinguish civil law systems from common law systems,

[63] For a critique of the "no-method method" and "no-politics politics" of mainstream comparative law, see D. Kennedy, The Methods and the Politics, in P. Legrand and R. Munday (eds.), *Comparative Legal Studies: Traditions and Transitions* (Cambridge: Cambridge University Press, 2003), pp. 345–434.

[64] We thank Thiago Amparo for this comment and formulation.

[65] For a critique of such arguments, see D. Kennedy, The Bitter Ironies of Williams v. Walker-Thomas Furniture Co. in the First Year Law School Curriculum, Unpublished Working Paper, 2023.

but the concept of legal heterodoxy captures more than the distinction between common law and civil law. According to the economists behind the influential "legal origins" literature, a critical distinction between common law and civil law systems is that the latter are more likely to use private law to pursue policy objectives besides encouraging private contracting and protecting property rights.[66] Although we may disagree with aspects of their legal analysis, we agree that civil law institutions in Continental Europe are generally less modular than corresponding institutions in the United States and the United Kingdom.[67] At the same time, the European civil law institutions appear more modular than some of their counterparts in the Global South.

The idea that legal heterodoxy resembles but cannot be assimilated to distinctively civilian approaches to business law is consistent with several of the studies in our volume. Weitseng Chen's contribution on contract law in China (Chapter 4) and Jorge Esquirol's account of property and security interests in Latin America (Chapter 7) both argue that these jurisdictions have followed the civil law's greater amenability to antimodularity in their respective fields. At the same time, both chapters describe heterodox approaches that are not captured by the spectrum of solutions represented in Europe. Moreover, the contributions on corporate law in India by Vikramaditya S. Khanna (Chapter 9) and on India and South Africa by Mariana Pargendler (Chapter 10) reveal significant high-level commonalities between heterodox approaches in common law (India), civil law (Brazil and Colombia), and mixed jurisdictions (South Africa[68]) in embracing heterodox modes of stakeholder protection through corporate law. These shared features of legal institutions in the Global South have been obscured by comparative efforts, in both academic works and the World Bank's Doing Business reports, based on "hypermodular" metrics derived from a certain view of the US and UK common law experiences.

If there are significant commonalities among legal institutions in the Global South, then it may be time to reconsider the traditional method of classifying legal systems. For over a century, comparative lawyers have grouped legal systems into legal families defined by a dichotomy between the common law and civil law and,

[66] R. La Porta et al., Law and Finance (1998) 106 *Journal of Political Economy* 1113–55; La Porta, Lopez-de-Silanes, and Shleifer, The Economic Consequences of Legal Origins.

[67] H. Spamann, The "Antidirector Rights Index" Revisited (2010) 23 *The Review of Financial Studies* 467–86.

[68] Curiously, the "legal origins" literature classifies South Africa as a common law jurisdiction. See La Porta, Lopez-de-Silanes, and Shleifer, The Economic Consequences of Legal Origins. However, comparative law scholars typically categorize South Africa as a mixed legal system that blends elements of English common law, Dutch law, and local customary law. See, e.g., J. Du Plessis, Comparative Law and the Study of Mixed Legal Systems, in M. Reimann and R. Zimmermann (eds.), *The Oxford Handbook of Comparative Law* (Oxford: Oxford University Press, 2006), pp. 477–512.

within those two broad categories, proximity to the laws of individual European colonizing powers.[69] If our findings on heterodox stakeholder approaches to corporate law are replicated in other areas of law, then perhaps the traditional classification scheme should be revised to place large economies in the Global South in a class of their own.[70]

1.5.7 *Resistance to International Influence*

Legal heterodoxy marks a form of resistance to international forces that, more or less forcefully, aid in the diffusion of orthodoxy around the world. Those forces include, historically, colonialism. More recent examples include exercises of "soft" (and not so soft) power by modern states and international organizations such as legal technical assistance, harmonization projects, and governance indicators.[71] In recent years, international actors have often pressed countries in the Global South to embrace a distinctively neoliberal orthodoxy that favors providers of financial capital over other economic actors, and economic actors in the Global North over actors in the Global South. For instance, the orthodox view of debtor–creditor and bankruptcy law rejects its use to achieve objectives such as favoring specific industries (as described in Chapter 7 by Jorge Esquirol) or giving workers' claims priority over secured creditors.[72] Meanwhile, Pargendler argues in Chapter 10 that upholding limited liability of parent companies vis-à-vis the protection of stakeholders may systematically favor Global North companies and investors at the expense of Global South victims.

Legal heterodoxy in the Global North sometimes emerges as a direct reaction to international forces. The experience of South Africa described in Chapter 10 is illustrative in this regard. In 2010, a foreign investor filed suit under a bilateral

69 Pargendler, The Rise and Decline of Legal Families.

70 Cf. E. A. Farnsworth, A Common Lawyer's View of His Civilian Colleagues (1996) 57 *Louisiana Law Review* 227–238, 228 (noting "differences between industrialized and the developing countries," as well as differences "between the free market economies and the socialist countries").

71 T. C. Halliday and B. G. Carruthers, The Recursivity of Law: Global Norm Making and National Lawmaking in the Globalization of Corporate Insolvency Regimes (2007) 112 *American Journal of Sociology* 1135–202; K. Davis et al. (eds.), *Governance by Indicators: Global Power through Quantification and Rankings* (Oxford: Oxford University Press, 2012); Pargendler, The Rise of International Corporate Law.

72 See, e.g., The World Bank, *Principles and Guidelines for Effective Insolvency and Creditor Rights Systems: Introduction, Executive Summary and Principles* (Washington: World Bank Group, 2001) ("Any priority placed ahead of the secured party represents a substantial cost, which is generally transferred back to borrowers in the form of higher interest rates and transaction costs. Often the public policy represented by the priority (say, benefiting workers) receives a minor and occasional benefit at a substantial cost to the entire commercial system. Such priorities should be eliminated, reduced, and, where public policy concerns are compelling, addressed *by other legal reforms* that do not compromise the system for secured lending").

investment treaty, claiming that one of South Africa's initiative of Black Economic Empowerment initiatives (which required the transfer of 26 percent of mining assets to historically disadvantaged South Africans) constituted an expropriation and violated the obligation of fair and equitable treatment. While the case was settled before a final decision on the merits, it contributed to South Africa's decision to terminate various bilateral investment treaties and adopt the more heterodox Protection of Investment Act of 2015. The new legislation not only provides for dispute resolution in domestic courts, as opposed to international arbitral panels, but also recognizes considerations of "historical, social and economic inequalities" to "achieve the progressive realization of socio-economic rights."[73]

1.6 OVERVIEW OF THE VOLUME

The chapters in this volume document examples of legal heterodoxy in contract, property, tort law, as well as in the concept of legal personality in several parts of the Global South. As noted, the selection of countries and areas of law was determined in part by our knowledge of the authors and their availability. Consequently, this collection of studies is intended to be illustrative and provocative rather than comprehensive and definitive. In this section we summarize the chapters and their key findings.

1.6.1 *Summary of the Contributions*

Chapter 2 ("Contract Law and Inequality in the Global South"), by Kevin Davis and Mariana Pargendler, describes how courts in South Africa, Brazil, and Colombia have recently deviated from orthodoxy to embrace the task of using contract law to address societal inequality (as opposed to inequality between the parties to a contract). In a series of decisions, the Constitutional Court of South Africa has held that contract terms must conform to constitutional values, including the African value of *ubuntu*. *Ubuntu*, which relates to values of humanness, social justice, and solidarity, operates to infuse contract law with distributive considerations. For instance, the Court cited the legacy of racism and apartheid in disavowing prejudgment interest, noting its potentially catastrophic effect on consumer debtors. Brazilian courts repeatedly appeal to "social justice" in contract disputes, and have developed distinct doctrines to benefit weaker parties, such as by allowing consumers to terminate contracts for the purchase of real estate in installments through the payment of a limited judicially-imposed fine – thereby switching labor and real estate market risks from consumers to construction companies.

[73] M. A. Forere, The New South African Protection of Investment Act: Striking a Balance between Attraction of FDI and Redressing the Apartheid Legacies, in F. Morosini and M. R. S. Badin (eds.), *Reconceptualizing International Investment Law from the Global South* (Cambridge: Cambridge University Press, 2017), pp. 251–83, p. 252.

In Colombia, constitutional review applies to contract disputes potentially impinging on fundamental rights such as life, health, or the vital minimum, at least when affecting "subjects of special constitutional protection," such as the elderly, the ill, minors, the disabled, female heads of households, and persons earning less than the minimum wage. While the statute generally allows interruption of public service for nonpayment, the Court found that denial of water to a 54-year old woman who was the head of her household, physically incapable of working, and responsible for two minor sons, was disproportionate and unconstitutional. This chapter suggests that mounting inequality can increase the appeal of contract law heterodoxy and that the dominance of current contract law orthodoxy is neither universal nor inevitable.

In Chapter 3 ("Reducing Inequality in Consumer Transactions"), María Guadalupe Martínez Alles contrasts the different approaches to consumer protection in the European Union and in Latin America. Even though EU consumer law has been hailed as too interventionist compared to US law in this area,[74] it is more timid and far less imbued with distributive considerations than the laws of Latin American jurisdictions. Martínez describes EU consumer law as traditionally focused on *consumer empowerment* based on the paradigmatic *average consumer* – with the primary goal of EU law in this area being regulatory harmonization in service of economic integration. By contrast, consumer protection in Argentina, as in Latin America more generally, centers on the broader goal of *consumer protection* based on a paradigm of the *vulnerable consumer*, a concept that both pays greater heed to inequality and is more sensitive to context-specific forms of vulnerability. Recent reforms in Argentine consumer protection law have accentuated its heterodox traits by introducing a regime of enhanced protection for *hypervulnerable* consumers, defined as those in a situation of aggravated vulnerability due to age, gender, physical or mental state, or social, economic, ethnic, and/or cultural circumstances. At the same time, European scholars have begun advocating for the concept of "structural vulnerabilities" in the context of the digital economy, which happens to be dominated by US companies.

Chapter 4, by Weitseng Chen ("Contracts, Inequality, and the State"), examines contract disputes in China during the pandemic. He argues that, in many respects, Chinese legal responses resembled those implemented elsewhere in Asia and in other civil law jurisdictions. For instance, to the extent they applied contract law doctrine, Chinese courts used the change in circumstances provision of the Civil Code to alter or waive contractual obligations that would result in unfairness or inequality. Similarly, like their counterparts in other countries, Chinese regulators required lenders to grant temporary, procedural relief to debtors and encouraged

[74] For a critical appraisal of European consumer protection from an orthodox US perspective, see O. Bar-Gill and O. Ben-Shahar, Regulatory Techniques in Consumer Protection: A Critique of European Consumer Contract Law (2013) 50 *Common Market Law Review* 109–26.

landlords to reduce rents for tenants. Chen's ultimate argument, however, is that Chinese courts, the Party and government officials used distinctive "ultra-heterodox" measures to alter or nullify contractual terms in cases that raised serious concerns about inequality, social unrest, or systemic financial risk. Specifically, courts would refer such disputes to either mediation, insolvency, or a "macro-prudential" proceeding that involved courts collaborating with government agencies, party officials, and stakeholders of firms experiencing financial distress to negotiate and implement resolutions of disputes. These procedures allow the party-state to achieve its objectives of preventing market disruption, social unrest, and financial crisis triggered by unfair and unequal contracts. These objectives may diverge from the interests of either party to the contract, which would be the focus of orthodox contract doctrine.

Chen argues that Chinese ultra-heterodoxy can be explained in part by distinctive elements of the Chinese situation, namely, the dominance of the party-state and widespread acceptance among contracting parties of a communitarian understanding of liability and responsibility. He also points out that having courts and state actors determine risk allocation at the enforcement stage relieves contracting parties of the costs of allocating risks at the contract formation stage. Chen also suggests that this shift in responsibility for risk allocation may be efficient in emerging markets where there are a relatively large number of material risks to address.

In Chapter 5 ("Tort Law Heterodoxy in China"), Benjamin Liebman, Rachel Stern, Eva Wenwa Gao, and Xiaohan Wu explore how Chinese courts use concepts of fairness and justice to impose liability in tort cases. China's civil code provisions on "equitable liability" allowed courts to impose liability on defendants who had the ability to pay even if they had tenuous links to the accident and were neither negligent nor within the limited set of cases subject to strict liability. These provisions, which reflected China's socialist legal heritage, produced significant debate in China, and were curtailed by the Civil Code that came into effect in 2021. Liebman et al. read over 2,000 cases, including a representative sample drawn from a dataset of over 9,000 cases released between 2013 and 2018 that cited the equitable liability provisions. They also read cases that used phrases associated with fairness or dealt with child drowning or death-by-drinking, several of which did not cite the provisions on equitable liability. They identified two broad types of cases in which Chinese courts relied on fairness as a basis for imposing liability: "participant liability" and "space-based liability." In cases of the first type the parties were participating in the same activity. In the second type of case the parties were either businesses and their customers or employees, or public institutions and their users. They found that courts continued to impose liability on these bases in the years immediately after the Civil Code came into effect. Liebman et al. describe these forms of loss sharing as "blunting the sharp edges of inequality by redistributing wealth." They interpret these judicial practices as a form of "socialist tort law heterodoxy" that may survive the shift of formal law toward orthodoxy.

In Chapter 6 ("Evictions during the Pandemic"), Bianca Tavolari and Saylon Alves Pereira compare the regimes that govern evictions of residential tenants in the United States and Brazil during the COVID-19 pandemic. It shows how seemingly heterodox and activist decisions by a Global South court can in fact represent substantive convergence (if imperfect) to Global North solutions – with the judiciary effectively compensating for the legislature's failure to act. Tavolari and Pereira describe how the US Congress enacted a temporary evictions moratorium as part of the CARES Act, which was signed into law by President Trump on = March 27, 2020. Initially valid for 120 days, the federal moratorium was successively extended by Congress until July 2021. When the legislative moratorium expired in 2021, the Centers for Disease Control announced a new moratorium, though its authority to do so was successfully challenged before the US Supreme Court.

Ironically, it was precisely in July 2021 – well into the second year of the pandemic – that the Brazilian Supreme Court placed restrictions on evictions, despite the absence of legislative action. The interim decision by Justice Luis Roberto Barroso is heterodox in appealing to the constitutional right to health and housing of vulnerable persons during the COVID-19 pandemic to impose restrictions on evictions. From a functional standpoint, however, the decision was "too little, too late" compared to the US response. The decision came only after it became clear that the legislature would not act to address this problem, since a timid statutory provision suspending fast-track evictions – for example, a special procedure for eviction in 15 days without hearing the tenant – expired in October 2020 after being in force for only two months. Moreover, far from offering a broad moratorium on evictions, the Brazilian Supreme Court's decision (like the previous short-lived statutory response) only prevented *fast-track* evictions. Interestingly, Tavolari and Pereira show how flawed distributional arguments were invoked to frustrate a more ambitious response, by both the legislature and the judiciary. While opponents of the eviction ban and Justice Barroso expressed concern about how a moratorium on evictions could have perverse distributional consequences in harming vulnerable landlords, Tavolari and Pereira challenge this argument with data showing that tenants are on average far poorer and more numerous than landlords.

In Chapter 7 ("Heterodox Legal Informality"), Jorge L. Esquirol describes different strands of heterodoxy in property law and the law of security interests in Latin America. He notes that heterodox approaches to property law have a long historical pedigree in the region, ranging from a right to extinguish title without compensation in Colombia in the early twentieth century to the constitutional protection of *campesino* lands in Mexico which lasted until recently. Esquirol observes that what counts as heterodoxy is historically and geographically contingent, with some of these earlier manifestations of socially-inspired legal innovation following the globalization of "social law" in the first part of the last century.

Esquirol then spotlights two recent developments in the law governing property and security interests in the region. On the one hand, he identifies an orthodox turn in the law of security interests, resulting from pressures by international organizations (such as the Organization of American States, the World Bank, and UNCITRAL) to adopt the US liberal and "nonselective" model. This illustrates how international organizations seek to promote modularity through private law. Prior to the reforms, selective models of secured lending – which offered a favored regime to certain sectors – served as channels for the implementation of industrial policy through private law, both in Latin America and in continental European jurisdictions such as France and Italy. On the other hand, Esquirol describes new emerging forms of legal heterodoxy in Latin America, as exemplified by Colombia's transitory property regime adopted in 2011 to address the wrongs of property's despoilment generated by the country's civil conflicts. In lieu of command-and-control regulation, Colombia modified the basic private law rules of ownership to introduce modified presumptions and burdens of proof. Esquirol also formulates a broader critique of the use of "informality" as a label that proponents of orthodoxy use to disqualify heterodox features of legal systems in the Global South as antiquated and dysfunctional. Instead, he shows that elements of formality and informality in property rights coexist both in Global North and Global South legal systems, even if the precise locus of informality can differ in each case.

Chapter 8, by Carlos Portugal Gouvêa ("Heterodoxy of the Brazilian Supreme Court"), considers intellectual property law. He focuses on a decision of the Brazilian Supreme Court overturning a statute that he describes as "ultra-orthodox" because it allowed patent terms to be extended for a period longer than any patent law regime in the world. Portugal Gouvêa explains the Brazilian legislature's support for ultra-orthodoxy by reference to the influence of foreign economic interests, specifically the international pharmaceutical industry. He also notes that some of the dissenting judges defended the statute based on the works of foreign law-and-economics and constitutional scholars without citing any supporting empirical evidence.

Portugal Gouvêa identifies several heterodox features of the Court's reasoning and procedure, such as its attention to distributional considerations, reliance on human rights norms, reference to comparative and empirical analyses that included experiences in the Global South, and openness to interventions by academics independent of interested parties. Portugal Gouvêa acknowledges that the effects of the decision may yet be undone by legislative and judicial backlash. Moreover, even in the absence of effective backlash, the ultimate effect of the decision may be only to bring Brazilian law into line with the provisions of the TRIPS agreement, a quintessentially orthodox instrument. In that case the court's heterodoxy will have merely balanced out a legislative tendency toward ultra-orthodoxy, echoing the argument made by Tavolari and Pereira in Chapter 6.

In Chapter 9 ("The Political Economy of India's Corporate Social Responsibility Reforms"), Vikramaditya S. Khanna examines India's pioneering decision to mandate corporate spending on corporate social responsibility (CSR). The new provision introduced in the Companies Act of 2013 required companies exceeding certain thresholds to either spend 2 percent of average profits on CSR activities defined by the government or explain why they did not do so. Khanna aims to address an apparent puzzle: why did India opt for a CSR spending requirement rather than using a tax on the same firms to fund increased social spending? He argues that India's heterodox CSR spending rules responded both to considerations of limited state capacity (relative to the capacity of private firms) and to the optics of the reform. Prior to the reform, there was rising concern that the previous wave of market-oriented liberalization had led to rising income and wealth inequality. In this context, the CSR spending requirement was superior to a tax in making it *look like* firms, rather than the state, were benefitting the citizenry. The chapter thus illustrates how, in contexts of mounting inequalities, legal heterodoxy may serve to legitimate – and therefore buy political support for – market-based institutions.

In Chapter 10 ("Corporate Law in the Global South"), Mariana Pargendler documents and analyzes the incorporation of a diverse array of policy and distributional objectives in the corporate laws of developing countries, an approach she terms "heterodox stakeholderism." The instances of heterodox stakeholderism in the Global South include the mitigation of limited liability in India and its elimination in Brazil vis-à-vis various stakeholders, such as workers, consumers, and victims of environmental harm; the adoption of mandatory corporate social responsibility in Indonesia and India; the requirement of social responsibility committees in India and South Africa; workers' and unions' rights to enforce directors' duties in South Africa; and a large-scale program of Black corporate ownership and empowerment in South Africa, among many others. Beyond addressing inequality and externalities, Pargendler argues that heterodox stakeholderism in the Global South also responds to distributional implications of corporate law rules along North–South lines. For instance, limited liability for environmental harm caused by corporate subsidiaries tends to enrich Global North companies and investors at the expense of Global South victims. She also suggests that the dearth of South–South comparison has produced an "odd-duck syndrome" in the comparative literature, to the effect that the heterodox regimes of individual developing jurisdictions are described as unique, even if similar responses exist in other Global South countries. Pargendler then describes the recent resurgence of stakeholderism in corporate laws of developed countries as a form of "reverse convergence," with Global North regimes converging to approaches previously embraced in the Global South, rather than the other way around.

Last but not least, Daniel Bonilla Maldonado's Chapter 11 ("Global Legal Pluralism and the Rights of Nature") considers a particularly striking example of heterodoxy: legal recognition of rights of nature. Several countries have recognized natural objects as legal subjects entitled to protection of their rights and have created systems of representation to enable those rights to be defended. This development is a radical departure from the orthodox view that only human beings and legal entities established by human beings or other legal entities can be legal subjects and that nature is only an object to be dominated by human beings. Bonilla Maldonado argues that rights of nature are a hybrid legal product that reflects the expression of indigenous traditions in the grammar and vocabulary of modern law.

Bonilla Maldonado's focus in this chapter is on the emergence and diffusion of discourse about rights of nature. He identifies three distinct types of discourse about the topic: poietic, mimetic, and resistance. Poietic patterns define and support recognition of rights to nature and emerged in the legal systems of Ecuador, Bolivia, and New Zealand (although, interestingly, a US NGO played an important role). Mimetic patterns reproduce and sometimes modify the poietic patterns. These discourses have appeared in several countries in the Global South, as well as in countries such as Australia, Canada, and Spain. Finally, discourses of resistance oppose recognition of rights of nature and are particularly prevalent in Europe. Bonilla Maldonado argues that the diffusion of discourse supporting rights of nature from peoples and countries which tend to be peripheral in global legal dialogue to countries in both the Global North and South upsets the traditional view that legal knowledge typically diffuses from central actors in the Global North.

1.6.2 *Key Findings*

The main contribution of these chapters is to illustrate the variety of forms that legal heterodoxy can take. For instance, many of the chapters describe developments in substantive doctrines and underlying conceptions of legal personality that lead to deviations from orthodox outcomes in contract, tort, and property law. Some chapters focus on heterodox reasoning rather than the outcomes, such as the Brazilian courts' reliance on human rights norms to supplement or challenge legislation governing rights over real and intellectual property. These Brazilian cases also highlight the fact that seemingly heterodox legal developments might simply offset the orthodoxy-enhancing effects of other components of the legal systems. This possibility calls into question the feasibility of assessing the overall level of orthodoxy or heterodoxy of a legal system.

Some of the examples of heterodoxy involve deviations from the orthodox procedures used to generate private law norms and to resolve private disputes. These include the use of mediation, insolvency, and macro-prudential approaches in China.

The chapters also display the range of policy objectives, or combinations of objectives, which can be embodied in heterodox approaches. Some of the examples of heterodoxy involve attempts to protect or benefit vulnerable groups in society. These sorts of distributional objectives appear to underlie the contract law doctrines discussed by Davis and Pargendler and Martínez Alles, the protections against eviction discussed by Tavolari and Pereira, and the corporate law initiatives described by both Pargendler and Khanna. Khanna raises the possibility that

India's reliance on corporate law to induce private firms to help achieve distributional objectives might have been an efficient response to the Indian state's limited capacity to achieve those ends on its own.

The chapters in this volume also contain indications that legal heterodoxy can be used to pursue other objectives, including objectives that seem to be especially important in societies in the Global South. Esquirol explains how heterodox sector-specific versions of the law of secured transactions can be used to pursue industrial policy by influencing the cost of credit in certain sectors. He also explains how property law in Colombia has been deliberately altered to compensate for the effects of civil conflict. Pargendler suggests that certain aspects of corporate law in the Global South represent efforts to influence the distribution of wealth between domestic actors and actors based in the Global North. Chen argues that the ultra-heterodox elements of Chinese contract law may qualify as an efficient response to a risky environment, but he also suggests they are designed to maintain social, political, and financial stability. Liebman argues that Chinese tort law is also designed to provide social stability, but also serves as a form of social insurance.

Some of the chapters point out that heterodox legal developments serve to express distinctive local values and to legitimate certain institutions as opposed to merely influencing behavior or the distribution of resources.[75] For instance, Davis and Pargendler identify respect for the African value of *ubuntu* as part of the underpinning for the reasoning in South African contracts cases. Chen and Liebman et al. suggest that Chinese courts' decisions in contracts and torts cases, respectively, are consistent with local communitarian values. And Bonilla Maldonado emphasizes that recognition of rights of nature is grounded in the practices and beliefs of indigenous peoples in Ecuador, Bolivia, and New Zealand. Meanwhile, Khanna argues that India's mandatory corporate social responsibility law helped to legitimate the Indian state at a critical juncture.

Most of the chapters focus on challenging the traditional view that orthodoxy fully captures formal laws in the Global South by documenting and explaining the emergence of legal heterodoxy in a single country's legal system, but some go further and discuss South–South diffusion or convergence between the Global North and Global South. Bonilla Maldonado's chapter documents an example of legal heterodoxy diffusing from the Global South and the periphery of the Global North to other sites in both the Global South and the Global North. After evaluating various instances of "heterodox stakeholderism" in the corporate laws of Global South jurisdictions, Pargendler suggests that the current renaissance of stakeholder approaches in the Global North represents an unforeseen form of "reverse

[75] There are, to be sure, numerous non-instrumental and value-oriented accounts of private laws in the Global North. See, e.g., J. C. P. Goldberg and B. C. Zipursky, *Recognizing Wrongs* (Cambridge, MA: Harvard University Press, 2020); D. Markovits, Contract and Collaboration (2004) 113 *Yale Law Journal* 1417–518.

convergence." As the Global North faces growing socio-economic and environmental challenges it will look more like the Global South and may resort to similar legal responses. Likewise, the analysis by Maria Guadalupe Martínez Alles of consumer protection in Latin America and the European Union suggests that reverse convergence may well be on the horizon, with EU scholars increasingly calling for a more protective approach based on "structural vulnerabilities" in the digital economy.

1.7 A RESEARCH AGENDA

An important aim of this volume is to stimulate additional research on legal heterodoxy in the Global South and beyond. The hope is that, by providing examples of studies of legal heterodoxy, we will inspire scholars to pay more attention to the distinctive attributes of the work being done by courts, legislators, and regulators in the Global South. The fruits of these efforts will benefit both scholars and lawmakers.

The focus of the contributions in this volume is on describing rather than explaining instances of legal heterodoxy. Many of the chapters also identify basic structural conditions that explain the emergence of legal heterodoxy. However, in most of the cases there is additional room to explore the sociology and political economy that have led to specific legal developments, as well as their economic consequences. To what extent is legal heterodoxy a bottom-up or a top-down process? What are the roles of elites and social movements? What processes led to the adoption of heterodox doctrines? What is the degree of South–South or South–North diffusion (or suppression) of legal heterodoxy? What are the relevant actors and institutional channels? What are the economic consequences of legal heterodoxy? Do heterodox rules help transform the allocation of wealth and power, legitimize and maintain the status quo, or instead have the perverse effects of reinforcing poverty, inequality, and injustice?

Subsequent stages of the research agenda should strive to go beyond description or explanation and attempt to evaluate legal heterodoxy and predict its future course. We suspect, however, that moving on to those modes of analysis will be challenging. Lawmakers in the Global South embrace a diverse set of objectives and values that diverge not only from those embedded in legal orthodoxy but also, potentially, from the ones favored by other lawmakers in the Global South. This normative diversity creates a significant probability that any given heterodox approach will be designed to pursue objectives that diverge from the values or objectives favored by the person evaluating them.

Turning to prediction, the challenge will be to sort through the many possible futures of legal heterodoxy. One possible future, as suggested by Bonilla Maldonado's study of rights of nature, is diffusion. We have documented several examples of legal heterodoxy that respond to conditions that are widespread in the

Global South and suspect that there are many more. It seems plausible to expect that such responses will diffuse to countries that experience similar conditions, particularly if they receive positive evaluations. Another possibility is convergence across the North–South divide. This seems especially plausible when we consider that many of the conditions that stimulate heterodoxy are also present in the Global North. Moreover, as Esquirol, Bonilla Malsonado, and others point out, some examples of legal heterodoxy represent approaches that have been considered and rejected in the Global North. This last point suggests yet another possibility: legal heterodoxy will be resisted and eventually defeated by the forces of orthodoxy.

All these predictions about whether jurisdictions will converge upon or reject heterodoxy seem likely to depend, at least in part, upon whether the relevant form of heterodoxy receives positive evaluations from key actors. Consequently, the tasks of prediction and evaluation appear to be inextricably linked.

Finally, while our principal goal is to extend the scholarly literature, research on legal heterodoxy is also potentially valuable to lawmakers. Like other branches of comparative law, research on legal heterodoxy promises to expand the range of possibilities that lawmakers consider when contemplating reforms. Expanding the imagination in this way is particularly important for lawmakers in the Global South who might otherwise only consider orthodox options that are poorly suited to local conditions.

1.8 RELATIONSHIP TO EXISTING LITERATURE

The research agenda sketched in this chapter relates to, and builds on, several strands of existing literature. Scholars associated with legal pluralism, comparative constitutional law and TWAIL, as well as critical or decolonial approaches to comparative law have all documented deviations from legal orthodoxy in developing countries.[76] The line of scholarship on "varieties of capitalism" explores the role of institutional complementarities in various areas of law, suggesting that different bundles of institutional features produce comparative advantages in different modes of production.[77] While Alisha Holland has characterized forbearance from enforcement of legal norms as a form of politically motivated redistribution, we explore how distributional objectives have shaped the very content of legal rules in the Global

[76] Maldonado, Legal Barbarians. Salaymeh and Michaels, Decolonial Comparative Law.

[77] P. Hall and D. Soskice, *Varieties of Capitalism: The Institutional Foundations of Comparative Advantage* (Oxford: Oxford University Press, 2001); B. R. Schneider, *Hierarchical Capitalism in Latin America: Business, Labor, and the Challenges of Equitable Development* (Cambridge: Cambridge University Press, 2013). The concept of institutional complementarities refers to the idea that the effectiveness of an institution depends on its relationship to other institutions. An institution is complementary to another institution when it raises the returns from the former. Hall and Soskice famously argued that certain private law institutions, such as corporate law and contract law, are complementary to legal institutions in other fields, such as institutions of industrial relations, education and training, and labor and employment laws.

South.[78] In addition, the burgeoning literature on Chinese law yields many insights about both justifications for and potential consequences of deviating from legal orthodoxy.[79] The literature on critical legal studies (CLS) and law and political economy (LPE) draws attention to the conformation of power and wealth distribution through private law rules.[80]

Our proposed research agenda diverges from these other approaches in terms of emphasis and object of study. The literature on legal pluralism and, perhaps to a lesser extent, decolonial approaches, tends to emphasize the importance of non-state law. TWAIL is, naturally, focused on international law. The literature on comparative constitutional law is, of course, focused on constitutional law. Holland's research on regulatory forbearance focuses on variations in levels of enforcement, rather than on the content of legal doctrine. Beyond discursive contributions, both CLS and LPE are highly US centric, and have largely neglected comparative law, in general, and Global South legal institutions, in particular. The literature on varieties of capitalism leaves aside multiple areas of private law, such as property, torts, and consumer protection, and pays little attention to legal doctrines and judicial decisions, even in areas that it examines more closely, such as corporate, contract, and labor laws. By contrast, we propose to focus on domestic law and doctrines, including those of central areas of private law, emanating from state sources. We focus on the content of legal norms rather than how they are enforced. We also propose to emphasize the production of scholarship aimed at international audiences in order to explore potential opportunities for mutual learning across countries. Finally, our project is inspired by and arguably subsumed within critical approaches to comparative law devoted to documenting deviations from legal orthodoxy. However, we focus on a specific class of deviations that are consistent with a specific set of theoretical explanations.

BIBLIOGRAPHY

Acemoglu, D. et al., Institutional Causes, Macroeconomic Symptoms: Volatility, Crises and Growth (2003) 50 *Journal of Monetary Economics* 49–123.

Acuña, R. M., Comparación Jurídica desde el Sur Global: Genealogía de un Proyecto Crítico (2018) 73 *Themis Revista de Derecho* 131–45.

Alfaro, L., Gains from Foreign Direct Investment: Macro and Micro Approaches (2017) 30 *The World Bank Economic Review* S2–15.

78 A. C. Holland, *Forbearance as Redistribution: The Politics of Informal Welfare in Latin America* (Cambridge: Cambridge University Press, 2017).

79 D. Kennedy and J. Stiglitz (eds.), *Law and Economics with Chinese Characteristics: Institutions for Promoting Development in the Twenty-First Century* (Oxford: Oxford University Press, 2013).

80 Unger, The Critical Legal Studies Movement; J. Britton-Purdy et al., Building a Law-and-Political-Economy Framework: Beyond the Twentieth-Century Synthesis (2020) 129 *Yale Law Journal* 1784–1835.

Alfaro, L. and Chauvin, J., Foreign Direct Investment, Finance and Economic Development, in M. Spatareanu (ed.), *Encyclopedia of International Economics and Global Trade* (Singapore: World Scientific, 2020), vol. I, pp. 231–58.

Bahamón, G. Z., Constitucionalización y Protección de Derechos Fundamentales en el Contrato de Seguros. Análisis Jurisprudencial-Corte Constitucional de Colombia (2016) 25 *Revista Ibero-Latinoamericana de seguros* 233–68.

Bar-Gill, O. and Ben-Shahar, O., Regulatory Techniques in Consumer Protection: A Critique of European Consumer Contract Law (2013) 50 *Common Market Law Review* 109–26.

Barriola, I., Deffains, B., and Musy, O., Law and Inequality: A Comparative Approach to the Distributive Implications of Legal Systems, Working Paper 114037, Munich Personal RePEc Archive (2022).

Basheer, S., Trumping Trips: Indian Patent Proficiency and the Evolution of an Evergreening Enigma (2018) 18 *Oxford University Commonwealth Law Journal* 16–45.

Benoit, P., China Is Developing and Developed at the Same Time, *Foreign Policy*, May 23, 2023.

Black, B. and Kraakman, R., A Self-Enforcing Model of Corporate Law (1996) 109 *Harvard Law Review* 1911–82.

Blanchet, T., Chancel, L., and Gethin, A., Why Is Europe More Equal than the United States? (2022) 14 *American Economic Journal: Applied Economics* 480–518.

Bozio, A. et al., Predistribution vs. Redistribution: Evidence from France and the US, Working Paper 24, Center for Research in Economics and Statistics (2020).

Britton-Purdy, J. et al., Building a Law-and-Political-Economy Framework: Beyond the Twentieth-Century Synthesis (2020) 129 *Yale Law Journal* 1784–835.

China Africa Research Initiative, *Chinese Investment in Africa*, Johns Hopkins School of Advanced International Studies, 2022.

Chua, A. L., The Paradox of Free Market Democracy: Rethinking Development Policy (2000) 41 *Harvard International Law Journal* 287–380.

Dann, P., Riegner, M., and Bönnemann, M., The Southern Turn in Comparative Constitutional Law: An Introduction, in P. Dann, M. Riegner, and M. Bönnemann (eds.), *The Global South and Comparative Constitutional Law* (Oxford. Oxford University Press, 2020), pp. 1–36.

Davis, K., Legal Universalism: Persistent Objections (2010) 60 *University of Toronto Law Journal* 537–53.

Davis, K. and Kruse, M. B., Taking the Measure of Law: The Case of the Doing Business Project (2007) 32 *Law & Social Inquiry* 1095–1119.

Davis, K. and Pargendler, M., Contract Law and Inequality (2022) 107 *Iowa Law Review* 1485–1541.

Davis, K. et al. (eds.), *Governance by Indicators: Global Power through Quantification and Rankings* (Oxford: Oxford University Press, 2012).

Dincecco, M., *State Capacity and Economic Development: Present and Past* (Cambridge: Cambridge University Press, 2017).

Du Plessis, J., Comparative Law and the Study of Mixed Legal Systems, in M. Reimann and R. Zimmermann (eds.), *The Oxford Handbook of Comparative Law* (Oxford: Oxford University Press, 2006), pp. 477–512.

Easterly, W. and Levine, R., The European Origins of Economic Development (2016) 21 *Journal of Economic Growth* 225–57.

Easterly, W., Islam, R. and Stiglitz, J. E., Shaken and Stirred: Explaining Growth Volatility, in B. Pleskovic and N. Stern (eds.), *Annual World Bank Conference on Development Economics 2000* (Washington: The World Bank, 2001), pp. 191–211.

Esquirol, J. L., *The Fictions of Latin American Law and Their Strategic Uses: Legitimacy and Failure in Latin American Legal Systems* (Cambridge: Cambridge University Press, 2019).

Farnsworth, E. A., A Common Lawyer's View of His Civilian Colleagues (1996) 57 *Louisiana Law Review* 227–38.

Fiorentini, F., Legal Transplants in the Law of Secured Transactions. Current Problems and Comparative Perspectives, in F. Fiorentini and M. Infantino (eds.), *Mentoring Comparative Lawyers: Methods, Times, and Places: Liber Discipulorum Mauro Bussani* (New York: Springer, 2020), pp. 3–23.

Forere, M. A., The New South African Protection of Investment Act: Striking a Balance between Attraction of FDI and Redressing the Apartheid Legacies, in F. Morosini and M. R. S. Badin (eds.), *Reconceptualizing International Investment Law from the Global South* (Cambridge: Cambridge University Press, 2017), pp. 251–83.

Frankenberg, G., Critical Comparisons: Re-thinking Comparative Law (1985) 26 *Harvard International Law Journal* 411–56.

Comparative Law as Critique (Northampton: Edward Elgar, 2016).

Gilson, R. J., Globalizing Corporate Governance: Convergence of Form or Function (2001) 49 *The American Journal of Comparative Law* 329–57.

Gilson, R. J., Hansmann, H., and Pargendler, M., Regulatory Dualism as a Development Strategy: Corporate Reform in Brazil, the United States, and the European Union (2011) 63 *Stanford Law Review* 475–537.

Goldberg, J. C. P. and Zipursky, B. C., *Recognizing Wrongs* (Cambridge, MA: Harvard University Press, 2020).

Greenleaf, G., Global Data Privacy Laws 2021: Despite Covid Delays, 145 Laws Show GDPR Dominance (2021) 169 *Privacy Laws & Business International Report* 1, 3–5, UNSW Law Research Paper No. 21-60, Available at SSRN: https://ssrn.com/abstract=3836348 or http://dx.doi.org/10.2139/ssrn.3836348

Hall, P. and Soskice, D., *Varieties of Capitalism: The Institutional Foundations of Comparative Advantage* (Oxford: Oxford University Press, 2001).

Halliday, T. C. and Carruthers, B. G., The Recursivity of Law: Global Norm Making and National Lawmaking in the Globalization of Corporate Insolvency Regimes (2007) 112 *American Journal of Sociology* 1135–202.

Hirschl, R., *Comparative Matters. The Renaissance of Comparative Constitutional Law* (Oxford: Oxford University Press, 2014).

Holland, A. C., *Forbearance as Redistribution: The Politics of Informal Welfare in Latin America* (Cambridge: Cambridge University Press, 2017).

Horwitz, M. J., *The Transformation of American Law, 1870–1960, The Crisis of Legal Orthodoxy* (New York: Oxford University Press, 1992).

Kaplow, L. and Shavell, S., Why the Legal System Is Less Efficient than the Income Tax in Redistributing Income (1994) 23 *Journal of Legal Studies* 667–81.

Kennedy, D., Distributive and Paternalist Motives in Contract and Tort Law, with Special Reference to Compulsory Terms and Unequal Bargaining Power (1982) 41 *Maryland Law Review* 563–658.

The Bitter Ironies of Williams v. Walker-Thomas Furniture Co. in the First Year Law School Curriculum, Unpublished Working Paper, 2023.

The Methods and the Politics, in P. Legrand and R. Munday (eds.), *Comparative Legal Studies: Traditions and Transitions* (Cambridge: Cambridge University Press, 2003), pp. 345–434.

Three Globalizations of Law and Legal Thought: 1850–2000, in D. Trubek and A. Santos (eds.), *The New Law and Economic Development: A Critical Appraisal* (Cambridge: Cambridge University Press, 2006), pp. 19–73.

Kennedy, D. and Stiglitz, J. (eds.), *Law and Economics with Chinese Characteristics: Institutions for Promoting Development in the Twenty-First Century* (Oxford: Oxford University Press, 2013).

King, A. S. and Bookman, P. K., Traveling Judges (2022) 116 *American Journal of International Law*, 477–533.

Kordana, K. A. and Blankfein-Tabachnick, D. H., Rawls and Contract Law (2005) 73 *The George Washington Law Review* 598–632.

Kovvali, A., Stakeholderism Silo Busting (2022) 90 *University of Chicago Law Review* 203–60.

Kraakman, R. et al., *The Anatomy of Corporate Law: A Comparative and Functional Approach*, 2nd ed. (Oxford: Oxford University Press, 2009).

The Economic Consequences of Legal Origins (2008) 46 *Journal of Economic Literature* 285–332.

Legrand, P., The Impossibility of "Legal Transplants" (1997) 4 *Maastricht Journal of European and Comparative Law* 111–24.

Levander, C. and Mignolo, W., Introduction: The Global South and World Dis/Order (2011) 5 *The Global South* 1–11.

Loayza, N. V. et al., Macroeconomic Volatility and Welfare in Developing Countries: An Introduction (2007) 21 *The World Bank Economic Review* 343–57.

Maldonado, D. B. (ed.), *Constitutionalism of the Global South: The Activist Tribunals of India, South Africa, and Colombia* (Cambridge: Cambridge University Press, 2013).

Legal Barbarians: Identity, Modern Comparative Law and the Global South (Cambridge, Cambridge University Press, 2021).

Mallat, C., Comparative Law and the Islamic (Middle Eastern) Legal Culture, in M. Reimann and R. Zimmermann (eds.), *The Oxford Handbook of Comparative Law*, 2nd ed. (Oxford: Oxford University Press, 2019), pp. 624–651.

Markovits, D., Contract and Collaboration (2004) 113 *Yale Law Journal* 1417–518.

Mattei, U., Three Patterns of Law: Taxonomy and Change in the World's Legal Systems (1997) 45 *The American Journal of Comparative Law* 5–44.

Michaels, R., The Functional Method of Comparative Law, in M. Reimann and R. Zimmermann (eds.), *The Oxford Handbook of Comparative Law* (Oxford: Oxford University Press, 2006), pp. 339–82.

Milhaupt, C. and Pargendler, M., Related Party Transactions in State-Owned Enterprises: Tunneling, Propping, and Policy Channeling, in L. Enriques and T. Tröger (eds.), *The Law and Finance of Related Party Transactions (International Corporate Law and Financial Market Regulation)* (Cambridge: Cambridge University Press, 2019), pp. 245–59.

Morosini, F. and Badin, M. R. S. (eds.), *Reconceptualizing International Investment Law from the Global South* (Cambridge: Cambridge University Press, 2017).

OECD, *Revenue Statistics in Latin America and the Caribbean – Brazil* (Paris: OECD, 2023).

Pargendler, M., Análise Econômica e Comparada do Art. 40, Parágrafo Único, da Lei de Propriedade Industrial, in A. Frazão, R. R. Monteiro de Castro, and S. Campinho (eds.), *Direito Empresarial e suas Interfaces – Homenagem a Fabio Ulhoa Coelho* (São Paulo: Quartier Latin, 2023), vol. II, pp. 65–106.

Pargendler, M., Controlling Shareholders in the 21st Century: Complicating Corporate Governance beyond Agency Costs (2020) 45 *Journal of Corporation Law* 953–75.

The Grip of Nationalism on Corporate Law (2020) 95 *Indiana Law Journal* 533–90.
Politics in the Origins: The Making of Corporate Law in Nineteenth-Century Brazil (2012) 60 *The American Journal of Comparative Law* 805–50.
The Rise and Decline of Legal Families (2012) 60 *The American Journal of Comparative Law* 1043–74.
The Rise of International Corporate Law (2021) 98 *Washington University Law Review* 1765–820.
Paschel, T. S., *Becoming Black Political Subjects: Movements and Ethno-Racial Rights in Colombia and Brazil* (New Jersey: Princeton University Press, 2016).
Pistor, K., *The Code of Capital: How the Law Creates Wealth and Inequality* (Princeton: Princeton University Press, 2019).
Polanyi, K., *The Great Transformation: Economic and Political Origins of Our Time* (New York: Rinehart, 1944).
Posner, R. A., Creating a Legal Framework for Economic Development (1998) 13 *The World Bank Research Observer* 1–11.
Roe, M. J., Backlash (1998) 98 *Columbia Law Review* 217–41.
Salaymeh, L. and Michaels, R., Decolonial Comparative Law: A Conceptual Beginning (2022) 86 *Rabel Journal of Comparative and International Private Law* 166–88.
Santos, T. D., The Structure of Dependence (1970) 60 *American Economic Review* 231–6.
Schneider, B. R., *Hierarchical Capitalism in Latin America: Business, Labor, and the Challenges of Equitable Development* (Cambridge: Cambridge University Press, 2013).
Schneider, N., Between Promise and Skepticism: The Global South and Our Role as Engaged Intellectuals (2017) 11 *The Global South* 18–38.
Shaffer, G., *Emerging Powers and the World Trading System: The Past and Future of International Economic Law* (Cambridge: Cambridge University Press, 2021).
Sieder, R., Indigenous Peoples' Rights and the Law in Latin America in C. R. Garavito (ed.), *Law and Society in Latin America: A New Map* (London: Routledge, 2014), pp. 143–56.
Siems, M., *Comparative Law*, 3rd ed. (Cambridge: Cambridge University Press, 2022).
The Power of Comparative Law: What Types of Units Can Comparative Law Compare? (2019) 67 *The American Journal of Comparative Law* 861–88.
Spamann, H., The "Antidirector Rights Index" Revisited (2010) 23 *The Review of Financial Studies* 467–86.
Contemporary Legal Transplants: Legal Families and the Diffusion of (Corporate) Law (2009) 2009 *Brigham Young University Law Review* 1813–77.
Unger, R. M., The Critical Legal Studies Movement (1983) 96 *Harvard Law Review* 561–675.
Vieira, O. V., Baxi, U., and Viljoen, F. (eds.), *Transformative Constitutionalism: Comparing the Apex Courts of Brazil, India and South Africa* (Pretoria: Pretoria University Law Press, 2013).
The World Bank, *Principles and Guidelines for Effective Insolvency and Creditor Rights Systems: Introduction, Executive Summary and Principles* (Washington: World Bank Group, 2001).
Zweigert, K. and Kötz, H., *An Introduction to Comparative Law*, 3rd ed. (Oxford: Oxford University Press, 1998).

2

Contract Law and Inequality in the Global South

Brazil, Colombia, and South Africa

Kevin E. Davis and Mariana Pargendler

2.1 INTRODUCTION

Economic inequality is one of the most pressing problems facing modern societies, but it remains an open question whether it is one that contract law has any role to play in addressing. The orthodox answer to this question is no – contract law should pursue autonomy, efficiency, or justice in exchange, but not distributive objectives. This orthodoxy is rooted in the idea that pursuit of distributive objectives through contract law is both illegitimate and ineffective, particularly when initiated by judges as opposed to legislators. Accordingly, distribution should be pursued principally through the fiscal system – taxes and public spending – rather than through courts' rulings in contractual disputes. Critiques of the prevailing orthodoxy struggle with an inconvenient fact: Existing literature suggests that legal systems around the world have converged on contract law doctrines that are insensitive to distributive considerations, part of a broader trend that leaves very few differences of economic significance among contract laws. The absence of concrete experiences with alternatives to contract law orthodoxy casts doubt on the appeal and viability of heterodoxy.

This chapter explores examples of contract law heterodoxy in the legal systems of the Global South. Although the potential uses of contract law to mitigate inequality have long been the subject of heated scholarly debate,[1] the comparative dimension of this controversy has been neglected, even though inequality in the Global South is an especially pressing concern.[2] Our analysis unveils how courts in select Global South jurisdictions have recently diverged from orthodoxy and begun to embrace

This chapter is an abridged and slightly modified version of the article, originally published as K. E. Davis and M. Pargendler, Contract Law and Inequality (2022) 107 *Iowa Law Review* 1485–542.

[1] See Section 2.2.

[2] For exceptions, cf. A. Bagchi, The Political Economy of Regulating Contract (2014) 62 *The American Journal of Comparative Law* 687–738, 704 (examining how inequality ought to and

heterodoxy: the use of contract law to reduce inequality. In particular, we document important instances in which courts in South Africa, Brazil, and Colombia have adopted distinctly heterodox approaches to contract law. The decisions cover an eclectic mix of topics, including general rules on the calculation of prejudgment interest as well as more specific doctrines governing the purchase and sale of real estate and the provision of health insurance, life insurance, and water.

We do not claim that legal heterodoxy prevails in all Global South jurisdictions or even that it is dominant in the Global South jurisdictions we focus on in our case studies; indeed, we believe that this is not the case. We also do not maintain that heterodox contract laws actually achieve their intended distributive objectives; they may well be ineffective or backfire. Nevertheless, the greater incidence of contract law heterodoxy in several large Global South jurisdictions is noteworthy and likely consequential from an economic standpoint.

The existence of contract law heterodoxy in Global South jurisdictions has both practical and scholarly implications. From an economic perspective, heterodox approaches to contract law have the potential to alter pricing schemes, contract design, the choice of contracting partners, and incentives for vertical integration. From a theoretical standpoint, the finding of greater contract law heterodoxy in Global South jurisdictions has important implications for scholarship on comparative contract law, law and development, and contract theory.

To begin, these findings contradict the frequent assumption that contract laws do not differ substantially around the world.[3] The consensus in the literature on comparative law has been that the traditional distinctions between contract law in civil and common law systems are either waning or have limited economic significance.[4] As for comparisons between Global North and Global South countries, the focus of the literature on the role of contract institutions in development has been on differences in contract enforcement. When institutional economists and

will influence contract law in the United States and Europe and arguing that greater "income inequality increases the cost of mandatory terms"); Helen Hershkoff has examined the closely related topic of the use of contract law to protect rights to education and healthcare services in selected Global South jurisdictions. H. Hershkoff, Transforming Legal Theory in the Light of Practice: The Judicial Application of Social and Economic Rights to Private Orderings, in V. Gauri and D. M. Brinks (eds.), *Courting Social Justice: Judicial Enforcement of Social and Economic Rights in the Developing World* (Cambridge: Cambridge University Press, 2008), pp. 268–302, 290–94.

3 For such assumptions, see F. Jiménez, Against Parochialism in Contract Theory: A Response to Brian Bix (2019) 32 *Ratio Juris* 233–50, 236; J. Smits, *The Making of European Private Law: Toward a Ius Commune Europaeum as a Mixed Legal System* (Cambridge: Intersentia, 2002), p. 187.

4 See, e.g., H. Spamann, Contemporary Legal Transplants: Legal Families and the Diffusion of (Corporate) Law (2009) 2009 *BYU Law Review* 1813–78, 1814–75. But see generally M. Pargendler, The Role of the State in Contract Law: The Common–Civil Law Divide (2018) 43 *The Yale Journal of International Law* 143–90 (explaining the rationale behind the existing distinctions between the common and civil law of contracts).

international agencies, such as the World Bank, have attempted to assess the quality of contract institutions across the globe, they have focused exclusively on measures of enforcement (such as the time and costs of legal proceedings and the competence and integrity of courts), completely neglecting potential variations in contract law doctrines.[5] Scholars who have commented on substantive divergences between private law in Global South and Global North jurisdictions have posited that jurisdictions in Latin America and Africa embody "the rule of political law," in which distribution is led by political actors who are susceptible to influence by wealthy as well as poor groups.[6] In contract law at least, the possibility of progressive judicially-led innovations in the Global South – a well-known phenomenon in constitutional law[7] – has been overlooked.

Contract law heterodoxy in the Global South also destabilizes the theoretical foundations of contract law orthodoxy, namely, arguments that distribution through contract law as opposed to the fiscal system is always illegitimate or ineffective. Our findings suggest that the practical appeal of these arguments is contingent rather than universal. Even if contract law orthodoxy is optimal for Global North jurisdictions, contract law heterodoxy may, in economic parlance, constitute an attractive second-best approach in the Global South, given the limitations of other institutional alternatives in tackling inequality.

We argue that three key features of the countries we study favor the use of contract law to achieve distributive objectives and explain the emergence of heterodox approaches. First, widespread poverty and inequality make the distributions of income and wealth more salient. The fact that these inequalities are often traced to historical injustices such as slavery and colonial exploitation enhances the perceived legitimacy of distributive objectives. Second, the fiscal system has failed to meaningfully reduce persistent inequality. Third, consideration of inequality in contract disputes is often viewed as a constitutional imperative in view of legal commitments to equality. For all these reasons, arguments against consideration of distributive concerns in contract law have recently won less traction in Brazil, South Africa, and Colombia than in the Global North.

Finally, our examination of contract law heterodoxy in the Global South has a deeper methodological implication. Specifically, it illustrates the potential benefits of looking beyond the usual Global North suspects as sites for contract law

[5] World Bank Group, Doing Business 2020: Comparing Business Regulation in 190 Economies (2020), 19. For a discussion of the economic literature's exclusive focus on procedural criteria to measure contract institutions, see M. Pargendler, Comparative Contract Law and Development: The Missing Link? (2017) 85 *The George Washington Law Review* 1717–38, 1719.

[6] U. Mattei, Three Patterns of Law: Taxonomy and Change in the World's Legal Systems (1997) 45 *The American Journal of Comparative Law* 5–44, 28.

[7] See M. Versteeg, Can Rights Combat Economic Inequality? (2020) 133 *Harvard Law Review* 2017–61, 2020, 2059 (describing how courts in various Global South jurisdictions, as well as a few Global North jurisdictions, have employed constitutional law to tackle economic inequality).

scholarship and comparative analysis. Explorations of how and why contract law varies from one environment to another can shed a great deal of light on empirical assumptions and prevailing normative and explanatory theories. At the very least, this kind of inquiry can help address the question of whether Global South jurisdictions are best served by rules of contract law that diverge from those which are suitable for the Global North. We show that analysis of innovations in the Global South can also illuminate how contract law might respond to problems that affect a broader range of countries.

As inequality becomes an increasingly pressing problem around the world, deviations from contract law orthodoxy in the Global North become more plausible. In fact, the highly explicit instances of heterodoxy in the developing world draw attention to the significant – if less salient and often downplayed – elements of heterodoxy in the contract laws of the United States and European jurisdictions. In the real-world operation of different legal systems, the distinction between contract law orthodoxy and heterodoxy is a continuum rather than a dichotomy. Orthodoxy is not, contrary to frequent assumptions, the inevitable or universal "end of history" for contract law. Mounting inequality raises the prospect of public policy interventions through contract law in all jurisdictions – regardless of whether one believes they constitute clever remedies or misguided populist responses.

Before proceeding, two caveats are in order regarding the scope of the analysis that follows. First, our analysis leaves out agreements governed by labor and employment law. In contrast to prevailing assumptions of similarities in general contract laws, scholars have documented significant cross-country variations in the law of employment agreements.[8] Excluding employment agreements from the scope of this chapter likely understates the degree of contract law heterodoxy in the Global South to a significant extent.

Second, contract law heterodoxy is not a unitary phenomenon. Just as we define contract law orthodoxy broadly enough to encompass distinct (and conflicting) normative goals, contract law heterodoxy is used as an expansive category that covers different strategies to address diverse and potentially conflicting conceptions of inequality. Heterodox approaches may be more or less tailored to the circumstances of the particular contract parties, or instead operate based on untailored (categorical) assumptions about the majority of similar cases.[9] Contract law heterodoxy may focus on factors such as income, wealth, ability, capabilities, opportunity, poverty, exclusion, race, gender, or historical injustice – and these are only a few of the possible

8 See generally, e.g., B. Ahlering and S. Deakin, Labor Regulation, Corporate Governance, and Legal Origin: A Case of Institutional Complementarity? (2007) 41 *Law & Society Review* 865–908; J. C. Botero et al., The Regulation of Labor (2004) 119 *The Quarterly Journal of Economics* 1339–82.

9 I. Ayres and R. Gertner, Filling Gaps in Incomplete Contracts: An Economic Theory of Default Rules (1989) 99 *Yale Law Journal* 87–130 (detailing the classical distinction between tailored and untailored default rules in contract law).

dimensions. While we focus on how contract law heterodoxy in South Africa, Brazil, and Colombia differs from contract law orthodoxy in the Global North, the case studies reveal "varieties of heterodoxy," rather than a single monolithic approach.

2.2 CONTRACT LAW ORTHODOXY

2.2.1 *Defining Contract Law Orthodoxy*

Although there are profound disagreements about the aims and purposes of contract law, the orthodox view is that generally contract law is not and should not be concerned with the distribution of wealth in society.[10] Liberals and libertarians argue that contract law should instead be motivated by the value of individual autonomy, that is, the value of allowing individuals to make the momentous decision to bind themselves legally or, more broadly, by making it possible for them to pursue their own conceptions of the good in collaboration with others.[11] Law and economics scholars argue that contract law should be designed to promote efficiency, primarily by facilitating mutually beneficial (Pareto-efficient) exchanges.[12] Finally, scholars writing in the Aristotelian tradition focus on how contract law can help to preserve the existing distribution of wealth – which is presumed to be just – by promoting equality in exchange, which entails, among other things, ensuring that the terms of contracts are substantively fair.[13]

Although there is a fair amount of tension between these different intellectual traditions, they all view the pursuit of distributive objectives as beyond the domain of contract law, at least as that body of law is traditionally defined by teachers and scholars. Distributive considerations appear prominently in anti-discrimination law and bankruptcy law, which clearly bear upon the enforcement of contracts. But those bodies of law are traditionally understood to fall outside the bounds of contract law. Teachers and scholars also tend to define the domain of contract law in ways that exclude the statutory schemes that govern specific types of contracts, turning the field into a "law of leftovers."[14] Those statutory schemes may well contain

[10] See, e.g., H. Collins, Distributive Justice through Contracts (1992) 45 *Current Legal Problems* 49–67, 49; R. E. Scott, A Joint Maximization Theory of Contract and Regulation, in H. Dagan and B. C. Zipursky (eds.), *Research Handbook on Private Law Theory* (Northampton: Edward Elgar, 2020), pp. 22–38, p. 22. For a different, though now somewhat dated, assessment, see D. Kennedy, Distributive and Paternalist Motives in Contract and Tort Law, with Special Reference to Compulsory Terms and Unequal Bargaining Power (1982) 41 *Maryland Law Review* 563–658, 586–88.

[11] For a survey of autonomy-based theories of contract law see, H. Dagan and M. Heller, *The Choice Theory of Contracts* (Cambridge: Cambridge University Press, 2017), pp. 19–47.

[12] M. J. Trebilcock, *The Limits of Freedom of Contract* (Cambridge, MA: Harvard University Press, 1993), pp. 15–17.

[13] See generally, J. Gordley, Equality in Exchange (1981) 69 *California Law Review* 1587–1656.

[14] The expression comes from L. M. Friedman, *Contract Law in America: A Social and Economic Case Study* (Madison: University of Wisconsin Press, 1965), p. 193. It relates to the frequent

underappreciated amounts of heterodoxy. In any event, the dominant view, however accurate, is that distribution does not, and should not, influence the core contract law doctrines of general applicability concerning which promises are enforceable, how to determine when promises have not been performed and therefore need to be enforced, or the remedies available to the party seeking enforcement.[15]

Admittedly, there are points of contact between the orthodox and heterodox approaches when different objectives overlap. For instance, systemic disadvantage may be correlated with the presence of factors that undermine the promotion of autonomy, efficiency, or equality in exchange – factors such as coercion, imperfect information, or substantive unfairness. Within the orthodox position, examples of judicial solicitude for disadvantaged groups may be explained by concern about whether enforcement will promote autonomy or efficiency or equality in exchange, rather than about systemic disadvantage in its own right. It can often be difficult, in practice, to ascertain whether a certain exception to freedom of contract for the benefit of a disadvantaged party is attributable to orthodox or distributive considerations. Orthodox rhetoric may mask distributive objectives, and vice versa.

Moreover, it is important to recognize that the same tenets of contract law orthodoxy may lead to distinct patterns of adjudication owing to differences in factual circumstances. For instance, greater prevalence of inequality and market concentration in developing jurisdictions could prompt more frequent findings of unconscionability for the benefit of the weaker party, even under orthodox contract doctrines. The differences in dominant fact patterns are an important, though often overlooked, element in understanding the landscape of contract adjudication in the Global South. We argue, however, that there is more to the story: Beyond variations in the incidence of similar doctrines across jurisdictions due to distinct fact patterns, there are noticeable differences in contract law rules and doctrines as well.[16]

In practice, a legal system may embrace orthodoxy in relation to some types of transactions but not others, or place varying amounts of weight on distributive considerations. Therefore, the distinction between what we term orthodox and heterodox approaches to contract law constitutes a spectrum rather than a binary division. As is the case in comparative law more generally, our goal here is to

tendency in common law to characterize related fields of highly regulated contracts as something other than contract law. The effect of this artificial compartmentalization is to downplay the actual degree of heterodoxy in US law and beyond.

15 For discussion of the historical emergence of this view in US law, see A. Fleming, The Rise and Fall of Unconscionability as the "Law of the Poor" (2014) 102 *The Georgetown Law Journal* 1383–442, 1436–37 (discussing how, by the 1970s, the concerns of the poor were addressed through antidiscrimination laws and statutory disclosure requirements while unconscionability was no longer characterized as part of the "law of the poor" and was reconceptualized as a response to defects in reasoning).

16 It may also be that Global North jurisdictions offer greater regulation of specific types of contracts through dedicated regulatory schemes, thereby addressing certain fact patterns and relieving pressure on contract law (as it is conventionally defined) to tackle them. See discussion of functional equivalence in Section 2.4.3.1.

examine differences in emphasis between the contract laws of certain Global North and Global South jurisdictions rather than to identify stark contrasts.

2.2.2 *Orthodoxy and Heterodoxy in the United States*

The common law of contracts in the United States is overwhelmingly orthodox.[17] While there are several doctrines consistent with contract law heterodoxy in that they may be used to protect weaker parties, an orthodox reading of those doctrines is that they are triggered when the potential beneficiary is less informed or is being coerced by the opposing party or when the transaction deviates significantly from prevailing notions of a fair bargain.[18] They do not key upon whether the person is disadvantaged relative to society as a whole nor do they explicitly refer to the role of contract law in promoting social justice more generally.

There are important exceptions to the prevailing orthodoxy in US contract law. As far as judicial decisions are concerned, the most famous example of heterodoxy is Judge Skelly Wright's opinion in *Williams v. Walker-Thomas Furniture*.[19] That opinion endorsed the use of the doctrine of unconscionability to avoid enforcement of a sweepingly broad security agreement by a furniture store against a woman who was identified as being on public assistance and responsible for seven children.[20] Although her race was not mentioned in the opinion, it is safe to assume that the court was aware that the customer was Black, as were most of the store's other customers. Judge Wright ruled that the unconscionability doctrine applies when the party seeking relief faces "an absence of meaningful choice ... together with terms which are unreasonably favorable to the other party."[21] This language could be interpreted to reflect purely orthodox concerns about asymmetric information, coercion, and unfair exchange, which is now the mainstream understanding of the unconscionability doctrine in the United States.[22] However, in extrajudicial

[17] See note 10 and accompanying text.

[18] M. A. Eisenberg, The Theory of Contracts, in P. Benson (ed.), *The Theory of Contract Law: New Essays* (Cambridge: Cambridge University Press, 2001), pp. 206–64, p. 257; see, e.g., The American Law Institute, Restatement of the Law of Consumer Contracts, 1 (Tentative Draft, 2019) (characterizing the fundamental challenge of consumer contract law – including the doctrine of unconscionability – as protection of consumers who lack information about the terms of agreements).

[19] *Williams v. Walker-Thomas Furniture Co.*, 350 F 2d 445, 449–50 (D.C. Cir. 1965).

[20] Ibid., 449–50.

[21] Ibid., 449.

[22] On the modern scholarly understanding of unconscionability, see Fleming, The Rise and Fall of Unconscionability as the "Law of the Poor," 1386 (arguing that unconscionability "is rarely invoked to protect low-income borrowers" today) and The American Law Institute, Restatement of the Law of Consumer Contracts. Whether interpreted in orthodox or heterodox terms, the conventional view is that the actual application of the doctrine of unconscionability is exceedingly rare. There is emerging evidence, however, of a resurgence in the use of unconscionability by courts. See, e.g., J. H. Russell, Unconscionability's Greatly Exaggerated

writings, Wright characterized the *Williams* decision as part of the "law of the poor," a decidedly heterodox label.[23]

The "law of the poor" has not featured prominently in judicial decisions for contract cases in the United States – with the important exception of the implied warranty of habitability in residential landlord–tenant law.[24] One of the leading decisions in that field is another opinion authored by Judge Skelly Wright, *Javins v. First National Realty*.[25] Judge Wright announced that the decision was motivated in part by a desire to give effect to the expectations of the typical tenant, and in part by concerns about inequality in bargaining power arising from the use of standardized contracts.[26] Attention to these factors is consistent with orthodox concerns about autonomy, efficiency, and justice in exchange. But Judge Wright said that another compelling reason to adopt the implied warranty was to address the inequality in bargaining power caused specifically by "racial and class discrimination."[27] He made it clear that the decision was motivated by systemic concerns, saying "that poor housing [was] detrimental to the whole society, not merely to the unlucky ones who must suffer the daily indignity of living in a slum."[28] And, in private correspondence, Judge Wright described the *Javins* decision as part of an effort "to ameliorate, if not eliminate, the injustice involved in the way many of the poor were required to live in the nation's capital."[29] Unlike *Williams v. Walker-Thomas Furniture*, the decision in *Javins* endorsed a form of heterodoxy that is now an established feature of US law. Most states have legislation that codifies implied warranties of repair and habitability in residential leases, typically motivated, at least in part, by concerns about poverty and inequality.[30]

There are also notable historical examples of legislative interventions enacted in times of economic crisis that have fairly obvious distributive motivations. For instance, there is a long history of US states passing laws that impose moratoria on

Death (2019) 53 *UC Davis Law Review* 965–1026, 967 (challenging the conventional view by documenting how "the doctrine has quietly flourished in courts in recent years").

23 See Fleming, The Rise and Fall of Unconscionability as the "Law of the Poor," 1385, n. 1, citing Letter from Hon. J. Skelly Wright to William E. Shipley, The Lawyers Cooperative Publ'n Co. (July 12, 1967) (J. Skelly Wright Papers, 1962–1987, Box 77, Folder 1965 September term, Manuscript Division, Library of Congress).

24 See ibid., 1386, 1389.

25 See generally *Javins v. First Nat'l Realty Corp.*, 428 F 2d. 1071 (D.C. Cir. 1970) (holding that the warranty of habitability is implied by operation of law through the Housing Regulations for the District of Columbia).

26 Ibid., 1075–77.

27 Ibid., 1079.

28 Ibid., 1079–80.

29 Letter from Hon. J. S. Wright to Professor E. H. Rabin, U.C. Davis Sch. Law (October 14, 1982), in E. H. Rabin, The Revolution in Residential Landlord–Tenant Law: Causes and Consequences (1984) 69 *Cornell Law Review* 517–84, 549.

30 See D. A. Super, The Rise and Fall of the Implied Warranty of Habitability (2011) 99 *California Law Review* 389–463, 402–4; M. A. Glendon, The Transformation of American Landlord–Tenant Law (1982) 23 *Boston College Law Review* 503–76, 523–24.

enforcement of creditors' rights, especially during economic downturns and particularly for the benefit of farmers.[31] The US Supreme Court upheld the constitutionality of the moratoria by arguing that "the legislation was not for the mere advantage of particular individuals but for the protection of a basic interest of society."[32] The Court endorsed the Supreme Court of Minnesota's finding that "the economic emergency which threatened 'the loss of homes and lands which furnish those in possession the necessary shelter and means of subsistence' was a 'potent cause' for the enactment of the statute."[33] There are, of course, also more recent examples of US legislation pertaining to contracts that have had significant distributive effects, even if that was not their ostensible purpose.[34]

2.2.3 *Orthodoxy and Heterodoxy in Continental Europe*

We now turn to continental Europe, another setting in which contract law orthodoxy largely prevails. The well-known differences between consumer contract law in the European Union and in the United States can be interpreted as divergent responses to concerns about consumer behavioral biases or inequality of exchange. To that extent, both jurisdictions are merely pursuing different versions of contract law orthodoxy.[35]

The closest instance of a heterodox approach to contract law is the famous 1993 decision by the German Constitutional Court (*Bundesverfassungsgericht*) in the *Bürgschaft* case, which became the poster child for the consideration of fundamental rights in the interpretation and enforcement of private contracts.[36] The case involved the provision of a hefty personal guarantee (surety) by a 21-year-old daughter for the bank's extension of credit to her father. When she entered into the agreement, the daughter, who lacked either a professional education or a full-time job, earned 1,150 DM per month in a fish factory. By the time her father defaulted

[31] L. M. Friedman, *A History of American Law*, 4th ed. (New York: Oxford University Press, 2019), pp. 229–30; see generally L. J. Alston, Farm Foreclosure Moratorium Legislation: A Lesson from the Past (1984) 74 *The American Economic Review* 445–57 (discussing previous legislative attempts at mitigating farm foreclosures).

[32] *Home Building & Loan Association v. Blaisdell*, 290 US, 445.

[33] Ibid.

[34] See, e.g., S. Agarwal et al., Regulating Consumer Financial Products: Evidence from Credit Cards (2015) 130 *The Quarterly Journal of Economics* 111–64, 114 (arguing that the Credit Card Accountability Responsibility, and Disclosure Act of 2009 generated significant savings for consumers, especially those with low credit scores).

[35] For a critical appraisal of European contract law from a mainstream US law-and-economics perspective, see, for example, O. Bar-Gill and O. Ben-Shahar, Regulatory Techniques in Consumer Protection: A Critique of European Consumer Contract Law (2013) 50 *Common Market Law Review* 109–25, 109–10.

[36] The description of the case comes from Pargendler, The Role of the State in Contract Law, 179–80.

and the bank sued her for 160,000 DM, she was a single mother on social security. Her appeal argued that "courts should deny recognition to contracts that so strongly reduce the freedom of action of one of the contracting parties that she can no longer live with dignity."[37]

The German Constitutional Court found that the enforcement of an agreement characterized by a significant imbalance in bargaining power and resulting in such harsh consequences for the weaker party violated the constitutional rights to human dignity and free development of personality, as well as the principle of the social State (*Sozialstaatsprinzip*).[38] While the court's reasoning in the *Bürgschaft* decision stands out for its appeal to the social State and for its concern about the weaker party, the same result of full discharge would occur in other jurisdictions through different doctrinal routes.[39]

A prominent 1996 decision by the French *Cour de cassation* invoked fundamental rights to adjudicate a landlord–tenant dispute.[40] The agreement in question between the tenant and the city of Paris provided for the exclusive use by the tenant and her two children. However, the tenant also accommodated her children's father as well as her sister, leading to a notice of termination by the city. The Court invalidated the termination as a violation of the right to private and family life recognized by Article 8 of the European Convention of Human Rights.[41] At any rate, while noteworthy and widely cited, these cases from the 1990s failed to spur a revolution in contract law toward greater attention to social justice and inequality.

Although we do not see significant deviation from contract law orthodoxy in either continental Europe or the United States, there is greater support for heterodoxy in the European discourse about contract law. On balance, continental European scholars appear to be more likely than their US or UK counterparts to defend the role of contract law in the pursuit of social justice. It is common in continental Europe to regard contract law as striking a balance between the fundamental values of autonomy and solidarity,[42] a framing that differs from US scholars' primary focus on efficiency, autonomy, and fairness in exchange.[43]

37 Bundesverfassungsgericht [BVerfG] [Federal Constitutional Court] October 19, 1993, 89 Entescheidungen des Bundesverfassungsgerichts [BVerfGE] 220 (1994) (Germany) (translated by authors).

38 Ibid., 89, 232.

39 Pargendler, The Role of the State in Contract Law, 180–1.

40 Ibid., 154, citing Cour de cassation [Cass.] [Supreme Court for Judicial Matters] 3e civ., March 6, 1996, 93-11.113, Bull. 1996, Civ. III, No. 60, 41 (France).

41 Ibid.

42 See, e.g., M. Hesselink, The Horizontal Effects of Social Rights in European Contract Law (2003) 1 *Europa e Diritto Privato* 1–18, 11.

43 See generally D. Caruso, The Baby and the Bath Water: The American Critique of European Contract Law (2013) 61 *American Journal of Comparative Law* 479–91, 487.

2.2.4 *The Impact of the COVID-19 Pandemic*

The COVID-19 pandemic threatened to exacerbate inequality in most countries. The pandemic prompted not only moratoria on evictions of residential tenants in the United States, as discussed in Chapter 6 by Bianca Tavolari and Saylon Pereira, but also new manifestations of contract law heterodoxy in Europe. The German statute "to mitigate the consequences of the Coronavirus crisis" allowed consumers to refuse payment of essential continuing obligations if they would not be able to pay for the service without risking either their own subsistence or that of their dependents.[44] A temporary right to refuse performance was also extended to microbusinesses, provided that its exercise does not "endanger the creditor's [] subsistence[,] ... the reasonable subsistence of [the creditor's] dependents or the economic basis of [the] business" (in which case the debtor may seek to terminate the contract).[45] In linking contract rights to the particular economic situation of the parties – and not to the fairness of the exchange – this special German legislation reflects a new manifestation of contract law heterodoxy in a Global North jurisdiction, even if it was only a temporary response to a time of significant economic crisis and dislocation. We now turn to the description of contract law heterodoxy in the Global South, contexts where economic crisis, dislocation, and inequality are particularly commonplace.

2.3 CONTRACT LAW HETERODOXY IN THE GLOBAL SOUTH

In this section we describe instances in which contract law in three Global South jurisdictions – South Africa, Brazil, and Colombia – diverges from orthodoxy. Each example involves a doctrine formulated by one of the apex courts of the country which covers an economically important class of transactions. None of our examples involve the law of employment agreements because, as noted in the introduction, that is one of the few areas of contract law where scholars have already documented economically significant divergence.[46] Still, our collection of illustrations is eclectic. The contracts in dispute range from agreements for purchase and sale of residential real estate to insurance contracts to agreements for the provision of water. The different examples reveal that contract law heterodoxy, that is the endorsement of contract doctrines which embrace distributional goals, has made important inroads into the legal systems of these three countries. They are not, however, intended to suggest that contract law heterodoxy is dominant in any of these legal systems. In fact, even in the areas of law that we canvass, we document tension and conflict between proponents of orthodox and heterodox approaches.

44 For a description of the German statute, see N. Brunotte and L. Elsaß, The German Bundestag Resolves Amendments to Contract Law to Mitigate the Consequences of the Coronavirus Crisis, DLA Piper, May 6, 2020.

45 Ibid.

46 See note 8.

2.3.1 *South Africa*

South Africa is perhaps the leading example of a jurisdiction which has recently taken a heterodox approach to the relationship between contract law and inequality.[47] Much of the change has been driven by the incorporation of constitutional principles into contract law. This kind of horizontal application of constitutional principles is expressly required by the South African Constitution which states: "[W]hen developing the common law or customary law, every court, tribunal or forum must promote the spirit, purport and objects of the Bill of Rights."[48]

In a prominent series of decisions, the Constitutional Court of South Africa has taken the position that both principles of contract law and decisions about whether to enforce specific contractual terms must conform to constitutional values,[49] which might entail departing from "colonial legal tradition represented by English law, Roman law and Roman Dutch law."[50] Among those constitutional values is "*ubuntu*," an African concept which "emphasises the communal nature of society and 'carries in it the ideas of humaneness, social justice and fairness' and envelopes 'the key values of group solidarity, compassion, respect, human dignity, conformity to basic norms and collective unity.'"[51]

2.3.1.1 Prejudgment Interest

In *Paulsen v. Slip Knot Investments 777 Ltd.*, the Constitutional Court explicitly stated that limits on the principle of freedom of contract must be fashioned in light of socio-economic realities that include substantial amounts of economic inequality and poverty.[52] The appeal concerned the scope of the ancient *in duplum* doctrine, a rule which limits the interest that a creditor can recover on debts in arrears to an amount equal to the principal of the debt. At issue in *Paulsen* was whether the rule

[47] This is a recent development. As late as 2010, progressive commentators criticized the South African courts for their unduly orthodox approach to contract law. See D. M. Davis and K. Klare, Transformative Constitutionalism and the Common and Customary Law (2010) 26 *South African Journal on Human Rights* 403–509, 468–81, criticizing "the freedom-of-contract cases."

[48] Constitution of the Republic of South Africa, 1996 § 39(2).

[49] See *Barkhuizen* v. *Napier* (5) SA 323 (CC) (2007), para. 30 (South Africa); *Everfresh Market Virginia* v. *Shoprite Checkers* (1) SA 256 (CC) (2012), para. 48 (South Africa).

[50] *Everfresh Market Virginia* v. *Shoprite Checkers*, para. 23; see ibid., para. 71 (Moseneke, J., concurring).

[51] Ibid., para. 71 (footnote omitted).

[52] See *Paulsen v. Slip Knot Investments 777 Ltd.* (3) SA 479 (CC) (2015), para. 66 (South Africa) ("We need to look at South Africa's socio-economic realities. A large percentage of the providers of credit are large, established and well-resourced corporates. On the other hand, although there may be what the dissenting judgment refers to as 'stout-boned' credit consumers, it would be ignoring our country's economic reality to suggest that there is any comparison between these corporates and most credit consumers").

applied to interest that accrued after the institution of legal proceedings but before the date of judgment (there was no dispute that interest could accrue after judgment).[53] In a 1997 decision called *Oneanate*, South Africa's Supreme Court of Appeal decided that the *in duplum* rule should be suspended during the pendency of litigation.[54]

The debtors in *Paulsen* were sureties for a property developer which had defaulted on a debt of R12 million.[55] The loan agreement specified that interest was to accrue at the rate of 3 percent per month. Under the traditional *in duplum* rule, the creditor could not have a judgment for more than R24 million. Under the narrower version of the rule favored in *Oneanate*, the creditor was entitled to a judgment for R72 million.[56]

In a split decision, the Constitutional Court in *Paulsen* decided to reinstate the traditional *in duplum* rule. In the main opinion, Justice Madlanga wrote that the court in *Oneanate* misread the relevant authorities and ignored relevant public policy considerations. The overlooked considerations were the risks that modification of the rule would prejudice debtors and inhibit their constitutional right of access to the courts. Justice Madlanga reasoned that "debtors, despite a genuinely held belief that they have a valid defence, may sooner opt to settle a claim than face the potentially financially ruinous interest that would again commence to pile up once court process was served."[57]

Justice Madlanga acknowledged that there were competing policy considerations. In particular, the traditional rule would encourage debtors to prolong litigation by raising frivolous defenses or employing other delaying tactics. This might in turn raise a constitutional concern if it caused creditors to abandon claims against defaulting debtors because the value was eroded by inflation.[58] Pulling in the other direction, though, was the fact that creditors could protect themselves by charging relatively high rates of interest, avoiding lending to debtors who were bad risks, and litigating swiftly.[59] He also noted that debtors' delaying tactics could be addressed by means of summary judgment and punitive costs awards.[60] More importantly, he believed that bearing the costs of prolonged litigation would prejudice debtors more than creditors because, although the Paulsens appeared to be "stout-boned commercial parties," debtors generally were more likely to be financially vulnerable.[61]

[53] Ibid., para. 96 ("It is settled law that the in duplum rule permits interest to run anew from the date that the judgment debt is due and payable").

[54] See *Standard Bank of South Africa Ltd. v. Oneanate Investments Ltd.* (1) SA 811 (SCA) (1998), para. 50 (South Africa) ("[T]he in duplum rule is suspended pendente lite ..." (emphasis added)).

[55] *Paulsen v. Slip Knot Investments*, para. 2.

[56] Ibid., para. 63.

[57] Ibid.

[58] Ibid., para. 65.

[59] Ibid., paras. 81–85.

[60] Ibid., para. 84.

[61] See ibid., para. 135 (Cameron, J., dissenting); Ibid., para. 69 (Madlanga, J., majority opinion).

> We need to look at South Africa's socio-economic realities. A large percentage of the providers of credit are large, established and well-resourced corporates. On the other hand, although there may be what the dissenting judgment refers to as "stout-boned" credit consumers, it would be ignoring our country's economic reality to suggest that there is any comparison between these corporates and most credit consumers. To many credit consumers, who fall on the wrong side of this country's vast capital disparities, astronomical interest may mean the difference between economic survival and complete financial ruin. While in some cases creditors may lose money to inflation during litigation, this is very unlikely to have the same catastrophic effect on the creditor compared to what the accumulation of run-away interest will have on the debtor. If I were to be forced to make a choice between the two, it would be an easy one for me.[62]

Justice Madlanga went on to make it clear that he was particularly concerned about debtors who had been affected by apartheid and either remained financially vulnerable or were just emerging from the ranks of the financially vulnerable.

> It cannot be plausibly gainsaid that for our democracy to be meaningful, it is only fitting that those previously denigrated by racism and apartheid, confined to the fringes of society and stripped of dignity and self-worth must also enter the terrain of meaningful, substantial economic activity. Surely, our hard-fought democracy could not have been only about the change of the political face of our country and such upliftment of the lot of the downtrodden as the public purse and government policies permit. Entrepreneurship and the economic advancement of those with no history of being financially resourced must be given room to take root and thrive. This can hardly happen without finance. The sort of interest to which *Oneanate* exposes our legal system is deleterious to this necessary economic advancement.[63]

Accordingly, Justice Madlanga and the majority of the Constitutional Court decided to limit the creditor's judgment to R24 million.[64]

2.3.1.2 Installment Purchases of Land

South African jurisprudence also prescribes that constitutional principles inform the interpretation of statutory provisions regulating specific contractual provisions. A prominent example of this sort of application of constitutional principles is

[62] Ibid., para. 66 (citation omitted).

[63] Ibid., para. 75 (citations omitted).

[64] Ibid., para. 102. Justice Madlanga's judgment, which was joined by two other judges, characterized the decision as a reinstatement of a common law rule that had been abandoned in error. Ibid., paras. 89–90. He held that development of the common law in this area should be left to the Legislature. Ibid., para. 91. In a concurring opinion, Moseneke DCJ, joined by four other judges, preferred to say that the common law had been adapted to conform to public policy considerations and constitutional values and that this was a legitimate exercise of judicial power. Ibid., para. 109–10 (Moseneke, J., concurring).

Botha v Rich N.O., which concerned the statutory rights of purchasers of land who agree to pay in installments.[65] The Alienation of Land Act 1981 authorized a purchaser who paid more than 50 percent of the purchase price to demand that title be registered in their name, subject to the purchaser providing a mortgage in favor of the vendor to secure the purchaser's remaining obligations.[66] The central issue in *Botha* was what happens when a vendor fails to comply with a demand for a transfer. Was a purchaser who defaulted on her payments after paying more than 50 percent of the purchase price only entitled to cancel the contract and recover the amount she paid, or could she, in the alternative, demand specific performance of the obligation to register a transfer? The statute mentioned the possibility of cancellation and restitution but said nothing about specific performance.[67]

In *Botha*, the Court held that the purchaser was entitled to specific performance of the right to a transfer, conditional upon payment of arrears and amounts owed to the local municipality.[68] The Court could probably have reached this result based solely on ordinary principles of statutory interpretation. However, the Court went out of its way to say that the case raised a constitutional issue and that its decision was motivated by the constitutional duty to "promote the spirit, purport and objects of the Bill of Rights."[69] It pointed out that the statute was enacted to protect installment purchasers and was prompted by the collapse of several township development companies in the 1970s.[70] It could have, but did not, note that there was good reason to believe that, in the South African context, people who purchased real estate by installment were likely to be relatively poor.[71]

2.3.1.3 Equality Rights and the Enforcement of Contractual Terms

Concerns about inequality have also influenced the South African Constitutional Court's approach to the enforcement of contractual terms, but less profoundly than in cases concerned with the development of principles of contract law. Technically speaking, the Court does not evaluate contractual terms directly against constitutional norms. Instead, contractual terms are evaluated in light of public policy, which is in turn shaped by constitutional values along with more traditional

[65] *Botha v. Rich* N.O. 2014 (4) SA 124 (CC) (2014), para. 2 (South Africa).
[66] Alienation of Land Act 68 of 1981 § 27(1) (South Africa).
[67] Ibid., §§ 27(3), 28(1).
[68] *Botha v. Rich* N.O, paras. 37, 49.
[69] Ibid., para. 28.
[70] Ibid., paras. 30–31.
[71] *Sarrahwitz v. Maritz* N.O. (4) SA 491 (CC) (2015), para. 82 (South Africa) (Cameron and Froneman, JJ., concurring) ("[P]urchasers who have access to enough money to pay off a property purchase immediately, or within a year, are better-off than those who have to pay in instalments over a period of one year or more. Hence, they need less protection than those whose financial circumstances oblige them to pay off their property debt more arduously, over a longer period").

requirements of reasonableness and fairness. Significantly, the Constitutional Court has decreed that the relative bargaining power of the parties to the contract in question ought to be considered in determining whether contractual terms contravene public policy, stating, "[t]his is an important principle in a society as unequal as ours."[72] This contrasts with the approach taken in cases like *Paulsen*, in which the court ignored the fact that the parties seeking relief were "stout-boned" commercial actors.[73] It is not entirely clear, though, what counts as evidence of inequality of bargaining power. For instance, the seminal decision in *Napier v. Barkhuisen* was about whether a limitation of time for bringing claims under an automobile insurance policy was consistent with public policy. The majority in the Constitutional Court decided that there was insufficient evidence that enforcement of the clause was unreasonable.[74] However, the court noted below that the insured drove an expensive automobile (a BMW).[75]

The South African Constitutional Court continues to grapple with the challenges of using contract law to promote equality. Although most of the Court's members appear to be convinced of the legitimacy of the exercise, there remain serious questions about how far they are willing to depart from orthodoxy, as well as ongoing concerns about how to accurately identify disadvantaged parties and how to ensure that the potential benefits of decisions are not erased by changes in contracting practices.

All of these issues were raised, but not necessarily resolved, in *Beadica 231 CC v. Trustees for the time being of the Oregon Trust*.[76] In that case the trial judge allowed a set of franchisees to exercise options to renew their leases even though they failed to comply with a requirement that they give notice of intention to exercise the option more than six months prior to the initial termination date. The franchisees were black-owned enterprises and acquired their businesses as part "of a black economic empowerment [transaction]" funded by the National Empowerment Fund,[77] a public agency legislatively charged with "facilitat[ing] the redressing of economic inequality which resulted from the past unfair discrimination against historically disadvantaged persons."[78]

72 *Barkhuizen* v. *Napier*, para. 59. Cf. Ibid., para. 97 (Moseneke, J., dissenting) ("When one weighs whether a contractual term is at variance with public policy, it matters little, or perhaps matters not, what the personal attributes of the party seeking to escape the results of the time bar are. It is not inconceivable that the personal and social station of the claimant may have some bearing on the public policy evaluation, but ordinarily it is not decisive. It is the likely impact of the impugned stipulation that should be determinative of what public notions of fairness may tolerate").

73 *Paulsen v. Slip Knot Investments*, para. 73.

74 Ibid., para. 84.

75 *Napier v. Barkhuizen* (4) SA 1 (SCA) (2006), para. 15 (South Africa).

76 See generally *Beadica 231 CC v. Trustees* for the time being of the Oregon Trust (5) SA 247 (CC) (2020) (South Africa) (discussing when a court may refuse to enforce a contractual term on public policy grounds).

77 Ibid., para. 2.

78 National Empowerment Fund Act 105 of 1998, § 3 (South Africa).

The trial judge noted that the statutory initiative would be dealt a blow if the lease were cancelled.[79] He found that cancellation would be a disproportionate sanction.[80] He also referred to the competing policy considerations of, on the one hand, legal certainty and, on the other hand, the importance of infusing contract law with good faith and fairness and constitutional values such as *ubuntu*.

The trial decision in *Beadica* was overturned on appeal,[81] and that result was upheld by a divided Constitutional Court. The seven judges in the majority found that the renewal terms were written "in simple, uncomplicated language, which an ordinary person could reasonably be expected to understand" and so the franchisees failed to satisfy their onus of showing that enforcement would be unreasonable.[82] The majority were also unsympathetic to the franchisees' claim that strict enforcement of the renewal provision would violate public policy because it would be inconsistent with the constitutional right to equality.

In her majority opinion, Theron J. strongly rejected the proposition that enforcement of a contractual term would violate the constitutional right to equality merely because it would prejudice a member of a historically disadvantaged group. In fact, she suggested that refusing to enforce the contract would hurt rather than help the cause of equality, worrying that contracting parties would respond to such a legal rule by adjusting other terms of their contracts with members of disadvantaged groups, or refusing to contract with them altogether.[83] Her concern echoes a recurring theme in legal academics' defenses of contract law orthodoxy.[84]

The two dissenting judgments both argued that there was sufficient evidence to conclude that the franchisees were relatively unsophisticated and in a position of unequal bargaining power compared to the franchisors.[85] The dissenting judges would have found that enforcement in these circumstances was contrary to good

79 *Beadica 231 CC v. Trustees*, Oregon Unit Trust (1) SA 549 (WCC) (2018), para 39 (South Africa).

80 Ibid., para. 42.

81 *Beadica* 231 CC (5) SA, para. 12.

82 Ibid., paras. 93–95.

83 The passage merits quoting in full: "To hold that the failure of a black economic empowerment initiative financed by the Fund renders the enforcement of the renewal clauses deleterious to the constitutional value of equality would have the undesirable result of defeating the Funds own objects. This is because the effect of this finding would increase the risk of contracting with historically disadvantaged persons who benefit from the Fund. If the applicants were to succeed, it would establish the legal principle that enforcement of a contractual term would be inimical to the constitutional value of equality, and therefore contrary to public policy, where enforcement would result in the failure of a black economic empowerment initiative. This could, in turn, deter other parties from electing to contract with beneficiaries of the Fund, or force beneficiaries to offset the increased risk by making concessions on other contractual aspects during contract negotiations". Ibid., para. 101 (footnote omitted).

84 See the discussion of avoidance in Section 2.4.3.

85 *Beadica* 231 CC (5) SA, paras. 196–98, 202 (Froneman, J., dissenting); ibid., paras. 224–26 (Victor, A. J., dissenting).

faith, public policy, and *ubuntu*.[86] The majority's opinion, however, draws very important boundaries around heterodoxy in South African contract law.

2.3.2 *Brazil*

Brazil's contract law is heterodox, both in form and substance. Courts habitually note the "change in paradigm" in private law from a merely "liberal, individualistic, and patrimonial" view of private relations to one which emphasizes "good faith, the social function of contract and property and the valuing of the existential minimum."[87] The effect is that "the right to liberty and party autonomy needs to be weighed against the duty of social solidarity, in the sense that citizens must mutually help each other to preserve humanity and build a free, just, and solidary society that belongs to everyone indistinctly."[88] In this view, "solidarity is a guideline, an interpretative value, a guide to distributive justice," while "good faith is the translation of the respect to human dignity" and "represents the functionalization of private relations based on solidarity."[89] The scholarly push for the "constitutionalization of civil law" through horizontal effects of fundamental rights has been highly influential, even if the phenomenon is resented by doctrinal and law-and-economics scholars.[90]

Judicial and scholarly rhetoric on the role of human dignity, the social function of contract, and social solidarity in contract law disputes is pervasive. A search of abstracts (*ementas*) of contract opinions by Brazil's Superior Court of Justice (*Superior Tribunal de Justiça* ("STJ"))[91] alone returned over 1,700 results for "human dignity," over 13,000 results for "social function," and over 780 results for "social justice."[92] However, not all heterodox rhetoric translates into heterodox results, and not all heterodox results are based on heterodox rhetoric. While noting that heterodox rhetoric is widespread, this section will focus primarily on the distinct contours of the Brazilian contract law regime (heterodox results) that appear to set it apart from the international norm in the Global North.

86 Ibid., paras. 201–2 (Froneman, J., dissenting); ibid., paras. 230–31 (Victor, A. J., dissenting).

87 STJ, Agravo em Recurso Especial No. 1.681.421-RJ, Relatora: Ministra Maria Isabel Gallotti, 24.08.2020, 2980 Diario da Justiça [D.J.], 27.08.2020, 4 (Brazil) (quoting the decision by the Rio de Janeiro Court of Appeals in the case).

88 Ibid. The case in question concerned the abusive use of proxies by the administrator of a housing condominium to repeatedly elect himself and approve his accounts. Ibid.

89 Ibid., 5.

90 For a critique, see L. B. Timm, Ainda Sobre a Função Social do Direito Contratual no Código Civil Brasileiro: Justiça Distributiva versus Eficiência Econômica (2009) 2 *Revista da Associação Mineira de Direito e Economia* 1–39, 14.

91 The Superior Court of Justice is Brazil's court of last resort on federal law. Its jurisdiction encompasses all matters of private law, including contract law.

92 Search conducted on the website www.stj.jus.br on September 9, 2020. See www.stj.jus.br/sites/portalp/Inicio.

Brazilian scholars have long argued "that the *substance* of courts' approach to contract enforcement" – rather than the duration and cost of procedures, as assumed by the international literature and the World Bank – is potentially distinct and problematic.[93] According to a survey of Brazilian judges by political scientists in the early 2000s, only 48 percent of respondents argued that contracts must be respected independently of social repercussions, whereas 61 percent of them declared that the achievement of social justice justifies breaches of contract.[94] A famous 2005 article by some of Brazil's most prominent economists blamed the country's "extraordinarily high interest rates" for private credit on legal uncertainty due to courts' "anti-creditor bias," which they attributed, among other things, to "deep social differences and the high levels of income concentration in the country."[95] Since then, local literature has emerged to challenge both the existence and root causes of the alleged legal uncertainty and anti-creditor bias.[96] Nevertheless, the use of constitutional principles and social considerations in adjudicating contract disputes in Brazil is largely accepted as a descriptive matter, though contested from a normative standpoint.

2.3.2.1 Consumer Housing Purchases and Heterodox Contract Remedies

One notable instance of doctrinal heterodoxy appears in the judicial treatment of contracts for the acquisition of new housing from construction companies. A fairly common market practice is for consumers to acquire new housing through monthly installments before and during construction, effectively prepaying for their unit and helping to finance the housing project. As in South Africa, this longstanding practice likely responds, at least in part, to failures in the country's credit markets, leading to inordinately high interest rates in consumer and financial credit.[97]

93 See Pargendler, Comparative Contract Law and Development, 1736.

94 B. Lamounier and A. de Souza, *As Elites Brasileiras e o Desenvolvimento Nacional: Fatores de Consenso e Dissenso* (São Paulo: Instituto de Estudos Econômicos, Sociais e Políticos de São Paulo, 2002), p. 21. For another prominent survey result along the same lines, see generally A. C. Pinheiro, Judiciário, Reforma e Economia: A Visão dos Magistrados (2003) Instituto de Pesquisa Econômica Aplicada, Texto para Discussão No 966.

95 P. Arida, E. L. Bacha, and A. Lara-Resende, Credit, Interest, and Jurisdictional Uncertainty: Conjectures on the Case of Brazil, in F. Giavazzi, I. Goldfajn, and S. Herrera (eds.), *Inflation Targeting, Debt, and the Brazilian Experience, 1999 to 2003* (Cambridge, MA: MIT Press, 2005), pp. 265–93, pp. 265, 270, 286.

96 See, e.g., L. L. T. Yeung and P. F. de Azevedo, Neither Robin Hood nor King John: Testing the Anti-Creditor and Anti-Debtor Bias in Brazilian Judges (2015) 6 *Economic Analysis of Law Review* 1–21, 17–18.

97 The root causes of the financial market failures are contested. One prominent line of works attributes high interest rates to judicial bias toward debtors vis-à-vis creditors. P. Arida, E. L Bacha and A. Lara-Resende, Credit, Interest, and Jurisdictional Uncertainty, 274. Other commentators blame significant market concentration in the banking sector, as well as macroeconomic conditions. See, e.g., B. M. Salama, Spread Bancário e Enforcement Contratual: Hipótese de Causalidade Reversa e Evidência Empírica (2017) 71 *Revista Brasileira de Economia* 111–33, 120–25 (attributing the root of financial shortcomings to high interest rates).

In this context, a common fact pattern is the contractual breach by a consumer who is unable or unwilling to make the agreed upon installment payments. From an orthodox perspective, the legal treatment of this fact pattern should be reasonably straightforward. The construction company should be able to seek enforcement of the contract by demanding payment or to terminate the contract and seek either expectation damages or stipulated damages. In the case of a falling market, expectation damages could be substantial. Stipulated damages clauses in the sales contract could be subject to judicial scrutiny if excessive.

The resolution of this type of dispute in Brazil has differed sharply from the description given here. Courts have come to recognize consumers' rights to terminate the contract at-will and obtain restitution of circa 85 percent of the installment amounts paid.[98] This solution diverges from standard contract law insofar as the construction company has no right to demand performance, and the damages are fixed between 10 and 25 percent of the amounts paid in. In practice, this means that the sole remedy for breach is a court-imposed liquidated damages clause, which may easily be either over- or under-compensatory. In other words, the basic notion of contract as an agreement backed by expectation damages is no longer available in this highly significant segment of the Brazilian economy.[99]

No statutory rules prescribe this outcome. The Consumer Protection Code of 1990 (*Código de Defesa do Consumidor*) states that:

> In contracts for the purchase and sale of movable and immovable goods against payment in installments, as well as in fiduciary alienations in guarantee, clauses that establish the total loss of installments paid for the benefit of the creditor claiming the termination of the contract for breach and the repossession of the sold product are deemed to be null and void.[100]

This provision can be understood as a form of statutory constraint on penalty clauses and, as such, is largely consistent with contract law orthodoxy. Brazil's President vetoed another more heterodox provision of the Consumer Protection Code requiring the restitution of all amounts paid minus the economic benefit received.[101]

[98] See, e.g., STJ, Agravo Regimental no Recurso Especial 1.500.990-SP, 3a Turma, Rel. Moura Ribeiro, J. 26.04.2016, DJe 10.05.2016 (Brazil).

[99] This bears resemblance to the cancellation right afforded by statute in South Africa to installment purchasers of real estate. See text accompanying notes 65–70.

[100] Lei No. 8.078, de 11 de setembro de 1990, Diário Oficial da União [D.O.U.] de 12.9.1990, art. 53 (Brazil). European scholars have described Brazil's consumer contracts law as offering a comparatively "very high level ... of consumer protection, and [a] strong tendency to favour the so-called weaker party." O. L. R. Junior and S. Rodas, Interview with Reinhard Zimmermann and Jan Peter Schmidt (2015) 4 *Revista de Direito Civil Contemporâneo* 379–413, 403 (quoting Jan Peter Schmidt).

[101] Brazilian law permits Presidential line vetoes. The original provision approved by Congress (but vetoed by the President) provided that "the debtor will have the right to the compensation or restitution of installments paid by the time of contractual termination, adjusted for inflation,

The heterodox exit option granted to consumers followed from a series of incremental doctrinal steps based on somewhat traditional contract law principles.[102] In the first cases to reach the Superior Court of Justice, the Court held that "the defaulting debtor in principle has no right to request the termination of the contract," a conclusion to be altered only if "there is a supervening fact which is sufficiently strong to justify the breach."[103] The Court then found that currency devaluation and the application of various criteria for inflation adjustment under different national economic plans were supervening facts authorizing the termination of the contract because it was impossible, as a practical matter, for the consumer to perform.[104] The Court also found in such cases that contractual penalty clauses providing for the forfeiture of 90 percent of the amounts paid were abusive under the Consumer Protection Code – again not an outlandish conclusion in view of traditional suspicion of penalty clauses.[105]

In 2002 the Court settled a split between its chambers and confirmed that a consumer purchaser of real estate could unilaterally terminate the agreement due to the "insupportability" of installments. It also permitted the construction company to retain 25 percent of the amount paid "considering not only the costs of the company with the project but also the fact that, in this case, it was the plaintiff who took the initiative to breach the agreement."[106] The dissenting justices argued that the majority's interpretation was unreasonable in effectively implementing a vetoed statutory provision.[107]

Subsequent decisions did away with the requirement of changed circumstances or the impossibility or insupportability of payments by the purchaser, effectively

less the economic benefit obtained with use." This rule is similar to the result later embraced by courts, though it differed by not allowing consumers to sue for termination, and by requiring courts to ascertain the value of the economic advantage obtained by use (rather than universally applying a fixed rate such as 15 percent of payments made). It is noteworthy for offering restitution of benefits enjoyed by the purchaser as the sole remedy for this type of contract breach. The official message accompanying the Presidential veto specifically noted that, in disregarding the various costs incurred by sellers in installment contracts, the rule in question led to "unfair treatment" and "unforeseeable consequences for various sectors of the economy."

102 This form of exit rights bears little resemblance to the far narrower cancellation rights awarded by EU law (and also Brazil's Consumer Protection Code) for contracts negotiated on the doorstep or outside of a trader's establishment, which are limited in time to seven days following the purchase.

103 STJ, Recurso Especial No. 109.331-SP, Relator: Min. Ruy Rosado de Aguiar, 24.02.1997, D.J., 31.03.1997, 9638, 2 (Brazil).

104 Ibid., summary opinion 1 (ementa) ("[W]hen the breach is justified in view of supervening fact preventing contractual performance, with resulting imbalance due to the devaluation of the currency, the successive application of economic plans and different criteria to adjust the credit amount, the debtor may request the termination of the contract").

105 STJ, Recurso Especial No. 115.671, Relator: Min. Waldemar Zveiter, 08.08.2000, D.J., 02.10.2000, 161, 11 (Brazil).

106 STJ, Embargos de Divergência em Recurso Especial No. 59.870, Relator: Min. Barros Monteiro, 10.04.2002, D.J., 09.12.2002, 281, 6 (Brazil).

107 Ibid.

permitting home buyers to terminate purchase agreements at will. Courts also increasingly settled on the retention of a fixed percentage by the construction company, typically 10 or 15 percent of the amounts paid, without examining the particular benefits accruing to the consumer or damages incurred by the company. This form of remedial heterodoxy – in the form of judicially-imposed liquidated damages that dispense with proof of benefit or harm – likely responds to the massive caseload facing Brazilian courts. From a functional perspective, courts effectively implied a termination option subject to a small liquidated damages clause in all consumer contracts for the purchase of new housing.

Concerns about inequality and social justice likely played a role in the development of this line of opinions, which effectively shifted labor and real estate market risks from consumers to construction companies.[108] During the period of soaring house prices in the early 2000s, the implied exit option benefited consumers and construction companies alike, as the latter obtained financing from the first purchasers and then resold the units for a higher price if the initial purchasers were unable to pay. The termination agreements written in the shadow of the exit option case law were called "*distratos*" – a term which, according to the Civil Code, designates a mutual agreement to terminate a contract, even though not all terminations were entirely voluntary given the prevailing jurisprudence.[109] Nevertheless, when the housing market bubble exploded around 2014, demand for *distratos* – evidently encouraged by the heterodox jurisprudence – became a major problem for construction companies, some of which filed for bankruptcy during this period.

After significant lobbying from construction companies, a 2018 statute increased the maximum amount that could be retained in case of *distratos* to 50 percent of the amounts paid.[110] Strengthening the force of the contractual obligation was a step

[108] Brazilian courts have also protected purchasers of housing against the risk of insolvency on the part of construction companies. In the 1990s, Encol, one of the country's major construction companies, went bankrupt, causing great harm to consumers who had prepaid for their housing units. Even though many of Encol's units had been mortgaged to banks and duly registered, the Superior Court of Justice granted consumers who had paid the purchase price full title free of encumbrances, thus eliminating the banks' collateral. See STJ, Recurso Especial No. 415.667, Relator: Min. Aldir Passarinho Junior, 20.02.2003, 293 Diario da Justiça [D.J.], 07.04.2003, 1–2 (Brazil). Subsequent decisions concerning similar fact patterns invoked the social function of contracts to favor consumer purchasers, noting "the clear and systematic movement in the direction of correcting social distortions, in an attempt to reduce inequalities and afford mechanisms for the judge to seek the achievement of justice in the best possible way." STJ, Recurso Especial No. 691.738, Relatora: Min. Nancy Andrighi, 12.05.2005, 371, Diario da Justiça [D.J.], 26.09.2005, 8 (Brazil). This resulted in the enactment of a summary of the Court's uniform jurisprudence on the matter through súmula 308 in 2005, which states "the mortgage instituted by the construction company and the financing agent, before or after the preliminary agreement for the purchase and sale, has no effects vis-à-vis the purchasers of real estate." Ibid., 7–8.

[109] Código Civil (C.C.) (2002), art. 472 (Brazil).

[110] Lei No. 13.786, de 27 de Dezembro de 2018, DOU de 28.12.2018 (Brazil).

toward orthodoxy, although the reform is still heterodox in sanctioning now statutory liquidated damages in lieu of a default of expectation damages.

Brazilian law also provides other instances of heterodox approaches to contract remedies in the name of equality, such as imposing a requirement of symmetry in the application of penalty clauses. This means that, if a consumer contract only stipulates a penalty for a breach by the consumer (but not by the trader), the same penalty should apply for the benefit of the consumer in case of a breach by the trader. These decisions are generally based on notions of good faith, contractual equilibrium, and the social function of contract, as well as on the overarching purpose of consumer protection.[111] In one such opinion, the Court quotes a scholar noting that the "principle of equilibrium" emerging from the Consumer Protection Code results from "the protection of the consumer in view of their vulnerability" as well as the "protection of economic equilibrium," as a corollary of the principle of equality in the Brazilian Constitution.[112]

The so-called inversion of penalty clauses for the benefit of purchasers of housing under construction was the subject of a judgment by the STJ in a collective proceeding which became binding on lower courts.[113] The issue was whether the penalty clause imposed by the contract in the event of a late payment by the consumer may be applied for the benefit of the consumer if the construction company delays the conveyance of the housing unit. The judgment in question was preceded by a public hearing (*audiencia pública*) that included testimony by several civil law scholars, economists, as well as associations of consumers and construction companies.[114]

The public hearing dealt not only with technicalities regarding the doctrinal evolution of penalty clauses in Brazil, but also with the broader economic and social stakes of the issue in question. The attorney for the purchaser in the case defended the "heterointegration of the contract, by the judge" as a mechanism to achieve "social justice."[115] One public defender emphasized how it had become commonplace to sell real estate to the poor who could not afford the installments, leading to loss of amounts paid by the consumer when terminating the contract and profits by the construction company in subsequent sales. He argued that lack of proper

[111] See, e.g., STJ, Recurso Especial No. 1.614.721-DF, Relator: Min. Luis Felipe Salomão, 22.5.2019, Diário da Justiça Eletrônico [D.J.e], 25.6.2019 (Brazil).

[112] STJ., Recurso Especial No. 1.548.189-SP, Relator: Min. Paulo de Tarso Sanseverino, D.J.e, 6.9.2017 (Brazil), quoting B. Miragem, *Curso de Direito do Consumidor* (São Paulo: Revista dos Tribunais, 2014).

[113] Brazil's 2015 Code of Civil Procedure permits the Federal Supreme Court (Supremo Tribunal Federal) and the STJ to issue collective judgments that resolve multiple appeals addressing the same question of law – a mechanism designed to enhance efficiency in the adjudication of mass litigation in the country. See Lei No. 13.105, de 16 de Março de 2015, D.O.U. de 17.3.2015, arts. 1036–41 (Brazil).

[114] STJ, Recurso Especial No. 1.614.721-DF, Public hearing of August 27, 2018, Superior Tribunal de Justiça Jurisprudência [STJJ], 28.08.2018 (Brazil).

[115] STJ, Recurso Especial No. 1.614.721-DF, Public hearing of August 27, 2018, 6.

compensation for consumers in the case of delays would increase construction companies' incentives to make successive sales to persons unable to pay, leading to even greater harm to the poorest.[116] Gustavo Franco, a prominent economist and former president of the Brazilian Central Bank, appeared on behalf of an association of construction companies to argue against the inversion of penalty clauses, citing a "peril of populism" by which concerns about the disadvantaged and the weak would end up distorting the system and ultimately hurting the supposed beneficiaries of such a policy.[117] The STJ ultimately sided with consumers to issue a binding statement permitting the inversion of penalty clauses in all subsequent cases involving housing purchases.[118]

2.3.2.2 Health Insurance

There is also some evidence of heterodoxy in the field of insurance contracts. Brazilian courts have adopted pro-consumer approaches in prohibiting denial of coverage due to false statements or omissions of preexisting conditions by the insured, finding that insurance companies should bear the burden of requesting medical examinations. Numerous decisions also grant treatments deemed necessary for the realization of the insured's constitutional right to health despite clear contractual exclusions.[119] Commentators suspect that the near-disappearance of the market for individual (as opposed to collective) insurance contracts in Brazil is at least partly due to the excessively consumer-friendly case law of Brazilian courts.[120]

2.3.2.3 Legislative Backlash against Contract Law Heterodoxy

Brazil recently witnessed two legislative attempts to mitigate courts' heterodox approaches to contract law through new statutory rules on legal interpretation and

116 Ibid., 7.

117 Ibid., 64.

118 "In a contract of adhesion entered into between a buyer and the construction company, in case there is a penalty clause for the breach of the acquirer, the same shall be considered for the determination of damages for the breach of the seller." Tema Repetitivo 971, STJ Precedentes Qualificados (Tese Firmada for STJ, Recurso Especial No. 1.614.721-DF, Public hearing of August 27, 2018).

119 For a detailed analysis of the STJ's jurisprudence on health insurance contracts, see A. S. Guazzelli, A Busca da Justiça Distributiva no Judiciário Por Meio das Relações Contratuais: Uma Análise a Partir dos Planos de Saúde, Master's dissertation, University of São Paulo (2013) (finding support to the hypothesis that judges act in an arbitrary manner in favoring the weaker economic party, and concluding that "the judicial decisions may lead to undesirable effects, such as random wealth redistribution, favoring one individual to the detriment of the collectivity, and the incentive to opportunistic conducts").

120 The few companies that still offer individual health insurance plans charge a price that is 100 percent higher than those under group insurance plans. Ibid., 37.

application. A 2018 amendment to the Introductory Law to the Brazilian Legal System, which provides general standards of interpretation and choice of law, introduced a new rule which provides that "in the administrative, controlling and judicial spheres, one may not decide based on abstract legal values without considering the practical consequences of the decision."[121] The new provision is generally understood as an attempt to mitigate rising legal uncertainty due to an excessive use of broad principles (such as legality or human dignity) in legal decision-making in the country.

In 2019, the new "Law on Economic Freedom," initially enacted by President Bolsonaro as a provisional measure, sought to restrain state interference in economic activity, including private contracts.[122] Among other things, the statute amends the Civil Code to provide that contracts are to be interpreted in favor of economic freedom, that the allocation of contractual risks by the parties shall be respected, and that judicial rewriting of contract terms should only occur in an exceptional and limited manner. In specifically articulating implicit tenets of contract law's orthodoxy, it is difficult to make sense of these new rules except as a reaction to the prevailing heterodox approach of Brazilian courts. Nevertheless, the Law on Economic Freedom does not alter the protections of the Consumer Protection Code and, at any rate, its practical effects remain to be seen.

2.3.3 *Colombia*

Colombia's Constitutional Court expressly appeals to fundamental rights – such as the right to a vital minimum, health, housing, human dignity, and equality – in resolving disputes involving parties deemed to be weak and vulnerable with respect to contracts for the provision of public services. Colombia's Constitution, enacted in 1991, imposes on the state a duty to ensure the efficient provision of public services to all residents, which may be carried out by the state directly or by private parties subject to state regulation, control, and monitoring.[123] The Constitution goes on to provide that regulation of the provision of public services by statute should take into account the criteria of cost, solidarity, and, most notably for the present purposes, income redistribution.[124] However, the Constitutional Court of Colombia has intervened in contract disputes to promote the distributive concerns enshrined in the constitution even in the absence of statutory authorization. Some of its decisions can be justified as orthodox responses to concerns about imperfect information or substantive unfairness, but others appear to produce heterodox outcomes.

[121] Decreto-lei No. 4.657, de 4 de Setembro de 1942, as amended by Lei No. 13.655, de 25 de Abril de 2018, DOU de 26.4.2018 (Brazil).
[122] Lei No. 13.874, de 20 de Setembro de 2019, D.O.U. de 20.9.2019 (Brazil).
[123] Constitución Política de Colombia [C.P.], art. 365.
[124] See ibid., art. 367.

Contract cases typically reach the Constitutional Court through *tutela* claims, a type of action guaranteed by the constitution to protect fundamental rights against public authorities, as well as private parties in exceptional circumstances defined by statute.[125] While contract law disputes are generally subject to ordinary jurisdiction and remedies, *tutela* may be invoked by "subjects of special constitutional protection," such as the elderly, the ill, minors, the disabled, female heads of households, and persons earning less than the minimum wage.[126] Contract disputes potentially impinging on fundamental rights such as life, health, or the vital minimum are thus subject to *tutela* claims and constitutional review.[127] The Court's contract law jurisprudence has focused primarily on insurance and public utility contracts.

2.3.3.1 Health and Life Insurance

Colombia's Constitutional Court has decided several cases involving health and life insurance contracts in favor of disadvantaged plaintiffs based on constitutional principles protecting health and the vital minimum. In a 2005 *tutela* decision, the Court found that a private health insurer's refusal to renew a contract, while generally permissible, violated the constitutional right to health given the circumstances of the case. The plaintiff was an elderly person with multiple ailments that urgently required medical treatment, and the health insurance contract in question was in force for over four years. The Court rejected the argument that the social right to health applied exclusively against the state's social security framework, finding that "the contract's object has an inseparable relation to the effects of the constitutional right to health, so that the interpretation of the scope of contract clauses is contingent, in any case, on the need to guarantee the correct exercise of this right."[128] In a subsequent 2011 decision, the Court held that a health insurance company could not terminate a contract for the continued nonpayment of the monthly premium when the insured was HIV-positive, citing the fundamental rights to dignified life, health, personal integrity, social security, and equality.[129] It found that, even though the patient was receiving treatment through Colombia's standard health coverage, the relevant question was "the abuse of the company as the dominant party of the contract."[130]

[125] Ibid., art. 86.

[126] G. Z. Bahamón, Constitutionalización y Protección de Derechos Fundamentales en el Contrato de Seguros: Análisis Jurisprudencial-Corte Constitucional de Colombia (2016) 45 *Revista Ibero-Latinoamericana de Seguros* 233–68, 236.

[127] Ibid., 239.

[128] Corte Constitucional [C. C.] [Constitutional Court], julio 8, 2005, Sentencia T-724/05 (Colombia).

[129] C. C., October 27, 2011, Sentencia T-811-11.

[130] Ibid., 8. The Court also argued that the company had tolerated the insured's default and was therefore stopped from seeking termination of the contract (allanamiento a la mora).

2.3.3.2 Access to Water

The Court has also appealed to the fundamental rights to human dignity, life, health, and equality to limit a water company's ability to stop the provision of water due to nonpayment by "subjects of special protection."[131] The plaintiff in the case was a 54-year-old woman who was the head of her household, physically incapacitated to work, and responsible for two minor sons. While the Court upheld the statutory provision permitting the suspension of supply as a means to promote the efficient, continuous, and uninterrupted provision of public services to all, it also determined that denial of water to subjects of special protection was disproportionate and, therefore, unconstitutional. The Court held that, in response to nonpayment, the company should investigate the credit situation of the user and negotiate payment agreements consistent with their ability to pay. If the payment obligations were still not performed, the company could limit the water supply to 50 liters per person.[132]

2.4 EXPLAINING DIVERGENCE

The decisions and doctrines set out in Section 2.3 are difficult to reconcile with contract law orthodoxy. We first explain why defenders of orthodoxy would argue that these alternative approaches are either illegitimate or ineffective. We then identify ways in which economic, political, and legal features of Brazil and South Africa, and to a lesser extent Colombia, deviate from the assumptions that underpin contract law orthodoxy.

2.4.1 *The Case for Orthodoxy*

The orthodox view that contract law should not be designed to achieve distributive goals rests on two main sets of arguments. The first set focuses on *legitimacy*. One of those arguments rests on the libertarian proposition that forcible redistribution by the state generally cannot be justified, except, importantly, where it is required to rectify unjust transfers of resources.[133] Since contract law involves enforcement by the state, this view rules out redistribution through contract law in most cases.[134] Our impression is that relatively few modern legal scholars endorse this line of argument. A more widely accepted, though controversial, view is that judges lack the legitimacy to decide upon distributive objectives. According to at least some political theories, decisions about the distribution of resources in society are illegitimate

[131] C. C., October 3, 2011, Sentencia T-740/11 (Colombia).

[132] Ibid.

[133] R. Nozick, *Anarchy, State, and Utopia* (New York: Basic Books, 1974), pp. 151–53.

[134] A. T. Kronman, Contract Law and Distributive Justice (1980) 89 *Yale Law Journal* 472–512, 473–74.

unless made by democratically elected officials, which judges often are not.[135] This view is, to be sure, fiercely resisted by critical legal scholars.[136]

The second and arguably most central pillar of contract law orthodoxy is a set of pragmatic arguments about *effectiveness*. The common feature of these arguments is a claim that fiscal policy, meaning the rules and practices concerning taxation and public spending, is superior to contract law as a means of achieving distributive justice.[137] At least five distinct arguments support this conclusion.[138]

1. *Accuracy and predictability*. Fiscal policies can be conditioned on information – such as parties' income, location, profession, and number of dependents – that may not be available to either a tribunal adjudicating a contractual dispute or to parties when they enter into their contract.[139] This means that rules of contract law conditioned on distributive information would not only be inaccurate, but would also lead to inefficient uncertainty among contracting parties.[140]
2. *Comprehensiveness*. Redistribution through fiscal policy is likely to be more comprehensive.[141] Tax and spending programs can be applied to everyone in society, as opposed to just the parties subject to a given body of contract law. By contrast, when distribution is deliberately altered through regulation of contracts only people who participate in the relevant transactions will be affected.
3. *Efficiency*. Rules of contract law aimed at distributive objectives can induce inefficient behavior – meaning behavior whose costs exceed its

[135] K. A. Kordana and D. H. Tabachnick, Rawls and Contract Law (2005) 73 *George Washington Law Review* 598–632, 623–24.

[136] See, e.g., Kennedy, Distributive and Paternalist Motives in Contract and Tort Law 564–65; R. M. Unger, The Critical Legal Studies Movement (1983) *Harvard Law Review* 561–675, 565.

[137] See J. Rawls, *Political Liberalism: Expanded Edition* (New York: Columbia University Press, 2005), pp. 267–68; see also L. Kaplow and S. Shavell, Why the Legal System Is Less Efficient than the Income Tax in Redistributing Income (1994) 23 *The Journal of Legal Studies* 667–81 (arguing that redistribution of income through the income tax and welfare system can be more efficient than through other legal rules).

[138] D. A. Weisbach, Should Legal Rules Be Used to Redistribute Income? (2003) 70 *The University of Chicago Law Review* 439–53, 446–53.

[139] See Rawls, *Political Liberalism*, p. 267. Separate institutions are required to preserve background justice because "the rules governing individual agreements and ... transactions cannot be too complex, or require too much information to be correctly applied." Ibid.

[140] Ibid., pp. 267–68. See also M. Weber, *Economy and Society: An Outline of Interpretive Sociology* (New York: Bedminster Press, 1968), pp. 883, 886–87 (claiming that "the modern class problem" has led to demands for "social law" to be based on ethical postulates such as "justice" which, if accommodated, would undermine the formality and rationality and thus calculability of law that has supported capitalist economic development in Continental Europe).

[141] See Kaplow and Shavell, Why the Legal System Is Less Efficient than the Income Tax in Redistributing Income, 675.

benefits – that fiscal policy does not.[142] An example might be a warranty of habitability which requires sellers of buildings to make improvements whose costs exceed their value to certain buyers. In principle, policy-makers could confer the same benefit on the relevant buyers more efficiently by granting them a tax credit financed by an increase in income taxes.

4. *Avoidance*. Perhaps the most powerful argument against using contract law to achieve distributive objectives is that contracting parties may be able to avoid the effects of distribution-motivated rules. The law can mandate that one party to a contract confer a benefit on their counterparty, but the target of the regulation is likely to adjust the price or other terms of the contract, or refuse to contract altogether, in order to offset the costs of the mandate. The overall distributive effects of the intervention will depend on the effects of those adjustments.
5. *Interdependence*. Sometimes the welfare of the people burdened by an intervention motivated by distribution will be intertwined with the welfare of the intended beneficiaries. In the extreme case, distributive concerns are irrelevant to the resolution of contractual disputes because there is complete identity between the interests of the parties to the contract, as in the case where the parties are firms owned by diversified shareholders with equal interests in both firms.[143] One common critique is that it may be difficult to determine the overall effects of a measure that initially distributes wealth from firms to individuals. While also questionable in the United States, this concern tends to be less powerful in the Global South, where stock ownership tends to be much more concentrated, and lower among the general population, than in the United States.

2.4.2 *Explaining Heterodoxy*

Distributive demands, and the relative legitimacy and effectiveness of judges and fiscal institutions, all vary from time to time and place to place. Accordingly, as Anthony Kronman pointed out in a classic article, the case for contract law orthodoxy is highly contingent on the social and institutional context.[144] For instance, US scholars have occasionally recognized that contract law may be an appealing second

[142] Ibid., 669; S. Shavell, A Note on Efficiency vs. Distributional Equity in Legal Rulemaking: Should Distributional Equity Matter Given Optimal Income Taxation? (1981) 71 *The American Economic Review* 414–18.

[143] A. Schwartz and R. E. Scott, Contract Theory and the Limits of Contract Law (2003) 113 *Yale Law Journal* 541–620, 555–56 ("[I]t is difficult to create distributional benefits for the shareholders who own most business firms").

[144] Kronman, Contract Law and Distributive Justice, 508–10.

best mechanism for achieving distributive goals if the fiscal system cannot be counted on for that purpose.[145]

Contract law heterodoxy emerged in the Global South under social, economic, and institutional conditions that deviate substantially from the conditions assumed by the conventional justifications for the orthodox approach. First, substantial and unjustifiable inequality bolsters the legitimacy of state-led efforts to improve the welfare of disadvantaged groups. Profound inequality and segregation also make it easier to aim redistributive measures accurately at relatively privileged actors without affecting members of disadvantaged groups. Second, states that experience high levels of inequality may be unable to achieve adequate distribution solely through fiscal institutions. Third, leading judges in these countries have responded to these circumstances by embracing the idea of transformative constitutionalism, which expressly legitimizes pursuit of distributive objectives by the judiciary in the course of resolving private disputes.

The legal systems in which we observe contract law heterodoxy are also heterodox in other areas. In fact, Brazil, Colombia, and South Africa are well known among comparative lawyers for their embrace of a heterodox approach to constitutional law known as "transformative constitutionalism."[146] This term was coined to describe South Africa's distinctive approach to constitutional law and has subsequently been applied to Brazilian and Colombian constitutional law as well.[147]

As its name suggests, transformative constitutionalism starts from the premise that constitutional law should transform rather than simply reflect the society it governs.[148] Proponents argue that the project of social transformation would be doomed to failure if inequality and injustice in the private sphere were shielded

[145] Z. Liscow, Is Efficiency Biased? (2018) 85 *University of Chicago Law Review* 1649–718, 1664; L. A. Fennell and R. H. McAdams, The Distributive Deficit in Law and Economics (2016) 100 *Minnesota Law Review* 1051–130, 1053, n. 5; see B. H. McDonnell, The Economists' New Arguments (2003) 88 *Minnesota Law Review* 86–118, 111; R. S. Markovits, Why Kaplow and Shavell's "Double-Distortion Argument" Articles Are Wrong (2005) 13 *George Mason Law Review* 511–620, 556–57, 597–601; C. R. Sunstein, Willingness to Pay vs. Welfare (2007) 1 *Harvard Law & Policy Review* 303–30, 314–15; Z. Liscow, Reducing Inequality on the Cheap: When Legal Rule Design Should Incorporate Equity as Well as Efficiency (2014) 123 *Yale Law Journal* 2478–511, 2502, n. 52.

[146] See generally O. V. Vieira, U. Baxi, and F. Viljoen (eds.), *Transformative Constitutionalism: Comparing the Apex Courts of Brazil, India and South Africa* (Pretoria: Pretoria University Law Press, 2013); D. Bonilla Maldonado (ed.), *Constitutionalism of the Global South: The Activist Tribunals of India, South Africa, and Colombia* (Cambridge: Cambridge University Press, 2013).

[147] K. E. Klare, Legal Culture and Transformative Constitutionalism (1998) 14 *South African Journal on Human Rights* 146–88, 150. But see D. W. Arguelhes, Transformative Constitutionalism: A View from Brazil, in P. Dann, M. Riegner, and M. Bönnemann (eds.), *The Global South and Comparative Constitutional Law* (Oxford: Oxford University Press, 2020), pp. 165–89, 167 (arguing that Brazil's Supreme Court has been a "late bloomer" compared to Colombia's, and that it has at best played a marginal role in fighting poverty and inequality).

[148] Klare, Legal Culture and Transformative Constitutionalism, 150.

from scrutiny. Accordingly, a key precept of transformative constitutionalism is that the constitution is to be used to reshape the laws that govern relations between private actors, including contract law.[149]

While there is debate about whether transformative constitutionalism only appears in the Global South, it definitely relates to societies that have undergone profound political changes.[150] In the paradigmatic cases, those changes included the adoption of new constitutional texts following nation-wide consultations and deliberations. Brazil underwent this process in 1988, in the course of transitioning to democracy after a long period of military rule. Colombia's 1991 Constitution was adopted in an effort to open up a two-party political system that was captured by a handful of powerful actors, leading to widespread popular frustration and political violence. In South Africa, the 1996 constitution was adopted to mark the end of the apartheid regime and the advent of multiracial democracy.

In each of these cases the reformed constitution was clearly designed to achieve economic as well as political change. The Brazilian constitution is the most explicit. It states that "[t]he fundamental objectives of the [state] are," among other things, "to eradicate poverty and substandard living conditions and to reduce social and regional inequalities."[151] Both the Brazilian and South African constitutions also make special provision for expropriation of rural land for the purpose of land reform.[152] In South Africa, the "commitment to land reform" is listed along with a broader commitment "to reforms to bring about equitable access to all South Africa's natural resources."[153] South Africa's constitution also guarantees, in qualified terms, equitable access to land.[154] Finally, all three constitutional texts guarantee access to key goods such as education, healthcare, housing, and social security.[155]

For the present purposes, the critical feature of transformative constitutionalism is that it allows courts charged with resolving contractual disputes to invoke constitutional norms as a basis for altering the distribution of resources in society, especially when the aim is to reverse inequality that can be linked to historic injustice. This directly contradicts the idea that it is illegitimate for judges to use

149 Davis and Klare, Transformative Constitutionalism and the Common and Customary Law, 410–11.

150 M. Hailbronner, Transformative Constitutionalism: Not Only in the Global South (2017) 65 *The American Journal of Comparative Law* 527–65. See generally Versteeg, Can Rights Combat Economic Inequality? (describing broader concerns about inequality in the constitutional jurisprudence of certain Global North countries).

151 Constituição Federal [C. F.] [Constitution] art. 3 (Brazil). See also ibid., art. 170 (specifying that the economic order must accord "with the dictates of social justice," "the social function of property," and "reduction of regional and social differences").

152 Ibid., art. 184; S. Afr. Const., 1996 art. 25.

153 S. Afr. Const., 1996 art. 25(2)–(4).

154 Ibid., art. 25(5).

155 C. F. art. 6 (Brazil); Constitución Política de Colombia [C.P.], art. 48, 51, 67; S. Afr. Const., 1996, art. 26, 27, 29.

contract law as a tool for promoting distributive objectives, a key intellectual foundation of contract law orthodoxy.

2.4.3 *The Significance of Heterodoxy*

To this point, our analysis has presumed that contract law heterodoxy matters from a practical standpoint. In this section, we examine three possible challenges to that conclusion. First, the divergence we observe may be formal rather than functional. Second, heterodox features of contract law may affect a relatively small proportion of the population. Third, firms might take steps to avoid the impact of distributive interventions.

2.4.3.1 Functional Convergence

A classic lesson of comparative law is that not all differences in legal doctrines and styles of legal reasoning translate into distinct outcomes of similar controversies. Instead, many comparative scholars believe that the opposite is true, with different doctrinal labels often bringing about similar or identical results. Prominent comparativists Konrad Zweigert and Hein Kötz famously argued for a presumption of functional similarity in the response of different legal systems to practical problems, despite apparent doctrinal differences.[156] That presumption may well apply to the problems addressed by contract law heterodoxy, even though Zweigert and Kötz limited their analysis to "advanced" legal systems, perhaps in an effort to exclude the Global South.

Our case studies deal primarily with legal arguments about the role of inequality and social rights in the adjudication of contract disputes. As noted throughout the country narratives, we believe that an orthodox approach could lead to the same result in at least some of the cases examined. Although prevalent, functional similarity does not appear to be universal, to the effect that contract law heterodoxy is, in many cases, consequential from an economic standpoint. Moreover, the greater tendency to invoke distributive or social justice considerations in contract law reasoning is interesting in its own right.

A more comprehensive approach to functional equivalence would consider not only whether courts across different jurisdictions would decide a given case in the same way by invoking different contract law doctrines, but also whether they might arrive at similar outcomes by invoking other bodies of law. This kind of functional substitution may well serve to limit the practical significance of contract law

[156] See K. Zweigert and H. Kötz, *Introduction to Comparative Law*, 3rd ed. (Oxford: Clarendon Press, 1998), p. 4. See generally R. Zimmermann and S. Whittaker (eds.), *Good Faith in European Contract Law* (Cambridge: Cambridge University Press, 2000) (finding significant convergence in the outcome of various hypotheticals).

heterodoxy. For instance, in the United States (and, to a lesser extent, other common law jurisdictions), bankruptcy offers vulnerable parties a fresh start from harsh bargains, while civil law jurisdictions are more likely to offer responses through contract law.[157] US bankruptcy law is considered to offer a safety net which at least partially compensates for a weak welfare state,[158] and several progressive scholars advocate using bankruptcy law to achieve social objectives beyond economic efficiency.[159] More generally, US law often tackles some of the same distributive concerns through specific legislative (rather than judicial) interventions, including in the realm of consumer finance, healthcare, and the provision of public services.[160]

2.4.3.2 Lack of Comprehensiveness

The project of relying on contract law to achieve distributive objectives presupposes a minimum degree of access to formal markets and courts. This means that the impact of contract law heterodoxy is generally limited to parties who were able to enter into contracts with nontrivial stakes and who have access to courts (as well as, arguably, future contracting parties whose contract terms are shaped by the courts' jurisprudence). The poorest of the poor, however, are likely to lack access both to significant contracts and to courts, especially when the effects of their poverty are compounded by a lack of information or other forms of vulnerability. Consequently, the primary beneficiaries of contract law heterodoxy presumably will be members of the middle class and lower middle class, not the poorest. This limitation of the potential effect of contract law heterodoxy is a concrete manifestation of the problem of comprehensiveness discussed in Section 2.3.

Lack of comprehensiveness is not a definitive indictment of contract law heterodoxy given growing global concern about the shrinking size and increasing precarity of the middle class. Moreover, the problem appears to be no more acute than the one observed in the context of transformative constitutionalism and the right to health. Various scholars argue that "the judicialization of the right to health" may be regressive in favoring relatively wealthy citizens with access to courts, unlike public health policies that would benefit the poorest segments of the population.[161]

[157] Pargendler, The Role of the State in Contract Law, 145–46, 175–76.

[158] See, e.g., R. M. Lawless and E. Warren, Shrinking the Safety Net: The 2005 Changes in U.S. Bankruptcy Law, 1 (2006) University of Illinois Law & Economics, Working Paper No. LE06–031.

[159] See generally D. A. Skeel Jr., Vern Countryman and the Path of Progressive (and Populist) Bankruptcy Scholarship (2000) 113 *Harvard Law Review* 1075–129.

[160] See R. Van Loo, Broadening Consumer Law: Competition, Protection, and Distribution (2019) 95 *Notre Dame Law Review* 211–62 (arguing that consumer law can and should be designed to have significant distributive effects); Patient Protection and Affordable Care Act, 42 U.S.C. § 18001(d)(3) (barring discrimination in provision of health insurance against individuals with preexisting conditions).

[161] See, e.g., C. Portugal Gouvêa, Social Rights against the Poor (2013) 7 *Vienna Online Journal on International Constitutional Law* 454–75, 465–68; V. A. Da Silva and F. V. Terrazas,

The fact that the impact of contract law heterodoxy depends on access to courts and formal contracting means that its prospects in any given jurisdiction will depend on a range of institutional arrangements. In the United States, for example, beyond the costs of legal proceedings (including legal representation), the widespread use and enforceability of arbitration clauses in consumer contracts limits the emergence and potential application of heterodox contract law.[162] By contrast, Global South jurisdictions such as Brazil generally resist the use of arbitration in consumer contracts, which remain subject to judicial review – a mode of dispute resolution more conducive to heterodoxy.[163]

2.4.3.3 Avoidance

A central critique of contract law heterodoxy is that it can backfire. As the argument goes, attempts to favor certain groups in contract disputes may lead to price increases or other unfavorable contract terms that hurt precisely such parties in the future (the risk of "hurting the people you are trying to help"). Courts in the Global South are increasingly cognizant of the distinct ex ante incentives caused by contract law decisions, which can lead judges to pause before seeking to help the disadvantaged party in any given case due to the risk of harming similarly situated parties in the future.[164] This may be why most of the examples of heterodoxy we document involve changes in contract law doctrines of relatively broad application – such as rules on prejudgment interest or recovery of partial payments for real estate – that disproportionately benefit members of disadvantaged groups, as opposed to rules targeted solely at members of those groups. These kinds of rulings cannot be avoided simply by discriminating against members of the disadvantaged groups because they apply to transactions with a more broadly defined group of people. Even if the effects of these sorts of heterodox rulings are neutralized by changes in contracting behavior, the intended beneficiaries will not be the only ones to suffer. Therefore, the breadth of these rulings dilutes both their positive effects on intended beneficiaries and the negative effects of any efforts at avoidance.

Claiming the Right to Health in Brazilian Courts: The Exclusion of the Already Excluded? (2011) 36 *Law & Social Inquiry* 825–53, 830–31; O. L. M. Ferraz, Harming the Poor through Social Rights Litigation: Lessons from Brazil (2011) 89 *Texas Law Review* 1643–68, 1651–68.

162 See K. V.W. Stone and A. J. S. Colvin, The Arbitration Epidemic: Mandatory Arbitration Deprives Workers and Consumers of Their Rights (2015) *Economic Policy Institute* 26; J. P. Nehf, The Impact of Mandatory Arbitration on the Common Law Regulation of Standard Terms in Consumer Contracts (2017) 85 *George Washington Law Review* 1692–716, 1695.

163 Lei No. 8.078, art. 51, § VII, de 11 de Setembro de 1990, Código de Proteção e Defesa do Consumidor [C.D.C.] de Setembro 1990 (Brazil) (deeming null and void the clauses that impose mandatory arbitration of consumer contracts disputes).

164 For an example of this concern, expressed by Judge Theron in *Beadica 231 CC (5) SA*, see text accompanying note 83.

Another concern is that contract law heterodoxy may impact industrial organization and market structure. By imposing an "equity tax" on the contract law system, heterodox contract laws may encourage firms to eschew contracts entirely, such as by embracing vertical integration. One study by Brazilian economists found that global fast-food chain McDonald's changed its strategy in Brazil from relying primarily on franchisees (as it does in most jurisdictions) to adopting a significant majority of company-owned stores.[165] The shift occurred after courts rewrote the economic terms of franchise agreements based on constraints of Brazil's landlord–tenant laws when franchisees sued following the devaluation of the country's currency in 1999.[166]

Yet increased vertical integration may not be a particularly attractive outcome for Global South jurisdictions whose economies are already dominated by large business groups. Scholars argue that weak contract institutions are one reason for the prevalence of family-owned business groups in the Global South, as vertical integration and the family's reputation substitute for formal contract enforcement.[167]

Paradoxically, at least some manifestations of contract law heterodoxy may favor relatively large business groups. Not only are they able to avoid market contracting to a greater extent through vertical integration, they may also be relatively attractive contracting partners because they are less likely to qualify for special legal treatment in the event of a dispute. In short, small businesses may benefit from heterodox contract adjudication, ex post, yet suffer from its expected effects ex ante through price adjustments and lost contracting opportunities. Conversely, firms belonging to large business groups could avoid both effects. What is perhaps even more troubling, by weakening private contracting as a commitment device, heterodox approaches to contract law could raise barriers to entry and again favor business groups with established reputations.

2.4.4 *Prospects for Convergence*

The conditions correlated with the emergence of heterodoxy in Brazil, South Africa, and Colombia are beginning to emerge in the United States and other Global North countries. There has been a tremendous rise in economic inequality in the United States and, to a lesser extent, other Global North countries, at the end of the twentieth century.[168] In many countries, including the United States, inequality is

165 V. L. Dos Santos Silva and P. F. de Azevedo, Contratos Interfirmas em Diferentes Ambientes Institucionais: O Caso McDonald's França Versus Brasil (2006) 41 *Revista de Administração* 381–93, 382, 389–90.

166 Ibid.

167 See e.g., R. J. Gilson, Controlling Family Shareholders in Developing Countries (2007) 60 *Stanford Law Review* 633–56, 641–45. See generally T. Khanna and Y. Yafeh, Business Groups in Emerging Markets: Paragons or Parasites? (2007) 45 Journal of Economic Literature 331–72.

168 See, e.g., T. Piketty, *Capital in the Twenty-First Century* (Cambridge, MA: The Belknap Press of Harvard University Press, 2017), pp. 297–98.

explained in part by a history of racial injustice. This has prompted increased calls for attention to distributive considerations by scholars and political leaders, and lamentations about the state's inability to achieve the desired levels of distribution through tax and transfer schemes.[169] The manifestations of contract law heterodoxy that have emerged in Germany and other countries during the COVID-19 pandemic may mark the beginning of a trend.[170]

If inequality continues to rise, the pressure to abandon contract law orthodoxy in the United States and similarly situated Global North countries will become stronger. If and when that happens, scholars and lawmakers in the Global North will benefit from studying the heterodox approaches that have emerged in countries such as South Africa, Brazil, and Colombia. Whether contract law heterodoxy is viewed as a promising policy alternative or as an ill-devised strategy, its real-world significance shows how inequality might affect the operation of foundational private law institutions.

2.5 CONCLUSION

Documenting examples of contract law heterodoxy in the Global South illuminates both the factors shaping legal developments in the Global South and the normative stakes of contract law more generally. Contrary to conventional understandings, private law in the Global South is not merely a flawed copy of foreign counterparts or a remnant of indigenous (and backward) customs. Nor do the differences between Global North and Global South countries exclusively concern the efficiency of judicial enforcement. Instead, the economic, social, and institutional challenges faced by Global South jurisdictions have promoted adaptations to contract law adjudication, including notably greater concern for distributive outcomes. While it is unclear whether this stance is beneficial, it is likely consequential from an economic standpoint.

The emergence of heterodox legal approaches in the Global South also draws attention to the potential link between inequality and the delegitimization of orthodox contract law doctrine. Economic dislocation during the Great Depression and the COVID-19 crisis also prompted more heterodox approaches to contract law in the Global North. For those opposing contract law heterodoxy, this may offer a warning on the importance of mitigating inequality through other means. For those favoring contract law heterodoxy, it may show the feasibility of a broader array of tools to fight social injustice. At any rate, the phenomenon reveals that contract law around the world is not as orthodox and uniform as scholars typically assume and that there are valuable lessons to be learned from turning the lens of legal scholarship toward the Global South.

[169] Fennell and McAdams, The Distributive Deficit in Law and Economics; Z. Liscow, Redistribution for Realists (2022) 107 *Iowa Law Review* 495–562.

[170] See Section 2.2.4.

BIBLIOGRAPHY

Agarwal, S. et al., Regulating Consumer Financial Products: Evidence from Credit Cards (2015) 130 *The Quarterly Journal of Economics* 111–64.

Ahlering, B. and Deakin, S., Labor Regulation, Corporate Governance, and Legal Origin: A Case of Institutional Complementarity? (2007) 41 *Law & Society Review* 865–908.

Alston, L. J., Farm Foreclosure Moratorium Legislation: A Lesson from the Past (1984) 74 *The American Economic Review* 445–57.

Arguelhes, D. W., Transformative Constitutionalism: A View from Brazil, in P. Dann, M. Riegner, and M. Bönnemann (eds.), *The Global South and Comparative Constitutional Law* (Oxford: Oxford University Press, 2020), pp. 165–89.

Arida, P., Bacha, E. L., and Lara-Resende, A., Credit, Interest, and Jurisdictional Uncertainty: Conjectures on the Case of Brazil, in F. Giavazzi, I. Goldfajn, and S. Herrera (eds.), *Inflation Targeting, Debt, and the Brazilian Experience, 1999 to 2003* (Cambridge, MA: MIT Press, 2005), pp. 265–93.

Ayres, I. and Gertner, R., Filling Gaps in Incomplete Contracts: An Economic Theory of Default Rules (1989) 99 *Yale Law Journal* 87–130.

Bagchi, A., The Political Economy of Regulating Contract (2014) 62 *The American Journal of Comparative Law* 687–738.

Bahamón, G. Z., Constitutionalización y Protección de Derechos Fundamentales en el Contrato de Seguros: Análisis Jurisprudencial-Corte Constitucional de Colombia (2016) 45 *Revista Ibero-Latinoamericana de Seguros* 233–68.

Bar-Gill, O. and Ben-Shahar, O., Regulatory Techniques in Consumer Protection: A Critique of European Consumer Contract Law (2013) 50 *Common Market Law Review* 109–25.

Bonilla Maldonado, D. (ed.), *Constitutionalism of the Global South: The Activist Tribunals of India, South Africa, and Colombia* (Cambridge: Cambridge University Press, 2013).

Botero, J. C., et al., The Regulation of Labor (2004) 119 *The Quarterly Journal of Economics* 1339–82.

Brunotte, N. and Elsaß, L., (2020). The German Bundestag Resolves Amendments to Contract Law to Mitigate the Consequences of the Coronavirus Crisis, DLA Piper, May 6, 2020.

Caruso, D., The Baby and the Bath Water: The American Critique of European Contract Law (2013) 61 *American Journal of Comparative Law* 479–91.

Collins, H., Distributive Justice through Contracts (1992) 45 *Current Legal Problems* 49–67.

Da Silva, V. A. and Terrazas, F. V., Claiming the Right to Health in Brazilian Courts: The Exclusion of the Already Excluded? (2011) 36 *Law & Social Inquiry* 825–53.

Dagan, H. and Heller, M., *The Choice Theory of Contracts* (Cambridge: Cambridge University Press, 2017).

Davis, D. M. and Klare, K., Transformative Constitutionalism and the Common and Customary Law (2010) 26 *South African Journal on Human Rights* 403–509.

Davis, K. E. and Pargendler, M., Contract Law and Inequality (2022) 107 *Iowa Law Review* 1485–542.

Dos Santos Silva, V. L. and de Azevedo, P. F., Contratos Interfirmas em Diferentes Ambientes Institucionais: O Caso McDonald's França Versus Brasil (2006) 41 *Revista de Administração* 381–93.

Eisenberg, M. A., The Theory of Contracts, in P. Benson (ed.), *The Theory of Contract Law: New Essays* (Cambridge: Cambridge University Press, 2001), pp. 206–64.

Fennell, L. A. and McAdams, R. H., The Distributive Deficit in Law and Economics (2016) 100 *Minnesota Law Review* 1051–130.

Ferraz, O. L. M., Harming the Poor through Social Rights Litigation: Lessons from Brazil (2011) 89 *Texas Law Review* 1643–68.

Fleming, A., The Rise and Fall of Unconscionability as the "Law of the Poor" (2014) 102 *The Georgetown Law Journal* 1383–442.

Friedman, L. M., *A History of American Law*, 4th ed. (New York: Oxford University Press, 2019).

Contract Law in America: A Social and Economic Case Study (Madison: University of Wisconsin Press, 1965).

Gilson, R. J., Controlling Family Shareholders in Developing Countries (2007) 60 *Stanford Law Review* 633–56.

Glendon, M. A., The Transformation of American Landlord–Tenant Law (1982) 23 *Boston College Law Review* 503–76.

Gordley, J., Equality in Exchange (1981) 69 *California Law Review* 1587–656.

Guazzelli, A. S., A Busca da Justiça Distributiva no Judiciário Por Meio das Relações Contratuais: Uma Análise a Partir dos Planos de Saúde, Master's dissertation, University of São Paulo (2013).

Hailbronner, M., Transformative Constitutionalism: Not Only in the Global South (2017) 65 *The American Journal of Comparative Law* 527–65.

Hershkoff, H., Transforming Legal Theory in the Light of Practice: The Judicial Application of Social and Economic Rights to Private Orderings, in V. Gauri and D. M. Brinks (eds.), *Courting Social Justice: Judicial Enforcement of Social and Economic Rights in the Developing World* (Cambridge: Cambridge University Press, 2008), pp. 268–302.

Hesselink, M., The Horizontal Effects of Social Rights in European Contract Law (2003) 1 *Europa e Diritto Privato* 1–18.

Jiménez, F., Against Parochialism in Contract Theory: A Response to Brian Bix (2019) 32 *Ratio Juris* 233–50.

Junior, O. L. R. and Rodas, S., Interview with Reinhard Zimmermann and Jan Peter Schmidt (2015) 4 *Revista de Direito Civil Contemporâneo* 379–413.

Kaplow, L. and Shavell, S., Why the Legal System Is Less Efficient than the Income Tax in Redistributing Income (1994) 23 *The Journal of Legal Studies* 667–81.

Kennedy, D., Distributive and Paternalist Motives in Contract and Tort Law, with Special Reference to Compulsory Terms and Unequal Bargaining Power (1982) 41 *Maryland Law Review* 563–658.

Khanna, T. and Yafeh, Y., Business Groups in Emerging Markets: Paragons or Parasites? (2007) 45 *Journal of Economic Literature* 331–72.

Klare, K. E., Legal Culture and Transformative Constitutionalism (1998) 14 *South African Journal on Human Rights* 146–88.

Kordana, K. A. and Tabachnick, D. H., Rawls and Contract Law (2005) 73 *George Washington Law Review* 598–632.

Kronman, A. T., Contract Law and Distributive Justice (1980) 89 *Yale Law Journal* 472–512.

Lamounier, B. and de Souza, A., *As Elites Brasileiras e o Desenvolvimento Nacional: Fatores de Consenso e Dissenso* (São Paulo: Instituto de Estudos Econômicos, Sociais e Políticos de São Paulo, 2002).

Lawless, R. M. and Warren, E., Shrinking the Safety Net: The 2005 Changes in U.S. Bankruptcy Law, Working Paper No. LE06–031, University of Illinois Law & Economics (2006).

Liscow, Z., Is Efficiency Biased? (2018) 85 *University of Chicago Law Review* 1649–718.

Redistribution for Realists (2022) 107 *Iowa Law Review* 495–562.

Reducing Inequality on the Cheap: When Legal Rule Design Should Incorporate Equity as Well as Efficiency (2014) 123 *Yale Law Journal* 2478–511.
Markovits, R. S., Why Kaplow and Shavell's "Double-Distortion Argument" Articles Are Wrong (2005) 13 *George Mason Law Review* 511–620.
Mattei, U., Three Patterns of Law: Taxonomy and Change in the World's Legal Systems (1997) 45 *The American Journal of Comparative Law* 5–44.
McDonnell, B. H., The Economists' New Arguments (2003) 88 *Minnesota Law Review* 86–118.
Miragem, B., *Curso de Direito do Consumidor* (São Paulo: Revista dos Tribunais, 2014).
Nehf, J. P., The Impact of Mandatory Arbitration on the Common Law Regulation of Standard Terms in Consumer Contracts (2017) 85 *George Washington Law Review* 1692–716.
Nozick, R., *Anarchy, State, and Utopia* (New York: Basic Books, 1974).
Pargendler, M., Comparative Contract Law and Development: The Missing Link? (2017) 85 *The George Washington Law Review* 1717–38.
The Role of the State in Contract Law: The Common–Civil Law Divide (2018) 43 *The Yale Journal of International Law* 143–90.
Piketty, T., *Capital in the Twenty-First Century* (Cambridge, MA: The Belknap Press of Harvard University Press, 2017).
Pinheiro, A. C., Judiciário, Reforma e Economia: A Visão dos Magistrados. Instituto de Pesquisa Econômica Aplicada, Texto para Discussão No 966 (2003).
Portugal Gouvêa, C., Social Rights against the Poor (2013) 7 *Vienna Online Journal on International Constitutional Law* 454–75.
Rabin, E. H., The Revolution in Residential Landlord–Tenant Law: Causes and Consequences (1984) 69 *Cornell Law Review* 517–84.
Rawls, J., *Political Liberalism: Expanded Edition* (New York: Columbia University Press, 2005).
Russell, J. H., Unconscionability's Greatly Exaggerated Death (2019) 53 *UC Davis Law Review* 965–1026.
Salama, B. M., Spread Bancário e Enforcement Contratual: Hipótese de Causalidade Reversa e Evidência Empírica (2017) 71 *Revista Brasileira de Economia* 111–33.
Schwartz, A. and Scott, R. E., Contract Theory and the Limits of Contract Law (2003) 113 *Yale Law Journal* 541–620.
Scott, R. E., A Joint Maximization Theory of Contract and Regulation, in H. Dagan and B. C. Zipursky (eds.), *Research Handbook on Private Law Theory* (Northampton: Edward Elgar, 2020), pp. 22–38.
Shavell, S., A Note on Efficiency vs. Distributional Equity in Legal Rulemaking: Should Distributional Equity Matter Given Optimal Income Taxation? (1981) 71 *The American Economic Review* 414–18.
Skeel, Jr., D. A., Vern Countryman and the Path of Progressive (and Populist) Bankruptcy Scholarship (2000) 113 *Harvard Law Review* 1075–129.
Smits, J., *The Making of European Private Law: Toward a Ius Commune Europaeum as a Mixed Legal System* (Cambridge: Intersentia, 2002).
Spamann, H., Contemporary Legal Transplants: Legal Families and the Diffusion of (Corporate) Law (2009) *BYU Law Review* 1813–78.
Stone, K. V. W. and Colvin, A. J. S., The Arbitration Epidemic: Mandatory Arbitration Deprives Workers and Consumers of Their Rights (2015) *Economic Policy Institute* 26.
Sunstein, C. R., Willingness to Pay vs. Welfare (2007) 1 *Harvard Law & Policy Review* 303–30.
Super, D. A., The Rise and Fall of the Implied Warranty of Habitability (2011) 99 *California Law Review* 389–463.

Timm, L. B., Ainda Sobre a Função Social do Direito Contratual no Código Civil Brasileiro: Justiça Distributiva versus Eficiência Econômica (2009) 2 *Revista da Associação Mineira de Direito e Economia* 1–39.

Trebilcock, M. J., *The Limits of Freedom of Contract* (Cambridge, MA: Harvard University Press, 1993).

Unger, R. M., The Critical Legal Studies Movement (1983) *Harvard Law Review* 561–675.

Van Loo, R., Broadening Consumer Law: Competition, Protection, and Distribution (2019) 95 *Notre Dame Law Review* 211–62.

Versteeg, M., Can Rights Combat Economic Inequality? (2020) 133 *Harvard Law Review* 2017–61.

Vieira, O. V., Baxi, U., and Viljoen, F. (eds.), *Transformative Constitutionalism: Comparing the Apex Courts of Brazil, India and South Africa* (Pretoria: Pretoria University Law Press, 2013).

Weber, M., *Economy and Society: An Outline of Interpretive Sociology* (New York: Bedminster Press, 1968).

Weisbach, D. A., Should Legal Rules Be Used to Redistribute Income? (2003) 70 *The University of Chicago Law Review* 439–53.

World Bank Group, *Doing Business 2020: Comparing Business Regulation in 190 Economies* (Washington: The World Bank, 2020).

Yeung, L. L. T. and de Azevedo, P. F., Neither Robin Hood nor King John: Testing the Anti-Creditor and Anti-Debtor Bias in Brazilian Judges (2015) 6 *Economic Analysis of Law Review* 1–21.

Zimmermann, R. and Whittaker, S. (eds.), *Good Faith in European Contract Law* (Cambridge: Cambridge University Press, 2000).

Zweigert, K. and Kötz, H., *Introduction to Comparative Law*, 3rd ed. (Oxford: Clarendon Press, 1998).

3

Reducing Inequality in Consumer Transactions

The Significance of Aggravated Vulnerabilities

María Guadalupe Martínez Alles

3.1 INTRODUCTION

Whether consumer law should address inequality has been approached from various perspectives in Latin America and Europe.[1] A central factor to consider in the effort to elucidate the place for inequality concerns in consumer transactions is the underlying concept of the consumer embraced in each jurisdiction. In Europe, EU consumer law has historically emphasized *consumer empowerment*, and the European Court of Justice has predominantly elaborated its jurisprudence around the interpretive benchmark of the *average consumer*, that is, one who is presumed "reasonably well informed, observant and circumspect." Conversely, consumer protection laws in Latin America start by emphasizing *consumer protection* and, by consequence, the courts have generally embraced the interpretive benchmark of the *vulnerable consumer*, that is, the party in the transaction who occupies, however relatively, a markedly vulnerable position in the regulatory structure of the marketplace.[2]

I am grateful to Kevin Davis and Mariana Pargendler for exceptionally helpful and detailed comments as well as editorial guidance, and to Sergio Verdugo and the participants of the NYU-UBA Legal Heterodoxy Conference, IE Law School Faculty Workshop and Sciences Po Workshop on Experimental Regulation and AI Governance for their very helpful comments and suggestions. All errors are my own.

[1] Note that most consumer protection laws in Latin America are influenced by a mix of approaches taken in other Latin American jurisdictions, European legal systems (mainly France and Spain) and, to a limited extent, United States jurisprudence (mainly involving class action lawsuits and punitive damages).

[2] Two clarifications are in order: First, by referring to "consumer protection laws in Latin America," I do not mean to undermine the diversity and distinctiveness of each national jurisdiction. Quite the contrary: my aim is to offer a reconstruction of the broader shared rationale on consumer law during the time when (in the 1980s and 1990s) most countries in the region enacted national consumer protection laws. This shared understanding does not directly contradict the many singularities that distinguish national consumer protection laws. Moreover, my focus on one particular jurisdiction, that of Argentina, for concrete, localized, and in-depth analysis reflects my respect for the distinctiveness of consumer protection laws'

The European emphasis on *empowerment* and the *average consumer* benchmark is informed by an underlying assumption that consumers are sovereign: they are rational actors who adequately process information and make informed decisions on their own. Following this particular assumption of rationality, EU consumer law has mainly taken the form of disclosure obligations and the recognition of consumers' correlative rights in order to make the information necessary for autonomous choices available to them. Put in the simplest form, the professional supplier is taken as the *informant* and the consumer as the *informed sovereign*. This means that, on one side, the focus is on whether the supplier discloses the information owed and, on the other, on whether the consumer has sufficient access to that information – an approach often characterized as "empowerment through information." Under this framework, information and empowerment are usually preferred to substantive regulation which, in principle, reflects reduced concern for vulnerable consumers. Indeed, cognitive vulnerabilities of consumers (the particular circumstances that impair decision-making) are primarily treated as exceptions (or deviations) from the default assumption of rational autonomy.

Contrarily, the Latin American emphasis on *protection* and the *vulnerable consumer* benchmark is informed by an underlying conception of the consumer as an imperfectly rational actor (one of "bounded rationality") whose structural relation to the provider and marketplace situates her in a position of relative vulnerability. The point of departure is precisely such structural vulnerability: all consumers are *potentially* vulnerable. Under this framework, consumers' vulnerabilities are the *norm* rather than the *exception*. This approach acknowledges the inherent complexity of market dynamics and consumer behavior, and the way in which professional suppliers and consumers relate to each other within that complex context. Part of the complexity derives from the dual objectives of the professional suppliers. Professional suppliers balance their obligation to inform potential customers against their primary objective of marketing their products or services to attract as many actual customers as possible. In other words, the professional supplier seeks to persuade the consumer that her product offers more advantages and benefits than her competitors, and to that end she invests resources and effort in gaining an understanding of her consumers' behavior that surpasses that of the consumers themselves. The persuasive angle of suppliers' exploitative behavior signals, on one hand, the insufficiency of the empowerment-through-information approach; and,

designs in Latin America. Second, bringing to light all the national differences in the design of consumer law regulation in Latin American jurisdictions or in Member States in Europe lies beyond the scope of this project. From time to time I resort to specific comparisons within Latin American jurisdictions or EU Member States in order to illuminate the line of argument of this chapter, however such references are not intended as exhaustive or comprehensive. For an example (in the context of corporate law) of a comprehensive scholarly approach to meaningfully address these (and other) questions, see M. Pargendler, The Grip of Nationalism on Corporate Law (2020) 95 *Indiana Law Journal* 533–90.

on the other hand, the need to display more sensitivity to particular circumstances that impair consumers' decision-making. The underlying principle is that consumer protection statutes should not limit themselves to remedying market imbalances because they can also provide a means for fostering substantive equality in consumer transactions, which becomes manifest where there is more substantive regulation coupled with more room for courts to intervene.

In this chapter, I demonstrate significant consequences of this distinctive emphasis: the more consumer law moves toward *empowerment* and embraces the *average consumer* default, the less sensitive it becomes to the vulnerabilities that impair consumer decision-making, which hinders this model's capacity to address substantive inequality in consumer transactions. The different starting points, consumer vulnerability as an *exception* in Europe versus consumer vulnerability as a *norm* in Latin America, are crucial in the determination of when a court may justifiably intervene in a contractual relationship in order to protect vulnerable consumers from detrimental agreements. Following an examination of the European experience, the article takes a closer look at consumer protection law in Argentina, where the courts embrace the task of using consumer law to reduce inequality. In particular, it focuses on the significant, recently introduced category of the hyper-vulnerable consumers – that is, consumers who find themselves in a situation of aggravated vulnerability due to age, gender, physical or mental state or social, economic, ethnic and/or cultural circumstances, any of which may cause special difficulty for the full exercise of their rights as consumers (Res. 139/2020). The choice of the Argentine case is motivated by the country's paradigmatic shift from a formal and abstract principle of equality to a substantive and situated conception that was introduced by Civil Code reform of 2015. The referred shift is also operative in the recently proposed Project of Reform of the Consumer Protection Law, which opens a path for novel regulation sensitive to inequality in consumer relations,[3] and was given momentum by the urgent need for responses from government, civil society, and social associations to the structural inequality that has become glaringly evident in the aftermath of the COVID-19 crisis.

Against this background, the traditional view that Latin American legal systems often represent outdated or failed transplants from Global North models becomes unsatisfactory. As this introduction suggests, the legal structures for consumer protection in Latin America differ from the approaches to consumer law which are currently considered "orthodoxy" in EU consumer law.[4] This deviation itself suggests that a more helpful or meaningful framework to address the development of "heterodox" legal approaches to consumer law in Latin America is greatly needed.[5]

[3] For an example of how the reform tackles consumer inequality, see M. G. Martínez Alles, Regulating Gender Stereotypes in Advertising: When Persuasion Reinforces Inequality (2019) 5 *Latin American Legal Studies* 287–312.

[4] "Orthodoxy" refers to legal doctrines designed by developed countries.

[5] "Heterodoxy" refers to legal doctrines that deviate from those designed by developed countries.

In this context, the legal heterodoxy framework introduced by Mariana Pargendler and Kevin Davis offers a promising alternative.[6] The close attention the legal heterodoxy framework devotes to the local circumstances (social, economic, and political) in developing countries makes it better equipped to unpack the variety of public policy objectives pursued within a range of different worldviews, each with its own order of values embraced. The conjugation of policy objective and local values yields the distinctive responses of consumer law in different jurisdictions to the problems common to all of them.

Moreover, by inviting scholars to tease out the underlying reasoning behind the divergent approaches to consumer law in developing jurisdictions, this methodology offers a unique opportunity not only to overcome the traditional unidirectional perspective of inquiry and learning (i.e., focusing on the degree to which Latin American institutions *converge* with their European counterparts), but also, and perhaps most importantly, it opens up an avenue for identifying "reverse convergence" (i.e., areas where Europe *converges* with Latin America). This broader perspective is particularly apt in the current rise of the global digital economy. The rapid development of Artificial Intelligence (and other new technologies), whose algorithms have a direct impact on consumers' rights to safety, privacy, and non-discrimination, is exacerbating the salience of the structural character of consumer vulnerability in the marketplace.

3.2 CONSUMER LAW AND INEQUALITY IN EUROPE AND LATIN AMERICA

3.2.1 *Between Empowerment and Protection Paradigms: A Matter of Emphasis*

Whether consumer law should be concerned with inequality is a multi-faceted question that depends to a certain extent on the particular vision and understanding of the aims of consumer law in play, as well as the base conception of the consumer in a given legal system. Europe and Latin America have approached the relationship between consumer law and inequality from various, distinct perspectives, which reflect different views on both the goals of consumer law and the role of the consumer in the marketplace.

In the European context, where the underlying objective was putting in place a set of rules for the creation and maintenance of a single, durable regional market, consumer protection law was predominantly understood from the outset in terms of its usefulness for market optimization, a one-sided, exclusive goal aiming for internal

[6] K. Davis and M. Pargendler, Legal Heterodoxy in the Global South: Adapting Private Laws to Local Contexts, Chapter 1.

market integration.[7] This unidimensional stance implied that *economic interests* and *social interests* are somehow fully separable.[8] The thinking behind the approach considered that EU consumer protection law should only concern the economic interests of the parties to any transaction, which are compatible with a market economy. Non-transactional interests, such as equality, social cohesion, or distributive concerns, which could conflict with market integration, were secondary.[9]

According to this stance, protecting consumers against their vulnerabilities that result from particular circumstances puts a limit on (liberal notions of) freedom of contract and party autonomy,[10] which could hinder rather than enhance market integration.[11] The underlying liberal position is that the right to free choice constitutes the core element of the individual rights of citizens to participate in cross-border transactions in accordance with European Community law – the notion that the internal market should maximize the capacities of both businesses and consumers to do business with each other across borders.

Following this logic, the main rationale behind consumer protection law became the empowerment of consumers to take sufficiently informed autonomous decisions on their own by focusing on the right to information and relying on information duties to facilitate consumer choices and autonomy.[12] This paradigm of empowerment-through-information embraced by the EU is based on the conceptualization of

[7] G. Davis, The Consumer, the Citizen, and the Human Being, in D. Leczykiewitz and S. Weatherill (eds.), *The Images of the Consumer in EU Law* (Oxford: Hart Publishing, 2016), pp. 325–38; M. Bartl, Internal Market Rationality, Private Law and the Direction of the Union: Resuscitating the Market as the Object of the Political? (2015) 21 *European Law Journal* 572–98. Moreover, see G. G. Howells, C. Twigg-Flesner, and T. Wilhelmsson (eds.), *Rethinking EU Consumer Law: Markets and the Law* (Oxfordshire: Taylor & Francis, 2018) (the underlying position of this book is that European consumer law and policy risked overemphasizing the internal market goal to the detriment of protections for the vulnerable).

[8] Davis, The Consumer, the Citizen, and the Human Being, 326 (criticizing the dominant view as factually wrong, distinctively un-European, and "potentially dangerous for the achievement of European societies, which are notable precisely for their commitment to the integration of the social and the economic").

[9] T. Wilhelmsson, *Social Contract Law and European Integration* (Aldershot: Dartmouth, 1995).

[10] C. Kirchner, Justifying Limits to Party Autonomy in the Internal Market: Mainly Consumer Protection, in S. Grundmann, W. Kerber, and S. Weatherill (eds.), *Party Autonomy and the Role of Information in the Internal Market* (Berlin: de Gruyter, 2001), pp. 173–96.

[11] V. Mak, The Consumer in European Regulatory Private Law, in D. Leczykiewicz and S. Weatherill (eds.), *The Images of the Consumer in EU Law* (Oxford: Hart Publishing, 2016), pp. 381–400, p. 382 ("The image of the weak consumer, however, does not sit well with the general framework for economic regulation of private law relationships in the EU . . .; nor does it fit with the general principle of party autonomy that underlies most national private laws").

[12] European Commission, A European Consumer Agenda: Boosting Confidence and Growth, COM/2012/0225 (2012), p. 225 final: "Empowering consumers means providing a robust framework of principles and tools that enable them to drive a smart, sustainable, and inclusive economy. Empowered consumers who can rely on robust frameworks ensuring their safety, information, education, rights, means of redress, and enforcement can actively participate in the market and make it work for them by exercising their power of choice and by having their rights properly enforced."

the consumer "as a rational actor who – like other private actors – makes autonomous decisions and for whom the law normally only offers a facilitative back-up, rather than protection."[13] The emphasis in the EU Directives on the mandatory disclosure of information and rights of withdrawal (a short cooling-off period following the transaction to allow consumers to re-evaluate and change their decision without penalty), which are designed for reasonably well-informed and circumspect consumers, clearly reflects this agenda of empowerment.[14]

Alongside the empowerment narrative is the rhetoric that *maximum harmonization* is needed in order to promote the internal market, with its corollary that *minimum harmonization* should be dismissed because it might harm the unity of the internal market by inhibiting the establishment of a level playing field for trade.[15] Whether accurate or not, this assertion implies that the success of the empowerment-through-information paradigm ultimately requires a ceiling on consumer rights for the sake of maximum harmonization. Achieving maximum harmonization, for its part, ultimately means that consumer protection must be determined by the EU, and that level of protection cannot be raised by national law (i.e. stricter national rules of consumer protection are disallowed).[16] This limits national choice

[13] Mak, The Consumer in European Regulatory Private Law, p. 382. Questioning the empowerment-through-information approach in the EU, see H.-W. Micklitz, The Expulsion of the Concept of Protection from the Consumer Law and the Return to Social Elements in the Civil Law: A Bittersweet Polemic (2012) 35 *Journal of Consumer Policy* 283–96. Questioning the assumption that the consumer is able to use the disclosed information in order to bargain more effectively and secure the benefits of a transparent and competitive market, see G. Howells, The Potential and Limits of Consumer Empowerment by Information (2005) 32 *Journal of Law and Society* 349–70. For research showing that consumers suffer from information overload and that highlights their limited information-processing capabilities, see B. Duivenvoorde, *The Consumer Benchmarks in the Unfair Commercial Practice Directive* (New York: Springer, 2015); H. Schebesta and K. Purnhagen, Island or Ocean: Empirical Evidence on the Average Consumer Concept in the UCPD (2020) 28 *European Review of Private Law* 293–310.

[14] Note that EU consumer law is mostly composed of disclosure rules that aim to provide consumers with all sorts of information not only during the precontractual stage but also once a contract has been concluded. Moreover, it is important to point out that The Consumer Rights Directive implements standardization of the information requirement across the EU. See e.g. Articles 5–6 of the Council Directive 2011/83/EU of October 25, 2011, on consumer rights, OJ 2011 No. L304, November 22, 2011 (CRD); Articles 4–6, 10–11 of the Council Directive 2008/48/EC of April 23, 2008 on credit agreements for consumers, OJ 2008 No. L133, May 22, 2008; Article 5 of the Council Directive 2001/95/EC of December 3, 2001 on general product safety, OJ 2002 No. L11, January 15, 2002 (GPSD).

[15] For a critical assessment of this assertion, see G. Howells, Europe's (Lack of) Vision on Consumer Protection, in D. Leczykiewicz and S. Weatherill (eds.) *The Images of the Consumer in EU Law: Legislation, Free Movement and Competition Law* (Oxford: Hart Publishing, 2016), pp. 431–46, p. 442 (arguing that the benefits of maximum harmonization have been overstated, since there is no convincing empirical evidence on the extent to which such uniformity increases cross-border trade).

[16] See, for instance, Case C-358/01, *Commission v. Spain* [2003] ECR I-13145 (where national measures related to labeling of products were deemed overly protective and struck down because they created unjustifiable barriers to trade in the Internal Market).

and flexibility in that the centralization does not allow sufficient space for national initiatives to protect groups of vulnerable consumers whose particular needs cannot be satisfactorily addressed by rules adopted at the EU level.[17] Moreover, *maximum harmonization* also means that if the maximum EU level of protection is lower than existing national standards, then the central EU determination causes a reduction in protection in those member states.[18]

Whether EU consumer law should leave room for member states to choose how they enhance protection of particular groups of vulnerable consumers is a contested issue subject to (ongoing) debate,[19] one that I do not engage in this piece.[20] My aim is distinct: I wish to show that, the more EU consumer law emphasizes *empowerment* and embraces *maximum harmonization*, the less sensitive it is to vulnerabilities that impair consumer decision-making, which hinders the

[17] S. Weatherill, Empowerment Is Not the Only Fruit, in D. Leczykiewicz and S. Weatherill (eds.), *The Images of the Consumer in EU Law: Legislation, Free Movement and Competition Law* (Oxford: Hart Publishing, 2016), pp. 203–21, p. 221 (arguing that "maximum harmonization should be regarded as the exception and minimum harmonization as the norm in order to preserve space for national initiatives that reflect the sheer diversity of consumer experience and preference across the regulatory terrain of the EU's internal market"). For an analysis of the divergence in rationalities of EU and national private law, see R. Michaels, Of Islands and the Ocean: The Two Rationales of European Private Law, in R. Brownsword et al. (eds.), *The Foundations of European Private Law* (Oxford: Hart Publishing, 2011), pp. 139–58. For an analysis of the effect of nationalism on the design of corporate laws, see Pargendler, The Grip of Nationalism on Corporate Law.

[18] An example of enhanced protection at the member state level is found in Spain's recent introduction of the general category of the "vulnerable consumer." According to Article 3, Law No 4/2022, vulnerable consumers are "those individuals who, individually or collectively, for their characteristics, needs or personal, economic, educational or social circumstances, are, even when only territorial, sectorial or temporarily, in a special situation of subordination, helplessness, or lack of protection that prevents them from exercising their rights as consumers under conditions of equality." This reform of the Spanish Consumer Protection Law mainly responded to the devastation caused by the pandemic on the basis of the constitutional mandate to grant protection to consumers (Art. 51.1, Spanish Constitution).

[19] For objections to excessive harmonization in European contract law, see T. Wilhelmsson, Private Law in the EU: Harmonised or Fragmented Europeanisation? (2002) 1(1) *European Review of Private Law* 77–94, 84. Similarly, see N. Reich, A European Contract Law or an EU Contract Law Regulation for Consumers? (2005) 28 *Journal of Consumer Policy* 383–407. For an analysis on the impact of maximum harmonization in contract law, see F. De Elizalde, Standarisation of Agreement in EU Law. An Adieu to the Contracting Parties?, in T. Tridimas and M. Durovic (eds.), *New Directions in European Private Law* (Oxford: Hart Publishing, 2021), pp. 29–59 (arguing that EU law is transforming core elements in contract formation by following a standardization approach – which, for instance, relies on legal standards such as the "average consumer" that ignores the individual characteristics of the contracting parties).

[20] For thoughts on this debate, see, for instance, H. W. Micklitz, The Full Harmonization Dream (2022) 11 *Journal of European Consumer and Market Law* 117–21; S. Weatherill, The Fundamental Question of Minimum or Maximum Harmonisation, in S. Garben and I. Govaere (eds.), *The Internal Market* 2.0 (Oxford: Hart Publishing, 2020), pp. 261–84; N. Reich, From Minimal to Full to "Half Harmonisation," in J. Devenney and M. Kenny (eds.), *European Consumer Protection Theory and Practice* (Cambridge: Cambridge University Press 2012), pp. 3–5.

empowerment-through-information model's capacity to address inequality in consumer transactions. To clarify, I am not implying that EU consumer policy solely involves empowerment.[21] It also recognizes the need for protection, and some concern for vulnerabilities is evident in the recognition that certain groups of consumers warrant enhanced protection.[22] For example, the Unfair Commercial Practice Directive (Directive 2005/29/EC) conveys (limited) concern for the vulnerable consumer by incorporating measures of consumer protection targeting specific disadvantaged groups ("mental or physical infirmity, age or credulity").[23] Other references to vulnerable consumers are made in the Consumer Rights Directive (Directive 2011/83/EU) and the General Product Safety Directive (Directive 2001/95/EC). The reference in the Consumer Rights Directive stipulates that traders should take into account the specific needs of "consumers who are particularly vulnerable because of their mental, physical or psychological infirmity, age or credulity" when providing consumers with pre-contractual information.[24] The General Product Safety Directive (Directive 2001/95/EC), for its part, mandates that categories of consumers "particularly vulnerable to the risks posed by the products under consideration, in particular children and the elderly" be taken into account when assessing product safety.[25] Together however, the original choice to (over)emphasize *empowerment* and the pervasiveness of the narrative on the advantages of *maximum harmonization* for the internal market have powerfully influenced the overly restrictive consideration of consumer vulnerabilities in EU law, which, as I will demonstrate in Section 3.2.2, are considered secondary (or subsidiary) protective interests.[26]

[21] See Weatherill, Empowerment Is Not the Only Fruit, pp. 203–4 (arguing that "[c]onsumer law needs to be about more than empowerment"; and that "[a] vision based exclusively on empowerment is too narrow").

[22] See Howells, Europe's (Lack of) Vision on Consumer Protection, p. 434 (arguing that there are many instances when the Commission and the Court of Justice have in fact shown sensitivity to consumer concerns).

[23] Article 5(3) of the Council Directive 2005/29/EC of May 11, 2005, on unfair business-to-consumer commercial practices in the internal market, OJ 2005 No L149, June 11, 2005 (UCPD) provides: "Commercial practices which are likely to material distort the economic behavior only of a clearly identifiable group of consumers who are particularly vulnerable to the practice or the underlying product because of their mental or physical infirmity, age or credulity in a way which the trader could reasonably be expected to foresee, shall be assessed from the perspective of the average member of that group. This is without prejudice to the common and legitimate advertising practice of making exaggerated statements or statements which are not meant to be taken literally."

[24] Article 34, CRD.

[25] Article 8, GPSD.

[26] On this point, see Howells, Europe's (Lack of) Vision on Consumer Protection, p. 434 ("In other words, I do not think the EU lacks a soul to its consumer policy, but its emphasis on the internal market and maximum harmonization has risked making people forget the core values and rights it has guaranteed EU citizens"). For a critical view, see Howells, Twigg-Flesner, and Wilhelmsson (eds.), *Rethinking EU Consumer Law*, p. 7 (arguing that "consumers should be recognized as a class who are structurally poorly positioned to protect themselves in the marketplace").

The situation is quite different in Latin America. There, the *protective* aim of consumer law has been emphasized over the empowerment one since the very beginning.[27] The prevailing underlying rationale at the time when most consumer protection laws were enacted in the region (the 1980s and 90s) prioritized the need for specific regulation from the state to properly address the contractual asymmetry of power between suppliers and consumers in the marketplace. This stance reveals the shortfall, at least in the realm of consumer law, of the classic assumption of formal equality between the contracting parties on the basis of which most nineteenth century Civil Codes were constructed. Consequently, consumer law has mainly been understood as a tool to counteract structural power imbalances between suppliers and consumers in the marketplace, with the aim of strengthening consumers' substantive rights. This stance is perhaps partially explained and, to some extent, reinforced by the constitutional status of consumer rights in most jurisdictions in the region.[28] Constitutional status complicates the simplicity of the widely professed solid line walling economic and social rights from the underlying logic of private law institutions, such as contracts, torts, and property law. Ultimately, constitutionalizing consumer rights means that the constitution can be invoked to reshape the legal relationship between consumers and suppliers in the marketplace.[29]

Following this line of thinking, the underlying idea was that consumer protection encompasses much more than empowerment because its concern is achieving adequate levels of substantive protection for all consumers, whether empowered or not. The underlying conception of the consumer thus departs markedly from the "reasonably well-informed and circumspect" rational actor that is assumed by the empowerment-through-information model. Instead, under the *protection* paradigm, the dominant depiction of the consumer is that of a *structurally vulnerable consumer*, that is, one who occupies a relatively although decidedly vulnerable position

[27] On the importance of starting points and narratives, see e.g. Weatherill, Empowerment Is Not the Only Fruit, pp. 203–204 ("It may seem a small shift to prefer to address 'consumer law' over 'consumer protection law', but it is a shift that carries with it an enormous risk that the protective instinct that underpins the development of the law, driven by the appreciation that in some circumstances the market will harm the consumer, or at least some consumers, will be diluted or even lost").

[28] Most modern Latin American Constitutions, such as those of Argentina (1994), Brazil (1988), Colombia (1991), and Peru (1993), enshrine consumer rights as fundamental rights. The Chilean Constitution (1980) is an important exception, although the Constitutional Court of Chile has recognized the importance and protective nature of rules for consumer protection. For a discussion on the inclusion of new rights in the new constitutions in Latin America, see R. Gargarella, Inequality and the Constitution: From Equality to Social Rights, in P. Dann, M. Riegner and M. Bönnemann (eds.), *The Global South and Comparative Constitutional Law* (Oxford: Oxford University Press, 2020), pp. 235–49.

[29] For research showing how courts in Brazil and Colombia have recently embraced using traditional contract law to address inequality, see K. E. Davis and M. Pargendler, Contract Law and Inequality (2022) 107 *Iowa Law Review* 1485–541.

in the market structure, which calls for a higher degree of protection than other transactional contexts involving private parties who negotiate on more equal footing.[30]

Under this distinctive structural narrative, the empowerment-through-information strategy (i.e., seeking to enable consumers to exercise their freedom of choice) appears, at least *a priori*, ill-suited for effective protection of consumers deemed, in principle, vulnerable to market power dynamics that (more often than not) impair their ability to inform themselves adequately or make free, autonomous choices. Consequently consumer protection statutes in many Latin American jurisdictions originally contained, in addition to the classic information duties and disclosure rules (which align well with the empowerment approach), more robust substantive protections, such as a consumer's right to compensation and stringent remedies (e.g., the broader availability of pain and suffering awards and increasing recourse to punitive damages awards),[31] a right to dignity and equitable treatment, a regime of strict liability, and the availability of class action mechanisms, free access to justice and protective principles (e.g., "*in dubio pro-consumer*"), all of which better serve the aim of shielding consumers from structural vulnerability. Again, the claim is not that consumer law in Latin America exclusively involves substantive protection and heightened concern for vulnerable consumers, for empowerment is certainly an objective too.[32] The point is that the original emphasis on *protection* has facilitated the model's capacity to address *inequality* in consumer transactions, by displaying much more sensitivity toward consumer vulnerabilities not only from legislators but also, and importantly, from courts – which I explore through reference to the particular case of Argentina in Section 3.3.

Examining the distinctive European and Latin American visions of consumer law reveals how the pervasive foundational narratives pit the aims of consumer law as dichotomous (empowerment *or* protection), leading to starkly contrasting default conceptions of the consumer in Europe and Latin America ("reasonably well-informed, observant and circumspect" versus "structurally vulnerable"). These different default assumptions then affect ensuing decisions on when, where, and how consumer vulnerability in the marketplace should be addressed. The problem with

30 For instance, the structural vulnerability of consumers in the marketplace is explicitly recognized in the consumer law of Brazil (Article 4 [I], Law 8078/1990), hereinafter "Brazilian Consumer Protection Code."

31 Note that punitive damages are available in the consumer protection laws of Argentina and Chile, see notes 114–118.

32 Consumer protection statutes in Latin America also establish and regulate duties of information. For instance, the Argentinian Consumer Protection Law provides as follows: "Art. 4: Information. The supplier is obliged to provide to the consumer, in a certain, clear and detailed manner, all the information related to the essential characteristics of the goods and services that it provides, and the conditions of its commercialization. The information must always be free for the consumer and provided with the necessary clarity that allows its understanding." Art. 4, Law No 24.240 (text according to Law No 26.361, B.O. 7/4/2008).

this dichotomous narrative is that consumer *protection* and consumer *empowerment* are not necessarily at odds. On the contrary, they may very well complement each other. Another problematic aspect of the empowerment *or* protection framework is that it diverts attention from the more relevant question (and challenge), which is the appropriate relative weight of each in the design of any given legal system's consumer law, not to mention the particular circumstances and contexts that might justify modifying that balance. In other words, the empowerment v. protection characterization overlooks the importance of recognizing and mapping out the interconnectedness and interaction between the two objectives, a relationship that is socially and culturally dependent – which will become clearer when I explore their interplay in the Argentinian context in Section 3.3.

However, the institutional choice on whether to emphasize *empowerment* or *protection* over the other has been assumed necessary from the outset in both Europe and in Latin America, perhaps without awareness of the extent of the practical ramifications that would actually transpire. In what follows, I explore one such ramification. In particular, I show how the initial emphasis on empowerment in Europe led the EU to embrace the "average consumer" as its interpretive benchmark, depicting consumer vulnerabilities as exceptions that occasionally require a higher degree of protection if properly justified; whereas the original Latin American emphasis on protection has led those jurisdictions to embrace the "vulnerable consumer" as their interpretive benchmark, positing structural vulnerability as the norm allowing greater room for the provision of enhanced protection in cases of "aggravated vulnerability," which intensifies structural vulnerability.

3.2.2 *The Significance of the Benchmark Adopted*

The European narrative emphasizing consumer empowerment-through-information assumes a particular understanding of the consumer that responds to the initial, overarching concern with providing the information needed by consumers to make well-informed decisions.[33] This implies that stringent consumer protection, meaning protection that goes beyond duties of information (e.g., mandatory substantive law, such as the control of standard contract terms) is only justified "when the information content cannot be shaped in such a way that a reasonably observant, circumspect consumer could digest it at a reasonable price or with reasonable effort."[34] This profile for the typical consumer in Europe was in fact established by the European Court of Justice (ECJ) itself, which described her as: "reasonably

[33] For a critical view of this constructed image, see Davis, The Consumer, the Citizen, and the Human Being, pp. 326–27 ("the Court does not look at Europeans as they are, but as a certain vision of the law would like them to be").

[34] S. Grundmann, Targeted Consumer Protection, in D. Leczykiewicz and S. Weatherill (eds.) *The Images of the Consumer in EU Law: Legislation, Free Movement and Competition Law* (Oxford: Hart Publishing, 2016), pp. 223–44, p. 238.

well-informed and reasonably observant and circumspect."[35] The ECJ then developed, through reference to this profile in its case law, the interpretive benchmark of the "average consumer" as the default standard in legal doctrine for judging "unfairness," for example, when assessing whether a contractual clause, in legal terms, is sufficiently clear.[36] Following this logic, the aim of consumer law is empowering the average, "reasonably well informed and reasonably observant and circumspect" consumer to exercise her choices, and to establish under which justifiable circumstances a heightened degree of protection may be *exceptionally* required.

Likewise, the Unfair Commercial Practice Directive (UCPD) has also adopted the "average consumer" benchmark as the standard to assess whether a specific practice (outside the forbidden) is unfair (e.g., whether it has misled or caused consumers to engage in a transaction that they would not have taken otherwise) and, as a consequence, whether consumers should be protected against it.[37] For example, in *Sony*,[38] the ECJ examined whether the economic behavior of the "average consumer" with regard to the product would be materially distorted by the commercial sale of a computer equipped with pre-installed software that affords no option for the consumer to purchase the same model of computer without the pre-installed software. Namely, would it significantly undermine the average consumer's ability to make an informed decision and lead to a transactional decision that the consumer would not have taken otherwise? In dealing with this question, the ECJ emphasized that the consumer had been duly informed prior to the purchase that the computer model in question did not come without pre-installed software. On the basis of that information in particular, the understanding was that the consumer was able to

[35] The ECJ formulated its standard definition of the concept in its 1998 judgment *Gut Springenheide*: case C-210/96, *Gut Springenheide GmbH v Oberkreisdirektor des Kreises Steinfurt* [1998] ECR I–4657. For further case law on the average consumer: case C-303/97, *Verbraucherschutzverein eV v Sektkellerei G. C. Kessler GmbH und Co.* [1999] ECR I–513; case C-220/98, *Estée Lauder Cosmetics GmbH & Co. OHG v Lancaster Group GmbH* [2000] ECR I–117; case C-465/98, *Verein gegen Unwesen in Handel und Gewerbe Kölv Adolf Darbo AG.* [2000] ECR I–2297; case C-3/99, *Cidrerie Ruwet SA v Cidre Stassen SA and HP Bulmer Ltd.* [2000] ECR I-8749, and many others. See also Recital 18, UCPD.

[36] Mak, The Consumer in European Regulatory Private Law, p. 383 (referring to "the average consumer of EU law as a benchmark but also as a means by which to mediate between EU law and national laws"). Similarly, see S. Weatherill, Who Is the "Average Consumer"?, in S. Weatherill and U. Bernits (eds.), *The Regulation of Unfair Commercial Practices under EC Directive 2005/29: New Rules and New Techniques* (Oxford: Hart Publishing, 2007), pp. 115–38, p. 135 (stating that the average consumer standard "is an attempt to navigate a course between the rich diversity of actual consumer behavior and the need for an operational regulatory benchmark"). For a critique of the normative model of the average consumer in credit and mortgage law, see I. Domurath, The Case of Vulnerability as the Normative Standard in European Consumer Credit and Mortgage Law: An Inquiry into the Paradigms of Consumer Law (2013) 2 *Journal of European Consumer and Market Law* 124–37, 133, 135.

[37] The UCPD is the only legal instrument that systematically employs the concept of the "average consumer," namely in Article 5 (contrary to provider's due diligence), Article 6 (misleading actions), Article 7 (misleading omissions), and Article 8 (aggressive practices).

[38] Case C-310/15, *Vincent Deroo-Blanquart v. Sony Europe Limited* ECLI:EU:C: 2016:633 (2016).

decide whether to accept the terms previously drawn up by the seller and was therefore, in principle, free to choose another model of computer, or another brand, of similar technical specifications that was sold without pre-installed software or came with different pre-installed software. In light of these considerations, the ECJ concluded that the commercial practice at issue did not in itself constitute an unfair commercial practice within the meaning of Article 5(2) of the UCPD. As is evident in the ECJ's approach, the consumer is treated in the abstract and the preponderant focus is on the quality (correctness) of the information provided.

Besides the "average consumer" benchmark, the UCPD includes two other categories of consumers: the "targeted (average) consumer" and the "vulnerable (average) consumer."[39] The "targeted consumer" refers to situations where a commercial practice is specifically aimed at a particular group of consumers, such as children.[40] The "vulnerable consumer" is meant to capture situations where "certain characteristics such as age, physical or mental infirmity or credulity make consumers particularly susceptible to a commercial practice or to the underlying product."[41] However, the Directive further establishes that those commercial practices "shall be assessed from the perspective of the *average member* of that group."[42] The fact that the reference point is the "average member" of the protected group means that, whether or not actual members of the "targeted" or the "vulnerable" group are misled by a certain practice, if the "assumed average member" would not be misled, there are no grounds for enhanced protection.

This theoretical construct, which contradicts the centrality of relational, situational, and highly contextual factors in the very definition of vulnerability, makes effective protection of vulnerable consumers difficult to ensure.[43] What it actually does is reconfirm the original, underlying intent of EU consumer law to facilitate market integration where consumers' vulnerabilities are seen as a destabilizing departure from informed autonomy rather than relevant interests that warrant heightened protection (i.e., vulnerabilities as interests of secondary consideration). Most importantly, these two categories end up consolidating and reinforcing the default standard of the "average consumer." First, consumer vulnerability is conceived as an exceptional deviation from the norm of the "average consumer" whose protection must be justified by additional substantive reasons beyond personal status as consumers.[44] Second, the "average" benchmark is embedded as a subsidiary consideration in the exceptional categories themselves, in that vulnerabilities are

[39] For an analysis of the average, targeted and vulnerable consumer of the UCPC, see Howells, Twigg-Flesner, and Wilhelmsson, *Rethinking EU Consumer Law*, pp. 66–73.

[40] Article 5(3), UCPD.

[41] Ibid.

[42] Ibid (my emphasis).

[43] For relational notions of consumer vulnerability, see N. Helberger et al., Choice Architectures in the Digital Economy: Towards a New Understanding of Digital Vulnerability (2022) 45 *Journal of Consumer Policy* 175–200.

[44] On this point, see Grundmann, Targeted Consumer Protection.

assessed in reference to the "average member" of the group. Moreover, it is not entirely clear what these category-based classifications are meant to address.[45] For instance, the exclusive focus on personal attributes (age, physical or mental infirmity or credulity) is questionable. They are narrow and flat attributes that fail to recognize that vulnerabilities are dynamic, not static: a person or group of persons may experience different kinds of vulnerabilities at different times. The manifestation of vulnerability depends on the particular circumstances (or contextual setting) in which consumers find themselves (situational vulnerability). For example, age does not in itself imply vulnerability. In many situations, an educated, resourceful elderly woman in Argentina can overcome hurdles of digital financial transactions that an illiterate poor elderly woman in the same country might not. Additionally, the categorical approach invites further criticism from those who argue that person-based categorizations not only stigmatize (or stereotype) groups of consumers, but also that they, perhaps most importantly, prevent us from identifying those from among the vulnerable category who are worse off than others (e.g., the illiterate and poor elderly woman when attempting to make a digital financial transaction).[46] Moreover, if these categories are meant to mitigate structural inequality in consumer transactions, they seem to present problematic shortfalls. For example, they do not capture other social, economic, ethnic, and/or cultural circumstances, which may very well impair consumers' decision-making and call for some sort of enhanced protection.[47] Admittedly, vulnerability is extremely complex and multi-layered.[48] However, reflecting it solely in terms of person-focused attributes, as EU consumer law does in a categorical, selective, and fragmented way, makes it even more difficult (if not impossible) to grasp.

The point is that using the benchmark of the average consumer reduces the space for consumer vulnerability to an exceptional departure from the norm.[49] The

45 There is also some discussion on whether the list is exhaustive or not, see e.g. Howells, Twigg-Flesner, and Wilhelmsson, *Rethinking EU Consumer Law*; B. Duivenvoorde, The Protection of Vulnerable Consumers under the Unfair Commercial Practices Directive (2013) 2 *Journal of European Consumer and Market Law* 69–79.

46 T. Wilhelmsson, The Informed Consumer vs the Vulnerable Consumer in European Unfair Commercial Practices Law: A Comment, in G. G Howells et al. (eds.), *Yearbook of Consumer Law 2007* (Hampshire: Ashgate Publishing, 2007), pp. 211–28, pp. 212–13. Moreover, see F. Luna, Identifying and Evaluating Layers of Vulnerability: A Way Forward (2019) 19 *Developing World Bioethics* 86–95, 87.

47 Weatherill, Who Is the "Average Consumer"?, p. 136. Similarly, Mak, The Consumer in European Regulatory Private Law, p. 386 (pointing out that these categories of consumers are not easy to apply in practice and may be underinclusive).

48 P. Cartwright, Understanding and Protecting Vulnerable Financial Consumers (2005) 38 *Journal of Consumer Policy* 119–38 (who developed a different taxonomy of vulnerability which seeks to account for said complexity by focusing on the particular circumstances creating vulnerabilities). For a layered understanding of vulnerability, see F. Luna, Elucidating the Concept of Vulnerability, Layers Not Labels (2009) 2 *International Journal of Feminist Approaches to Bioethics* 121–39.

49 For the opposite approach, see M. Fineman, The Vulnerable Subject: Anchoring Equality in the Human Condition (2008) 20 *Yale Journal of Law and Feminism* 1–23 (arguing for a default

influence of this framework has been widely discussed in the European scholarly work on the vulnerable consumer: most scholars depart from acknowledging and recognizing the average consumer as the unquestionable default and argue for *flexibilization* or *expansion* of that very notion in order to more accurately capture consumer vulnerabilities.[50] The few European scholars who have of late begun fundamentally questioning the average consumer default itself have thus far focused on the specific context of digital markets – persuasively arguing that "structural vulnerability" be taken as the *norm* in the digital economy and calling for higher levels of consumer protection and a reassessment of the information paradigm dominant in the EU.[51]

Conversely, in Latin America, the dominant narrative of consumer protection has paved the way for the original notion of the consumer as one who occupies a relatively yet markedly vulnerable position in the market structure. Consumer law's aim has thus concentrated on establishing when and under which circumstances consumers require protection, and when and under which circumstances an enhanced degree of protection is warranted or even required. The underlying rationale is that all consumers are potentially vulnerable (whether empowered or not) due to structural features that are characteristic of the market contextual dynamics: asymmetry of knowledge and systemic power imbalances between suppliers and consumers. The idea is that recognizing consumer vulnerability means acknowledging that consumers, for the mere fact of being consumers, might be exploited by suppliers under certain circumstances. Hence, the most relevant factor is the *possibility* of exploitation in the marketplace.

Following this logic, the idea of an "average consumer" presumed "reasonably well informed, observant and circumspect" who is therefore considered sufficiently protected by the disclosure of crucial information did not take root in Latin America. Instead, in addition to the asymmetrical advantages in terms of bargaining

universal understanding of vulnerability as "the ever-present possibility of harm, injury, and misfortune" that is a consequence of human embodiment).

50 See, for example, F. Esposito and M. Grochowski, The Consumer Benchmark, Vulnerability, and the Contract Terms Transparency: A Plea for Reconsideration (2022) 18 *European Review of Contract Law* 1–31.

51 See, for instance, Helberger et al., Choice Architectures in the Digital Economy, 182 (arguing that "vulnerability is not a state of exception, reserved for particular groups of consumers, but a universal condition [which] is particularly true of digital markets"). On this topic, it is important to point out the European Commission's new definition of the vulnerable consumer, which signals toward a more universal conception of vulnerability: "This new definition distinguishes five dimensions of consumer vulnerability. A vulnerable consumer could be defined as: A consumer, who, as a result of socio-demographic characteristics, behavioral characteristics, personal situation, or market environment: is at higher risk of experiencing negative outcomes in the market; has limited ability to maximize his/her well-being; has difficulty in obtaining or assimilating information; is less able to buy, choose or access suitable products; or is more susceptible to certain marketing practices." Cf. European Commission, Understanding Consumer Vulnerability in the EU's Key Markets, Factsheet (2016).

power and information that suppliers enjoy, another dimension of the unequal supplier–consumer relationship has been recognized: the imbalance caused by consumers' cognitive vulnerabilities.[52] The empirical evidence convincingly shows that people usually, when making decisions, do not behave as a *homo economicus* or a perfectly rational agent would.[53] On the contrary, as imperfectly rational agents, their behavior deviates from what rational choice theory predicts. Individual rationality is bounded because cognitive abilities are finite. This acknowledgment admits instances when, in certain contexts, and maybe even in a great many if not most of them, individuals who resemble the "average consumer" behave according to the postulates historically assumed by the prevailing economic models.[54] It also means, however, that sometimes individuals deviate from those models' predictions and act using mental shortcuts and alternative cognitive processes whose connection to logical deduction or standards of rational decision-making is tenuous. The responsibility for this behavior lies with the heuristics of intuitive thinking and cognitive biases.[55] Psychologists and economists have identified a large catalog of cognitive biases based on experiments and hypotheses, including availability, confirmation, *status quo* biases, and the bandwagon effect, among others.[56]

For their part, suppliers invest considerable resources and effort (into, for example, highly sophisticated neuromarketing techniques)[57] in order to gauge the cognitive biases of consumers better than the consumers understand them themselves, which increases the marketplace asymmetry already noted.[58] In the process of informing and persuading consumers, cognitive biases are used as a tool like any other to promote products. Even if it can be accurately said that suppliers do have a genuine interest in providing reliable information about their products, it is equally fair to say they do so with the clear aim of attracting as many consumers

[52] C. Jolls, C. R. Sunstein, and R. Thaler, A Behavioral Approach to Law and Economics (1998) 50 *Stanford Law Review* 1471–1550.

[53] Ibid.

[54] Ibid., 1477.

[55] The concept of heuristics and biases was originally proposed by A. Tversky and D. Kahneman, Judgment under Uncertainty: Heuristic and Biases (1974) 185 *Science* 1124–31. See also D. Kahneman, *Thinking, Fast and Slow* (London: Penguin, 2012); R. B. Korobkin and T. S. Ulen, Law and Behavioral Science: Removing the Rationality Assumption from Law and Economics (2000) 88 *California Law Review* 1051–144; J. J. Rachlinski, The Psychological Foundations of Behavioral Law and Economics (2011) 2011 *University of Illinois Law Review* 1675–96.

[56] Jolls et al., A Behavioral Approach to Law and Economics.

[57] Neuromarketing is the study of consumer behavior that makes use of neuroscientific techniques in order to obtain data on a person's consumption behavior and habits. For example, cameras, sensors, and wristbands are used to record expressions, changes in speech, and even the consumer's heart rate.

[58] See G. A. Akerlof and R. J. Shiller, *Phishing for Phools. The Economics of Manipulation and Deception* (New Jersey: Princeton University Press, 2015), pp. 52–54 (describing how advertisers use, through trial and error, persuasive techniques to secure and increase sales of their products).

as possible – the ultimate goal being increased sales, not necessarily fully informed consumers.[59] Furthermore, suppliers in competitive markets who are not willing to exploit the cognitive limitations of consumers are often quickly supplanted by those who are. Thus, according to Jon Hanson and Douglas Kysar, manipulation becomes an inescapable requirement for staying power in competitive markets.[60]

Consumer transactions are shaped by the interaction between market dynamics and consumer psychology.[61] Understanding the behavioral dynamics of the relevant actors in the marketplace further illuminates the structural dimension of consumer vulnerability. At the same time, it makes evident both the insufficiency of duties of information and rights of withdrawals as exclusive legal protective measures and the need for mechanisms to provide enhanced, substantive protection in especially impairing circumstances. Importantly, this approach acknowledges both the dynamism of consumers' vulnerabilities and the relational advantage of suppliers who are able to identify personal biases and characteristics of which consumers themselves are often unaware and the suppliers can exploit.

Regarding the former, the dynamism of consumer vulnerability means that consumer susceptibility to manipulation is not a static characteristic of a person (age, education, etc.) but rather often a product of the market dynamics designed to exploit cognitive biases and heuristics. While this implies that consumers are not inherently and irremediably vulnerable, the more important implication is that vulnerabilities are mainly relational, situational, and highly contextual. They are dependent on the particular circumstances' consumers are in when engaging in consumer transactions, which can exacerbate those vulnerabilities to the consumers' detriment (e.g., an elderly consumer may be vulnerable to certain commercial practices involving digital expertise that evoke familial duties, but not to ones that exploit a desire for fame, recognition, or romance).

As for the latter, the relational advantage of suppliers in the modern marketplace, the information on potential consumers' biases and vulnerabilities has multiplied by many orders of magnitude. Before the advent of the digital economy, for example, empirical evidence already showed that female consumers were often more vulnerable to (predatory) price personalization in car purchasing,[62] but the landscape thirty

[59] A. Kuenzler, *Restoring Consumer Sovereignty. How Markets Manipulate Us and What the Law Can Do About It* (Oxford: Oxford University Press, 2017), pp. xvii–xxi (describing how advertising from its beginnings served a dual purpose of informing and persuading).

[60] J. D. Hanson and D. A. Kysar, Taking Behavioralism Seriously: Some Evidence of Market Manipulation (1999) 112 *Harvard Law Review* 1420–1572 (focusing on the cigarette industry as a paradigmatic example of market manipulation strategies).

[61] On this point, see O. Bar-Gill, Consumer Transactions, in E. Zamir and D. Eichman (eds.), *The Oxford Handbook of Behavioral Economics and the Law* (Oxford: Oxford University Press, 2014), pp. 465–90, p. 466.

[62] For empirical research demonstrating that retail car dealerships systematically offered substantially better prices on identical cars to white men than they did to blacks and women, see I. Ayres and P. Siegelman, Race and Gender Discrimination in Bargaining for a New Car (1995) 85 *The American Economic Review* 304–21.

years after that research was conducted is almost unrecognizable. It is important to recall that we are not only talking about the information that consumers freely and publicly share on social media.[63] From the information on spending habits tracked by credit card companies to the internet browsing information shared by internet providers, suppliers' ability to identify and target personal circumstances and individual characteristics that make a consumer potentially more prone than others to enter into detrimental consumer transactions has grown exponentially.[64]

This is the background against which the point of departure for consumer protection statutes in Latin America, that of "structural vulnerability," becomes especially pertinent. Consumer protection statutes were envisioned as a key tool to counterbalance systemic power imbalances between suppliers and consumers with the aim to protect consumers' ability to fully exercise their substantive rights. Under this logic, improving standards for the disclosure of information and market transparency, however important and desirable, appear insufficient to compensate fully for consumers' structural disadvantages because informative measures hardly seem capable of empowering consumers to make wholly autonomous decisions.[65] Unlike EU consumer law, Latin American countries embraced from the start more substantive measures (e.g., rules of strict liability, broader availability of pain and suffering awards, recourse to punitive damages, among others) and protective principles (e.g., *in dubio pro consumer*)[66] that go beyond the mere duty to provide information and further developed these measures through the case law in individual cases involving consumer transaction disputes – which I explore further in the Argentinian context discussed in Section 3.3.

Moreover, the protective narrative of the "structurally vulnerable consumer" underlying the norm has made it possible for courts to play a dynamic and active role in interpreting whether and when to protect individual consumers from abusive or unfair commercial practices in the particular cases before them.[67] The courts do this by appealing to, among other legal resources, the underlying protective

[63] On reclaiming privacy in digital markets, see A. Kuenzler, On (Some Aspects of) Social Privacy in the Social Media Space (2022) 12 *International Data Privacy Law* 63–73.

[64] For a general account of such practices, see S. Zuboff, *The Age of Surveillance Capitalism: The Fight for a Human Future at the New Frontier of Power* (New York: PublicAffairs, 2019).

[65] See N. Reich, Vulnerable Consumers in EU Law, in D. Leczykiewicz and S. Weatherill (eds.), *The Images of the Consumer in EU Law: Legislation, Free Movement and Competition Law* (Oxford: Hart Publishing, 2016), pp. 139–58.

[66] I did not find an explicit reference to the principle of "*in dubio pro consumer*" in the UCPD Directive or a concrete application of that principle in the CJEU consumer protection case law. However, absence at the European level does not mean that protective principles are absent from the national laws of the Member States.

[67] Note that others have argued that the presumption of vulnerability of all consumers is a consequence of the *pro-consumer* principle on which consumer law is built, see P. V. López Díaz, The Hyper Vulnerable Consumer as a Weak Party in Chilean Law: A Taxonomy and Scope of the Applicable Legal Protection (2022) 10 *Latin American Legal Studies* 340–415, 342, fn 5.

principles already mentioned that transversally inform consumer protection law.[68] For instance, the practice of personalized pricing, which would normally be allowed under the "average consumer" benchmark as long as the provider complies with the requisite disclosure requirements (i.e., that it disclose in advance that the price has been personalized), might be found questionable under the "vulnerable consumer" benchmark together with the contextual sensitivity to the particular circumstances of the case usually involved in the operation of the *in dubio pro-consumer* principle. This is because one particular circumstance of personalized prices is that they are often the product of sophisticated profiling and manipulation, which make evident the shortcomings of an exclusive focus on the information disclosed and demand a meaningful assessment of the structural and situated factors potentially impairing consumers' decision-making in those specific contexts.

Furthermore, the protective narrative has facilitated the acknowledgment in some jurisdictions of what are called "aggravated vulnerabilities," which are individual characteristics (e.g., age, gender, disability) or personal circumstances (e.g., residency in rural or impoverished areas, limited access to technology or education, unemployment, poverty) that on their own or in the aggregate heighten the "structural vulnerability" affecting all consumers as such, in that they exacerbate particular consumers' odds to enter into detrimental economic transactions. Following this thinking, the debate in Latin America has recently progressed to assessing the desirability of adding the normative category of "hyper-vulnerable consumer" (which responds to "aggravated vulnerabilities") to the standard for the "vulnerable consumer" (which responds to "structural vulnerabilities") in order to reduce inequality in consumer transactions when certain exacerbating circumstances impairing individual consumers' decision-making are manifest – a debate I explore further in the Argentinian context discussed in Section 3.3.[69]

[68] Protective principles are similarly expressed in different jurisdictions in Latin America, such as: (i) "in case of doubt about the interpretation of the principles established by this law, the one most favorable to the consumer will prevail"; or (ii) "the interpretation of the contract will be made in the most favorable sense for the consumer. When there are doubts about the scope of its obligation, the one that is less burdensome will be followed." Arts. 3 and 37, Law No 24.240 (text according to Law No 26.361, B.O. 7/4/2008).

[69] S. S. Barocelli, Consumidores Hipervulnerables. Hacia Una Acentuación del Principio Protectorio (2018a) 57 *La Ley* 1–5. For a recent discussion in the context of consumer protection law in Chile, see López Díaz, The Hyper Vulnerable Consumer as a Weak Party in Chilean Law. Regarding the concern at regulating the hypervulnerable consumer category in Latin America, see, for instance, Article 39 of the Brazilian Consumer Protection Code prohibiting professional suppliers from "taking advantage of the weakness or ignorance of the consumer, considering his/her age, health, knowledge or social condition, to convince him/her to acquire his/her products or services"; and article IV, paragraph 4 of the Consumer Protection of Peru and article 15 of the general law of the rights of users and consumers, where they refer to "pregnant women, children and adolescents, the elderly, people with disabilities" and also incorporate into this hypervulnerable category "consumers in rural areas or in extreme poverty."

The impact of the default image of the consumer initially selected is doubtless significant in terms of consumer law's capacity to address inequality. As just described, the European "average consumer" benchmark hinders the model's capacity to meaningfully address inequality in consumer transactions. In contrast, the Latin American benchmark of the "vulnerable consumer" opens a path for substantive consumer protection laws that demonstrate more sensitivity to inequality concerns in consumer relations by recognizing room for courts to address inequality in the particular cases before them. Examining the divergence between the Latin American and European narratives on the role of consumer law and the default image of the consumer reveals a vital element in understanding the different attitudes toward the more fundamental question of whether consumer law *should* address inequality in those jurisdictions. The relevance of my claim is reinforced by the relative futility of simply looking at the wording of consumer protection provisions here and there without a broader understanding of the emphasis in each case. It is the underlying narratives embraced in those jurisdictions that ultimately give content to and inform the default interpretive benchmarks ("average" or "vulnerable") used by judges (and other relevant actors) in enforcing consumer protection laws. These benchmarks play an important role in assessing the different levels of protection ultimately granted to consumers. This suggests that the practical relevance of the specific concept of the consumer embraced in the different jurisdictions plays an important normative role.

3.3 CONSUMER LAW AND INEQUALITY IN ARGENTINA

3.3.1 *Structural Vulnerability as Default: An Explanation*

The initial rationale of consumer protection law in Argentina was to provide legal tools to counterbalance the factual asymmetry of information and negotiating power between consumers and suppliers in the marketplace, which is characteristic of consumer transactions.[70] The underlying wisdom behind the enactment of the Argentinian Consumer Protection Law (1993) was the aspiration to devise a normative microsystem which had as its primary objective creating legal tools to comprehensively and effectively account for the challenges faced by consumers in the marketplace. After all, the unequal bargaining positions between the parties in consumer contracts were already well known, inequality which in many instances throws into question the affirmation of a pillar of classic contract law, true consent. In many ways, the emergence of consumer protection law represented a fracture in the classic general theory of contract law, which has traditionally assumed contractual parties to be on equal footing. Instead, consumer protection law in Argentina acknowledged the power imbalance between the contracting parties from the very

[70] The first Argentinian Consumer Protection Law was sanctioned in 1993 (Law 24.240). It was then substantially reformed in 2008 (Law 26.361) and in 2015 (Civil Code Reform).

beginning with its recognition that consumers as such occupy a relatively although markedly vulnerable position in the market structure that calls for differentiated treatment and stringent substantive protection.[71]

This protective aim was substantively reinforced a year later by the reform of the Argentinian Constitution (1994), which expressly introduced consumers rights (such as protection of consumers' health, safety, and economic interests; right to access to adequate and truthful information; freedom of choice; and conditions of equal and dignified treatment) as constitutional rights,[72] and incorporated into Argentine law several International Treaties with constitutional status, many of which include (directly or indirectly) consumer protection measures.[73] Furthermore, this trend, which understands consumers as the subject of protection in as much as they are consumers, was first reinforced by the Supreme Court of Justice[74] and later confirmed by the paradigmatic shift from *formal* and *abstract* equality to a *substantive* and *situated* notion of the same that was transversally instituted by the recently reformed Argentinian Civil Code (2015). The 2015 reform introduced specific rules and principles directly aimed at protecting consumers' structural position of vulnerability in the marketplace within the general norms of contracts.[75] Moreover, the current *Project of Reform of the Argentinian Consumer Protection Law* explicitly introduces the "structural vulnerability of the consumer" as a fundamental principle of consumer law.[76]

Apart from the underlying protective rationale fundamentally inspired by the recognition of consumers' structural vulnerability in the marketplace as the norm, consumer law in Argentina is further informed by, among other principles, the normative principle of "*in dubio pro consumer*" – which prescribes that courts, "when in doubt," interpret the rules contained in the consumer statute "in favor of the consumer."[77] Importantly, the "*in dubio pro consumer*" principle is explicitly recognized as such in both the Consumer Protection Law[78] and the recently reformed Civil Code.[79] This normative principle, in conjunction with the

[71] See S. S. Barocelli, Hacia la Construcción de la Categoría de Consumidor Hipervulnerables, in S. S. Barocelli (ed.), *Consumidores Vulnerables* (Buenos Aires: El Derecho, 2018b), pp. 9–32, p. 11.

[72] Article 42 of the Argentine Constitution (justified by consumers' structural vulnerability in the marketplace).

[73] Article 75, Inc. 22 of the Argentine Constitution.

[74] CSJN, Fallos: 339:1077, Cons. 17°. Prevención, Asesoramiento y Defensa del Consumidor c/ Bank Boston N.A. (declaring that Art. 42 CN establishes the special protection that the Constitution recognizes to consumers due to their structural vulnerability in the marketplace).

[75] See S. S. Barocelli, Principios y Ámbito de Aplicación del Derecho del Consumidor en el Nuevo Código Civil y Comercial (2015) 5 *Revista de Derecho Comercial del Consumidor y de la Empresa* 64.

[76] Article 5, Anteproyecto de Ley de Defensa del Consumidor, 6/12/2018.

[77] Article 3 of the Consumer Protection Law (Law 24.240).

[78] Ibid.

[79] Article 1095 of the Civil Code: "Interpretation of the consumer contract. The contract is interpreted in the most favorable sense for the consumer. When there are doubts about the scope of their obligation, the one that is less onerous is adopted."

consumers' structural vulnerability standard, is being used by relevant legal actors, particularly judges, as a flexible interpretive tool (e.g., to fill in gaps or solve conflicts of rights in case of doubt) to justify measures deemed necessary to protect individual consumers in the cases brought before them, a tool that allows more sensitivity to context-specific forms of vulnerability.[80] For instance, the "*in dubio pro consumer*" principle has been applied to interpret normative conflicts within consumer law;[81] compliance with the duty to inform;[82] and deceptive, abusive, or discriminatory advertising, among many others cases. Judges have also resorted to it to assess relevant aspects of the particular relationship between the parties in order to uncover abusive clauses or fraudulent business practices.[83] Importantly, most of these cases show some sensitivity to individual consumers who find themselves in a particularly vulnerable situation vis-à-vis suppliers.[84]

80 For instance, CNACAF (Cámara Nacional de Apelación en lo Contencioso Administrativo) has adopted the *in dubio pro consumer* principle, interpreting that "the protection of the weakest party in the consumer relation is based on a 'presumption of legitimate ignorance.'" CNACAF, Sala II, Ombú Automotores S.A. c/Secretaría de Comercio e Inversiones: Disp. DNCI No 220/97, 23.921/1998, 4/03/1999.

81 For instance, in case of conflict regarding the applicable law (e.g., the Civil Code or the Consumer Protection Law), the provision that is most favorable to the consumer will prevail.

82 See, for instance, SCJ Mendoza, "Bloise de Tucci, Cristina c. Supermercado Makro S.A.," 2/7/2002, LLGran Cuyo, 2002–726 (where the advanced age of the plaintiff was taken into special consideration in order to determine that the information on the automatic doors [the "entrance" and "exit" signs] installed by the supermarket was not sufficient to protect her safety or that of the rest of the consumers).

83 For example, the advanced age of the consumer was considered when his car was stolen in a supermarket (CNCom., Sala C, 18/3/2016, "Luzuriaga, Julián Enrique c. COTO C.I.C.S.A.," La Ley Online Argentina); on the occasion of the execution of a promissory note against a retired woman (CCC de Córdoba de 5° Nominación, 9/5/2019, "Comercial Salsipuedes S.A. c/ Casanova, Miriam Nelly"); and in order to determine the interest rate and payment capacity of an elderly woman (CNCom, Sala C, 27/5/2019, "Fello, Elena Yolanda c/ Banco Piano S.A."). Similarly, smokers were protected "as a particularly vulnerable group, insofar as – for many of them – the habit of smoking has become an addiction." (CNCiv., Sala C, 09/09/2019, "Q., M. A. c. Nobleza Piccardo S.A. y otros s/ Daños y perjuicios," La Ley Online: AR/JUR/27633/2019), among many others. Similarly, special protection was also recognized to minors (CNCiv., Sala L, 6/13/2007, "Osorio, Marcela B. c, Alto Palermo S.A.," La Ley, Buenos Aires, 1/17/2008; CNCiv., Sala H, 6/2/2014, "G.R., J.H. y otros," La Ley Online: AR/JUR/44769/2014); and to consumers with disabilities (CSJN, 8/28/2007, "C.P. de N., C.M.A. y otros v. Centro de Educación Médica e Investigaciones Médicas," La Ley Online: 70039319: in this case the prepaid medical entity was ordered to cover the expenses required in a lawsuit in favor of the disabled minor).

84 For the leading Argentinian case in terms of dignified and equitable treatment in which punitive damages were imposed because the commercial premises of a telephone company lacked an access ramp, thus forcing the physically impaired plaintiff to be attended to on the sidewalk, see SCBA, 06/11/2012, "Machinandiarena Hernández, Nicolás c. Telefónica de Argentina SA s/ reclamo de actos de particulares." For another example in which punitive damages were imposed, see *G. I. T. v. Swiss Medical* S. A. (C. Nac. Com. Sala B, 2016), where a health insurance company deliberately delayed the payment of the urgent treatment required by the insured patient under the insurance policy coverage, openly jeopardizing his health and physical integrity.

Accordingly, besides looking at the wording of protective legislative measures (for instance, duty of information, rights of withdrawal, abusive clauses, free access to justice, and so on), observing the intervention and behavior of the courts in interpreting and enforcing consumer protection law is extremely important, since courts and judges play a relevant role in reducing inequality in consumer transactions by adjudicating case-by-case situations, and whether effective access to justice is granted to consumers ultimately lies in their hands. Certainly, this has not always been the scenario. In Argentina, the actual implementation and enforcement of the Consumer Protection Law only gradually began to gain traction around a decade after it was enacted. A cultural change had to be wrought because consumers were not sufficiently aware of their rights while, for their part, lawyers and civil law judges also unfamiliar with the new statutory regulation initially resisted its implementation. The major shift in the enforcement of consumer protection laws in Argentina occurred much later, in 2008, when, among other reforms, free access to justice, class action mechanisms, and punitive damages[85] were introduced in Argentina's Consumer Protection Law.[86] These substantive reforms, coupled with the implementation of more expeditious procedures, were key factors behind the expansion of consumer litigation in Argentina.[87]

3.3.2 *The Significance of Aggravated Vulnerabilities*

It seems clear at this point that the assumption of the consumer as a rational actor who processes information adequately in order to meet her individual preferences is altogether unsatisfactory. At the same time, an understanding of the consumer as someone who suffers from cognitive biases that make her completely vulnerable and subject to constant manipulation by suppliers is not fully satisfying either. The structural fact that all consumers are potentially vulnerable does not mean that actual vulnerabilities will always materialize for everyone in every transaction. Furthermore, even when actual vulnerabilities do often materialize in certain circumstances, it does not follow that all consumers will be rendered *equally* vulnerable, since vulnerabilities have differentiated impact on different persons in different situations – not everyone will experience the same type or the same degree (or level) of vulnerability.[88] Structural vulnerability thus suggests a rather simplistic

[85] For a detailed analysis of punitive damages in Argentina, see M. G. Martínez Alles, ¿Para Qué Sirven los Daños Punitivos? Modelos de Sanción Privada, Sanción Social y Disuasión Óptima (2012) 14 *Revista de Responsabilidad Civil y Seguros* 55–100.

[86] Note that, in Europe, the lack of a strict, harmonized approach to sanctions for infringements of substantive consumer protection rules has been repeatedly brought up as a weakness in its enforcement of consumer law.

[87] D. A. Chamatropulos, *Estatuto del Consumidor* (Buenos Aires: La Ley, 2019).

[88] On this point, see R. P. Hill and E. Sharma, Consumer Vulnerability (2020) 30 *Journal of Consumer Psychology* 551–70. Similarly, Luna, Identifying and Evaluating Layers of Vulnerability, 87.

answer to a more complicated problem: consumers are not uniform; diversity and heterogeneity better characterize consumers as a group – for they do not share the same abilities, characteristics, social circumstances, economic position, etc. In such a context, a richer understanding of the act of consumption and what it involves is needed, one that takes into account the social and cultural context within which consumer preferences are channeled, for a more accurate appreciation of consumer vulnerability, whose forms are distinctive for different individuals in different settings, and, as such, relational, situational, and highly contextual (i.e., we need to envision the "socially situated consumer").[89]

This more holistic and contextual understanding of the consumer necessarily leads to a logic that forecloses understanding consumer protection law as an eminently informative tool disconnected from the particularities of the social and cultural context of consumption. Within the broader universe of the structurally vulnerable consumer there are individual consumers who, on account of internal factors (e.g., age, gender, disability) and/or external circumstances (e.g., poverty, residency in rural or disadvantaged areas, limited access to technology or education, unemployment) find themselves in particularly disadvantageous situations of subordination, defenselessness, or lack of protection which, temporarily or permanently, prevent them from fully exercising their rights as consumers in equal conditions.[90] These consumers are known as "hyper-vulnerable consumers" (or "especially vulnerable consumers").[91] This means that, beyond the shared cognitive vulnerabilities potentially affecting all consumers, there are additional contingent factors – both internal (i.e., characteristics pertaining to oneself) and external (i.e., pertaining to the circumstances surrounding the transaction) – that might exacerbate consumers' relatively structural vulnerable position vis-à-vis suppliers, further impairing their decision-making.

This approach to vulnerability as a complex phenomenon requiring an exercise of internal and external contextualization fits well with "layered" concepts of vulnerability.[92] For instance, Florencia Luna has argued that vulnerability should be understood "dynamically and relationally" since we do not face "a solid and unique vulnerability" but rather "different vulnerabilities, different layers operating."[93] Moreover, she points out that "some of these layers may overlap: some of them

[89] On the notion of the consumer as a socially and culturally situated actor, see Kuenzler, *Restoring Consumer Sovereignty*, pp. 156–87.

[90] For a skeptical view on increasingly individualized consumer law in the EU, see G. G. Howells, Protecting Consumer Protection Values in the Fourth Industrial Revolution (2020) 43 *Journal of Consumer Policy* 145–75, 167. On personalized law more broadly, see O. Ben-Shahar and A. Porat, *Personalized Law. Different Rules for Different People* (Oxford: Oxford University Press, 2021).

[91] See S. S. Barocelli (ed.), *La Problemática de los Consumidores Hipervulnerables en el Derecho del Consumo Argentino* (Buenos Aires: Universidad de Buenos Aires, 2020).

[92] Luna, Elucidating the Concept of Vulnerability.

[93] Ibid., 128.

may be related to problems with informed consent, others to social circumstances." According to Luna, "the layered way of viewing vulnerability allows it to target differences or variations within the group and to consider different kinds of safeguards or empowerment tools targeting these different features."[94]

Admitting gradations of vulnerability that affect consumers differently allows us, in turn, to recognize the situational diversity of different social and cultural settings and to acknowledge the need for special and differentiated protections from the state. Treating everyone as equals when significant substantive cognitive and contextual differences exist can lead to unsatisfactory results and breakdowns in protection. Where different levels of inequality operate, the state should intervene in differentiated manners to protect consumers, according to the situated diversity at hand. Where the vulnerability is aggravated with respect to the standard, the law can account for this difference by providing more or less accentuated protection depending on the case – the intensity of the legal protection of vulnerable individuals should be proportional to the quantity and nature of the various layers of vulnerability in play. Ultimately, the underlying principle holds that all consumers are potentially vulnerable, but at distinct levels and in different contexts.

Regulating aggravated vulnerabilities has supporters and detractors. The critics argue that special rules stigmatize groups of individuals by identifying them as subsets of society who deserve exemptions based on a set of predetermined personal characteristics (e.g., age, gender, disabilities).[95] Others argue that such regulation goes against the very ideal of equality before the law, the ideal that requires courts to turn a blind eye to differences of, for instance, social status.[96]

Conversely, those who support normative recognition for special subsets believe positive discrimination is required in order to restore equality in consumer transactions – especially in societal contexts where pervasive conditions of socioeconomic inequality are patent. The underlying idea is that *highlighting* disadvantages by explicitly regulating them and providing differentiated treatment represents an important step forward in addressing inequality in consumer transactions by

[94] Luna, Identifying and Evaluating Layers of Vulnerability, 89.

[95] See, for instance, A. Cole, All of us Are Vulnerable, but Some Are More Vulnerable than Others: The Political Ambiguity of Vulnerability Studies, An Ambivalent Critique (2016) 17 *Critical Horizons* 260–77; G. Malgieri and J. Niklas, Vulnerable Data Subjects (2020) 37 *Computer Law and Security Review* 1–16; M. Fineman, Vulnerability and Inevitable Inequality (2017) 4 *Oslo Law Review* 133–49 (arguing that the concept of vulnerabilities is incorrectly used as "disadvantages" or "discrimination" since it ignores the inherently unequal relationship between consumers and providers).

[96] For a criticism of this conventional view in the context of civil litigation, see M. Shapiro, The Indignities of Civil Litigation (2020) 100 *Boston University Law Review* 501–79, 511 ("The conventional view in political and legal theory has long been that the ideal of equality before the law requires judicial blindness to differences of social status ... But it may well be that, in conditions of socioeconomic inequality, attending to, and even highlighting, differences of social status can promote legal equality, by helping level the playing field between socially weaker and more powerful parties").

directing the attention of relevant actors, such as judges, lawyers, and the state, to internal and external factors that impair consumers' decision-making and would not otherwise be weighted, factored in, or even perhaps considered relevant under the broader (more elusive) framework of structural vulnerability.[97] Moreover, the focus on identifying and understanding disadvantages would not only help to expose and raise awareness of undesirable commercial practices that would otherwise go unnoticed but also, and most importantly, to devise mechanisms to counteract them, mitigate their impact on hyper-vulnerable consumers, and ultimately restore equality in consumer transactions.

While regulation for aggravated vulnerabilities acknowledges these aspects and builds upon them, the broader framework of the structurally vulnerable consumer does not on its own assure that certain inequalities will be directly tackled and addressed by the relevant actors. Ultimately, the salience and significance of consumers' inequalities must be taken up by the legislator to obtain the consideration they deserved from judges, lawyers, and the state. Giving the framework statutory backing would help to level the playing field between socially vulnerable and more powerful parties in the specific context of certain consumer transactions.

More than discriminating or stigmatizing certain groups of consumers, identifying layers of vulnerability (e.g., poverty, illiteracy, gender, age, etc.) that impair individual consumer decision-making, directs our focus and attention to the existing institutional arrangements and the more fundamental question of how law and policy might more fairly balance vulnerabilities in the consumer–provider relationship. No meaningful answer to this question can be found without devoting attention to context and complexity and any meaningful answer will require responsive institutions and state architecture that acknowledge vulnerability – a responsive state with the capacity to take substantive action.[98]

3.3.3 *The Normative Category of the Hyper-Vulnerable Consumer*

The COVID-19 crisis not only made the already deep inequalities in Argentine society more salient but exacerbated many of them – the exceptionally long periods of lock-downs and social distancing measures increased the proliferation of online

[97] Similarly, see F. R. Cooper, Always Already Suspect: Revising Vulnerability Theory (2015) 93 *The North Carolina Law Review* 1339–79; Cole, All of us Are Vulnerable, but Some Are More Vulnerable than Others, 267, stressing the importance of acknowledging the differences within consumers (i.e., identifying the needs of specific groups and individuals) to tackle system inequalities.

[98] On this point, see M. Fineman, The Vulnerable Subject and the Responsive State (2010) 60 *Emory Law* 251–76. Similarly, see L. Peroni and A. Timmers, Vulnerable Groups: The Promise of an Emerging Concept in European Human Rights Convention Law (2013) 11 *International Journal of Constitutional Law* 1056–85 (showing how the acknowledgment of vulnerability status for particular groups in the case law of the European Court of Human Rights has led the court to find special positive obligations on the part of the state).

and digital tools to engage in economic transactions which created a "digital gap" for those with restricted access to the Internet and technology or little knowledge of how to use them, restricted access to basic health care and education, and increased the levels of unemployment and poverty, among other examples of the societal impact of the pandemic response.[99] The urgent need to reduce structural inequality from the government, civil society, and social associations became more pressing than ever.[100] If anything, it became evident that ignoring the vulnerabilities impairing consumers' decision-making would result in perpetuating and worsening inequality. In this context, the category of the hyper-vulnerable consumer, which had previously been discussed in scholarly circles,[101] acknowledged in the case-law[102] and explicitly introduced in reform draft proposals of the Consumer Protection Law,[103] was at last officially introduced in the Argentine legal system (Resolution SCI 139/2020).[104] The new category was formally introduced as a response to the constitutional mandate (Art. 75 Inc. 23) to promote positive action measures to guarantee consumers full enjoyment of their rights in conditions of actual equality of opportunity and treatment according to the National Constitution (Art. 42 CN; Art. 1094 CC) and other International Human Rights Treaties with constitutional status in Argentina (Art. 75 Inc. 22 CN; Arts. 1 y 2 CC).

The regulation establishes that hyper-vulnerable consumers are those who, in addition to their structural vulnerability as consumers, find themselves in other aggravated situations of vulnerability due to their age, gender, physical or mental state, or due to social, economic, ethnic, and/or cultural circumstances that cause special obstacles to the full exercise of their rights as consumers.[105] The category is dynamic, flexible, and relational in that it must be assessed in each particular situation. Furthermore, the regulation establishes a nonexhaustive list of situations that might be considered criteria of hypervulnerability: claims that involve the rights or interests of (i) children and adolescents; (ii) members of the LGBT+ collective; (iii) persons of over 70 years of age; (iv) persons possessing a certified disability; (v) individuals without permanent resident immigration status; (vi) those who belong to native communities; (vii) those who reside in rural areas; (viii) those who reside in impoverished neighborhoods (according to Law 27.453); and (ix) situations of

99 See R. A. Vazquez Ferreyra, La Pandemia y Los Nuevos Vulnerables (2020) 92 *La Ley* 1–7.

100 See E. N. Mendieta and C. D. Kalafatich, El Reconocimiento de los Consumidores y las Consumidoras Hipervulnerables en el Ordenamiento Jurídico Argentino (2020) 288 *El Derecho* 1–6.

101 See generally S. S. Barocelli, Los Consumidores Hipervulnerables como Colectivos de Especial Protección por el Derecho del Consumidor, in G. A. Stiglitz and F. Alvarez Larrondo (eds.), *Derecho del Consumidor* (Buenos Aires: Hammurabi, 2003), p. 165.

102 For examples, see note 83.

103 See generally C. A. Hernández et al., Antecedentes y Estado Actual del Proyecto de Código de Defensa del Consumidor (2020) 39 *La Ley* 1.

104 Resolution No 139/2020 of the Secretary of Internal Commerce.

105 Article 1, Resolution No 139/2020.

socioeconomic vulnerability. Situations of socioeconomic vulnerability include being a retiree, pensioner, or a worker in a dependency relationship whose gross income is less than or equal to twice the official minimum wage known as the Minimum Vital and Mobile Salary in Argentina; belonging to certain categories of tax contributors; being a beneficiary of pregnancy or child social allowances; and being included in the special social security scheme for domestic service employees (Law 26.844), among others.[106]

One of the concrete practical implications of being considered within the new normative category is facilitating access to justice, broadly understood, for hyper-vulnerable consumers. The regulation obliges the state to provide specialized legal assistance and more general support when needed, and to identify ex-officio the complaints filed by hyper-vulnerable consumers to give them expedited treatment and provide additional support for conflict resolution.[107] This is not only important in cases where the consumers' losses are not significant, which reduces the incentive to pursue redress but, most importantly, in order to overcome the enforcement costs barriers and generalized apathy toward consumer rights on the part of consumers themselves. Furthermore, the regulation establishes two additional protective principles that must be observed in all procedures involving a hyper-vulnerable consumer: (i) accessible language: all communication must use clear, colloquial language, expressed in a plain, concise, understandable, and appropriate manner to the conditions of hyper-vulnerable consumers; and (ii) a reinforced duty of collaboration: suppliers' conduct must be aimed at guaranteeing adequate treatment and an expedited solution of the conflict, and must demonstrate full collaboration to this end.[108] Apart from the reinforced duty of collaboration, the regulation does not contemplate any additional or stringent sanctions for suppliers who do not comply with the requirement of expedited and effective treatment of claims involving hyper-vulnerable consumers. However, the explicit recognition of a "reinforced duty of collaboration" might open a path in practice for stricter assessment of supplier behavior by judges in those cases.[109] For instance, judges might use their discretion to raise the monetary sanctions imposed in the particular case to account for the nature of those claims (i.e., higher amounts in cases of

[106] Article 2, Resolution No 139/2020.

[107] Article 3, Resolution No 139/2020 establishes the following positive acts that the authority must perform: (i) provide guidance and support to hypervulnerable consumers in filing their claims; (ii) identify ex-officio the claims filed by hypervulnerable consumers to give them priority and provide additional support in solving the conflict; (iii) articulate the intervention of free legal services when necessary; (iv) promote the imposition of necessary preventive measures; (v) propose actions oriented to educate consumers and measures to eliminate access barriers; and (vi) promote good practices in terms of supplier attentiveness, treatment and protection of hypervulnerable consumers.

[108] Article 4, Resolution No 139/2020.

[109] See, for instance, CN Com., Sala E, Asociación Coordinadora de Usuarios, Consumidores y Contribuyentes c. Despegar.com.ar S.A., 26/08/2020, LL AR/JUR/34616/2020; C. Fed. Apel., Sala I, Bahía Blanca, Reimondi, José Antonio c. Banco Nación Argentina, 27/05/2021.

hypervulnerability).[110] Indeed, a new reform grants discretion to the authority to double economic sanctions in certain situations where hyper-vulnerable consumers are involved.[111] Another possibility might be recourse by courts to the imposition of other stringent remedies (e.g., punitive damages).[112] As a matter of fact, judicial decisions where judges awarded higher punitive damages in cases involving hyper-vulnerability have already been handed down.[113] The availability of punitive damages in the realm of consumer relationships in Argentina is probably one of the most distinctive tools at the judiciary's disposal for consumer law enforcement.[114] Granted, the amounts of punitive awards are legally capped[115] and are in general

[110] Note that the Consumer Protection Law grants discretionary power to determine the graduation of sanctions (between established legal limits) in the particular case. Art. 49 LDC.

[111] Cf. Law 15.410/2022, Art 73 bis.

[112] For the first case invoking protections for a hypervulnerable consumer, see *M. M. A. v. Banco Patagonia S. A.* (2022). Mr. M, a retiree, received a confusing letter sent by his bank to his home address instructing him to provide details to confirm his identity and the validity of the operations he carried out peremptorily within 72 hours or the bank would close all the accounts and products that the bank held in his name. The bank's action caused the plaintiff deep discomfort, uncertainty, and fear because he could not think of any reason for the company where he had done his banking for more than fifty years would summon him, a retiree, in such an intimidating and exaggerated manner. In deploying the hypervulnerable consumer protections, the court emphasized that Mr. M was a seventy-two-year old retiree, the letter was confusing and unclear, the letter did not provide complete and detailed information about the request, the letter did not explain why the requested information was needed, and, when bank officials had a second opportunity to do so when the plaintiff sought them out at his local branch, they again failed to provide an explanation. Banco Patagonia was sentenced to pay compensation to the retiree for non-pecuniary damages ($30,000) and punitive damages ($50,000) for reprehensible behavior and violation of consumer dignity. For an analysis of using punitive damages to protect hypervulnerable consumers, see E. N. Mendieta, L. Colás, and S. Sansone, Los Daños Punitivos como Mecanismo de Protección de los Consumidores Hipervulnerables, in S. S. Barocelli (ed.), *Consumidores Hipervulnerables* (Buenos Aires: El Derecho, 2018), pp. 261–94.

[113] For an analysis of the case law along this line, see S. S. Barocelli, Incumplimiento del Trato Digno y Equitativo a Consumidores Hipervulnerables y Daños Punitivos: La Suprema Corte de Buenos Aires Confirma su Procedencia (2013) 29 *Diario Judicial* 3.

[114] The Consumer Protection Law regulates punitive damages through two main norms. The general basic rule is expressed in Art. 52bis and Art. 8bis which identify specific types of abusive conducts susceptible to the imposition of punitive damages. Art. 52bis: "Punitive Damages. To the supplier that does not comply with its legal or contractual obligations with the consumer, at the request of the injured party, the judge may apply a civil fine in favor of the consumer, which will be graduated according to the seriousness of the conduct and other circumstances of the case, regardless of other compensation that corresponds to the consumer." Art. 8bis states that suppliers' behavior revealing undignified or inequitable treatment or that places consumers in embarrassing, humiliating, or intimidating situations, may be subject to the imposition of punitive damages, without prejudice to the compensation that corresponds to the consumer. Arts. 8bis y 52bis, Law No 24.240 (text according to Law No 26.361, B.O. 7/4/2008).

[115] Note that the legal cap was recently reformed as follows: "The amount of the fine cannot be more than [2.100 basic baskets]" (Art. 119, Law No 27.701 B.O. 1/12/2022). This means that the limit of punitive damages as of 1 December 2022 is equivalent to USD 1,837,000.

relatively modest.[116] Nonetheless, punitive awards have played an important expressive[117] and indeed growing role in the increased enforcement of consumer law in Argentina, which is reinforced by the fact that they are fully awarded to individual consumers.[118]

All these measures combined under the normative force of the new category of hyper-vulnerable consumers could play an important role in altering the behavior by disincentivizing market actors from exploiting aggravated vulnerabilities in the first place, which might, hopefully, mitigate the inequality in contemporary consumer transactions. Certainly, for this regulation to be effective, efforts and resources must be allocated to creating the proper enforcement mechanisms and strengthening the state's capacity to adapt and respond to the challenges posed by the variety of situations involving hypervulnerability. The regulation is too recent for informed conclusions at this point; however, it holds promise as a complement to other government policies aimed at addressing inequality in Argentina.

3.4 CONCLUSION

The need to reduce societal inequality is not unique to the Global South, it is a pressing global problem that urgently demands attention. Europe and Latin America have much to learn from each other. The distinctive emphasis on either *empowerment* or *protection* adopted in those jurisdictions impacts the discussion on the relationship between consumer law and inequality: the more consumer law moves toward empowerment and embraces the average consumer standard, the less

[116] The average punitive award amounts to $200,000 Argentinian Pesos. Only recently have we seen higher amounts – $800,000 to $1,000,000 – which remain far below the legal limit. For an analysis of problems related to the practical implementation of punitive awards, see M. G. Martínez Alles, La Dimensión Sancionadora del Derecho de Daños. Los Daños Punitivos, in D. M. Papayannis (ed.), *Manual de Responsabilidad Extracontractual* (Mexico City: Suprema Corte de Justicia de la Nación de Mexico, 2022), pp. 601–47.

[117] For the expressive dimension of punitive damages, see M. G. Martínez Alles, Moral Outrage and Betrayal Aversion: The Psychology of Punitive Damages (2018) 11 *Journal of Tort Law* 245–303.

[118] See Note 114. Punitive damages offer an interesting example of the diffusion of ideas within Latin America. In fact, Chile joined in this trend by introducing punitive damages in the framework of its Consumer Protection Law passed in 2018 (Art. 53 [c], Law No 21.081, 13/09/2018, although it should be noted that the law does not expressly refer to the institution as "punitive damages"). In Mexico, meanwhile, punitive damages were directly introduced by the Supreme Court of Justice in 2014 (Amparo Directo 30/2013, Primera Sala, Suprema Corte de Justicia de la Nación, 26/02/2014). For comparative insights on the distinctive path followed by those jurisdictions, see M. G. Martínez Alles, Punitive Damages in Argentina and Mexico: Rethinking the Scope of the Public Policy Exception, in L. Meurkens and C. Vanleenhove (eds.), *The Recognition and Enforcement of Punitive Damages Judgments across the Globe: Insights from Various Continents* (The Hague: Eleven International Publishing, 2023), pp. 129–47. For a comparative analysis on the approach to punitive damages in Latin America and Europe, see M. G. Martínez Alles, Punitive Damages: Reorienting the Debate in Civil Law Systems (2019) 10 *Journal of European Tort Law* 63–81.

sensitive it is to the vulnerabilities that impair consumer decision-making, which hinders this model's capacity to address inequality in consumer transactions. The socially devastating aftermath of the COVID-19 pandemic, coupled with the rapid acceleration of the digital economy, globally compel an approach to consumer law that recognizes the default conception of consumers as occupying a relatively although markedly vulnerable position in the market structure. In this sense, the Latin American emphasis on structural vulnerability seems better equipped to address inequality in consumer transactions than the European emphasis on the average consumer. A fresh start for EU consumer law might thus begin with recalibrating its focus on the proper balance between empowerment and protection such that the law not only considers in the equation the relevance of addressing consumer inequality, but also the deep interconnectedness of economic and social interests. Whether EU law will refocus the concept of consumer vulnerability is unclear. However, reliance on the current standards of the average consumer (the default) and the vulnerable consumer (the exception) is becoming increasingly difficult to sustain, especially in the context of the emerging global digital economy.[119] Aggravated vulnerabilities are exacerbated in the digital age because the use of algorithms and big data collection allows providers to obtain much more information than ever before about their consumers' behavior.[120] Acknowledging the combination of the structural and situational factors that impair consumer decision-making could be an important step toward overcoming the (over)emphasis on empowerment and the (over)reliance on the benchmark of the average consumer as default.

BIBLIOGRAPHY

Akerlof, G. A. and Shiller, R. J., *Phishing for Phools. The Economics of Manipulation and Deception* (New Jersey: Princeton University Press, 2015).

Ayres, I. and Siegelman, P., Race and Gender Discrimination in Bargaining for a New Car (1995) 85 *The American Economic Review* 304–21.

Bar-Gill, O., Consumer Transactions, in E. Zamir and D. Eichman (eds.), *The Oxford Handbook of Behavioral Economics and the Law* (Oxford: Oxford University Press, 2014), pp. 465–90.

Barocelli, S. S., Consumidores Hipervulnerables. Hacia Una Acentuación del Principio Protectorio (2018a) 57 *La Ley* 1–5.

Hacia la Construcción de la Categoría de Consumidor Hipervulnerables, in S. S. Barocelli (ed.), *Consumidores Vulnerables* (Buenos Aires: El Derecho, 2018b), pp. 9–32.

Incumplimiento del Trato Digno y Equitativo a Consumidores Hipervulnerables y Daños Punitivos: La Suprema Corte de Buenos Aires Confirma su Procedencia (2013) 29 *Diario Judicial* 3.

[119] Similarly, see V. Mak, A Primavera for European Consumer Law: Re-birth of the Consumer Image in the Light of Digitalisation and Sustainability (2022) 11 *Journal of European Consumer and Market Law* 77–80.

[120] N. Bol et al., Vulnerability in a Tracked Society: Combining Tracking and Survey Data to Understand Who Gets Targeted with What Content (2020) 22 *New Media & Society* 1996–2017.

(ed.), *La Problemática de los Consumidores Hipervulnerables en el Derecho del Consumo Argentino* (Buenos Aires: Universidad de Buenos Aires, 2020).

Los Consumidores Hipervulnerables como Colectivos de Especial Protección por el Derecho del Consumidor, in G. A. Stiglitz and F. Alvarez Larrondo (eds.), *Derecho del Consumidor* (Buenos Aires: Hammurabi, 2003), p. 165.

Principios y Ámbito de Aplicación del Derecho del Consumidor en el Nuevo Código Civil y Comercial (2015) 5 *Revista de Derecho Comercial del Consumidor y de la Empresa* 64.

Bartl, M., Internal Market Rationality, Private Law and the Direction of the Union: Resuscitating the Market as the Object of the Political? (2015) 21 *European Law Journal* 572–98.

Ben-Shahar, O. and Porat, A., *Personalized Law. Different Rules for Different People* (Oxford: Oxford University Press, 2021).

Bol, N. et al., Vulnerability in a Tracked Society: Combining Tracking and Survey Data to Understand Who Gets Targeted with What Content (2020) 22 *New Media & Society* 1996–2017.

Cartwright, P., Understanding and Protecting Vulnerable Financial Consumers (2005) 38 *Journal of Consumer Policy* 119–38.

Chamatropulos, D. A. *Estatuto del Consumidor* (Buenos Aires: La Ley, 2019).

Cole, A., All of us Are Vulnerable, but Some Are More Vulnerable than Others: The Political Ambiguity of Vulnerability Studies, An Ambivalent Critique (2016) 17 *Critical Horizons* 260–77.

Cooper, F. R., Always Already Suspect: Revising Vulnerability Theory (2015) 93 *The North Carolina Law Review* 1339–79.

Davis, G., The Consumer, the Citizen, and the Human Being, in D. Leczykiewitz and S. Weatherill (eds.), *The Images of the Consumer in EU Law* (Oxford: Hart Publishing, 2016), pp. 325–38.

Davis, K. and Pargendler, M., Contract Law and Inequality (2022) 107 *Iowa Law Review* 1485–541.

De Elizalde, F., Standarisation of Agreement in EU Law. An Adieu to the Contracting Parties?, in T. Tridimas and M. Durovic (eds.), *New Directions in European Private Law* (Oxford: Hart Publishing, 2021), pp. 29–59.

Domurath, I., The Case of Vulnerability as the Normative Standard in European Consumer Credit and Mortgage Law: An Inquiry into the Paradigms of Consumer Law (2013) 2 *Journal of European Consumer and Market Law* 124–37.

Duivenvoorde, B., The Protection of Vulnerable Consumers under the Unfair Commercial Practices Directive (2013) 2 *Journal of European Consumer and Market Law* 69–79.

The Consumer Benchmarks in the Unfair Commercial Practice Directive (New York: Springer, 2015).

Esposito, F. and Grochowski, M., The Consumer Benchmark, Vulnerability, and the Contract Terms Transparency: A Plea for Reconsideration (2022) 18 *European Review of Contract Law* 1–31.

Fineman, M., The Vulnerable Subject and the Responsive State (2010) 60 *Emory Law* 251–76.

The Vulnerable Subject: Anchoring Equality in the Human Condition (2008) 20 *Yale Journal of Law and Feminism* 1–23.

Vulnerability and Inevitable Inequality (2017) 4 *Oslo Law Review* 133–49.

Gargarella, R., Inequality and the Constitution: From Equality to Social Rights, in P. Dann, M. Riegner and M. Bönnemann (eds.), *The Global South and Comparative Constitutional Law* (Oxford: Oxford University Press, 2020), pp. 235–49.

Grundmann, S., Targeted Consumer Protection, in D. Leczykiewicz and S. Weatherill (eds.) *The Images of the Consumer in EU Law: Legislation, Free Movement and Competition Law* (Oxford: Hart Publishing, 2016), pp. 223–44.

Hanson, J. D. and Kysar, D. A., Taking Behavioralism Seriously: Some Evidence of Market Manipulation (1999) 112 *Harvard Law Review* 1420–572.

Helberger, N. et al., Choice Architectures in the Digital Economy: Towards a New Understanding of Digital Vulnerability (2022) 45 *Journal of Consumer Policy* 175–200.

Hernández, C. A. et al., Antecedentes y Estado Actual del Proyecto de Código de Defensa del Consumidor (2020) 39 *La Ley* 1.

Hill, R. P. and Sharma, E., Consumer Vulnerability (2020) 30 *Journal of Consumer Psychology* 551–70.

Howells, G., Europe's (Lack of) Vision on Consumer Protection, in D. Leczykiewicz and S. Weatherill (eds.) *The Images of the Consumer in EU Law: Legislation, Free Movement and Competition Law* (Oxford: Hart Publishing, 2016), pp. 431–46.

Howells, G., The Potential and Limits of Consumer Empowerment by Information (2005) 32 *Journal of Law and Society* 349–70.

Howells, G. G., Protecting Consumer Protection Values in the Fourth Industrial Revolution (2020) 43 *Journal of Consumer Policy* 145–75.

Howells, G. G., Twigg-Flesner, C., and Wilhelmsson, T. (eds.), *Rethinking EU Consumer Law: Markets and the Law* (Oxfordshire: Taylor & Francis, 2018).

Jolls, C., Sunstein, C. R., and Thaler, R., A Behavioral Approach to Law and Economics (1998) 50 *Stanford Law Review* 1471–550.

Kahneman, D., *Thinking, Fast and Slow* (London: Penguin, 2012).

Kirchner, C., Justifying Limits to Party Autonomy in the Internal Market: Mainly Consumer Protection, in S. Grundmann, W. Kerber, and S. Weatherill (eds.), *Party Autonomy and the Role of Information in the Internal Market* (Berlin: de Gruyter, 2001), pp. 173–96.

Korobkin, R. B. and Ulen, T. S., Law and Behavioral Science: Removing the Rationality Assumption from Law and Economics (2000) 88 *California Law Review* 1051 144.

Kuenzler, A., *Restoring Consumer Sovereignty. How Markets Manipulate Us and What the Law Can Do About It* (Oxford: Oxford University Press, 2017).

Kuenzler, A., On (Some Aspects of) Social Privacy in the Social Media Space (2022) 12 *International Data Privacy Law* 63–73.

López Díaz, P. V., 'The Hyper Vulnerable Consumer as a Weak Party in Chilean Law: A Taxonomy and Scope of the Applicable Legal Protection (2022) 10 *Latin American Legal Studies* 340–415.

Luna, F. Elucidating the Concept of Vulnerability. Layers Not Labels (2009) 2 *International Journal of Feminist Approaches to Bioethics* 121–39.

Identifying and Evaluating Layers of Vulnerability: A Way Forward (2019) 19 *Developing World Bioethics* 86–95.

Mak, V., A Primavera for European Consumer Law: Re-birth of the Consumer Image in the Light of Digitalisation and Sustainability (2022) 11 *Journal of European Consumer and Market Law* 77–80.

Mak, V., The Consumer in European Regulatory Private Law, in D. Leczykiewicz and S. Weatherill (eds.), *The Images of the Consumer in EU Law* (Oxford: Hart Publishing, 2016), pp. 381–400.

Malgieri, G. and Niklas, J., Vulnerable Data Subjects (2020) 37 *Computer Law and Security Review* 1–16.

Martínez Alles, M. G., La Dimensión Sancionadora del Derecho de Daños. Los Daños Punitivos, in D. M. Papayannis (ed.), *Manual de Responsabilidad Extracontractual* (Mexico City: Suprema Corte de Justicia de la Nación de Mexico, 2022), pp. 601–47.

Moral Outrage and Betrayal Aversion: The Psychology of Punitive Damages (2018) 11 *Journal of Tort Law* 245–303.

¿Para Qué Sirven los Daños Punitivos? Modelos de Sanción Privada, Sanción Social y Disuasión Óptima (2012) 14 *Revista de Responsabilidad Civil y Seguros* 55–100.

Martínez Alles, M. G. Punitive Damages in Argentina and Mexico: Rethinking the Scope of the Public Policy Exception, in L. Meurkens and C. Vanleenhove (eds.), *The Recognition and Enforcement of Punitive Damages Judgments across the Globe: Insights from Various Continents* (The Hague: Eleven International Publishing, 2023), pp. 129–47.

Martínez Alles, M. G., Punitive Damages: Reorienting the Debate in Civil Law Systems (2019a) 10 *Journal of European Tort Law* 63–81.

Regulating Gender Stereotypes in Advertising: When Persuasion Reinforces Inequality (2019b) 5 *Latin American Legal Studies* 287–312.

Mendieta, E. N. and Kalafatich, C. D., El Reconocimiento de los Consumidores y las Consumidoras Hipervulnerables en el Ordenamiento Jurídico Argentino (2020) 288 *El Derecho* 1–6.

Mendieta, E. N., Colás, L., and Sansone, S., Los Daños Punitivos como Mecanismo de Protección de los Consumidores Hipervulnerables, in S. S. Barocelli (ed.), *Consumidores Hipervulnerables* (Buenos Aires: El Derecho, 2018), pp. 261–94.

Michaels, R., Of Islands and the Ocean: The Two Rationales of European Private Law, in R. Brownsword et al. (eds.), *The Foundations of European Private Law* (Oxford: Hart Publishing, 2011), pp. 139–58.

Micklitz, H. W., The Expulsion of the Concept of Protection from the Consumer Law and the Return to Social Elements in the Civil Law: A Bittersweet Polemic (2012) 35 *Journal of Consumer Policy* 283–96.

The Full Harmonization Dream (2022) 11 *Journal of European Consumer and Market Law* 117–21.

Pargendler, M., The Grip of Nationalism on Corporate Law (2020) 95 *Indiana Law Journal* 533–90.

Peroni, L. and Timmers, A., Vulnerable Groups: The Promise of an Emerging Concept in European Human Rights Convention Law (2013) 11 *International Journal of Constitutional Law* 1056–85.

Rachlinski, J. J., The Psychological Foundations of Behavioral Law and Economics (2011) 2011 *University of Illinois Law Review* 1675–96.

Reich, N., A European Contract Law or an EU Contract Law Regulation for Consumers? (2005) 28 *Journal of Consumer Policy* 383–407.

From Minimal to Full to "Half Harmonisation," in J. Devenney and M. Kenny (eds.), *European Consumer Protection Theory and Practice* (Cambridge: Cambridge University Press, 2012), pp. 3–5.

Vulnerable Consumers in EU Law, in D. Leczykiewicz and S. Weatherill (eds.), *The Images of the Consumer in EU Law: Legislation, Free Movement and Competition Law* (Oxford: Hart Publishing, 2016), pp. 139–58.

Schebesta, H. and Purnhagen, K., Island or Ocean: Empirical Evidence on the Average Consumer Concept in the UCPD (2020) 28 *European Review of Private Law* 293–310.

Shapiro, M. The Indignities of Civil Litigation (2020) 100 *Boston University Law Review* 501–79.

Tversky, A. and Kahneman, D., Judgment under Uncertainty: Heuristic and Biases (1974) 185 *Science* 1124–31.

Vazquez Ferreyra, R. A., La Pandemia y Los Nuevos Vulnerables (2020) 92 *La Ley* 1–7.

Weatherill, S., Empowerment Is Not the Only Fruit, in D. Leczykiewicz and S. Weatherill (eds.), *The Images of the Consumer in EU Law: Legislation, Free Movement and Competition Law* (Oxford: Hart Publishing, 2016), pp. 203–21.

The Fundamental Question of Minimum or Maximum Harmonisation, in S. Garben and I. Govaere (eds.), *The Internal Market 2.0* (Oxford: Hart Publishing, 2020), pp. 261–84.

Who Is the "Average Consumer"?, in S. Weatherill and U. Bernits (eds.), *The Regulation of Unfair Commercial Practices under EC Directive 2005/29: New Rules and New Techniques* (Oxford: Hart Publishing, 2007), pp. 115–38.

Wilhelmsson, T., Private Law in the EU: Harmonised or Fragmented Europeanisation? (2002) 1(1) *European Review of Private Law* 77–94.

Social Contract Law and European Integration (Aldershot: Dartmouth, 1995).

The Informed Consumer vs the Vulnerable Consumer in European Unfair Commercial Practices Law: A Comment, in G. G. Howells et al. (eds.), *Yearbook of Consumer Law 2007* (Hampshire: Ashgate Publishing, 2007), pp. 211–28.

Zuboff, S., *The Age of Surveillance Capitalism: The Fight for a Human Future at the New Frontier of Power* (New York: PublicAffairs, 2019).

4

Contracts, Inequality, and the State

Contract Law Ultra-heterodoxy in China

Weitseng Chen

4.1 INTRODUCTION

This chapter examines the role of contract law in tackling inequality unveiled by the COVID-19 pandemic, with a focus on China, where courts seem to have made the most drastic moves. Whether contract law has any role to play in addressing economic inequality is the focal point of a long-lasting debate among contract law scholars.[1] The orthodox view of contract law contends that contract law is expected to guarantee freedom of contract, individual autonomy, and efficiency rather than bearing extra burdens of pursuing distributive justice; for the latter, tax law and fiscal policies are more effective and legitimate tools.[2] In comparison, Kevin Davis and Mariana Pargendler have recently pointed out the trend of contract law heterodoxy in developing countries.[3] This heterodox approach to contract law moves beyond the conventional doctrines relating to the validity and enforceability of contracts of contracts, such as frustration, duress, and misrepresentation, to correct injustice on additional grounds.[4] Courts in countries such as Brazil, Colombia, and South Africa have been willing to alter or void unfair contract terms in order to protect weaker parties on the grounds of distributive justice. Against this backdrop, I find that neither orthodox nor heterodox approaches can explain Chinese courts' drastic

This chapter benefitted from comments by Donald Clarke, Damian Chalmers, Tze-Shiou Chien, Kevin Davis, Mike Dowdle, Matthew Erie, Christian Hofmann, Chih-Hsing Ho, Hualing Fu, Susan Finder, Dieter Grimm, Andrew Godwin, Ying Hu, Benjamin Liebman, Teng Li, Leo You Li, Mariana Pargendler, Tan Zhong Xin, and Umakanth Varottil. The author acknowledges the financial support of a NUS research fund (A-8001907-00-00) and excellent research assistance by Marcus Dee, Claire Khoo, Glenda Tan, and Zheqi Zhong.

1 K. E. Davis and M. Pargendler, Contract Law and Inequality (2022) 107 *Iowa Law Review* 1485–542.

2 It is argued that the US Constitution's Contract clause was designed to prevent laws that alter contracts for distributive purposes. Ibid, 1498.

3 Ibid.

4 M. Chen-Wishart, *Contract Law* (Oxford: Oxford University Press, 2012), p. 197.

approach to dealing with inequality. Chinese courts have gone further to espouse what I term "ultra-heterodoxy" to denote the greater latitude they enjoy in deciding cases that impact inequality.

The debate between contract law orthodoxy and heterodoxy has not received much attention in Asia. This is in part because of the civil law tradition existing in most Asian countries. Contract law in Asia usually gives judges broad discretion to review the validity of contracts according to public interest and fairness considerations, thereby approximating it to the type of legal heterodoxy that Davis and Pargendler describe in the Global South. For example, the Civil Codes of Japan, South Korea, Taiwan, and China all provide that contracts and other legal acts should be deemed void if they violate social morals, public order, and social customs.[5] Other cultural factors also contribute to the appeal of a more socially- and policy-oriented approach to contract law in Asia, including the country's political economy, people's communitarian values, the perception of the role of state, and even the paternalistic function of the legal system. As a result, compared to the common law of contract, contract law in Asian civil law countries allows much greater regulatory and legislative intervention, and subjects contracts to other special laws that amend contractual obligations for policy reasons, such as consumer protection, financial stability, fairness, and healthcare considerations. Such regulatory intervention in contract law reflects the perception of the state in civil law systems, which is generally expected to be the guardian of public interests and freedom rather than the enemy of liberty.[6] All in all, civil codes in Asia and the prevailing legal culture provide ample scope for heterodox approaches.

In view of the different role of state in private contract relationships, this chapter aims to examine contract disputes in China during the pandemic to explore how the strong Chinese party-state intervenes in the private sphere to tackle economic inequality. By way of background, inequality is a serious issue in China. In 2021, China's Gini coefficient reached a score of 0.46, which indicates a high level of income inequality.[7] Rich and powerful market actors have better capacity to engage with sophisticated contractual arrangements than weaker market actors do. In the case of financial products, for example, complex contractual arrangements, such as securitization of assets and prioritization of varying debts, could facilitate the persistence of inequality by exploiting weaker parties who do not have the capacity to understand the nuances of contract terms. In this regard, it is understandable that

5 For example, Art. 72, Civil Code of Taiwan (1929); Art. 153, Civil Code of The Republic of China (2020); Art. 103, Civil Code of South Korea (1958); Art. 90, Civil Code of Japan (1896).

6 For a general discussion, see M. Damaska, *The Faces of Justice and State Authority*: A Comparative Approach to the Legal Process (New Haven: Yale University Press, 1986), pp. 71–96; J. Whitman, 'The Two Western Cultures of Privacy: Dignity versus Liberty' (2004) 113 *Yale Law Journal* 1151–222.

7 C. Textor, Gini Index: Inequality of Income Distribution in China 2004–2021, *Statista* (September 29, 2023).

China's nascent legal system coupled with the limited access to it by lay people could help institutionalize and increase such inequality. Like elsewhere, the COVID-19 pandemic has worsened preexisting inequality in China.[8] Such inequality may well manifest itself in increasing contract disputes. As a matter of fact, during the latter part of the pandemic, disputes over contracts, which may or may not have been unequal and exploitative in nature, led to street protests by angry contract parties from time to time in the context of both consumer and commercial arrangements.[9] Such anger and frustration also destabilized the financial system because many financial institutions have been involved in those transactions in dispute.[10] As a result, the Chinese state, seriously concerned about spreading impacts, has tried hard to resolve such disputes.

It is not a secret that the Chinese state will intervene in political cases and in cases involving state interests.[11] Yet, in private contract disputes, the state also intervenes to tackle inequality. In doing so, the state faces a similar tension between contract law orthodoxy and heterodoxy, trying to strike a balance between exchange efficiency and distributive justice, both of which greatly affect the legitimacy of the party-state. This tension could be observed in some contract disputes that led to serious political challenges. In 2022, for example, massive numbers of home buyers in several provinces of China collectively refused to pay their mortgage loans as a way of protest on the ground that the contract terms with real estate developers and their banks had resulted in unfair and unbearable hardship during the pandemic.[12] Such protests struck a nerve for the Chinese government because these consumers legitimately called for economic justice but at the tremendous cost of stability of the financial system.

This chapter thus examines the ways in which the Chinese state and courts dealt with such contract disputes during the pandemic and describes their ultra-heterodox approaches to the relationship between contract law, inequality, and the state. The approaches to contract disputes within the Chinese state also reflect a unique construction of legality that I term "negotiated legality," in which all stakeholders subject legality to negotiations during the contract enforcement process with the goal of delivering substantive justice rather than demarcating strict winners and losers. I have identified three modes of ultra-heterodoxy applied by the Chinese

8 W. Wan, J. Wang, and W. Jiang, Does COVID-19 Exacerbate Regional Income Inequality? Evidence from 20 Provinces of China (2023) 15 *Sustainability* 1–16.

9 See, e.g., K. Slaten, Grassroots Protests Are Frequent in Xi Jinping's China, *Freedom House* (November 17, 2022); Bloomberg News, Sweeping Mortgage Boycott Changes the Face of Dissent in China, *Bloomberg* (August 3, 2022).

10 See, e.g., C. Lo, The Risks around China's Grassroots Mortgage "Boycott," *BNP Paribas* (July 26, 2022).

11 See K. Hang Ng and X. He, *Embedded Courts: Judicial Decision-Making in China* (Cambridge: Cambridge University Press, 2017).

12 I. Qian and A. Chang, They Poured Their Savings into Homes That Were Never Built, *New York Times* (January 24, 2023).

courts, in which continuing negotiations can be observed. Such negotiations over legality are only possible because of factors such as China's unique political economy that allows the party-state to intervene in private contractual relationships; various communitarian norms surrounding liability, which can be employed by judges; and the motivations behind state actors' efforts to secure broader policy goals, including maintaining economic stability and preventing social unrest.

This chapter explores how the Chinese party-state and courts tackled inequality in contract disputes during the pandemic and is organized as follows. Section 4.2 offers a brief comparison between China and other countries in terms of the general approach for dealing with contract disputes during the pandemic. Section 4.3 describes the three approaches that make China different from other countries, followed by Sections 4.4–4.6, which discuss each of the approaches. In Section 4.7, I analyze the implications on administration of justice in light of my case study in China – particularly, the "negotiated legality." Section 4.8 concludes.

4.2 DEALING WITH CONTRACT DISPUTES DURING THE PANDEMIC

4.2.1 *Procedural Approach vs. Substantive Approach*

During the peak of the pandemic, many counties passed legislation, much of which remains in force, to give breathing space for contract parties that faced financial difficulty.[13] Most laws seeking to provide relief from the effects of COVID-19 (including those of the United States, United Kingdom, Australia, and Singapore), provide temporary, procedural relief. Typically, companies or individuals are granted an extended grace period to repay their debts. It is also common for such COVID-19 legislation to raise the statutory threshold for creditors to apply for an injunction or file for bankruptcy against their debtors.[14]

COVID-19 legislation in Asia does not substantively revise the underlying rights and obligations between contract parties. For example, Singapore's COVID-19 (Temporary Measures) Act states that the monetary threshold for creditor companies to petition for an insolvency of a business increased from S$10,000 to S$100,000, but at the same time the regulators emphasized that the banks' contract rights to charge

[13] For example, Singapore's COVID-19 (Temporary Measures) Act 2020 (No. 14 of 2020) remains in effect as of February 2025. In Taiwan, the ordinance to mitigate defaults in construction contracts due to the pandemic also remains effective as of February 2025. See Public Construction Commission of Executive Yuan, The Guidelines for Non-Performance of Construction Contracts Caused by the Pandemic (2022); Public Construction Commission of Executive Yuan, Directive No. 1100100687o (2021).

[14] See, e.g., Section 20 of Singapore's COVID-19 (Temporary Measures) Act 2020. Australia also increased their threshold for bankruptcy notices issued by a creditor's petition from AUD 5,000 to AUD 20,000. For more information, see M. Murray, Managing the Insolvency Curve in Australia, *Oxford Business Law Blog* (April 20, 2020).

fees and interest for non-payment or late payment of loan obligations was not affected.[15] The Act mitigates the consequences of loan defaults only procedurally.

Notably, this procedural model still endorses market mechanisms as well as contract law orthodoxy in that it avoids compromising individual autonomy and freedom of contract. On the one hand, it strongly encourages contract parties to negotiate a solution; on the other, the regulators do not prescribe any substantive solution for parties. Regulators in several major Asian economies have issued directives to suggest that contract parties engage in negotiations under preexisting change in circumstances doctrine and the temporary procedural measures announced. For example, Taiwan's Public Construction Commission issued directives to instruct that the pandemic could be deemed as "force majeure" and hence qualify for the application of the contract law doctrine of "change in circumstances" to avoid related obligations.[16] Similarly, the Monetary Authority of Singapore suggested that small- and medium-sized enterprises work with their banks to explore solutions made available by individual banks and take into account any late charges and higher interest, as well as the possibility that they may end up paying more in the future. This is because, as in other jurisdictions, the country's COVID-19 Act only extends the grace period but does not substantively affect contract terms about late payment charges.[17] The final solution must remain subject to private negotiations.

By contrast, China employed a very different approach, which did not hesitate to substantively revise the rights and obligations of contract parties to solve disputes and address policy concerns during the pandemic. The People's Supreme Court of China and its intermediate courts have selected and published several exemplary cases as a form of guidance for judges to deal with COVID-related contract disputes.[18] By analyzing these precedents, this chapter identifies three different approaches that Chinese courts have employed. All of the three approaches not only echo contract law heterodoxy but also move beyond it. I call these approaches examples of "ultra-heterodoxy in contract law."

4.2.2 *Practices of Contract Law Heterodoxy*

China's ultra-heterodoxy appears only in certain types of contract disputes that seriously concern inequality and public policies; for less serious cases, Chinese judges behaved similarly to their counterparts in other Asian countries and adjudicated according to contract law doctrines as well as some ad hoc directives announced by regulators during the pandemic. For example, Articles 6, 7, and

[15] Monetary Authority of Singapore, Comments by MAS on Covid-19 (Temporary Measures) Bill, Monetary Authority of Singapore (April 1, 2020).

[16] Public Construction Commission of Executive Yuan, The Guidelines for Non-Performance of Construction Contracts Caused by the Pandemic.

[17] Monetary Authority of Singapore, Comments by MAS on Covid-19, 4.

[18] People's Supreme Court of China, Guidelines on Proper Trial of Civil and Commercial Cases related to Coronavirus Pandemic (May 2020).

8 of PRC Civil Code state the basic principles that a legal entity cannot violate social morals, fairness, and good faith in their legal transactions. As basic principles instead of mere legal doctrines, they serve as the overarching notions that bind legal interpretation and seal any legal loopholes.[19] Article 534 further empowers courts to monitor and regulate contracts that violate national interest and public interest. Under this doctrine, Chinese judges altered or voided the contractual obligations of contract parties, and sometimes required them to renegotiate a new contract.[20] The doctrine most commonly applied by Chinese judges in pandemic-related cases is the "change in circumstance" clause, which allows judges to amend or void contract obligations in the event of a change in circumstance that the parties did not foresee and that would result in unfairness and inequality.[21]

For example, face masks were in short supply during the pandemic, so disputes regarding mask production agreements were common. In such cases, courts frequently applied the doctrine of "change in circumstance" to alter contract terms in favor of weaker parties. While some cases were not inequality-related as the problems were caused by unexpected, volatile market conditions, many cases did involve strong market players taking advantage of their market position to exploit weaker parties, such as when price increases by a wholesaler caused defaults by small retailers, or when a manufacturers' willful blindness of their limited manufacturing capacity caused buyers' subsequent defaults in other resale contracts.[22]

For these less severe cases, Chinese regulators also behaved similarly to their counterparts in other Asian countries. The Chinese government issued COVID-related directives to offer temporary, procedural relief. For example, the China Banking and Insurance Regulatory Commission (CBIRC) required commercial banks to extend grace periods for individuals and small- and medium-sized enterprises that defaulted on their loan agreements.[23] Also, financial institutions were required to be less stringent about loan defaults by debtors in certain types of

[19] F. Yu, The Distinction between Basic Principles and General Clauses: The Interpretation Methodology for Interpreting the Principles of Good Faiths and Social Morals (2021) 4 *China Legal Science* 25–43 [于飛, 基本原則與概括條款的區分：我國誠實信用與公序良俗的解釋論構造, 中國法學].

[20] For example, People's Supreme Court of China, Selected Cases about Labor Employment Disputes, vol. 1, No. 6 (July 10, 2020) [最高人民法院联合发布第一批劳动人事争议典型案例之六：李某与某餐饮公司劳动争议纠纷案]; Jiangsu Wuxi People's Intermediate Courts, Ten Selected Precedents about Commercial Contract Disputes during the Pandemic, No. 4 (2020) [江苏省无锡市中级人民法院发布10起涉疫情商事合同纠纷典型案例之四：甲公司与乙公司、丙公司关于口罩买卖合同纠纷案].

[21] Art. 533 of the Civil Code of The Republic of China (2020).

[22] Jiangsu Wuxi People's Intermediate Courts, Ten Selected Precedents about Commercial Contract Disputes during the Pandemic.

[23] China Banking and Insurance Regulatory Commission (CBIRC), Notice about Offering Finance Services for Firms in Distress during the Pandemic, No. 64 (2022) [中国银保监会办公厅关于进一步做好受疫情影响困难行业企业等金融服务的通知, 银保监办发〔2022〕64号].

vulnerable industries, such as transportation, travel, and hotels, or by poor and underprivileged debtors such as peasants.[24]

Nonetheless, compared to Singapore and Taiwan, the Chinese state has gone further in some of its directives to substantially revise certain terms to reduce the legal consequences of contract defaults. For example, banks were required to not exercise their rights against debtors to ask for early repayment, lower debtors' credit lines, or terminate loan agreements altogether.[25] Accordingly, to compensate those banks for the rollback of their rights, CBIRC raised the allowable bad loans ratio in financial institutions up to 3 percent and promised not to hold such an increase in bad loans against the performance evaluation of bank managers.[26] The Chinese government also offered relief measures to prevent defaults on other types of contracts. For example, with respect to landlord and tenant agreements, landlords of state property were required to reduce rents for three to five months for their tenants[27]; in return state-owned banks would offer favorable loans with lower interest rates to such landlords. Landlords of private property who reduced rents for tenants could also enjoy similar financial benefits.[28] Here, the Chinese state utilized its leverage over strong market players to make them more lenient with weaker parties.

4.3 MOVING FROM HETERODOXY TO ULTRA-HETERODOXY OF CONTRACT LAW

With respect to contract disputes that seriously concern inequality and public policies, however, Chinese judges do not want to apply codified doctrines to exert their discretionary power. There are several reasons for this. A typical reason is the concern of their own legitimacy being questioned if they unilaterally alter the contract terms. There are cases in which the judges could have made a straightforward decision by relying on the doctrine of "change in circumstance," but they did not, due to worries that the decision would trigger backlash by upset parties.[29]

Another reason comes from the style of judicial administration in a civil law system. In civil law jurisdictions, it is an established norm that judges should apply concrete laws first to adjudicate before they resort to abstract doctrines including

[24] China Banking and Insurance Regulatory Commission Helongjian Branch, Directive about Further Leniency and Support for Financial System during the Pandemic, No. 3 (2020) [中国银保监会黑龙江监管局 关于进一步落实监管容忍政策 加大疫情期间金融支持力度的通知, 黑银保监发〔2020〕3号].

[25] Ibid.

[26] Ibid.; CBIRC, Notice about Offering Finance Services for Firms in Distress during the Pandemic, Art. 17.

[27] China Banking and Insurance Regulatory Commission (CBIRC), Support for Landlord that Reduced Rents, No. 64 (2022) [对减租人给予支持，银保监办发〔2022〕64号（十四）], Art. 14.

[28] Ibid.

[29] In this regard, the type of Chinese courts' behavior was in line with concerns expressed by the contract law orthodoxy. See Davis and Pargendler, Contract Law and Inequality.

their discretionary power that allows them to nullify a contract, for example, on the ground of violation of public morals and social customs. For instance, during the 2008 global financial crisis, the People's Supreme Court of China instructed district judges to work hard to stabilize the economic order by adjusting contract terms according to the "change-in-circumstance" clause under the General Principles of Civil Code (1987) but required them to not directly apply this doctrine unless higher courts approved.[30] Similarly, the Supreme Court of South Korea strictly limits the application of force majeure doctrine and holds that even the MERS (Middle East respiratory syndrome) outbreak and Asian Financial Crisis did not meet the threshold of force majeure.[31]

Most importantly, Chinese judges do not think the codified discretionary power, which provides room for contract law heterodoxy, is sufficient for dealing with cases that raise serious concerns about inequality. Here, both contract law orthodoxists and Chinese judges reject heterodoxy but differ strikingly on their rationales. The orthodoxists argue that courts should refrain from using contract law to deal with inequality for various reasons, such as respect for individual autonomy, lack of legitimacy to intervene, freedom of contract, or the existence of other better tools. In comparison, Chinese judges believe the opposite – they should try all possible legal means to alter or bypass contract terms that have caused inequality and its consequences. Being generally reluctant to invalidate contracts, Chinese judges are instead instructed, as per the People's Supreme Court of China's guidance, to alter contract terms to achieve greater societal goals. In short, contract law heterodoxy is not good enough for Chinese judges; they need ultra-heterodoxy.

By examining the selected exemplary cases issued as guidance, I have identified three approaches through which courts have been able to alter or circumvent contracts in order to obtain greater latitude in addressing inequality and its impact on public order. I relied on the Peking University legal database (Pkulaw.cn) to collect 123 selected precedents and cases by searching broadly under several key words: the pandemic, inequality, change-in-circumstance, contract disputes.[32]

The first approach is mediation, through which judges would not be strictly bound by contract terms. The mediation approach is used to deal with disputes that require remedies not entirely in accordance with legal rights but impose externalities on social and financial stability. When judges foresaw that the lengthy

[30] People's Supreme Court, Notice about Correct Application of PRC Contract Law for Serving the Party and National Macro-Policies, *Law* (2009) No. 165 (2009).

[31] As in many civil law countries, the main doctrinal threshold is whether the risk is unforeseeable and whether the risk is beyond the realm of control by the default party. In practice, however, the threshold actually seems higher. It is a stretch to say that a MERS outbreak is foreseeable. See Kim & Chang, COVID-19: Force Majeure under Korean Law Considered in Wake of COVID-19 Pandemic, Kim & Chang (April 4, 2020).

[32] My collection of cases overlaps with the batches of guiding cases published by the People's Supreme Court of China and its Intermediate Courts to guide judges to adjudicate COVID 19-related contract disputes.

litigation process would be harmful for social and economic order, or that adjudication would create backlash, from either stronger parties or weaker parties, they would move disputes from litigation to mediation. In China, judges can act as mediators in cases they are hearing as judges. They also adopt an evaluative approach, under which they actively present strategies for resolving the dispute at hand, as opposed to facilitative mediation, which focuses more on neutrality and facilitating negotiations.[33] In relation to pandemic disputes, the People's Supreme Court of China also issued guidance to encourage mediation.[34]

The second approach is insolvency procedure. Courts will press companies/debtors to move disputes into insolvency procedure if they involve large numbers of weaker parties in great frustration and could trigger significant social unrest. Judges are mainly concerned about the political consequences of economic inequality. The insolvency approach allows judges to bring all stakeholders and respective contracts into a single legal proceeding, thereby finding a holistic solution. Under the insolvency approach, government officials and cadres of the Chinese Communist Party ("the Party") are also involved to play a complementary role.

The last approach is the macro-prudential approach, which echoes the macro-prudential policy developed after the 2008 global financial crisis to address systematic risks inherent in financial systems. If the contract disputes have triggered serious concerns about financial stability, this approach will be applied. Here, time is essential, and risks have to be contained as soon as possible. The government and the Party would put themselves forward to lead the dispute resolution. Initially, the party-state bypasses not only contract terms but also the legal procedure but, at a later point, it brings the case back to the courts to seek judicial endorsement. In contrast to the insolvency approach, the courts play only a complementary role.

Before proceeding to examine these three approaches, it is worth highlighting two ways in which the findings reported below diverge from the existing literature on the Chinese legal system. First, collaboration between courts and the government has long existed in China and elsewhere in Asia. For example, as Frank Upham and John Haley have pointed out with respect to Japan, where the judiciary has been highly capable and independent, the implicit collaboration between the executive branch and the judiciary allows social problems to be identified and solved in a timely manner.[35] Similarly, in the case of Singapore, which has been ranked as one of the top rule-of-law countries, Thio Li-Ann has described the existence of a

[33] A. Godwin, Judicial Mediation, *China Business Law Journal* (online) (October 12, 2018). https://law.asia/judicial-mediation/.

[34] People's Supreme Court, Guidance about Rightfully Dealing with Civil Disputes during the Pandemic, No. 1 (April 20, 2020) [关于依法妥善审理涉新冠肺炎疫情民事案件若干问题的指导意见（一）].

[35] F. K. Upham, Reflection on the Rule of Law in China (2011) 6 *National Taiwan University Law Review* 251–68; J. Haley, Constitutional Adjudication in Japan: History and Social Context, Legislative Structures, and Judicial Values (2011) 88 *Washington University Law Review* 1467–92.

collaborative, rather than adversarial, relationship between the executive and judicial branches of the government.[36] That being said, the level of government–court collaboration in China is the most extensive. Since 2021, the government and courts have begun to officially promote the so-called Government-Court Collaboration Model (府院聯合模式), which deems the doctrines of separation of power and judicial independence incompatible with the Chinese context.

The second point worth noting is that the ownership structure of parties in dispute does not seem to matter to the application of the three approaches. In other words, courts and government do not take into account whether contract parties are state-owned enterprises (SOEs), private firms, governmental agencies, or individuals. Rather, the merit of cases and their impacts are the key factors in choosing which approach to apply. Traditionally, Chinese courts, whose budgets come from local governments, would practice regional protectionism and thereby take a favorable position toward SOEs and state actors in the region. However, through an evaluation of the selected cases, it does not appear that the identity of the parties in disputes play a role in determining the applicable approach. As long as a contract dispute may cause externalities in the form of social and financial instability, judges will choose one suitable approach to apply. Hence, this judicial policy seems more impersonal than before, although it may be limited to pandemic-related contract disputes only. Nonetheless, it remains to be observed whether the three approaches may evolve into a more general model of justice administration and continue to operate in the post-pandemic era.

4.4 ULTRA-HETERODOX MODE ONE: THE MEDIATION APPROACH

In 2022, Chinese courts settled a total of 8.95 million disputes through mediation, up by 46.6 percent year on year, and this is approximately one third of the disputes brought to courts.[37] Courts use the mediation approach under several circumstances. The most common scenario is caused by the difficulty under the pandemic that rendered a normal legal proceeding impractical. For example, a property management company had a dispute against twenty-one property owners during the time when the whole housing complex was put under quarantine. Given the imposed quarantine order, the judges advised all parties to switch to mediation and used telephones and WeChat, the Chinese version of WhatsApp, to complete the mediation.[38] Here, courts tried to use mediation to gain more flexibility and did not have to be bound by formal procedure.

36 L. A. Thio, We Are Feeling Our Way Forward, Step by Step, in Albert Chen (ed.), *Constitutionalism in Asia in the Early Twenty-First Century* (Cambridge: Cambridge University Press, 2014), pp. 270–94.

37 Xinhua, 'Chinese Courts See Increase in Pre-litigation Mediation', *China Org* (February 16, 2023).

38 High Court of Inner Mongolia, Selected Cases on the Online Resolution of Covid-19 Disputes, No. 6 (March 26, 2020) [内蒙古高院发布首批新冠肺炎疫情期间在线化解纠纷典型案例之六：某物业服务公司与刘某等21名业主物业服务合同纠纷案].

What is more relevant for the purposes of this chapter is that courts use mediation not only to circumvent procedural requirements but also to bypass substantive contract terms in order to facilitate renegotiation between the parties. Notably, contracts in China do not necessarily reflect the outcome of due diligence and business negotiations; rather, contracts merely represent the beginning of a long-term business relationship. A boilerplate contract could be quickly executed by parties without being thoroughly reviewed. Subsequently, the terms of contract are subject to renegotiation between the parties when they realize the terms do not work practically. Therefore, when disputes arise, it is a norm that renegotiation is allowed. In a dispute, judges are expected to facilitate renegotiation, instead of being an adjudicator. Contract terms remain as a mere default position for further negotiation rather than a binding legal undertaking. Parties are looking for a solution acceptable by all major stakeholders, instead of a one-sided solution. Hence, mediation offers the most suitable platform for such renegotiations and also provides judges flexibility to address contract inequality.

4.4.1 *Discretion beyond Contract Terms*

Specifically, courts have proceeded beyond enforcement of contract terms via mediation for two main reasons. First, mediation allowed courts to carry out their policy mandate during the pandemic. Second, mediation allowed courts to accommodate extralegal business customs that failed to function during the pandemic.

To begin with, the political embeddedness of the judiciary renders the courts an extension of the state itself; therefore, courts are also tasked with executing the state's policy objectives aside from merely adjudicating disputes.[39] During the COVID crisis, the mandate of judges was to support business operations such that production could continue and unemployment would not increase. This mandate was unlikely to be achieved if judges adjudicated disputes according to contract terms and civil procedure law. Some district courts even issued their own directives as to how to maintain and restore market order during legal proceedings.[40] Most parties involved in this type of mediation are firms that played a vital role in providing public services (such as wastewater treatment,[41] road pavement and

[39] B. Ahl, Why do Judges Cite the Party? References to Party Ideology in Chinese Court Decisions (2020) 18 *China: An International Journal* 175–85, 185.

[40] For example, Xuzhou Intermediate Court, 15 Measures to Protect Small and Medium-Sized Firms' Development under the Covid Control Policy (2020) [徐州中院，出台疫情防控形势下服务保障中小微企业发展的15项举措]; Qindao City Jimou District Court, Suggestion on Judicial Protection and Services under the Covid-Control Situation (2020) [青岛市即墨区人民法院,关于为新型冠状病毒肺炎疫情防控工作提供司法保障和服务的意见].

[41] People's Supreme Court of China, Selected Cases on Ensuring the Resumption of Operations by Companies, Vol. 3, No. 5 (April 22, 2022) [最高人民法院发布第三批13个全国法院服务保障疫情防控期间复工复产典型案例之五：湖北荆州某水业有限公司执行案].

repairs,[42] or telecommunication),[43] offering local jobs, and contributing to local tax revenues. Employees and workers were not necessarily parties to the disputes, but they suffered significantly when the employers stopped operations. Interestingly, courts seemed to be more concerned with how to get their employees back to work than with the merit of disputes. This reflects how the courts used mediation to give effect to the government's policy mandate of continuing operations and curbing unemployment. In contrast, if the dispute would not have a significant economic impact, courts were more likely to adjudicate it.[44]

As such, judges realized that adjudication procedures, such as injunctions against the companies' assets and bank accounts, would only further disrupt the firms' operations. Employees cannot be paid and raw materials cannot be purchased if the trial proceeds.[45] In some cases, judges even had to help to remove injunctions already imposed on companies' assets during the pre-trial procedure,[46] or restore the defaulting parties' credit rating.[47] Adjudication, coupled with various injunctions during formal civil procedure, would worsen public services and negatively affect the local economy, thereby frustrating the courts' mandate.

In such cases, courts were not shy in expressing the rationale of their decisions to move cases from trial to mediation. For example, one case involved a large meat processing company that defaulted on its loan agreements with a local bank during the pandemic. Consequently, an early repayment clause was triggered. After the dispute was brought to court, the district court engaged in mediation instead of

[42] People's Supreme Court of China, Selected Cases on Ensuring the Resumption of Operations by Companies, Vol. 3, No. 8 (April 22, 2022) [最高人民法院发布第三批13个全国法院服务保障疫情防控期间复工复产典型案例之八：贵州某路面有限公司买卖合同纠纷执行案].

[43] People's Supreme Court of China, Selected Cases on Ensuring the Resumption of Operations by Companies, Vol. 1, No. 6 (6 March 2020) [最高人民法院发布首批十个全国法院服务保障疫情防控期间复工复产民商事典型案例之六：苏州资产管理有限公司诉苏州德威系关联企业金融借款纠纷系列案].

[44] For example, a dispute between a movie theater operator and its contractors caused the closing of the movie theater. As such a closing would not have any significant impact on social and economic order, the court went ahead to adjudicate it rather than switching it to mediation.

[45] In a case involving a high-tech company, the court realized that 2,000 employees could not receive their salary because of an injunction made to the firm's all bank accounts during the pre-trial proceeding. The court quickly move the case into mediation so that such injunctions can be removed. People's Supreme Court of China, Selected Cases on Ensuring the Resumption of Operations by Companies, Vol. 1, No. 8 (March 6, 2020) [最高人民法院发布首批十个全国法院服务保障疫情防控期间复工复产民商事典型案例之八：东证融汇证券资产管理有限公司诉光一科技股份有限公司等质押式证券回购纠纷案].

[46] People's Supreme Court of China, Selected Cases on Ensuring the Resumption of Operations by Companies, Vol. 1, No. 3 (March 6, 2020) [最高人民法院发布首批十个全国法院服务保障疫情防控期间复工复产民商事典型案例之三：上海丽景针织制衣有限公司诉合玺（上海）服装有限公司等买卖合同纠纷系列案].

[47] Ningbo Medical Instrument Co. Case (2019) [宁波某医疗器械有限公司], available at F. Dou, S. Cheng, and A. Zhang, *Analysis of Legal Issues Related to Bankruptcy of Enterprises under the Influence of the Epidemic* [疫情影响下与企业破产相关的法律问题解析], Allbright Law Offices (February 14, 2020).

adjudication. During the mediation, instead of reviewing the loan agreement terms, judges emphasized the moral principle of "being sympathetic and being accommodating to one another."[48] The mediation quickly helped restore the firm's credit record, resume contract performance, and continue the business operation after the firm agreed to provide additional loan guarantees. The People's Supreme Court endorsed the decision by emphasizing the decision of the District Court as a model of how to use court proceedings to support major employers and taxpayers.[49]

Second, by using mediation, courts can accommodate and sustain some extralegal or even illegal contractual agreements. In such cases, the original written contracts usually do not reflect the genuine intention of contract parties. Their business could be based on some extralegal arrangements which are part of common business customs in China. Such noncompliance is considered a violation of law and policies set by the central government but might be viewed as beneficial and even necessary for business at the local level. Courts as part of local government would be sympathetic and therefore try to accommodate such extralegality that facilitates local business. For example, it is a common practice that sellers issue receipts of payments and deliver goods to buyers before buyers actually make the payment. Sellers often agree with buyers that payment can be made at a later point in time, probably after the sale of goods. In this way buyers can obtain better liquidity while sellers could be more competitive by offering this favorable condition. However, such an agreed term is not stipulated in contracts because issuing receipts without actual payments can be viewed as tax evasion and subject to criminal prosecution.[50] Later, when buyers experienced financial difficulty during the pandemic, they claimed, based on the receipts sellers issued, that full payment had been made.[51] In such cases, it would not help solve the dispute if judges stuck to formal contract documents and ignored the illegal side agreement. Judges would have to accommodate such business customs rather than take these contract terms at their face value. Considering the difficulty in rebuking the validity of receipts due to years of complicated payment records between buyers and sellers, courts used mediation procedures to bypass written contract terms and avoid unjust enrichment.

48 People's Supreme Court of China, Selected Cases on Ensuring the Resumption of Operations by Companies, Vol. 1 (March 6, 2020) [最高人民法院发布首批十个全国法院服务保障疫情防控期间复工复产民商事典型案例之五：中国农业银行股份有限公司浮梁县支行诉景德镇康源农业发展有限公司金融借款合同纠纷案].

49 Ibid.

50 It could be a serious crime for sellers to issue receipts without receiving the exact amounts stated in the receipts. Such fake receipts with inflated numbers could be used for the purpose of tax deduction and therefore considered as tax evasion. Xin Hua News, *Strict Prohibition on False Receipts and Tax Evasion in order to Maintain a Fair Market* [我國嚴打虛開發票和騙稅行為維護市場公平], Finance People (September 2, 2018).

51 Beijing Fentai District People's Court, The Right Way to Construct the [Business] Model of "Receipt First, Payment Later" [先开票后付款的正确打开方式], Fentai District People's Court (April 30, 2021).

Other typical extralegal arrangements are designed to bypass China's capital controls. For example, a firm based in China would collaborate with a trustworthy overseas partner that is willing to issue an invoice with a contract price higher than the actual price of goods it sells. In this way, the company in China could obtain a legitimate reason to wire extra money overseas. Today, this strategy has been widely adopted by Chinese companies, foreign or local, to circumvent capital control regulations. Chinese regulators have tolerated or simply do not have the capacity to correct this industry custom. From time to time, such extralegal contracts would give rise to disputes when the collaboration goes sour. The overseas partner would claim the inflated consideration according to the written contract and refuse to return the extra payment according to the parties' illegal side agreements. By the same token, it does not help to solve the underlying issue if judges simply nullify such illegal agreements and inform the tax bureau to prosecute these parties for tax evasion. Courts at the local level are concerned more about the business environment and market order in the localities than the capital control policies set by regulators in Beijing. Hence, judges would adjudicate beyond contract terms to accommodate such business norms that maintain economic stability. Mediation once again is the platform to prevent one party from obtaining unjust enrichment by taking advantage of the other party subject to capital control.

In short, while typical mediation focuses on determining liability through an alternative procedure, Chinese courts do not use mediation to determine winners and losers in a clear and concise fashion, but rather to seek greater flexibility and discretion necessary for carrying out their policy mandate. The extralegal transactions in dispute might violate the Civil Code and other national regulations, but they support the local economy and market order, and therefore prompt judges to resolve disputes beyond the contract terms. But, as no one can be sure whether an extralegal business model can be upheld in the long-term, the courts' attitude could create market uncertainty.

4.4.2 *Collective Risk Sharing through Communitarian Norms*

Among the selected mediation cases, judges have resorted to moral persuasion to press the parties to compromise, instead of using the codified discretionary power to revise contract terms. They emphasize communitarian norms that subsume parties' individual rights within the larger social good.[52] For example, the popular Chinese saying "going through hardship together" (共體時艱) is often stated in the reasoning. Judges also often cited other Chinese sayings such as "be sympathetic," and "collective risk sharing." The other policy-specific norm the courts often used was "to restore business as usual." With this norm, judges suggest to the creditors

[52] G. B. Chen, *Law without Lawyers, Justice without Courts: On Traditional Chinese Mediation* (Oxfordshire: Routledge, 2002), p. 8.

that they should not be overly aggressive so that debtors could continue their business. This is in line with the typical Chinese saying that denounces people for being "unforgiving and aggressive simply based on legitimate positions" (得理不饒人). All of these norms encompass a communitarian value requiring collective sharing of risks and losses during hardship.

By resorting to communitarian narratives through mediation, judges legitimize their decisions even without the support of the black letter law, thus persuading the stronger party to yield and avoid backlash from weaker parties. Although a clear decision is possible by using the equitable principles codified in the Civil Code, judges might foresee how adjudication would not solve but rather provoke more disputes. As such, Shanxi People's Intermediate Court emphasized that "judges should actually avoid a simple decision and enforcement, because that may add fuel to the fire from the perspective of the firms in distress."[53] For example, a disappointed sport fan sued a travel agency because it failed to execute the travel service for the plaintiff to support her favorite volleyball team at the 2020 Tokyo Olympics games.[54] If the Court relied on traditional legal principles, a straightforward decision based on force majeure principle could have easily decided on the justice as the travel agent should not be held liable for losses caused by travel bans and the closed-door policy of the 2020 Olympics Games under the pandemic. However, the judge decided to switch to mediation anyway to comfort this sport fanatic, who already submitted multiple suits, and persuaded the travel agency to share losses. Eventually, the plaintiff dropped all the claims. In this case, the court emphasized the need to "be sympathetic," and the concepts of "collective risk sharing," and "going through hardship together." By avoiding the strict adjudication of the dispute, which may cause losses to the aggrieved person, the court implicitly recognized the limitations of contract law in effectively solving disputes.

What underlies those communitarian norms is ex post renegotiation about loss sharing.[55] In some contract disputes, especially in those concerning extralegal or illegal business models, parties in fact had foreseen such future renegotiation at the time when they signed contracts. Knowing various risks and inevitable uncertainty in their contractual relationships, they took collective loss sharing as an implicit contract term, even without judges persuading them to do so. This challenges existing literature about China's communitarian norms in torts, which focuses on

[53] Shanxi Intermediate Court, 'Announcement on Selected Cases about Covid-19 Control and Preservation of Economic and Social Development' No. 4 (April 24, 2020) [陕西高院发布服务保障疫情防控和经济社会发展典型案例之四：胡某等诉陕西某实业有限公司商品房销售合同纠纷案].

[54] Chengdu Court, Selected Seven Types of Cases during the Pandemic, Vol. 3, No. 1 (October 14, 2020) [成都法院第三批涉新冠肺炎疫情七大典型案例之一：因新冠肺炎疫情致东京奥运会延期旅游合同纠纷调解案].

[55] See, e.g., B. L. Liebman, 'Ordinary Tort Litigation in China: Law versus Practical Justice?' (2020) 13 *Journal of Tort Law* 197–228; R. Stern et al., Liability beyond Law: Conceptions of Fairness in Chinese Tort Cases (2023) *Asian Journal of Law and Society* 1–24.

how courts require the community members to collectively share in losses.[56] In the context of contract disputes, however, the communitarian norm appears to operate in the earlier phase. Parties in commercial transactions seem to have made the implicit agreement on potential ex post renegotiation about risks and losses sharing when they enter into agreement. Later, when judges switch to the mediation procedure, this renegotiation norm enables judges to smooth the contract terms to achieve their policy mandate.

4.5 ULTRA-HETERODOX MODE TWO: THE INSOLVENCY APPROACH

The second approach the courts utilize to address issues of unequal contractual agreements is the insolvency procedure. Compared to the mediation approach, the insolvency approach is aimed at dealing with contract disputes that involve large numbers of contracting parties. For example, a dispute between real estate developers and home buyers could involve thousands of home buyers, developers, land sellers, banks, guarantors, mortgagors, contractors, and workers. It is not uncommon for a single case to involve more than 10,000 parties. Take the example of Evergrande, the largest real estate developer in China, which defaulted in 2021. Evergrande was infamous for its highly leveraged investment. Its employees were given lucrative monetary incentives to secure funding domestically and globally. Some funds were secured at the very early stage of development projects to compensate rural villagers from whom the company acquired land, but much of the funds were used neither for compensation nor construction, but for other investments, including those in shadow banking businesses. When the firm encountered crisis, most victims were economically weaker parties, including house buyers who handed over their life savings for houses that were never built, depositors who hoped to receive high interest payments promised by the shadow banking arm of the company, or land sellers who had not received their full compensation.[57]

Obviously, real estate developers in China are economic and political power players. They are able to obtain large pieces of land under China's state-owned land system and conduct highly leveraged investment within and beyond their core business. During the real estate market boom in China, many home buyers acted like American shoppers during the Black Friday sale. They waited in a long queue, rushed into developers' showrooms, and spent only a few minutes to choose a unit from a display map of the housing project.[58] After that, contracts of sale and mortgage were swiftly arranged and signed, usually without being informed of the deal structure and detailed terms. Most home buyers were required to pay in

56 Stern et al., Liability beyond Law.

57 H. J. He, Evergrande Debt Crisis; Stocks become Wallpaper?, *Wealth Magazine* (September 17, 2021); L. C. Wei and Y. Giao, CEO of Evergrande under Investigation, *Yicai* (January 7, 2023).

58 Qian and Chang, They Poured Their Savings into Homes.

advance before developers began any construction work and had little say in contract terms and payment conditions. Buyers' payments were usually not properly protected by security interest, whereas the rights of developers, mortgage banks, and other project investors were well protected by a security package. Furthermore, with the protection of firms' limited liability and the business judgment rule, and without any personal pledge agreement signed, corporate leaders of these firms were able to avoid personal liability in these contract disputes and walked away safely when projects failed. By contrast, as shown in many disputes, buyers were required to continue to pay their mortgages to avoid default even after developers had long ceased construction due to financial difficulty.

The extremely unequal positions between creditors and debtors in such disputes have led to social unrest in China during the pandemic. In the summer of 2022, massive protests by home buyers across various provinces began to emerge. Protesters resorted to property rights and equitable principles and mobilized other home buyers to refuse to pay mortgages collectively. These protests struck a nerve with the Chinese government. As a result, the insolvency approach began to be widely used by courts to address this type of contract dispute. By comparison, in other similar cases about real estate development but involving fewer people and tensions, courts still adjudicated or used mediation.[59]

4.5.1 *Capacity beyond Civil Procedure*

In contract disputes, it is an established rule that judges are not allowed to unilaterally invite any third party to join the proceeding as a plaintiff or defendant. Neither can their judicial decisions bind any third party who is not a party to the contract in dispute. This *in personam* nature of contract, however, constrains judges' capacity to deal with contract disputes that involve massive numbers of stakeholders. Although Chinese judges have broad discretion under the Civil Code, which provides great scope for contract law heterodoxy, it is not good enough as judges need not only possess greater discretion but also greater institutional capacity for such types of cases.

Against this backdrop, judges found China's Enterprise Insolvency Law a better platform to resolve such multi-stakeholder disputes than mediation and the law of contracts. Procedure-wise, the insolvency law offers a 3-in-1 advantage as it has a built-in mediation procedure, corporate reorganization procedure (for firms that still have business potential), and bankruptcy procedure (for firms without any business prospects). During the pandemic (i.e., since 2019), insolvency cases increased by at least five- to ten-fold according to my interviews with bankruptcy lawyers in China. It should be noted that the majority of insolvency cases start with mediation and

59 For example, Shanxi Intermediate Court, Announcement on Selected Cases about Covid-19 Control and Preservation of Economic and Social Development.

reorganization as these two procedures preserve the possibility to rescue the firms and maintain employment. The objective of reorganization is to resume business as usual by deviating from existing contract terms.

During the litigation process, judges would instruct parties that they may choose to stay in litigation or switch to mediation or insolvency.[60] Before the procedure started, in most cases, large numbers of weaker parties had already begun their petition to regulators and governmental agencies. Some petitions may have turned into protests, and such antagonistic circumstances are the last thing that the local officials want to see. Under financial and public pressure, defendants would usually accept the switch to the insolvency procedure, albeit reluctantly. Plaintiffs would also agree with this switch as they would feel empowered by standing together with other creditors. Once the insolvency procedure kicks off, the court may inform and involve all creditors and stakeholders in the dispute resolution process.[61]

In the insolvency procedure, courts can gain more authority over debtors, thereby adding pressure on stronger parties to yield to the demands of weaker parties. For example, judges forbid debtors from making payment to any other third party[62] and from leaving their residence area without the court's permission.[63] Per judges' discretion, courts could also nullify any contract made prior to the insolvency, where such contracts concern actions by debtors to conceal their assets and evade debt obligations.[64] Most importantly, courts could suspend the exercise of priority rights and security interest by preferred or secured creditors (e.g. financial institutions and major investors).[65] With such additional authority and discretion, judges can thereby bypass the terms and conditions of existing contracts, including those of contracts in dispute and those of other contracts not being contested.

With this leverage, judges are able to demand that secured creditors relinquish their security interest for the benefit of weaker creditors.[66] A study shows that the resistance from powerful secured creditors is the most challenging task during reorganization and the bankruptcy procedure.[67] This is understandable as these secured creditors, such as banks and other major lenders, usually have few

60 See cases, e.g., the Second Batch of Commercial Law Precedents about Courts Restoring Production during the Pandemic [全国法院服务保障疫情防控期间复工复产民商事典型案例（第二批）], Case No. 7: Sichuan Southwest Medical Equipment Co.'s Switch from Contract Enforcement to Insolvency [案例7：四川西南医用设备有限公司执转破案] (April 20, 2020); Case No.1, Guandong Xingang Cement Company Settlement (April 26, 2020) [广东新港兴混凝土有限公司和解案].

61 Enterprise Bankruptcy Law of the People's Republic of China (2006), Art. 14.

62 Ibid, Art. 16

63 Ibid, Art. 15.

64 Ibid, Arts. 31 and 33.

65 Ibid, Arts. 75 and 77.

66 Interview with a senior partner of a leading law firm in China (February 23, 2023).

67 L. Shuguang and W. Zuofa, The Gap between Expectation of Legislation and Judicial Practice and Its Resolution: Empirical Analysis of Bankruptcy Law's Three-years Implementation (2011) 2 *Chinese University of Political Science and Law Review* [中国政法大学学报] 58–79.

incentives to rescue the firm and yield interest for weaker parties. They could have exercised their priority rights and got repaid first before unsecured creditors, rather than bearing the risk of resuming the company's operation. But for the remaining thousands of unsecured creditors and weaker parties, the insolvency procedure represents the form of justice they expect from courts despite the fact that the average haircut of creditors made during the insolvency procedure in China is still as high as 60 or 70 percent[68]

Furthermore, the insolvency procedure provides a vital platform for courts to fulfill the government's policy – to minimize the economic impact caused by these disputes. Once the insolvency procedure begins, for example, courts can cancel all existing injunctions over debtor's property imposed by previous litigation.[69] Injunctions and subsequent enforcement actions (such as the sale of machinery) could disrupt the process and result in an increase in unemployment, which could subsequently result in social unrest. Unsurprisingly, in many selected precedents by Chinese high courts, judges always emphasized the mandate of "making business as usual" after switching to insolvency and thereby lifted the injunctions that had frozen the firms' assets and bank accounts, stopped salary payments, and ceased business operations.[70]

Notably, the government and the Party play a vital role in insolvency procedures. While court documents have recorded the presence of Party officials in various meetings, the summary of selected precedents have also emphasized their participation and contribution. Interestingly, the government and Party involvement does not serve to diminish the courts' authority; on the contrary, it helps to empower the courts. The local officials and party cadres issue orders to require other agencies, SOEs, and banks to disclose information that courts and reorganization managers (who are usually lawyers) demand.[71] Occasionally, they even pay service fees to law firms to deal with SOE insolvency cases.[72]

It should be noted that plaintiffs, weaker parties, judges, and lawyers always welcome the Party and government's involvement, instead of worrying about a lack of judicial independence. In some cases, lawyers would not have taken the cases if the government had not promised to be involved.[73] That being said, governmental

[68] H. X. Chian and J. Y. An, Choices, Mechanisms, Economic Efficiency, and Legal Grounds of Listing Companies' Bankruptcy and Reorganization (2006) 7 *Management World* 130 [何旭强, 周业安, 上市公司破产和重整的选择, 机制、经济效率及法律基础].

[69] Enterprise Bankruptcy Law of the People's Republic of China (2006), Art. 19.

[70] People's Supreme Court of China, Selected Cases on Ensuring the Resumption of Operations by Companies.

[71] Interview with a senior partner of a leading law firm in China (February 13, 2023).

[72] Usually, this is about what are commonly called "zombie SOEs," which refer to SOEs that ceased to operate prior to the pandemic. The State-owned Assets Supervision and Administration Commission (SASAC) of the State Council required these zombie SOEs to go into insolvency procedure as well. While the government paid the service fees, law firms charged only minimal service fees as such cases are effectively deemed as pro bono services.

[73] Note 66.

officials and Party cadres do not intervene directly in actual administration of insolvency and reorganization. Rather, they let courts and lawyers run the insolvency procedure for a strategic reason: the insolvency procedure led by judges and lawyers can contain and dissolve the tensions of social unrest. Judicialization of social unrest and regional financial crises can protect local officials and Party cadres from direct pressure that they could have potentially encountered in dealing with weaker parties directly.

4.5.2 *Social Unrest and Contract Disputes*

Inequality could be one of the underlying causes of massive numbers of contract disputes and resulting social unrest in China. It concerns distributive justice and the performance of the government. A shared feature of cases dealt with under the insolvency approach is their large scale. One real estate dispute could involve several thousand, or up to more than ten thousand, home buyers. One of the law firms I interviewed has more than twenty such cases ongoing at any one point in time. The largest cases involve consolidated insolvencies, where the parent company is amalgamated with several dozens of "zombie subsidiaries" that have ceased operations even prior to the pandemic.

The insolvency approach is strategic in that it offers a sense of entitlement to comfort weaker parties. Each phase of the insolvency procedure offers a symbolic milestone that creditors' rights seem to have been further confirmed and protected by the legal system. With creditors' anger being channeled into the insolvency procedure, the government will not have to undergo the difficulty of dealing with thousands of angry creditors chanting in front of government buildings. At the end of the day, however, courts cannot generate revenues to fulfill the legal claims of creditors and other weaker parties. A certificate of credit has little meaning if such credit cannot be honored by debtors eventually. Nonetheless, the lengthy insolvency procedure can help to allay tensions with most of the angry protesting creditors. Once their anger has been channeled into an insolvency procedure, they would be amenable to following the courts' order to proceed. "Eventually, they will come to realize that they will not be able to get their money back," said a bankruptcy lawyer.[74]

Nonetheless, courts indeed tried to address weaker parties' grievances and find a way to protect their rights. Judges have leveraged their discretion and authority to persuade secured creditors to give up some of their legal entitlement for the benefit of weaker parties. Sometimes, judges would impose real pressure. Courts would refuse to approve secured creditors' motion to sell debtors' assets or other collateral if they do not yield to demands of weaker parties.[75] Courts could also refuse to remove

[74] Interview with a Chinese bankruptcy lawyer (February 1, 2023).

[75] Note 66.

injunction over the pledged assets to prevent secured creditors from exercising their security interests. Sometimes, courts have resorted to moral persuasion. For example, judges often emphasize in their judgments a Chinese saying that "we should share hardship together during difficult time" (共體時艱), which again represents a communitarian, collective value about social responsibility and risk-sharing.

The government is aware that the success of this approach requires institutional capacity of the courts and legal professionals. They have empowered and collaborated with courts and lawyers involved in facilitating the process, but they would never put themselves forward to lead the procedure directly. As a bankruptcy lawyer described, he spent more time in comforting those anxious small creditors than in dealing with legal issues, and still received phone calls from them from time to time even after he left the firm.[76] Nonetheless, the government has acted quite legalistically in that it required such disputes to be resolved through legal processes. That being said, it has solved the problem of inequality by circumventing contract terms, which is far from legalistic behavior.

4.5.3 *Limitations*

The courts and governments do manage to address inequality through the insolvency approach, but whether this approach is effective remains a separate issue. It is common for weaker parties, who are usually unsecured creditors, to discover that their credits were not protected by any security interest. On the contrary, power players such as financial institutions, formal or informal, and other guarantors have obtained priority rights at the early stage of transactions. Judges could put pressure on secured creditors to relinquish their priority rights but only to a limited extent. Consequently, through the insolvency procedure, unsecured creditors, common shareholders, and other weaker parties might secure but not materialize their rights eventually. In a case that involves a shadow bank defaulting on its contracts with large numbers of depositors, the creditors settled the disputes by accepting a 70 percent haircut after months of protests that compelled the government to intervene. Although the government's direct intervention accounted for the successful settlement, creditors were still unable to receive any of their scheduled payments.[77]

Under the insolvency approach, the main challenge of tackling inequality in contract disputes is the complexity of transactions. Any transaction involves multiple contracts that construct various degrees of priority rights and involve a large number

[76] Note 74.

[77] Interview with a lawyer based in Hong Kong who has close contact with victims of financial product default in China (December 12, 2022).

of institutional and individual stakeholders. Some of those contracts could be viewed as unfair, but most of them are in line with market practices and are not in dispute in the proceedings. For instance, when a real estate developer fails to perform its contracts with home buyers, the mortgage contracts between home buyers and their banks nonetheless remain valid. Also, banks that have offered lines of credit to the real estate developer can also validly claim their priority rights over other unsecured creditors as their contracts are valid. Even though Chinese judges have engaged in insolvency procedures to circumvent some unfair contract terms, they still cannot address inequality in a fundamental way, unless they can revise other contractual agreements beyond the original scope of dispute. However, that would go too far and affect the core function of contracts in market transactions. At the end of the day, contract law heterodoxy as well as ultra-heterodoxy, even justifiable, seems to be able to play only a complementary role.

Under the insolvency approach, inequality would be addressed but seems to be an ancillary benefit compared to the state's main objective of preventing social unrest. Due to its strategic considerations, the government behaves legalistically in terms of the insolvency procedure. The judicial system has proved to be an effective tool to tackle the social and political consequences of inequality, but not necessarily the economic consequences per se. In fact, China's approach is not uncommon. During its authoritarian era, Taiwan relied on its judicial system to dissolve social and economic tensions, while Japan's courts have also worked with the executive branch to identify and solve disputes that would disrupt social and economic order.[78] Additionally, at its nascent stages of economic development, Singapore created an illiberal welfare state and had lawyers step in to reduce the risk of violent protests and channel tensions into the judicial system.[79] Similarly, during 1997 Asian financial crisis, law firms in Korea also played a vital role and benefited significantly from a rapid increase in insolvency cases.[80] However, economic inequality remains an issue in both Singapore and South Korea today, although the trickle-down effects of economic development together with their mature legal systems have largely prevented any disruptive consequences of inequality from coming to the fore. Without political determination and broader policies, the judiciary could only address the tip of the iceberg.

[78] W. Chen and H. Fu (eds.), *Authoritarian Legality in Asia* (Cambridge: Cambridge University Press, 2020); W. Chen, Twins of Opposites: Why China Will Not Follow Taiwan's Model of Rule of Law Transition Toward Democracy (2018) 66 *The American Journal of Comparative Law* 481–535; Upham, Reflection on the Rule of Law; Haley, Constitutional Adjudication in Japan.

[79] Y. Dezalay and B. Garth, *Asian Legal Revivals: Lawyers in the Shadow of Empire* (Chicago: University of Chicago Press, 2010), pp. 117–31, pp. 247–62, p. 251.

[80] K. S. Hyun, The Democratization and Internationalization of the Korean Legal Field, in Y. Dezalay and B. Garth (eds.), *Lawyers and the Rule of Law in an Era of Globalization* (Oxfordshire: Routledge, 2011), pp. 223–46, pp. 223–24.

4.6 ULTRA-HETERODOX MODE THREE: THE MACROPRUDENTIAL APPROACH

The last approach is designed to deal with contract disputes that may trigger the most undesirable scenario for the Chinese government during an economic downturn such as the pandemic financial crisis. Here, the main risk is not social unrest, but the systemic risk inherent in the financial system. Such systemic risk arises from how intertwined these entities are with the wider Chinese financial ecosystem, including entities such as real estate developers, non-bank financial institutions, and large banks. The macroprudential approach is thus focused on such institutions. Inequality problems were exposed by such types of contract disputes, and hence petitions and protests by contract parties also took place.

Considering the larger impacts, the government and Party would take the lead in containing the crisis instead of relying on lengthy judicial proceedings to borrow time and dissolve social tensions. The solution is still constructed in a legal way, although courts are relegated to a more secondary role. For example, after relevant parties and the governmental agencies have reached a solution, usually involving corporate restructuring, haircut of debts, additional loans and bailout, and creations of trust, they would register their solutions as a "reorganization by agreement" with the court in the insolvency procedure.

4.6.1 *Systemic Risks Triggered by Contract Disputes*

In China, the most serious problem during the pandemic, other than the pandemic per se, was likely the regional financial crises. Before the pandemic, mounting debts of local governments, prevailing shadow banking, real estate bubbles, and speculative and wasteful investments had already constituted the perfect recipe for crises if a trigger happened. The pandemic, together with China's long lockdown, added more pressure to China's banking and financial system, which saw rapidly increasing bad loans, quick depreciation of Chinese yuan, and disruptions to funding in the interbank market.[81] Such conditions could result in a liquidity mismatch and bank run, which could be further amplified by existing contract terms such as cross-default provisions and escalate into a systemic crisis. Since the pandemic, observers have been paying close attention to the situation to assess the possibility of a financial crisis.

Financial crises are usually caused by systemic risks triggered by a series of contract defaults. Unlike the risk of individual entities that can be contained largely through legal and economic measures, such as mandatory disclosure, systemic risks are usually triggered by one entity in distress and followed by domino effects that

[81] N. Borst, Has Covid-19 Led to Financial Instability in China?, *Seafarer* (April 2020).

would bring down other financially healthy entities.[82] The transmission of such risks is possible due to the highly interconnected and interdependent nature of modern financial systems. One firms' liquidity shortage can be transmitted to other financially healthy firms through preexisting legal arrangements such as cross-guarantees, cross-default, and cross-shareholding. China is no different in this regard.[83] Due to the potential for the transmission of systemic risk, these domino effects have to be stopped through a coordinated and swift intervention by state agencies, regulators, and stakeholders before a systemic financial crisis breaks out.

Systemic risks of the financial system did not attract sufficient attention of scholars and regulators until after the 2008 global financial crisis. Thereafter, macroprudential policies have been developed to address systemic risks inherent to the markets and financial system, as opposed to micro-prudential polices popular prior to 2008, which focus on risks of individual market players and use legal measures such as corporate governance and disclosure requirement under securities regulations to prevent such risks. China is a latecomer to such policies but appears to have quickly adapted to the existing literature set out in macroprudential policy discussions. Compared to the mediation and insolvency approaches, the government, the Party, and the courts have adopted the macroprudential policy to prevent financial crisis during the pandemic.[84] This approach also involves multiple stakeholders and regulators in the process and operates within and beyond the judicial system. I call it "the macroprudential approach."

While the insolvency procedure aims to prevent social unrest as a result of unequal contractual relationships, the macroprudential approach is aimed at dealing with broader financial consequences. Three other differences between insolvency and macroprudential approaches exist. To begin with, the main difference lies in the length of time to solve the contract disputes. While the insolvency approach utilizes a lengthy legal procedure to mitigate the tension among massive numbers of unhappy creditors, the macroprudential approach seeks to solve the disputes as soon as possible to the extent that the transmission of systemic risks could be stopped.

The second difference is the role of the government and the Party. In the insolvency approach, the Party, together with relevant departments of local governments such as the land and accounting bureaus, operates behind the scenes and demands courts and lawyers take the frontline in dealing with unhappy creditors. In contrast, the macroprudential approach involves the state putting itself forward and actively

[82] W. Chen, China's Long March to Dismantling the Financial Great Wall: Renminbi's Internationalization, Systemic Risks and Macro-prudential Regulations, in A. Anand (ed.), *Systemic Risk, Institutional Design and the Regulation of Financial Markets* (Oxford: Oxford University Press, 2016), pp. 143–74.

[83] W. Chen, Lost in Internationalization: The Rise of China's Renminbi, Macroprudential Policy, and Global Impacts (2018) 21 *Journal of International Economic Law* 31–66.

[84] People's Bank of China, Guidelines on Macroprudential Policy (Temporary), The State Council of the People's Republic of China (January 1, 2022).

leading the process, with courts playing a complementary role. As time is of essence, the state leverages its power over all stakeholders to solve disputes during a brief window of time before any domino effect could take root.

The last difference is the respective legal instruments each approach engages with. The insolvency approach uses the reorganization process built into the insolvency procedure to protect the poor by circumventing contract terms altogether. In comparison, the macroprudential approach moves beyond the insolvency procedure, using multiple legal tools including renegotiation, contractual agreements, reorganization, and trust, together with financial bailouts, to address the issues. But, eventually, these multi-faceted solutions, once finalized, would be formulated as a legal scheme so that courts can follow up and help out with implementation. In any case, similar to the insolvency approach, the original contract terms were bypassed or amended in order to address inequality and its impacts.

4.6.2 *Macroprudential Policy in Law*

China started its adoption of macroprudential policies fairly late; however, now, courts have been asked to play a more involved role in implementing macroprudential policies. Specifically, macroprudential policies in the areas of financial regulation usually require counter-cyclical measures to prevent economic bubbles and restrain banks from over-lending. Inter-agency monitoring and information sharing are crucial to provide a holistic assessment of potential systemic risks.[85]

Not only are Chinese courts recognized as a key agency for enforcing macroprudential policy but also Chinese contract law plays a crucial tool in this regard. In 2021, the People's Supreme Court issued guidance stating that a contract should be nullified if its primary purpose is to circumvent China's macroprudential policy.[86] In 2023, a Supreme Court judge further emphasized that a contract contradicting the macroprudential policy could be deemed in violation of social morals and public order under Chinese contract law, leading to its nullity.[87] Additionally, judges have the authority to adjudicate cases based on administrative orders or directives related to macroprudential policy and other financial market regulations, even in the absence of specific applicable laws.[88]

At the moment, the macroprudential approach remains tied with the insolvency procedure but subject to a very different dynamic. For example, in a reorganization

85 Chen, Lost in Internationalization.

86 People's Supreme Court, 'Opinion about Streamlining Lawsuits that Cover Illegal Purposes' [关于深入开展虚假诉讼整治工作的意见] No. 281 (2021).

87 H. Zhang and S. S. Wu, The Direction for Adjudicating Financial Disputes? Highlights of Financial Law Adjudication of National Courts [金融纠纷审判何处去？ —全国法院金融审判会议热点探讨], *AnJie Broad* (March 2, 2023). Also, People's Supreme Court, Notice on the Summary of the Conference on Civil and Commercial Adjudication by National Courts ["全国法院民商事审判工作会议纪要"的通知], No. 254 (November 8, 2019).

88 Zhang and Wu, The Direction for Adjudicating Financial Disputes?.

case in Tianjin City, a large construction company fell into distress and triggered a chain of defaults.[89] The city government as well as the local Party officials quickly intervened to prevent further complications. They took the leading role and gathered more than forty banks to discuss a possible reorganization plan for the company. Government agencies and Party officials that were involved included those from the local branches of People's Bank of China, Chinese Banking Regulation Commission, City Land Bureau, City Natural Resources Bureau, City Development and Reform Bureau, Tax Bureau, Accounting Bureau, Electricity and Power Bureau, and the City Legal Office. Various priority rights held by pledgees and guarantees were rearranged and a trustee was appointed to manage valuable assets and execute the reorganization plan. From the beginning the government invited legal advisers to join but not the courts. Only when all parties had reached a settlement agreement were the courts involved, after the company registered their plan as a "reorganization by agreement" under the Enterprise Insolvency Law.[90] In this way, the courts can monitor and help enforce the settlement plan.

It is understandable that the government leads the courts in this process. What the government and courts did in such type of cases are in line with what the macroprudential policy suggests. The government exerts its power to order other stakeholders, such as state-owned banks, to act in a certain way to preserve the markets. Despite scant discussions before, Chinese regulators were swift in adapting and implementing macroprudential policy best practices during the pandemic. Most notably, Beijing required the courts to collaborate and carry out macroprudential policies as well. In 2021, the emphasis on the extensive coordination between the courts and regulators was spelled out in the language of the 2021 Central Economic Work Conference:[91] "combining the responsibilities of local authorities, financial regulatory authorities, industry authorities and other parties, and strengthening the self-rescue responsibility of enterprises."[92] The necessity of such coordination was also spelled out in the Guidelines on Macro-Prudential Policies ("Guidelines") which emphasize intra-branch coordination mechanisms.[93] Unlike in Western

89 Reorganization of Tianjin Municipal Construction Group.

90 Note 66.

91 Fangda Partners, The Annual Report of Financial Law Compliance [金融法律监管年度报告] (2022).

92 In 2021, for example, the China Securities Regulation Commission (CSRC) established a working group to crack down on illegal capital markets activity. This group consisted of the Ministry of Public Security, the Supreme Court, and the Supreme Procuratorate. The Supreme Procuratorate also set up a procuratorial office branch in the CSRC. The cases investigated by this working group include corporate entities involved in large-scale market manipulation. Additionally, the court's reliance on the preceding administrative procedure was abolished to give the courts greater freedom to reach their own judgments and not to be bound by a predecision of the CSRC. See General Office of the Central Committee of the CPC and the General Office of the State Council, Opinions on Strictly Cracking Down on Securities-related Illegal Activities [关于依法从严打击证券违法活动的意见] (2021).

93 Note 84, Art. 34.

countries where courts are independent of the implementation of the macroprudential policy, the Guidelines emphasize the courts' role as the primary entity for adjudicating illegal activities in the capital market and underscore the importance of collaboration between the courts and the leading regulators of macroprudential policy.[94]

The involvement of courts is quite unique compared to the practices in the United Kingdom and the United States. In the United Kingdom, the Bank of England is assigned full responsibility for macroprudential policy. Within the Bank, the Financial Policy Committee, chaired by the Governor, is the main body charged with identifying, monitoring, and addressing risks to the financial system as a whole.[95] In the United States, a Financial Stability Oversight Council has been formed as a result of the Dodd-Frank Act, comprising all US financial regulators and chaired by the Secretary of the Treasury.[96] In both the United Kingdom and the United States, courts are not included in this regulatory body, nor do they play any role in implementing these regulations. In China, by contrast, courts are actively involved in macroprudential policies. This indicates that courts are deemed as part of the government body and expected to share the administrative workload. Separation of powers is not the norm.

Under the macroprudential approach, the original contract terms only serve as a reference point for the negotiation among all parties to settle the reorganization plan for the company in default. Contracts are selectively enforced to the extent that any enforcement or non-enforcement should not worsen the financial crisis and instead should be readjusted for the sake of restoring the financial order. This selective enforcement approach is not unprecedented. During the 2008 global financial crisis, to preserve the market and halt the financial crisis, the Federal Reserve discharged several selected financial firms from their contractual obligations as stringent enforcement would have brought down the whole financial system. Such a selection is based on the value of individual firms for preserving the financial system.[97] Those that constituted the core of the financial system were not only freed from their contractual obligations but also received governmental bailouts.[98] Similar to China's macroprudential approach here, these decisions were made by the US government while courts only played a secondary role.

4.6.3 *Government–Court Collaboration*

More generally, in addition to the courts' involvement in macroprudential policy implementation, China has been promoting a model called "Government–Court

94 Ibid., Art. 12.

95 United Kingdom, Stationary Office, The Financial Services Bill: The Financial Policy Committee's Macro-Prudential Tools (2012).

96 European Central Bank, Financial Stability Review (December 2010).

97 K. Pistor, A Legal Theory of Finance (2013) 41 *Journal of Comparative Economics* 315–30.

98 Ibid.

Collaboration" (府院聯動模式) since 2021. Local governments and courts have issued guidelines and organized workshops to promote this model. The People's Supreme Court of China has also been evolving its own judicial policies to accommodate and implement party-related pandemic policies.[99] The idea of this model is to have courts work with local governments to preemptively solve business disputes which have been identified as potentially having wider impacts on local social order and economic markets. On the one hand, the government and the Party facilitate the legal proceeding. On the other, the solution should be framed legalistically and enforced by the court. This model is derived from administrative law principles immediately prior to the pandemic, with the purpose of demanding related governmental agencies to participate in the procedure. Subsequently, during the pandemic, the model was expanded, as discussed herein.

In cases that may trigger a financial crisis, local governments have strong incentives to proactively participate in legal proceedings. This is because large companies which conduct operations in the localities usually have significantly contributed to job markets and tax revenues, serving as an indicator of good performance and governance.[100] Contracts involved in such cases, like those dealt with by the other two approaches, involve many economically weak parties. Fixed terms were not allowed for negotiations before parties signed the contracts. But, once disputes arise out of these types of contracts, the scale of economic impacts is wider, the number of parties involved larger, and the financial and political risks higher. Interestingly, although local officials do not want the formal legal proceedings to prolong the crisis, they nonetheless appreciate the value of the law in standardizing and institutionalizing the crisis management process.

As a result, courts and local governments began to "institutionalize and normalize this model" and vowed to "improve communication and collaboration with local party secretaries and government agencies" and jointly solve disputes based on "the market principle and legalistic approach."[101] In early 2023, for example, Shanxi Provincial Governments enacted "Guidance for Government–Court Collaboration Mechanism for Insolvency Cases," which demands various collaboration mechanisms between district governments and courts to be created, including joint task forces, regular meetings, information sharing, preemptive monitoring, assessment of corporate risks, and proposed settlement proposition.[102]

99 People's Supreme Court of China, Guidelines on Proper Trial of Civil and Commercial Cases.

100 Shuguang and Zuofa, The Gap between Expectation of Legislation and Judicial Practice and its Resolution.

101 Y. Shan, Heilongjang Fonglin District Court Explored New Mechanisms for Bankruptcy Practices through Government-Courts Collaboration [黑龙江丰林县法院，积极推动"府院联动"探索破产审判新机制], *China Court Org.* (November 30, 2022).

102 Shanxi People's Government, Enterprise Bankruptcy and the Creation of Government–Court Collaboration Mechanisms [企业破产处置建立府院联动机制], *Datong Municipal People's Government Portal* (January 6, 2023).

Given China's political economy, the government's direct involvement is arguably inevitable and even necessary for tackling these problems. Now, the involvement has been formalized by this government–court collaboration model. In the insolvency process, secured creditors and preferred shareholders (most are rich and powerful banks) have a higher claim on the firm's assets than unsecured creditors and common shareholders, respectively, and therefore they have fewer incentives to reorganize the firm in default. They do not necessarily benefit from reorganization but have to bear the risks of it. As such, renegotiation about contract terms cannot be completed through market mechanisms, as such mechanisms favor the prevailing power players.[103] It requires pressure from the government to press these priority rights holders to give in and work with other normal creditors and the management team, as judges have little bargaining power in the face of powerful market players.

While the legal procedure and contract terms are largely bypassed, both courts and the government tackle the corporate problems legalistically by framing it in the context of legal rules and frameworks. The government and Party take the leading role in the macro-prudential approach, but eventually they would frame the solutions in a legalistic way. For instance, a trust is usually created to hold the firms' assets, with an appointed trustee to execute the reorganization plan under the courts' monitoring. In short, it serves the central government's interests for the courts to stick to established insolvency and legal procedures as it promotes social stability and order.

4.7 NEGOTIATED LEGALITY

The fact that these various approaches work in China offers us an opportunity to observe a peculiar perception of legality in China, which I name "negotiated legality." The perception of legality is closely associated with the legitimacy of the state and courts. The Chinese government's political legitimacy does not lie in any bottom-up democratic procedure, but rather in its substantive performance.[104] Political scientists have empirically demonstrated that, in China as well as in other Asian countries, both democratic and authoritarian, citizens' perceptions about "democracy" and "accountability" concerns mainly economic development rather than human rights, policymaking participation, or democratic election, all of which instead reflect the perception of democracy and accountability in the West.[105] In this

[103] Shuguang and Zuofa, The Gap between Expectation of Legislation and Judicial Practice and Its Resolution, 68.

[104] W. Chang, *In Search of the Way: Legal Philosophy of the Classic Chinese Thinkers* (Edinburgh: Edinburgh University Press, 2016); F. Fukuyama, *Political Order and Political Decay: From the Industrial Revolution to the Globalization of Democracy* (New York: Farrar, Straus and Giroux, 2014); S. Cook, The Debate over Coercive Rulership and the "Human Way" in Light of Recently Excavated Warring States Texts (2004) 64 *Harvard Journal of Asiatic Studies* 399–440.

[105] M. H. Huang, Cognitive Involvement and Democratic Understanding, in T. J. Cheng and Y. H. Chu (eds.), *Routledge Handbook of Democratization in East Asia* (Oxfordshire: Routledge, 2017), pp. 219–313; P. Goedde, The Making of Public Interest Law in South

regard, it is not a surprise that many Chinese people view China as a democracy as long as they are economically better off. This strange phenomenon existed in Taiwan, Singapore, and South Korea during their authoritarian era too.[106]

Such understanding of accountability therefore exerts pressure on the Chinese government to deliver good performance. In courts, people do not necessarily trust the judicial system but may have trust in individual judges and exert similar pressure and expectation. When inequality issues arise in contract disputes, good performance is about the delivery of distributive justice. Otherwise, the problems of unfairness, inequality, social unrest, and financial crisis will directly harm the legitimacy of the government and the Party, without resorting to any periodic election. On the other hand, the Party-state's use of courts and the legal system to solve disputes also constitute an alternative form of bottom-up accountability in that people are willing to participate in legal proceedings to voice their concerns and the government in turn responds through the proceedings to address their grievances. A resilient authoritarian regime cannot rely solely on top-down coercion but has to create some bottom-up mechanisms to strengthen its legitimacy.

Negotiated legality in China is unique in that all stakeholders including the courts subject legality to negotiations during contract enforcement. As shown in my case studies, dispute resolution is more about delivering substantive justice, even just symbolically, than determining winners and losers according to the law of contract. Judges are more concerned about seeing the final resolution of a dispute where parties are satisfied with the outcome. Legality is not determined according to the law and existing contract terms fixed during contract formation. Rather, legality is determined through subsequent negotiations during the contract enforcement process. Examples of how substantive justice is promoted occurs across all three ultra-heterodox modes, where all parties' (including dominant market players and weaker individual creditors) reasonable expectations are safeguarded, to a degree deemed appropriate, through court-led renegotiation about risks and losses sharing. Original contract terms serve merely as a starting point for all parties to renegotiate risk distribution and damage-sharing. All stakeholders share the same understanding of legality, and hence those involved in negotiations are not limited to contract parties but also involve many non-contract parties.

Negotiated legality contrasts with the concept of "relational contract," which describes how contract parties could rely on the reputation mechanism and reciprocity norms to form and enforce their informal contracts, and thereby maintains a long-term relation in a cost-efficient fashion.[107] The process usually involves

Korea via the Institutional Discourses of Minbyeon, PSPD and Gonggam, in H. Yang (ed.), *Law and Society in Korea* (Cheltenham: Edward Elgar, 2013), pp. 131–49.

[106] See, e.g, Huang, Cognitive Involvement and Democratic Understanding.

[107] S. Johnson et al., Courts and Relational Contracts (2002) 18 *Journal of Law, Economics, & Organization* 221–77; L. Bernstein, Opting Out of the Legal System: Extralegal Contractual Relations in the Diamond Industry (1992) 21 *The Journal of Legal Studies* 115–57; M. J.

frequent negotiation between contract parties due to the nature of their incomplete contracts. What I unveil in this essay offers a different picture. Negotiation is not just a process for maintaining a long-term relationship between contract parties. Much more fundamentally, it demonstrates a continuing process to determine legality *ex post*.

While the operation of both negotiated legality and relational contracts primarily takes place during contract enforcement, the mechanisms that possibly drive negotiation appear differently through the lens of negotiated legality. My case studies show that, without the Party-state's intervention, negotiations between strong and weaker parties would not necessarily happen even though a long-term relationship exists. In the case of extremely unequal contracts, stronger parties with priority rights (such as banks and secured creditors), especially those based on other valid contracts not in dispute, do not have the incentive to negotiate. Many of those contracts are also the products of long-term relationships, for example, contracts about long-term supply of manufacturing materials, financial credit line, or business alliances. Even if those stronger parties such as secured creditors negotiate with their underprivileged counterparties, such private negotiation would allow them to largely keep their market advantages by sticking to the contract terms. Inequality would remain and even be strengthened by the law to the extent the validity of existing contract terms is upheld.[108]

As such, it requires a third-party to intervene in this unequal contractual relationship rather than rely on markets or private negotiation. In other words, relational contracts might correctly account for the reality of contract enforcement in some countries, but they also lead to inequality that requires a different approach to address. Considering the current political economy in China, this unfair setting arguably has to be brokered by the government, together with courts. The Party-state is the main dominant power that has sufficient political and legal clout over those stronger parties in contractual relationships. To judges and Party-state officials, the wide discretion delegated by Chinese contract law is still not good enough, so they resort to the more drastic approaches I have identified to circumvent the contract terms in dispute.

Moreover, while the relational contract literature suggests that the self-interest of the parties drives negotiations, the negotiations under the three ultra-heterodox modes in China are rather policy-driven through significant external pressure from the government and courts. Through the exercise of legal discretion, moral persuasion, or sheer power, the judges and the Party-state pressed creditors, and sometimes debtors too, to concede. These negotiations are about the state actors' efforts to prevent market disruption, social unrest, and financial crisis, which private contract parties are not particularly concerned about. Contract parties do not necessarily

Trebilcock and J. Leng, The Role of Formal Contract Law and Enforcement in Economic Development (2006) 92 *Virginia Law Review* 1517–80.

108 See K. Pistor, *The Code of Capital: How the Law Creates Wealth and Inequality* (Princeton: Princeton University Press, 2019).

benefit from such negotiations either; for example, secured creditors would be compelled by judges to give up their priority rights. Most likely, their counterparties alleging unfair contracts would not gain significantly from such negotiations either. Through insolvency, the weaker parties may receive certificates of credit, but such certificates are not cash and most likely would not be redeemed eventually. Their money was long gone through complex and wasteful networks of speculation activities long before the disputes arose. At the end of the day, they would come to realize that credit certificates and negotiation outcomes only offer a symbolic and emotional comfort.[109] Arguably, the main beneficiaries are those who benefit from the stabilization policies that drive the ultra-heterodox approaches, such as the community at large, government agencies, and, eventually, the Party-state, all of which demand social and economic stability as the paramount objective.

Negotiated legality works in China because of the country's political economy, culture, and economic efficiency calculation. To begin with, the strong Party-state, dominant both in public and private sectors, has the capacity to intervene in private contractual relationships. Stakeholders either welcome or cannot reject such intervention. Secondly, there exist various communitarian norms for judges to employ. In Western-style democracy, justice will be delivered through procedural formalism, with injustice generally stemming from not adhering to the procedures or terms agreed upon. In contrast, negotiated legality treats the agreed contract terms at issue merely as a reference point for subsequent negotiations during contract enforcement. Contract parties in China, regardless of their status in a contractual relationship, do share a communitarian understanding of liability and responsibility, such as "going through hardship together."[110] Judges believe such norms can solve contract disputes in cases concerning inequality better than the law of contract. Lastly, negotiated legality could be more cost efficient in emerging markets in that contract parties can postpone the costly risk identification process and lengthy negotiation about risk allocation from the contract formation phase to enforcement stage. In this way, the initial stage of deal making could be faster and less costly. From the Party-state's perspective, it could be efficient too if they delegate to local participants and market actors the power to clarify and debate about legality through their market practices and concretize some abstract legal doctrines. The Party-state can always intervene at a later point when necessary. In short, negotiated legality, which underlies various communitarian norms, are not just a cultural phenomenon but also closely tied with the country's political economy and cost-benefit calculation.

[109] This is the view often expressed by insolvency lawyers I interviewed.

[110] Literature on the communitarian norms in China is scant but has pointed out such communitarian norms in the field of torts, constitutional law, and property law. As shown in this essay, this communitarian view exists in the area of contract law too. See, e.g., B. Liebman, 'Leniency in Chinese Criminal Law? Everyday Justice in Henan' (2015) 33 *Berkeley Journal of International Law* 153–222; T. Li-ann, 'Varieties of Constitutionalism in Asia' (2021) 16 *Asian Journal of Comparative Law* 285–310; Stern et al., Liability beyond Law.

It remains to be observed whether China's statist model will be sustainable in the long-term, although in the short-term it seems justifiable by some positive outcomes. Within the legal academia in China, criticism against such government involvement is not uncommon.[111] Negotiated legality offers room for policy intervention and serves as a mechanism to correct the failure of market mechanisms to address inequality. But it is also vulnerable for manipulation under authoritarianism and populism.

4.8 CONCLUSION

A civil law system comes closer to contract law heterodoxy in preserving room to deal with inequality through various doctrines that enable judges to nullify contracts in violation of communitarian values such as social morals and public order. Such doctrines indicate that the state preserves the authority to correct unfairness and inequality in certain contracts in dispute, although as a last resort. In China, as well as elsewhere, the pandemic has unveiled economic inequality in many contractual agreements. Have Chinese judges increased their use of these codified doctrines to correct contract inequality accordingly? Oddly, the number of cases in reliance to those doctrines did not increase during the pandemic; rather, it seemed to drop significantly.[112]

Chinese judges did not seem to use these doctrines under their contract law at a time when most extensive inequality had been exposed in contract disputes. Why not? My case study shows that Chinese judges endorse the spirit of the contract law heterodoxy, but do not think it is good enough to address inequality. Rather, they have developed three alternative approaches, depending on the merit and impact of various cases, to deal with contract disputes that are of inequality nature: the mediation, insolvency, and macro-prudential approaches. Interestingly, judicial independence is never a concern. As in all three approaches, the state and courts collaborate closely and work hand-in-hand to solve disputes and weaker parties welcome such intervention.

There are several takeaways from Chinese practices. First, the idea of contract law heterodoxy is valuable, but its effectiveness may be limited. Most transactions have to be constructed by multiple contracts, such as real estate transactions that could involve purchase agreements, mortgage agreements, guarantee agreements, pledge

[111] Shuguang and Zuofa, The Gap between Expectation of Legislation and Judicial Practice and Its Resolution.

[112] According to China Judgments Online, the judicial database maintained by the People's Supreme Court of China, the number of cases adjudicated based on the "change in circumstance" clause dropped by 34 percent during the pandemic (between January 2000 and December 2022), compared to the same period of time prior to the pandemic (between January 2017 and December 2019). However, it should be noted that it is unclear whether such statistics of reported cases are complete and correct.

agreements, and other understandings when necessary. Inequality, when existing, does not necessarily result from only the specific contract in dispute, but rather from other related contracts too between third parties and the parties in dispute. The negative impact of each contract varies at different degrees and what is not justifiable is the accumulative effect of inequality caused by multiple contracts, including those not in dispute (yet) and thus not subject to judicial scrutiny. Unless courts are allowed to further conduct a holistic review and correct some terms of other contracts, they cannot address inequality effectively.

Second, the role of the government remains vital in addressing inequality, although the specific Chinese model is difficult to replicate. Driven by concerns about social stability, Chinese courts seem more adamant than courts of other countries about addressing inequality, instead of letting tax or fiscal policies deal with inequality as opponents to contract law heterodoxy suggest. If courts in a democracy try to mirror the approach of Chinese courts, however, they would face severe challenges against its legitimacy as contract freedom and individual autonomy would have been seriously compromised. Chinese courts do not have to face legitimacy challenges from either the executive or the legislative branches, because they are viewed as an integral part of the state apparatus. By endorsing and empowering the courts, the government prevents inequality issues from escalating into social unrest and financial crises. The general public supports the government's intervention because of its clout over those strong parties in such unfair contract relationships. With support, courts could extensively apply communitarian norms, such as "going through hardship together," "collective risk sharing," or "be sympathetic to your counter-party," to demand stronger parties to negotiate and compromise. This process is fluid and smooth due to the peculiar perception of legality in China – negotiated legality.

The last takeaway is centered around the interesting finding that the Chinese government has framed its actions legalistically, despite bypassing legal procedure and contract terms, and is adamant that the courts and legal professionals play a key role in solving those disputes concerning inequality. In contrast to the general impression that the Chinese Party-state acts against the law, my findings reveal more nuances about the dynamics of China's legal system development and shed light on how the Party-state treats legality strategically.[113] Apparently, even as an authoritarian regime, the Chinese state has come to appreciate the institutionalization of combating inequality through the legal system. Also, in its view, existing institutional settings and doctrines do not seem sufficient; rather they sometimes strengthen the unequal status quo. Such perception leads to the ultra-heterodox approach the Chinese courts have developed, together with the state's further intervention in

[113] C. Minzner, China's Turn against Law (2011) 59 *The American Journal of Comparative Law* 935–84. C.f. T. Zhang and T. Ginsburg, China's Turn toward Law (2019) 59 *Virginia Journal of International Law* 306–89.

dispute resolution. Their drastic approaches might not be replicated elsewhere, but the general lesson is meaningful: To combat inequality, it is necessary to move beyond the existing legal framework and further regulatory intervention will be required.

BIBLIOGRAPHY

Ahl, B., Why Do Judges Cite the Party? References to Party Ideology in Chinese Court Decisions (2020) 18 *China: An International Journal* 175–85.

Bernstein, L., Opting Out of the Legal System: Extralegal Contractual Relations in the Diamond Industry (1992) 21 *The Journal of Legal Studies* 115–57.

Bloomberg News, 'Sweeping Mortgage Boycott Changes the Face of Dissent in China', Bloomberg (August 3, 2022).

Borst, N., Has Covid-19 Led to Financial Instability in China?, *Seafarer* (April 2020).

Chang, W., *In Search of the Way: Legal Philosophy of the Classic Chinese Thinkers* (Edinburgh: Edinburgh University Press, 2016).

Chen, G. B., *Law without Lawyers, Justice without Courts: On Traditional Chinese Mediation* (Oxfordshire: Routledge, 2002).

Chen, W., China's Long March to Dismantling the Financial Great Wall: Renminbi's Internationalization, Systemic Risks and Macro-prudential Regulations, in A. Anand (ed.), *Systemic Risk, Institutional Design and the Regulation of Financial Markets* (Oxford: Oxford University Press, 2016), pp. 143–74.

Lost in Internationalization: The Rise of China's Renminbi, Macroprudential Policy, and Global Impacts (2018) 21 *Journal of International Economic Law* 31–66.

Twins of Opposites: Why China Will Not Follow Taiwan's Model of Rule of Law Transition toward Democracy (2018) 66 *The American Journal of Comparative Law* 481–535.

Chen, W. and Fu, H. (eds.), *Authoritarian Legality in Asia* (Cambridge: Cambridge University Press, 2020).

Chen-Wishart, M., *Contract Law* (Oxford: Oxford University Press, 2012).

Chian, H. X. and An, J. Y., Choices, Mechanisms, Economic Efficiency, and Legal Grounds of Listing Companies' Bankruptcy and Reorganization (2006) 7 *Management World* 130 [何旭强, 周业安, 上市公司破产和重整的选择, 机制、经济效率及法律基础].

Cook, S., The Debate over Coercive Rulership and the "Human Way" in Light of Recently Excavated Warring States Texts (2004) 64 *Harvard Journal of Asiatic Studies* 399–440.

Damaska, M., *The Faces of Justice and State Authority: A Comparative Approach to the Legal Process* (New Haven: Yale University Press, 1986), pp. 71–96.

Davis, K. E. and Pargendler, M., Contract Law and Inequality (2022) 107 *Iowa Law Review* 1485–542.

Dezalay, Y. and Garth, B., *Asian Legal Revivals: Lawyers in the Shadow of Empire* (Chicago: University of Chicago Press, 2010).

Dou, F., Cheng, S., and Zhang, A., *Analysis of Legal Issues Related to Bankruptcy of Enterprises under the Influence of the Epidemic* [疫情影响下与企业破产相关的法律问题解析], Allbright Law Offices (February 14, 2020).

Fukuyama, F., *Political Order and Political Decay: From the Industrial Revolution to the Globalization of Democracy* (New York: Farrar, Straus and Giroux, 2014).

Godwin, A., Judicial Mediation (October 12, 2018) *China Business Law Journal* (online). https://law.asia/judicial-mediation/.

Goedde, P., The Making of Public Interest Law in South Korea via the Institutional Discourses of Minbyeon, PSPD and Gonggam, in H. Yang (ed.), *Law and Society in Korea* (Cheltenham: Edward Elgar, 2013), pp. 131–49.

Haley, J., Constitutional Adjudication in Japan: History and Social Context, Legislative Structures, and Judicial Values (2011) 88 *Washington University Law Review* 1467–92.

Hang Ng, K. and He, X., *Embedded Courts: Judicial Decision-Making in China* (Cambridge: Cambridge University Press, 2017).

He, H. J. Evergrande Debt Crisis; Stocks become Wallpaper?, *Wealth Magazine*, September 17, 2021.

Huang, M. H., Cognitive Involvement and Democratic Understanding, in T. J. Cheng and Y. H. Chu (eds.), *Routledge Handbook of Democratization in East Asia* (Oxfordshire: Routledge, 2017), pp. 219–313.

Hyun, K. S., The Democratization and Internationalization of the Korean Legal Field, in Y. Dezalay and B. Garth (eds.), *Lawyers and the Rule of Law in an Era of Globalization* (Oxfordshire: Routledge, 2011), pp. 225–46.

Johnson, S. et al., Courts and Relational Contracts (2002) 18 *Journal of Law, Economics, & Organization* 221–77.

Kim & Chang, COVID-19: Force Majeure under Korean Law Considered in Wake of COVID-19 Pandemic, Kim & Chang (April 4, 2020).

Li-ann, T., Varieties of Constitutionalism in Asia (2021) 16 *Asian Journal of Comparative Law* 285–310.

Liebman, B., Leniency in Chinese Criminal Law? Everyday Justice in Henan (2015) 33 *Berkeley Journal of International Law* 153–222.

Liebman, B. L., Ordinary Tort Litigation in China: Law versus Practical Justice? (2020) 13 *Journal of Tort Law* 197–228.

Lo, C., The Risks around China's Grassroots Mortgage "Boycott," *BNP Paribas* (July 26, 2022).

Minzner, C., China's Turn against Law (2011) 59 *The American Journal of Comparative Law* 935–84.

Murray, M., Managing the Insolvency Curve in Australia, *Oxford Business Law Blog* (April 20, 2020).

Pistor, K., A Legal Theory of Finance (2013) 41 *Journal of Comparative Economics* 315–30.

The Code of Capital: How the Law Creates Wealth and Inequality (Princeton: Princeton University Press, 2019).

Qian, I. and Chang, A., They Poured Their Savings into Homes That Were Never Built, *New York Times* (January 24, 2023).

Shan, Y., Heilongjang Fonglin District Court Explored New Mechanisms for Bankruptcy Practices through Government-Courts Collaboration [黑龙江丰林县法院，积极推动"府院联动"探索破产审判新机制], *China Court Org*. (November 30, 2022).

Shuguang, L. and Zuofa, W., The Gap between Expectation of Legislation and Judicial Practice and Its Resolution: Empirical Analysis of Bankruptcy Law's Three-years Implementation (2011) 2 *Chinese University of Political Science and Law Review* [中国政法大学学报] 58–79.

Slaten, K., *Grassroots Protests Are Frequent in Xi Jinping's China*, Freedom House (November 17, 2022)

Stern, R. et al., Liability Beyond Law: Conceptions of Fairness in Chinese Tort Cases (2023) 11 *Asian Journal of Law and Society* 70–93.

Textor, C., Gini Index: Inequality of Income Distribution in China 2004–2021, *Statista* (September 29, 2023).

Thio, L. A., We Are Feeling Our Way Forward, Step by Step, in A. Chen (ed.), *Constitutionalism in Asia in the Early Twenty-First Century* (Cambridge: Cambridge University Press, 2014), pp. 270–94.

Trebilcock, M. J. and Leng, J., The Role of Formal Contract Law and Enforcement in Economic Development (2006) 92 *Virginia Law Review* 1517–80.

Upham, F. K., Reflection on the Rule of Law in China (2011) 6 *National Taiwan University Law Review* 251–68.

Wan, W., Wang, J. and Jiang, W., Does COVID-19 Exacerbate Regional Income Inequality? Evidence from 20 Provinces of China (2023) 15 *Sustainability* 1–16.

Wei, L. C. and Giao, Y., CEO of Evergrande under Investigation, *Yicai* (January 7, 2023).

Whitman, J., The Two Western Cultures of Privacy: Dignity versus Liberty (2004) 113 *Yale Law Journal* 1151–222.

Xin Hua News, *Strict Prohibition on False Receipts and Tax Evasion in order to Maintain a Fair Market* [我國嚴打虛開發票和騙稅行為維護市場公平], Finance People (September 2, 2018).

Yu, F., The Distinction between Basic Principles and General Clauses: The Interpretation Methodology for Interpreting the Principles of Good Faiths and Social Morals (2021) 4 *China Legal Science* 25–43 [于飛, 基本原則與概括條款的區分：我國誠實信用與公序良俗的解釋論構造, 中國法學].

Zhang, H. and Wu, S. S., The Direction for Adjudicating Financial Disputes? Highlights of Financial Law Adjudication of National Courts [金融纠纷审判何处去？—全国法院金融审判会议热点探讨], *AnJie Broad* (March 2, 2023).

Zhang, T. and Ginsburg, T., China's Turn toward Law (2019) 59 *Virginia Journal of International Law* 306–89.

5

Tort Law Heterodoxy in China

Benjamin L. Liebman, Rachel E. Stern, Eva Wenwa Gao, and Xiaohan Wu

5.1 INTRODUCTION

Mr. Zhang drowned in a fishpond on the property of the Huludao Jinhui Agricultural Industrial and Commercial Group Company, in Liaoning Province in China's northeast. Zhang's family sued, arguing that the company was negligent in failing to take adequate safety precautions. On appeal, the Huludao Intermediate Court rejected the family's legal claim, finding that Zhang was mentally ill and that there was no way that the company could have completely prevented the tragedy.[1] The court concluded that Zhang's guardians had failed in their responsibility to supervise him, and thus "to hold others responsible ... has no legal basis."

Nevertheless, the court proceeded to order the defendant company to pay 50,000 yuan in compensation to the family. "It cannot be denied that Zhang's ... accidental death has given his family huge suffering and economic harm," the court wrote. "In particular, the deceased has elders above and a minor child below, and they are deserving of sympathy." The court's anger at the defendants' conduct was clear. The decision noted that the plaintiffs had accepted an initial settlement offer from the company arrived at through court mediation and expressed frustration that the company had added a new condition to its offer, insisting that the family transfer a piece of land in exchange for compensation. The court noted that the company's decision to withdraw its offer was in accordance with "formal justice," but was "out

[1] (2014) 葫民终字第00645号. The trial court found that the fishpond was a public place, akin to a place of entertainment or any other location open to the public, and thus that Zhang's family had heightened responsibility for supervising him. Although the trial court found that Zhang's family members bore primary responsibility, the decision still ordered the defendant to pay 20 percent of damages, roughly 65,000 yuan. On appeal by the company, the appellate court rejected the analogy to a public place. Portions of this chapter first appeared in R. E. Stern et al., Liability beyond Law: Conceptions of Fairness in Chinese Tort Cases (2023) *Asian Journal of Law and Society* 1–24. Although cases sometimes include the full names of parties, the rules governing online publication call for names of litigants to be redacted so that only family names are listed. In this chapter, we thus include only the family names of litigants.

of step with substantive justice" and "would cause harm to the creation of a spirit of peace and order and public order and morals."[2] The court concluded:

> In light of the above, this court believes that although [defendant company] subjectively was without fault, nevertheless starting from the perspective of taking the people as the basis, our nation's national circumstances, and positive village customs, giving some compensation in light of the circumstances will better reveal the substantive justice of law.[3]

The Huludao court's embrace of substantive justice and "the people as the basis"[4] as grounds for awarding compensation was not unusual for Chinese courts. In cases that involve bad luck, catastrophic loss, and even commonplace accidents, Chinese courts routinely ask defendants to pay damages without evidence of negligence. At times, courts make such arguments explicitly, as with the Huludao court. In others, courts use less direct terms, including "reason," "discretion," or "actual circumstances," or cite legal provisions that allow courts to adjust outcomes based on equity. Prior to 2021, Chinese courts that did so often relied on a legal provision that explicitly authorized payment of damages based on "actual circumstances," regardless of fault. Commonly referred to as the "equitable liability" provision of the 1986 General Principles of Civil Law and the 2010 Tort Liability Law, Chinese law authorized courts to impose liability by relying on fairness, not just fault. But courts often went beyond the provisions of statutory law. And they have continued to do so even after China's new Civil Code, which became effective in 2021, curtailed the use of the provisions.

China's use of equitable liability provisions and references to concepts such as substantive justice or discretion demonstrates how tort law can serve heterodox policies and goals. Comparative scholarship on tort law has long noted the range of different goals that tort law may seek to achieve, from corrective justice to deterrence to loss spreading to supplementing a weak social safety network.[5] In many ways Chinese tort law resembles legal orthodoxy in the Global North: in most situations, tort compensation is awarded either due to the negligence of a tortfeasor or based on the application of strict liability to a specific, limited subset of cases. Yet Chinese law, both on the books and in practice, has gone further,

2 (2014) 葫民终字第00645号.

3 Ibid.

4 The phrase "taking the people as the basis" (以人为本) is commonly attributed to Guan Zhong, a Legalist thinker who lived in the seventh century BCE. The phrase re-emerged as a key CCP slogan under General Secretary Hu Jintao, after he used it in a speech at the Third Plenum of the 16th Communist Party Congress in 2003, and became a key part of Hu's Theory of Scientific Outlook on Development. China Central Television, 中国共产党第十六届中央委员会第三次全体会议公报 [*Report of the Third Plenum of the 16th Party Congress of the Chinese Communist Party*] (2021).

5 For an overview of the contested goals of US tort law, see K. Abraham, *The Forms and Functions of Tort Law* (St. Paul: Foundation Press, 2022), pp. 17–23. Abraham notes that, in the United States, compensation alone is not a goal of tort law.

awarding damages even when little or no link is established between a victim's injuries and a defendant, or when a victim appears to be entirely at fault. Chinese courts often use tort cases to spread losses, redistribute wealth, supplement a weak social safety network, build social cohesion, and ensure that losses are compensated and acknowledged. Beyond these specific goals, Chinese tort law often appears to embrace an unwritten principle: that losses should be compensated, even when they occur without negligence.

This chapter explores one example of legal heterodoxy in practice by examining how Chinese courts operationalize fairness and justice (公平公正) in published decisions involving personal injuries that either directly use such language, or reference closely related ideas and legal provisions, most importantly the "equitable liability" provisions of Chinese tort law. We do this by exploring a database of 10,000 judicial decisions, mostly tort cases, that include language about fairness, or the need to take account of actual circumstances or cite provisions of Chinese law that authorize courts to look beyond which party is at fault. We also read and coded at least 250 cases in three categories – injuries to students at school, child drownings, and death due to excessive alcohol consumption – to investigate whether the legal reasoning and outcomes we saw in the larger dataset were also prevalent in a broader swath of similar cases that did not necessarily include the same direct references to fairness, equity, and discretion.[6] To examine the effect of changes resulting from the 2021 adoption of China's Civil Code, which curtailed judicial discretion in tort cases, we also explore a smaller dataset of child-drowning and death-by-drinking cases that arose after the adoption of the Civil Code.

What we find is that Chinese courts try to smooth misfortune by imposing costs on parties with ethical, but not legal, obligations to the victims. The legal reasoning in these decisions reflects two de facto doctrines, or common judicial solutions to recurrent fact patterns, that assign liability to people linked through a relationship. We identify two types of relationship-based liability: participant liability, which assigns liability to those participating in a shared activity, and space-based liability, which assigns liability to those who control a physical space. Sometimes courts are acting within the broad discretion granted to them by Chinese law. Other times, as with the Huludao court already mentioned, Chinese courts expand or reach beyond heterodox legal provisions to resolve disputes in ways that ensure that victims of accidental injury receive compensation. The theme is that judges share an impulse

6 We did this to address concerns about a self-selected sample, at least partly. In these three categories, we drew a sample based on facts of the case or, in the case of school injury cases, citations to school-specific provisions of Chinese tort law. Using this second pool of cases, we were able to compare legal reasoning and outcomes in decisions that reference fairness directly or cite the fairness-based provisions of Chinese tort law, with those that do not. Of course, questions remain about when and why judges directly discuss fairness in their decisions, and when they do not. Due to missing data, we are also unable to make any frequency claims about how often Chinese courts impose costs on parties with ethical, but not legal, obligations to victims. The number of cases we were able to turn up, however, suggests that this is common.

to assign legal responsibility to certain social relationships and to spread economic losses through a community. The damages imposed range from a de minimis acknowledgment of trauma in cases in which the victim was largely or entirely at fault to substantial sums. When sizable amounts of money are awarded, courts are also acting as agents of redistribution, fashioning an ad hoc social safety net for victims and their families. Together, these cases reflect both the pursuit of specific policy goals and a worldview that appears prevalent within Chinese courts. We also find that Chinese courts continued to decide cases by relying on fairness or equity after the adoption of the Civil Code, either through appeals to fairness or equity or by finding defendants negligent even when they appeared to have only tangential links to the harm that occurred. Heterodox practices persist even after the written law tries to eliminate it by becoming closer to the orthodoxy in the Global North.

Recognizing and detailing how tort law can serve heterodox goals in China raises three questions about the practice and concept of legal heterodoxy. First, how do China's legal traditions fit into the orthodoxy/heterodoxy framework that is the focus of this volume? China's embrace of legal heterodoxy in tort law may not be a rejection of the legal orthodoxy of the Global North but rather may reflect an attempt to combine China's socialist and pre-revolutionary legal traditions with the need for flexibility in practice in a rapidly changing society. Second, China's tort law heterodoxy raises questions about the relationship between legal provisions and legal practice. In particular, when and how do heterodox practices outlive shifts toward legal orthodoxy? The curtailment of the equitable liability provisions in China's new Civil Code suggests that orthodox criticism of such practices may have had an effect in China, even as China's leadership argues that it is developing a uniquely Chinese approach to law-based governance.[7] Those seeking to bring China more into line with orthodox tort law principles of requiring either fault or strict liability as a basis for imposing damages may have won the argument in China's legislature. Yet heterodoxy lives on in actual court practice, suggesting that in at least some situations heterodoxy can outlive changes to written law. Third, is regime type relevant to the idea of legal heterodoxy? Chinese courts' practice of appealing to equitable principles, substantive justice, or just "actual circumstances" is not simply an effort to maintain social stability or avoid protest or escalation.[8] But ensuring that victims of accidental injury receive compensation, that social ties are maintained, and that loss is acknowledged may nevertheless serve both bureaucratic interests and Party-state goals in China. This raises the question of whether a legal

[7] Xinhua News, 20th Congress of the Communist Party of China (2022) 高举中国特色社会主义伟大旗帜 为全面建设社会主义现代化国家而团结奋斗 – 在中国共产党第二十次全国代表大会上的报告 [Hold High the Great Banner of Socialism with Chinese Characteristics and Strive for the Comprehensive Construction of a Socialist Modernized Country – Report at the 20th National Congress of the Communist Party of China], *Xinhua News*, October 25, 2022.

[8] We make this argument more directly elsewhere. See Stern et al., Liability beyond Law.

practice is heterodox if it achieves not just social policy goals but also the goal of maintaining political control and authority, as well as whether the practice of legal heterodoxy differs in authoritarian systems (or countries undergoing democratic backsliding) compared to democracies.

5.2 FAIRNESS IN LAW AND EQUITABLE LIABILITY

Chinese law includes numerous provisions that give courts discretion to consider fairness (公平) in their decisions, from contract law, to takings law, to intellectual property law.[9] Yet two of the most controversial legal provisions in Chinese language scholarship do not actually use the term "fairness" – the equitable liability provisions of the 1986 General Principles of the Civil Law and the 2010 Tort Liability Law.[10] Most legal systems impose liability for personal injuries based on negligence, strict liability, or a combination of the two. Prior to 2021, Chinese tort law included a third category: liability based on the "actual circumstances." Both Article 24 of the Tort Liability Law and Article 132 of the General Principles of the Civil Law state that if none of the parties are at fault for damages, they can nevertheless share liability "according to the actual circumstances."[11] These "equitable liability provisions" authorized courts to allocate damages based on fairness in situations in which a defendant's actions had contributed to harm but the defendant was not found to be negligent or strictly liable.

The 1986 equitable liability provision had explicitly heterodox roots. Scholars reported that the 1986 provision was inspired by a mixture of the 1900 German Civil

9 Article 533 of the Civil Code (2020). The provision governs court determinations that a contract should be modified because it is impractical, and states, in part, "the people's court or an arbitration institution shall rectify or rescind the contract in compliance with the principle of fairness, taking into account the actual circumstances of the case." Along similar lines, Article 117 of the Civil Code requires "fair and reasonable" compensation in takings cases, and Article 47 of the Patent Law requires patent-related fees to be refunded when a patent that had been in use was subsequently and nonretroactively declared invalid, if "the principle of equity" is contravened.

10 Article 132 of the General Principles of the Civil Law (1986); Article 24 of the Tort Liability Law (2009).

11 The phrasing of the two provisions differs slightly. Article 24 of the Tort Liability Law stated that "when the injured party and the actor both lack negligence regarding the injury, both parties may share the loss according to the actual circumstance." Article 132 of the General Provisions of the Civil Law, adopted twenty-four years before the Tort Liability Law, stated that "when neither party has been negligent in respect to the harm that has occurred, the parties may share civil liability in accordance with the actual circumstances." The Tort Liability Law's phrasing is narrower than that in the General Provisions, referring specifically to "the actor" and suggesting that a causal link is required between the defendant's non-negligent actions and the harm to the plaintiff. The phrasing in the General Principles allows someone whose actions had no causal link with the victim's injuries to be partially or fully liable. In accordance with the general principle that specific laws are meant to prevail over general laws, courts are supposed to rely on Article 24 of the Tort Liability Law in tort cases rather than Article 132 of the General Provisions of the Civil Law. In the cases we read, courts sometimes cited both provisions.

Code as well as Yugoslav and Soviet civil law.[12] The provision also reflected the relative lack of development of Chinese tort law in the mid-1980s[13] and thus the need for courts to be flexible in adjudicating cases. One influential scholarly discussion of Yugoslav law at the time, authored by the primary drafter of the General Principles of the Civil Code, made clear that the Yugoslav provision that served as a model for those drafting the General Principles was intended to reject the norms of capitalist systems.[14] The article argued that the adoption of the equitable liability provision in the General Principles reflected a fundamental shift in when and how damages are awarded: "in the conditions of modern technological and civilized society, the basis for liability is no longer exclusively fault-based, but rather, liability is established without the need for a connection to fault. The emergence of liability is due to the occurrence of harm."[15]

The equitable liability provisions were unusual when placed in a comparative perspective. Although other legal systems permit the parties' circumstances (including relative wealth) to be considered in determining damages in some circumstances, these factors come into play only after liability is established. In China (and apparently in Yugoslavia), in contrast, courts were authorized to look to "actual circumstances" to impose liability, even absent negligence or strict liability. This reflected the view, that "under no circumstances can the causer of harm be exempt from liability by proving the absence of fault for the occurrence of the harm."[16] The link to socialist ideology was also made clear in the explanation that "socialist fairness and unity ... sometimes require not applying provisions that exclusively mandate compensation from the responsible party."[17] In the view of Chinese scholars, this "fairness" or "equitable liability" provision became an independent form of socialist tort liability, in addition to liability based on fault and strict liability.

[12] Z. Wang, 我国侵权法上"公平责任"源流考 [An Examination of the Origins of "Equitable Liability" in Chinese Tort Law] (2008) 3 *甘肃政法学院学报 [Journal of the Gansu Institute of Political Science and Law]* 138–44; C. Liu, Socialized Liability in Chinese Tort Law (2018) 59 *Harvard International Law Journal* 16–44; X. Cheng, 中国民法典侵权责任编的创新与发展 [The Innovation and Development of Tort Liability in the Chinese Civil Code] (2020) 3 *中国法律评论 [China Law Review]* 46–61.

[13] Cheng, 中国民法典侵权责任编的创新与发展 [The Innovation and Development of Tort Liability in the Chinese Civil Code].

[14] The article first appeared in 1980 in the journal *Legal Studies Translation Series* and was later republished in a 1983 book, *Selected Foreign Civil Law Materials*, published by the Editorial Department of Legal Textbooks. The book had a print run of 20,000 copies – extremely large for a legal publication at the time. Wang, 我国侵权法上"公平责任"源流考 [An Examination of the Origins of "Equitable Liability" in Chinese Tort Law].

[15] Ibid., quoting Editorial Department of Law Textbooks, Compilation Group of Materials on Civil Law Principles, 外国民法资料选编 [Selected Foreign Civil Law Materials] (Beijing: Law Press, 1983).

[16] Ibid.

[17] Ibid.

The equitable liability provisions have been controversial in China.[18] By the early 2000s, scholars had begun to recognize that the vagueness of the provision made it open to misuse in practice. Nevertheless, the provision was maintained, albeit in a slightly different form, when China adopted its Tort Liability Law in 2009, despite calls from leading scholars to limit the use of equitability liability to specific situations. More detailed criticism followed in the 2010s. Much of the criticism centered on how equitable liability has been applied outside of its intended sphere of torts cases,[19] or misapplied. For example, a study of a hundred cases citing the provision found that nearly half involved a finding of fault, even though the provision is only supposed to apply when neither party is at fault.[20] Another criticism is that the language of "actual circumstances" in the law is stretched by courts to impose liability based on a wide range of factors, including the severity of damages, parties' financial status, ethical concerns, and the goal of achieving social harmony.[21] Courts sometimes ignore causation to impose liability on defendants with only tenuous links to an accident because they have the ability to pay.[22]

[18] The Supreme People's Court appeared to recognize the possibility that the provision was excessively vague when it issued its "1988 Opinions on Several Issues Concerning the Implementation of the General Principles of the Civil Law." The Opinions stated that article 132, the equitable liability provision, should be limited to situations where one party acts for the benefit of the other party or the parties have mutual interests. Supreme People's Court, 最高人民法院印发《关于贯彻执行<中华人民共和国民法通则>若干问题的意见 （试行）》的通知 [Notice of the Supreme People's Court on Issuing the Opinions on Several Issues Concerning the Implementation of the General Principles of the Civil Law of the People's Republic of China (For Trial Implementation)] (1988). Yet the Opinions appear to have had limited impact on court practice.

[19] For example, D. Mao writes that the principle has been applied "with no limits" and has often been used beyond what is legally permitted. See D. Mao, 公平责任典型案例探析 [Analysis of Typical Cases Involving Equitable Liability] (2019) 9 *法制与经济 [Legal System and Economics]* 15–16. See also X. Yu, 公平责任"是否"公平" – 以二十世纪新侵权法理论为视角 [Is "Equitable Liability" Really "Equitable" – A Perspective from New Tort Liability Theory in the Twentieth Century] (2017) 12 *政治与法律 [Politics and Law]* 107–22, 107; G. Shi and C. Xie, 前民法典时代公平责任的适用: 裁判误区与应然路径 [Application of Equitable Liability in the Pre-Civil Code Era: Adjudicatory Errors and the Normative Path] (2019) 9 *河南社会科学 [Henan Social Sciences]* 25–37, 31.

[20] K. Chen, 公平责任一般条款的司法适用: 以100份侵权案件判决书为分析样本 [Judicial Application of Ordinary Provisions Employing Equitable Liability: Using 100 Tort Cases as a Sample for Analysis] (2015) 1 *法律适用 [Applied Law]* 11–16, 12. For more criticism of equitable liability, see also X. Cheng, 民法典侵权责任编的体系结构及总则部分的完善 [The Systematic Structure of the Civil Code's Tort Liability Book and Improvements to the General Provisions] (2018) 6 *财经法学 [Economic and Financial Legal Studies]* 5–22, 11–12.

[21] H. Dou, 侵权法中公平分担损失规则的司法适用 [Judicial Application of Equitable Loss-Sharing Rules in Tort Law] (2016) 5 *法商研究 [Research into Law and Commerce]* 125–36, 129; Y. Zhang, 论公平责任的不当适用及其规范 [Discussing Erroneous Application of Equitable Liability and Its Regulation] (2019) 4 *法制与社会 [Legal System and Society]* 14–15.

[22] Dou, 侵权法中公平分担损失规则的司法适用 [Judicial Application of Equitable Loss-Sharing Rules in Tort Law], 127–28; Zhang, 论公平责任的不当适用及其规范 [Discussing Erroneous Application of Equitable Liability and Its Regulation]; Shi and Xie, 前民法典时代公平责任的适用 [Application of Equitable Liability in the Pre-Civil Code Era], 26.

Chinese scholars' criticism of the equitable liability provisions appears largely to have been rooted in their belief that courts were misapplying the provisions—not that the provisions did not conform to global practices. Widespread misapplication of the law likewise appears to have been the primary factor that led legislative drafters to curtail the use of equitable liability provisions under China's new Civil Code (which came into effect in 2021), limiting it to cases explicitly authorized by law.[23] The revision attracted little scholarly or media attention in China. Nevertheless, the larger project of adopting the Civil Code was clearly linked to China's pursuit of legal modernization and the goal of having a "complete legal system." Part of this effort involved removing legal provisions viewed as outdated.[24] The Civil Code was also in significant part an effort to reduce judicial discretion by clarifying (and in some cases limiting) existing legal provisions.

China has also maintained some other provisions in the torts section of the Civil Code that reflect its communitarian or socialist traditions. Most notably, Article 1254 of the Civil Code provides that, when objects falling from a building cause harm and the specific source of the object cannot be identified, all residents or the building shall share in compensating the victim. Leading Chinese scholars have also noted that the fundamental purpose of Chinese tort law is to "care for victims and provide relief for them."[25]

In contrast to the robust debate over equitable liability in Chinese language scholarship, however, the provisions have attracted scant attention in the English language literature on Chinese law. One notable exception is a 2018 article by Chenglin Liu, who sees the "primary purpose" of equitable liability provisions as

[23] Article 1186 of the Civil Code states that equitable liability shall only be permitted where specifically authorized by law. "Where neither the victim nor the actor is at fault for the occurrence of a damage, both of them may share the damage according to the provisions of the law." Article 1190 is one example of a specific provision authorizing the continued use of equitable liability. The provision states that in situations in which a person causes harm due to temporary loss of consciousness or control, a defendant who is not at fault may nevertheless be asked to pay compensation "according to the actor's economic circumstances." The Civil Code likewise authorizes the imposition of damages based on fairness in cases involving defendants with limited capacity. In commentary that accompanied the issuance of the draft Civil Code, the Standing Committee of China's National People's Congress stated that the vagueness of the equitable liability provisions had resulted in "excessively broad application of the provision, with negative social effects." National People's Congress Standing Committee, 关于《民法典各分编（草案）》的说明 [Explanations of Each Separate Part of the Civil Code (Draft)] (2018).

[24] The official explanation issued by China's legislature, the National People's Congress, alongside the Civil Code noted that the Civil Code "involves the compilation and revision of existing civil legal norms, the modification and improvement of provisions that are no longer in line with the current reality, and the formulation of targeted new regulations to address emerging situations and issues in economic and social life." National People's Congress Standing Committee, 关于《中华人民共和国民法典（草案）》的说明 [Explanations of the Civil Code of the People's Republic of China (Draft)] (2020).

[25] L. Wang, *侵权责任法研究（上卷）[Research on Tort Liability Law (Volume I)]* (Beijing: China Renmin University Press, 2010).

"maintaining social stability."[26] Liu's interpretation accords with a good deal of empirical work on Chinese tort law, which documents how courts sometimes stretch the law to ensure compensation. This is especially likely when cases are prone to give rise to instability[27] and in cases involving insurance companies, hospitals, or other institutions seen as having deep enough pockets to help shoulder the cost of injuries.

Although prior work in both Chinese and English offers important insight into the origin and use of the equitable liability provisions, this scholarship has also tended to focus on cases in which the equitable liability provisions are cited directly. In practice, however, courts often rely on equitable principles without citing the provisions, through reference to principles such as "taking the people as the basis," "actual circumstances," or simply basing an outcome on a court's discretion.[28] Indeed, one of the insights gained from the methods we use in this article is that the use of equitable principles extends far beyond cases that cite the specific equitable liability provisions. Prior scholarship has generally also focused on the types of situations in which courts apply equitable liability and has not discussed the norms and relationships courts uphold in such cases.

5.3 DATA AND METHODS

Our primary source of data is 44.2 million Chinese court decisions, publicly released between 2013 and 2018 on a website run by the Supreme People's Court called "China Judgements Online" (中国裁判文书网).[29] In order to navigate a dataset this large, we combined computer-assisted content analysis with close reading. To start, we identified 9,485 court decisions citing either the equitable liability provisions of the Tort Liability Law or the General Principles of the Civil Law.[30] These were all cases we were confident would be concerned with substantive justice and equity-based adjudication. Then, we applied topic modeling, a text-mining tool that is frequently used to discover topics in large collections of documents, to the 9,485

26 Liu, Socialized Liability in Chinese Tort Law, 36.

27 Medical disputes are a prime example of this. See B. L. Liebman, Malpractice Mobs: Medical Dispute Resolution in China (2013) 113 *Columbia Law Review* 181–264.

28 Traffic accidents are another area in which courts frequently ignore or stretch the law in the interests of fairness but virtually never cite the equitable liability provisions while doing so. B. L. Liebman, Ordinary Tort Litigation in China: Law versus Practical Justice? (2020) 13 *Journal of Tort Law* 197–228.

29 We believe that our dataset includes all cases made public on the China Judgements Online website between July 1, 2013, when the website was launched, and September 2, 2018. For more on why China began requiring courts to upload decisions to a centralized website, see B. L. Liebman et al., Mass Digitization of Chinese Court Decisions: How to Use Text as Data in the Field of Chinese Law (2020) 8 *Journal of Law and Courts* 177–201.

30 These cases represent all civil cases in our database that cite either Article 24 of the Tort Liability Law or Article 132 of the General Principles of the Civil Law. Our database includes 25,395,376 civil cases. Of these, 2,070,498 cite the Tort Liability Law.

decisions.[31] Topic modeling gave us a way to group this still-sizable corpus into themes to select cases for close reading. Our topic model yielded seventy-one topics.[32] Since these topics are generated by a computer, a close read is needed to understand the context of each topic. Research assistants helped us assign each topic a label (e.g., worker injury cases, sports-related injury cases) by reviewing the high-frequency words associated with each topic and reading twenty cases associated with each topic.[33]

In addition to topic modeling, we selected cases for close reading in two ways. First, we read decisions that included two specific phrases associated with fairness in the holding section of the opinion ("substantive justice" and "taking the people as the basis"). We read all 77 decisions that included the phrase "substantive justice" (实质正义), and a random sample of 200 of the 1,507 decisions that included "taking the people as the basis" (以人为本). Second, we read and coded a sample of 250 cases in three types of cases in which our own background knowledge, conversations with legal professionals in China, or reading of the topic model suggested that courts were likely to give strong consideration to substantive justice: cases involving injuries to students at school,[34] child drownings,[35] and death due to excessive alcohol consumption.[36] We took this second step to try to uncover cases

[31] For a brief introduction to how topic modeling works, and a discussion of how it can be used as a tool of discovery to surface themes in a large corpus, see Liebman et al., Mass Digitization of Chinese Court Decisions.

[32] We estimated the number of topics from the data using an algorithm developed by M. Lee and D. Mimno, Low-dimensional Embeddings for Interpretable Anchor-based Topic Inference (2014) *Proceedings of the 2014 Conference on Empirical Methods in Natural Language Processing*, implemented in the STM package in R. See also M. E. Roberts, B. M. Stewart, and D. Tingley, STM: An R Package for Structural Topic Models (2019) 91 *Journal of Statistical Software* 1–40.

[33] For each topic, we draw the ten documents that the model determines are most representative of the topic, as well as a random sample of an additional ten documents that have an estimated topic proportion above 0.3, meaning that 30 percent or more of the words in the case were estimated to be from the topic. We explain this methodology in more detail in Liebman et al., Mass Digitization of Chinese Court Decisions.

[34] We read a random sample of 250 cases that cite two articles of the Tort Liability Law that specifically apply to injuries at school (Articles 38 and 39). Article 38 of the Tort Liability Law concerns injuries at school to younger children who lack civil capacity. Article 39 concerns injuries at school to older children deemed to have limited civil capacity. Our dataset includes 6,202 cases that cite Article 38 and 8,283 cases that cite Article 39.

[35] We searched for the cases through a combination of terms reflecting drowning (溺水身亡,溺水死亡,溺亡) and terms suggesting that the victim or one of those involved in the case was a minor (限制民事行为能力人,无民事行为能力人,未成年,监护人). The search yielded 5,273 cases. In the random sample, 231 cases were tort claims arising from child drownings. The remaining cases involved adult drownings, non-tort claims, or were duplicate cases. Six of the 231 cases were decisions on whether to grant a rehearing and thus did not include information on whether or not the defendant was ordered to pay compensation.

[36] In searching for death by drinking cases we ran two searches that sought to identify cases in which drinking had occurred in social contexts, by combining a search for terms relating by death by drinking (死亡, 猝死, 过量饮酒, 醉酒) with terms suggesting of drinking in a public

where courts were strongly concerned with substantive justice, but did not cite the equitable liability provisions directly. Indeed, our coding suggests that this happens fairly frequently. Although both child drowning and death-by-drinking cases do appear in the topic model of equitable liability cases, the samples of cases that we read suggest that court decisions often reference to the "actual circumstances" of the case or the court's discretion to justify outcomes, without citing the equitable liability provisions. Altogether, our research team read 2,170 cases.[37] We are not aware of any prior scholarship that has attempted to look at these cases on this scale.

To examine court practices after the adoption of the Civil Code, we also examined a separate database of 100 million cases uploaded during the years 2018 through 2022. Because this dataset was obtained from a commercial data provider, not directly from the SPC website, we cannot be sure that it precisely mirrors cases made public on the China Judgements Online website. Yet a rough look at the total numbers per year suggests that the dataset includes most such cases. Within this dataset, we looked for cases involving two of the common fact patterns we discuss, cases involving death-by-drinking and cases involving child drownings, that arose after the Civil Code came into effect in 2021. We located 85 relevant child drowning cases and 116 death-by-drinking cases that arose under the new Civil Code.

The advantage of our approach was it yielded a large and transsubstantive set of legal decisions, virtually all of which directly or indirectly considered fairness in resolving the case. The cases we read also came from across China, and included hundreds of cases from China's rich provinces and big cities as well as from poorer, more rural areas, refuting the common argument that better-financed urban courts adhere closely to the law and would be more reluctant to consider amorphous, non-legal notions of fairness.[38] Although our primary focus is cases involving physical injuries in tort law, the topic model reveals how concerns about fairness have spread into other areas of the law as well, including employment law and sexual

place, such as a restaurant, bar, or hotel (房间, 包厢, 酒吧, KTV). The two searches we ran yielded 1,169 cases. We read a combined random sample of 250 cases. Twenty-three of the cases did not relate to death-by-drinking. Our analysis thus relies on 227 cases. We also explored several other categories of cases where we thought that fairness considerations might also be apparent. Not all of these searches were successful. We read random samples of 500 cases involving financial products, 220 cases involving peer-to-peer lending, and 200 contract disputes that referred to either the phrases "manifestly unfair" (显失公平) or "major error" (重大误解) in the holding section – substantive areas that we expected might likewise show strong signs of equity-based reasoning. Examination of these cases did not reveal dynamics similar to the cases we examine in this chapter, and these cases are not included in the total number of cases we read.

37 We read a total of 1,420 cases from the topic model of cases citing to the equitable liability provisions of the General Principles of the Civil Law or the Tort Liability Law.

38 At least in our dataset, courts in big cities and rich provinces frequently cite to the equitable liability provisions of the Tort Liability Law or the General Principles of the Civil Law. Our topic model includes 706 cases from Jiangsu province and 402 cases from Zhejiang province, as well as a sizeable number of decisions from Beijing (382), Chongqing (244), Tianjin (106), and Shanghai (55).

relations.[39] The disadvantage of our methodology is that written court decisions only tell us how cases turned out, and the public justifications judges choose to offer for their decisions. They cannot tell us how judges thought about a case, or what a judicial panel discussed in private. We also cannot see cases that are settled or withdrawn prior to the issuance of a final court judgment; judges may pressure litigants to do so by signaling likely outcomes if litigants do not settle or withdraw their cases. Further research interviewing judges, or observing court proceedings, is needed to better understand when and why judges frame their decisions in terms of fairness, and whether that language cloaks other concerns.[40] But court decisions are not a bad place to start, as the primary place where judges offer public rationales for their decisions. In the cases we examine, courts often acknowledge fairness, equity, and justice as an explicit justification for their decisions, despite the risk that discussing values may open up the court to criticism for going beyond the law.

5.4 SUBSTANTIVE JUSTICE IN AND BEYOND THE LAW: COURT PRACTICE

Reading thousands of cases through a topic model and guided reading suggests that what is fair depends at least in part on the underlying relationship between the parties. We divide the cases we read into two categories of relationship-based liability: participant liability and space-based liability (Table 5.1).[41] Neither type of liability is specifically recognized in Chinese law. Rather, they are what we call de facto doctrine, or common judicial solutions to a recurrent similar fact pattern. Below, each type of liability is illustrated with typical cases, followed by a discussion of the judicial rationale we see as implicit in the text of these decisions. Although it is difficult to know whether court-ordered compensation counts as a significant amount of money to the parties involved, we differentiate between two different logics of court-ordered compensation, depending on how much money changes hands. We see smaller awards where plaintiffs receive 20 percent or less of what they

39 To limit scope, this chapter does not look at the fairness provisions of the Contract Law, which have also been controversial. Rather, our focus instead is on the cases in which courts overlay legal obligations onto noncontractual relationships. In other words, the cases in this chapter are all situations in which the court – rather than a contract – imposes legal obligations onto everyday interactions.

40 Interviews with judges were not possible due to the travel restrictions created by the COVID-19 pandemic. Another limitation is that our dataset is unlikely to be comprehensive. There are well-documented problems with missing cases on China Judgements Online. Liebman et al., Mass Digitization of Chinese Court Decisions. In addition, many tort cases are likely to be resolved through court-brokered mediation and mediated cases are not released to the public. It is also likely that courts are concerned with substantive justice in areas of law not picked up by or included in the topic model or in our guided reading.

41 In tort law scholarship in English, "participant liability" is sometimes used to discuss liability arising from shared participation in a sporting event. We use the term more broadly here, to refer to liability resulting from participation in any shared activity.

TABLE 5.1 *Types of relationship-based liability*

Type of Liability	Relationship between parties	Implicit rationale
Participant Liability	People participating in the same activity.	Terrible things happen and those present share in the loss.
Space-based Liability	Businesses and their customers or employees.	If you profit off people, you should share the loss when customers or employees suffer harm.
	Public institutions and their users.	Harm requires compensation, and those who can pay should pay, in particular when in a custodial relationship (schools, hospitals).

requested as a de minimis acknowledgment of trauma and understand larger awards to be a form of redistribution that shifts significant sums to victims and their families.

5.4.1 *Participant Liability*

5.4.1.1 Social Companions

In September 2016, a group of retirees went on a road trip together to Zhumadian, in Henan. At lunch, the owner of a restaurant warned the group about wasps in the area. While hiking later in the day, two of the retirees, a married couple surnamed Li and Cui, suffered wasp stings and died. The trip had been organized informally through a "senior university" (老年大学), a social organization for retirees, but the court found no evidence that the senior university had done anything wrong. Instead, the court noted that all of the participants had shared the costs of the trip. Although there was no negligence and no way to anticipate the accident, the court reasoned that, because the participants were members of a "temporary mutual self-assistance group," they should share a portion of the loss and compensate the surviving family members. Citing the equitable liability provisions of the Tort Liability Law, the court ordered each defendant to pay 10,000 yuan in compensation.[42]

The Zhumadian case is representative of a common theme that emerges from reading equitable liability cases: presence at the scene is often enough to give rise to a duty to compensate when a fellow participant is injured. We refer to this court-imposed obligation to share losses among a group of fellow participants as "participant liability." In some cases, the defendant's actions contributed to the plaintiff's injury, but courts find no negligence. In others, there is no causal link, only presence at the scene. Nevertheless, courts rely on arguments about fairness to

[42] (2018) 豫17民终290号. The court found that the "senior university" was not legally registered, but that fact did not appear to affect how the court assessed liability.

ensure that plaintiffs receive some compensation. In a similar case to the bee sting case, but this time involving surfing, the court ordered three defendants to pay compensation after their surfing companion drowned.[43] The court found no evidence that the defendants were negligent or had contributed to the accident, stating that the death was the result of an accident. Nevertheless, the court ordered each defendant to pay 10,000 yuan in compensation in accordance with the equitable liability provisions of the Tort Liability Law, noting that they had shared the costs of the trip.[44]

5.4.1.2 Drinking and Illicit Activities

Heavy social drinking is another shared social activity that likewise often gives rise to loss-sharing, even when the court finds the deceased to be wholly responsible for their own death. Thus, for example, in a case from Shenyang,[45] Mr. Zhao died from a car accident after drinking with friends. The court found that Zhao's friends, who had been eating and drinking with him to celebrate a birthday, were not responsible for the death, and that Mr. Zhao was "solely responsible" for the accident. Nevertheless, the court ordered the two defendants to pay Zhao's surviving family members 40,000 yuan as "appropriate economic compensation" (应适当补偿经济损失为宜).[46] Similarly, in a case from Shandong,[47] Mr. Xiao died of suffocation after drinking heavily with friends and riding his motorbike home. The court found that there was no evidence showing that defendants' behavior caused the death, but nevertheless ordered each of the defendants to pay 33,900 yuan in compensation.

In other cases, courts appear to impose liability in part because defendants were engaged in a common illicit activity, such as gambling, despite there being no link between the injury and the activity. In a case from Inner Mongolia,[48] the victim was

43 (2018) 粤1323民初422号.

44 In a somewhat similar case from Sichuan, two victims were found dead on a rafting trip after disappearing one morning. After a night of heavy drinking, the victims had set up tents on a riverbank, while others in the group slept in rooms they had rented for the night. Local villagers found their bodies in the river three days later. The court ordered the other eleven participants on the trip to pay compensation of 2,500 yuan each. The court noted that there was no evidence of negligence, that the co-travelers had acted appropriately in searching for the victims and calling the police, and that no one had gained financial benefit from the trip. Nevertheless, the court stated that the members of the group "bore certain responsibility for caring for each other" as they had formed a "temporary mutual self-assistance group" and thus should pay compensation according to Article 24 of the Tort Law (2014) 都江民初字第11号; (2014) 都江民初字第10号. See also (2016) 渝05民终2577号, holding that a defendant who was knocked into the plaintiff by a wave in the ocean was not negligent but should share 10 percent of the plaintiff's loss.

45 (2016) 辽0122民初583号.

46 Ibid. See also (2014) 濂民初字第644号 (in which the victim died of suffocation after heavy drinking).

47 (2015) 梁民初字第2584号.

48 (2016) 内25民终27号.

gambling with three other people, including one of the defendants, when a second defendant knocked on the door, pretending to be the police. The victim and one of the defendants then jumped out of the apartment window, apparently out of fear that they would be arrested for gambling. The victim died from a brain injury suffered during the fall. The court stated that there was no evidence that the defendants were at fault for the plaintiff's death, but nevertheless ordered the defendants each to pay 40,000 yuan compensation, stating that it was doing so in consideration of the conduct of the two defendants and the "economic situation of the parties."[49]

5.4.1.3 Children

Courts' emphasis on communal sharing of loss is even clearer when the victim is a child. In a series of cases, courts use equitable liability to order compensation to the parents of children who drowned while swimming, despite the lack of causal link between the actions of the surviving children and the accident. Thus, for example, in a case from Sichuan,[50] a 15-year-old boy surnamed He drowned on a hot Friday afternoon in June while swimming in the river with four friends. Contrary to the claims of He's parents, who brought the lawsuit, the court found that swimming had been He's idea. None of his friends had goaded him into the water, or to the dangerous middle of the river. Even so, the court ordered the families of the four other boys to pay compensation in order to "provide comfort" to He's parents in light of their suffering and economic loss.[51] Even the family of the boy who spent the whole time playing games on his phone, and never left the river bank, was asked to pay 1,000 yuan. In cases like He's, it is not clear that significant sums are changing hands. Rather, courts seem to be focused less on meeting the economic needs of the victim's family than on publicly acknowledging catastrophic emotional loss.[52]

49 Ibid. In other cases, participating in an argument was sufficient to give rise to liability. In a case from Guangdong, a woman surnamed Shen died following an argument about a parcel of land. The court stated that there was insufficient evidence to show that the argument directly caused Shen's death, but held that the defendant should pay compensation "according to the actual situation of the case." (2018) 粤02民终89号 (appellate decision quoting trial court decision).

50 (2014) 旺苍民初字第110号.

51 The court decision noted that the families of the four defendants had agreed to pay compensation prior to litigation but could not agree on an amount.

52 Chinese courts also use participant liability to ensure compensation for the loss of a child in cases involving suicide. In a case from Gansu, for example, the plaintiffs' son killed himself after being accused of stealing a phone from his friends. The court ordered each of his friends, who were defendants in the case, to pay compensation of 30,000 yuan because the death caused emotional and financial distress to the parents. The court provided little explanation for this imposition of liability, other than stating that they should pay "in accordance with fairness principles." See (2014) 成民初字第26号.

5.4.1.4 Sexual Relationships

The idea that certain types of social interaction result in an obligation to compensate extends to sexual relationships. A good example comes from the city of Dalian, in a 2015 case brought by the parents of a woman surnamed Zhang who died of a sudden cerebral hemorrhage while her boyfriend was at work.[53]Although the court found no connection between the boyfriend's behavior and the victim's death, the "great suffering" (很大痛苦) caused by Zhang's death was enough reason for the court to order Zhang's boyfriend to pay the parents 40,000 yuan.[54] Even a one night stand can be enough to trigger de facto legal liability for the death of a sexual partner. In a 2016 case from Hunan province, Ms. Zhan was found dead in a hotel room after having sex with a former elementary school classmate, Mr. She. The two had gone to a Changsha hotel following a dinner the previous night, and Mr. She called for help when Ms. Zhan did not wake in the morning. Should he have noticed that Ms. Zhan was making unusual noises in her sleep and sought help earlier? Mr. She argued that the two were not a couple, and he had no way of knowing how she ordinarily slept. He also suggested that her death was the result of drug use. A police report found no evidence of foul play, and the court ultimately decided that there was no evidence of negligence on She's part. Regardless, the decision noted that Zhan was a widow, and she left behind a son as well as an aging parent. In light of the family's financial situation, the court ordered She to pay 60,000 RMB in compensation.[55]

Disputes over who should pay for an abortion are another context in which courts layer financial obligations on top of an extramarital sexual relationship. These cases also show how courts sometimes extend and blend tort law references to equitable liability with contract law claims based on fairness. Men are typically ordered to pay part of the cost of an abortion based on "the principle of fairness" (公平的原则), a phrase drawn from contract law, even when the court decides neither party is legally at fault. These disputes are especially tricky because they often take place against the backdrop of a strained relationship. One such estranged couple came to a district court in Guangxi Province in 2012, having already lived through the death of a first premature child because they could not pay for an incubator, fighting over who should pay for a subsequent abortion. Relying on the equitable liability provisions from tort law, the court asked Mr. Wu, the defendant in the case, to pay half the costs of terminating the pregnancy under the umbrella "principle[s] of fairness and upholding women's rights."[56] Notably, the court cited the equitable liability provision of tort law to justify its decision.[57]

53 (2015) 沙民初字第5830号.

54 Ibid.

55 (2016) 湘0105民初1855号.

56 (2012) 南民初字第1474号.

57 Abortion cases were common enough to manifest as a specific topic in the topic model (Topic 54), with a topic proportion of 1.12 percent, meaning that, on average, 1.12 percent of the words in all documents related to the topic.

5.4.1.5 Rationales

What explains courts' efforts to impose participant liability in such a wide range of social interactions, from social outings, to heavy drinking and illicit activities, to children playing together, to sexual relationships? Certainly it is not the law. Many of these cases do not fit the equitable liability provisions of the Tort Law, which required a causal link between defendants' conduct and plaintiffs' injuries. Stability also falls short as a full explanation, unless stability is defined to include every potentially unhappy litigant. It seems unlikely that the illicit gambler, or the family of the deceased sexual partner, was genuinely perceived as a likely petitioner or protester. What emerges in these cases is a particular view of relationship-based liability, which is that certain social interactions give rise to obligations beyond specific legal requirements. Rather than letting losses fall where they may absent a finding of negligence, Chinese courts send a strong message that participation in shared social activities requires a collective sharing of losses.

How predictable are the outcomes in these cases? To get traction on this question, we read and coded 250 cases of each of two types of cases that involve participant liability: child drowning and death-by-drinking. What we found is that courts overwhelmingly allocate at least some compensation to victims, or the families of victims. Across a sample of 250 child drowning cases, courts awarded damages 75 percent of the time.[58] In a sample of 250 death-by-drinking cases, plaintiff success was even more likely, with 85 percent of the cases resulting in damages paid to plaintiffs.[59] Victims also recover in both rural and urban courts.[60] Although victims are slightly more likely to be awarded compensation in rural courts, perhaps because a more communitarian logic holds sway in the tighter-knit communities of the countryside, plaintiffs are likely to receive compensation regardless of the location of the court (Table 5.2). The vast majority of lower court decisions across the country treat participant liability as a de facto doctrine and ensure that plaintiffs recover at least some money in recognition of their losses.

58 Courts generally find negligence in child drowning cases, but such findings often read as strained, with courts simply mentioning a failure on the part of defendants to supervise without pointing to any specific act of negligence. The logic often appears to be that, because misfortune has occurred, someone must have been negligent. In the 126 decisions that referenced fairness or equity, all but two awarded damages to plaintiffs. In contrast, in cases in which courts did not mention fairness or equity, defendants were more likely to prevail, winning 56 percent of the cases in the sample (55 of 99 cases).

59 As in the drowning cases, courts that made reference to fairness virtually always awarded damages: only 4 of the 154 cases that made reference to fairness denied recovery. In most cases, courts found negligence, with courts often finding negligence either on the part of drinking companions or the restaurant or bar that served the alcohol. In general, courts found those who drank with the deceased to be liable. Those who refrained from drinking, who were seated at a different table, or who departed before the final round of drinks were not held liable.

60 There were also no significant differences by level of court.

TABLE 5.2 *Percentage of decisions that award compensation to plaintiffs*

	District courts (mostly urban)	County courts (mostly rural)
Death-by-drinking	82%	92%
Child drowning	69%	74%

Typically, plaintiffs only receive a portion of what they requested. In our sample of child drowning cases, plaintiffs received less than half of what they requested in 82 percent of cases, and less than a quarter of what they requested in 55 percent of cases.[61] In the death-by-drinking cases, plaintiffs received less than half of their request in 85 percent of cases, and less than a quarter in 57 percent of cases.[62] Clearly, courts are trying to split the difference between plaintiffs and defendants. Yet fairly substantial sums are also changing hands. The average award in a death-by-drinking case in our sample was 143,720 yuan and the average award in a child drowning case was 118,274 yuan.[63] We also see little evidence that defendants are better placed than plaintiffs to shoulder losses, at least from what we can gather from the clues sprinkled throughout the text of decisions, particularly occasional references to defendants' occupations. Rather, these cases generally appear to involve parties from the same economic background. Ordering damages in these cases, then, involves sharing the burden of loss within a community rather than channeling money from haves to have-nots. Do Chinese judges think about this kind of loss-spreading as part of their role in society, or do they take a harder-nosed view of it as a tactic to appease grief-stricken plaintiffs so that they neither appeal nor complain? It is impossible to say without interviewing judges, and judicial attitudes are also likely to vary with the circumstances of the case. At least some cases are likely to be influenced by the moral judgment of judges and their views of activities such as drinking, gambling, and sex outside of marriage. But, regardless of the view judges take of the parties involved in the case, or even how they view their role in society, the decisions in these cases are strikingly consistent: Chinese courts routinely

[61] This analysis is limited to the 203 cases that included information on how much plaintiffs initially requested.

[62] In the drinking cases, 202 of the 227 cases included data on amounts claimed and awarded.

[63] In making these award determinations, Chinese courts likely had in mind national standards for how much compensation to award in cases involving injury or death, which vary by province and are based on the per capita income in each province (prior to 2019 each province had separate standards for rural and urban areas). Death compensation is fixed at twenty times local income in each province. The relatively high awards in these cases reflect the fact that they typically involved the death of the victim. Supreme People's Court, 最高人民法院关于审理人身损害赔偿案件适用法律若干问题的解释 [Interpretation of the Supreme People's Court of Some Issues Concerning the Application of Law for the Trial of Cases on Compensation for Personal Injury] (2003).

impose an implied social compact that requires those present at the scene to share the burden of loss when things go awry.

5.4.2 *Space-based Liability: Businesses and Institutions as Insurers*

5.4.2.1 Businesses: Bars, Hotels, and Bathhouses

Mr. Song died following heavy drinking at the somewhat innocuously named Latte Bar, in Beijing.[64] Instead of suing his drinking companions, as in the participant liability cases above, Song's parents sued the bar, arguing that its employees failed to meet their obligations to protect their customers.[65] But the bar's employees had called an ambulance and had waited outside for it to arrive, leading the court to find no negligence or causal link between the conduct of bar employees and Song's death. Nevertheless, the court noted that Song was a frequent customer at the bar, including the night of his death, and that the bar had profited from Song's presence. The court thus ordered the Latte Bar to pay 120,000 yuan in compensation to Song's survivors "according to equitable liability principles."

Song's case is emblematic of a second category of court-imposed obligation in tort cases: liability based on physical presence, most often from accidents that occur at a place of business or large institutions. Business owners, employers, schools, and hospitals are often ordered to share losses with their customers, employees, or students, even when there is no finding of negligence or even a causal link to the defendants' actions. As in cases involving participant liability, courts use arguments about fairness to impose an implied social contract that businesses and institutions must share in the losses of those off whom they profit, or those over whom they have control, even absent negligence.

Courts sometimes make the economic benefit rationale explicit. In a similar case to the Beijing case, from Henan Province,[66] the Yiyun Hotel was ordered to pay 20,000 yuan to the family of Mr. Shang, who died in the hotel after checking in drunk. The hotel's proprietor found Shang dead in his room the next morning. The cause of death was unknown, and the family rejected an autopsy. The court stated that the hotel was not at fault, but nevertheless cited the fact the hotel was financially benefiting from the victim's presence and said the hotel had failed to meet its "ethical obligation to provide humanistic care" to its guests.[67]

64 (2015) 朝民初字第04635号.

65 The court decision made no mention of drinking companions and, thus, it is not clear whether the victim was drinking alone or with others.

66 (2014) 泌民初字第94号.

67 In a similar case, a customer died in an internet cafe. The court noted that the death was due to an underlying physical condition, not excessive internet surfing, and that there was no evidence of negligence by the cafe. Nevertheless, the court noted that the staff had failed to discover the body until the next morning, and thus should pay "appropriate compensation" of 140,000 yuan. (2015) 朝民初字第68370号.

In the drinking cases, courts imply that businesses have some duty to care for their customers, or at least supervise them. In other cases, however, courts impose damages even when customers die of a heart attack on the premises. In a case from Liaoning Province, a court imposed liability on a public bathhouse, the Shenyang Dijia Women's Club, after a 72-year old customer, Ms. Xu, died of cardiac arrest.[68] The family declined an autopsy, and the court noted that the bathhouse had acted properly in calling an ambulance. Although the court said that the bathhouse had made "management errors" by failing to enforce the sign at the door refusing service to elderly customers in poor health bathing alone, it clearly stated that these errors did not cause Xu's death. Nevertheless, the court stated that the bathhouse had an obligation to pay because it was financially benefiting from her presence. The court ordered 20,000 yuan in "appropriate compensation" to "balance the rights and obligations of the parties." Similarly, a court in Guangdong Province ordered a health product shop to pay compensation to the family of a customer who died shortly after getting in a heated argument with the shopkeeper.[69] The shop had promised a free bag of eggs to anyone who attended a lecture about its products, and an argument developed when the shop refused to give a bag of eggs to both the decedent and his spouse. Although the court found that the plaintiff failed to show that the shop caused the death, the decision used the Tort Liability Law's fairness principle to order the shop to bear 20 percent of the plaintiffs' loss "according to the actual situation" of the case. The court also appeared to be signaling that it disapproved of the shop's marketing tactics, even if there was no direct link to the victim's death.

5.4.2.2 Employers

Courts also routinely rely on arguments about fairness based in the equitable liability provisions of the Tort Liability Law to impose liability on employers for injuries or deaths to employees, even when the harm is unrelated to employment. The implied argument is that the employer benefited from the victim's labor, and also that whoever has physical control over a workplace is responsible for anything that happens there, regardless of cause. Thus, for example, after a bus driver became sick and died on the job, the court asked both the company and the subcontractor who hired the decedent to pay damages, even though there was no link between the death and the employee's job.[70] The decision noted that the decedent was working for the subcontractor at the time of his death, and that he acted to the benefit of the company and its subcontractor when he managed to stop the bus without harming passengers when he became ill.[71] Similarly, a court in Jiangxi relied on arguments

68 (2017) 辽0105民初5490号.
69 (2017) 粤02民终1127号.
70 (2014) 陈民初字第02004号.
71 The court ordered the company to pay 20,000 yuan and the subcontractor who hired the decedent to pay 30,000 yuan. Ibid.

about fairness when a worker died of a hornet sting while working on a construction site.[72] The court ordered the employer to pay 110,000 yuan in compensation.[73] In similar cases involving sudden deaths at work, courts likewise found no negligence or causation on the part of the employer, but awarded damages "according to the actual circumstances"[74] or based on "fairness."[75] These cases place employers in a custodial or quasi-parental role vis-a-vis their employees, and hold them responsible for anything that happens to workers on the job.[76] In so doing, they extend far beyond law and regulations on work-related injuries.[77]

Other cases extend employers' obligations to compensate even beyond the workplace. In one such case, the victim was murdered on her way to work at a Henan internet cafe. The court found no connection between the murder and the employer, but relied on equitable liability principles to award 20,000 yuan in damages.[78] The court justified compensation "according to the actual circumstances" of the case, and included a note that the murderer had been executed without paying any compensation to the victim's family.[79]

[72] (2016) 赣07民终61号.

[73] There were three defendants in the case: two individuals and a company. The company had subcontracted the work to one defendant, who had then subcontracted the work to a second defendant, who had hired the decedent. The court ordered the individual who had directly hired the decedent to pay 50,000 yuan and the two other defendants to pay 30,000 yuan each.

[74] (2016) 鲁民终757号, holding the defendant liable when the employee died of an underlying heart condition suddenly while working on defendant's fishing boat.

[75] (2018) 新2325民初208号, in which the employee died suddenly while acting as a driver for the defendant, and neither party submitted evidence showing cause of death.

[76] In one such case, an employee was injured in a fight at work with a co-worker. Although finding no negligence, the court nevertheless ordered the employer to share 10 percent of the damages. (2017) 鄂96民终680号. Chinese law includes a provision explicitly imposing liability on beneficiaries of work carried out by victims. But the provisions apply to work undertaken for free where the injury or death results from the work, not employment situations or unrelated injuries. Supreme People's Court, 最高人民法院关于审理人身损害赔偿案件适用法律若干问题的解释 [Interpretation of the Supreme People's Court of Some Issues Concerning the Application of Law for the Trial of Cases on Compensation for Personal Injury].

[77] State Council regulations state that, in situations involving sudden death, or death within 48 hours of an emergency at work, compensation should be paid from workers compensation insurance rather than directly by the employer. In addition to covering workplace injuries, the regulations state that workers compensation funds shall only cover injuries occurring on the way to and from work arising from traffic accidents that are not primarily due to the worker's negligence. See State Council, 工伤保险条例 [Regulation on Work-related Injury Insurance] (2003).

[78] The court ordered the four shareholders in the café to split the compensation. The appellate court increased damages from 8,000 yuan to 20,000 yuan, noting the amount awarded by the trial court was "inappropriate" given the harm suffered. (2016) 豫07民终4414号.

[79] In another case involving an injury off-premises, the victim died of heart disease while traveling from work to the hospital. The court found no negligence or link to employment and noted that the employer had sent the employee to the hospital when he reported not feeling well. The court ordered both the defendant company and a subcontractor that had directly hired the decedent to each pay 20,000 yuan in compensation. The court stated it was "starting from the

5.4.2.3 Large Institutions

A third example of a space-based relationship giving rise to an obligation to compensate is between large public institutions, such as schools and hospitals, and the people who use them.[80] The principle is that injuries that occur on the premises of public institutions, or that befall those under their supervision, deserve compensation, even when there is no link to defendants' conduct. Litigation resulting from injuries suffered by children at school is a central and common[81] example of how courts have extended tort law to force certain public institutions to serve as virtual insurers of harm suffered on their watch.

Chinese law has clear provisions regarding injuries to children at school. For injuries to children who are eight years old or younger (ten or younger prior to 2017), schools have the burden of proof to show that they were not negligent.[82] For older children, the burden of proof is on the plaintiffs.[83] In practice, however, courts considering claims made on behalf of children injured during the school day virtually always order the school to pay compensation, even in cases involving older children in which plaintiffs fail to introduce evidence that schools were at fault.

In numerous cases, courts find that schools were not responsible for harm suffered by students, but nevertheless order compensation according to principles of equity. Thus, for example, in a case from Xixiang County in Shaanxi,[84] a fifth-grade student surnamed Xu injured his arm when he fell while running in an 800 meter race. He was hospitalized for ten days. Upon returning to school, Xu re-injured his arm when another student collided with him while exiting the classroom, leading to a second hospitalization and surgery. The court found that the school had taken all necessary steps to ensure the safety of its students and was not negligent. Nevertheless, the court ordered the school to assume 30 percent of the cost of the first injury, roughly 11,000 yuan, "in accordance with the actual situation."[85]

point of balancing the financial situation and property loss of each party" in compelling compensation. (2017) 粤13民终3235号.

80 Most schools and hospitals in China are public, and we did not see significant numbers of private large institutions in the cases we reviewed.

81 Two topics were primarily cases involving injuries at schools, with a combined topic proportion of 1.94 percent.

82 Articles 19 and 20 of the General Principles of the Civil Law, and Articles 1200 and 1201 of the Civil Code. Revisions to the General Principles in 2017 shifted the boundary between those who have diminished civil capacity and those who are deemed to lack civil capacity from ten to eight years old. Those who are sixteen or older are considered to have full capacity and are treated as adults.

83 Article 40 of the Tort Liability Law; Article 19 of the General Provisions of the Civil Law; Article 1200 of the Civil Code.

84 (2014) 西民初字第01035号.

85 The student who collided with Xu was held fully responsible for the second injury.

Similarly, in a case from Nanjing,[86] a first grader surnamed Chen was injured on the playground. He was running away from a child who was chasing him and collided with another classmate, suffering an injury to the nose which led to a five-day hospitalization. The court found that the school had not acted negligently, noting also that the children "were playing a game and their play should not be restricted," but nevertheless ordered the school and the guardians of each of the two children involved in the accident to each pay 2,000 yuan in compensation.

In some cases, courts explicitly acknowledge that they are guided by the view that those who suffer an injury should receive compensation, regardless of whether anyone acted negligently. In a case from Chongqing,[87] plaintiff Fan injured his arm while training for a high-jump competition and spent 48 days in the hospital. The court found that Fan himself was primarily responsible for the accident, due to his own lack of ability, rather than anything related to the quality of school facilities or oversight. Nevertheless, the court relied on "substantive justice" to assign secondary responsibility to the school and ordered them to pay 40 percent of the harm suffered. A situation in which there is no one to "settle the bill" for Fan's injury (无人买单的情形), the decision explicitly stated, would violate the principle that "where there are damages, there should be remedies" (有损害则应有救济).[88]

Schools are at times held liable even for injuries that occur outside of school, reinforcing the idea that they bear broad responsibility for their students' wellbeing. In September 2014, a nine-year-old child surnamed Wang drowned in a river flooded by heavy rain while walking home from school at lunchtime. Although a Henan court found that the death was not connected to the school, it nevertheless ordered the school to pay 50,000 yuan in compensation to Wang's family, noting that the death had caused "very large emotional harm" to his parents.[89] Likewise, in

86 (2015) 栖民初字第175号. See also (2016) 粤2072民初9006号 (ordering 10,000 yuan compensation "according to the actual circumstances" to a fourteen-year-old student who fell while running at school); (2013) 涪民初字第7035号 (ordering a school to pay 30 percent of the harm suffered when the plaintiff fell during gym class); (2017) 川1521民初1026号 (ordering a school to shoulder part of the cost of damages resulting from injuries sustained when an elementary school student cut in front of another student in the lunch line). In all of these cases, courts found no evidence of negligence on the part of the school.

87 (2015) 永法民初字第08225号.

88 Ibid. The court went on to suggest that, although the school was not directly negligent, it failed in its "safety protection obligations." This reasoning, invoking a vague reference to an obligation to supervise or to maintain safety, is common in school injury cases.

89 (2014) 确民初字第01570号. On appeal, the intermediate court ordered a retrial. On retrial, the county court found that the school was negligent because it dismissed students during a rainstorm without adequately warning them of the risks of walking home in the rain. The trial court also increased the damages from 50,000 yuan to 90,000 yuan. (2016) 豫1725民初256号. In its original decision, the trial court had found that there was no causal link between the school's decision to cancel afternoon classes and the injury, as the school had dismissed students at lunchtime as usual. The case suggests that courts may sometimes use equitable liability to avoid finding a defendant negligent, and thus to reduce damages.

a case from Beijing,[90] the plaintiffs' son was a student at a boarding school on the outskirts of the city. After returning home for the weekend he failed to return to school on Sunday. He was found drowned six days later, and the police concluded that there was no evidence of a crime. The court noted that the victim's death had not occurred at school, but that, in accordance with the "case situation," it was using its discretion to order the school to pay 20,000 yuan in compensation.

To check the representativeness of these cases, we read and coded 250 cases that discussed injuries that occurred at school. Courts awarded damages in 95 percent of cases (207 of 217 cases with data on outcomes),[91] confirming that schools are virtually always asked to pay for injuries that occur to children at school. Students, and the families of students, also recover fairly significant sums. In the school injury cases, plaintiffs received 50 percent or more of their demands in 60 percent of cases,[92] with an average award of 81,800 yuan.[93] The takeaway of this coding exercise is clear: schools assume responsibility for most of the damages suffered by children at school, at least during the time period covered by our dataset. Legal provisions that state that schools are not responsible if they can disprove negligence (for injuries to younger children) or if the plaintiff fails to show that schools were negligent (in cases involving older children) appear largely irrelevant. Typically, courts stretch to find some negligence, often relying on a general statement that schools failed to fulfill their duty to adequately supervise.[94]

Following the same logic as schools, courts also often push hospitals into the role of social insurer. Two topics in the topic model concerned medical disputes,[95] with courts generally imposing compensation on hospitals for catastrophic harm to patients, even absent evidence demonstrating negligence or medical malpractice. In a case from Jilin,[96] for example, the court imposed liability on a hospital that had initially treated a patient who had been hit by a car while walking home after drinking. The court found that the hospital had "made some mistakes," though the mistakes did not contribute to the patient's death. However, the court also noted the importance of balancing the interests of hospitals with "the weak position of

90 (2016) 京0105民初67665号.

91 The random sample was selected from cases citing to Articles 38 or 39 of the Tort Liability Law, the two primary provisions relating to injuries at school. Ten of the 250 cases were either duplicates or did not relate to school injuries. Twenty-three cases lacked information on amounts claimed or awarded.

92 Only 20 percent of cases (43 of 217 cases) awarded 25 percent or less of plaintiffs' demands.

93 School injury cases typically involve injuries rather than death. This explains the lower awards compared to the child drowning and death-by-drinking cases.

94 Only four cases cited the equitable liability provisions of the Tort Liability Law directly. This is not surprising, given that the Tort Liability Law included specific provisions governing injuries to children at school. But courts did frequently include language relating to fairness or equity, doing so in 45 percent of the cases (ninety-seven cases in total). Courts awarded damages in all of these cases.

95 The topic proportion of the two topics related to medical disputes was 2.48 percent.

96 (2015) 江林民初字第33号.

patients" and the importance of preventing patient–hospital conflict.[97] Likewise, in a case from Inner Mongolia, plaintiffs sued after a man died while waiting for an ambulance. The court found no evidence that the delay contributed to the victim's death. Nevertheless, the court ordered the hospital to pay compensation because the ambulance "should have been more prompt" and the plaintiff's family was in a "difficult financial condition."[98]

5.4.2.4 Rationales

In these cases, courts treat liability as a spatial concept. Sharing physical space triggers financial obligations. Businesses are asked to pay for accidents to customers on their premises, just as ordinary people are asked to pay when they are present at the scene of an accident. Courts are particularly likely to invoke space-based liability when the space is being used for profit, or when the space-owner is a public-facing institution such as a school or a hospital.[99] In both situations, courts ask defendants to assume custodial responsibility for those who enter their space, including sometimes injuries that happen off-site. In the case of businesses, part of the logic appears to be that profiting off customers and employees triggers an obligation to care for them. In cases involving state-run institutions, the assumption that the state will pay is anchored in a long history of state paternalism that predates the Chinese Communist Party (CCP), and is also a recurrent theme of CCP governance and contemporary civil litigation.[100]

Reading a range of space-based liability cases highlights variation in the amount of money that changes hands. Sometimes, especially when defendants are closer to struggling mom-and-pop shops than deep-pocketed corporations, courts award fairly minimal sums. In these cases, courts' logic appears similar to the vision of collective loss spreading that animated the participant liability cases. But more substantial awards are possible. Especially in cases involving (relatively) rich business-owners or state-run institutions, courts shift a fair amount of money from society's haves to its have-nots. Court-ordered redistribution effectively creates a social safety net for families experiencing emotional trauma and economic loss and, as legal scholars

97 In another example, the court awarded 20,000 yuan in damages for the death of an infant strangled by its umbilical cord during birth. The court found no negligence on the part of the hospital but nevertheless relied on equity provisions to ensure the parents of the child received compensation. (2018) 桂08民终382号.

98 (2015) 昆民初字第3413号.

99 Another good example is the landlord–tenant relationship. Our dataset includes a number of cases in which landlords are asked to pay compensation to tenants for injuries that happen on their properties, even absent evidence of negligence. One such case involved a tenant who died of carbon monoxide poisoning. The court found no evidence of negligence but held that requiring the plaintiffs – the parents of the deceased tenant – to bear the loss on their own "obviously would violate principles of fairness." (2014) 管民初字第902号.

100 For discussion of this dynamic, see B. Liebman, Legal Reform: China's Law-Stability Paradox (2014) 143 *Daedalus* 96–109; Liebman, Malpractice Mobs, 250–54.

writing in Chinese have noted, helps plaintiffs recover in situations where neither party has insurance.[101]

Another way of thinking about participant liability and space-based liability are as two implicit rationales Chinese courts use to adjudicate cases involving bad luck and catastrophic loss. To determine who should pay – and how much – Chinese courts look to the law, but also to unwritten expectations about the responsibilities triggered by certain types of relationships. Some types of cases can also be decided according to either logic. Although the vast majority of decisions in child drowning cases, for example, impose participant liability on the families of other swimmers, we also encountered a few space-based liability cases in which courts asked adjacent property owners with no link to the accident to pay compensation. In one such case, which involved a local boy who drowned in a river, a Hunan court ordered a nearby business that had profited from selling stones taken from the river to pay 50,000 yuan in compensation to the victim's family. The court acknowledged that there was no link between the stones and the death, but noted the massive loss suffered by the parents, whose fourteen-year-old child "had left the world without first repaying his parent's kindness and upbringing."[102]

To be sure, neither participant liability nor space-based liability are entirely new ideas. Legal culture is hardy and, at a minimum, Chinese courts are drawing on a centuries-old practice of attaching legal obligations to dyadic relationships as well as a twentieth-century socialist tradition of using law to strengthen social solidarity. The Qing Dynasty Code, to take one well-known historical antecedent, adjusted criminal penalties depending on the relationship between the parties. A son who struck a parent, for example, was punished far more harshly than an assault on a nonparent.[103] In the more recent past, twentieth-century socialist states leaned heavily on law to strengthen social solidarity,[104] a legacy that resurfaces in Chinese courts' impulse to ask the community collectively to share in catastrophic loss. Legal historians, of course, would expect to see these continuities, and could doubtless identify many more connections between past and present. For observers who are less attuned to history, however, these historical continuities serve as an important corrective to the idea that China is forging an entirely new model of justice under Xi Jinping. At the same time, too, the cases we read also show Chinese courts innovating as society changes, particularly by starting to assign legal responsibility in

[101] Y. Zhang notes the role that equitable liability provision plays in providing remedies where social insurance is lacking. See Zhang, 论公平责任的不当适用及其规范 [Discussing Erroneous Application of Equitable Liability and Its Regulation].

[102] (2017) 湘12民终592号.

[103] D. Bodde and C. Morris, *Law in Imperial China* (Philadelphia: University of Pennsylvania Press, 1967), p. 37.

[104] I. Markovitz, *Justice in Lüritz: Experiencing Socialist Law in East Germany* (Princeton: Princeton University Press, 2010). Professor Markovitz also notes, however, that over time "the East German goal of forging social solidarity by means of law over the years increasingly looked forced and artificial." Ibid. p. 201.

a wider range of relationships, such as sexual relationships outside marriage. Another emergent dyad is the relationship between schools and businesses, and the people who either use them or are employed by them. Chinese courts routinely ask schools and businesses to take financial responsibility for accidents that involve their employees, customers, or students beyond what is legally required, or take place on their premises (or even just nearby). The Chinese courts reflect – and also reinforce – a worldview that social order is sustained by family, community, commercial, and institutional relationships, and that part of their role is to make sure these relationships are maintained.

5.4.3 *Continuing Heterodoxy? Cases Adjudicated after the Adoption of the Civil Code*

How did courts respond to the changes to the Civil Code that restricted the use of equitable liability? To check, we ran the same term searches for cases involving child drownings and death-by-drinking cases in our database of cases uploaded from 2018–2022, looking at cases decided after January 1, 2021. For child drowning cases we read all 158 such cases; for death-by-drinking cases, we read a random sample of 500 cases decided in 2021 and all 151 cases decided in 2022.[105] We excluded cases that were not relevant, either because they involved irrelevant fact patterns or because the facts arose prior to January 1, 2021. In total we located eighty-five relevant child-drowning cases that arose after the implementation of the new Civil Code,[106] and 116 death-by-drinking cases that similarly arose under the new Civil Code.

In the drowning cases, courts awarded damages in sixty-four of the eighty-five cases, or 75 percent of cases, the same percentage success rate as in our initial sample of cases. In most of these cases – fifty-nine cases – courts did so by finding negligence, suggesting that courts are shifting from relying on fairness to finding negligence. In many of these cases, the finding of negligence appeared to be a stretch, imposing obligations on landowners to both warn of dangers and construct fences around their property.[107] In one case, a child fell into a ditch that had

[105] The decline in the number of cases decided in 2022 likely reflects both decreased rates of posting cases online and also the fact that not all cases had been uploaded by the time we obtained our dataset. We looked at 500 cases from 2021 (instead of the 250 we used in our original search) because we expected a significant number of cases to have arisen before the Civil Code came into effect. We did not rerun our searches for school injury cases because those cases are governed by specific legal provisions that did not change substantively in the new Civil Code.

[106] We located ninety-three court decisions relating to child drownings, reflecting eighty-five unique disputes. Eight of the judgments were either appeals from first-instance cases also in our database, or judgments against multiple defendants from disputes arising from the same incident.

[107] Other cases involved insufficient numbers of lifeguards at public swimming pools, or failure to warn of water hazards, or the partial demolition of bridges with no warnings posted. These cases appeared to be straightforward applications of negligence standards.

allegedly been dug by defendants.[108] In another, an unattended child drowned in a rice paddy; the court found that there should have been a fence around the field.[109] Damage awards were also significant, averaging 220,000 yuan in cases in which courts awarded damages.[110]

One court explicitly refuted arguments regarding fairness. The court rejected compensation to the family of a child against the local government after a fifteen-year-old drowned while fishing after ignoring posted warning signs, stating that "sympathy and mercy are not the same as judgment, and cannot be made into a duty."[111]

Yet other courts continued to apply fairness principles without citing to the equitable liability provision or noting the change in the law. Five decisions, or 7 percent of the new drowning cases, included reference to fairness principles. In one case, for example, a child drowned when an upstream power plant released water. The court noted that the release of water was a daily occurrence that local villagers knew about, and thus that there was no negligence.[112] But the court nevertheless awarded 40,000 yuan in damages, commenting that it was doing so in light of the fact that the defendant derived economic benefit from its activities and in light of "the parties' ability to pay." Another court noted that "although there was no clear negligence [on the part of two of the defendants], in consideration of the special circumstances of this case and according to principles of fairness, appropriate damages should be awarded."[113] In yet another case in which a child drowned while swimming, the court found no negligence but enforced a prior promise by the families of the surviving children to pay damages, noting that payment of "appropriate compensation" was in line with "socialist core values."[114]

In the death by drinking cases, courts awarded compensation in 91 of the 116 cases, or 78 percent of cases. This figure was slightly lower than the 85 percent success rate in our original dataset. In general, courts did so by finding that defendants were negligent. Yet particularly noteworthy were fifteen cases in which courts declared that defendants had not been negligent, but nevertheless imposed

[108] (2022) 鲁01民终884号.

[109] (2022) 黔2635民初105号.

[110] Average damages were thus significantly higher than the average payouts of 118,274 yuan in child drowning cases in our original dataset. Much of this increase likely reflects increases in income levels, as damage awards in tort cases are scheduled with reference to annual average provincial incomes.

[111] (2022) 宁0202民初956号. Courts awarded damages in only two of the eight cases where government actors were defendants, perhaps suggesting some reluctance to find government actors negligent or responsible.

[112] (2022) 赣10民终314号.

[113] (2022) 陕06民终871号. The court ordered each, both government entities, to pay 5 percent. Two other government defendants were found negligent, and the decision thus distributed the damage payment among additional government actors.

[114] (2021) 豫0225民初6094号.

liability. In twelve of these cases, courts made explicit reference to terms like "fairness," without citing a specific legal provision.

The themes of space-based liability and participant liability continued to manifest in the cases decided after the new Civil Code. Most of the cases involved courts holding drinking companions liable. In one case, for example, a court held drinking companions liable when a man committed suicide after drinking. The court noted that the defendants had physically restrained the defendant when he tried to jump off a bridge and then had taken him home. When the deceased fled they pursued him and notified the police and family. The court nevertheless found the defendants negligent and ordered compensation.[115] Some courts also imposed space-based liability on businesses. In one case,[116] for example, a court imposed liability on a hotel when hotel staff found a guest passed out from drinking. The court noted that the employees failed to seek help, and also noted that it was imposing liability based on the court's "discretion."

As with the child drowning cases, there were some signs of courts becoming stricter in the application of fairness provisions in the death-by-drinking cases. One appeals court explicitly overturned a judgment against a drinking companion by noting that courts may not rely on fairness principles without applying a specific legal provision.[117] Lawsuits against bars, restaurants, and hotels were much less common than they were in our original dataset.

Taken together, cases decided under the new Civil Code suggest that Chinese courts continue to seek equitable outcomes. To some degree, courts have used the broad discretion they have in making determinations about defendants' negligence to do so. But some courts have also continued to make explicit reference to fairness principles or have shifted from relying on fairness arguments to citing "socialist core values." Legal heterodoxy in tort cases may be more muted under the Civil Code, but it nevertheless persists in practice.

5.5 CONCLUSION

Looking at a large number of tort cases that involve largely accidental misfortune reveals that courts consistently stray from or stretch the law to achieve outcomes that recognize the ethical as well as legal obligations that arise out of relationships. When cases involving misfortune arise in the Chinese legal system, courts often turn to two de facto doctrines – participant liability and space-based liability – to craft solutions that appeal both to notions of fairness and to practical needs to ensure victims receive some compensation. The range of cases this chapter examines reveals that

[115] (2021) 豫1381民初6635号.
[116] (2021) 湘3125民初438号.
[117] (2022) 鲁11民终402号. Co-defendants did not appeal, and thus the trial court's fairness-based decision against them was not reversed.

courts stretch the law to ensure that compensation is paid and loss is acknowledged. Courts have continued to do so even after China's Civil Code restricted fairness-based adjudication.

Worldwide, restoring equilibrium in a community has long been recognized as an important part of what courts do, particularly in small towns where disputants will remain neighbors long after the case concludes.[118] It is also a familiar theme in the literature on twentieth-century socialist legal systems, which tended to view trials as an educational opportunity to reinforce societal values by punishing outcasts.[119] Stretching the law to ensure communal sharing of losses has remained an important strand of Chinese legal culture even following decades of urbanization, a wide range of legal reforms that have in significant part been based on adapting legal norms from the Global North into the Chinese legal system, and a tightening of political control under General Secretary Xi Jinping. It routinely happens in big cities, such as Beijing and Shanghai, as well as in rural areas. And when courts engage in loss-spreading, the economic and social implications take on a new dimension in the twenty-first century. On the economic side, court-ordered redistribution backstops state benefits and smooths the pain of rising income inequality. On the social side, treating catastrophic loss as a community event marks a renewed attempt to create social solidarity through law. In some cases the sums awarded are substantial; in others, the awards appear to be primarily symbolic. But the cases suggest that there is also value in this symbolism, an understanding that even symbolic awards may play a role in fostering social cohesion.

Is this practice of Chinese courts looking to fairness and equity as they seek to spread and acknowledge losses through tort cases heterodox? In many respects, yes. Courts have developed consistent legal doctrine based on a specific legal provision that helps to smooth the rough edges of some of China's most pressing policy problems: rising economic inequality and a weak social safety system. Particularly when significant sums change hands, the courts are blunting the sharp edges of inequality by redistributing wealth. Even when awards are modest, court decisions that treat catastrophic loss as a community event may send important signals recognizing tragic loss and the social obligation to support others. This practice has persisted despite a legal system (and legal academia) dominated for much of the reform era by the importation of foreign ideas and models, and in particular

118 One classic discussion of this dynamic is L. Nader, *Harmony Ideology: Justice and Control in a Zapotec Mountain Village* (Redwood City: Stanford University Press, 1993).

119 Many socialist legal systems drew inspiration from how the USSR used courts to try to help mold new Socialist citizens. In his 1959 report to the 21st Communist Party Congress, Party Secretary Nikita Khrushchev called for an overhaul of the courts in order to focus "on questions of everyday behavior and morality … [and] deviations from the standards of public order … It is necessary to undertake such measures as would prevent and then completely eliminate the appearance in individuals of any misdemeanors which cause harm to society" (quoted in H. J. Berman and J. W. Spindler, Soviet Comrades' Courts (1963) 38 *Washington Law Review* 842–910, 854–55).

scholarship and practice from the United States and Western Europe. China's practice of tort law heterodoxy reflects both a particular worldview and the pursuit of specific policy goals.[120] The fact that tort law heterodoxy has persisted in China despite the lack of economic volatility or crisis, and in a system with a very different colonial history than many of the countries examined in this volume,[121] demonstrates that legal heterodoxy may persist and flourish across a wide range of legal systems. It is also a reminder that, despite the focus of much scholarship on the Chinese legal systems on either economic development or social stability and regime survival, other non-modular goals also shape how Chinese courts adjudicate cases.[122]

The Chinese legal system's willingness to award compensation without fault also raises questions about the nature of legal heterodoxy. First, how do socialist legal systems fit into a framework that focuses on differences between the Global North and Global South? China's tort law heterodoxy is a reminder to take socialist legal systems seriously in any discussion of legal heterodoxy in the Global South. What we see in practice in China is not just courts relying on heterodox legal provisions to address inequality or provide social welfare on the cheap, but also to pursue a particular social vision. Chinese courts are active participants in the broader state project of creating a particular conception of a good society.[123] Comparative law scholarship too often views socialist legality as a historical relic. Regardless of whether China is viewed as a developing or developed legal system, the practice of tort law in China shows that the socialist legal tradition persists and remains central to the role courts play. Understanding tort law heterodoxy as part of this tradition also helps to explain why China does not fit perfectly into the framework of this book: scholars who criticized the equitable liability provisions were pushing back against a different sort of orthodoxy, one rooted in China's socialist traditions (although they rarely do so directly). Yet, even if not a perfect fit, socialist tort law heterodoxy helps to illuminate an important contribution of the theory of legal heterodoxy. Much scholarship on China's courts focuses on whether courts follow

[120] K. Davis and M. Pargendler, Chapter 1.

[121] Although China had its own experience with colonialism, including colonial law, China's modern legal development started in 1978 with the reconstruction of the legal system from the ground up after the Cultural Revolution.

[122] On the concept of modularity, see Davis and Pargendler, Chapter 1.

[123] To be sure, this is not a new view of Chinese courts. Nearly four decades ago, comparative law scholar Mirjan Damaska wrote about how activist states strive "toward a comprehensive theory of the good life," such that law is "directive, even hectoring, . . . tell[ing] citizens what to do and how to behave." See M. R. Damaska, *The Faces of Justice and State Authority: A Comparative Approach to the Legal Process* (New Haven: Yale University Press, 1986), pp. 80 and 82. In the 1980s, when Damaska was writing, Maoist China would have been an archetypal example of an activist state. Today, our findings suggest that this activist orientation toward law persists, even if the CCP's theory of "the good life" has blurred to the point where it is hard to discern much beyond the oft-repeated public commitments to socialist core values, Communist Party leadership, and continued economic growth.

the law or ignore it: scholars look for legality, sometimes at the expense of understanding what courts actually do. Legal heterodoxy reminds us that focusing on consistent legal patterns of adjudication – examining what courts actually do – is more important than the legal/nonlegal binary that often dominates evaluation of court practice in China (and elsewhere in the Global South).

Second, how and when does legal heterodoxy continue even when formal law shifts toward orthodoxy? China's experience highlights the importance of continuing to examine legal heterodoxy in practice. Substantive law certainly matters – it was the basis on which Chinese courts relied for equity-based decisions, even when they did not cite the specific provisions of the General Principles of the Civil Law or the Tort Liability Law. Yet initial evidence also suggests that legal heterodoxy has persisted even after the equitable liability provisions were significantly curtailed. At one level this is not surprising: the interests of lawmakers and scholars advocating changes to the formal law were clearly different from the interests of judges who not only must adjudicate cases but also meet societal and Party-state expectations and demands. But the deeper point is that as scholarship on legal heterodoxy evolves, comparing when and where heterodoxy persists even when written law shifts toward orthodoxy may yield insights across jurisdictions. In particular, scholars may want to examine differences in approaches among judges based on education, location, age, or other factors.

Third, to what degree does regime type affect theories of legal heterodoxy? On the one hand, there is nothing particularly authoritarian about the practice of tort law heterodoxy in China: other legal systems at times adjudicate cases in very similar ways.[124] But in a world characterized by resurgent authoritarianism and democratic backsliding, is legal practice equally heterodox if it is the product of democratic or nondemocratic processes? One insight that comes from studying tort cases in China is that it is a mistake to view everything that seems unusual when placed in comparative perspective (in particular when compared to the Global North) as due to China's political system and its obsession with social stability. Other legal systems similarly consider fairness and social impact in deciding civil cases. Another insight is that regime type is not irrelevant, either in understanding the roots of heterodox laws or actual court practice. Indeed, much of what appears to be non-modular in China can be explained by a focus on social stability and regime survival. Yet our findings also demonstrate how courts can pursue other nonmodular goals. Our discussion of Chinese tort litigation raises the question of why tort law – and private law generally[125] – have become the site where issues regarding equity and fairness are contested and adjudicated in China. One answer may be the lack of a divide between private

[124] See, for example, the discussion of Brazilian practice in Davis and Pargendler, Chapter 1.

[125] Scholarship on Chinese law has noted a range of areas, from family law to contract to labor disputes, in which courts similarly pursue goals that seek to ensure both stability and fairness. Stern et al., Liability beyond Law.

and public law in China combined with the weakness of public law. Asking the same question across a range of countries in the Global South may yield insights into the sources of legal heterodoxy. As scholarship on legal heterodox continues to develop, scholars may want to consider in greater depth how politics shapes legal heterodoxy – and how our views and understanding of heterodoxy may be dependent on the political systems in which such norms and practices develop.

BIBLIOGRAPHY

Abraham, K., *The Forms and Functions of Tort Law* (St. Paul: Foundation Press, 2022).

Berman, H. J. and Spindler, J. W., Soviet Comrades' Courts (1963) 38 *Washington Law Review* 842–910.

Bodde, D. and Morris, C., *Law in Imperial China* (Philadelphia: University of Pennsylvania Press, 1967).

China Central Television, 中国共产党第十六届中央委员会第三次全体会议公报 [*Report of the Third Plenum of the 16th Party Congress of the Chinese Communist Party*] (2021).

Chen, K. 公平责任一般条款的司法适用: -以100份侵权案件判决书为分析样本 [Judicial Application of Ordinary Provisions Employing Equitable Liability: Using 100 Tort Cases as a Sample for Analysis] (2015) 1 *法律适用 [Applied Law]* 11–16.

中国民法典侵权责任编的创新与发展 [The Innovation and Development of Tort Liability in the Chinese Civil Code] 2020 3 *中国法律评论 [China Law Review]* 46–61.

民法典侵权责任编的体系结构及总则部分的完善 [The Systematic Structure of the Civil Code's Tort Liability Book and Improvements to the General Provisions] (2018) 6 *财经法学 [Economic and Financial Legal Studies]* 5–22.

Damaska, M., *The Faces of Justice and State Authority: A Comparative Approach to the Legal Process* (New Haven: Yale University Press, 1986).

Dou, H., 侵权法中公平分担损失规则的司法适用 [Judicial Application of Equitable Loss-Sharing Rules in Tort Law] (2016) 5 *法商研究 [Research into Law and Commerce]* 125–36.

Editorial Department of Law Textbooks, *Compilation Group of Materials on Civil Law Principles*, 外国民法资料选编 [*Selected Foreign Civil Law Materials*] (Beijing: Law Press, 1983).

Lee, M. and Mimno, D., Low-dimensional Embeddings for Interpretable Anchor-based Topic Inference (2014) *Proceedings of the 2014 Conference on Empirical Methods in Natural Language Processing*, Doha, Qatar, 1319–28.

Liebman, B., Legal Reform: China's Law-Stability Paradox (2014) 143 *Daedalus* 96–109.

Liebman, B. L., Malpractice Mobs: Medical Dispute Resolution in China (2013) 113 *Columbia Law Review* 181–264.

Ordinary Tort Litigation in China: Law versus Practical Justice? (2020) 13 *Journal of Tort Law* 197–228.

Liebman, B. L. et al., Mass Digitization of Chinese Court Decisions: How to Use Text as Data in the Field of Chinese Law (2020) 8 *Journal of Law and Courts* 177–201.

Liu, C., Socialized Liability in Chinese Tort Law (2018) 59 *Harvard International Law Journal* 16–44.

Mao, D., 公平责任典型案例探析 [Analysis of Typical Cases Involving Equitable Liability] (2019) 9 *法制与经济 [Legal System and Economics]* 15–16.

Markovitz, I., *Justice in Lüritz: Experiencing Socialist Law in East Germany* (Princeton: Princeton University Press, 2010).

Nader, L., *Harmony Ideology: Justice and Control in a Zapotec Mountain Village* (Redwood City: Stanford University Press, 1993).

Roberts, M. E., Stewart, B. M., and Tingley, D., STM: An R Package for Structural Topic Models (2019) 91 *Journal of Statistical Software* 1–40.

Shi, G. and Xie, C., 前民法典时代公平责任的适用：裁判误区与应然路径 [Application of Equitable Liability in the Pre-Civil Code Era: Adjudicatory Errors and the Normative Path] (2019) 9 *河南社会科学 [Henan Social Sciences]* 25–37.

Stern, R. E. et al., Liability beyond Law: Conceptions of Fairness in Chinese Tort Cases (2023) 11 *Asian Journal of Law and Society* 1–24.

Wang, L., *侵权责任法研究（上卷）[Research on Tort Liability Law (Volume I)]* (Beijing: China Renmin University Press, 2010).

Wang, Z., 我国侵权法上"公平责任"源流考 [An Examination of the Origins of "Equitable Liability" in Chinese Tort Law] (2008) 3 *甘肃政法学院学报 [Journal of the Gansu Institute of Political Science and Law]* 138–44.

Xinhua News, 20th Congress of the Communist Party of China (2022) 高举中国特色社会主义伟大旗帜 为全面建设社会主义现代化国家而团结奋斗 – 在中国共产党第二十次全国代表大会上的报告 [Hold High the Great Banner of Socialism with Chinese Characteristics and Strive for the Comprehensive Construction of a Socialist Modernized Country – Report at the 20th National Congress of the Communist Party of China], *Xinhua News*, October 25, 2022.

Yu, X., 公平责任"是否"公平" – 以二十世纪新侵权法理论为视角 [Is "Equitable Liability" Really "Equitable" – A Perspective from New Tort Liability Theory in the Twentieth Century] (2017) 12 *政治与法律 [Politics and Law]* 107–22.

Zhang, Y., 论公平责任的不当适用及其规范 [Discussing Erroneous Application of Equitable Liability and Its Regulation] (2019) 4 *法制与社会 [Legal System and Society]* 14–15.

6

Evictions during the Pandemic

An Empirical Discussion from the Brazilian Law Perspective

Bianca Tavolari and Saylon A. Pereira

6.1 INTRODUCTION

On the morning of July 31, 2021, a demonstration in front of the US Capitol drew the attention of those passing through the city center. Unlike the events of January 6th of the same year, which further exposed the social divide of an already divided country, the August protest was small in number, peaceful, and silent. Faced with the impending congressional recess, Democratic Representative Cori Bush from Missouri, serving in her first term, decided she would not leave the demonstration until lawmakers voted to extend the eviction moratorium adopted in response to the COVID-19 pandemic. The decision to sleep in front of the building for five days in a folding chair, with her orange sleeping bag, was extreme.[1] But for Bush, the Congressional decision to go on a seven-week summer recess without discussing the suspension of evictions that was about to expire, and would therefore allow the immediate eviction of thousands of families who could not afford to pay their rent, was even more serious.[2] The *sit-in*, an activist tactic widely employed by the civil rights movement in the United States throughout the 1960s, gained supporters: at the beginning of August protesters joined the congresswoman in solidarity with the cause of preventing evictions. Congress left on recess without extending its moratorium. In response, on August 3rd, the Biden administration's Centers for Disease Control and Prevention (CDC) announced a 60-day extension of the eviction moratorium in light of the escalation of infections associated with the Delta variant.[3]

[1] N. Fandos, With Capitol Sit-In, Cori Bush Galvanized a Progressive Revolt over Evictions, *The New York Times*, August 4, 2021.

[2] V. Stracqualursi, House Democrat Sleeps on Capitol Steps as She Blasts Lawmakers over Expiring Eviction Moratorium, *CNN*, August 2, 2021.

[3] J. Eballos-Roig, Biden Administration Rolls Out 60-Day Targeted Eviction Ban Aimed at Protecting Millions of Renters from Losing Their Homes, *Insider*, August 3, 2021.

The executive measure would soon be challenged by the US Supreme Court, putting an end to the federal eviction moratorium.[4]

In the United States, the eviction moratorium was created as an emergency measure in response to the pandemic. It was part of the CARES Act, a federal law passed by the US Congress on March 27, 2020.[5] Section 4024, titled *Temporary moratorium on eviction filings*, prevented landlords both from filing eviction actions to regain possession of rented properties and from collecting rent or even fines from tenants.[6] The measure was initially established for 120 days, with successive extensions by Congress, and was in effect until July 31, 2021. The initial response from the legislature was very different from the position expressed by then-President Donald Trump, who declared that landlords would "take it easy," suggesting that rental relationships did not need any course correction in the midst of the pandemic.[7]

Among the many impacts of the COVID-19 pandemic, the impact on housing was a central concern. While vaccines were not yet available, social isolation was a fundamental measure to prevent and reduce virus contamination. Staying at home became a matter of life or death. The necessary condition was, of course, to have a place to live. But not only that: it was necessary to ensure some security of permanence, that is, that housing would be a point of security and not instability while the health risks persisted. As a result, governments in several countries adopted emergency policies to prevent the worsening of the housing crisis, which meant, in many cases, changing the rules governing rental contracts, especially residential ones. The solutions found to avoid evictions and mitigate the housing impacts of the health crisis involved different legal and institutional arrangements, including suspension of landlords' ability to enforce their rights, creation of public funds to pay the rent of vulnerable people, adoption of rules permitting installment payments or requiring negotiation, and even combined measures.[8]

4 The main basis of the decision by the US Supreme Court was the CDC's lack of authority to declare a nationwide eviction moratorium. See *Alabama Association of Realtors et al. v. Department of Health and Human Services et al.*, 141 S. Ct. 2485 (2021). Cori Bush, Alexandria Ocasio-Cortez, and ninety-two other lawmakers signed a manifesto against the Supreme Court's decision the following day, addressed to Nancy Pelosi, Speaker of the House, and Charles Schumer, then Majority Leader in Congress: A. Pressley et al., Eviction Moratorium Extension Letter, Congress of the United States, August 27, 2021. Local eviction moratoriums were not affected by the decision.

5 For the processing of the Coronavirus Aid, Relief, and Economic Security Act, see Congress. Gov, S.3548 – CARES Act, www.congress.gov/bill/116th-congress/senate-bill/3548.

6 For the specific text of section 4024, see Digital Library – National Consumer Law Center, Sec. 4024. Temporary Moratorium on Eviction Filings, https://library.nclc.org/sec-4024-temporary-moratorium-eviction-filings.

7 For an analysis, see B. Tavolari, O Aluguel no Centro da Crise, *Novos Estudos*, May 13, 2020.

8 For a comparison of policies adopted by OECD member countries during the pandemic, see The Organization for Economic Cooperation and Development, HC3.3. Evictions, OECD Affordable Housing Database, May 27, 2021.

The United States was one of the first countries to approve legislative measures regarding rent. In a country where over 44 million households rented in 2020 – with historically underreported numbers for rental housing, as stated by the Census Bureau[9] – movements under the banner of "*cancel the rent*" began to form during the pandemic, demanding the incorporation of redistributive justice criteria and state intermediation in contracts between landlords and tenants.[10]

If in the United States the response from Congress was immediate and the Supreme Court only ruled against extension of the eviction moratorium in the middle of its second year and after Congress had allowed the moratorium to expire, the Brazilian case followed a similar script, but with completely inverted signs. In Brazil, even though the initial attempt to establish transition rules for rent came from the federal legislature, the first enforceable protective regulation would only be established on June 3, 2021, in the middle of the second year of the pandemic, through the interim decision of Justice Luís Roberto Barroso in the Action for Noncompliance with a Fundamental Precept (*Ação de Descumprimento de Preceito Fundamental*) 828 (or simply ADPF 828).

The inverted signals are both temporal and institutional. The protection against evictions in Brazil effectively begins when the eviction moratorium *ends* in the United States, which means that the Brazilian government did not adopt any transitional measure during the most critical period of the pandemic, when vaccines were not yet available. The timing of the decision-making process was also reversed: the urgent approval of the protective measure as a federal law in the United States contrasts with the inaction from the Brazilian legislature. In addition, the supreme courts of both countries had opposite roles: The US Supreme Court decided to end the moratorium while the Brazilian Supreme Court decided to initiate protective rules.

6.2 LEGAL HETERODOXY AND ORTHODOXY BETWEEN NORTH AND SOUTH

Heterodoxy is a relational concept. As Kevin Davis and Mariana Pargendler describe in Chapter 1, legal heterodoxy is employed to address a deviation from what has been conventionally adopted by countries of the Global North, in a very specific sense: deviations that incorporate distinct public policy objectives beyond economic efficiency into law, demonstrating a greater concern with distributive goals, taken

[9] For data from the 2020 US Census, see United States Census Bureau, 2020 Census Results,: www.census.gov/programs-surveys/decennial-census/decade/2020/2020-census-results.html. For systematized data on housing and rental, see National Multifamily Housing Council, Quick Facts: Resident Demographics, www.nmhc.org/research-insight/quick-facts-figures/quick-facts-resident-demographics/.

[10] K. Y. Taylor, Cancel the Rent, *The New Yorker*, May 12, 2020; M. Brady et al., Why We (Still) Need to Cancel the Rent, Movement Policy Brief Series, *NYU Urban Democracy Lab*, June 24, 2020.

forward not only in the legislative arena, but especially by courts. There is, therefore, a twofold dimension. First, the recognition by law of concern with inequalities – a *content* dimension – and, second, the fact that courts play a decisive role in this recognition – a *procedural* or *institutional* dimension. Due to its relational nature, determining legal heterodoxy implies an opposition to an established legal orthodoxy. The conceptual opposition is useful if understood not in purely descriptive or normative terms, but as an analytical tool.

When it comes specifically to contract law, legal orthodoxy may be characterized by a formal notion of equality between parties and by the argument that contracts should not be designed to address any kind of distributive goals.[11] The orthodox paradigm admits some leeway for the inclusion of social aims other than efficiency: if contract law is to have any role in combating economic inequalities, it should be explicitly designed by elected lawmakers rather than courts.[12] Thus, contract law orthodoxy has a two-dimensional character: formal equality and *pacta sunt servanda* as the main *content*, and a rejection of courts as the legitimate site for changing the rules that govern the contract as the main *institutional* claim. Conversely, heterodoxy is characterized by contract interpretation and adjudication guided by external public and collective values determined by courts.

Given these initial definitions, we interpret Brazil as a case of legal heterodoxy and the United States as a case of legal orthodoxy regarding protection from evictions during the pandemic. Both contract law and property law are at the center of the discussion on lease or rental contracts, as private agreements that govern the rules of use, access, and distribution to a bundle of rights linked to private property, specifically to ownership of real estate.[13]

In the case of Brazil, this legal heterodoxy may be explained by a set of decisive legal and political features. The Brazilian 1988 Constitution is characterized by its dirigisme, with a constitutional text deeply influenced by the constitutional movements of the nineteenth century – the extensive list of social rights and transformative objectives that bind the state, such as poverty eradication and reducing social and regional inequalities, are evocative of this point. The 1988 Constitution has also granted a central role to the Brazilian judiciary in the structure of the state apparatus, with an especially prominent role assigned to the Brazilian Supreme Court (*Supremo Tribunal Federal*). The Brazilian Supreme Court is, at the same time, a constitutional court, and a court of appeal. The comparative ease of access to courts

[11] See K. E. Davis and M. Pargendler, Contract Law and Inequality (2022) 107 *Iowa Law Review* 1485–41.

[12] See K. E. Davis and M. Pargendler, Contract Law Heterodoxy (2022) 4 *Revue Européenne du Droit* 92–97.

[13] For one of the main accounts of the bundle of property rights, see J. Waldron, What Is Private Property? (1985) 5 *Oxford Journal of Legal Studies* 313–49. For an analysis of how property and contract are decisive legal instruments to create and distribute wealth, see K. Pistor, *The Code of Capital: How Law Creates Wealth and Inequality* (Princeton: Princeton University Press, 2020).

of law in general has transformed the Brazilian judiciary into a privileged arena for several legal political disputes.

Moreover, housing is a constitutional right in Brazil, as one of the social rights enshrined in Article 6. However, it was not a guaranteed social right in the constitution's original text of 1988. It was incorporated twelve years later, in 2000, by a constitutional amendment.[14] Nonetheless, the original constitutional text established the "social function" of property as a fundamental right with the same status as the right to private property and, even before that, since at least 1916 housing had been recognized on an infra-constitutional level by the Brazilian Civil Code. We have, therefore, the grounds for what we are calling legal heterodoxy: The Constitution recognizes housing as a social right and guarantees broad access to courts authorized to apply and enforce the right. The constitutional recognition is also a reference in cases that involve the enforcement of private agreements.[15]

This does not mean, however, that the right to housing is fully enforced in all private legal relations or that courts consistently and regularly apply the right to housing to compensate for or correct inequalities in housing.[16] As we will discuss further in Section 6.3, the Brazilian bill on the Emergency and Transitional Legal Regime for private law relations during the pandemic period was not at all protective of the right to housing in private agreements, indicating a mismatch between enshrined constitutional rights and specific protections discussed and established by the legislative chambers. But the fact that the right to housing is a constitutional social right changes the *legal grammar* of the discussion: it can be claimed as a legal argument in specific lawsuits, and its lack of recognition by the state may be legitimately criticized as a violation of a fundamental right. The right to housing is, therefore, a yardstick for immanent critique of legal reasoning, judicial decisions, legislative decision-making and measures adopted by the executive, in all three levels of the Brazilian federation, encompassing the Union, States, and municipalities.

This legal and institutional scenario deviates quite drastically from the one in the United States, where the right to housing is not guaranteed by the federal constitution, the country has not signed the International Covenant on Economic, Social, and Cultural Rights, and, as a consequence, there is relatively little scope for using

[14] Constitutional Amendment No. 26/2000. The amendment was originally proposed in 1998 (*Proposta de Emenda à Constituição* No. 601/1998). For an analysis of the changes in the legal protection of the right to housing in Brazil from 1992, when Brazil signed the International Covenant on Economic, Social and Cultural Rights, which includes the right to housing in an international human rights perspective, until 2004, after the constitutional amendment, see M. P. Morais et al., Monitorando o Direito à Moradia no Brasil (1992–2004) (2006) 12 *IPEA Políticas Sociais – Acompanhamento e Análise* 230–41.

[15] See V. A. Silva, *A Constitucionalização do Direito: Os Direitos Fundamentais nas Relações entre Particulares* (São Paulo: Malheiros, 2005).

[16] For a discussion of the Brazilian Housing Financial System and how courts systematically deny the right to housing in mortgage contracts, see M. Schapiro and S. Alves, Developmental State with Neoliberal Tools: A Portrait of the Brazilian Housing Financial System (2019) 12 *Law and Development Review* 457–93.

the courts to protect shelter needs in private agreements.[17] As we will see, the United States is, in relation to Brazil, characterized as a case of legal orthodoxy since the protection against evictions during the pandemic was enacted by Congress. But, even if the legal and institutional conditions are so different as to establish the deviation, there are several similar aspects that bring both countries together when it comes to the pandemic. The United States and Brazil are on the top tier of the most populated countries and among the most severely hit by COVID-19 when it comes to death tolls.[18] Politically, both countries had presidents with autocratic tendencies who downplayed the impact of the virus, the importance of science and vaccines, and tried to delegitimize the recommendations of the World Health Organization. We have, therefore, legal, and institutional deviation, which makes the case for a legal heterodoxy/orthodoxy relational analysis.

By establishing an even stronger link between the right to housing and the right to life, the COVID-19 pandemic placed pressure on countries that previously did not incorporate rental housing into redistributive public policies to do so. Prior to the pandemic, both the United States and Brazil lacked substantive public policy arrangements that addressed rental relations in view of distributive objectives – with perhaps the exception of some municipal initiatives that establish housing units with rent control, such as in New York, or still-timid social rental housing policies for specific vulnerable groups, such as in São Paulo.

We aim to show that, unlike the United States, which prevented the filing of eviction actions through legislative means and, therefore, followed a path close to legal orthodoxy, the Brazilian case is a clear example of heterodoxy in establishing distributive and protective objectives for rental contracts through the judiciary after failing to adopt safeguarding conditions via legislation. In addition, although there is a tradition in Brazil of enforcing social rights through the Supreme Court,[19] cases related to the right to housing were still very concentrated on specific issues – such as the possibility of seizing a guarantor's family property in residential and

[17] C. Hartman, The Case for a Right to Housing (1998) 9 *Housing Policy Debate* 223–46; M. Foscarinis, The Growth of a Movement for a Human Right to Housing in the United States (2007) 20 *Harvard Human Rights Journal* 35–40; C. Lamb, Congress, the Courts, and Civil Rights: The Fair Housing Act of 1968 Revisited (1982) 27 *Villanova Law Review* 1115–62.

[18] According to the World Health Organization Database, the death tolls for the United States and Brazil were the most acute in absolute numbers: there have been 1,127,152 deaths by COVID-19 in the United States and 704,659 in Brazil. See World Health Organization, WHO COVID-19 Dashboard, https://covid19.who.int/. In terms of COVID-19 daily confirmed cases, the comparison of both countries shows a very similar timeline, with coinciding peaks. See Our World in Data, Daily New Confirmed COVID-19 Cases per Million People, https://encurtador.com.br/ehozF.

[19] This is especially the case for the social right to health. See D. W. L. Wang, Courts and Health Care Rationing: The Case of the Brazilian Federal Supreme Court (2013) 8 *Health Economics, Policy and Law* 75–93; O. L. M. Ferraz, The Right to Health in the Courts of Brazil: Worsening Health Inequities? (2009) 11 *Health and Human Rights Journal* 33–45. For a specific case of enforcement of the social right to health regarding intellectual property rights, see Chapter 8, by Carlos Portugal Gouvêa.

commercial rental agreements, for example[20] – and not on a broad discussion of evictions and displacement. Thus, as in other fundamental areas, such as criminal justice, the pandemic can be seen as a "critical juncture" for the constitutional right to housing, a moment which partially alters the functioning of institutions, with important reinterpretations.[21] The Supreme Court's decision on ADPF 828 may be regarded simultaneously as an innovative rupture with its previous jurisprudence on social rights, which did not comprehensively cover the right to housing,[22] and a continuation of the Court's general tradition of enforcing social rights.

This chapter is part of a broader and ongoing research project on protections for the right to housing during the pandemic in Brazil. The project covers (i) legislative discussions surrounding transition rules for rent, which were weakened during the passage of Law No. 14,010 of June 10, 2020, creating the Emergency and Transitional Legal Regime for private law relations during the pandemic period;[23] (ii) legislative discussions that led to the proposal of several bills, initiated by lawmakers from different positions in the Brazilian political spectrum, aimed at creating protective rules to prevent evictions and repossessions, which ultimately culminated in the approval of Law No. 14,216, promulgated only on October 7, 2021, months after the Supreme Court's decision;[24] (iii) an analysis of Minister Luís Roberto Barroso's decision in ADPF No. 828 of June 3, 2021, as well as constitutional complaints filed from them,[25] the deference of lower courts to the decision, and the legal arguments

[20] See T. Acca, Uma Análise da Doutrina Brasileira dos Direitos Sociais: Saúde, Educação e Moradia entre os Anos de 1964 e 2006, Master's Thesis, University of São Paulo Law School (2009); N. C. Campos, A Efetividade do Direito à Moradia no Judiciário Brasileiro: Uma Análise Comparativa da Jurisprudência, Thesis, Escola de Formação da Sociedade Brasileira de Direito Público – SBDP (2010); M. Silva, Colisão de Direitos Fundamentais: Como o STF faz a Ponderação entre o Direito à Propriedade e o Direito Social à Moradia em Contratos de Locação na Área Urbana?, Thesis, Escola de Formação da Sociedade Brasileira de Direito Público – SBDP (2020).

[21] For this diagnosis, see M. R. Machado, and N. P. Vasconcelos, Uma Conjuntura Crítica Perdida: a COVID-19 nas Prisões Brasileiras (2021) 12 *Revista Direito e Práxis* 2015–43.

[22] The scenario is composed of a few cases collectively decided by the Supreme Court's plenary on the right to housing, with another scenario not yet systematically mapped regarding monocratic decisions at the appellate level. In the case concerning the protection of the guarantor's family property in lease contracts, the Supreme Court held that the inclusion of the right to housing in 2000 did not alter the interpretation of Federal Law No. 8,009 of 1990, which had determined the possibility of seizure of the family property in this circumstance, whether in residential or commercial contracts. No other case has been decided by the plenary on rental agreements, which leads to understanding ADPF 828 as a landmark: it is the first protective decision on rent for more vulnerable individuals interpreted from the perspective of the fundamental right to housing.

[23] Lei No. 14.010, de 10 de junho de 2020. D.O.U. de 12.6.2020 (Brazil).

[24] Lei No. 14.216, de 7 de outubro de 2021. D.O.U de 8.10.2021 (Brazil).

[25] We have published two empirical studies on constitutional complaints based on ADPF No. 828 in the form of Technical Notes: B. Tavolari, S. Alves, and V. Nisida, Nota Técnica: Ação de Descumprimento de Preceito Fundamental n. 828 (2021) *Núcleo de Questões Urbanas – Insper*; B. Tavolari, V. Nisida, and S. Alves, Nota Técnica: Ação de Descumprimento de Preceito Fundamental n. 828 – Atualização 31/01/22: período de Dezembro de 2021 a Janeiro de 2022 (2022) *Núcleo de Questões Urbanas – Insper*.

mobilized by those courts; and (iv) finally, an analysis of a "transition regime" for ADPF No. 828, in a decision of October 31, 2022, which established procedural and institutional conditions for collective removals but immediately ended protective measures for rental agreements.[26]

Thus, this chapter is the first systematic formulation of different research findings on protective measures for rent in Brazil during the pandemic. Additionally, it points to some research paths that are still being developed. At this moment, our aim is to discuss the main arguments, in the initial legislative debate, in favor and against the inclusion of criteria of redistributive justice in the interpretation of rental contracts in Brazil. The comparative perspective is mainly analytical – it provides a conceptual tool to investigate the Brazilian case but will not lead us to a detailed comparative analysis of Brazil and the United States in this chapter. The remainder of this chapter will examine (i) the first Brazilian legislative attempt to establish eviction and rental protection as part of a legal transitional regime for private relations in response to the pandemic, in March 2020; (ii) the empirical assumptions made by members of Congress in refusing to accept the vulnerability of tenants vis-à-vis landlords, and how data may help us to shed light on the actual distributive implications, and (iii) the justifications presented by former president Jair Bolsonaro for blocking even very mild protective legislation.

6.3 FIRST ATTEMPT AT CREATING PROTECTION AGAINST EVICTIONS: THE EMERGENCY AND TRANSITIONAL LEGAL REGIME FOR PRIVATE LEGAL RELATIONS

In Brazil, the first initiative to create distinct parameters for rental contracts in view of the pandemic originated in the federal legislature. On March 30th, Senator Antonio Anastasia filed Bill No. 1179/2020, which established the emergency and transitional legal regime for private law relationships during the pandemic. The original text contained two specific articles regarding rent.[27] The proposed changes relate to the structural elements of eviction actions (*ações de despejo*) in Brazil.[28]

[26] Since ADPF No. 828 has suspended forced evictions, ending its validity abruptly had a high potential to trigger concentrated effects of evictions nationwide. Therefore, a "transition regime" was established to put an end to the protection. The regime included, for instance, changing courts' institutional architecture, as Justice Barroso determined the obligation to create specific bodies, internal to the courts, for mediating collective conflicts arising from the end of the protection period. See B. Tavolari, A Volta dos Despejos e Remoções, *Folha de São Paulo*, November 9, 2022.

[27] Senado Federal, Projeto de Lei n. 1179, de 2020 (2020).

[28] Eviction (*despejo*) is a term widely used in public debate to designate individual and collective forced removals of all kinds. However, from a technical legal point of view, evictions refer to a specific type of judicial action derived from a rent agreement, as distinct. Other removals may occur in other types of legal proceedings, such as repossession actions, actions resulting from expropriation or reclamation, public civil actions, and other types of actions to defend possession and property.

Eviction actions are regulated by Law 8,245/1991 (Law of Tenancy). Article 59 paragraph 1 provides a *fast track* for eviction in certain circumstances, authorizing the judge to issue an injunction for eviction of the tenant within fifteen days, without the tenant being heard in the process, so long as the landlord provides a deposit in the amount equivalent to three months' rent. This fast-track eviction action applies in case of nonpayment of rent or other amounts due when the contract is not subject to guarantees. In other words, if the tenant does not pay the rent on time and the agreement is not subject to any formal guarantee – features that are common in contracts with low-income tenants – they can be evicted from the property in fifteen days without even being heard. In these cases, the decision is provisional, meaning it can be reversed by a decision on the merits. The landlord's deposit of a security in the amount of three months' rent serves as potential compensation if the eviction proves to be improper.

The first article of the bill on the Emergency and Transitional Legal Regime suspended the possibility of fast-tracking evictions during the pandemic, which did not mean, in any way, that evictions would be suspended *tout court*. Nothing in the bill prevented eviction actions from proceeding using the regular procedure, with eviction by means of a final judicial decision. The second article of the bill provided a specific transition rule for tenants who had suffered economic and financial changes resulting from dismissal or reductions in workload or remuneration, allowing negotiation between landlords and tenants to pay the amounts due in installments.

When we compare the proposed bill with the legislation enacted in the United States, the former is much more modest. While in the United States landlords were prohibited from filing eviction actions and collecting past due rent payments from the outset, the Brazilian proposal allowed for evictions and required the payment of unpaid amounts, even if deferred over time. The Brazilian proposal only prevented fast-track eviction.

The Senate justified the initial proposal as follows:

> In general terms, the project establishes that: …
>
> (iv) Evictions of residential properties are suspended until December 31, 2020, but tenants are not exempt from paying rent, although payment can be deferred in case of loss of income due to unemployment. The landlord may repossess the property either for their own use or for that of their family. …
>
> Today, both the Civil Code and the Consumer Protection Code have adequate rules for resolving or revising contracts due to unforeseeable events and excessive burden, respectively. It is now necessary to contain excesses in the name of the occurrence of fortuitous events and force majeure, but also to allow vulnerable segments such as urban tenants not to suffer restrictions on their right to housing.[29]

The public justification is structured as a two-fold argument. First, the official justification is mistaken in stating that evictions are suspended. As explained, only

[29] Senado Federal, Projeto de Lei n. 1179, p. 12–14.

the fast-track form of eviction through a preliminary injunction would have been affected if the bill had been approved. Second, there is explicit mention of general provisions of Brazilian law that supposedly address situations that cause excessive imbalance between parties. However, the bill recognizes that existing rules allowing courts to rewrite agreements in view of changed circumstances for contractual revision were insufficient – if they were, it would not be necessary to approve specific measures. The justification revolves around the constitutional right to housing, whose protection should be ensured ("It is now necessary to contain excesses in the name of the occurrence of fortuitous events and force majeure, but also to allow vulnerable segments such as urban tenants not to suffer restrictions on their right to housing").

Nevertheless, the wording of the bill was disputed and contested during the legislative process. On April 3, 2020, a new text was presented and approved by the Senate's Constitution and Justice Committee. The points regarding rent were removed from the approved text. The rapporteur Simone Tebet made amendments to the provision on suspension of injunctions in evictions and, moreover, removed the entire article that dealt with installment payments of rent (see Table 6.1). The justification used is that the text assumed that tenants would not be able to pay rents and disregarded the situation of landlords who live on these incomes:[30]

> The ideal approach would be to leave this matter to private negotiations, with the reminder that the legal system already has tools to authorize, depending on the specific case, contractual revision, as exemplified by articles 317 and 478 of the Civil Code.[31]

There are two justifications for the Committee's amendments. First, there is an empirical claim. According to Senator Simone Tebet's report, one may not assume that tenants are the weaker side of the rental contract and, therefore, should be protected by specific rules. It challenges the idea of including distributive objectives in the transition rule on the grounds that cases of owners who rely solely on rental income would need to be considered in the equation, which would indicate that vulnerability could also be located on the landlord's side. The second point builds on the first one: if there are no elements to presuppose vulnerability of only one side, there would be insufficient reasons for the state to provide rules seeking to protect tenants. Any imbalances could be resolved through the general rules of contractual interpretation already provided for in the Brazilian Civil Code – an assumption that had been expressly rejected in the original formulation of the proposal.

Thus, within the conceptual framework employed so far, the original Senate bill could be read as an orthodox variant of contract law, insofar as it provided for the need to weigh economic inequalities, but expressly through legal provision, that is, via approval of the Emergency and Transitional Legal Regime of Private Legal Relations. The proposal reformulated in the Constitution and Justice Committee is

[30] "Article 10 deserves to be suppressed as it provides an absolute presumption that tenants will not be able to pay rents and disregards that there are cases of landlords who survive only on these incomes." Senado Federal, Parecer n.18 de 2020 (2020), p. 18.

[31] Ibid.

TABLE 6.1 *Comparison of proposed text*

Bill No. 1179/2020, authored by Antonio Anastasia	Report n.18/2020, which approves the substitute in the Commission of Constitution and Justice, by the rapporteur Simone Tebet
CHAPTER VI On Urban Property Rentals Article 9. An injunction for eviction from urban property in eviction actions referred to in Article 59, § 1, I, II, V, VII, VIII, and IX, of Law No. 8,245, of October 18, 1991, shall not be granted until December 31, 2020. Paragraph 1. The provisions of this Article shall only apply to actions filed from March 20, 2020. Paragraph 2. The right of repossession of the property is guaranteed in the cases provided for in Article 47, items I, II, III, and IV of Law No. 8,245, of October 18, 1991, and the restrictions of the caput shall not apply to such cases. Article 10. Residential tenants who undergo economic and financial changes resulting from dismissal, reduction of work hours, or decrease in remuneration, may fully or partially suspend the payment of due rents from March 20, 2020, until October 30, 2020. §1. In the event of exercising the rent payment suspension as referred to in the caput, overdue rents must be paid in installments starting from October 30, 2020, on the due date, adding to the payment of future rents, the monthly percentage of 20% of overdue rents. §2. Tenants must notify the lessor of the suspension exercise provided in the caput. §3. The communication provided for in §2 may be carried out by any act that can be legally proven.	CHAPTER VI On Urban Property Rentals Article 9. No preliminary injunction for eviction from urban property shall be granted in eviction proceedings referred to in Article 59, § 1, I, II, V, VII, VIII, and IX, of Law No. 8,245, of October 18, 1991, until October 30, 2020. Sole Paragraph. The provisions of this article apply only to actions filed from March 20, 2020, onward.

orthodox both from an institutional and a functional perspective,[32] insofar as it denies the distributive role of contract law in this specific case by refuting the claim that there would be a more vulnerable side. If there is no side that is evidently more vulnerable, protections by means of law would not be justifiable – and would therefore need to be altered, as they were.[33]

Table 6.1 compares both formulations.

[32] For this distinction, see Davis and Pargendler, Contract Law and Inequality.

[33] From a comparative perspective, the Senate's response could even be understood as ultra-orthodox, in the sense that it even goes against any minimum social protection and distributive goal that has been adopted by countries that have not enshrined the right to housing as a constitutional guarantee. For the notion of legal "ultra-orthodoxy", see Chapter 4 by Weitseng Chen and Chapter 8 Carlos Portugal Gouvêa.

TABLE 6.2 *Income distribution by class: All families, rent-paying families, and rent-receiving families*

Income classes	All families (A)	Rent-paying families (B)	Rent-receiving families (C)
Up to 2 min wages	24.3%	29.0%	5.8%
More than 2 up to 3 min wages	19.0%	19.2%	9.3%
More than 3 up to 6 min wages	30.6%	28.9%	26.1%
More than 6 up to 10 min wages	13.8%	12.7%	19.4%
More than 10 up to 15 min wages	6.2%	5.0%	14.9%
More than 15 up to 25 min wages	3.8%	3.6%	12.4%
More than 25 min wages	2.5%	1.6%	12.1%
Total	100%	100%	100%

Source: Household Budget Survey (*POF*) (2018).

6.4 ARE THE RELATIONS BETWEEN LANDLORDS AND TENANTS MARKED BY STRUCTURAL ECONOMIC INEQUALITIES IN BRAZIL?

The empirical argument about the lack of clear asymmetry between landlord and tenant in a rent contract lacked data and evidence that could support the diagnosis. In view of this absence, we gathered data on who pays and who receives rent in Brazil, based on the 2018 Household Budget Survey, the most up-to-date at the time. The data shows that, out of the 69 million Brazilian families, 11.7 million, or 17 percent, had some monetary expenditure on rent. In aggregate, the families spent just over R$6.5 billion on rent, in 2018 values. This amount, distributed among the 11.7 million families that had expenditures on rent, equals a monthly average expenditure of R$555, or 58 percent of the minimum wage at the time. For these families, this represented 20 percent of their monthly income.[34] For the purposes of the Household Budget Survey, rent does not necessarily need to be formal, established by a duly agreed contract between the parties – it is sufficient that there is some declared expenditure on rental housing, even if in an informal manner. Accordingly, the data allows us to visualize the situation of extremely vulnerable and informal renters.

Table 6.2 shows the proportion of Brazilian families in each income bracket, as well as how families who pay and receive rent are distributed across income brackets. The distribution of rent-paying families across income brackets is highly heterogeneous, reflecting to a large extent the country's unequal income distribution. Among the 11.7 million families who had any expenditure on rent, 77 percent have a monthly income of less than six times the minimum wage, and 29 percent have a total monthly income of less than two times the minimum wage. Only 10 percent of families who pay rent have an income greater than ten times the minimum wage.

[34] See S. Firpo and B. Tavolari, Políticas de Moradia em Momentos de Crise: a Centralidade do Aluguel, in L. M. Machado (ed.), *Legado de uma Pandemia: 26 Vozes Conversam sobre os Aprendizados para a Política Pública* (Rio de Janeiro: Autografia, 2021), pp. 56–69.

The number of families who pay rent is proportional to their representation in each of the income brackets that encompass more than two minimum wages and less than twenty-five minimum wages. The biggest discrepancy is in the tails, that is, in the income brackets of less than two minimum wages and more than twenty-five minimum wages. We are talking about more than 3.4 million families in the first case and a little less than 190,000 in the second. Although families tend to spend on rent according to their income, the expenses are relatively high for the poorest. As a fraction of income, these expenses are also quite unequal, both among and within groups. Among families earning up to two minimum wages, rent expenses represent 34 percent of their income. For the richest group, these expenses do not exceed 4 percent of the family's total monthly income. Even though the expenditure in Brazilian real is almost five times higher, as a fraction of income, the rental expenditure of the richest is only 13 percent of what the poorest spend.[35]

To build a complete picture of rental relationships, it is also necessary to look at the other side, that is, the landlords. Table 6.3 shows how families that receive rent are distributed across income brackets. Out of the 69 million Brazilian families, 3.4 million, or 4.9 percent, generate monetary income from rent.[36] In total, these families received a little over R$6.1 billion, in 2018 values. Distributed among the 3.4 million families, this corresponds to an average monthly income of R$1,827, or 1.9 minimum wages at the time, which was equivalent to 17 percent of their income. The distribution of these values is also highly unequal.

The proportion of families receiving rental income varies immensely with income. It ranges from 1.2 percent among the poorest to 23.8 percent among the richest. Additionally, rental income is highly concentrated: 12.1 percent of families with rental income receive 43.8 percent of all rental income received by families in the country. This shows that favoring landlords over tenants may have a regressive effect on income distribution, which is contrary to what was suggested in the Senate Judiciary Committee's justification.

The majority of Brazilian families neither have expenses on rent (83%) nor receive rental income (95%). Expenses on rent represent less than 0.1 percent of GDP. Despite these small numbers, it is worth remembering that 11.7 million families have rental expenses and almost 50 percent of them have a total family income of up to three minimum wages. Moreover, for every two families earning rental income, there are seven that pay rent. The data from the Household Budget Survey is from prior to the pandemic. The poorest families suffered an even greater impact from the pandemic as their sources of income were the most affected – in poorer families, 79 percent of employed adults are informal workers.

35 Ibid.

36 It is important to mention that this information does not take into account families who receive rental income indirectly, intermediated by their participation in companies that are landlords. Since data is limited to individuals and families and does not include corporate landlords, this is only a partial view of the broader picture of rental relations.

TABLE 6.3 *Incidence of monetary rent income by income class*

Income Classes	Number of Consumer Units (Families)	Number of CUs with Positive Rent Income	Frequency of CUs with Positive Rent Income
Up to 2 min wages	16,737,438	197,252	1.2%
More than 2 up to 3 min wages	13,079,821	315,031	2.4%
More than 3 up to 6 min wages	21,099,497	882,031	4.2%
More than 6 up to 10 min wages	9,509,008	653,105	6.9%
More than 10 up to 15 min wages	4,256,727	501,108	11.8%
More than 15 up to 25 min wages	2,629,450	418,530	15.9%
More than 25 min wages	1,705,764	406,818	23.8%
Total	69.017,704	3,373,845	4.9%

Source: Household Budget Survey (*POF*) (2018).

Therefore, it is necessary to contrast both poles – those who pay and those who receive rent – to have a representative picture of the relationships between landlords and tenants. One way to measure such inequalities relates to the number of families who pay rent compared to the number of families who receive it: property-owning families are smaller in number and much more concentrated in higher-income brackets. But inequality also relates to the amounts paid and received, as well as the proportion of these amounts in family income. This picture does not exclude the counterexample raised by Senator Simone Tebet: the argument claimed that the absolute presumption of vulnerability of tenants is not sustained in the face of cases of families whose only source of income would be rental income. It is true that these cases exist. However, public policies should not be based on exceptional cases. The data shows that there is a distributive conflict between the poles of the rental relationship in Brazil. Cases of landlords whose only source of income would cease to exist with eventual legislative protection for tenants should be treated as distortions and also addressed by public policy, as was done, for example, in Spain, where differentiation was made between small and large landlords.[37]

6.5 THE FINAL WORDING OF LAW 14,010 OF 2020 AND THE CONFLICTS BETWEEN THE LEGISLATIVE AND EXECUTIVE BRANCHES

The Emergency and Transitional Regime statute was only approved by Congress on June 10, 2020. On June 15, then-president Jair Bolsonaro decided to veto the entire

[37] For a discussion of the distortion and institutional arrangements aimed at addressing it, see Firpo and Tavolari, Políticas de Moradia em Momentos de Crise: a Centralidade do Aluguel.

section of the statute that included rules on rent, even in its diluted version. The justification for the veto was as follows:

> The legislative proposal, by prohibiting the granting of injunctions in eviction actions, goes against the public interest by suspending one of the instruments of coercion for the payment of obligations established in the rental agreement (eviction), for a substantially long period of time, therefore providing excessive protection to the debtor at the expense of the creditor, as well as promoting the incentive for non-payment and disregarding the reality of several landlords who depend on the receipt of rent as a complementary or even exclusive form of income for their own sustenance.[38]

If we were to formulate a kind of scale of contractual orthodoxy, the justification for the veto of the law would certainly be in one of the positions closest to the maximum of orthodoxy. Here, the public interest is not the protection of more vulnerable people in the pandemic, who may lose their homes, impacting their rights to housing and life. The declared public interest is exactly the opposite, in the protection of the owner and creditor – it is even spoken of as "excessive protection to the debtor," a claim with questionable empirical basis. The argument that the rule would favor noncompliance also falls short, as only evictions through injunction would be suspended and evictions through the common procedure would continue to be judged normally by the Brazilian judiciary. Finally, the dimension of "disregarding reality" is, in fact, a caricature that disregards the evidence about who pays and who receives rent in Brazil, based on the creation of a strawman: the poorer landlord who depends solely and exclusively on rental income to survive.

However, the veto was not the final word on the law. In an atypical reaction, Congress partially overturned the presidential vetoes, keeping part of the article that provided protective rules for rent during the pandemic. On August 20, with 64 votes against 2 in the Senate, and 409 votes against 7 in the Chamber of Deputies, Congress overruled the veto on the main provision of the article on rent. The remaining final wording was as follows:

> Article 9. No preliminary injunction shall be granted for eviction from urban real estate in eviction actions referred to in Article 59, paragraph 1, items I, II, V, VII, VIII and IX, of Law No. 8,245, of October 18, 1991, until October 30, 2020.[39]

Therefore, in its first legislative attempt at the federal level, Brazil approved a transitional rule for rental relationships during the pandemic that prevented eviction through a preliminary injunction, within 15 days and without hearing the tenant. The paths were still open for eviction through a final judgment. In addition, the suspension period until October 30th gave the rule a period of validity of only two months.

38 Congresso Nacional, Estudo do Veto n. 20/2020 (2020), p. 7.

39 Lei No. 14.010, de 10 de junho de 2020. D.O.U. de 12.6.2020 (Brazil).

The rocky path in the legislative branch and the executive veto led to a division of efforts. On the one hand, lawmakers chose to present individual bills on evictions and removals, outside the framework of the transitional legal regime developed for the pandemic. On the other hand, a large part of organized civil society turned to the Supreme Court, and in particular through ADPF 828. ADPF 828 was filed on April 15, 2021, by the Socialist and Freedom Party, in the second year of the pandemic, when expectations regarding the legislative branch had already been exhausted. Its scope extended beyond rental relationships to encompass judicial and administrative collective evictions.

The first interim decision by Justice Luís Roberto Barroso on the scope of the ADPF came on June 3, 2021. This judicial decision, which was grounded on the constitutional right to housing and health of vulnerable individuals, granted a six-month valid precautionary measure, suspending, during this period, administrative or judicial actions resulting in evictions, displacements, forced removals, or repossessions of a collective nature in properties used as residences or productive areas for vulnerable populations. This suspension applied to cases of occupations that occurred before the onset of the pandemic, from March 20, 2020, onward.

Furthermore, the measure suspended the granting of summary evictions, without hearing from the opposing party, in cases of residential leases involving tenants considered vulnerable. However, the eviction action due to non-payment remained possible, provided it followed the regular and adversarial procedure. The opinion argued that a "minimalist" form of judicial intervention was warranted, given the concern that "the income resulting from rent is, in many cases, also vital to the sustenance of landlords."

The precautionary measure allowed for some exceptions. These included premises located in areas at risk of landslides, floods, or similar processes, where removal could take place as provided by the law. Other exceptions addressed situations related to combating organized crime, the removal of invaders from indigenous lands, and the application of local laws more favorable to protecting the right to housing, provided they were in accordance with the Constitution. Previous judicial decisions that provided greater protection to specific vulnerable groups were also preserved and would prevail over the ADPF 828 decision.

The effects of this decision were extended until October 31, 2022, when the resumption of eviction and removal actions was authorized due to the easing of the pandemic's effects. However, this resumption was subject to a series of procedures – such as the establishment by the courts of land conflict committees and the conduct of judicial inspections and mediation hearings before any eviction decision – aimed at reducing housing and humanitarian impacts in the face of the serious housing insecurity situation in the country.

This decision, albeit relatively late in the course of the pandemic, was used by several groups and social movements, and became one of the main tools for defending vulnerable populations against evictions and removals during the pandemic, placing the Judiciary as the primary actor in ensuring the right to housing in this extremely critical context.

6.6 CONCLUSION

In this chapter, we have characterized the protection against eviction during the pandemic in Brazil as a case of legal heterodoxy, mainly because it was established by the Federal Supreme Court in June 2021, via ADPF No. 828, based directly on the social rights to housing and health in the Brazilian Constitution. The Brazilian legal system as a whole has many characteristics of a heterodox system, including a systematic set of norms that project principles of public law onto private relations, the protection of the right to life and housing as positive social rights enshrined in the Constitution, along with a highly active and accessible judiciary to ensure the enforcement of these rights. Nonetheless, Brazilian institutions do not appear to have responded to a crisis more effectively than US institutions in terms of response time and the scope of protection. In other words, even a heterodox system – at least within the limits of the concept outlined in this chapter – although legally capable of offering institutions a range of resources and tools to implement public policies, may encounter significant difficulties in enforcing social rights, especially in reaction to crises such as the COVID-19 pandemic.

BIBLIOGRAPHY

Acca, T., Uma Análise da Doutrina Brasileira dos Direitos Sociais: Saúde, Educação e Moradia entre os Anos de 1964 e 2006, Master's Thesis, University of São Paulo Law School (2009).

Brady, M. et al., Why We (Still) Need to Cancel the Rent, Movement Policy Brief Series, *NYU Urban Democracy Lab* (June 24, 2020).

Campos, N. C., A Efetividade do Direito à Moradia no Judiciário Brasileiro: Uma Análise Comparativa da Jurisprudência, Thesis, Escola de Formação da Sociedade Brasileira de Direito Público – SBDP (2010).

Davis, K. E. and Pargendler, M., Contract Law and Inequality (2022a) 107 *Iowa Law Review* 1485.

Contract Law Heterodoxy (2022b) 4 *Revue Européenne du Droit* 92–97.

Eballos-Roig, J., Biden Administration Rolls Out 60-Day Targeted Eviction Ban Aimed at Protecting Millions of Renters from Losing Their Homes, *Insider*, August 3, 2021.

Fandos, N., With Capitol Sit-In, Cori Bush Galvanized a Progressive Revolt over Evictions, *The New York Times*, August 4, 2021.

Ferraz, O. L. M., The Right to Health in the Courts of Brazil: Worsening Health Inequities? (2009) 11 *Health and Human Rights Journal* 33–45.

Firpo, S. and Tavolari, B., Políticas de Moradia em Momentos de Crise: A Centralidade do Aluguel, in L. M. Machado (ed.), *Legado de uma Pandemia: 26 Vozes Conversam sobre os Aprendizados para a Política Pública* (Rio de Janeiro: Autografia, 2021), pp. 56–69.

Foscarinis, M., The Growth of a Movement for a Human Right to Housing in the United States (2007) 20 *Harvard Human Rights Journal* 35–40.

Hartman, C., The Case for a Right to Housing (1998) 9 *Housing Policy Debate* 223–46.
Lamb, C., Congress, the Courts, and Civil Rights: The Fair Housing Act of 1968 Revisited (1982) 27 *Villanova Law Review* 1115–62.
Machado, M. R. and Vasconcelos, N. P., Uma Conjuntura Crítica Perdida: a COVID-19 nas Prisões Brasileiras (2021) 12 *Revista Direito e Práxis* 2015–43.
Morais, M. P. et al., Monitorando o Direito à Moradia no Brasil (1992–2004) (2006) 12 *IPEA Políticas Sociais – Acompanhamento e Análise* 230–41.
Pistor, K., *The Code of Capital: How Law Creates Wealth and Inequality* (Princeton: Princeton University Press, 2020).
Schapiro, M. and Alves, S., Developmental State with Neoliberal Tools: A Portrait of the Brazilian Housing Financial System (2019) 12 *Law and Development Review* 457–93.
Silva, M., Colisão de Direitos Fundamentais: Como o STF faz a Ponderação entre o Direito à Propriedade e o Direito Social à Moradia em Contratos de Locação na Área Urbana?, Thesis, Escola de Formação da Sociedade Brasileira de Direito Público – SBDP (2020).
Silva, V. A., *A Constitucionalização do Direito: Os Direitos Fundamentais nas Relações entre Particulares* (São Paulo: Malheiros, 2005).
Stracqualursi, V., House Democrat Sleeps on Capitol Steps as She Blasts Lawmakers over Expiring Eviction Moratorium, *CNN*, August 2, 2021.
Tavolari, B., A Volta dos Despejos e Remoções, *Folha de São Paulo*, November 9, 2022.
O Aluguel no Centro da Crise, *Novos Estudos*, May 13, 2020.
Tavolari, B., Alves, S., and Nisida, V., Nota Técnica: Ação de Descumprimento de Preceito Fundamental n. 828 (2021) *Núcleo de Questões Urbanas – Insper*.
Tavolari, B., Nisida, V., and Alves, S., Nota Técnica: Ação de Descumprimento de Preceito Fundamental n. 828 – Atualização 31/01/22: período de Dezembro de 2021 a Janeiro de 2022 (2022) *Núcleo de Questões Urbanas – Insper*.
Taylor, K. Y., Cancel the Rent, *The New Yorker*, May 12, 2020.
Waldron, J., What Is Private Property? (1985) 5 *Oxford Journal of Legal Studies* 313–49.
Wang, D. W. L., Courts and Health Care Rationing: The Case of the Brazilian Federal Supreme Court (2013) 8 *Health Economics, Policy and Law* 75–93.

7

Heterodox Legal Informality

Some Examples from Latin America

Jorge L. Esquirol

7.1 INTRODUCTION

Legal heterodoxy is hard to sustain, especially in developing countries. When transnational interests are at stake, the geopolitical pressures are great and opposite forces are usually prevalent. Legal harmonization predominates. The European Union may be the best example among developed countries. There, visions of a common market drive the reduction of national legal differences. In the developing world, promises of development and foreign investment propel hegemonic models. Institutions like the Organization for Economic Cooperation and Development, the United Nations Commission on International Trade Law, Unidroit, as well as the World Bank and the International Monetary Fund, each in their own way promotes the global standardization of national laws. International development assistance by powerful countries also works by conditioning aid on national legal reform, often in the style if not exact copy of donor laws and institutions. Foreign investors equally demand familiar laws and legal institutions providing for the maximum of profits and guarantees.

By contrast, critiques of "one-size-fits-all" solutions are routinely rebuffed by assertions of "best practices," proven solutions, investor rights, efficiency, and lower transaction costs. Alternatives more responsive and representative of local conditions, potentially more sustainable, are mostly undermined or ignored. This is not simply because they are not known. Powerful interests often stand against them. In this environment, the developing world is the least capable of resisting. Such countries often depend on international loans, trade treaties, bilateral assistance, and foreign investment tied to legal harmonization. If that were not enough, the main

My sincere thanks to Kevin Davis, Michele Graziadei, Heather Hughes, Mariana Pargendler, and all the coauthors of this volume and participants at the NYU/University of Buenos Aires meeting in Buenos Aires in 2023. All errors and omissions are of course mine.

experts on law and development, and their sponsoring institutions, similarly applaud the benefits of one model over multiple alternatives.

Despite the adverse currents, Latin American countries enjoy a long history of legal innovation, whether the result of autonomous development, explicit adaptations of foreign models, or *de facto* variation on the ground of the law-in-the-books. For most international observers, many of these developments remain relatively obscure, unless they involve transnational interests or geopolitical attention. Indeed, most comparative law on Latin America stems from law-and-development work. It is these projects that have garnered the most attention. Local legal differences – when considered at all – mostly figure as diagnoses of legal underdevelopment. They generally become targets for reform, "modernization," and inevitably elimination.

Regardless, differences persist. And not all Global South differences can be simply dismissed as either dysfunctional or indefensible. However, the law-and-development literature has helped consolidate a hierarchical ordering between developed and developing. This makes it harder to take developing country law seriously and to examine its features at face value. It is not simply a question of making these legal systems, and their latest developments, better known to an international audience. Even when amply shown, skepticism quickly emerges over their lack of effectiveness, relative unacceptance by the broader population, origins in a foreign parent jurisdiction, and even their drafters' misunderstanding of their own laws. Pretending that this hierarchical structure does not exist will not make it go away. An array of geopolitical interests, and an extensive development assistance industry, depend on it existentially.

As such, in addition to making heterodox laws and legal institutions better known in the legal literature, the structural bias against their recognition must be frontally addressed. The elements that keep it in place must be critically assessed. To the extent these are not defensible distinctions, they must be challenged and rejected – repeatedly, until a new paradigm is in place. It may not be inalterably structural, but it is also not just ephemerally discursive. This chapter contributes to that work by challenging one of the main elements of this hierarchical arrangement: specifically, legal informality as a marker of underdevelopment.

Surely, recognizing different policy objectives and distributional effects within developing country law allows for more sober consideration of alternatives. This is not possible, however, if they are summarily dismissed. Certainly, not all differences will be useful or positive. Some examples of heterodoxy may turn out to be norms and institutions from a different era – uniformly regarded as unsuitable to address contemporary problems. Some may represent unjustifiable advantages for a single group or class in society, enacted through pork-barrel politics common throughout the world's legislatures. However, some legal heterodoxy may more valuably signal a defensible technique, policy preference, and distribution of resources than those offered by hegemonic prescriptions.

This chapter is divided into two sections and two examples. Section 7.2 examines the notion of legal heterodoxy itself and introduces the theory of *heterodox legal informality*. The latter, I argue, is Latin America's pre-eminent contribution to modern law. It represents alternative arrangements of legal formality and informality, combined. Section 7.3 examines two instances of heterodoxy in Latin America. The first is secured transactions laws. These are laws that enable transfers of property rights from debtors to creditors to guarantee debts. They have undergone a neo-liberal revolution in the past decades. Almost all countries in the region have replaced, or are under pressure to replace, their chattel mortgage laws. Whatever laws were previously in place, the reforms enact the liberalizing approach to security rights modeled by the Uniform Commercial Code in the United States. The second example is specifically from Colombia. That country has adopted an innovative property law regime within the context of private law transitional justice. Its objective is to restore landed property to those physically displaced from their homes by that country's guerrilla war. It turns the traditional mix of formality and informality in property law on its head, by switching presumptions and shifting burdens of proof. Both of these are examples of heterodoxy: the first waging a rearguard action and mostly losing, the second recently extended by Colombia's legislature for a second ten-year period until 2031.

7.2 LATIN AMERICAN LEGAL HETERODOXY

Uncovering legal heterodoxy, from a constructive perspective, may yield some defensible alternatives to dominant global models. Of course, the first distinction to make concerns the meaning of the term "heterodoxy" itself. What is considered heterodox or divergent from the hegemonic changes over time, as dominant global positions themselves change. Features that may seem heterodox today may have been hegemonic in their day, when initially introduced. Heterodoxy also depends on the type of orthodoxy that it militates against – whether global, local, sectorial.

From today's perspective, legal heterodoxy was rife in Latin America in the early twentieth century. An example is the area of property rights. Panama developed a form of rural property not subject to foreclosure.[1] Colombia established the power to extinguish title *without compensation* on large, un-utilized tracts of agricultural land for redistribution to landless farmers.[2] Mexico, until a recent reform, constitutionally protected collective ownership of *campesino* farmlands.[3] Brazil recognized different

[1] Law No. 1 of March 20, 1941, on *Patrimonio Familiar* (Panamá); J. L. Esquirol, Titling and Untitled Housing in Panama City (2008) 4 *Tennessee Journal of Law and Policy* 243–302.

[2] Agrarian Reform Law No. 200 of 1936 (Colombia); J. L. Esquirol, Formalizing Property in Latin America, in M. Graziadei and L. Smith (eds.), *Comparative Property Law: Global Perspectives* (Northampton: Edward Elgar, 2017), pp. 333–54.

[3] K. Karst and N. Clement, Legal Institutions and Development: Lessons from the Mexican Ejido (1969) 16 *UCLA Law Review* 281–303.

property types, distinct from full title, for squatters on public land.[4] And, in many countries, indigenous territories have long constituted a different type of landholding.

Most of these laws when enacted were not counter-hegemonic *per se*. They benefitted from the globalization of "social law" in the early twentieth century, equally impacting Latin America.[5] The specific formulas adopted in the region were in some cases unique, but they were supported by a broader transnational *zeitgeist* generating models and authoritative ideas. These were generally directed at protecting the most vulnerable from the unequal harms produced by industrialization and capitalism. Some of the laws and models from that era remain on the books. And these are certainly heterodox today, from the perspective of a contemporary neoliberal order.

Faced with the increasing power of multinational agribusiness and foreign investors, however, even obscure agrarian laws on the books have come under fire. Promoted by the World Bank and the Inter-American Development Bank, titling programs for squatters and parcelization of collective farming have had this effect. They substitute full-title property for the social relations and legal forms previously in place – consolidating a singular form of property. Indeed, "orthodox" legal rules – to which powerful transnational actors are committed – are hard to deviate from. A significant amount of geopolitical pressure accompanies the push for uniform rules for foreign creditors and investors.

7.2.1 *Legal Informality*

Probably the most significant example of legal heterodoxy in Latin America however is the role played by informality in the legal system.[6] This is not generally perceived as a positive, though.[7] Rather the opposite is true. In fact, it figures as an element in

4 Law No. 10.406 of 2002 (Brazil), Art. 1.225, inc. XI and XII (originally 1967) ("concessão de uso especial," "concessão de direito real de uso").

5 Du. Kennedy, Three Globalizations of Law and Legal Thought, in D. Trubek and A. Santos (eds.), *The New Law and Economic Development: A Critical Appraisal* (Cambridge: Cambridge University Press, 2006), pp. 17–73; see also Du. Kennedy, A *Critique of Adjudication: Fin de Siècle* (Cambridge: Harvard University Press, 1997), pp. 92–95.

6 The focus here is on legal informality and not the informal sector per se defined by social scientists. See generally, B. Guha-Khasnobis, R. Kanbur, and E. Ostrom, Beyond Formality and Informality, in Linking the Formal and Informal Economy, in B. Guha-Khasnobis, R. Kanbur, and E. Ostrom (eds.), *Linking the Formal and Informal Economy: Concepts and Policies* (Oxford: Oxford University Press, 2006), pp. 1–18, p. 3 ("formal and informal are better thought of as metaphors that conjure up a mental picture of whatever the user has in mind at that particular time"); R. La Porta and A. Shleifer, Informality and Development (2014) 28 *Journal of Economic Perspectives* 109–26 (reporting that the main obstacles of informal firms are underskilled entrepreneurs and access to finance).

7 K. J. Fandl, The Role of Informal Legal Institutions in Economic Development (2008) 32 *Fordham International Law Journal* 1–31, 3 ("When we begin to examine how legal reform can

law-and-development's diagnosis of underdevelopment.[8] In development circles, legal informality goes hand in hand with legal formal*ism*, which has a different meaning than informality's opposite, "formalization."[9] Legal formalism refers to excessive rigidity in the drafting and application of legal rules and categories.[10] This is generally associated with raising form over substance. And the forms *prereform* in Latin America are generally perceived as backward, connected to (old) European models, inherent to political economies less conducive to economic development, and generally unaligned with contemporary policy goals. The formalistic training of lawyers is blamed for the reproduction of a legal consciousness steeped in doctrinal categories, traditions, and *idées fixes*. These get in the way of implementing policy and functionality.

Indeed, both excessive legal formalism and rampant informality are closely associated with law in the region. One is typically tied to the other: legal formalism breeds informality. However the two are interconnected, they mark the hard divide between developed and developing country law. Developed countries are not formalistic (or much less so), and they do not have significant informality, so this thinking goes. I have critiqued the diagnosis of excessive legal formalism in Latin America, elsewhere.[11] My focus here is on informality. In this context, the high incidence of legal informality is perceived as related to economic stagnation, political instability, lawlessness, and other evils.[12] It may be expressed as a gap between law and society, lack of penetration of the formal legal system, or some other way. The basic concept, however, is routinely misused. And informality has no singular meaning.[13] It has been stretched to include a broad array of phenomena – that is, as a euphemism for illegality; abuse of discretion in official decision-making;

be provided to all people in a developing country, we run up against a significant issue that is often sidestepped – informality").

8 See generally, J. L. Esquirol, *Ruling the Law: Failure and Legitimacy in Latin American Legal Systems* (Cambridge: Cambridge University Press, 2019).

9 See some of the classics on Latin America: K. Karst and K. Rosenn, *Law and Development in Latin America: A Casebook* (Berkeley: University of California Press, 1975); K. Karst, Rights in Land and Housing in an Informal Legal System: The Barrios of Caracas (1971) 19 *American Journal of Law* 550–74; K. Rosenn, The Jeito: Brazil Institutional Bypass of the Formal Legal System and Its Development Implications (1971) 19 *American Journal of Comparative Law* 514–49; all the way to contemporary repetition of these same ideas, H. De Soto, *The Mystery of Capital: Why Capitalism Triumphs in the West and Fails Everywhere Else* (New York: Basic Books, 2000); M. G. Villegas, *La Eficacia Simbólica del Derecho: Examen de Situaciones Colombianas* (Bogotá: Uniandes, 1993).

10 For a discussion of legal formalism, see Du. Kennedy, *A Critique of Adjudication: Fin de Siècle*; *contrast* L. Grossman, Langdell Upside Down: James Coolidge Carter and the Anticlassical Jurisprudence of Anti-codification (2007) 19 *Yale Journal of Law and Humanities* 149–220.

11 Esquirol, Ruling the Law.

12 Ibid., see also Esquirol, Titling and Untitled Housing in Panama City.

13 A. Sindzingre, The Relevance of the Concepts of Formality and Informality: A Theoretical Appraisal, in B. Guha-Khasnobis, R. Kanbur, and E. Ostrom (eds.), *Linking the Formal and Informal Economy: Concepts and Policies* (Oxford: Oxford University Press, 2006), pp. 58–74, p. 58.

social norms operating instead of legal norms; gaps, conflicts, and ambiguities in the positive law; impunity; the gap between law and enforcement; and other possibilities. In reality, these represent commonplace phenomena in all modern legal systems, although not normally labeled that way.[14] Nonetheless, the diagnosis of informality – in its various forms – drives much development reform.[15] It works by undermining the defensibility of existing arrangements – described as informal – and, in their place, advancing development reforms.

7.2.2 *The Stigma of Informality*

The preference for formalization is strong and long-standing. It hails back to at least Max Weber and his authoritative analysis of developed legal systems.[16] According to him, their hallmark was the superior level of formalization and bureaucratization attained. It was a legal system's dis-embeddedness from traditional and charismatic authorities that distinguished it. It was able to garner legitimacy through routinization and regularization. Legal norms and institutions stand apart because of their character as general rules applied uniformly. Weber may have fallen prey to an overly narrow reading of his texts, considering his more nuanced views.[17] It is not surprising, however, that Western legal professionals would have internalized this definition.

Law and development experts easily extended it to the developing world.[18] There, the prevalence of non-formalization or different formalization helps explain

[14] M. Granovetter, The Social Construction of Corruption, in V. Nee and R. Swedberg (eds.), *On Capitalism* (Redwood City: Stanford University Press, 2007), pp. 152–72 ("it is common in human history that groups with conflicting interests present different sets of standards for what behavior is appropriate, and label behavior that benefits competing groups as illegitimate or more specifically 'corrupt'").

[15] J. E. Larson, Informality, Illegality, and Inequality (2002) 20 *Yale Law & Policy Review* 137–82, 142–43 (noting the negative valence of informality: "... fundamental values of legal culture stand in the way of a productive engagement with informality in the United States. Informality contradicts legality, and especially equality, as we conceive these values. From within this tradition, informality is an abuse of law, as well as tolerance of exploitation and inequality. Accordingly, informality creates the best argument for stepped-up regulation").

[16] M. Weber, *From Max Weber: Essays in Sociology*, C. Wright Mills and H. H. Gerth (eds.) (London: Routledge, 2014), pp. 216–17 ("The 'rational' interpretation of law on the basis of strictly formal conceptions stands opposite the kind of adjudication that is primarily bound to sacred traditions"). But note Weber's recognition that "Even today in England ... a broad substratum of justice is actually Kadi-justice to an extent that is hardly conceivable on the continent"; M. Weber, *Economy and Society: An Outline of Interpretive Sociology*, G. Roth and C. Wittich (eds.) (New York: Bedminster Press, 1968).

[17] D. Trubek, Max Weber's Tragic Modernism and the Study of Law and Society (1986) 20 *Law and Society Review* 573–604, 590 ("Weber can and has been read as asserting the superiority of a formal legal order").

[18] See e.g., L. M. Friedman, On Legal Development (1970) 24 *Rutgers Law Review* 11–64, 12 (arguing that legal developmentalists had no theory); J. H. Merryman, Comparative Law and Social Changes: On the Origins, Style, Decline & Revival of the Law and Development

underdevelopment.[19] It encapsulates the distinction between developed and underdeveloped law. Not limited to informality, the discursive divide is created by an array of familiar observations about underdevelopment: the arcaneness of laws on the books, backwardness of institutions, an extraordinary gap between the law-on-the-books and the law-in-action, law's lack of penetration in society, excessive legal formalism, *as well as extensive informality*. These generalized beliefs consolidate the view that legal development reform depends on formalization of the informal.

However, what may be appropriately considered informal is far from clear. There is a tendency to find a plethora of informality in developing countries and to characterize such phenomena as negative. The designation may effectively express, in any given instance, a preference for rules over standards on a certain question; judicial review instead of administrative discretion; state law instead of social (or extralegal) norms; and the repression – or conversely regularization – of illegal or quasi-illegal activities. Regardless, the finding of informality becomes an argument for reform. Whatever gets tagged as "informal" appears deficient and in need of modernizing and changing.

Quixotically, some of the same phenomena when noted in developed countries are rarely labeled "informal." Instead, they are validated and legitimated within the legal system as expressing some other value. Extralegal phenomena simply become private ordering, self-regulation, legislated deference to commercial practices, decision-making based on standards, official tolerance for residual non-enforcement, self-help remedies, and other concepts of this type. Some of the equivalent phenomena in the developing world are not so generously described. Regardless, law and sociology scholars have abundantly demonstrated the gap between the law in the books and the law in action *in developed countries*.[20] In a famous 1971 article by Stewart Macaulay, the informal practices of businesspeople, car dealers in Wisconsin, were examined.[21] Despite the mythology of commercial law as a regulator of business transactions, business actors actually transact in the shadow of the law. Moreover, their behavior varies significantly depending on whether they are dealing with repeat actors or one-time transactions. Repeat actors are better able to interact with the legal system to their benefit.

Movement (1977) 25 *American Journal of Comparative Law* 457–91, 466, and 481 ("The law and development movement, primarily a U.S. phenomenon, has incorporated a view of the role and consequences of lawyers that is unfamiliar to and inconsistent with the legal cultures of most developing societies ... [it] was bound to fail and has failed").

19 F. K. Upham, Speculations on Legal Informality: On Winn's Relational Practices and the Marginalization of Law (1994) 28 *Law & Society Review* 233–42, 235 ("It is natural, then, [for developmentalists] to conclude that there is a causal connection between the existence of some kind of formal legal system on the one hand and economic growth and social order on the other ... this easy and intuitive conclusion is most likely fundamentally wrong").

20 See, e.g. O. W. Holmes, The Path of the Law (1897) 10 *Harvard Law Review* 22–36; R. Pound, Law in Books and Law in Action (1910) 44 *American Law Review* 12–36, 24.

21 S. Macaulay, Non-Contractual Relations in Business: A Preliminary Study (1963) 28 *American Sociology Review* 55–67.

The Macaulay piece is significant for many reasons. Primarily, however, it demonstrates the informality prevalent within developed legal systems. No need to go to the developing world or other locations to find it. It exists in plentiful form throughout developed country law. Authoritative descriptions, such as certain interpretations of Weber, obfuscate the real workings of these legal systems. They present a fictionalized narrative, in which evidence of informality is relegated to the exceptions or not even clearly seen for what they are. For example, trial court judges have significant latitude in a range of decisions. They may have the power to assess monetary responsibility for harms produced in society through their views on duties of care and proximate cause of events. In fact, numerous areas of the law require that government officials rely on standards and not black-letter law. Likewise, the Uniform Commercial Code frequently relies on industry standards and commercial practices as the source of law.[22]

What might be condemned as informality in one context can be seen quite differently in another. Indeed, it may approvingly reflect private parties independently pursuing their contractual remedies rather than submitting to judicial management. Or, the repossession and sale of collateral in a secured credit transaction may allow for efficient (if relatively unchecked) self-help remedies rather than mandated judicial intervention. Such powers nonetheless allow for significant amounts of informality on the part of creditors, pushing against if not overstepping the bounds of legality when repossessing collateral. Regardless, self-help is a lauded feature of US secured transactions law, the premier global model.

Additionally, there are differences in terms of doctrinal formality and informality. While formal categories like "contract" and "property" may have legal significance, the distinction may not matter at all or matter only for specific questions. The latter suggests a form of doctrinal informality. In an example, the difference between a "true sale" of an account receivable – and its transfer as collateral – does not matter for most purposes in the Uniform Commercial Code (UCC). But it critically matters *upon default* of the debtor.[23] If the transaction is deemed retrospectively a secured loan and not a sale *based on formal indicia*, the debtor may be able to get its surplus value back after the loan is paid off. As such, within the same law in the same code, formal legal categories are determinative for some purposes, but not so for others.[24] Another example is the effect of public registration for property transfers. This formal requirement may generate a favorable legal presumption for some

[22] L. Bernstein, Merchant Law in a Merchant Court: Rethinking the Code's Search for Immanent Business Norms, 144 *University of Pennsylvania Law Review* 1765 (1996).

[23] See Article 9-601(g) and 9-607(c); *Major's Furniture Mart, Inc.* v. *Castle Credit Corp., Inc.*, 602 F 2d 538 (3rd Cir. 1979) (requiring the court to devise a definition of "property" ownership).

[24] See H. Hughes, Robots, Markets, and the Value of Deal Lawyers (2024) 49 *Journal of Corporation Law* 833–71, Compare UCC Article 9-109, which provides that Article 9 applies to "a transaction, regardless of its form that creates a security interest", and Ohio Revised Code Annotated §1109.75 (West 2016), which provides that in securitization transactions, assignments are true sales if they are labeled as such, regardless of actual function and intent of parties.

transactions or, quite differently, certain facts on the ground may be assigned (by courts or legislatures) the superior legal presumption. All of these scenarios involve alternative allocations of formality/informality within the legal system as discussed next.

7.2.3 *Locating Legal Informality*

Examples abound in Latin America, and elsewhere, that much legal informality is not outside the legal system but rather within it. It is ordered directly by legislation and enabled indirectly through the mix of background rules. This is what I am calling *legislated informality*. Moreover, legal systems may allocate – or allow for – informality at different points within legal relationships, substantive law requirements, the legal process, and official decision-making. As already noted, it is not as if any legal system in the world has eliminated all forms of informality altogether. That would not be possible or advisable. Developed country law relies on substantial standards-based official decisions, discretion of the parties, self-help remedies, legal ambiguity, function over form, and a host of similar phenomena.

Moreover, if one were to accept certain legal realist insights, the differences between inside and outside the legal system are not substantial.[25] Legislating informality (authorizing private practices, etc.) is not much different than allowing its reign without such explicit approval. Thus, de jure and de facto deference to private ordering – for example – is rather indistinguishable. Deregulating and legislative silence are functionally equivalent. There is nothing truly outside the law or essentially extralegal, the latter being one of the standard understandings of "informality." One could unilaterally insist on a narrow *formal* definition of informality to attempt to cabin its usage. However, that would not reflect functional reality nor how the term gets used expansively.

Indeed, the intention here is not to nail down a definitive meaning for the term "legal informality," once and for all. One could certainly insist on a narrow definition of "informality" in the hopes of policing its expansive and instrumental use. But that is not the project here. Nor is my objective to track down all the many meanings attached to the term "informality." That would certainly be useful but beyond my scope. Rather, this chapter examines a few ways in which the notion has been used. I am not espousing any particular definition myself. I am simply selecting some of its usages in Latin America in order to turn the gaze back on developed country law. How about if developed country law were viewed through the same wide lens of legal informality used to diagnose underdevelopment?

[25] R. L. Hale, Coercion and Distribution in a Supposedly Non-Coercive State (1923) 38 *Political Science Quarterly* 470–94 (legislated coercion and background norms producing coercion are indistinguishable).

When viewed from this angle, informality – in its expanded use – is alive and present throughout the developed world. Most of it is just not typically characterized as *negative*. Instead, it is legitimated by alternative terms and concepts that normalize it. Moreover, the locus of informality – when comparing laws and legal systems – is different from legal community to legal community. And that is not always a sign of dysfunction (of either one or the other). Informality is simply a legal device employed with different policy and distributional consequences.

7.2.4 *Heterodox Legal Informality*

Latin America has historically produced different allocations of legal informality – different from hegemonic models. This is what I am calling *heterodox legal informality*. It has been the region's main contribution to modern law. To take it seriously, however, legal informality requires destigmatization and differentiation among its varieties. It is not just an epithet to be used against things we don't like. And, distinguishing among the different meanings is crucial to developing better policy. The specific type of informality foregrounded here is located within law itself, whether overtly legislated or produced indirectly through the intersection of background rules.

In a number of legal domains in Latin America, the locus of informality is – or has been – simply different than where global hegemonic models prescribe. For example, local criminal procedure may place investigative and charging authority in the hands of a "judge of instruction," rather than a public prosecutor. However, both involve significant quotients of discretion to the officials designated. And this kind of standards-based, relatively unaccountable decision-making is one of the possible definitions of "informality." But this kind of informality is obtained in either case. It is simply allocated differently, to different officials in different offices.

Indeed, over the past twenty years in Latin America, the United States Agency for International Development (USAID) and other foreign assistance have been heavily involved in promoting the transformation of criminal procedure codes in the region.[26] The change is characterized as moving from an inquisitorial to an adversarial system. One of the main indictments of the inquisitorial system is the wide discretion it vests in the "judge of instruction." In civil law systems, a judge is in charge of the investigation phase of a criminal proceeding. They should lead an effective investigation but also safeguard the rights of defendants. This type of "informality" lying within the entire discretion of the judge of instruction has been highlighted as exceptional and intolerable. It is damningly perceived as providing no accountability for decisions made, unchecked by defense counsel, a "secretive" process, and increasing the likelihood of outside influence and corruption.

[26] M. Langer, Revolution in Latin American Criminal Procedure: Diffusion of Legal Ideas from the Periphery (2007) 55 *American Journal of Comparative Law* 617–76.

However, the big change made in many Latin American countries was to move those decisions to a public prosecutor, along the lines of the model of the United States. The prosecutor has broad discretion in deciding whether or not to take on a criminal case, what charges to press, whether or not to enter into a plea deal, and a number of other questions throughout the life of a criminal case. All the same discretion remains, if not more. In fact, judges of instruction had in some cases less discretion. They had to process all cases brought to them and could not choose to drop a case. However, prosecutorial discretion – no less a form of informality – within the legal system appears more natural to USAID funders than the civil law analogue. Informality has not been eliminated. It has just been relocated.

Legal informality in developed and developing countries is, in fact, not so dissimilar. The difference, I am arguing, is its location. Some countries locate their informality under the auspices of different officials, allow certain social or economic groups to exercise their particular norms and practices, and sanction explicitly or not certain activities or individuals to undertake self-help remedies. Whether these allocations are justified or not, should be reformed or not, is certainly a topic of debate and contestation. They should not, however, be simply refuted or reformed on the basis of the practice being stigmatizingly labeled informal, or that the informality happens to be located differently than "developed country" models. Indeed, the strong belief in Weber's reputed characterization has obscured the fuller picture.[27] Developed legal systems are riddled with instances of informality, whether legislated directly or indirectly through background rules or meaningful omissions and lacunae.

When examining Latin American legal systems, however, these heterodox phenomena are often lumped together as harmful informality, especially when placed in the hands of unexpected actors and situations. Unexpected because the informality is assigned differently than where informality occurs in hegemonic models. By contrast, within hegemonic models, the given allocations of informality are normalized as acceptable – if not preferable – and may not even be fully understood as examples of informality. Indeed, as already noted, instances of informality are routinely described more positively as standards-based decision-making, deference to commercial practice, functionalism, self-help remedies, alternative interpretations, legal pragmatism, and other such legitimating characterizations. By contrast, the over-inclusive epithet of "informality" for these same and other phenomena is mostly reserved for developing countries.

Certainly, informality assigned *de jure* or *de facto* to unexpected parties and situations appears, from an external perspective, as extralegal. It looks like social norms prevailing over legal norms, pragmatic workarounds to ineffective legal systems and outright law breaking. Such informality seems to be taking place wholly

[27] See generally, E. Ehrlich, *Fundamental Principles of the Sociology of Law*, W. L. Moll (ed.) (Cambridge: Harvard University Press, 1936).

outside the legal system. From this angle, the greater the informality, the greater the gap appearing to exist between law and society. The greater the gap between law and society, the greater the perceived failure of law. The greater the perceived failure of local law, the more compelling the exhortations to adopt hegemonic models.

Ideological filters that normalize informality generally fall away when examining foreign legal systems. Unless the lines separating formality and informality are drawn exactly the same way, foreign informality assigned to different actors and situations appears strikingly prominent and out of place. In these foreign contexts, informality has not been normalized, especially from an outsider perspective. Rather, it stands out. It stands out from the baseline normal, or what is unreflexively considered normal from an external legal consciousness. The observed legal community may indeed have developed its own modes of legitimating specific allocations of informality and formality. However, as is often the case in developing countries, there is frequently much less self-legitimating discourse surrounding those systems. And foreign observers are indubitably less attuned to – or interested in – its affirmative construction.

Indeed, in any liberal-legalist system, reinforcing the rationality and justification of legal institutions and legal outcomes requires substantial resources – both discursive and economic. Legal scholars and legal commentators are on the front lines of this societal and institutional function. Overall, their job is to justify and legitimate the workings of liberal legal systems, often in the face of contradictory values and inevitable failures and shortcomings. The objectives of neutrality, objectivity, and universality that these systems aspire to, however, are tall bills to fill. The inevitable shortcomings are mitigated through explanations and post-hoc rationalizations by supportive – or relatively supportive – legal experts and commentators.

In developing countries, this task of social construction is less well sustained, or less well prioritized, as an essential element of liberal-like legal systems. Latin American countries, in particular, have constructed national legality as relatively continuous with continental European and in some cases US law. Local legitimating discourse often piggybacks on foreign scholars from those same source countries. Such foreign sources and commentators, however, are principally focused on their own legal systems and their particular composition. Justifying the mix of formality and informality chosen, or – when seen as a whole – in place, in a given Latin American country, is not at the forefront of concerns for foreign legal scholars or international observers.

As such, there is no institutionalized rebuttal, defense, or justification generally available to defend Latin America's particular allocations of formality and informality. This is not to say that *all* informality – wherever and of whatever type – is justified and should be maintained. But, some of it might. They are not simply social norms interfering with otherwise formal legal systems, not simply a gap between the law on the books and law in action, not simply an unjustifiable transaction cost or inefficiency. Rather, they are an integral legal device. However, it is not possible to perceive them as such – or credibly argue in defense of a particular configuration – if they are summarily denounced. If they are automatically diagnosed as the product of failed legal systems.[28]

In the examples in Section 7.3, one can better appreciate the various generations of law-and-development as a preference for one combination of formalization/informality over another. The mix of formality and informality is simply different: different from pre-reform law and different across the various generations of law and development itself. They are differences, however, that have major policy and distributional implications.

7.3 EXAMPLES FROM LATIN AMERICA

This section discusses two examples of legal heterodoxy from Latin America. The first concerns secured transactions law and the "heterodox" secured lending previously in place. It has been substituted almost in its entirety by reforms based on UCC Article 9. It is a story of the difficulties of sustaining and articulating a credible defense for heterodoxy in the Global South. The second example concerns the special private–law transitional justice scheme enacted in Colombia. It is an exceptional measure to address that country's long-standing guerrilla war and displacement of people. It transforms the traditional rules of property. Admittedly, it is an exceptional measure with a limited duration, twenty years. However, the model has the potential to be extended to other policy concerns and potentially made permanent or of long duration.

7.3.1 *Secured Transactions Laws*

Laws enabling personal property guarantees for debts are another example of the travails of legal heterodoxy. In an area of law highly relevant to transnational financial interests, secured credit in recent years has been a major topic. Indeed, secured lending has widely caught the attention of the US government, international financial institutions, development experts, and legal scholars. It is considered an essential aspect of economic development, presumably enabling additional resources in the form of debt to support business development. With liberalized security laws, the thinking goes, creditors would be encouraged to lend more freely on the strength of debtor's economic resources. And they would do so at lower rates of interest. Anything of value could potentially serve as collateral. And creditors could easily enforce property rights to obtain those resources upon the debtor's default.

[28] J. L. Esquirol, The Failed Law of Latin America (2008) 56 *American Journal of Comparative Law* 75–124.

The ostensible objective of reforms is thus to make credit more readily available to all debtors, from all creditors, and guaranteed by anything of value. The model overwhelmingly pursued is Article 9 of the Uniform Commercial Code, adopted in all fifty US states. It is the preeminent model for secured transactions worldwide. International financial institutions and proponents of harmonization widely promote it. It has at this point influenced numerous legal reforms around the world.[29] It is a model directly or indirectly, in its essential terms, pursued by international institutions, including in the Organization of American States's (OAS) Model Inter-American Law on Secured Transactions.[30] The UNCITRAL (United Nations Commission on International Trade Law) Model Secured Transactions Law,[31] and the recommendations of the International Finance Corporation, which is part of the World Bank Group, equally follow this same approach.

Many Latin American countries have followed suit. They have modified their laws to resemble Article 9. Some have adopted the OAS Model Law, in part or outright.[32] The latter is also patterned on Article 9.[33] Vestiges of differences and distinctions from earlier secured transactions models may remain in certain countries.[34] However, the reforms move in the direction of making anything of value the potential object of collateral, the creation of a single security device to do so, and a centralized registry to record these consensual liens.[35] Latin American countries have not been able to resist this type of uniformization.[36] After all, providing

[29] Article 9, internally, contains its own imperial ambitions. It limits recognition of debtor-located applicable law to jurisdictions with similar filing provisions. UCC 9-307(c), Comment 3. Absent that, the applicable law is Washington, DC.

[30] The Model Inter-American Law on Secured Transactions ("Model Law") was approved by the Sixth Inter-American Specialized Conference on Private International Law (CIDIP-VI) on February 8, 2002.

[31] F. Fiorentini, Legal Transplants in the Law of Secured Transactions. Current Problems and Comparative Perspectives, in F. Fiorentini and M. Infantino (eds.), *Mentoring Comparative Lawyers: Methods, Times, and Places* (Cham: Springer, 2020), pp. 3–23, p. 3 and 13 (describing the heavy influence of US-based Commercial Financial Association in the drafting of the UNCITRAL model law, and corresponding Article 9 similarities).

[32] Guatemala (Decree No. 51 of 2007), Honduras (Legislative Decree No. 182 of 2009), Colombia (Law No. 1,676 of 2013), El Salvador (Decree No. 488 of 2013), Panama, some provisions (2013), Costa Rica (Law No. 9,246 of 2014), Peru (2018); Mexico (Reform to Ley General de Títulos y Operaciones de Crédito, May 23, 2000 and June 13, 2003); Dominican Republic (2020).

[33] A. M. Garro, Exportability of North American Chattel Security Regimes: The Inter-American Model Law on Secured Transactions (2006) 43 *Canadian Business Law Journal* 200–7.

[34] A. M. Garro, La Ley Modelo Interamericana sobre Garantías Mobiliarias: Primeros Desafíos en su Implementación, in *The Organization of American States – Inter-American Juridical Committee, Curso de Derecho Internacional XXXVII (2010)* (Rio de Janeiro: OAS, 2011), pp. 127–70 (discussing implementation in Peru, Guatemala, and Honduras).

[35] M. Dubovec, UCC Article 9 Registration System for Latin America (2011) 28 *Arizona Journal of International and Comparative Law* 117–42, 142 (arguing that Latin American states – other than Honduras – fail the test of international model instruments for secured transactions registration reform).

[36] At the Organization of American States Commission meeting adopting the OAS Model Secured Transactions law, which incorporated the US delegations essential 7 principles based

unconditional market access, without government limitations, is an essential part of the neoliberal recipe – at least when it comes to some markets and for some market actors.

The international campaign began in the 1970s with funding by the Rand Corporation and the United States Agency for International Development.[37] Recipient of this funding, Professor Boris Kozolchyk's National Law Center for Inter-American Free Trade at the University of Arizona has led the charge throughout Latin America. Many commentators note his oversized influence and direct involvement with reform proposals in Latin American legislatures.[38] His center produced the Arizona Project, modeled on Article 9, which served as the first draft, and substantially final, for the OAS Model Law.

Other legal scholars have also forcefully argued for Article 9 as the model for Latin America-wide harmonization.[39] Among them, Professor Alejando Garro at Columbia Law School has been instrumental with extensive publications and consulting, critiquing Latin America's selective model and praising Article 9.[40] Moreover, liberalized secured transactions laws are heavily endorsed by the United States government, international financial institutions, the European Union, and other promoters of Article 9. Legal heterodoxy in this realm has been explicitly targeted for elimination, which makes the defending and maintaining of alternative models quite improbable.

Such reforms and the discourses that propel it have been, nonetheless, critiqued from certain quarters. To some extent, Latin America's alternative political economy and modes of regulation have been championed. For example:

> [T]here are consistent assertions that Mexico's secured transactions and bankruptcy laws are not just deficient, but pre-modern, archaic, and backwards. These same voices contend that Mexico's economic development will remain retarded as long as the Mexican government fails to adopt protections of creditors modeled after the U.S. Uniform Commercial Code. These discourses are propagated by elite

on Article 9 of the UCC, only Guatemala declared the right to not approve the model law on the grounds that enforcement provisions were "exclusively thought for the benefit of creditors." D. Fernández Arroyo, La CIDIP VI ¿Cambio de Paradigma en la Codificación Interamericana de Derecho Internacional Privado, in *The Organization of American States – Inter-American Juridical Committee, Curso de Derecho Internacional XXIX (2002)* (Rio de Janeiro: OAS, 2002), pp. 465–600, p. 475.

37 Garro, Exportability of North American Chattel Security Regimes.

38 Crediting Kozolchyk as the intellectual author of the OAS Model Law, and indefatigable activist, Fernández Arroyo, La CIDIP VI, p. 8.

39 A. M. Garro, The Reform and Harmonization of Personal Property Security Law in Latin America (1990) 59 *Revista Jurídica de la Universidad de Puerto Rico* 1–156.

40 See e.g., A. M. Garro, Security Interests in Personal Property in Latin America: A Comparison with Article 9 and a Model for Reform (1987) 9 *Houston Journal of International Law* 157–242; A. M. Garro, The Difficulty of Obtaining Secured Lending in Latin America: Why Law Reform Really Matters (1996) 1 *Yearbook of International Financial and Economic Law* 97–116; Garro, Exportability of North American Chattel Security Regimes.

corporate groups within the U.S. that have vested interests in altering particular aspects of Mexico's legal system.[41]

Critiques of this type, however, remain vastly in the minority. Alternatives – heterodoxies – are hard to sustain.[42] The analysis that follows focuses on the interests disfavored by Article 9 reforms. It also examines the preconceptions and discredit associated with alternative legal devices. Part of the campaign in favor of reform rides on critiques of the particular mix of formalism and informality. It is especially this latter dimension that I consider here.

The following sections describe the heterodox model previously in place in Latin America. And, they examine the allocations of informality inherent in both this model and in Article 9. My argument is that the selective "Latin American" model simply assigns informality differently than Article 9 does. The latter could be equally faulted on grounds of "informality." Indeed, I provide three different examples of *legislated informality* within Article 9. However, these are not perceived as signs of its weakness but of its strength. This is evidence of the structural bias operating within developed and developing country discourse. It is not about whether or not there is informality. It is about where informality is preferably located and by whom it is exercised. And, ultimately, whose preferences prevail on these questions.

7.3.1.1 Selective Secured Transactions Laws

Latin American countries began from a different starting point. They generally pursued a model of *selective* secured lending. Historically, the civil codes in these countries limited personal property security to the traditional pledge. That legal device requires the transfer of physical possession of the collateral to the creditor. Only in this way are these asset guarantees (for other than publicly *registered* personal property) enforceable against all others. Certainly, this is an unworkable solution for debtors that must handle those assets on a regular basis. Only in some countries did commercial codes relax this requirement.[43] They enabled nonpossessory security interests for merchants. In the past, however, for most countries of the

[41] T. A. Canova, Banking and Financial Reform at the Crossroads of the Neoliberal Contagion (1999) 7 *United States – Mexico Law Journal* 85–120, 94–95 ("A very ethnocentric mind-set permeates these dominant discourses. They conveniently overlook the flaws in the US legal system and in US bankruptcy law. In addition, there seems to be no formal modeling or empirical support for the more dramatic assertions that Mexico's commercial code is the primary and direct cause of the country's economic plight. Finally, these dominant development discourses also overstate the deficiencies in Mexican law").

[42] C. R. P. Pouncy, Contemporary Financial Innovation: Orthodoxy and Alternatives (1998) 51 *SMU Law Review* 505–90, 510 and 575 ("heterodox (economic) concerns (lie) with greater risk taking, increased speculation and diminished monetary control").

[43] Garro identifies these countries as Colombia, Panama, Costa Rica, Mexico's capital district, and Paraguay. Garro, Security Interests in Personal Property in Latin America; See e.g. Colombia (Commercial Code, Decree No. 410 of 1971, Article 1200).

region nonpossessory security interests were only available through *special enabling legislation*.

7.3.1.1.1 SPECIAL LAWS In civil law countries generally, not just Latin America, special legislation has historically supported a selective approach to secured credit.[44] Specific industries and products have been singled out for the benefits of this private law instrument. Special laws were created over time for specific types of personal property. These include assets commonly serving as security, such as automobiles, vessels, and generally registered property. But, more creatively, special legislation can target specific assets, industries, and creditors.

Selective secured credit is not simply pre-modern, archaic, and backward – as development reformers insist. It does promote some defensible goals. Selectively enabling *non-possessory* security interests provides opportunities for enacting industrial policy. It allows governments to conduct differential credit policy through a private law mechanism. Moreover, it allows them to do so without state aid or subsidies, which could violate contemporary international trade treaties. These special laws are not government subsidies or exemptions from amounts owed to government. Rather, this scheme mobilizes the rules of private law, commercial law specifically. It does so in a way such as to create segmented credit markets. Some actors are capable of accessing – through the relevant legislation – secured credit markets. Others are not. Only certain industries or products are granted such exceptions, in this case "private law" benefits. Additionally, certain conditions may be imposed in order to qualify for the exception, whether certain products, production methods, environmental sustainability, or other.

Both France and Italy, for example, developed this sectorial approach over time.[45] Secured credit was not indiscriminately made available in the civil code. Rather, certain sectors of the economy were selected legislatively to benefit from this legal privilege. The laws in each of these countries developed over time, dependent on economic exigencies and the importance of certain industries or sectors of the economy. Probably the most recent example of this is Italy's enactment of special legislation for the wine and alcoholic beverage industry. As part of its COVID-19 emergency measures to support the economy, it extended these norms to these industries in its 2021 *Cura Italia* decree.[46] Previously, collateral enabling legislation had been directed to the prosciutto industry in 1985 and aged-cheese industry in

[44] Along with common law developments, such was the case in the United States as well, prior to UCC Article 9.

[45] J. L. Esquirol, Les Outils Juridiques en Matière de Politique Économique: L'Exemple de la Réforme du Droit des Sûretés en France (2022) 22 *Revue des Juristes de Sciences Po* 4–11; J. L. Esquirol, Credit Supports for Italian Specialty Products: The Case of Prosciutto and Long-Aged Cheese (2021) 14 *FIU Law Review* 589–614.

[46] Decree 23 of 2020 (Italy).

2001.[47] These laws allow producers to grant their stock of products, warehoused during the ageing process, as collateral without transfer of possession to the creditor. These provisions are limited to certified Italian origin denominated goods. And, they are conditioned on producers following the traditional production protocols required by their industry association. In short, selectively – rather than liberally – enacting secured lending laws functions as a sort of industrial policy. Whether thought out comprehensively over any one point in time, or the accretion of past decisions of industrial policy, the overall model in the history of civil law countries is one of selective enabling laws.

Latin America followed this selective approach.[48] Most countries in the region, starting in the late nineteenth and early twentieth century, opted for the French model of *warrants* and *gages sans dépossession*.[49] The *warrants* were new legal instruments that combined a negotiable instrument and chattel mortgage over specifically defined assets. The *gages sans dépossession* constituted a nonpossessory pledge with registration. There is considerable similarity among the region's twenty plus countries.[50] A discernible pattern of economic policy emerges at historical inflection points.[51] Like in France, the earliest laws were in the agricultural sector.

47 Law No. 401 of 1985 (Italy), Law No. 122 of 2001 (Italy).

48 A useful summary is provided by Garro, Security Interests in Personal Property in Latin America, 162 and 175–99.

49 A *warrant* consisting of a warehouse receipt, see Esquirol, Les Outils Juridiques en Matière de Politique Économique.

50 Notably, Mexico did not follow this course. They have a *guaranty trust* that preceded the 2001/2003 reforms, remains unrevoked by reforms, and by all accounts functions well as a guarantee device. Debtors transfer title on collateral to a guarantee trust for the benefit of one or multiple creditors. No official or judicial intervention is required for foreclosure. Additionally, the general warehouse receipt long exists as a form of real right guarantee. General Law on Negotiable Instruments and Credit Transactions of 1932 (Mexico), Article 229; See also, A. Lopez-Velarde and J. M. Wilson, A Practical Point-by-Point Comparison of Secured Transactions Law in the United States and Mexico (2004) 36 *Uniform Commercial Code Journal* 3–65, 14–15.

51 Argentina: Law No. 928 of 1878 (initially for any goods deposited in customs houses); Law No. 9,643 of 1914 (available for national agricultural, ranching, forestry, mining, and manufacturing products warehoused in third part depositories with the exception of wine); Bolivia: Civil Code, amended by Decree Law No. 12,760 of 1975 (providing for nonpossessory agricultural, hotelier, and industrial pledges); Brazil: Decree No. 3,272 of 1885 (nonpossessory agricultural pledge with registration on crops, machinery and others with prior consent of real property mortgage holder); Law No. 492 of 1937 (rural pledges over agricultural products and animals without transfer of possession and with registration in real estate registries); Decree Law No. 1,271 of 1939 (extending nonpossessory pledge with registration to industrial machines and apparatuses), replaced by Decree Law No. 413 of 1969 (creating *cédula de crédito industrial*, a promissory note with security interest including guarantees of industrial personality without dispossession and with registration); Chile: Law No. 497 of 1926 (agrarian nonpossessory pledge), Law No. 4,702 of 1929 (nonpossessory purchase money security interest with registration over specific items of personalty); Law No. 5,687 of 1935 (nonpossessory industrial pledge); Colombia: Law No. 24 of 1921 (nonpossessory agrarian pledge including working machinery, animals and products of national mining and industry); Decree No. 553 of 1932 (nonpossessory industrial pledge extending to industrial machinery, tools, raw materials,

Such laws enabled pledges without transfer of possession, so-called agrarian pledges. They defined the permissible scope of assets, debtors, and creditors. These later led to industrial pledges: extending the same legal device to industrial debtors and their particular assets. The conditions and terms of legislation certainly vary across countries. The terminology may also be slightly different. Overall, though, the differences between this selective model and Article 9 are highlighted next.

7.3.1.1.2 HETERODOX INFORMALITY The reform campaign for secured transactions in Latin America has relied mostly on critiques of *legal formalism*, not informality per se. The variety of laws pertaining to different industries, different debtors, and different registries are condemned as part of Latin America's typical, excessive formalism. Yet, as this same thinking goes, that leads to a sort of informality for those not benefiting from the legislation. They must resort to a combination of contractual means, legal subterfuges, and official complicity to simulate their desired legal outcomes. Excessive formalism and informality here work together discursively. Debtors excluded from selective enabling laws must recur to other devices to achieve comparable yet less favorable results.

Certainly, private parties can transact into nonpossessory secured transactions. They can operate under the general rules of contract law – in relation to either official or ad hoc creditors. However, these are not recognized as property rights enforceable against third parties and the bankruptcy trustee. Historically in the civil law, there has been a limitation on contractual arrangements for asset guarantees, and the parties need careful drafting to avoid such pitfalls.[52] However, the difference between formal and *informal* is precisely the point. It is the relative advantage made available to the law's intended beneficiaries. Only the former may assuredly engage in secured credit transactions, backed by assets employed in the operation of business, enforceable by creditors, *against all others*.

Certainly, credit market segmentation is quite controversial from a neo-liberal economics perspective. Differentiation is precisely what hegemonic secured transactions reform is intended to eliminate. The latter is championed as opening up

products); Peru: Law No. 2,402 of 1916 (nonpossessory agricultural pledge available only to farmers and ranchers); Law No. 23,407 of 1982 (nonpossessory industrial pledge over machinery, tools, raw materials, and products).

[52] The doctrine of *pacto comisorio* is a civil code prohibition that limits the ability of parties to contingently transfer property rights upon default by simple contract. It effectively works to bar self-help strict foreclosure (permitted by UCC Article 9-620 in which the secured party transfers ownership to itself upon debtor's default without returning any surplus value of collateral to debtor, over amount owed, but disallowing deficiency claims against the debtor in case of insufficient value to cover the debt). The doctrine is meant, among other possibilities, to protect the debtor from rapacious creditors or the debtor itself. It creates a pitfall for the unwary contract drafter but does not prevent contractual arrangements altogether. That discussion, however, is beyond the scope here. See Fiorentini, Legal Transplants in the Law of Secured Transactions; M. Bussani, *Il Problema del Patto Commissorio: Studio di Diritto Comparato* (Torino: Giappichelli, 2000), pp. 10–94.

credit to all on equal terms and on anything considered by the parties to be of value. Article 9 does indeed provide a singular security device for all industries in the real economy. However, this does not mean that it does not differentiate among markets. It focuses on financial assets – with different rules depending on financial type and deviations from standard priority rules. It is economic policy tailored to the financial industry. Wall Street not Main Street.

Still, defenders of the state's need to undertake industrial policy remain steadfast. This is especially so in developing countries where "Main Street" is the principal, or only, economy. Beliefs about the ability of completely undirected markets to create development, sustainable and equitable, are very much disputed. Sectorial differentiation – rather than financial asset differentiation – may be even more important there. In light of that economic debate, *selective* secured credit is not necessarily anachronistic but rather an alternative legal device that enables a different economic policy prescription.

The disagreements over economics may be debated on their own merits. The economic reasoning may certainly be challenged from a neo-liberal perspective. Nonetheless, selective enabling is an approach with a long pedigree in Western countries and an articulable rationale in its favor. Credit markets are segmented.[53] And the private law rules enable this differentiation. However, the arguments are obscured by erroneously characterizing it as arcane legal tradition, cumbersome technique, or even legal informality. Disagreements over these policy differences cannot genuinely be resolved by simple appeals to formalizing the informal, or conversely reducing formalism. That shortcut would circumvent the economic and distributional decisions being made. It is tantamount to deregulation and liberalization without transparent discussion.

7.3.1.2 "Liberalized" Secured Transactions

The transformation to "liberalized" secured transactions upends the selective model. At its utmost, liberalization means enabling anything of value, from any debtor, to be conveyed to any creditor, preferentially against all others, with minimal recording requirements, enforceable privately without recourse to the courts. The reforms are promoted as pro-development, pro-modernization, good for small- and medium-sized businesses, and a win–win. It portends to place all potential debtors on equal footing. In effect, it restructures how the state implements credit policy. Government is deprived of the use of multiple legal devices, tailored to specific industries, to devise and implement industrial policy through private law. Regardless

[53] The dual economy hypothesis in developing countries has been reaffirmed by authoritative studies such as La Porta and Shleifer, Informality and Development. They see duality as between formal and informal. But, even within what is considered formal, rejecting segmentation is neither realistic nor conducive to good policy necessarily.

of one's economic theory or political preferences, the change is not merely one of modernization over tradition, development over stagnation. Rather, it reflects divergent opinions with respect to industrial policy, and it generates different distributional outcomes.[54]

Latin America is not the only region to feel the pressure to "liberalize," nor is it just developing countries. Italy passed liberalizing reform in 2016, coming into effect just this past 2022.[55] France has gone through two stages of liberalization in 2006 and 2021, while still retaining some nominal distinctions.[56] Regardless, the Article 9 model contains its own mix of formality and informality.[57] This is not the place for a detailed description of the workings of the UCC. Suffice it to say that Article 9's provisions create a singular legal device for all non-realty consensual guarantees.[58] The result serves as an example of the political and economic indeterminacy of critiques of formalism. In this case, formalism's opposite – functionalism – is placed at the service of the financial industry.[59] Anything of value can be *preferentially* conveyed to creditors as collateral.[60] As to its particular types of "informality," I point out three dimensions: private action (self-help) based on social norms; informal types of property; and related transactions outside the law's scope.

54 Article 9 does not eliminate the state's ability to conduct industrial credit policy through private (commercial) law. It merely replaces the technique of doing so through multiple security devices. It favors a singular device (the security interest), while allowing for differential rules related to different asset types and effects of perfection in its many specialized provisions.

55 Decree Law No. 59 of 2016 (Italy), *Disposizioni urgenti in materia di procedure esecutive e concorsuali, nonché a favore degli investitori in banche in liquidazione*, converted into Law No. 119 of 2016 (Italy).

56 Ordinance No. 2006-346 of 2006 (France) relating to sureties; Ordinance No. 2021-1192 of 2021 (France) reforming the law of sureties. See J. F. Riffard, The Reform of the French Law on Security Interests (Droit des sûretés): A Second and Final Season? (2022) *Zeitschrift für Europäisches Privatrecht* 565–84 (explaining that the French Reforms which commenced in 2006 and retaken in 2021, were instigated by pressure from the World Bank's Doing Business Reports, ranking France low).

57 Consider G. Gilmore, *Security Interests in Personal Property*, vol. I (Boston: Little, Brown & Company, 1965), pp. 24–25 (describing the relaxation of the transfer-of-possession to creditor requirement in the Anglo-American tradition, as passing from a conclusive presumption of retention of possession by seller/creditor to one of a rebuttable presumption, and then a variety of independent security devices).

58 K. Llewellyn, Problems of Codifying Security Law (1947) 13 *Law and Contemporary Problems* 687–702, 694 ("Codifiers in the field of secured commercial transactions are not planners of an economy, they are but shapers of legal tools to be used at will").

59 A. R. Kamp, Downtown Code: A History of the Uniform Commercial Code 1949–1954 (2001) 49 *Buffalo Law Review* 359–476, 361 ("In the words of Soia Mentschikoff, 'special interests' won over the drafters' desire to protect small merchants and consumers ... They (business representatives on drafting committee) wanted, for example, the unified article 9 security interests that allows a financier to have priority on almost all the debtor's assets but did not want any provisions for consumer disclosures or limitations of obtaining or realizing on a security interest").

60 Llewellyn, Problems of Codifying Security Law, 694 ("I as a person feel that the tendency of full legal availability of the assets of an enterprise to serve as security will *expand* net credit materially less than it will *secure* that credit" (original emphasis)).

7.3.1.2.1 SELF-HELP REMEDIES Article 9 deploys informality in several ways. Most prominently, it authorizes self-help remedies for repossession of collateral and foreclosure of a debtor's property rights. Creditors can seize debtors' property without any prior judicial notice or supervision. Private parties may seize the collateral and dispose of the property to satisfy the underlying debt. The only limitation is that creditors not "breach the peace" as part of the physical act of seizing the property. And the only remedies for debtors are post hoc. They may be able to sue for wrongful repossession, if they can prove damages. And, they may defend against a deficiency judgment – that is, a judgment for the remaining amount of the debt beyond the proceeds of the foreclosure sale – if the repossession and foreclosure are not conducted by the creditor in a commercially reasonable manner.

There can be no greater example of legal informality than this.[61] The legal process is seconded to private actors.[62] Creditors and their agents may carry out the entire procedure of seizing assets and terminating debtor's rights. All of this under the most general and cursory admonition to creditors to not "breach the peace" and to proceed under "commercially reasonable" standards. These post hoc restraints have proven very malleable and are interpreted in wildly different ways. It leads to conflicting and even absurd results. In some cases, simply saying no to a repossessor entails a breach of peace if the latter proceeds anyway.[63] In another reported case, two male repossessors could legitimately proceed in the middle of the night against a single mother with two small children, living in a trailer park, contrary to her physical overtures to enter her car and the disturbance caused to neighbors.[64] And, most perplexingly, a repossession carried out with the accompaniment of paid law enforcement *does* constitute a breach of the peace even where there was no disruption or violence, because the debtor was inhibited from becoming violent – ironically.[65] Moreover, the post hoc check of commercial reasonableness only works to eliminate deficiency judgments against debtors. As such, the actions of creditors and their agents are constrained, if anything, by *social norms and personal limits*. The line of illegality is frequently grazed if not outright breached with impunity. Notably, this is an area in which social norms reign in the place of law. It is legislated informality.

61 See Rosenn, The Jeito (providing a typology of good and bad legal informality in Latin America. Self-help remedies would certainly fall under more than one of these categories).

62 Courts have found no due process for debtors because no state action is involved. See W. M. Burke and D. J. Reber, State Action, Congressional Power and Creditors' Rights: An Essay on the Fourteenth Amendment (1973) 47 *Southern California Law Review* 1–57.

63 *Hollibush* v. *Ford Motor Credit Co.*, 508 N.W.2d 449 (Ct. App. 1993); *Dixon* v. *Ford Motor Credit Co.*, 391 N.E.2d 493, 497 (Ill. App. Ct. 1979).

64 *Williams* v. *Ford Motor Credit Co.*, 674 F 2d 717 (8th Cir.1982); see also *Chrysler Credit Corp.* v. *Koontz*, 661 N.E. 2d 1171 (Iil. App. Ct. 1996).

65 *Stone Machinery Co.* v. *Kessler*, 463 P.2d 651 (Wash. Ct. App. 1970); see also Comment 3 to UCC §9-609.

Globalization of Article 9 on this very point has met with significant resistance. Even countries that have in principle adopted "self-help" remedies have built in protections.[66] Secured creditors must repossess under the supervision of a notary public or public official. Moreover, the debtor may stop creditor's self-help remedies if there is disagreement on the default, amount of debt, or right to repossess. These safeguards for debtors have provoked a hail of criticism from Article 9 harmonizers. Only the most extensive informal version is considered economic and efficient. Indeed, in the case of Mexico, for example, it has led to the complaint:

> The Mexican legislator seems to harbor a fundamental distrust of the marketplace, wary of the secured creditor's capacity to restrain himself from abuses against his debtor if foreclosure is made too easy and of the debtor's capacity to assert himself when he has a valid defense or cooperate in an expeditious foreclosure when appropriate.[67]

Formalization here is rather a global inclination, if not the hegemonic one.

7.3.1.2.2 INFORMAL PROPERTY Another example of informality relates to the scope of Article 9. The latter is primarily a property statute governing chattel mortgages. But it also includes contractual payment rights and treats them increasingly like property. It accomplishes the latter by muddying the differences between contract and property.[68] This is especially poignant in the case of accounts receivable.[69] The elision has become so normalized in US legal culture that it is hard to see. It is a two-step operation. First, payment rights are deemed to be "property." What that means is not a given, however. Second, the full range of property features are presumed.

Article 9 principally advances the second step. It extends the *power* to convey "preferential rights against all others" to contract right-holders.[70] A contract right-

66 D. B. Furnish, Mexico's Emergent New Law of Secured Transactions: Recent Developments 2000–2010 (2011) 28 *Arizona Journal of International and Comparative Law* 143–82, 169 ("the Mexican foreclosure procedure … established excessive safeguards for the debtor, creating a high-cost, time-consuming process that favored the debtor at the expense of the creditor, thus raising the cost of credit by increasing the risks associated with default").

67 Ibid., 171.

68 Article 9-109(a) ("creates a security interest in personal property" and "sale of accounts, chattel paper, payment intangibles or promissory notes." The original Article 9 included the term "contract rights" specifically as objects of collateral). Secured Transactions: Sales of Accounts, Contract Rights and Chattel Paper, UCC 229 (1951). Currently, those not covered by the definition of accounts are included as payment intangibles; see G. Gilmore, Security Law, Formalism, and Article 9 (1968) 47 *Nebraska Law Review* 659–77, 671 ("Almost nothing new was added"); see G. Gilmore, The Assignee of Contract Rights and His Precarious Security (1964) 74 *Yale Law Journal* 217–61, 218 ("Security assignments of executory contract rights have been widely used only in recent years").

69 An account receivable is simply money owed to a party, whether under a contract or simple sales transaction. Article 9 differentiates among the types of rights to payment, but that is not necessary for the discussion here.

70 See W. N. Hohfeld, *Fundamental Legal Conceptions as Applied in Judicial Reasoning and Other Legal Essays* (New Haven: Yale University Press, 1919), pp. 35–42. Distinctive features of

holder does not have a "preferential right against all others" with respect to its debtor. But it can nonetheless convey one to its own creditor.[71] Admittedly, the contract right and the derivative preferential right are enforceable by different parties. Still, the logic runs counter to the fundamental property principle that one cannot convey more than one has.[72] Much less the contract rule that assignees stand in the shoes of their assignors.

In the world of Article 9, however, this all makes perfect sense. The objects of security interests need not consist of full title. *Any right* held by a debtor will suffice.[73] Conveyed to a creditor, it becomes a full preferential right. In this way, Article 9 sanctions a sort of *informal* property creation;[74] that is, contract rights with property characteristics. Notably, Article 9 does not codify a new property type. Nor does it change the definition of "personal property." Nor does it explicitly announce a *power* to convey greater rights.[75] Rather, it simply operates *as if* it already existed. It is not that the distinction between contract and property does not matter in the common law[76]: it does, throughout the legal system, including other sections of Article 9.[77] On this particular point, however, doctrinal "informality" flourishes.

property are priority against all others and the right to pursue in the hands of others. Security interests under Article 9 share these two characteristics, see § 9-117/§ 9-322 and § 9-315.

[71] Including contractual rights in Article 9 enables additional preferential rights for secured creditors. Specifically, expected income flows from contract payments need not be sold outright but rather granted as collateral. The latter produces a legally valid conveyance at the time concluded and perfected. Such act marks the priority ranking of preference of creditors. And, it grants creditors immunity from later fraudulent conveyance challenges, when the actual transfer to creditor really takes place upon default (likely near the bankruptcy date). This "perfected" transfer also ensures that the conveyance is enforceable against all others, including the bankruptcy trustee. Extending this property rule to contracts potentially excludes yet another source of repayment by the debtor away from the unsecured voluntary and the involuntary creditors.

[72] Compare UCC 2-403 that expressly grants greater rights to the transferee from the transferor with voidable title; Hughes, Robots, Markets, and the Value of Deal Lawyers.

[73] Art. 9-203(b)(2) and Comment 6.

[74] See generally Y. Emerich, La Nature Juridique des Sûretés Réelles en Droit Civil et en Common Law: Une Question de Tradition Juridique? (2010) 44 *Revue Juridique Themis* 95–142, 103–13, 125–28 (describing the predominantly essentialist perspective of civil law secured transactions law: "[It] creates a situation relatively heretical for the civilian in that a concept is preserved whilst associating it with the legal regime of a different concept").

[75] Article 9 does recognize such powers may derive from other law, such as UCC Article 2-403 (explicitly granting better title to transferee over transferor's voidable title); and Article 3-305(b) (holder in due course of negotiable instrument has greater rights than transferor subject to claims and defenses); UCC Article 9-617 expressly authorizes the transfer of greater rights to the transferee in a foreclosure sale, since the Secured Party is not an "owner" and the Debtor is not voluntarily transferring. See W. D. Warren and S. D. Walt, *Secured Transactions in Personal Property*, 10th ed. (New York: Foundation Press, 2019), p. 319 ("Although the selling secured party does not 'own' the collateral after repossession, 9-617(a) (1) empowers it to make a transfer of all of the debtor's rights to the transferee").

[76] Ibid., pp. 130–31.

[77] See Emerich, La Nature Juridique des Sûretés Réelles en Droit Civil et en Common Law, 125–28; see also, UCC Article 9-607 distinguishes between a true sale and a security assignment for transfers of accounts receivable in the application of the commercially reasonable standard

Admittedly, accounts receivable have long been considered "property" in the United States.[78] They have been extensively assigned and used as collateral since the 1920s and expanding after WWII.[79] Assignments of such accounts were first popularized in the textile industry. In turn, assignments of long-term contract rights became popular during World War II, to finance inputs for US government procurement contracts. Such transactions assumed a property-like nature, at least with respect to assignor–assignee conveyances and debtor–creditor collateral.[80] Doctrinalists in the United States have gone as far as claiming that contract rights are property, *tout court.*[81]

Regardless, the fact that contract rights have some property features does not mean that they have to have them all. Contract rights serving as property-guarantees *enforceable against all others*, especially against the bankruptcy trustee and all involuntary creditors, is an additional step. Yet, it passes relatively unremarked.[82] In this way, Article 9 effectively adds more property features to contract

for disposition. On the one hand, Article 9's inclusion within its scope of the sale of financial assets – such as accounts, instruments, chattel paper, and payment intangibles – blurs the distinction of ownership and other rights. On the other, the formal distinction re-emerges as legally meaningful, in which commercial lawyers and courts must grapple with the meaning of "ownership." Comment 4, UCC Article 9-109 ("That issue is left to the courts"); Here is an example of the significance elsewhere based on the "nature" of the transaction: "The question for the court then is whether the *nature* of the recourse, and the true nature of the transaction, are such that the legal rights and economic consequences of the agreement bear a greater similarity to a financing transaction or a sale." *Major's Furniture Mart, Inc.* v. *Castle Credit Corp., Inc.*, 602 F 2d 538 (3rd Cir. 1979); see also, J. Moringiello, False Categories in Commercial Law: The (Ir)Relevance of (In)Tangibility (2007) 35 *Florida State University Law Review* 119–66, 120 (arguing that tangibility and traditional conceptions of property re-enter Article 9 enforcement attempts and argue for collapsing the tangible/intangible distinction in Article 9 in favor of the "legal qualities of those assets").

78 A. L. Corbin, Assignment of Contract Rights (1926) 74 *University of Pennsylvania Law Review and American Law Register* 207–34; Gilmore, The Assignee of Contract Rights and His Precarious Security, 221 and 259 ("It is assumed, and there is no modern authority to the contrary, that such rights can be effectively assigned ... We have been discussing the assignee's righemerts on the assumption that only the original parties to the financing transaction are involved. Against third parties such rights might be of doubtful worth").

79 M. S. Boas, Legal and Economic Aspects of Accounts Receivable Financing and Factoring (1954) 59 *Commercial Law Journal* 65–67.

80 Commentators continue to support this formula, without explicit distributive analyses. See Moringiello, False Categories in Commercial Law, 132–33, "For the purpose of creditors' rights laws, this inquiry remains current; if a right can be transferred for value (or in exchange for a 'fund'), then it should be capable of serving as collateral ... It remains necessary to give those rights a property label because Article 9 defines collateral in property terms." In the 1940s, many US states regulated the assignment of receivables confirming the same stature. 'Comment', (1958) 67 *Yale Law Journal* 402, 410–1 (twenty-three states requiring recordation).

81 A. Corbin, *Corbin on Contracts: A Comprehensive Treatise on the Working Rules of Contract Law* (Saint Paul: West Publishing Company, 1951), vol. IV, p. 418 (§ 860 Is a Contract Right "Property"?).

82 Article 9-318 rejects prior US Supreme Court invalidation (based on fraudulent conveyances New York law) of enforceability against bankruptcy trustee of accounts receivable assignment because of non-notification to account debtors (retention of dominium by debtor), *Benedict*

rights.[83] It extends the power to grant enforceability against all others.[84] And, it does so informally by fudging the distinction between assignment of contract and mortgage of property. It subsumes both types of transactions indistinctly within its scope.[85] The differences between contract and property are thus blurred.[86]

It is not incidental that Article 9 avoids all mention of property rights, opting instead for the term security "interest." The UCC drafters admit, in an obscure comment on licenses:

> Neither this section nor any other provision of this Article determines whether a debtor has a property interest ... the debtor's *property interest* may be confined solely to its interest in the promises made by the licensor in the license agreement (e.g. a promise not to sue the debtor for its use of the software) (italics mine).[87]

This insouciance about formal categories is no doubt a testament to the UCC's legal realist pedigree.[88] Surely, there are strong arguments for function over form. A debtor's contractual rights to payment from a third party is a definable value over which a creditor *could* be assigned priority.[89] Nothing materially impedes it. Not wholly dissimilar situations in Latin America have been labelled "informal"

v. *Ratner* 268 U.S. 353 (1925). Article 9 comments state that it "makes explicit what was implicit, but perfectly obvious."

83 As an additional example, Article 9 extends additional property-like protections to accounts receivable by rendering ineffective any contractual restriction on the alienation of accounts receivable, as impermissible restraints on alienation. Article 9-406(d), Comment 5 ("the policies ... under this section build on common law developments").

84 S. Posel, Factoring Accounts Receivable in France: Some Legal Aspects and American Comparisons (1982–1983) 57 *Tulane Law Review* 292–327, 293. ("Free from the restrictions and doubts which once surrounded its legal status, such a loan *(secured by accounts receivable)* is no longer the expensive practice it was during and between the World Wars. Governed by article 9 (secured transactions), which specifically includes accounts as available collateral security"); see also G. Gilmore, Article 9: What It Does for the Past (1966) 26 *Louisiana Law Review* 285–99, 295 ("a sixth part [of Article 9], on long-term contract rights financing as distinguished from short-term accounts receivable financing, was projected but never reached draft stage"). Subsequent reforms have extended the definition of accounts and payment intangibles to the point long-term payment rights are also included.

85 UCC 9-109(a); 9-309(2) (retaining the ambiguous "assignments" language for accounts and payment intangibles).

86 Gilmore, *Security Interests in Personal Property*, pp. vii–ix (extending the "property rule," Gilmore transforms the question into: "what types of claims or choses in action ..., can be presently transferred ... with the result that today's assignee will have priority?"); but see Corbin, Assignment of Contract Rights, 229 ("the right of the assignee is the same right as that previously held by the assignor").

87 Article 9-408, Comment 3.

88 Llewellyn, Problems of Codifying Security Law, 694; Gilmore, Security Law, Formalism, and Article 9; P. Winship, An Historical Overview of Article 9, in L. Gullifer and O. Akseli (eds.), *Secured Transactions Law Reform: Principles, Policies and Practice* (Oxford: Hart Publishing Ltd, 2016), pp. 21–48.

89 Comment, Contract Rights as Commercial Security: Present and Future Intangibles (1958) 67 *Yale Law Journal* 847–92, 861 ("A criterion of identifiability would accordingly appear a more realistic standard").

property, that is, private contractual arrangements that are treated like property.[90] At the same time, enabling the proliferation of informal property priorities through private ordering contradicts the contemporary development mantra on the need for "clear property rights."[91] Functionality and informality may be different sides of the same coin.[92]

In any case, "functionalist" deconstruction of the property–contract distinction does not address its distributive effects. The fact that contractual and other rights can be treated as property *functionally/informally* does not mean that they should be. Function here is not neutral.[93] The doctrinal distinction has major policy implications. How much of debtor's economic value can be prioritized for some obligations and not others? Privileged are consensual creditors – without limits on the economic value available for their prioritized claims.[94] In the process, contractually produced judgment-proof debtors may leave non-self-adjusting involuntary creditors without any recourse whatsoever.[95] Think workers, pensioners, tort judgment creditors, tradespeople, and the like. They may be left with no assets to satisfy their claims. These considerations may be particularly relevant to developing countries where Article 9 is exported, which may not have social safety nets like workers compensation or pension guaranty trusts.

90 Karst, Rights in Land and Housing in an Informal Legal System (contractual arrangements coupled with de facto acquiescence by the state labeled informal property). Notably, Karst ascribes a positive development value to informality of this type. Subsequent law and development reverses that: targeting it for formalization; B. Kozolchyk and C. Castaneda, Invigorating Micro and Small Businesses through Secured Commercial Credit in Latin America: The Need for Legal and Institutional Reform (2011) 28 *Arizona Journal of International and Comparative Law* 43–116, 89 (contractual arrangements simulating a registered business association).

91 Esquirol, Titling and Untitled Housing in Panama City; Da. Kennedy, Some Caution about Property Rights as a Recipe for Economic Development (2011) 1 *Accounting, Economics & Law* 1–62.

92 See Hughes, Robots, Markets, and the Value of Deal Lawyers (Article 9 endorses unclear conveyances, contradictorily styled both sales and security interests in the securitization context. Article 9 legislates this informality by conflating (1) sales of payment rights and (2) transfers of security interests in payment rights. Investment bankers are allowed to exploit the ambiguity – or informality – of blurred legal categories: pretending they are sales to induce maximum investor assurances while knowing the seller/debtor will claim they are security interests upon a default).

93 Kamp, Downtown Code, 362 ("The reality is that the Code is a political document – the product of political realities of the early 1950s on the state level").

94 Ibid., 374 ("They (business representatives on drafting committee) wanted, for example, the unified article 9 security interests that allows a financier to have priority on almost all the debtor's assets but did not want any provisions for consumer disclosures or limitations of obtaining or realizing on a security interest").

95 Involuntary creditors are creditors that do not choose to be creditors. They are simply owed money from a past debt, court judgment, or outstanding legal claim. They are nonadjusting because it is not in their power to negotiate for better terms, raise the interest rate, etc., since this is not a voluntary anticipated relationship. The list in the next sentences provides some examples.

In the civil law tradition including Latin America, this operation is much more debated.[96] Civilians are more punctilious and insistent about "formalities." The *conceptual* question has bedeviled commentators and courts.[97] Can "obligations" be property? Property rights over contractual obligations have been controversial, if not an outright anomaly. They are like apples and oranges.[98] Likely, it is because the civil law world is more categorical about legal distinctions.[99] It defies the quintessential logic of contract and property, personal and real rights. In Latin America, security interests over floating stocks, proceeds, and uncertificated accounts receivable, for example, have been a particularly thorny issue.[100] A property right over a contractual right appears quite anomalous, and a contractual right such as an account receivable is not property. It is only in the latter half of the twentieth century that certain property rights over contract rights became admitted.[101] But, even so, it remained mostly a minority position in doctrinal circles.[102] It has been

[96] Some civilian jurisdictions abide by the doctrine of *numerus clausus* that limits "real" rights. Property rights are limited to those enumerated in the civil code or, alternatively, legislation. The topic is beyond the scope here, but see generally B. Akkermans, The Numerus Clausus of Property Rights, in M. Graziadei and L. Smith (eds.), *Comparative Property Law: Global Perspectives* (Northampton: Edward Elgar, 2017). Article 9 provides that legislative authority – although as I am arguing here *informally*.

[97] See S. Praduroux, Objects of Property Rights: Old and New, in M. Graziadei and L. Smith (eds.), *Comparative Property Law: Global Perspectives* (Northampton: Edward Elgar, 2017), pp. 51–70 ("It is widely debated whether claims – especially monetary claims for a fixed sum of money – can be classified as things that can be the object of property rights. This issue is controversial especially in legal systems which restrict property law to corporeal things; but even under legal systems that recognize property rights over intangible things, there is no consensus among legal scholars as to whether claims can be the objects of ownership or other rights of property"). It is beyond the scope here to discuss the differences *across* civil law systems.

[98] The differences between property and contract may be approached in – at least – three different ways: either nominally, functionally, or distributionally. Nominally, historical characterizations of legal relationships and their traditional objects are paramount. Functionality looks past nominal differences to the role the device serves, or can serve, in real transactions. Distributionally, who wins and who loses takes precedence in the analysis. Both nominal and functional arguments sidestep the real stakes.

[99] Some of the main proponents of the indistinguishability of credits (i.e., personal obligations) and real rights were the French legal realists described by M. C. Belleau, The Juristes Inquiets: Legal Classicism and Criticism in Early Twentieth Century France (1997) 1997 *Utah Law Review* 379–424; Y. Emerich, *La Propriété des Créances: Approche Comparative* (Paris: Librairie Générale de Droit et de Jurisprudence, 2007) (citing Josserand, Saleilles, Bonnecase); see specifically, J. Bonnecase, La Condition du Créancier Chirographaire: Sa Qualité D'ayant-Cause à Titre Particulier (1920) 19 *Revue Trimestrielle de Droit Civil* 103–50; R. Saleilles, *Etude sur la Théorie Générale de l'Obligation d'Après le Premier Projet de Code Civil pour l'Empire Allemand*, 3rd ed. (Paris: Librairie Générale de Droit et de Jurisprudence, 1925).

[100] See Garro, Security Interests in Personal Property in Latin America, 197–98; Furnish, Mexico's Emergent New Law of Secured Transactions, 153–54.

[101] S. Ginossar, *Droit Réel, Propriété et Créance: Elaboration d'un Système Rationnel des Droits Patrimoniaux* (Paris: Librarie de Droit et de Jurisprudence, 1960).

[102] The solutions arrived at in civil law jurisdictions are, nonetheless, not diametrically opposed to the UCC – even before the influence of Article 9 worldwide. Some jurisdictions had settled on

asserted that certain contractual obligations have a dual nature.[103] Defenders of "credits" or contractual rights, as property, have also upheld this classification on functional grounds.[104] Rights to payment, the argument goes, can be appropriated and conveyed just like property.[105]

Not surprisingly, the question of "property" was one of the stumbling blocks over the Article 9-inspired Arizona Project first presented as the OAS model law by the United States. Early on, Mexican commentators noted the Anglo-American particularity of the text that did not fit with Latin American legal codifications precisely for this reason:

> Typical *personal rights* will now be the axis upon which previously real rights transited. Or said in different words, assets today have a different value than assets conceived under the structure of real rights.[106]

These objections led, in response, to Mexico's co-presidency (along with the United States) of the OAS Commission that approved that institution's model law. It ultimately produced the same informalization of property evident in Article 9, possibly with a "Latin American" twist. Specifically, the discussion of "real" rights – the civilian term for property rights – was simply set aside, given the insistence by reformers for property-like priority over personal rights and credits.[107] The doctrinal conundrum between real and personal rights could not be formally resolved, so it was informally settled by not calling them property rights.

7.3.1.2.3 INFORMAL OTHERS Finally we come to closely-related parties and transactions that Article 9 leaves out. These other legal relations operate in a realm of relative informality. In this regard, I channel the work of Peruvian economist Hernando de Soto specifically. He draws a hard line between formals and informals. Formals are those that operate within the formal legal structure. Informals are all those that operate outside, for whatever reason. The costs of formal transactions may be too high. They may not be convenient for them. There may be too many

a comparable formula. *Certain* contractual rights to payment may be the object of a property right as a guarantee. In France, for example, the 1980 Loi Dailly initiated this path, taken further by the 2021 reforms to the Civil Code. Law No. 81-1 of 1981 (France), amended January 24, 1984. Monetary and Financial Code (France), Articles L. 313-23.

[103] Emerich, *La Propriété des Créances*.

[104] Ibid.; J. Flour, J. L. Aubert, and E. Savaux, *Les Obligations: L'Acte Juridique*, t. 1, 10th ed. (Paris: Dalloz, 2002); Ginossar, *Droit Réel, Propriété et Créance*.

[105] Riffard, The Reform of the French Law on Security Interests, with respect to accounts, "the ordinance [of 2021] aligns the rules of effectiveness against third parties of pledge and assignment." Essentially extending that rule to collateral transactions – like Article 9 does.

[106] L. Pereznieto Castro, Comentarios al 'Proyecto México -Estadounidense para una Ley Modelo en Materia de Garantías Mobiliarias (2001) 10 *Revista Mexicana de Derecho Internacional Privado* 59–66 (translation mine).

[107] Compare the Chilean Law, however, which specifically accepts the "real right" of guarantee over future goods and rights. Article 9, Law No. 20,190 of 2007 (Chile).

bureaucratic steps to fulfill. They may be subject to an alternative set of rules, functionally similar but distinct. Regardless, de Soto's prescription for development is to turn informals into formals. This means, in effect, lowering or eliminating legislative and regulatory conditions that treat them differently, whether that requires unconditionally titling squatters, automatically licensing street vendors, or condition-free regularizing of workers. No differentiations – or only minimal ones.

This conceptualization merely serves, however, to redraw the regulatory lines. Anything outside the existing lines can be labeled "informal." The conditions for it, and the reasons those operating outside may want to remain so, as well as policy reasons for having more than one line, are dismissed or simply ignored. Informality, once identified, must be formalized – according to this prescription. In the case of de Soto, the new lines proposed happen to coincide with neo-liberal preferences.

Yet, Article 9 could be described in similar ways. It draws its own regulatory lines, not always in functional ways.[108] Agricultural liens are included, but not other nonconsensual liens.[109] Consumer deposit accounts cannot serve as original collateral, but they can when they are the proceeds of a different type of collateral.[110] The centralized registration system excludes nonconsensual liens (with the exception of agricultural liens).[111] All of these are subject to complicated rules beyond the scope here, but the point is that Article 9 makes significant policy distinctions.

Additionally, security agreements need not be recorded or even written. Loan amounts are not public information, nor is meaningful documentation of collateral provided, especially in the case of accounts and contract rights.[112] The latter must be forensically reconstructed when bankruptcy or other issues arise, requiring proof

[108] See H. Hughes, Aesthetics of Commercial Law – Domestic and International Implications (2007) 67 *Louisiana Law Review* 689–750; see also, Kamp, Downtown Code, 435–48 (reporting politics of secured transactions provisions).

[109] S. C. Turner et al., Agricultural Liens and the UCC: A Report on Present Status and Proposals for Change (1991) 44 *Oklahoma Law Review* 9–70.

[110] Up until 2001, deposit accounts were excluded altogether. UCC Article 9-109; W. E. Gibson, Banks Reign Supreme under Revised Article 9 Deposit Account Rules (2005) 30 *Delaware Journal of Corporate Law* 819–62; G. T. McLaughlin, Security Interests in Deposit Accounts: Unresolved Problems and Unanswered Questions under Existing Law (1988) 54 *Brooklyn Law Review* 45–94; see also W. F. Kroener III and S. L. Sepinuck, Report of the Subcommittee on the Use of Deposit Accounts as Original Collateral, Working Document No. M6–44, in Permanent Editorial Board for the Uniform Commercial Code, *PEB Study Group Uniform Commercial Code Article 9 Report* (Philadelphia: PEB for UCC, 1992).

[111] Agricultural liens – created independently by state law – are incorporated within the registration and priority system of Article 9. All other statutory liens as well as judgment liens are not included. These others have their own separate state-prescribed procedures. And they are addressed by Article 9 only within general provisions on the relative priority of other "lienholders," defined as statutory and judgment liens.

[112] G. A. Moglia Claps and J. B. McDonnell, Secured Credit and Insolvency Law in Argentina and the U.S.: Gaining Insight from a Comparative Perspective (2002) 30 *Georgia Journal of International and Comparative Law* 393–442, 416 ("describing the Argentine system as more formal than the U.S. system does not in any way establish that the Argentine system is bad and the U.S. good. Formality is a normal feature of the legal order as indeed the Argentine hipoteca

such as invoices, bank statements, ledgers, and oral testimony. All of these features may be characterized as *informality* of various types.[113]

Indeed, distributing the remaining assets of an insolvent debtor may be seen as requiring a wholistic formal legal regime. Latin American systems have been faulted precisely for failing at that.[114] But, the scope of wholistic reform under the model of Article 9 extends only so far. For example, the silence on involuntary creditors effectively downgrades their remedies, if not eliminates them altogether. Their rights and powers are dependent on sources outside of Article 9 – for their different creation, priority, and enforcement. This is not unlike Hernando de Soto's "informals." Indeed. their relative order of preference is not pegged to a pre-emptive "perfection" or *notice* filing date, but in the best of cases after the legal process runs its course and a valid judgment is rendered.[115]

Surely, another way to perceive this is not as a gap or informality but as deliberate and justifiable, a conscious political or policy decision. Employees, pensioners, and other involuntary creditors – no matter how meritorious – have little or no priority and may only collect after everyone else. The priority date for these creditors is when a judgment is obtained. Surely, that is the case in the United States. Still, a relative informality – or an alternative formality if you will – is the way of achieving this result. These are matters of deliberate choice. As is evident, the mantra of comprehensive formalization alone cannot neutrally decide the question.

7.3.1.3 Section Summary

The transformation from selective to liberalized secured transactions law rearranges the elements of formality and informality. In the process, it distributes resources differently. The two models both allow for informality but at different stages and assign it to different actors. It would be hard to choose one model over the other based merely on *preferring formalization*. Both have elements of formality and informality. And arguments based merely on the equating "formalization" – or the model effectively labeled as representing formalization – with development are misleading. Indeed, the choice cannot be made as a technical legal matter. Rather, it requires understanding the relative benefits assigned to different parties under different regulatory regimes.

The informality of Article 9 may be no greater than that denounced in developing countries, although of a different type. The difference is that Article 9's text remains

and U.S. mortgage reflect. The critical issue in each case is whether the appropriate formalities are in place. That issue involves the weighing of competing values").

113 Ibid.

114 Furnish, Mexico's Emergent New Law of Secured Transactions, 156–59.

115 Contrast to the singular exception provided by Art. 9-333, addressing and giving priority to statutory *possessory* liens – where the goods subject to lien are in the possession of the involuntary creditor.

relatively unchallenged, indeed hegemonic.[116] As such, it can effectively elide the question of superior rights granted to priority secured creditors over all economic value of the firm. It blurs the distinction between property and contract and effectively makes these rights property. The latter squarely involve economic and social policy questions. These should be debated specifically, not as either "transcendental" legal categories, disembodied functional equivalents, or informal property rights.

7.3.2 *Real Property Laws*

In a quite different example of legal heterodoxy, a 2011 Colombian law introduced a transitory property regime.[117] It was intended to right the wrongs of property despoilment generated by that country's civil conflict. Even though the conflict was not yet over, nor is it still completely now, the state acted to restore property to those displaced by the war, at least in areas where it was secure to do so.[118] The new law was meant to operate for 10 years, which was later extended another ten years, now in effect until 2031.[119] It sets up a separate state bureaucracy to deal with restitution cases. It has achieved some notable success. It is an elaborate scheme of new actors and new government offices.

For our immediate purposes, the more interesting points are the heterodoxy it introduced into property law. In the context of transitional justice, it modified the basic rules of ownership. Rather than employ command and control public legislation, it amended the rules of private law for cases of involuntary displacement. Restitution claims are judged based on alternative criteria, modified presumptions, and shifted burdens of proof. Indeed, this property restitution scheme offers another example of re-arranging formal and informal elements in the legal system. It is an instance of heterodox informality.

7.3.2.1 Traditional Property Law

Normally, property law in Colombia – like in most modern legal systems – grants superior rights to registered property owners.[120] Real property formalization in the

[116] See Hughes, Aesthetics of Commercial Law.

[117] Law No. 1,448 of 2011 (Colombia), Art. 74; For a general description of the law, see N. Summers, Colombia's Victims' Law: Transitional Justice in a Time of Violent Conflict? (2012) 25 *Harvard Human Rights Journal* 219–35.

[118] For a detailed history of reparation efforts to displaced persons, see A. J. Bautista Revelo, *La Restitución de Tierras en Colombia: ¿Realidad o Ficción?* (Quito: Universidad Andina Simón Bolívar / Corporación Editora Nacional, 2015); D. L. Attanasio and N. C. Sánchez, Return within the Bounds of the Pinheiro Principles: The Colombian Land Restitution Experience (2012) 11 *Washington University Global Studies Law Review* 1–54; R. Uprimny-Yepes and N. C. Sánchez, Los Dilemas de la Restitución de Tierras en Colombia (2010) 12 *Revista Estudios Socio-Jurídicos* 305–42.

[119] Law No. 2,078 of 2021 (Colombia) (extending Law 1,448's effectiveness from 2021 to 2031).

[120] M. R. Gardeázabal, *Teoría General de la Propiedad* (Bogotá: Themis, 2011).

civil law tradition typically takes one of two forms. Either it conditions property rights on public registration or it conditions enforceability of property rights against all others on the act of registration. Colombia recognizes ownership without registration but makes it subject to superior rights of registered owners. This step, registration, is considered the epitome of formalization. Registered right-holders receive all the legal procedural advantages.[121] They enjoy a presumption in their favor. Opponents, mounting a challenge, must rebut the presumption and carry the burden of proof demonstrating better rights.

In recent years, a wave of development projects has swept the developing world which purports to extend this type of formalization to all land holdings. Indeed, international financial institutions have embraced the formula of titling all forms of landholding. Squatters, irregular tenants, and others have been made eligible to receive full title ownership. Along with that presumably come the benefits of legal presumptions in their favor and shifted burdens of proof.[122] The formula has been advanced as a social justice measure for the landless and a development project for the economy. The locked-up capital of irregular holdings may become more freely alienable and available for mortgage loans. In both cases, markets are expected to expand.

Formal property in this mold, in the full-title civil code form, is not bereft of informality however.[123] Legal systems throughout the world recognize a quintessentially *informal* method of land transfer. Adverse possession is an integral part of property law in both common law and civil law countries. Open and notorious irregular possession of another's land (but not state land) over an extended period of time vests superior rights in the informal holder. Two types of adverse possession are recognized: adverse possessors in good faith who presumably had good title but there is a defect, and adverse possessors lacking good faith. Both of these periods have been repeatedly shortened over the past century: They currently stand at five and ten years, respectively.[124]

Adverse possession is not the only type of legislated informality.[125] Irregular possessors of state land may also be eligible for ownership rights. Under agrarian reform laws, the state may assign certain lands to landless farmers meeting eligibility guidelines. One of the requirements, under one of the procedures, is occupation of those lands for a period of time. Once again, informality is legislated and sanctioned. Meeting the formal requirements for both adverse possession and allocation of state

[121] Hale, Coercion and Distribution in a Supposedly Non-Coercive State.

[122] P. S. Pinheiro (Special Rapporteur on Housing and Property Restitution in the Context of the Return of Refugees and Internally Displaced Persons), *Principles on Housing and Property Restitution for Refugees and Displaced Persons* (New York: United Nations Economic and Social Council, 2005), princ. 15.7.

[123] Esquirol, Titling and Untitled Housing in Panama City.

[124] Law No. 791 of 2002 (Colombia).

[125] Esquirol, Formalizing Property in Latin America, 333 (discussing presumption shifting in the Colombian 1936 Agrarian Reform Law).

lands requires informality. It requires the irregular occupation of land. Indeed, the initial Colombia agrarian reform law of 1936, Law 200, provided for superior rights to occupants of state land working the soil for a period of two years.[126] No registration was required or expected. Indeed, this legislated informality worked as the pre-eminent legal fact. It carried primary legal significance. Possibly in an era, and at a time, where extensive cartography and registration were not feasible, raising alternative acts to the level of legal significance made perfect sense. Regardless of the differences in time and resources, however, these quick examples demonstrate the deliberate uses of informality within the law.

Moreover, property theorists have demonstrated the equally property-like nature of competing claims to formal ownership.[127] Disputes over the use of land, for example, may thus be best understood as consisting of property claims on both sides. Squatters may have colorable property claims based on adverse possession or agrarian reform laws. Neighbors may have a legal privilege to challenge nuisances on adjoining property based on city ordinances. Long-time licensees of land may have accrued property interests in the development decisions of formal owners. The task for adjudicators is not identifying an owner based on strictly formal indicia and then excluding all others. Rather, the issue when more realistically approached requires resolving competing property claims (including both formal and informal elements) to determine who is in fact the "owner" of the specific *entitlement* in question.

Furthermore, formal property rights in both civil and common law systems are subject to a number of well-known limitations and restrictions.[128] They are certainly not absolute and are subject to the discretional state power of eminent domain; dependent on zoning laws in the area and their potential modification; and restricted by nuisance doctrines and other local rules and regulations. Many of these are subject to formal processes themselves (e.g. amending zoning laws and declaring eminent domain). They are subject to wide swaths of official discretion and unanticipated variability as evident for example in the determination of what qualifies as a nuisance or differences about takings for a public purpose.

Finally, full title is not the only type of formal property in modern legal systems. Both civil law codes and common law estates demonstrate multiple property forms: Fee simple, mere possession, life estates, fee tails, emphyteusis, servitudes, etc. These are made formally available within the positive law. And not all of them rely on public registration. As such, for example, possessors are recognized as having a property status. They have rights, just different or less than full owners. They may seek judicial assistance against intruders in Colombia for a one-year period.

[126] Ibid.

[127] J. W. Singer, *Entitlement: The Paradoxes of Property* (New Haven: Yale University Press, 2000), pp. 91–94 (distinguishing between the bundle-of-rights approach and entitlements approach to property).

[128] Hohfeld, *Fundamental Legal Conceptions*, pp. 35–42.

However, as initially noted, registered owners have paramount rights. They enjoy all legal presumptions in their favor and the burden is on opponents to dispute their rights. This is what the Colombian transitional justice regime changes.

7.3.2.2 Private Law Transitional Justice

The *traditional* property scheme is vastly unsatisfactory for remedying the particular situation of forcible displacement in Colombia's countryside. There, residents lost their homes and farms due to: Fighting nearby requiring them to abandon their holdings; coercive and below-market purchases by unscrupulous individuals, guerrilla fighters, and organized crime figures taking advantage of the situation; and fraudulent sales at gunpoint or other forms of intimidation. Moreover, some of the displaced had registered title to their lands. Others were mere possessors or occupants of private or state lands. While some cases resulted from harried abandonment and flight, other transfers were formally registered conveyances. These various fact patterns, equally considered as forcible displacement by the law, could not be easily addressed by formal property law. Unless traditional duress can be proven, the sale would not be overturned. Moreover, if adverse possession periods had run against displaced persons, even prior registered owners would lose their rights. Furthermore, possessors and occupants are quickly impeded, by the short statute of limitations, from a return of possession. In all cases, claimants would have to carry the burden of proof in individual cases. All in all, standard property law could not satisfactorily address the multitude of cases. Nor could it effectively restore lands to those unjustly displaced.

More specifically, traditional property raises the formal element of registration as the *sine qua non*. All legal presumptions and preponderance of proof tilt in the favor of registered owners. Other property rights are at best informal. For example, the adverse possessor is informal in that they have no adjudicated rights. At best they have an executory claim to seek adjudication of the land in their favor. By comparison, occupants on state land may not adversely possess under private law rules. Instead, they may seek an adjudication of the land under administrative law, agrarian reform proceedings. However, they are not entitled to such land until the procedure is concluded and rights are granted. Thus, any property claimant seeking to disrupt that status quo has presumptions stacked against them and must carry the burden of proving better rights against the registered owner, satisfaction of adverse possession requirements, or compliance with state land distribution conditions.

As such, everyone other than the registered owner starts from a position of informality. Squatters are normally considered "informal," but so are mere possessors and occupants (even those waiting out adverse possession periods and occupant residency requirements). Past registered owners barred by adverse possession running against them – or those having sold at unfair prices or under coercion not easily proved – may all be seen as holders of informal claims. Faced with a new registered owner, or adverse possessor running the required period, restitution claimants are all *informals* – or informal petitioners. Their particular combination of formal and informal indicia of property rights are insufficient to award restitution – to prevail over new property holders.

Law 1448 changes that. It works by re-arranging the formal and informal elements of property law. Preeminence is assigned to informal indicia of superior property rights. The law itself sets out four fact patterns that are elevated and prioritized: displacement arising from generalized violence, forced collective displacement or serious human rights violations in the area; property concentration of land abutting armed conflict; property transfers to narco-traffickers; and excessively below-market sales (below 50 percent). The law provides a bit more detail and the special land courts, set up by the law, have further refined its application. In any case, demonstrating these facts – with the assistance of the special bureau established to assist claimants – is of preeminent legal significance. It is not property registration that primes all else. It is a particular arrangement of facts on the ground that is awarded superior rights. Registration is only another element of the complicated picture. Still, subsequent purchasers may demonstrate utmost good faith in the transfer and may, as a result, be eligible for state compensation. However, it is not determinative of whether or not they will be able to keep the property.

7.3.2.3 Heterodox Informality in Transitional Property Law

In this manner, facts on the ground – a form of legislated informality – have primary legal significance. The particular circumstances surrounding the transfer, the abandonment, or displacement are what give rise to the superior position of claimants. They are then vested with a legal presumption in their favor. They have a presumptive right to restitution. Subsequent occupants must carry the burden of proof of their own "good faith without fault." If proven, these secondary occupants (as described in the law) may receive compensation, or in some cases alternate property.

This particular arrangement is surely not without faults. It does attempt, however, to get at the problem of manipulation of registration systems to effectuate fraud. And, it has the capacity of setting up a dual or multiple property market. Indeed, its mechanisms could be extended to other domains. In this case, it is the public policy determination to restore land to displaced persons. The subjects of fact patterns identified in the law are assigned a priority. The informal, multiple and fact-driven situations enjoy presumptions and shifted burdens of proof which prevail over formal registration. But displacement is not the only public policy issue which could potentially be addressed this way.

Low-income housing and small-scale farming may also be considered. The scarcity and unaffordability of these proprieties arise from market competition. Merely one single market for urban housing or agricultural land places great pressure on lower income residents and small farmers. It also tends to displace them. As such, a re-allocation of formality and informality – not unlike that in Law 1448 – could be extended to these sectors. Even duly registered transfers of housing and land could be subject to informal requirements. Transferees would need to meet such need or use requirements. Otherwise, transferees – even those duly registered – would be confronted with a reversed legal presumption and shifted burdens of proof. This would act to keep a pool of designated properties within their segment of differentiated markets. The penalty for transfers out would be a private law remedy – a cloud on title and possible reversal of the transaction.

In any case, consideration of other applications must remain for another day. For now, land restitution has been proceeding at a steady pace in Colombia. Even large corporations have been subject to the land courts' orders of restitution.[129] As noted, the program was extended for a second ten-year period. The ultimate merits may surely be better assessed then. However, reconcentration of land is a continuing issue in Colombia. It may be the primary issue in fact. Land restitution only indirectly gets at that. Some restitution claimants are small landholders, but some of them are not. Restitution to the latter only exacerbates the problem of land concentration. As such, other mechanisms of maintaining sectors of low income housing and small scale farming will be needed. Whether the mechanisms contained in Law 1448, or other modes of legal heterodoxy, will crucially need to be devised and implemented.

7.4 CONCLUSION

Legal heterodoxy presents in a variety of ways. Alternative laws, different institutional arrangements, and special procedures may all be discovered in different places. For developing countries, these are not always easy to maintain, even if patently suitable to their particular concerns and constraints. Geopolitical pressures have a large role to play. International institutions, powerful states, and foreign investors forcefully advance their own interests and preferred models. In a hegemonic arrangement, these interests primarily coalesce around a limited set of orthodox types. Thus, heterodoxy that stands out is often condemned, as underdeveloped or dysfunctional.

This is even more the case with informality, or alternative assignments of informality within the legal system. Informality appears like a marquis sign of underdevelopment. Regardless of the fact that all legal systems make use of substantial levels of informality, in the development community it is evidence of dysfunction and a rallying cry for formalization. Of course, informality within the legal system – in the sense of discretion lying with certain public officials, self-help remedies,

[129] H. S. Villota, En 9 Años de Restitución de Tierras se han Condenado 66 Empresas del País, *Caracol Radio*, March 6, 2020; see also Pares, Magistrados Condenan a Reconocidas Empresas a Devolver Tierras, *Pares*, November 6, 2016; Colprensa, Estas Son las Empresas que han Sido Condenadas a Restituir Tierras, *El Universal*, November 2, 2016 (indicating that these nineteen cases add up to approximately 53,821 hectares of land returned).

private dispute resolution, tolerated areas of nonenforcement of law, and other forms – is an intrinsic aspect of liberal legal systems. When those instances of informality arise in unexpected places – especially from the perspective of external observers – they stand out, seem excessive or outright unlawful. Surely, outside observers have internalized the particular mix of formality and informality in their home legal systems. It is those arrangements that seem natural and right. Developed country legal systems dedicate significant resources to normalizing the inherent anomalies of their own versions of liberal legality.

Regardless, probably the most significant type of legal heterodoxy that Latin America produces is its particular arrangements of legal informality. This is not a defense of all of its uses – wherever they may appear. To recall how I began, the term informality is overused. Sometimes it is just a euphemism for illegality. However, in many cases, the mobilization of discretion, private action, self-help remedies, and the like are just differently arranged. As such, a project for continuing work is analyzing the heterodox informality that proliferates in Latin America, and the developing world generally – without negative preconceptions.

BIBLIOGRAPHY

Akkermans, B., The Numerus Clausus of Property Rights, in M. Graziadei and L. Smith (eds.), *Comparative Property Law: Global Perspectives* (Northampton: Edward Elgar, 2017), pp. 100–20.

Attanasio, D. L. and Sánchez, N. C., Return within the Bounds of the Pinheiro Principles: The Colombian Land Restitution Experience (2012) 11 *Washington University Global Studies Law Review* 1–54.

Bautista Revelo, A. J., *La Restitución de Tierras en Colombia: ¿Realidad o Ficción?* (Quito: Universidad Andina Simón Bolívar / Corporación Editora Nacional, 2015).

Belleau, M. C., The Juristes Inquiets: Legal Classicism and Criticism in Early Twentieth Century France (1997) 1997 *Utah Law Review* 379–424.

Boas, M. S., Legal and Economic Aspects of Accounts Receivable Financing and Factoring (1954) 59 *Commercial Law Journal* 65–67.

Bonnecase, J., La Condition du Créancier Chirographaire: Sa Qualité D'ayant-Cause à Titre Particulier (1920) 19 *Revue Trimestrielle de Droit Civil* 103–50.

Burke, W. M. and Reber, D. J., State Action, Congressional Power and Creditors' Rights: An Essay on the Fourteenth Amendment (1973) 47 *Southern California Law Review* 1–57.

Bussani, M., *Il Problema del Patto Commissorio: Studio di Diritto Comparato* (Torino: Giappichelli, 2000).

Canova, T. A., Banking and Financial Reform at the Crossroads of the Neoliberal Contagion (1999) 7 *United States – Mexico Law Journal* 85–120.

Corbin, A., *Corbin on Contracts: A Comprehensive Treatise on the Working Rules of Contract Law*, vol. IV (Saint Paul: West Publishing Company, 1951).

Comment, (1958) 67 *Yale Law Journal* 402.

Comment, Contract Rights as Commercial Security: Present and Future Intangibles (1958) 67 *Yale Law Journal* 847–92.

Corbin, A. L., Assignment of Contract Rights (1926) 74 *University of Pennsylvania Law Review and American Law Register* 207–34.
De Soto, H., *The Mystery of Capital: Why Capitalism Triumphs in the West and Fails Everywhere Else* (New York: Basic Books, 2000).
Dubovec, M., UCC Article 9 Registration System for Latin America (2011) 28 *Arizona Journal of International and Comparative Law* 117–42.
Ehrlich, E., *Fundamental Principles of the Sociology of Law*, W. L. Moll (ed.) (Cambridge: Harvard University Press, 1936).
Emerich, Y., La Nature Juridique des Sûretés Réelles en Droit Civil et en Common Law: Une Question de Tradition Juridique? (2010) 44 *Revue Juridique Themis* 95–142.
La Propriété des Créances: Approche Comparative (Paris: Librairie Générale de Droit et de Jurisprudence, 2007).
Esquirol, J. L., Credit Supports for Italian Specialty Products: The Case of Prosciutto and Long-Aged Cheese (2021) 14 *FIU Law Review* 589–614.
The Failed Law of Latin America (2008) 56 *American Journal of Comparative Law* 75–124.
Formalizing Property in Latin America, in M. Graziadei and L. Smith (eds.), *Comparative Property Law: Global Perspectives* (Northampton: Edward Elgar, 2017), pp. 333–54.
Les Outils Juridiques en Matière de Politique Économique: L'Exemple de la Réforme du Droit des Sûretés en France (2022) 22 *Revue des Juristes de Sciences Po* 4–11.
Ruling the Law: Failure and Legitimacy in Latin American Legal Systems (Cambridge: Cambridge University Press, 2019).
Titling and Untitled Housing in Panama City (2008) 4 *Tennessee Journal of Law and Policy* 243–302.
Fandl, K. J., The Role of Informal Legal Institutions in Economic Development (2008) 32 *Fordham International Law Journal* 1–31.
Fernández Arroyo, D., La CIDIP VI ¿Cambio de Paradigma en la Codificación Interamericana de Derecho Internacional Privado, in *The Organization of American States – Inter-American Juridical Committee, Curso de Derecho Internacional XXIX (2002)* (Rio de Janeiro: OAS, 2002), pp. 465–600.
Fiorentini, F., Legal Transplants in the Law of Secured Transactions. Current Problems and Comparative Perspectives, in F. Fiorentini and M. Infantino (eds.), *Mentoring Comparative Lawyers: Methods, Times, and Places* (Cham: Springer, 2020), pp. 3–23.
Flour, J., Aubert, J. L., and Savaux, E., *Les Obligations: L'Acte Juridique*, 10th ed. (Paris: Dalloz, 2002)
Friedman, L. M., On Legal Development (1970) 24 *Rutgers Law Review* 11–64.
Furnish, D. B., Mexico's Emergent New Law of Secured Transactions: Recent Developments 2000–2010 (2011) 28 *Arizona Journal of International and Comparative Law* 143–82.
Gardeázabal, M. R., *Teoría General de la Propiedad* (Bogotá: Themis, 2011).
Garro, A. M., The Difficulty of Obtaining Secured Lending in Latin America: Why Law Reform Really Matters (1996) 1 *Yearbook of International Financial and Economic Law* 97–116.
Exportability of North American Chattel Security Regimes: The Inter-American Model Law on Secured Transactions (2006) 43 *Canadian Business Law Journal* 200–7.
La Ley Modelo Interamericana sobre Garantías Mobiliarias: Primeros Desafíos en su Implementación, in *The Organization of American States – Inter-American Juridical Committee, Curso de Derecho Internacional XXXVII (2010)* (Rio de Janeiro: OAS, 2011), pp. 127–70.

The Reform and Harmonization of Personal Property Security Law in Latin America (1990) 59 *Revista Jurídica de la Universidad de Puerto Rico* 1–156.

Security Interests in Personal Property in Latin America: A Comparison with Article 9 and a Model for Reform (1987) 9 *Houston Journal of International Law* 157–242.

Gibson, W. E., Banks Reign Supreme under Revised Article 9 Deposit Account Rules (2005) 30 *Delaware Journal of Corporate Law* 819–62.

Gilmore, G., Article 9: What It Does for the Past (1966) 26 *Louisiana Law Review* 285–99.

The Assignee of Contract Rights and His Precarious Security (1964) 74 *Yale Law Journal* 217–61.

Security Interests in Personal Property, vol. I (Boston: Little, Brown & Company, 1965).

Security Law, Formalism, and Article 9 (1968) 47 *Nebraska Law Review* 659–77.

Droit Réel, Propriété et Créance: Elaboration d'un Système Rationnel des Droits Patrimoniaux (Paris: Librarie de Droit et de Jurisprudence, 1960).

Granovetter, M., The Social Construction of Corruption, in V. Nee and R. Swedberg (eds.), *On Capitalism* (Redwood City: Stanford University Press, 2007), pp. 152–72.

Grossman, L., Langdell Upside Down: James Coolidge Carter and the Anticlassical Jurisprudence of Anti-codification (2007) 19 *Yale Journal of Law and Humanities* 149–220.

Guha-Khasnobis, B., Kanbur, R., and Ostrom, E., Beyond Formality and Informality, in Linking the Formal and Informal Economy, in B. Guha-Khasnobis, R. Kanbur, and E. Ostrom (eds.), *Linking the Formal and Informal Economy: Concepts and Policies* (Oxford: Oxford University Press, 2006), pp. 1–18.

Hale, R. L., Coercion and Distribution in a Supposedly Non-Coercive State (1923) 38 *Political Science Quarterly* 470–94.

Hohfeld, W. N., *Fundamental Legal Conceptions as Applied in Judicial Reasoning and Other Legal Essays* (New Haven: Yale University Press, 1919).

Holmes, O. W., The Path of the Law (1897) 10 *Harvard Law Review* 22–36.

Hughes, H., Aesthetics of Commercial Law – Domestic and International Implications (2007) 67 *Louisiana Law Review* 689–750.

Robots, Markets, and the Value of Deal Lawyers (2024) 49 *Journal of Corporation Law* 833–71.

Kamp, A. R., Downtown Code: A History of the Uniform Commercial Code 1949–1954 (2001) 49 *Buffalo Law Review* 359–476.

Karst, K., Rights in Land and Housing in an Informal Legal System: The Barrios of Caracas (1971) 19 *American Journal of Law* 550–74.

Karst, K. and Clement, N., Legal Institutions and Development: Lessons from the Mexican Ejido (1969) 16 *UCLA Law Review* 281–303.

Karst, K. and Rosenn, K., *Law and Development in Latin America: A Casebook* (Berkeley: University of California Press, 1975).

Kennedy, Da., Some Caution about Property Rights as a Recipe for Economic Development (2011) 1 *Accounting, Economics & Law* 1–62.

Kennedy, Du., *A Critique of Adjudication: Fin de Siècle* (Cambridge: Harvard University Press, 1997).

Three Globalizations of Law and Legal Thought, in D. Trubek and A. Santos (eds.), *The New Law and Economic Development: A Critical Appraisal* (Cambridge: Cambridge University Press, 2006), pp. 17–73.

Kozolchyk, B. and Castaneda, C., Invigorating Micro and Small Businesses through Secured Commercial Credit in Latin America: The Need for Legal and Institutional Reform (2011) 28 *Arizona Journal of International and Comparative Law* 43–116.

Kroener III, W. F. and Sepinuck, S. L., Report of the Subcommittee on the Use of Deposit Accounts as Original Collateral, Working Document No. M6–44, in Permanent Editorial Board for the Uniform Commercial Code, *PEB Study Group Uniform Commercial Code Article 9 Report* (Philadelphia: PEB for UCC, 1992), pp. 1–49.

La Porta, R. and Shleifer, A., Informality and Development (2014) 28 *Journal of Economic Perspectives* 109–26.

Langer, M., Revolution in Latin American Criminal Procedure: Diffusion of Legal Ideas from the Periphery (2007) 55 *American Journal of Comparative Law* 617–76.

Larson, J. E., Informality, Illegality, and Inequality (2002) 20 *Yale Law & Policy Review* 137–82.

Llewellyn, K., Problems of Codifying Security Law (1947) 13 *Law and Contemporary Problems* 687–702.

Lopez-Velarde, A. and Wilson, J. M., A Practical Point-by-Point Comparison of Secured Transactions Law in the United States and Mexico (2004) 36 *Uniform Commercial Code Journal* 3–65.

Macaulay, S., Non-Contractual Relations in Business: A Preliminary Study (1963) 28 *American Sociology Review* 55–67.

McLaughlin, G. T., Security Interests in Deposit Accounts: Unresolved Problems and Unanswered Questions under Existing Law (1988) 54 *Brooklyn Law Review* 45–94.

Merryman, J. H., Comparative Law and Social Changes: On the Origins, Style, Decline & Revival of the Law and Development Movement (1977) 25 *American Journal of Comparative Law* 457–91.

Moglia Claps, G. A. and McDonnell, J. B., Secured Credit and Insolvency Law in Argentina and the US: Gaining Insight from a Comparative Perspective (2002) 30 *Georgia Journal of International and Comparative Law* 393–442.

Moringiello, J., False Categories in Commercial Law: The (Ir)Relevance of (In)Tangibility (2007) 35 *Florida State University Law Review* 119–66.

Pares, Magistrados Condenan a Reconocidas Empresas a Devolver Tierras, *Pares*, November 6, 2016.

Pereznieto Castro, L., Comentarios al 'Proyecto México–Estadounidense para una Ley Modelo en Materia de Garantías Mobiliarias (2001) 10 *Revista Mexicana de Derecho Internacional Privado* 59–66.

Pinheiro, P. S., *(Special Rapporteur on Housing and Property Restitution in the Context of the Return of Refugees and Internally Displaced Persons), Principles on Housing and Property Restitution for Refugees and Displaced Persons* (New York: United Nations Economic and Social Council, 2005).

Posel, S., Factoring Accounts Receivable in France: Some Legal Aspects and American Comparisons (1982–1983) 57 *Tulane Law Review* 292–327.

Pouncy, C. R. P., Contemporary Financial Innovation: Orthodoxy and Alternatives (1998) 51 *SMU Law Review* 505–90.

Pound, R., Law in Books and Law in Action (1910) 44 *American Law Review* 12–36.

Praduroux, S., Objects of Property Rights: Old and New, in M. Graziadei and L. Smith (eds.), *Comparative Property Law: Global Perspectives* (Northampton: Edward Elgar, 2017), pp. 51–70.

Riffard, J. F., The Reform of the French Law on Security Interests (Droit des sûretés): A Second and Final Season? (2022) *Zeitschrift for Europäisches Privatrecht* 565–84.

Rosenn, K., The Jeito: Brazil Institutional Bypass of the Formal Legal System and Its Development Implications (1971) 19 *American Journal of Comparative Law* 514–49.

Saleilles, R., *Etude sur la Théorie Générale de l'Obligation d'Après le Premier Projet de Code Civil pour l'Empire Allemand*, 3rd ed. (Paris: Librairie Générale de Droit et de Jurisprudence, 1925).
Sindzingre, A., The Relevance of the Concepts of Formality and Informality: A Theoretical Appraisal, in B. Guha-Khasnobis, R. Kanbur, and E. Ostrom (eds.), *Linking the Formal and Informal Economy: Concepts and Policies* (Oxford: Oxford University Press, 2006), pp. 58–74.
Singer, J. W., *Entitlement: The Paradoxes of Property* (New Haven: Yale University Press, 2000).
Summers, N., Colombia's Victims' Law: Transitional Justice in a Time of Violent Conflict? (2012) 25 *Harvard Human Rights Journal* 219–35.
Trubek, D., Max Weber's Tragic Modernism and the Study of Law and Society (1986) 20 *Law and Society Review* 573–604.
Turner, S. C. et al., Agricultural Liens and the UCC: A Report on Present Status and Proposals for Change (1991) 44 *Oklahoma Law Review* 9–70.
Upham, F. K., Speculations on Legal Informality: On Winn's Relational Practices and the Marginalization of Law (1994) 28 *Law & Society Review* 233–42.
Uprimny-Yepes, R. and Sánchez, N. C., Los Dilemas de la Restitución de Tierras en Colombia (2010) 12 *Revista Estudios Socio-Jurídicos* 305–42.
Villegas, M. G., *La Eficacia Simbólica del Derecho: Examen de Situaciones Colombianas* (Bogotá: Uniandes, 1993).
Villota, H. S., En 9 Años de Restitución de Tierras se han Condenado 66 Empresas del País, *Caracol Radio*, March 6, 2020.
Warren, W. D. and Walt, S. D., *Secured Transactions in Personal Property*, 10th ed. (New York: Foundation Press, 2019).
Weber, M., *Economy and Society: An Outline of Interpretive Sociology*, G. Roth and C. Wittich (eds.) (New York: Bedminster Press, 1968).
Weber, M., *From Max Weber: Essays in Sociology*, C. Wright Mills and H. H. Gerth (eds.) (London: Routledge, 2014).
Winship, P., An Historical Overview of Article 9, in L. Gullifer and O. Akseli (eds.), *Secured Transactions Law Reform: Principles, Policies and Practice* (Oxford: Hart Publishing Ltd, 2016), pp. 21–48.

8

Heterodoxy of the Brazilian Supreme Court

Setting a New Precedent in Response to Ultra-orthodoxy of the Patent Law System

Carlos Portugal Gouvêa

8.1 INTRODUCTION

This chapter proposes an investigation of the landmark ruling by the Brazilian Supreme Court (*Supremo Tribunal Federal*) declaring the unconstitutionality of the patent extension mechanism provided by the Brazilian Patent and Trademark Law at the time. The challenged mechanism extended the term of patents to a much longer period than any other patent regime in the world. The case became known as the "*Artigo 40*" case, referring to the challenged section of the statute, or alternatively, "ADI 5529," referring to the docket number of the case.[1]

This chapter argues that the challenged extension mechanism was the result of a phenomenon I call ultra-orthodoxy, which is the adoption of radically neo-liberal legal institutions in developing countries as a result of the lobbying efforts of

I am grateful for the comments on earlier versions of this chapter received from the participants of the IDGlobal Seminar, organized by the Instituto de Direito Global (Global Law Institute). I am also grateful to the participants in the workshop on Legal Heterodoxy in the Global South, organized by Fundação Getúlio Vargas Law School in May 2023, for helpful comments and discussions. I also acknowledge the detailed and generous comments received from Mariana Pargendler and Kevin Davis on the various versions of this chapter. I thank Calixto Salomão Filho and the researchers from the Law and Poverty Group at the University of São Paulo for their dedication to research and inspiration for this chapter: Gustavo H. Kastrup, Victor Barone, Vitor Ido, Bernardo Castro, Cynthia Maria Santos Bezerra, Gustavo Manicardi Schneider, Joyce Ricarte, Laura Pereira Feitoza, Maria Clara Vieira Câmara, Marina Kanarek, Michelle Baruhm Diegues, Paloma Casanovas Reis, Paulo Fucci, Pietra Christinne Caramalac Braga, Tárik Jarouche, and Thaís Calixto De Abreu. All errors are my own.

[1] STF, ADI 5529/DF, *en banc*, rap. Justice Dias Toffoli, j. 06/05/2021, DJe 01/09/2021. The case challenged the sole paragraph of Section 40 of the Brazilian Patent and Trademark Law as being unconstitutional for violating the principle of legal security, the temporality of patents (Art. 5°, XXIX, Brazilian Constitution), the social function of intellectual property (Art. 5°, XXIX and Art. 170, III, Brazilian Constitution), the reasonable duration of the process (Art. 5°, LXXVIII, Brazilian Constitution), the efficiency of public administration (Art. 37, Brazilian Constitution), free competition (Art. 170, IV, Brazilian Constitution), consumer protection (Art. 170, V, Brazilian Constitution), and the right to health (Art. 196, Brazilian Constitution).

industries with substantial economic power. These institutions are not orthodox, in the sense of merely reproducing legal structures from the Global North, but also are not heterodox, in the sense of trying to respond to economic inequality in the Global South. In the case investigated here, the Brazilian patent law system adopted in the 1990s was not merely a copy of the model proposed by multilateral organizations, such as the World Trade Organization but, rather, a hyperbolic version of the orthodox model which granted foreign enterprises patent rights which were not granted in their countries of origin.[2]

The Brazilian Supreme Court's landmark ruling in ADI 5529[3] declared the automatic patent extension mechanism unconstitutional, mainly on account of its undeniable negative distributive effects, and provided a framework for reversing the damaging effects of ultra-orthodoxy.

Section 8.2 discusses the characteristics of orthodoxy and heterodoxy in the fields of constitutional law, intellectual property law, and the right to health. Section 8.3 focuses on the theoretical groundings of ultra-orthodoxy, using the legislative process that led to the Brazilian Patent and Trademark Law[4] as an example of the development of ultra-orthodoxy. Section 8.4 is dedicated to a detailed analysis of the ruling of the Court on the matter of the patent extensions, highlighting the positions of the different Justices.

The ruling by the Brazilian Supreme Court revealed the ultra-orthodox features of Brazilian patent law and provided a precedent for heterodox responses to ultra-orthodoxy. The ruling had several distinctive features. First was the recognition that Section 40 of the Patent and Trademark Law had negative distributive effects in society and that such effects amounted to a violation of the right to health. A second distinctive feature of the ruling was the value given to independent academic

[2] Such extensions were granted based on the sole paragraph of Section 40 of the Brazilian Patent and Trademark Law, Federal Law No 9,279/1996, which provided the following "Section 40. The patent for invention shall be valid for a period of 20 (twenty) years, and the utility model patent for a period of 15 (fifteen) years, both counted from the filing date. Sole Paragraph. The validity period shall not be less than 10 (ten) years for the patent for invention and 7 (seven) years for the utility model patent, counted from the date of grant, except in cases where the Brazilian National Institute of Industrial Property (INPI) is unable to carry out the substantive examination of the application due to proven judicial conflict or force majeure." In the original Portuguese: "Art. 40. A patente de invenção vigorará pelo prazo de 20 (vinte) anos e a de modelo de utilidade pelo prazo 15 (quinze) anos contados da data de depósito. Parágrafo único. O prazo de vigência não será inferior a 10 (dez) anos para a patente de invenção e a 7 (sete) anos para a patente de modelo de utilidade, a contar da data de concessão, ressalvada a hipótese de o INPI estar impedido de proceder ao exame de mérito do pedido, por pendência judicial comprovada ou por motivo de força maior."

[3] STF, ADI 5529/DF.

[4] Federal Law No 9,279/1996. The statute deals with patents, industrial designs, and trademarks. Copyrights, software, and other specific intellectual property are regulated by other statutes. In Portuguese, this statute is usually referred to as the *Lei de Propriedade Industrial*, or the industrial property law. In order to make such reference clearer for an international audience, in this chapter I will reference it as the Brazilian Patent and Trademark Law.

opinions, not funded by any of the interested industries (the international pharmaceutical industry and the local generic drugs industry), which highlighted the negative distributive effects and identified human rights violations. The court's decisions also illustrated the value of comparative law, particularly with regard to the law of other developing countries, as a means of identifying ultra-orthodoxy.

Section 8.5 is dedicated to analyzing a potential backlash against the decision. A few months after the Brazilian Supreme Court's decision, the Brazilian Congress repealed the sole paragraph of Section 40 of the Federal Patent and Trademark Law. The move seemed to respond to pressures from the international pharmaceutical industry designed to limit the effects of the Supreme Court's decision. The purpose of this final section is simply to analyze whether the fact that Congress and private parties may circumvent the ruling by the Supreme Court, thereby delaying production of generic drugs, also undermines the argument that the ruling is an important heterodox precedent. My conclusion is that the heterodoxy of the ruling resides in its challenge to private law institutions on distributive grounds. The importance of this challenge is not negated by the potential ineffectiveness of the ruling itself. The ineffectiveness of the ruling suggests that ultra-orthodoxy may not only be a feature of Brazilian statutes or caselaw, but a broader characteristic of the whole legal system. This may explain the persistence of economic inequality as a major feature of Brazilian society at the beginning of the twenty-first century.

8.2 ORTHODOXY AND HETERODOXY IN INTELLECTUAL PROPERTY RIGHTS, THE RIGHT TO HEALTH AND CONSTITUTIONAL LAW

Before analyzing the decision by the Brazilian Supreme Court on the unconstitutionality of the patent extension regime, it is important to define the concepts of legal orthodoxy and heterodoxy in the fields of intellectual property law, the right to health, and constitutional law. Based on those definitions, I will propose the concept of ultra-orthodoxy.

In the areas of intellectual property, the right to health, and constitutional law, I consider legal orthodoxy to be the legal institutions that Duncan Kennedy regarded as characteristic of the "third globalization of law" initiated in the 1980s. Those would be legal institutions resulting from a combination of (i) liberal constitutionalism regarding human rights and public law in general and (ii) the doctrine of law and economics regarding private law and regulation of private economic agents, and exported to developing countries as a supportive legal discourse for neo-liberal economic reforms.[5]

In previous work I have argued that the hallmarks of orthodoxy are disregarded for the distributive effects of legal reforms and celebration of legal transplants, departing

[5] Du. Kennedy, Three Globalizations of Law and Legal Thought, in D. Trubek and A. Santos (eds.), *The New Law and Economic Development: A Critical Appraisal* (Cambridge: Cambridge University Press, 2006), pp. 17–73.

from the premise that legal institutions adopted by developed countries are inherently efficient.[6] My argument is that, when legal institutions from the Global North are segregated for export, the rest of the legal infrastructure that provides economic equality is usually forgotten. As an example, neo-liberal reforms were implemented in the United States and the United Kingdom, on top of institutions of the welfare state. In many countries of the Global South such institutions still do not exist. The result is that neoliberal legal reforms in countries of the Global South tend to have negative distributive effects, because only the legal institutions that increase inequality were exported and not those that compensate for such effects. That is the core of my critique of neo-liberal reforms in developing countries in general and Brazil in particular.

Regarding intellectual property law, the orthodox approach is the intellectual movement that supported the adoption of the framework of the Agreement on Trade-Related Aspects of Intellectual Property Rights (TRIPS), without questioning its distributive consequences and, in particular, failing to consider the implications for inequality. Conversely, a heterodox approach in this field recognizes certain problematic aspects of the TRIPS agreement and the World Trade Organization (WTO) structure, particularly in countries marked by social and economic inequality.

As Yugank Goyal noted, the traditional "legal architecture" of intellectual property rights established by the legal framework of the TRIPS agreement tried to "synonymize trade with development."[7] This agreement originated from the bargaining power of the United States and pressure from the pharmaceutical industry, which developing countries could not resist due to their lack of economic power and sufficient knowledge regarding the use and effects of such standardized intellectual property regimes.[8] Countries that wanted to be members of the WTO had to adhere to the TRIPS and thereby grant broad intellectual property protection for a general period of twenty years, without any detailed analysis of which local industries would be affected and which parts of the population would pay the cost of such legal protection.[9]

By contrast, a heterodox approach to intellectual property law questions the consequences of the protection of certain intellectual property rights in countries marked by social and economic inequality, recognizing, for example, that when governments fail to regulate the pricing of medicinal drugs by pharmaceutical

6 C. Portugal Gouvêa, *Análise dos Custos da Desigualdade: Efeitos Institucionais do Círculo Vicioso de Desigualdade e Corrupção* (São Paulo: Quartier Latin, 2020), p. 227. Cf. R. A. Posner, Creating a Legal Framework for Economic Development (1998) 13 *The World Bank Research Observer* 1–11.

7 Y. Goyal, "Death of a Discipline": Locating Heterodoxy in Law (2014) 56 *Journal of the Indian Law Institute* 493–522, 502.

8 Ibid, 503. See also R. C. Bird, Defending Intellectual Property Rights in the BRIC Economies (2006) 43 *American Business Law Journal* 317–63, 327–29.

9 Goyal, "Death of a Discipline," 503.

companies this interferes directly in individuals' health.[10] As noted by Sandra Fredman, the international protection of intellectual property rights under the TRIPS has been particularly problematic in this sense. The concern is that the TRIPS allows pharmaceutical companies to patent drugs and therefore maintain high prices insulated from market competition,[11] not only in the markets where the drugs were originally developed, but also in poor countries with extreme levels of inequality. This means that, in such poor countries, either most of the population is left without access to modern medicine, or there is a tremendous burden on the budget of the government to buy such drugs, sometimes at prices higher than in the countries of origin. In the second scenario a substantial part of the country's tax revenue is transferred abroad to pay for patented pharmaceuticals instead of supporting a more general health policy.

Concerning the right to health, it is slightly easier to define the orthodox and heterodox approaches. Fredman analyzes how the right to health is understood in different jurisdictions, examining the substantive content given to the right to health and how this determines the duties of the State.[12] Fredman identifies three different approaches relating to the right to health. However, for clarity, I will here present them as four different legal treatments of the matter. The first, second, and third approaches, as detailed here, I consider as part of the orthodoxy. The fourth approach, incorporating the right to equality in the access to health care, I will define as the heterodoxy.

The first approach prevails in jurisdictions with no express constitutional right to health. This would include most developed countries, such as the United States, the United Kingdom, and many countries that followed the Westminster constitutional model of parliamentary democracy, along with most of continental Europe.

The second approach applies in jurisdictions where the right to health is not clearly provided for in the constitution but courts have held that the right to health is implied, derived from other rights that are constitutionally protected. Apex courts in India and Canada, along with the European Court of Human Rights, have provided examples of such departures from the orthodox approach to the right to health. The Indian Constitution includes language related to health in Article 47 of the "Directive Principles of Social Policy," but does not expressly provide for a right that is enforceable in courts.[13] In the case of the Canadian Charter of Rights and Freedoms and the European Convention on Human Rights (ECHR) there are no explicit references to health or the right to health.[14] Despite that, Fredman shows that courts in India and Canada, as well as the European Court of Human Rights, have derived aspects of the right to health from other rights, such as the right to life and personal integrity.[15] This

[10] S. Fredman, *Comparative Human Rights Law* (Oxford: Oxford University Press, 2018), p. 232.
[11] Ibid., p. 233.
[12] Ibid.
[13] Ibid., p. 237.
[14] Ibid.
[15] Ibid., p. 237.

intermediate approach shall still be regarded as orthodox since it does not regard the right to health as independently actionable before the courts but only as a consideration that informs decisions based on other grounds.

The third approach includes jurisdictions with an express right to health in their human rights instruments[16] but which recognize the right as a purely individual right. There are several ways in which an express right to health might be understood. It could be an individually justiciable right to medication or other medical intervention for individual illness. Alternatively, the right to health could be based on a broader framework which includes, for example, a right to access to health care or a right to be healthy that is implemented through public policy and collective enforcement.[17] The orthodox approach would be the individualistic one. For instance, in the case of limited access to medication, the individualistic approach favors litigation by individuals to force governments to buy pharmaceutical products. This approach favors the interests of pharmaceutical companies, preventing governments from having any bargaining power to negotiate the prices of such patented products. Also, it ends up having a negative distributive effect, since the haves typically gain more from mechanisms that rely on individual litigation than the have-nots. Hence, free drug distribution would benefit the middle classes and exclude the poorest of the poor.[18] Taking into account my own previous investigation of the litigation for the free distribution of pharmaceutical products in Brazil, based on the right to health, I would include Brazil in this third category.

What I previously concluded, studying the case of Brazil, is that this approach, based on formal equality before the law and favoring individual cases, ends up benefiting wealthier individuals in the urban middle classes, since those would be the ones with greater access to private medical and legal resources to support individual litigation.[19] Even if such an individualistic approach does not necessarily favor the super-wealthy individuals but only the middle-classes, in highly unequal countries, such as Brazil, because the middle-class is a small group, privileging those individuals to the detriment of the much larger group of poor people has a tremendously negative distributive effect.[20] Those effects usually go unnoticed, since underprivileged individuals suffer quietly, forgotten by the mass and social media.

I recognize that this third approach might be better described as the ultra-orthodox approach, more than just a variation of orthodoxy.[21] This would require

[16] Ibid., p. 243.

[17] Ibid.

[18] I previously discussed that issue in detail regarding a study of the Brazilian litigation on free access to drugs. See C. Portugal Gouvêa, Social Rights against the Poor (2013) 7 *Vienna Journal on International Constitutional Law* 454–75.

[19] See ibid.

[20] See ibid.

[21] I am grateful to Kevin Davis for this analysis, which provides an interesting question for more detailed comparative law analysis with other countries that adopted the individualized litigation of the right to health as its constitutional practice.

further analysis of other jurisdictions where ultra-orthodoxy might also be present in order to support this hypothesis, and in the further sections of this chapter I will attempt to offer more subsidies that may ground such an endeavor.

The fourth approach protects the human right to health based on a principle of material equality, departing from the more formalistic approach implemented through individual litigation. This approach would focus on how public policies are implemented and would include statistical analysis of, for example, access to specific treatments. In general, violations of the right would be brought to the courts by means of collective actions, such as direct constitutional challenges or class actions. I call this view the heterodox approach to the right to health because it only recognizes the right to health as an actionable constitutional right when it is applied with a positive distributive effect, meaning, for the benefit of the poorest individuals in society and not just the ruling elites and middle classes.[22] The heterodox approach to a right to health already recognizes, from a methodological point of departure, that individuals or groups might be marginalized because of their race, age, gender, disability, religion, and, as a result, will have disadvantages in access to justice and health care.[23]

A decision from the Colombian Constitutional Court offers a striking example of the heterodox approach to the right to health. In this case, decided in 2008, the Constitutional Court of Colombia ordered a massive restructuring of the country's health system, providing that "courts can enforce access to health goods and services as a matter of fundamental rights."[24] The case collected 22 *tutelas*[25] selected to demonstrate the systemic problems in the Colombian health system that had led to the overuse of the *tutela*. Instead of only granting relief to individuals, the court demanded a more extensive reform of the health system in order to grant access to healthcare to the poorest individuals in Colombian society. The success of the case lies not in putting the constitutional court in the position of implementing public policies, but in preventing the kind of individual litigation over the right to health that became endemic in countries such as Brazil.

In the field of constitutional law, legal orthodoxy is characterized by neoformalism,[26] as described by Duncan Kennedy, which appeals "to supposedly transcendent, but also positively enacted values in constitutions or treaties, against the status quo."[27] Moreover, the neoformalism "is unreflective in a way diametrically opposite to policy analysis."[28] Hence, the orthodox approach to the right to health is in line

22 Fredman, *Comparative Human Rights Law*, p. 250.

23 Ibid.

24 A. Yamin and O. Parra-Vera, How Do Courts Set Health Policy? The Case of the Colombian Constitutional Court (2009) 6 *PLoS Medicine* 0147–50, 0148.

25 Ibid., 0149.

26 Kennedy, Three Globalizations of Law and Legal Thought, 63.

27 Ibid., 64.

28 Ibid., 65.

with this broader approach to orthodox constitutionalism in the sense that it favors individual and not collective litigation.

The central aspect of constitutional law orthodoxy is the focus on the analysis of general principles. Ronald Dworkin, from an Anglo-Saxon perspective, and Robert Alexy, from a German perspective, are authors who exemplify this turn toward formalism and who "focus on law application," especially on "legal reasoning and the justification of judicial decisions."[29] Insofar as they remain concerned with either the application of "abstract principles directly, without any intermediation, to any given specific problem" as "the best way to reason about questions of rights,"[30] as in Dworkin's approach, or harmonizing the application of principles with rationality, as in the case of Alexy's theories of argumentation and principles,[31] their perspective appears to neglect completely, or at least not sufficiently value,[32] distributive consequences of the interpretation of constitutional law. In this respect, Dworkin's and Alexy's works exemplify the orthodox approach to constitutional law, which focuses on a formalistic and supposedly neutral balancing of principles, instead of adopting as a guiding methodology the distributive analysis of how constitutional rights are applied in practice.

By contrast, the heterodox approach to constitutional law can be seen in the paradigm of "transformative constitutionalism," first introduced by Karl Klare in his analysis of certain decisions of the South-African constitutional court.[33] The concept means a "project of constitutional enactment, interpretation and enforcement"[34] directed to a "large-scale, egalitarian social transformation," being, thus, not neutral, but "frankly intended to carry a positive valence, to connote a social good."[35] This project is aimed at "transforming a country's political and social institutions and power relationships in a democratic, participatory, and egalitarian direction."[36]

At the time he coined the term, Karl Klare used it "to describe both what South African constitutionalism" was at the time "and what it ought to be" in the

[29] A. V. Bogdandy et al., Ius Constitutionale Commune en América Latina: A Regional Approach to Transformative Constitutionalism, in A. V. Bogdandy (ed.), *Transformative Constitutionalism in Latin America: The Emergence of a New Ius Commune* (Oxford: Oxford University Press, 2017), pp. 3–26, p. 17.

[30] K. Möller, Dworkin's Theory of Rights in the Age of Proportionality (2018) 12 *Law & Ethics of Human Rights* 281–99, 286.

[31] R. Alexy, A *Theory of Constitutional Rights* (trans. Julian Rivers) (Oxford: Oxford University Press, 2002). See also A. V. Bogdandy et al., Ius Constitutionale Commune en América Latina, p. 38.

[32] Möller, Dworkin's Theory of Rights in the Age of Proportionality 286.

[33] K. E. Klare, Legal Culture and Transformative Constitutionalism (1998) 14 *South African Journal on Human Rights* 146–88, 150. J. Fowkes, Transformative Constitutionalism and the Global South: The View from South Africa, in A. V. Bogdandy et al. (eds.), *Transformative Constitutionalism in Latin America: The Emergence of a New Ius Commune* (Oxford: Oxford University Press, 2017), pp. 97–121, p. 99.

[34] Klare, Legal Culture and Transformative Constitutionalism.

[35] Ibid.

[36] Ibid.

future.[37] South Africa had adopted "a Constitution with massively egalitarian commitments."[38] These would be, however, only "progressive aspirations" if the lawyers did not engage in harmonizing judicial method and legal interpretation with the Constitution's rules.[39] In spite of the Constitution's potential, the dominant legal culture in South Africa, which was regarded by Klare as formalistic,[40] liberal,[41] and lacking a "strong tradition of substantive political discussion and contestation through the medium of legal discourses,"[42] could represent a barrier to a transformative project focused on the distributional effects of constitutional adjudication.[43]

According to Klare, the text of the South African Constitution, rather than being liberal,[44] was focused on social concerns and redistributive policies.[45] As he emphasized, "the Constitution contains a pervasive and overriding commitment to equality, specifically comprehending a substantive (redistributive), not just formal, conception of equality."[46] This approach assumed that the South African legal system could not be "neutral with respect to the distribution of social and economic power and of opportunities for people to experience self-realization."[47] Consequently, the courts ought not to be reluctant to interrogate its distributive consequences in all aspects of economic life,[48] including, as a result, the right to property, contractual rights, and torts regimes.

Based on this understanding of what orthodoxy and heterodoxy mean with regards to the constitutional right to health, I will discuss whether this form of transformative constitutionalism may be applicable to the Brazilian constitution and if the Brazilian Supreme Court adopted such a doctrine in ADI 5529.[49] However, in order to set the stage for this discussion I must first present the details of the decision itself. With this in mind, we now turn to the debate regarding how Section 40 of the Brazilian Patent

[37] Fowkes, Transformative Constitutionalism and the Global South, p. 100.

[38] Klare, Legal Culture and Transformative Constitutionalism, 188.

[39] Ibid.

[40] Ibid.

[41] Fowkes, Transformative Constitutionalism and the Global South, p. 101.

[42] Klare, Legal Culture and Transformative Constitutionalism, 188.

[43] D. M. Davis and K. Klare, Transformative Constitutionalism and the Common and Customary Law (2010) 26 *South African Journal on Human Rights* 403–509, 405.

[44] M. Hailbronner, Transformative Constitutionalism (2017) 65 *The American Journal of Comparative Law* 527–65, 536.

[45] Klare, Legal Culture and Transformative Constitutionalism, 153.

[46] Ibid., 153–54.

[47] Ibid., 154.

[48] Davis and Klare, Transformative Constitutionalism and the Common and Customary Law, 509.

[49] Brazilian commentators have been clear in their analysis that, at least prior to the decision on ADI 5529, the Brazilian Supreme Court has not adopted the doctrine of transformative constitutionalism neither explicitly or implicitly in its body of case law. See D. W. Arguelhes, Transformative Constitutionalism: A View from Brazil, in P. Dann, M. Riegner, and M. Bönnemann (eds.), *The Global South and Comparative Constitutional Law* (Oxford: Oxford University Press, 2020), pp. 165–87.

and Trademark Law came to exemplify what I will characterize as legal ultra-orthodoxy.

8.3 ULTRA-ORTHODOXY IN BRAZILIAN INTELLECTUAL PROPERTY LAW

I have already defined ultra-orthodoxy as the adoption of radically neo-liberal legal institutions in developing countries as a result of the lobbying efforts of industries with substantial economic power. The main characteristic of ultra-orthodox institutions is that they are not mere transplants of legislation and case law existing in Europe and the United States. They are truly radicalized versions of such legal institutions. When I say radicalized, I mean regarding their distributive effects. Hence, those ultra-orthodox institutions have, on face value, characteristics that increase their negative distributive effects. I believe that this phenomenon is substantially different from what has been documented in the literature on legal transplants,[50] since in this literature there is usually the expectation that legal institutions will be relatively similar with regards to their distributional effects. In this section, I will argue that the Brazilian Patent and Trademark Law provides at least two outstanding examples of ultra-orthodoxy: the provisions on patent extensions and the so-called pipeline regime. In order to demonstrate how those examples were developed, I will provide the context in which the Brazilian Patent and Trademark Law was approved by the Brazilian Congress, in the mist of the neo-liberal reforms of the 1990s, and of the legislative process involving what I regard as the ultra-orthodox features of such statute.

The current status of legal orthodoxy in intellectual property rights, the right to health and constitutional law in general is the result of a historical process of economic and legal transformations that erupted after the end of the Cold War that I will generally describe here as the neoliberal reforms. Despite its prevalence in the debates regarding legal reform in developing countries, neoliberalism can only be correctly understood as a construction of a specific historical context,[51] in which, with the fall of the Soviet Union and the end of the Cold War, the focus on integrating countries previously excluded from the process of economic globalization, such as Eastern European and Latin American countries, became central to the international public debate.[52]

[50] See, e.g., D. Berkowitz, K. Pistor, and J. F. Richard, The Transplant Effect (2003) 51 *The American Journal of Comparative Law* 163–203, 168; D. Berkowitz, K. Pistor, and J. F. Richard, Economic Development, Legality, and the Transplant Effect (2003) 47 *European Economic Review* 165–95; Posner, Creating a Legal Framework for Economic Development. Besides, for the concept of legal implants, see M. Pargendler, The Rise of International Corporate Law (2021) 98 *Washington University Law Review* 1765–820.

[51] H. J. Wiarda, *Cracks in the Consensus: Debating the Democracy Agenda in US Foreign Policy* (Westport: Praeger, 1997), p. 15.

[52] Ibid.

Central to the debate was the so-called Washington Consensus, a list, made in 1989, of ten policy actions that were supposedly "desirable in just about all the Latin American countries."[53] Its pillars were the "consensus on democracy and elections," "free trade," and "open markets."[54] Those policies were based, however, as Joseph E. Stiglitz once asserted, "on a simplistic model of the market economy"[55] in which there was no need for governmental intervention to achieve perfect market functioning. That is why these policies of the Washington Consensus were designated as neoliberal.[56] The concept of deregulation, which appeared frequently in the neoliberal discourse was, according to John Williamson, used in the sense of a facilitation of the entry of new companies in a country through the "abolition of barriers."[57] It was also argued that an excess of government regulation could be harmful to small businesses and might even encourage corruption.[58] The whole list was perhaps better labeled a "Liberalization Consensus." The policies were not free choices of the democracies in Latin America, as the term "consensus" might suggest, but impositions from Washington. This neoliberal model, imposed on Latin American countries without regard for their interests and their political, social, and historical peculiarities, failed to be implemented successfully.[59]

Establishment of an intellectual property rights regime was not a component of the original "Washington Consensus" but it later became a cornerstone of the effort to facilitate business entry in the Global South. Nonetheless, few areas of law have a more secure place in the canon of orthodoxy than intellectual property law. In the context of intellectual property law, for a country to follow a neoliberal or orthodox approach it has to adhere fully to the World Trade Organization's TRIPs model, which, according to Hans Löfgren and Owain David Williams, "marked the highpoint of neoliberalism."[60]

Brazil's Patent and Trademark Law created an exceptional intellectual property regime even more protective of the interests of transnational businesses than the TRIPS's regime. The head of Section 40 provides that patents for invention shall, as a general rule, be valid for a period of twenty years counted from the filing date. Up until this point, the Brazilian statute only followed the standard provisions of the TRIPS Agreements. The innovation came in its sole paragraph, which created an

53 J. Williamson, The Strange History of the Washington Consensus (2005) 27 *Journal of Post Keynesian Economics* 195–206, p. 196.

54 Wiarda, *Cracks in the Consensus*, p. 13.

55 J. E. Stiglitz, *Globalization and Its Discontents* (New York: W. W. Norton, 2002), p. 74.

56 Ibid.

57 Williamson, The Strange History of the Washington Consensus.

58 M. Naím, Washington Consensus or Washington Confusion? (2000) *Foreign Policy* 87–103, 89.

59 Wiarda, *Cracks in the Consensus*, p. 17.

60 H. Löfgren and O. D. Williams, Conclusion: TRIPS, Drug Production in the Global South and Access to Medicines, in. H. Löfgren and O. D. Williams (eds.), *The New Political Economy of Pharmaceuticals: Production, Innovation and TRIPS in the Global South* (Basingstoke: Palgrave Macmillan, 2013), pp. 246–50, p. 247.

exception for the terms provided in the head of the Section (*caput*). The sole paragraph provided that the term of the patent should not be less than ten years, counted from the date of grant, except in cases where the Brazilian National Institute of Industrial Property (*Instituto Nacional da Propriedade Industrial*) (INPI), the Brazilian patents and trademarks office, was unable to carry out the substantive examination of the application due to proven judicial conflict or force majeure.

Hence, if the INPI were to take, for example, almost twenty years to grant the patent, the total term of the patent would be thirty years. No other patent regime in the world had an equivalent provision, both among countries in the Global North and Global South.[61] Extensions in other jurisdictions are granted for only a few months, taking into consideration, for example, any real delay that the approval proceedings might have caused to taking the product into the market. No other patent law regime provides an automatic extension, much less of a minimum period of ten years.

I do not believe that the extraordinary character of the sole paragraph Section 40 can be explained only by the asymmetry of political power in the international arena between Brazil and developed countries or as a result of a lack of understanding on the part of Brazilian lawmakers. Brazil has one of the most sophisticated professional diplomatic bodies in the world, with substantial experience in multilateral organizations. Moreover, unlike most other countries in the Global South, Brazil has a very sizable economy, which grants it considerable bargaining power in international arenas, even when acting alone. Nor can it be said that Brazilian authorities were misled and that they had no idea that the patent system in Brazil was divergent. As a Brazilian diplomat recognized at the time, the "additional privileges" granted by the Brazilian Congress to patent holders[62] mostly favored foreign companies since, at the time, Brazil did not have a highly sophisticated research and development environment in the local private sector.

Local pharmaceutical companies were aware of the likely effects of Section 40 of the Brazilian Intellectual Property Statute and opposed its adoption. According to a speech in Congress from Dante Alário Junior, former President of the Association of National Pharmaceutical Laboratories, patent terms would be, if the bill was approved as it was proposed at the time, exactly "as the transnationals want"[63] and,

[61] C. S. Filho et al., A Inconstitucionalidade do Artigo 40, Parágrafo Único, da Lei de Propriedade Industrial sob uma Perspectiva Comparada (2020) 1–64, 33. On the concept, see also, B. Yang and H. Kwon, TRIPS and New Challenges for the Pharmaceutical Sector in South Korea, in H. Löfgren and D. O. Williams (eds.), *The New Political Economy of Pharmaceuticals: Production, Innovation and TRIPS in the Global South* (Basingstoke: Palgrave Macmillan, 2013), pp. 204–20, p. 211.

[62] P. N. Batista, Patentes – Como Chegar ao Primeiro Mundo, *Folha de São Paulo*, April 17, 1993, p. 2.

[63] República Federativa do Brasil, Diário do Congresso Nacional. Seção I. Ano XLVIII – Suplemento ao N° 42–A. Quarta-feira, 17 de março de 1993. Sessão Plenária transformada em Comissão Geral para Debate do Projeto de Lei n° 824–B, de 1991, que regula direitos e obrigações relativos à propriedade industrial (1993), p. 24.

consequently, would just unnecessarily increase "the time of the foreign private monopoly, which would not benefit Brazil at all."[64] The Federation of Industries of the State of São Paulo (FIESP) observed that these terms were "excessive," "creating a reserved market for too long," which could "discourage technological renewal."[65] In particular, FIESP believed that the automatic extension of patent terms due to eventual delay on the review process, which would later be enshrined in Section 40 of the Brazilian Intellectual Property Statute, should be eliminated.[66]

The automatic extension of the patent term provided by the sole paragraph of Section 40 was not even the aspect of the Patent and Trademark Law that ignited the most active public debates. Another controversial issue was the so-called pipeline provision, which became Sections 230 and 231 of the Patent and Trademark Law. The "pipeline" system allowed holders of foreign patents to register their patents in Brazil and obtain protection for the remaining period of validity under foreign law, despite the fact that such patents were in the public domain under the previously existing Brazilian legislation.[67] This mechanism was not provided for in the TRIPS agreements and was peculiar to the Brazilian legal system. It caused a great deal of concern among local public health specialists,[68] since it was estimated that 340 medicines that were not previously protected by patents in Brazil would be suddenly granted protection.

It was clear that protecting pipeline patents would cause a sudden and drastic increase in the prices of Brazilian pharmaceuticals.[69] According to Cassandra M. Sweet, referring to a study from Tahir Amin,[70] "total deposits through the pipeline system resulted in 1,182 applications (45% from the US, 13% from the UK, 10% from Germany, 9.6% from Japan, and 7.7% from France), over 700 (or well over half) were granted."[71] Consequently, Brazil had to pay "between 704% and 5,622% more for" some of these medicines "than it would have spent on

64 Ibid.

65 Ibid., p. 35.

66 Ibid.

67 Legal Opinion of Prof. Calixto Salomão Filho in STF, ADI 4234, en banc, rap. Justice Carmen Lúcia, p. 1781.

68 C. M. Sweet, The Political Economy of Pharmaceutical Production in Brazil, in H. Löfgren and O. D. Williams (eds.), *The New Political Economy of Pharmaceuticals: Production, Innovation and TRIPS in the Global South* (Basingstoke: Palgrave Macmillan, 2013), pp. 29–47, p. 34.

69 Ibid., p. 35.

70 T. Amin, Re-Visiting the Patents and Access to Medicines Dichotomy: An Evaluation of TRIPS Implementation and Public Health Safeguards in Developing Countries, in O. Aginam, J. Harrington, and P. Yu (eds.), *The Global Governance of HIV/Aids: Intellectual Property and Access to Essential Medicines* (Cheltenham: Edward Elgar, 2010), pp. 109–30, p. 114.

71 Sweet, The Political Economy of Pharmaceutical Production in Brazil, p. 38. See, in this regard, Amin, Re-Visiting the Patents and Access to Medicines Dichotomy.

equivalent generic medicines."[72] In gross values, from 2001 to 2007, it was estimated that Brazil paid "between US$420 and US$519 million more, when compared with the reference prices from the World Health Organization or Doctors without Borders, respectively."[73] These are striking numbers for a poor and unequal country. It was not without reason that pipeline patents were, throughout the discussion of the bill in Brazil, called "abject and despicable"[74] as well as a "legal aberration."[75]

The pipeline provisions were challenged before the Brazilian courts almost immediately after they were enacted. On April 24, 2009, the Federal Attorney General, urged on by the National Federation of Pharmacists and the Brazilian Network for the Integration of Peoples,[76] proposed before the Federal Supreme Court a direct action for the declaration of unconstitutionality of Articles 230 and 231 of the Patent and Trademark Law, which, as mentioned, provided for pipeline patents.[77] The Supreme Court, however, failed to rule promptly on that matter and all "pipeline" patents expired without being challenged.

The fact that the Intellectual Property Law was approved by Congress over the objections of local elites might be explained by the fact that it was supported by substantial lobbying activity from foreign actors. At the time, Brazil was facing political pressure from the United States,[78] which had companies holding a large number of patents to be protected. Fernando Henrique Cardoso, the then President of Brazil, even assured a US trade official, according to Folha de São Paulo, a Brazilian newspaper, that the bill met "85% of the demands of the international community."[79] In parallel, Interfarma, the association of the international pharmaceutical industry located in Brazil, dedicated to following parliamentary activities, among other things, participated actively in the discussion of the bill.[80] According to

72 C. T. Scopel and G. C. Chaves, Initiatives to Challenge Patent Barriers and their Relationship with the Price of Medicines Procured by the Brazilian Unified National Health System (2016) 32 *Cadernos de Saúde Pública* 1–11, 6.

73 Ibid.

74 República Federativa do Brasil, Diário do Congresso Nacional, p. 4, "O instituto do pipeline é tão abjeto e desprezível . . .

75 Ibid., p. 10, A pipeline é apenas uma aberração jurídica.

76 78 Complaint from the Federal Attorney General in STF, ADI 4234, *en banc*, rap. Justice Cármen Lúcia, p. 58.

77 79 STF, ADI 4234, *en banc*, rap. Justice Cármen Lúcia.

78 L. G. Santos, Tecnologia, Natureza e a "Redescoberta" do Brasil, in H. R. Araújo (ed.), *Tecnociência e Cultura: Ensaios sobre o Tempo Presente* (São Paulo: Estação Liberdade, 1998), pp. 26–30.

79 C. E. L. Da Silva, Patentes: Fernando Henrique Defende Lei nos EUA, *Folha de São Paulo*, May 11, 1993, p. 6.

80 F. Tozi, Intellectual Property Protection and Drug Patents in Brazil (2020) 19 *Mercator* 1–13, 5, "The legislative process enables the monitoring of other social agents' participation, such as INTERFARMA (Association of the Pharmaceutical Research Industry), which has participated publicly since the 10/12/1991 meeting of the Special Commission." República Federativa do Brasil, Diário do Congresso Nacional, p. 20. On this subject, according to a Master's dissertation published in Brazil, INTERFARMA would be the association "that represents the largest number of multinational pharmaceutical companies operating in Brazil." According to this

Laymert Garcia dos Santos, there was even speculation that the bill was originally drafted by Interfarma.[81] Unfortunately, the Brazilian political system does not regulate lobbying and so it is not possible to analyze the amounts different interest groups invested in lobbying around the adoption of the Patent and Trademark Law.

The automatic patent extension and the pipeline provisions of Brazil's Patent and Trademark Law are examples of ultra-orthodoxy, in contrast to the orthodoxy embodied in the terms of the TRIPS agreements. As used here, this concept refers to radical interpretations of nonliberal legal institutions that threaten to have negative distributive effects when implemented in countries in the Global South with high levels of inequality. As such, ultra-orthodoxy leads to worse distributive effects than simply importing or transplanting orthodox legal institutions in accordance with the Washington Consensus.

8.4 THE BRAZILIAN SUPREME COURT RULING ON PATENT EXTENSIONS

This section will consider the Brazilian Supreme Court's response to the ultra-orthodox patent extension provisions of the Patent and Trademark Law to evaluate if it deviated from the traditional orthodox approach by incorporating the distributive effects of private law in its decision on the ADI 5529, and, as a result, if such a ruling may be an example of legal heterodoxy. Kevin Davis and Mariana Pargendler have discussed in detail "how courts in select developing countries have recently diverged from orthodoxy and begun to embrace heterodoxy," using, for instance, "contract law to reduce inequality."[82] Davis and Pargendler define heterodoxy as divergence from institutional arrangements in countries in the Global North, a subset of which involve divergences adopted by courts and motivated by concerns about economic inequality.

The exceptional patent extension regime adopted by Brazil diverges from models favored in the Global North but in other respects fits awkwardly with Davis and Pargendler's conception of heterodoxy. I characterize the Brazilian regime as an example of ultra-orthodoxy because, even though it involves a departure from legal standards imported from the Global North, it does not have the heterodox feature of attempting to reduce or adapt to the effects of high economic inequality.

research, INTERFARMA has "48 multinational pharmaceutical companies associated, 19 of which are American, 24 European and 5 Asian." See K. C. Sousa, Estratégias de Avaliação de Desempenho dos Propagandistas de Medicamentos Utilizados pela Indústria Farmacêutica no Nordeste do Brasil, Master's Dissertation, Universidade Federal do Rio Grande do Norte (2013), p. 46–47.

81 Santos, Tecnologia, Natureza e a "Redescoberta" do Brasil, p. 27, "Segundo algumas indicações, o projeto Ney Lopes teria sido escrito pela Interfarma, uma associação de laboratórios americanos e europeus, cujo objetivo principal era a promoção do sistema de patentes no Brasil."

82 K. E. Davis and M. Pargendler, Contract Law and Inequality (2022) 107 *Iowa Law Review* 1485–541, 1487.

This section will consider whether the ruling by the Brazilian Supreme Court which declared the sole paragraph of Section 40 of the Brazilian Patent and Trademark Law unconstitutional[83] should be regarded as an example of legal heterodoxy, in the sense used by Davis and Pargendler. Some features of this ruling could be regarded as "heterodox," such as the attention paid to distributive concerns, the interpretation of the right to health as a human right that should be interpreted collectively, the value given to independent academic opinions, not funded by any of the interested industries (the international pharmaceutical industry and the local generic drugs industry), and, lastly, the attention paid to comparative law, particularly involving other countries from the Global South.[84] At the same time, it could be argued that the Supreme Court's decision does not qualify as heterodox since its results represent only a return to the TRIPS standard – the sole paragraph of Section 40, being a "TRIPS-plus mechanism."[85] Hence, the ruling of the court in favor of considering Section 40 unconstitutional would only put the Brazilian system in the "orthodox" category, by complying with the TRIPS agreement, which, as described in Section 8.2, represents orthodoxy in intellectual property law. The Court's position might be seen in that light as a repudiation of only those exaggerated aspects of legal ultra-orthodoxy. A more detailed assessment of the arguments presented by the opinion of the court may enlighten this discussion.

First, the opinion of the Rapporteur of the case, Justice Dias Toffoli, makes it clear that the decision was based on the right to health[86] in the midst of a global pandemic[87], which highlighted "the damage resulting from an undue and unconstitutional exclusivity."[88] Many Justices, besides Justice Toffoli, also endorsed consideration of evidence based on comparative law.[89] As summarized in the headnote of

[83] STF, ADI 5529/DF.

[84] For a comparative study of the Section 40, see also M. Pargendler, Análise Econômica e Comparada do Art. 40, Parágrafo Único, da Lei de Propriedade Industrial, in A. Frazão, R. M. Castro, and S. Campinho (eds.), *Direito Empresarial e suas Interfaces – Homenagem a Fabio Ulhoa Coelho* vol. II (São Paulo: Quartier Latin, 2023), pp. 65–106, which is based on an expert opinion commissioned by FarmaBrasil, an association of Brazilian pharmaceutical manufacturers.

[85] Filho et al., A Inconstitucionalidade do Artigo 40, Parágrafo Único, da Lei de Propriedade Industrial sob uma Perspectiva Comparada, 33; Yang and Kwon, TRIPS and New Challenges for the Pharmaceutical Sector in South Korea, p. 211.

[86] STF, ADI 5529/DF, p. 3.

[87] M. A. M. Cabral, Automatic Patent Term Extensions Ruled Unconstitutional in Brazil: Better Late Than Never? (2022) 53 *IIC – International Review of Intellectual Property and Competition Law* 160–68, 161, "Among the arguments presented by the Justice was the pandemic crisis," in regard to the preliminary injunction conceded by Justice Toffoli. See also, ibid, p. 167, "[a] different legal framework for an industry with specificities (pharmaceutical, for instance) is justified in order to protect legitimate values, such as public health, particularly in the context of a pandemic."

[88] Ibid., 161.

[89] As an example, see STF, ADI 5529/DF, pp. 43–48 (Justice Dias Toffoli, "Para uma análise sob a perspectiva do direito comparado . . ."); 66–69 (Justice Dias Toffoli, "Análise comparativa dos prazos de vigência efetiva das patentes no Brasil em relação ao cenário internacional"); 144 (Justice Nunes Marques, "Outro gráfico traça comparativo entre Brasil, Suécia, Estados

the decision, the Court concluded that the sole paragraph of Section 40 "does not derive from the TRIPS Agreement; nor does it find a parallel in other jurisdictions, in which the additional exclusivity rights follow a logic essentially different from that adopted by the Brazilian legislation, having a reduced application, being limited to specific cases and not being automatic rights."[90]

In reaching these conclusions, the court took into consideration research produced by the Law and Poverty Group of the University of São Paulo Law School, coordinated by Professor Calixto Salomão Filho and me. The report was prepared based on the work of several highly dedicated and talented students, without financial support from any of the parties involved in the litigation, including the foreign pharmaceutical industry (arguing against the declaration of unconstitutionality) and the Brazilian producers of generic pharmaceuticals (in favor). The report adopted an approach that is unusual in constitutional argument, focusing mainly on a comparative perspective with a strong empirical approach. Typically, the Brazilian Supreme Court, like other constitutional courts, refuses to ground its decisions on comparative law analysis because of sovereignty concerns. The Brazilian Interdisciplinary AIDS Association (ABIA), the first organization to make a statement as *amicus curiae* in the lawsuit, filed the report with the court on December 16, 2020.

The Law and Poverty Group's study included an analysis of process of extension of patents in Brazil and across twenty-nine other jurisdictions[91] and concluded that there was no other legal system in which the extension was automatic for a fixed number of years and operated as set forth in Section 40, sole paragraph.[92] The study represented the most extensive comparative analysis of the matter at the time. The study also concluded that there were no grounds for the argument that the provision was adopted by Brazil as a response to "an obligation under the TRIPS Agreement."[93] The study found that, in all cases in which a country allowed the extension of patent terms due to delays in the approval process, it imposed at the

Unidos, Reino Unido, Itália e Suíça"); 257–58 (Justice Rosa Weber, "Estudo comparativo publicado em 2016 apontou o Brasil como o país com o maior intervalo médio (dez anos e um mês) entre o depósito e a concessão de um pedido de patente, entre onze países selecionados . . .").

[90] STF, ADI 5529/DF, p. 4. In the original: "não deriva do Acordo TRIPS; tampouco encontra paralelo em outras jurisdições, nas quais os direitos adicionais de exclusividade seguem uma lógica essencialmente diversa da adotada pela legislação brasileira, por terem aplicação reduzida, limitada a casos específicos e não serem direitos automáticos."

[91] Filho et al., A Inconstitucionalidade do Artigo 40, Parágrafo Único, da Lei de Propriedade Industrial sob uma Perspectiva Comparada, 2, "Nesse sentido, com o objetivo de contribuir para o julgamento da presente ADI, o Grupo realizou pesquisa comparativa sobre a concessão de patentes no Brasil e em outras vinte e nove jurisdições." In English, "In this regard, with the aim of contributing to the judgment of the present ADI, the Group conducted a comparative study on patent granting in Brazil and twenty-nine other jurisdictions."

[92] Ibid., 60.

[93] Ibid.

same time a series of limitations. As mentioned in the previous section, such countries take into consideration the testing period of new drugs required by health authorities and if the delay in the approval caused a delay in taking the medicaments to the market. If there is no actual delay or if the cause cannot be singled out as being related to the approval process by the patent office, or even if the party concurred in the delay in any form, such elements may prevent the granting or reduce the extension period. The study demonstrated that such detailed analysis in other jurisdictions usually resulted in insignificant increases in the patent terms, of only a few months, for example. The Brazilian provision, on the contrary, had no limitations based on the specificities of the case, which meant that Brazil ended up having the longest effective patent terms of all the jurisdictions studied.[94]

This initial finding led the Law and Poverty Group to take a step further in the research and identify not only the applicable law in each jurisdiction but also the average effective duration of the patent terms, to determine whether differences in the legal framework created differences in practice. The results of the survey were absolutely striking. When comparing the effective term of the ten longest-lasting patents in the pharmaceutical sector with comparable patents in other jurisdictions, the difference is clear: "while the average term of the ten Brazilian patents indicated is 29.61 years, their counterparts in the other countries present average protection a little longer than the twenty years suggested by the TRIPS agreement."[95] In general, as highlighted by Mário André Machado Cabral, in his review of the court ruling and the study of the Law and Poverty Research Group, "the average patent term in Brazil is 24.305 years. This is the highest average term among the BRICS countries (Brazil, Russia, India, China and South Africa), Latin American countries, as well as the six countries with the highest average terms (Brazil, Switzerland, Italy, UK, US and Sweden)."[96] The study did not identify one single country in which the average surpassed twenty-one years, meaning that, in all other countries that adopted any kind of extension mechanism, such extensions did not surpass a few months on average. In Brazil it surpassed the TRIPS agreements term of twenty years by more than four years. This meant that Brazilian customers were paying monopolistic prices for, or being excluded from access to, patented products for many years after those patents were in the public domain in other jurisdictions. The study also included many jurisdictions in the Global South, breaking with the traditional approach in comparative law of looking only for standards from countries in the

94 Ibid.

95 Ibid., 56.

96 Cabral, Automatic Patent Term Extensions Ruled Unconstitutional in Brazil, 163. See also, Filho et al., A Inconstitucionalidade do Artigo 40, Parágrafo Único, da Lei de Propriedade Industrial sob uma Perspectiva Comparada, 42. In the original: "O Brasil, em razão do uso do artigo 40, parágrafo único, LPI, destaca-se por apresentar o maior período de proteção quando comparado aos demais, sendo que o tempo médio entre o início da vigência legal de uma patente e seu termo é de 24,305 anos."

Global North. Based on this overwhelming evidence, several of the Supreme Court justices stressed how extremely the country's patent system was tilted in favor of global monopolies and against the poorest of the poor.[97]

The study of the Law and Poverty Group concluded that these excessively long patent terms – which were also indeterminate, since the rule imposed no limits upon extensions after the patent was granted[98] – created disincentives to innovation since it prevented investments in new products based on technologies that would otherwise have been in the public domain.[99] Furthermore, by granting exclusive privileges in an indeterminate manner, the rule also violated the constitutional provision on free competition.[100] The study further concluded that, especially in the context of the COVID-19 pandemic, the rule interfered, without justification, with the population's access to health, since it influenced the price and, consequently, access to medicines.

In its references to the study by the Law and Poverty Group, the justices of the Supreme Court highlighted two aspects of the study in ways that may be regarded as heterodox. First, Justice Lewandowski emphasized that the research was "disinterested,"[101] recognizing that the report was carried out by a public university without resources from any of the industries involved in the litigation and in the legislative process that proceeded it. He affirmed emphatically: "I understand that the conclusions of the empirical and disinterested research of the Law and Poverty Group leave no room for doubt as to the total dysfunctionality and inadequacy of the device under analysis."[102]

Second, in his opinion, Justice Dias Toffoli regarded the study as "extremely relevant" because of its comparative analysis[103] and devoted an entire page of his opinion to quoting excerpts from the research focused on comparative law issues, which included countries in the Global South.[104] Right after this analysis, Justice Dias Toffoli concluded: "In other words, the term provided for in the sole

97 As an example, see STF, ADI 5529/DF, pp. 66–69 (Justice Dias Toffoli, "Análise comparativa dos prazos de vigência efetiva das patentes no Brasil em relação ao cenário internacional"); 144 (Justice Nunes Marques, "Outro gráfico traça comparativo entre Brasil, Suécia, Estados Unidos, Reino Unido, Itália e Suíça").

98 Filho et al., A Inconstitucionalidade do Artigo 40, Parágrafo Único, da Lei de Propriedade Industrial sob uma Perspectiva Comparada, 9.

99 Ibid., 58.

100 Free competition is one of the principles of the economic order provided by the Brazilian Constitution in its Article 170. "Article 170. The economic order, founded on the appreciation of human labor and free enterprise, aims to ensure a dignified existence for all, according to the dictates of social justice, observing the following principles: … IV – Free competition."

101 STF, ADI 5529/DF, pp. 1–2 of his opinion. In the original: "pesquisa empírica e desinteressada do Grupo Direito e Pobreza."

102 Ibid.

103 Ibid., p. 13 of his opinion.

104 Ibid., pp. 14–15 of his opinion.

paragraph, Section 40, is not justified."[105] Other Justices also emphasized the comparative law aspect in their opinions. Judge Nunes Marques, quoting from the report, stressed that "the average effective term of pharmaceutical patents in Brazil is the longest even in comparison with countries in the BRICS group."[106] This breaks the mold with regard to orthodox constitutional analysis, which usually understands matters of constitutional law to concern only domestic matters, refusing to rely upon comparative law arguments.

Justice Dias Toffoli also emphasized in his opinion the impact of the patent term extension on the Brazilian National Health System (SUS) – one of the largest public health systems in the world – and the pharmaceutical industry.[107] In his guiding opinion he cited[108] a study from the Institute of Economics of the Federal University of Rio de Janeiro, added to the case files by the Brazilian Interdisciplinary AIDS Association, and also quoted by the Attorney General,[109] which claimed that the Ministry of Health spent "about 1.9 billion [reais] per year on just nine drugs whose patents would have expired between 2010 and 2019."[110] Similarly, Justice Lewandowski pointed out, based on the data from the research of the Law and Poverty Group, that the rule had a "major impact" on public health.[111]

Justice Dias Toffoli was well aware of the importance of the ruling for the foreign pharmaceutical industry. He noted that Interfarma, the lobbying organization of the international pharmaceutical companies which participated intensively in the law-making process, as described above, also participated in the legal proceeding before the Supreme Court as *amicus curiae* and filed opinions in defense of its interests.[112] He made it clear that the sole paragraph of Section 40 of the Patent and Trademark Law was unconstitutional in great part because of "the undue extension of the term of effectiveness of pharmaceutical patents," creating an unjustified privilege for the private interest of one group "to the detriment of the collectivity, having an extreme impact on the provision of public health services in the country and, consequently, going against the constitutional right to health (art. 196 of the 1988 Constitution)."[113]

105 Ibid., p. 20 of his opinion. In the original: "Ou seja, o prazo previsto no parágrafo único, art. 40, não se justifica."

106 Ibid., p. 20 of his opinion. In the original: "Também nesse sentido, estudo realizado pela Faculdade de Direito da USP, constante dos autos, aponta que o prazo médio de vigência efetiva de patentes farmacêuticas no Brasil é o maior mesmo em comparação com países do bloco dos BRICS."

107 Ibid., pp. 5–6. In the original: "O impacto da extensão do prazo de vigência de patentes no Sistema Único de Saúde (SUS) é digno de atenção, pois, sendo ele um dos maiores sistemas de saúde pública do mundo ..."

108 Ibid., pp. 7 and 43–45.

109 PETIÇÃO AJCONST/PGR N° 51667/2021 in STF, ADI 5529/DF, p. 6.

110 Ibid.

111 STF, ADI 5529/DF, p. 2 of his opinion.

112 Ibid., p. 302.

113 Ibid., p. 6. In the original: "O prolongamento indevido dos prazos de vigência de patentes farmacêuticas reveste-se de caráter injusto e inconstitucional, por privilegiar o interesse

This recognition by the court that the decision would affect interest groups and that there was a distributional matter to be resolved among those interest groups is another feature of the ruling which suggests it represents a step in the direction of a heterodox approach to constitutional adjudication.

The opinion of Justice Toffoli adopted the language and methodology of the heterodox interpretation of the right to health, described in Section 8.2. He interpreted the right to health as a right to be protected by means of public policies rather than individual litigation, since the individuals who were being hurt by the patent extensions were not even part of the proceedings. This represented a clear departure from approaches to the right to health previously favored by the Brazilian Supreme Court. This was further clarified by the modulation decision, in which the court explained certain aspects of the main decision. The Brazilian Supreme Court developed this methodology of ruling constitutional cases first on the merits and then issuing a supplementary decision to decide on procedural matters such as the time in which the decision will be effective. The Brazilian Supreme Court refers to this process as "modulation" (*modulação*) of the ruling of unconstitutionality. In the ADI5529, Justice Toffoli provided in his modulation decision that, while the ruling generally would be applicable only to new patent filings, in the case of patents of pharmaceutical products it also would apply to patents filed before the ruling. This decision was also followed by the majority of the court.[114]

The analysis of the right to health in the leading opinion was intertwined with distributive concerns, reflecting an unprecedented adherence to a transformative constitutionalist approach. Citing the Law and Poverty Group's report, Justice Rapporteur Dias Toffoli stressed that, since Brazil was a developing country, the effects on poor people who were excluded from access to treatments due to the high costs for medicines were particularly harsh.[115] Consequently, the public health system enshrined in the Constitution would be severely affected and harmed, especially in relation to those who depend on the system "to ensure their physical integrity and their survival."[116]

particular em detrimento da coletividade, impactando de forma extrema a prestação de serviços de saúde pública no país e, consequentemente, contrariando o direito constitucional à saúde (art. 196 da Constituição de 1988)."

[114] Ibid., p. 7 of the decision regarding the modulation of the effects. In the original: "Em relação aos produtos e aos processos farmacêuticos e a equipamentos e/ou materiais de uso em saúde – repito –, deixo de modular os efeitos da decisão, tendo em vista a situação excepcional de emergência de saúde pública decorrente da Covid-19, a qual aumentou dramaticamente a demanda por medicamentos e por equipamentos de saúde de forma global, com elevação dos ônus financeiros na aquisição desses itens pela Administração Pública, pelo setor privado suplementar e complementar de saúde e pelo cidadão."

[115] Ibid., p. 68 of the decision.

[116] Ibid., p. 80 of the decision. In the original: "Verifica-se, dessa forma, que a extensão do prazo de vigência das patentes afeta diretamente as políticas públicas de saúde do país e obsta o acesso dos cidadãos a medicamentos, ações e serviços de saúde, causando prejuízos não apenas a

The extent to which the opinions of Justice Dias Toffoli and the Justices who concurred with him were based on distributive concerns was evident in the headnote of the ruling prepared by the Court. The headnote's summary of the main rulings in the case focused mainly on its distributive aspects. It noted, for example, that the Court relied upon the idea of the "social function of intellectual property," according to which property rights concern "the community and the development of the country."[117] The extension of patent terms would, therefore, be "unfair and unconstitutional," as it privileged "private interest to the detriment of the community,"[118] affecting access to medicines and the rights of competitors, consumers and those "who depend on the Unified Health System to guarantee their physical integrity and survival."[119] The Court also noted, as consequences of the extension of the terms, that there would be an "arbitrary increase in profits, deepening the inequality between economic agents and transforming what was justifiable and reasonable into something unconstitutional, thus constituting an offense to the social function of intellectual property," "free competition," and "consumer protection."[120]

The individual opinions provided more details regarding the reasoning of the Court on distributive matters. Justice Lewandowski noted that the rule hinders "overcoming poverty, contributes to Brazil's technological backwardness and discourages development" "in favor of multinational companies that obtain benefits" in Brazil "that they cannot achieve either in their countries of origin or in any other nation in the world."[121]

The Court also took into account the fact that the case took place against the backdrop of a pandemic. Justice Toffoli stressed this factor when granting a provisional remedy in the case.[122] The Court agreed with this perspective, emphasizing, in the words of the headnote, that the burden on "public authorities" and "society" had become even more serious and urgent "in view of the international health emergency resulting from the COVID-19 pandemic."[123]

As expected, the decision was not unanimous. Some of the dissenting opinions offered arguments in support of the "ultra-orthodox" legal approach. This was clear in the opinion of Justice Luiz Fux, who affirmed that he was inclined toward "analyzing the Law under the prism of economic analysis, of systemic risk, of

concorrentes e consumidores, mas, principalmente, àqueles que dependem do Sistema Único de Saúde para garantir sua integridade física e sua sobrevivência."

117 Ibid., p. 3.

118 Ibid., p. 6.

119 Ibid.

120 Ibid., p. 8.

121 Ibid., p. 297 of the decision.

122 STF, ADI 5529/DF, rap. Justice Dias Toffoli, j. 07/04/2021, DJe 09/04/2021 (Provisional Remedy Decision), pp. 56–57 and 85. Cabral, Automatic Patent Term Extensions Ruled Unconstitutional in Brazil, 161 and 166.

123 STF, ADI 5529/DF, p. 6.

'Brazil Risk', of investor flight."[124] He argued, if the rule was found unconstitutional, Brazil would face systemic risk, because contracts would be breached, and investors would be caught by surprise.[125] According to him, quoting Richard A. Posner,[126] such systematic consequences should not be underestimated by a judge. Justice Fux presented these arguments in a very formalistic manner, without citing empirical evidence to support his claims. The absence of empirical support was particularly striking considering the evidence submitted by the Law and Poverty Group showing that no other country in the world had a legal regime for patent extension similar to the Brazilian one. It is not reasonable to mention "investor flight" when even the countries with the largest pharmaceutical industries, such as the United States, Germany, and Switzerland, placed substantially greater restrictions on patent extensions than Brazil.

Justice Fux's reference to the economic analysis of law[127] provided his opinion with a scientific veneer, and he emphasized the foreign pharmaceutical companies' economic argument that longer patent terms would stimulate innovation by rewarding investment in inventions, however, without any empirical evidence. This exemplifies the "ultra-orthodox" approach because it bases its reasoning on what may be regarded as neo-liberal arguments. The generic use of economic analysis of law by Brazilian courts usually overlooks the fact that application of economic analysis of law by courts in the United States and Europe generally requires empirical analysis. In the case at hand, empirical work was required to determine the costs and benefits of such extraordinarily long patent terms, the benefits of potential innovation, and the potential costs to the right to health of the general population. The parties opposed to the declaration of unconstitutionality never presented such an analysis, and, as a result, Justice Fux relied only upon a theoretical approach. On the other hand, as mentioned in the beginning of this section, several *amicus curiae* reports presented data related to the costs of such patents to the health of the Brazilian population.[128] This led him to conclude that

[124] Ibid., p. 5 of his opinion. In the original: "Tenho um vezo de analisar o Direito sob o prisma da análise econômica, do risco sistêmico, do 'Risco Brasil', da fuga de investidores."

[125] Ibid., p. 356 of his opinion. In the original: "Vejam como o risco sistêmico é grave: contratos serão rompidos; investidores serão pegos de surpresa com essa declaração de inconstituciona lidade, já firmada."

[126] Ibid., p. 376 of his opinion. In the original: "O juiz constitucional não pode decidir com base em arroubos de vontade, desconsiderando os efeitos sistêmicos. No ponto, são valiosas as lições de Richard Posner ..."

[127] Ibid., pp. 358–78 of the appellate decision.

[128] A study from the Institute of Economics of the Federal University of Rio de Janeiro compared the projections of additional expenses from the Ministry of Health due to the extension of the patent with the projections of expenses for the acquisition of the respective generic drugs that hypothetically could be available in the national market. By January 2016, the loss amounted to a total value of R$2,139,243,073.30. See ibid., pp. 7 and 43–45. Besides, in 2020, an academic study provided new data for assessing the cost of extending the validity of patents for such drugs in the SUS. The research concluded that, compared to what would be paid for generic drugs,

the only solution to the effects of the patent terms on health would be the mechanism of compulsory license, which would be less drastic than a ruling of unconstitutionality.[129]

Following a similar approach, Justice Barroso also drew attention to the "systemic effects of decisions."[130] In response to the evidence based on comparative law, he pointed out that cross-country differences may be justified by the fact that each country deals with its own circumstances.[131] In this respect, Justice Barroso also resonated orthodox constitutional law, calling for the balancing of principles following Dworkin's and Alexy's approach, arguing that a decision only on the grounds of its distributive effect could break the equilibrium of the constitutional system and that principles related to the protection of intellectual property rights should also be taken into consideration.

The common feature in the opinions of Justices Fux and Barroso is that they failed to support their arguments with any empirical evidence to counter the studies by public universities that grounded the opinions by the majority. This also highlights the normative and antiscientific bent of supporters of ultra-orthodox legal arrangements. It has been a feature of law and economics in certain parts of the Global South that general concepts become dogmas, abandoning the idea that such arguments need to be based on scientific evidence. The fact that "a" patent system, well adapted to a particular economy, "may" further development does not mean that "any" and "all" patent systems will further economic development. There is no rule about it and finding a response to such a question would require detailed research.

Dissenting opinions often say more about the actual thinking of the court than the leading opinion itself. In this case, since the dissenting opinions were so clearly aligned with what I described as "ultra-orthodoxy," it is difficult not to recognize that the court's ruling is more about repudiating legal reforms with excessively negative distributive effects than about taking a more proactive role in supervising the implementation of public policies, whether in the public health or in the patent systems. In any case, this ruling already qualifies as one of the "most important decisions" in the history of the Brazilian Supreme Court,[132] and certainly "the case of most relevance and impact" on intellectual property law in the country, as noted

the excess cost borne by the public sector due to the patent extensions amounted to R$1.2 billion. See J. Paranhos, E. Mercadante, and L. Hasenclever, O Custo da Extensão da Vigência de Patentes de Medicamentos para o Sistema Único de Saúde (2019) 36 *Cadernos de Saúde Pública* 1–13.

129 STF, ADI 5529/DF, pp. 358–78 of the appellate decision.

130 Ibid., pp. 190–91 of the appellate decision. In the original: "Tenho grande preocupação quanto aos efeitos sistêmicos de decisões que envolvam áreas sensíveis e que refogem ao conhecimento estritamente jurídico."

131 Ibid., p. 186 of the appellate decision. In the original: "cada país lida com suas próprias circunstâncias."

132 Cabral, Automatic Patent Term Extensions Ruled Unconstitutional in Brazil, 160.

by Justice Nunes Marques.[133] It was also, in my opinion, the most important decision by any court in the world on health and intellectual property rights in the midst of the global pandemic, particularly for recognizing the distributive effects of the patent system and overcoming the traditional divide between public and private law in this area. By bridging that divide, the court challenges an important pillar of orthodox law and economics and neo-liberal thinking, namely the ideas that distributive matters are only of concern for public law, to be dealt with exclusively through tax and transfer policies, and that private law should not be changed on account of negative distributive effects.[134] The decision set a landmark by being the first Supreme Court ruling to adopt a clearly heterodox discourse, with its focus on distributive matters, its public policy-based approach to the right to health, and extensive use of comparative law with a focus on Global South countries.

It would be unfortunate if this decision ended up being understood as an isolated case, motivated only by the context of the pandemic. After all, the COVID-19 pandemic only highlighted[135] certain processes of deterioration of human rights protection caused by the global economic system that must be corrected by increasing the focus on distributive effects of the legal private order. The relevance of the case in the future as a true "heterodox" decision will depend on the willingness of the Supreme Court to apply the core aspects of the ruling in other cases, making it a true precedent on preventing the worst negative distributive effects of ultra-orthodox approaches to private law in Brazil. It will also depend on the capacity of scholars and judges in Brazil to recognize the transformative potential of the new heterodox approach to private law scholarship and adjudication, for which this ruling might be only a starting point. The chapter has the purpose of serving as a first step in this intellectual endeavor.

8.5 THE BACKLASH AGAINST THE RULING

The Supreme Court's ruling on ADI 5529 has generated backlash, by which I mean attempts to circumvent its effects.[136] Backlash may take many forms, including sham litigation to prevent competitors from beginning to produce generic drugs; filing a web of patent applications with similar names and descriptions, to confuse

[133] STF, ADI 5529/DF, p. 3 of his opinion. In the original: "Julgamos hoje, nesta Suprema Corte, possivelmente o caso de maior relevância e impacto para delinear os contornos da propriedade intelectual no País."

[134] For a detailed account of how the orthodox law and economics tradition developed this argument and how central it was for this school of thought, see D. Kennedy, Law and Economics from the Perspective of Critical Legal Studies, in P. Newman (ed.), *The New Palgrave Dictionary of Economics and the Law* (London: Macmillan Reference Limited, 1998), pp. 465–74, p. 465.

[135] Cabral, Automatic Patent Term Extensions Ruled Unconstitutional in Brazil, 161, "In a crisis such as that of CoVID-19, the need to manage scarce healthcare resources was clear."

[136] STF, ADI 5529/DF.

competitors; attempting to delay public procurement of generic drugs; and lobbying for new legislative initiatives in Congress. This section considers evidence of such backlash, the possibility that it could render the Supreme Court's ruling ineffective, and whether that would undermine the ruling's importance as a heterodox precedent.

The first evidence of backlash appeared in the Brazilian Congress. Three months after the Court's ruling, Congress repealed the sole paragraph of Section 40.[137] The repeal took place through the approval of Law 14,195/2021,[138] later informally known as the "doing business law," which generally addressed the process of company formation and other corporate law matters unrelated to intellectual property.

The decision to repeal a provision that had already been declared unconstitutional by the Supreme Court was, at least, puzzling. It is implausible that Congress's motivation was simply to do a "clean up" of the Patent and Trademark Law. It is reasonable to suspect that Congress was motivated by the lobbying of foreign pharmaceutical companies. But, again, to what end?

The explanation might lie in the fact that the repeal creates legal uncertainty. The uncertainty regards the effectiveness of the ruling by the Supreme Court, and in particular its decision (set out in the modulation decision) that the ruling would apply retroactively to pharmaceutical patents filed in the past, not only to new ones. Hence, the legal uncertainty created by the repeal of the sole paragraph of Section 40 of the Patent and Trademark Law is the following: what should be now applied: (i) the Court's modulation decision, including the holding that the ruling would put into the public domain patents already filed for pharmaceutical products, or (ii) ordinarily applicable rules regarding the temporal scope of legislation, which could be interpreted to mean that the change in the law would be applied only to patents filed after the sole paragraph of Section 40 of Federal Law No 9,279/1996 was repealed, meaning that previously filed pharmaceutical patents would be protected?

In my opinion, the repeal of Section 40, sole paragraph, of the Brazilian Patent and Trademark Law should not be interpreted as having limited the effects of the ruling by the Supreme Court because, according to the tenets of separation of powers, Congress could not change the law to circumvent the effects of a decision by the Supreme Court. However, other legal scholars, judges, and lawyers could have different opinions on the matter, creating legal uncertainty. The well-established scholarship on sham litigation demonstrates that all that it requires is legal uncertainty.[139] Private parties involved in such litigation are only buying time.

[137] This was done through Art. 57, XXVI, of Law No. 14,195 of August 26, 2021. The STF decision dates back to May 12, 2021.

[138] See ibid.

[139] See, e.g., T. A. Balmer, Sham Litigation and the Antitrust Laws (1980) 29 *Buffalo Law Review* 39–71; C. Klein, The Economics of Sham Litigation: Theory, Cases, and Policy (1989) *Bureau of Economics Staff Report to the Federal Trade Commission* 1–83; I. Lianos and P. Regibeau, "Vexatious"/"Sham" Litigation in EU and US Antitrust Law: A Mechanism Design Approach (2017) *CLES Research Paper Series* 1/2017 1–60.

To delay the production of generic drugs is already a major victory since it creates a de facto extension of patents. In the case of Brazil, it might be decades before this matter is settled by the Supreme Court, unless the court is challenged to take a more active role in the process.

It is unclear if the repeal was a result of lobbying by foreign pharmaceutical companies. Again, the lack of transparency in Brazilian legislative proceedings plays a part. The information that is publicly available shows that the original proposal to repeal the sole paragraph of Section 40 of the Patent and Trademark Law predates the ruling of the Supreme Court on the matter by a few months. A bill proposing the amendment of the Patent and Trademark Law was introduced in the final stages of the litigation, when it was clear that the Court would soon issue its opinion.[140] It was introduced by a member of Congress from a conservative party.

However, Congress approved the repeal only after the ruling of the Supreme Court and Congress' members used the Supreme Court's ruling as grounds to justify their support for the repeal.[141] It was a formal justification, since there is no public record of relevant debates in Congress about that repeal and opposition was modest.[142]

There is more evidence of looming backlash. Numerous pharmaceutical companies initiated legal proceedings with the aim of extending the duration of individual patents, thereby preventing the manufacturing of generic drugs.[143] By May 2023, thirty-nine lawsuits had already been filed by pharmaceutical companies seeking patent extensions.[144] The pharmaceutical companies argued, for example, that the INPI unreasonably postponed the patent application evaluation process, resulting in financial losses by curtailing the time during which the companies could enjoy exclusivity. They argued that this issue could be remedied by prolonging the patent terms, a course of action that the Supreme Court ruling on the ADI 5529 explicitly declared unconstitutional,[145] since it was the exact purpose of the extension of patents provided by law. The claim is wrong on its face value. These lawsuits are requesting lower court judges to grant the companies the same kinds of extensions contemplated by the unconstitutional provision based on general equity arguments, which are not admissible in cases in which there is a specific law that regulates patent rights. Clearly wrong arguments presented to courts like that are the hallmark of sham litigation. One strategy is to file several claims with bogus legal grounds under the belief that at least some lower court judges without sufficient information

[140] The proposal for repeal was made, in the form of an amendment, on April 5, 2021, by Congressman Hugo Leal (from the PSD Party, from Rio de Janeiro).

[141] Congressman Marco Bertaiolli noted, when approving the amendment, that it would be "in line with the understanding expressed by the Supreme Court in ADI 5529". See ibid., p. 22.

[142] Senator Humberto Costa attempted to exclude this repeal, by proposing an amendment.

[143] N. Felizardo, Não Tem Remédio: Farmacêuticas Movem Máquina de Processos para Barrar Genéricos de Medicamentos para Câncer, Diabetes e HIV, *Intercept Brasil*, August 21, 2023.

[144] Ibid.

[145] Ibid.

or knowledge of the matter will make mistakes, such as granting injunctions. In this case, what the pharmaceutical companies are requesting from the lower courts is to create caselaw that is directly contrary to a ruling of the Supreme Court. Even if the cases end up being decided against the international pharmaceutical companies, injunctions may be issued. Lawsuits in Brazil may take several years to have a final decision so obtaining an injunction may be a major victory, since it has the practical effect of extending the patent.

According to a survey conducted by Grupo Farma Brasil, all cases that reached the Appellate Courts resulted in the denial of patent extension requests. However, injunctions were issued in a few cases granting the international pharmaceutical companies the right to keep their patents while the case is decided without appeal. Such injunctions are also experiencing high rates of rejection – only 20 percent have been granted.[146] Nonetheless, the fact that injunctions were granted in about 20 percent of the cases is already astonishing and, as discussed, considering that those cases may take decades to have a decision that is not subject to appeal given the slowness of Brazilian courts, the injunction itself may represent a definitive victory with regard to certain patents. It will be important to keep track of the progress of these cases through the Brazilian courts.

In the years to come, we will see whether the Supreme Court's decision in ADI 5529 was effective in terms of increasing distribution of generic drugs to the Brazilian population. If backlash prevents the decision from having a positive distributive effect then we may infer that ultra-orthodoxy is a feature of the entire Brazilian legal system rather than of specific legal provisions. In that case, the role of courts and scholarship will be to identify the elements and sources of this ultra-orthodoxy.

8.6 CONCLUSION

The aspects of the Brazilian patent law regime that were declared unconstitutional by the Brazilian Supreme Court in ADI 5529 due to their negative distributive effects represented a phenomenon that I have labeled ultra-orthodoxy. Section 40, sole paragraph, of the Brazilian Patent and Trademark Law did not simply follow the orthodox approach, implementing rules provided in the TRIPs agreement, but in fact adopted a hyperbolic version of it. The negative distributive effects of such an arrangement are undeniable, since it was determined that Brazilian patents were extended, on average, for about four more years than all other jurisdictions in the world. As a consequence, pharmaceutical companies could charge monopolistic prices for their patented products in Brazil while such technologies were already in the public domain elsewhere. This chapter has demonstrated that the ruling by the Brazilian Supreme Court in ADI 5529 was grounded on the understanding that the patent extension mechanism provided by Section 40, sole paragraph, of the

[146] Ibid.

Brazilian Patent and Trademark Law was an outlier with no parallel in any other jurisdictions around the world, and that this had negative distributive effects for the Brazilian population, violating, most significantly, the right to health with regards to access to medicines. No other country in the world, as emphasized by the Brazilian Supreme Court, allowed such a long period of monopolistic exploitation of innovation. The main innovation of this ruling by the Supreme Court, in a departure from its own precedents, was to treat negative distributive effects as grounds for the declaration of unconstitutionality of a private law reform. In doing so, the Court rejected orthodox approaches, according to which courts should not engage in the analysis of the distributive effects of private law arrangements, since distribution should be accomplished through public law.

There are several heterodox elements of the Supreme Court ruling on ADI 5529. The first and foremost is its clear adoption of distributive analysis as grounds for declaring private law institutions unconstitutional, breaking with the neoliberal orthodoxy as incorporated in the canons of economic analysis of law. Second, the Brazilian Supreme Court made extensive use of comparative law and empirical analysis, including analysis of not only jurisdictions from the Global North but also from the Global South. Third, the Supreme Court made substantial use of amicus opinions which were regarded as independent of the economic interests at stake, coming mainly from research institutes located in Brazilian public universities. This aspect of the decision responds to the concern that distribution of wealth might also affect the way that expert opinions are presented to the court in high-stake cases. Last, but not least, the court clearly evaluated private law institutions in light of their impact on public interests and regarded them as means to implement social and economic rights such as the right to health. All these elements, grounded in the use of distributive analysis, put the ruling on ADI 5529 in the pantheon of significant heterodox precedents, not only in Brazil but also internationally.

The case also generated substantial backlash, including sham litigation designed to prevent competitors from producing generic drugs. The fact that this backlash may mute the potentially beneficial distributive effects sought by the Supreme Court in no measure reduces the relevance of the case and its heterodox character.

BIBLIOGRAPHY

Alexy, R., *A Theory of Constitutional Rights* (trans. Julian Rivers) (Oxford: Oxford University Press, 2002).

Amin, T., Re-Visiting the Patents and Access to Medicines Dichotomy: An Evaluation of TRIPS Implementation and Public Health Safeguards in Developing Countries, in O. Aginam, J. Harrington, and P. Yu (eds.), *The Global Governance of HIV/Aids: Intellectual Property and Access to Essential Medicines* (Cheltenham: Edward Elgar, 2010), pp. 109–30.

Arguelhes, D. W., Transformative Constitutionalism: A View from Brazil, in P. Dann, M. Riegner, and M. Bönnemann (eds.), *The Global South and Comparative Constitutional Law* (Oxford: Oxford University Press, 2020), pp. 165–87.

Balmer, T. A., Sham Litigation and the Antitrust Laws (1980) 29 *Buffalo Law Review* 39–71.

Batista, P. N., Patentes – Como Chegar ao Primeiro Mundo, *Folha de São Paulo*, April 17, 1993.

Berkowitz, D., Pistor, K., and Richard, J. F., Economic Development, Legality, and the Transplant Effect (2003) 47 *European Economic Review* 165–95.

The Transplant Effect (2003) 51 *The American Journal of Comparative Law* 163–203.

Bird, R. C., Defending Intellectual Property Rights in the BRIC Economies (2006) 43 *American Business Law Journal* 317–63.

Bogdandy, A. V. et al., Ius Constitutionale Commune en América Latina: A Regional Approach to Transformative Constitutionalism, in A. V. Bogdandy (ed.), *Transformative Constitutionalism in Latin America: The Emergence of a New Ius Commune* (Oxford: Oxford University Press, 2017), pp. 3–26.

Cabral, M. A. M., Automatic Patent Term Extensions Ruled Unconstitutional in Brazil: Better Late Than Never? (2022) 53 *IIC – International Review of Intellectual Property and Competition Law* 160–68.

Da Silva, C. E. L., Patentes: Fernando Henrique Defende Lei nos EUA, *Folha de São Paulo*, May 11, 1993.

Davis, D. M. and Klare, K., Transformative Constitutionalism and the Common and Customary Law (2010) 26 *South African Journal of Human Rights* 403–509.

Davis, K. E. and Pargendler, M., Contract Law and Inequality (2022) 107 *Iowa Law Review* 1485–541.

Felizardo, N., Não Tem Remédio: Farmacêuticas Movem Máquina de Processos para Barrar Genéricos de Medicamentos para Câncer, Diabetes e HIV, *Intercept Brasil*, August 21, 2023.

Filho, C. S. et al., A Inconstitucionalidade do Artigo 40, Parágrafo Único, da Lei de Propriedade Industrial sob uma Perspectiva Comparada (2020) *Social Science Research Network* 1–64. https://doi.org/10.2139/ssrn.3745372

Fowkes, J., Transformative Constitutionalism and the Global South: The View from South Africa, in A.V. Bogdandy et al. (eds.), *Transformative Constitutionalism in Latin America: The Emergence of a New Ius Commune* (Oxford: Oxford University Press, 2017), pp. 97–121.

Fredman, S., *Comparative Human Rights Law* (Oxford: Oxford University Press, 2018).

Goyal, Y., "Death of a Discipline": Locating Heterodoxy in Law (2014) 56 *Journal of the Indian Law Institute* 493–522.

Hailbronner, M., Transformative Constitutionalism (2017) 65 *The American Journal of Comparative Law* 527–65.

Kennedy, D., Law and Economics from the Perspective of Critical Legal Studies, in P. Newman (ed.), *The New Palgrave Dictionary of Economics and the Law* (London: Macmillan Reference Limited, 1998), pp. 465–74.

Kennedy, D., Three Globalizations of Law and Legal Thought, in D. Trubek and A. Santos (eds.), *The New Law and Economic Development: A Critical Appraisal* (Cambridge: Cambridge University Press, 2006), pp. 17–73.

Klare, K. E., Legal Culture and Transformative Constitutionalism (1998) 14 *South African Journal of Human Rights* 146–88.

Klein, C., The Economics of Sham Litigation: Theory, Cases, and Policy (1989) *Bureau of Economics Staff Report to the Federal Trade Commission* 1–83.

Lianos, I. and Regibeau, P., "Vexatious"/"Sham" Litigation in EU and US Antitrust Law: A Mechanism Design Approach (2017) *CLES Research Paper Series 1/2017* 1–60.

Löfgren, H. and Williams, O. D., Conclusion: TRIPS, Drug Production in the Global South and Access to Medicines, in. H. Löfgren and O. D. Williams (eds.), *The New Political*

Economy of Pharmaceuticals: Production, Innovation and TRIPS in the Global South (Basingstoke: Palgrave Macmillan, 2013), pp. 246–50.

Möller, K., Dworkin's Theory of Rights in the Age of Proportionality (2018) 12 *Law & Ethics of Human Rights* 281–99.

Naím, M., Washington Consensus or Washington Confusion? (2000) 118 *Foreign Policy* 87–103.

Paranhos, J., Mercadante, E., and Hasenclever, L., O Custo da Extensão da Vigência de Patentes de Medicamentos para o Sistema Único de Saúde (2019) 36 *Cadernos de Saúde Pública* 1–13.

Pargendler, M., Análise Econômica e Comparada do Art. 40, Parágrafo Único, da Lei de Propriedade Industrial, in A. Frazão, R. M. Castro, and S. Campinho (eds.), *Direito Empresarial e suas Interfaces – Homenagem a Fabio Ulhoa Coelho*, vol. II (São Paulo: Quartier Latin, 2023), pp. 65–106.

Pargendler, M., The Rise of International Corporate Law (2021) 98 *Washington University Law Review* 1765–820.

Portugal Gouvêa, C., *Análise dos Custos da Desigualdade: Efeitos Institucionais do Círculo Vicioso de Desigualdade e Corrupção* (São Paulo: Quartier Latin, 2020).

Social Rights against the Poor (2013) 7 *Vienna Journal on International Constitutional Law* 454–75.

Posner, R. A., Creating a Legal Framework for Economic Development (1998) 13 *The World Bank Research Observer* 1–11.

Santos, L. G., Tecnologia, Natureza e a "Redescoberta" do Brasil, in H. R. Araújo (ed.), *Tecnociência e Cultura: Ensaios sobre o Tempo Presente* (São Paulo: Estação Liberdade, 1998), pp. 26–30.

Scopel, C. T. and Chaves, G. C., Initiatives to Challenge Patent Barriers and Their Relationship with the Price of Medicines Procured by the Brazilian Unified National Health System (2016) 32 *Cadernos de Saúde Pública* 1–11.

Sousa, K. C., Estratégias de Avaliação de Desempenho dos Propagandistas de Medicamentos Utilizados pela Indústria Farmacêutica no Nordeste do Brasil, Master's dissertation, Universidade Federal do Rio Grande do Norte (2013).

Stiglitz, J. E., *Globalization and Its Discontents* (New York: W. W. Norton, 2002).

Sweet, C. M., The Political Economy of Pharmaceutical Production in Brazil, in H. Löfgren and O. D. Williams (eds.), *The New Political Economy of Pharmaceuticals: Production, Innovation and TRIPS in the Global South* (Basingstoke: Palgrave Macmillan, 2013), pp. 29–47.

Tozi, F., Intellectual Property Protection and Drug Patents in Brazil (2020) 19 *Mercator* 1–13.

Wiarda, H. J., *Cracks in the Consensus: Debating the Democracy Agenda in US Foreign Policy* (Westport: Praeger, 1997).

Williamson, J., The Strange History of the Washington Consensus (2005) 27 *Journal of Post Keynesian Economics* 195–206.

Yamin A. and Parra-Vera, O., How Do Courts Set Health Policy? The Case of the Colombian Constitutional Court (2009) 6 *Plos Medicine* 0147-50.

Yang, B. and Kwon, H., TRIPS and New Challenges for the Pharmaceutical Sector in South Korea, in H. Löfgren and D. O. Williams (eds.), *The New Political Economy of Pharmaceuticals: Production, Innovation and TRIPS in the Global South* (Basingstoke: Palgrave Macmillan, 2013), pp. 204–20.

9

The Political Economy of India's Corporate Social Responsibility Reforms

Vikramaditya S. Khanna

9.1 INTRODUCTION

India's Companies Law underwent a set of significant reforms in 2013, but the provision that has attracted perhaps the greatest attention is Section 135. It appears to be one of the first, if not the first, attempt in the world to mandate corporate spending on Corporate Social Responsibility (CSR) initiatives in certain circumstances. The law required that Indian firms above certain profit, sales, or net worth thresholds either spend 2 percent of their average profits over the last three years on activities deemed to be CSR by the government or publicly explain why they did not do so (with penalties increasing for noncompliance over time). Studies have explored the effects of these reforms on the market value of Indian firms impacted by them and on CSR spending by Indian firms, among other issues, but few have explored the genesis of the reforms. This chapter begins to examine that question with a central puzzle: The CSR requirement could have been written as a CSR tax rather than a CSR spending requirement, so why would the Government choose the latter, more heterodox, option?

The analysis suggests that the CSR reforms did not primarily arise from philanthropic considerations. Rather, the motivation for the reforms reflects a blend of political optics and state capacity or efficiency considerations informed by historical experiences with market-oriented reforms. On the efficiency and state capacity front, the Indian state might not have been as well placed to enforce a CSR tax as Indian firms might have been able to manage a CSR spending requirement in 2013. This is largely due to the incentives and constraints faced by private sector employees compared to public sector employees in the Indian context. On the political optics side there was a perception in government (and apparently a sizable part of the citizenry) that the liberalization efforts had primarily benefited only a very small sliver of the country. The CSR reforms were a way for the government to prod firms to engage in activities that benefited the citizenry in a manner that made it *look like* the firms, rather than the state, were doing it. If the state had explicitly used the tax system, it suggests that economic liberalization (which largely reduced the role of the state in managing the economy) was not working for the citizenry at large and that the state had to come back in to steer the economy. It would also have led businesses to question the state's commitment to liberalization. This might have undermined support for further liberalization reforms that were being put forward at that time. However, if corporations were engaged in CSR then it might *look like* the gains from economic liberalization were beginning to find their way from India Inc. (the colloquial label for corporate India) to the general citizenry. This latter account might enhance support for economic liberalization reforms that were contained in the 2013 Act and perhaps future reforms. This blended account provides interesting insights about this rather unique set of reforms and considerations that may be helpful in exploring developments following on from those reforms.

Section 9.2 begins the inquiry by detailing the current legal regime governing CSR activities in India. Section 9.3 examines the scholarly work that discusses the impact of the CSR reforms. This covers a remarkably broad terrain that is still evolving. Section 9.4 then examines the political economy and history behind these reforms and describes the blended account just mentioned. Section 9.5 delves into post-2013 CSR developments and Section 9.6 concludes.

9.2 OVERVIEW OF LEGAL DEVELOPMENTS RELATED TO CSR IN INDIA

India's Corporate Social Responsibility (CSR) provision was enacted as part of many other reforms in its Companies Act 2013. At the time of its enactment, it was one of the first provisions, if not the first, in any country to require that some firms spend a percentage of their profits on "socially responsible" activities or explain why they did not. These heterodox CSR reforms, however, were not the end of efforts in this realm. There have been further amendments – one in 2019 and one in 2021 – that have moved the regime from the "comply-or-explain" regime of 2013 toward a "comply-or-else" regime. This section describes the original 2013 reforms and 2014 rules and what changes were brought by the 2019 and 2021 amendments. In addition, it briefly discusses the limited case law that has emerged thus far.

Section 135 of the Companies Act 2013 operates in two steps. First, it creates conditions under which firms are subject to Section 135. Second, once a firm is subject to Section 135, it lays out the obligations that apply.

The first step is met when a firm meets at least one of three thresholds in any financial year – either sales (called "turnover") exceeding INR 10 billion (~USD 125 million), net profits exceeding INR 50 million (~USD 625,000), or net worth exceeding INR 5 billion (~USD 62.5 Million).[1] All firms with operations in India

[1] Section 135 (1), Companies Act 2013. Net worth is based on a firm's "paid up share capital" (the number of shares outstanding, multiplied by the face value at which the share certificates were

(including publicly traded firms, private firms, and foreign firms) are subject to Section 135 when they cross any of these thresholds.[2]

Assuming that a firm crosses any of these thresholds, then a number of obligations arise under the original Section 135 in the 2013 Act. In particular, the firm must:

i) constitute a "Corporate Social Responsibility" (CSR) committee with three directors where at least one must be independent,[3]
ii) disclose the composition of the CSR committee,[4]
iii) formulate a CSR policy (via the CSR committee) recommending the kinds and amounts of CSR spending the firm is to pursue and the CSR committee must monitor that policy,[5]
iv) publicize the firm's CSR policy, once it has been approved by the Board after taking into account the CSR committee's recommendations, and the Board must ensure that the policy is followed,[6] and
v) ensure, via Board action and monitoring, that it spends at least 2 percent of the firm's average net profits (over the last three years) on activities listed in the firm's CSR policy or provide reasons for why it did not (i.e., a "comply-or-explain" rule).[7]

Although this was called a "comply-or-explain" rule, it is only the amount of CSR spending (i.e., item (v) above) that is subject to a "comply-or-explain" requirement, while all the others (items (i) to (iv) above) are mandatory and failing to meet them triggers liability.[8] An explanation for failing to meet the 2 percent spending requirement (item (v)) might avoid liability if that explanation was thought to be *acceptable*, but the statute did not provide guidance on what might be acceptable or to whom

originally issued), but also takes account of the face value of preferred stock and adjusts for retained earnings and various reserves. See D. Dharmapala and V. Khanna, 'The Impact of Mandating Corporate Social Responsibility: Evidence from India's Companies Act 2013' (2018) 56 *International Review of Law and Economics* 92–104. The US Dollar totals are based on an exchange rate of 1 USD = 80 INR.

2 Ministry of Corporate Affairs, Companies (Corporate Social Responsibility Policy) Rules (2014) (hereinafter "CSR Rules").

3 Section 135 (1), Companies Act 2013.

4 Section 135 (2), Companies Act 2013.

5 Section 135 (3), Companies Act 2013.

6 Section 135 (4), Companies Act 2013.

7 Section 135 (5), Companies Act 2013. Section 135 (5) suggests that firms should give preference to CSR spending in its local areas, which has generated some negative commentary. See A. Afsharipour and S. Rana, The Emergence of New Corporate Social Responsibility Regimes in China and India (2014) 14 *UC Davis Business Law Journal* 175–230.

8 Arcot, Bruno, and Faure-Grimaud have argued that "comply-or-explain" provisions can lead to broad-based compliance, even if enforcement is limited. See S. Arcot, V. Bruno, and A. Faure-Grimaud, 'Corporate Governance in the UK: Is the Comply or Explain Approach Working? (2010) 30 *International Review of Law and Economics* 193–201.

such an explanation should be provided.[9] The penalty for violations of Section 135 was INR 100,000 (~USD 1,250) on the firm and every officer of the firm for the first day of the violation and an incremental INR 1,000 (~USD 12.50) per day for as long as the violation continues.[10]

As drafted, Section 135 did not provide guidance on what activities amounted to CSR and what did not. The Ministry of Corporate Affairs (MCA) provided this initial guidance later through a set of rules approved in February 2014.[11] The rules designated a broad array of activities as amounting to acceptable CSR, including education, arts, health, poverty eradication, environment, some designated government programs, funds for technology incubators in government academic institutions, reducing gender inequality and other inequalities, and more.[12] This left firms with considerable scope and discretion in deciding where to engage in CSR spending. Nonetheless, the MCA's rules did exclude certain items such as spending undertaken in the normal course of business, to benefit employees or political parties, or relating to foreign activities (i.e., activities occurring outside of India).[13] Over time there has been an increase in the number of government programs that are designated as counting for CSR purposes.

Section 135 was then amended in 2019 and 2021. The 2019 amendments made several technical changes but, for our purposes, perhaps the most important were changes that:

i) required firms to keep funds earmarked for CSR spending, but not spent, in a separate account for up to three years until the funds are spent and if they still are not spent after three years, then the funds must go to an activity in Schedule VII of the Act (e.g., the Prime Minister's Relief Fund),[14] and
ii) stated that failure to comply with the provisions (including the spending requirement) would not have a defense of an acceptable explanation and could result in *criminal liability* for the firm and relevant officers.[15]

9 The explanations typically provided by firms for noncompliance are that the CSR rule was novel and they did not have the time or expertise to respond promptly, they found it difficult to identify worthy causes, or that they will do more spending in future years. See Dharmapala and Khanna, The Impact of Mandating Corporate Social Responsibility.

10 Section 450, Companies Act 2013 (also attaching liability to other persons who are in default). Who is to enforce Section 135 is not entirely clear from its wording but one might assume it is the Ministry of Corporate Affairs. If the firm repeats the violation within three years, then it might suffer double the fine – see Section 451, Companies Act 2013.

11 CSR Rules (2014). Schedule VII of the Companies Act 2013 now contains these rules.

12 CSR Rules (2014).

13 Ibid. The rules provide for the CSR activities to be undertaken by the firm or through certain other third parties such as a registered society or trust (see Section 8, Companies Act) or through collaboration with other firms.

14 See Section 135(6).

15 See Section 135(7).

Unsurprisingly, the criminalization of noncompliance generated considerable consternation in Corporate India, leading to more amendments in 2021.[16] These involved:

i) decriminalizing noncompliance with CSR requirements (which are now only civil) while increasing the civil monetary penalties compared to the 2013 legislation. These penalties were capped at INR 10 million for firms (~USD 125,000) and INR 200,000 (~USD 2,500) for officers;[17]
ii) weakening some requirements for smaller firms;[18]
iii) excluding additional items from the list of acceptable CSR activities so that advertising or marketing and spending to fulfill other statutory obligations did not count toward the CSR requirement;[19]
iv) a requirement for firms who should spend more than INR 10,000,000 (~USD 125,000) on CSR, under the CSR rules, to conduct independent impact assessments and present them to the board;[20] and
v) a series of changes relating to the implementation process for the rule.[21]

In addition to these statutory and regulatory changes, the Government of India and private parties have created CSR tracking websites, which are quite detailed, and other resources that might facilitate greater and more effective spending on CSR.[22]

These changes are quite numerous and were enacted with considerable speed. However, judicial developments do not appear to have reflected that kind of urgency. There are few cases adjudicating significant issues associated with the CSR rules and even fewer that impose penalties for noncompliance. One case resulted in a fine of INR 100,000 (~USD 1,250) where the firm failed to meet the CSR committee and spending requirements in the first year they were bound (without any explanation).[23] The firm's justification was that it was not prepared in that first year, but has met the requirements since then.[24] Other cases have

[16] See K. S. Thomas, Corporate India Irked at New CSR Rules, *The Week*, August 3, 2019; D. Sikarwar, Government Won't Go Ahead with New CSR Rules, *The Economic Times*, August 14, 2019.

[17] See Section 135(7).

[18] For instance, under Section 135(9) firms with CSR spending requirements of INR 5,000,000 (~USD 62,500) or less did not need to form a CSR committee and the Board of such firms acts as the CSR committee.

[19] See Rule 2(d), CSR Rules (2014).

[20] See Rule 8(b), CSR Rules (2014).

[21] Examples abound, but a sampling may be illustrative. Under Rule 4(1) CSR Rules (2014) firms can implement the spending either themselves or through outside agencies and under Rule 7 (1) firms cannot charge more than 5 percent of the total CSR spend for administrative overheads.

[22] See, e.g., Ministry of Corporate Affairs, History (2023); Ministry of Corporate Affairs, CSR in India (2023). There are also national awards for CSR – see Ministry of Corporate Affairs, *Compendium on Corporate Social Responsibility in India* (New Delhi: Ministry of Corporate Affairs, 2022).

[23] See In re Parikh Enterprises Private Ltd., C.P. No. 4/441/NCLT/AHM/2017.

[24] Ibid.

revolved around whether decisions made by Income Tax Assessors were accurate (for determining whether the amounts spent count toward the CSR rule)[25] and whether some expenditures should not be counted toward the CSR requirements (e.g., spending on tobacco-related matters).[26]

The CSR rules generated a great deal of discussion, with many praising the reforms but many also criticizing them. A common response was that this rule had turned essentially a voluntary activity into a mandatory one, going against the very nature of CSR.[27] Others thought the reforms were in essence revolutionary, suggesting a new way forward in the inclusive development debate.[28] However, these arguments were often made before the reforms came into effect and hence were not often based on the effects of the reforms. It is to those effects that I now turn.

9.3 STUDIES ON THE EFFECTS OF CSR REFORM

The structure of the CSR reforms provided scholars with a rather nice empirical design to test some of the effects of the reforms. In particular, the substantive obligations only applied if the firm crossed certain thresholds (e.g., net profit, sales, net worth). This meant that firms just above and below the relevant thresholds might be very similar in most respects except that one set of firms (those just below the threshold) would not be subject to the substantive regulations and another set (those just above the threshold) would be subject to them. This provided for plausible control (just below the threshold) and treatment (just above the threshold) groups assuming these firms were otherwise similar, which they appeared to be. Several papers used this feature of the reforms to test their empirical effects.

9.3.1 *Firm Value Effects?*

Some conducted event studies and found that the stock market prices of the treatment firms (just above the threshold) declined on the earliest announcement of the reforms relative to control firms (just below the threshold).[29] This is perhaps not that surprising because the reforms in essence imposed a cost on firms subject to

[25] See NTPC-SAIL Power Co. Ltd. v. Deputy Commissioner of Income Tax, ITA No. 2146/Del/2017.

[26] See S. Cyril Alexander v. Union of India, Writ Petition No. 9955 of 2014, High Court of Madras.

[27] See e.g., A. Karnani, Mandatory CSR in India: A Bad Proposal, *Stanford Social Innovation Review*, May 20, 2013.

[28] See Afsharipour and Rana, The Emergence of New Corporate Social Responsibility Regimes in China and India. For an analysis of CSR obligations being imposed via regulation versus a voluntary mechanism see U. Varottil, Analysing the CSR Spending Requirements under Indian Company Law, in J. J. du Plessis, U. Varottil, and J. Veldman (eds.), *Globalisation of Corporate Social Responsibility and Its Impact on Corporate Governance* (Cham: Springer International Publishing, 2018), pp. 231–53.

[29] See Dharmapala and Khanna, The Impact of Mandating Corporate Social Responsibility; H. Manchiraju and S. Rajgopal, Does Corporate Social Responsibility (CSR) Create

the rules reflecting the increased CSR spending and the costs associated with creating a CSR committee and meeting the other requirements. This might be balanced by some benefits (e.g., goodwill, higher sales) that might accrue to the firm from these activities. However, the results of the early studies suggest that, at that time, the market did not appear to think those benefits were sufficiently large to overcome the costs.

More recent work suggests that there might have been benefits at the time of the earliest announcement of the reforms for foreign firms and for firms in controversial sectors in India because the government was providing greater clarity on what might amount to CSR and in turn what might generate goodwill for these firms.[30] This more recent work uses different event dates for its tests so its analyses are not directly comparable to earlier work but nonetheless the results are interesting.[31]

9.3.2 *CSR Spending Effects?*

Reformers might also be interested in whether firms actually complied with the additional spending and other requirements. This was not a given in light of the "comply-or-explain" rule and a somewhat less aggressive attitude toward enforcement by Indian regulators and courts in the corporate governance space at that time.[32]

The earliest empirical paper examining this issue found that soon after the reforms came into effect CSR spending for firms below the threshold began to increase and many more firms were reporting CSR spending when they had not done so before.[33] This was, however, accompanied by a reduction in advertising expenses at these firms (suggesting some substitutability between CSR and advertising spending).[34] Additionally, the paper found – somewhat counterintuitively – that firms that were engaged in active CSR spending prior to the reforms (e.g., spending more than 2 percent of profits on CSR before it was required) reduced their post-reform spending to 2 percent.[35] This presumably unintended consequence suggested that the pre-reform high-CSR spenders found the reputational advantage from that level of spending to be less valuable when CSR spending appeared mandated.[36]

Shareholder Value? Evidence from the Indian Companies Act 2013 (2017) 55 *Journal of Accounting Research* 1257–300.

[30] See R. Panwar et al., Did India's CSR Mandate Enhance or Diminish Firm Value? (2023) 62 *Business & Society* 401–33.

[31] Of course, it is also possible that over time the market may come to value CSR more than it did initially.

[32] See D. Dharmapala and V. Khanna, Corporate Governance, Enforcement, and Firm Value: Evidence from India (2013) 29 *Journal of Law, Economics, and Organization* 1056–84.

[33] See Dharmapala and Khanna, The Impact of Mandating Corporate Social Responsibility.

[34] Ibid.

[35] Ibid. Many of these larger firms had opposed the reforms.

[36] Ibid. It may also be that announcing a 2 percent rule might operate as an anchor for CSR spending (i.e., a ceiling and a floor). See ibid.

However, this study was early in the postreform period and it appears that, since then, the level of CSR spending by firms in India has grown substantially. The most recent data from the Government of India's CSR tracker website suggests that CSR spending is now quite significant, with most firms complying with the 2 percent spending requirement.[37] This not only suggests growth in actual CSR spend, but also heightened compliance, which is impressive given the fairly thin levels of official enforcement intensity thus far.

A recent paper argues that firms initially spending more than 2 percent of profits on CSR are likely to increase beyond that level if the law does not confine their choices too much.[38] In other words, initially larger CSR spenders are likely to increase their spending as the law gets clearer.

Another recent paper explores what the main CSR strategies of Indian firms appear to be.[39] These authors suggest that there are two main strategies. First, most firms follow a "narrow" strategy where their CSR spending tracks issues such as education and healthcare in high population density areas.[40] They do this directly rather than relying on nongovernmental organizations (NGOs). The authors suggest this reflects the concerns most likely relevant to the stakeholders of these more urban firms.[41] Second, the larger firms and state-owned enterprises tend to target "broader" issues by green-lighting many different projects and relying on NGOs to implement their plans.[42] Their findings suggest that firms' CSR expenditures are attuned to their likely stakeholders concerns rather than the potential efficiencies firms might provide in CSR activity.[43]

9.3.3 *CSR Spending and Politics?*

In recent years, concerns have been mounting about the interactions between the CSR rules, CSR spending, and politics. For instance, a recent paper argued that local politicians are heavily influencing the selection and spending on CSR projects in order to enhance their chances of winning the next set of elections.[44] It also finds

[37] See Ministry of Corporate Affairs, History; Ministry of Corporate Affairs, CSR in India. See also KPMG, India's CSR Reporting Survey 2019 (2020).

[38] See S. Jai et al., Choosing beyond Compliance over Dormancy: Corporate Response to India's Mandatory CSR Expenditure Law (2023) 19 *Management and Organization Review* 594–623.

[39] See A. Gatignon and C. Bode, When Few Give to Many and Many Give to Few: Corporate Social Responsibility Strategies under India's Legal Mandate (2023) 44 *Strategic Management Journal* 2099–127. The authors examine data on CSR spending and CSR projects from 2014 to 2017 (representing 12,086 firms and 86,755 projects) and how it maps out in terms of the social causes it targets, the geographies in which it operates, implementation channels, and number of projects.

[40] See ibid.

[41] See ibid.

[42] See ibid.

[43] See ibid.

[44] See N. Koya and J. Roper, Legislated CSR in Practice: The Experience of India (2022) 22 *Journal of Public Affairs* 1–10.

that, in addition to local politicians, local stakeholders and community activists have become more active in approaching firms for CSR spending since the reforms were enacted.[45]

In addition, some scholars have expressed concerns that CSR policy at the national level may reflect the ruling party's electoral concerns in pivotal states.[46] This is because contributions to certain government schemes can count toward the CSR spending requirements and the set of approved government schemes seems to be rising. Moreover, there is some evidence that state-owned enterprises are also contributing to these government schemes in fairly large amounts.[47]

This then raises the intriguing prospect that firms and politicians might trade off political contributions for lower levels of CSR spending. This is explored in another recent paper which finds that poorly governed firms in India use CSR spending and political donations as partial substitutes.[48] Its findings suggest that firms with more opaque governance (e.g., family group membership) or headquartered in high-corruption states are less likely to meet CSR targets around elections yet they tend to increase political donations at that time.[49]

These sets of papers suggest that it is worthwhile to further explore the interactions between CSR and politics. More generally, an analysis of how private CSR efforts and public efforts interact in the provision of public goods and social services would be valuable.

Although the empirical work on the CSR reforms is growing rapidly, that still leaves open the question at the heart of this chapter – what led to these reforms and are the effects of the reforms consistent with those motivations? Understanding the history and political economy of these reforms is critical in better understanding the reforms.

9.4 POLITICAL ECONOMY SURROUNDING CSR REFORM IN INDIA

The CSR reforms in India are puzzling in some respects because it appears that a simpler way to get firms to contribute to social causes would be for the government to impose a CSR tax on them. Indeed, one might argue that the CSR rules are, in effect, a 2 percent tax on firms above certain thresholds, with the decision on how to spend those funds being delegated to firms within boundaries established by the

45 See ibid., reporting results of interviews with some CSR professionals at firms.

46 See P. Sundar, Using CSR Funds for Political Gain, *The Wire*, December 22, 2018.

47 See KPMG, India's CSR Reporting Survey 2019.

48 See D. Aggarwal, The Politics of Mandatory Corporate Philanthropy (2023) Northwestern Law & Econ Research Paper No. 23-14. It is perhaps worth noting that firms could have made these trade-offs with other expenditures too (e.g., advertising and political donations), but it is possible the CSR spending allows this more easily.

49 The author also reports that business group firms' cash ratios tend to increase around this time, perhaps indicating that the firms are preparing to make political contributions with this increased cash. See ibid.

government. That then raises the question of why the government adopted this more heterodox approach to CSR – was this thought to be more efficient in some sense, more politically attractive, or something else?[50] Although one can imagine many possible responses, a deeper appreciation of the political and historical background against which the choice was made is likely to be illuminating. I approach this in two steps – first, what led to the heightened desire for corporations to give back to society?; and second, what led the reforms to take the specific shape that they did? (i.e., a CSR spending requirement as opposed to a CSR tax).

9.4.1 *Heightened Need to Give Back to Society?*

Business in the Indian subcontinent has a long history of contributing to social activities,[51] but the factors that were most important in leading to the CSR rules appear to be of more recent vintage. The Companies Act 2013, of which Section 135 is but a part, was envisioned as a major overhaul of India's 1956 Companies Act. These reforms were primarily based on the J. J. Irani Committee Report of 2005 commissioned by the Government of India.[52] The report came after India's securities market regulator (the Securities and Exchange Board of India (SEBI)) had

[50] For further discussion see Dharmapala and Khanna, The Impact of Mandating Corporate Social Responsibility.

[51] See P. Sundar, *Beyond Business: From Merchant Charity to Corporate Citizenship. Indian Business Philanthropy through the Ages* (New Delhi: Tata McGraw-Hill Publishing Company, 2000); R. S. Rungta, *The Rise of Business Corporations in India: 1851–1900* (New Delhi: Cambridge University Press, 1970); V. Khanna, Business Organizations in India Prior to the British East India Company, in H. Wells (ed.), *Research Handbook on the History of Corporate and Company Law* (Cheltenham: Edward Elgar, 2018), pp. 33–64. Although these are historical accounts, it is noteworthy that some Indian businesses have even in recent times supported such activities and some have even conducted social audits as early as the 1970s. See A. Sood and B. Arora, The Political Economy of Corporate Responsibility in India (2006) Technology Business and Society Program Paper No. 18, United National Research Institute for Social Development; M. Herdeck and G. Piramal, *India's Industrialists* (Washington, DC: Three Continents Press, 1985), vol. I. Business responsibility in more modern times is also tied to Mahatma Gandhi's notion of "trusteeship" where firms are conceptualized as trustees who manage resources on behalf of society (which in turn is connected to some ancient justifications for the charitable activities of business in India). See A. Afsharipour, Directors as Trustees of the Nation? India's Corporate Governance and Corporate Social Responsibility Reform Efforts (2011) 34 *Seattle University Law Review* 995–1024; See Afsharipour and Rana, The Emergence of New Corporate Social Responsibility Regimes in China and India; B. N. Balasubramanian, 'Governing the Socially Responsible Corporation – A Gandhian Perspective', in A. Das Gupta (ed.), *Ethics, Business and Society: Managing Responsibly* (New Delhi: Sage Publications, 2009), pp. 157–80. It is also noteworthy that one of India's most well-known conglomerates – the Tata Group – takes two-thirds of the profits it makes and places them in charitable trusts supporting a variety of social activities and institutions. See Afsharipour and Rana, The Emergence of New Corporate Social Responsibility Regimes in China and India, 165.

[52] See J. J. Irani Committee Report, Report on Company Law, Ministry for Company Affairs (2005).

promulgated a watershed corporate governance reform (known as Clause 49 of the listing agreement) that adopted many global best practices in corporate governance.[53] The Irani committee report appeared designed to move India away from the more "mandatory" model of the 1956 Act and toward a more "enabling" corporate law and to be generally more consistent with global trends.[54] The overall sense was that India was modernizing its corporate laws.[55] However, the Irani committee report contained no mention of CSR reforms.

The CSR reforms were first mentioned in the Companies Bill in the middle of 2011,[56] but that was not the first time that the debate over CSR had reached the national stage in India. The Ministry of Corporate Affairs (MCA) had put forward a set of voluntary guidelines on CSR in late 2009 that were designed to persuade Indian firms to engage in more CSR activities.[57] It was these voluntary guidelines that set the stage for the CSR reforms that would eventually get enacted into the Companies Act 2013. Thus, the genesis of these guidelines forms a key area of inquiry for this chapter.

There were many forces at play that appear to have set the stage for the 2009 Guidelines. Perhaps one of the most consistent was a growing sense that India's liberalization efforts had only really benefited a small segment of society and not the common person. Indeed, in 2007 the then-Prime Minister Manmohan Singh expressed concern that rising levels of executive compensation in India against a background of rising wealth and income inequality could cause social unrest.[58] He suggested that firms should curb this level of compensation and undertake more socially responsible activities that were consistent with more inclusive development.[59] Soon thereafter the global financial crisis led to even more concerns about income and wealth inequality, among other things.

[53] See V. Khanna, Corporate Governance in India: Past, Present & Future? (2009) 1 *Jindal Global Law Review* 171–95; V. Khanna and B. S. Black, Can Corporate Governance Reforms Increase Firms' Market Values?: Event Study Evidence from India (2007) 4 *Journal of Empirical Legal Studies* 749–96; N. Balasubramaniam, B. S. Black, and V. Khanna, The Relation between Firm-Level Corporate Governance and Market Value: A Study of India (2010) 11 *Emerging Markets Review* 319–40.

[54] See Khanna, Corporate Governance in India.

[55] See ibid.

[56] See The Companies Bill (Proposed), 2011, No. 121, Lok Sabha, Clause 135.

[57] See Ministry of Company Affairs, Government of India, Voluntary Guidelines on Corporate Social Responsibility (2009).

[58] See J. Johnson, Inequality Fears Sting Indian Business, *Financial Times*, May 28, 2007. In another context then-Prime Minister Singh suggested that rising inequality was adding fuel to insurgency and terrorism in India. See K. Mukherjee, Manmohan Says Development Threatening Security, *Reuters*, December 20, 2007. See generally S. Sharma, Corporate Social Responsibility in India; The Emerging Discourse & Concerns (2013) 48 *Indian Journal of Industrial Relations* 582–96.

[59] See Sharma, Corporate Social Responsibility in India: The Emerging Discourse & Concerns, 586.

By 2009, the Indian political landscape had mounting concerns over the distributional aspects of the liberalization efforts. However, these concerns became more prominent when India suffered its largest corporate scandal in the form of the Satyam fraud at the start of 2009. It appeared that India's fourth largest Information Technology Services Firm – Satyam – had its prime assets siphoned off and sent to entities owned by its controller, Ramalinga Raju, and his family and kin.[60] The Government of India had to step in and essentially pick up the pieces. This, unsurprisingly, left a sour feeling about the private sector in early 2009. This rising skepticism was also a key theme in the national elections of 2009 where the ruling coalition – the United Progressive Alliance (UPA), led by the Indian National Congress Party – was looking rather shaky. The UPA eventually won the election by joining forces with a set of resurgent left-leaning parties who seemed to also find the liberalization efforts too limited in their benefits.

Thus, by the middle of 2009, there were concerns about the economic and distributional effects of liberalization, the ethics of the corporate sector,[61] and rising income and wealth inequality. Against this context the MCA drafted and released its voluntary guidelines on corporate social responsibility in late December 2009.

These guidelines exhorted firms in India to engage in more CSR activities. The then-Minister of Corporate Affairs Salman Khurshid said in the introduction to the guidelines:

> [T]he corporate sector is also standing in the midst of a sustainability crisis that poses a threat to the very existence of business. What we have before us is a cross-road where one path leads us to inclusive growth and the other may lead to unsustainable future. However, the first path will require careful nurturing for which all stakeholders need to assume and discharge their respective responsibilities . . . The corporate growth is sometimes seen as widening the gap between the India and Bharat through its income-skewing capability. This gap needs to be bridged. While the Government undertakes extensive developmental initiatives through a series of sectoral programmes, the business sector also needs to take the responsibility of exhibiting socially responsible business practices that ensures the distribution of wealth and well-being of the communities in which the business operates.[62]

This suggests that a key motive behind the guidelines was to encourage business to undertake more CSR activities or else there may be threats to the "very existence

[60] See Khanna, Corporate Governance in India; Afsharipour, Directors as Trustees of the Nation?

[61] Some scholars noted that before the CSR guidelines and reforms it appeared – based on an analysis of communications between CEOs and shareholders – that Indian firms had moved much more toward a shareholder orientation than in the past. See T. Jain, R. V. Aguilera, and D. Jamali, Stakeholder Orientation in an Emerging Country Context: A Longitudinal Cross Industry Analysis (2017) 143 *Journal of Business Ethics* 701–19. Relatedly some scholars argued that Indian firms' modern philanthropy efforts seem to be falling short given the significant economic profits obtained. See B. Arora and R. Puranik, A Review of Corporate Social Responsibility in India (2004) 47 *Development* 93–100.

[62] See Ministry of Company Affairs, Government of India, Voluntary Guidelines on Corporate Social Responsibility, Introduction.

of business." Presumably, this was a reference to rising calls to restrain business and curtail further liberalization efforts.[63]

This was matched, and perhaps expanded upon, in the introductory note by the Chief Secretary to the MCA, R. Bandyopadhyay, who said:

> A number of initiatives are underway on the legislative, service delivery and capacity building sides so that the corporate sector is provided with a buoyant and enabling regulatory environment for its growth. Simultaneously, the Ministry is also focusing on various issues related to inclusive growth in relation to the development of corporate sector.[64]

Here the connection between further reforms and inclusive growth seems more clearly drawn. This suggests that political elites within the government were keen to encourage firms in India to engage in more CSR activities in a more visible manner.[65]

In spite of these appeals, it appears that the guidelines had little effect.[66] Soon thereafter the Ministry decided it was going to propose reforms to India's Companies Laws that would install CSR as a requirement. The earliest inkling of this came in August 2010 with reports that the Government was thinking of inserting a mandatory provision into the draft Companies Bill requiring CSR in some circumstances.[67]

This generated negative responses from the business elites in the Indian corporate sector (often known collectively as "India Inc.") suggesting some tension on this point between the business and political elites.[68] Key industry trade associations,

63 This bears some similarity to the political backlash argument in M. J. Roe, Backlash (1988) 98 *Columbia Law Review* 217–41.

64 See Ministry of Company Affairs, Government of India, Voluntary Guidelines on Corporate Social Responsibility, Comments by Chief Secretary.

65 Although the voluntary guidelines did not *require* firms to engage in CSR, they brought into focus concerns that had been percolating for some time. Absent some attempts to balance these effects (such as a CSR initiative), continuing liberalization was likely to face some strong political headwinds. See C. Van Zile, India's Mandatory Corporate Social Responsibility Proposal: Creative Capitalism Meets Creative Regulation in the Global Market (2012) 13 *Asian-Pacific Law & Policy Journal* 269–303. Moreover, academic discussion in India seemed to be moving toward a "trusteeship" model of governance that appeared more likely to facilitate CSR regulation. See, e.g., Balasubramanian, Governing the Socially Responsible Corporation.

66 See Standing Committee on Finance, Twenty-First Report (The Companies Bill, 2009), *Lok Sabha*, Clause 49 (2010). See also Richa Gautam and Anju Singh, Corporate Social Responsibility Practices in India: A Study of Top 500 Companies (2010) 2 *Global Business and Management Research: An International Journal* 41–56. See also V. Sundaram, Vinod Khosla to Donate Half His Fortune to Charity, *New America Media*, May 18, 2011; Afsharipour, Directors as Trustees of the Nation?; Van Zile, India's Mandatory Corporate Social Responsibility Proposal.

67 See Money Control, Mandatory CSR Not a Great Idea, Feels India Inc., *CNBC-TV18 News*, August 6, 2010. This was also discussed in a closely followed Blog website on corporate matters in India. See U. Varottil, Viability of Mandatory CSR, *IndiaCorpLawBlog*, August 7, 2010.

68 As early as the first news reports on August 6, 2010, Indian firms responded with concerns about mandating CSR. See Money Control, Mandatory CSR Not a Great Idea, Feels India Inc. It is noteworthy that even those who support firms being more involved in philanthropy expressed skepticism of CSR as being a Western import. See Sharma, Corporate Social Responsibility in

including the Confederation of Indian Industry (a very influential and large trade group), opposed the proposed rule. They did not necessarily oppose the notion of firms having social responsibilities, but rather were concerned that turning what had traditionally been voluntary into a mandated behavior was wrong and likely to be counterproductive, and also that the desire for a CSR mandate may be a signal that the support for liberalization efforts was weakening.[69] Their opposition appeared to have some effect because, by December 2010, there were reports that the government was backing away from mandating CSR spending and moving toward a "comply-or-explain" rule.[70] By 2011, the draft Companies Bill had a provision in it mandating that firms above certain thresholds spend 2 percent of their net profits on activities designated as CSR or explain why they did not (i.e., a "comply-or-explain" rule) along with mandating the formation of a CSR committee and other requirements that track the final provisions in the 2013 Act.[71]

Along with the proposed bill there were other developments indicating a concerted push toward CSR initiatives from the government. In April 2010 the Department of Public Enterprises issued "Guidelines for Corporate Social Responsibility for Central Public Sector Enterprises."[72] These tracked in large measure the voluntary guidelines from 2009, but with additional requirements and limitations for Public Enterprises. In 2011, the MCA issued the "National Voluntary Guidelines on Social, Environmental & Economic Responsibilities of Business," which also stressed the importance of CSR-oriented activities among other things.[73] Further, in 2012, SEBI required the 100 largest firms in India to file Business Responsibility Reports which required disclosure of CSR activity.[74]

Thus, by 2012, there was a draft Companies Bill with CSR provisions, guidelines for public sector enterprises on CSR, and a requirement for India's 100 largest firms (regardless of net worth, sales, or profits) to disclose their CSR activities. Clearly, the government was pushing for CSR to be an important issue across virtually all sectors of corporate activity in India underscoring the importance of India Inc. and India's business elites contributing to India's development in a visible manner.

India: The Emerging Discourse & Concerns; Balasubramanian, Governing the Socially Responsible Corporation.

69 See A. Vijayaraghavan, Indian Industries Oppose Mandatory CSR Reporting, *Just Means*, August 16, 2010; Times of India, IT CEOs back Premji against Mandatory CSR, *Times of India*, March 26, 2011; ENS Economic Bureau, CSR Spend on Cards for India Inc., *Indian Express*, February 9, 2011.

70 See Times of India, It's Their Business, *Times of India*, December 24, 2010.

71 The Companies Bill (Proposed), 2011, No. 121, Lok Sabha, Clause 135.

72 See Department of Public Enterprises, Government of India, DPE Guidelines (2010). In addition, see S. Pingola, Towards Strategic Corporate Social Responsibility in Cpsus': Positive Transformation through DPE Guidelines (2012).

73 See Ministry of Corporate Affairs, National Voluntary Guidelines on Social, Environmental & Economic Responsibilities of Business (2011).

74 See SEBI Circular CIR/CFD/DIL/8/2012, August 13, 2012.

9.4.2 *Why Not a CSR Tax?*

That brings us back to the question which began this section – if the government wanted to enhance the provision of public goods and services through funds provided by India Inc. it could have enacted a CSR spending requirement (as it eventually did) or it could have enacted a CSR tax (which was considered). Why then choose the relatively more heterodox CSR spending requirement? Although there could be multiple explanations (and indeed they need not be mutually exclusive), the two that I focus on are: (i) that a CSR spending requirement was more efficient in some sense than a CSR tax and (ii) that a CSR spending requirement would suit the political economy of the times better than a CSR tax.

The efficiency argument is premised on the notion that the Indian private sector may have some advantages in providing public goods and services over the Government in India. For instance, if private sector employees have greater expertise than government employees on where to spend funds for the greatest impact for certain activities (e.g., ITC's efforts for farmers in villages).[75] Also, we might think that private sector employees are more strongly motivated to make some decisions because they might generate business goodwill that inures more directly to their benefit. On a different note, we might be concerned that government employees in certain environments are more likely to siphon off funds than private sector employees. Of course, one might imagine circumstances in which government employees might have better incentives than private sector employees (e.g., where the CSR activity has more long-term payoffs, government employees have greater experience, or where the risk of siphoning funds is greater in the private sector). In addition, there may be areas where public and private sector employees working together might generate better outcomes than just one set of employees.[76] In essence, the question depends on the relative advantages of one set of employees making decisions compared to another.

Such arguments also suggest that limits on state capacity – for instance, in the state's ability to police its own employees or to enforce its tax rules[77] – might have played a role in the choice of reform (as has been discussed in Chapter 2). If the state is limited in its ability to enforce tax rules or police its own employees then relying on a CSR tax where government collects and disburses funds is likely to run into many problems and a more heterodox CSR spending requirement may be better. Indeed, commentary after the enactment of Section 135 stressed that the CSR spending requirement might have advantages because it was attempting to push

75 See ITC e-Choupal, Agribusiness (2023).

76 Cf. F. Guarini and G. Nidasio, CSR Role in Public–Private Partnerships: Models of Governance (2002).

77 Indeed, the Government of India loses the vast majority of its tax enforcement cases. See V. Khanna, Reducing Losses in India's Tax Cases, unpublished manuscript, 2024.

the private sector into doing activities that it might do better (i.e., more efficiently) than the public sector.[78]

Such an efficiency or state capacity argument is certainly a compelling account for why the government might prefer a CSR spending requirement over a CSR tax. Moreover, there are occasional hints that the government did not think it could meet the goals for inclusive development by itself,[79] which is consistent with concerns over state capacity and efficiency. Having said that, this may not have been the only motivation for the CSR reforms at the time. Much of the discussion and news reports leading up to the voluntary guidelines, the 2011 Bill, and the Companies Act 2013 did not emphasize state capacity or efficiency considerations.[80] Indeed, even later studies found that much CSR spending in India does not take advantage of the potential efficiencies provided by firms, suggesting that even if enhanced efficiency and addressing state capacity concerns were primary considerations their promise has yet to be fulfilled.[81]

Another explanation – one that is not inconsistent with the state capacity or efficiency argument – relates to the political economy of the times. This was hinted at in Minister Khurshid's statement as well as that of the MCA's Chief Secretary. In particular, it appears that the Government was keen for it to *look like* the firms were providing these public goods or services to the citizenry rather than it looking like the state was doing it. Moreover, a CSR tax is more likely to face opposition from business.

To better appreciate why the optics of the benefits coming from the corporate sector are important we need to note what the economic liberalization reforms in India were advertised to do. In essence, the reforms involved the state pulling itself back from managing large parts of the economy and society. Prior to the early 1990s the state occupied the "commanding heights" of the economy and social life.[82] However, by the late 1980s and early 1990s, it was becoming clear that the state's management of the economy was not what had been advertised.[83] On many metrics of development, India seemed to have stalled or, worse yet, regressed from just two

78 See, e.g., M. Mahapatra, CSR Practices among Public and Private Sector Companies: A Community Development Approach in Indian Context (2019) 10 *Journal of Management and Public Policy* 33–42. For a study on the impact of private firms as compared to publicly traded firms in the United States, see J. Li and D. Wu, Do Corporate Social Responsibility Engagements Lead to Real Environmental, Social and Governance Impact? (2020) 66 *Management Science* 2564–88.

79 This can be seen in the See Ministry of Company Affairs, Government of India, Voluntary Guidelines on Corporate Social Responsibility.

80 See discussion in Section 9.3.1.

81 See Gatignon and Bode, When Few Give to Many and Many Give to Few.

82 See Government of India, Industrial Policy Resolution (1956). This was later adopted into the Second Five Year Plan which was to operate from 1956 to 1961. See generally, S. Tharoor, *Nehru: The Invention of India* (New York: Arcade Publishing, 2011).

83 See A. O. Krueger (ed.) *Economic Policy Reforms and the Indian Economy* (Chicago: The University of Chicago Press, 2002); S. Tharoor, *India From Midnight to Millenium* (New York:

decades earlier.[84] There was a sense that, to improve the situation, the State needed to pull back and allow market forces and the business sector to grow with less of the "old" style state regulation.[85] The belief was that this would engender economic growth by fueling the market (or mixed-market) economy and that, although there would be gains to business, many gains would accrue to the general citizenry as well.[86] One must note that this was not an easy case to make in India, where many believe that so-called free market policies during the British Raj led to the impoverishment of the subcontinent.[87] Thus, it was essential that whatever market-oriented reforms were adopted actually provided benefits to the citizenry rather than appearing to be a repeat of earlier policies.

By 2009, it was clear that economic growth had certainly improved, but there was a strong sense that the growth had not been well distributed, with the lion's share of growth going to a small sliver of society.[88] Concerns were mounting that this was not sustainable and that further economic reforms were likely to face significant headwinds if some of the promised gains to the citizenry had not materialized after nearly two decades of reforms.[89] Indeed, much of the national election in 2009 turned on issues related to the effects of economic reforms on the general citizenry. These concerns were underscored by the global financial crisis in 2008 and the Satyam fraud – India's largest – in early 2009.

Arcade Publishing, 1997); M. S. Ahluwalia, Economic Reforms in India since 1991: Has Gradualism Worked? (2002) 16 *Journal of Economic Perspectives* 67–88.

84 See Krueger (ed.), *Economic Policy Reforms and the Indian Economy*; Ahluwalia, Economic Reforms in India since 1991.

85 See A. J. Goulding, Retreating from the Commanding Heights: Privatization in an Indian Context (1997) 50 *Journal of International Affairs* 581–612.

86 See Krueger (ed.), *Economic Policy Reforms and the Indian Economy*; Ahluwalia, Economic Reforms in India since 1991; Goulding, Retreating from the Commanding Heights: Privatization in an Indian Context.

87 There is a vast literature (and a somewhat contested one). For a sampling see S. Tharoor, *Inglorious Empire: What the British Did to India* (London: Hurst, 2017); S. Broadberry and B. Gupta, Cotton Textiles and the Great Divergence: Lancashire, India and Shifting Competitive Advantage, 1600–1850 (2005) Centre for Economic Policy Research Discussion Paper No. 5183; S. Broadberry, J. Custodis, and B. Gupta, India and the Great Divergence: An Anglo–Indian Comparison of GDP per capita, 1600–1871 (2015) 55 *Explorations in Economic History* 58–75; I. Ray, *Bengal Industries and the British Industrial Revolution (1757–1857)* (New York: Routledge, 2011); D. Clingingsmith and J. G. Williamson, Deindustrialization in the 18th and 19th Century India: Mughal Decline, Climate Shocks and British Industrial Ascent (2008) 45 *Explorations in Economic History* 209–34. For a different view see N. Ferguson, *Empire: How Britain Made the Modern World* (London: Allen Lane, 2003).

88 Atul Kohli's book provides an insightful discussion related to this point. See A. Kohli, *Poverty amid Plenty in the New India* (Princeton: Princeton University Press, 2012). See also S. Ahuja et al., *Economic Reform in India: Task Force Report* (Harris School of Public Policy University of Chicago, 2006).

89 See Ministry of Company Affairs, Government of India, Voluntary Guidelines on Corporate Social Responsibility; Kohli, *Poverty amid Plenty in the New India*; Van Zile, India's Mandatory Corporate Social Responsibility Proposal.

The government could surely tax corporations in order to provide those benefits,[90] but that would involve the government essentially getting more involved in managing economic matters (the opposite of what economic reforms were sold as doing) and that might send mixed (or contradictory) messages about whether the general reform effort (to reduce and reimagine the role of the state) was worth it and undermine support for existing and proposed reforms from citizens and business. On the other hand, if the government could persuade or cajole corporations to spend resources to benefit the citizenry then the optics would probably be better for future economic reforms.[91] After all, a citizenry that was told economic reforms reducing the role of the state will benefit them are unlikely to find further economic reforms palatable unless those benefits emerge. Indeed, if the emergence of those benefits depended in a visible manner on state involvement, then the case for further reducing the role of the state would not be easy. Moreover, businesses might also question the state's commitment to reform if a CSR tax was put forward.

It would then appear that, for further economic reforms reducing the role of the state to have stronger support, the last generation of reforms reducing the role of the state needed to provide tangible benefits that did not appear as if they depended on the state. Optically, it would be helpful if it appeared as if the benefits were coming from the activity of the corporations rather than the activity of the state, and a tax does not send that message. A nudge via voluntary guidelines or a comply-or-explain rule just might.

In addition, a CSR tax is more likely to raise the ire of India Inc. Although a CSR spending requirement was not cheered on by India Inc., one suspects that a CSR tax would be received much more negatively. Indeed, India Inc.'s reactions to the 2019 amendments (which moved CSR closer to a tax) reflected substantial opposition and led to the 2021 amendments that back-tracked.[92] Trying to enact a CSR tax in the earlier 2011–2013 window seems like it would have faced even more opposition.

One suspects that a mix of political optics and anticipated opposition to a CSR tax likely influenced the government in designing the CSR reform as a spending requirement rather than a tax. This, combined with potential state capacity and

[90] Note that the OECD suggests using the tax system for more inclusive growth, see OECD, Tax Policies for Inclusive Growth in a Changing World, Report to G-20 Finance Ministers and Central Bank Governors (2018).

[91] This tracks Van Zile, India's Mandatory Corporate Social Responsibility Proposal, but is also consistent with several informal conversations I have had with Government of India officials. Note that the Van Zile argument does not explain why the CSR provisions needed to be in the form of CSR spending requirements rather than a CSR tax.

[92] See Thomas, Corporate India Irked at New CSR Rules; Sikarwar, Government Won't Go Ahead with New CSR Rules. See also A. Prasad, India's New CSR Law Sparks Debate among NGOs and Businesses, *The Guardian*, August 11, 2014 (stating that noted Indian Industrialist Azim Premji of Wipro was concerned that the comply-or-explain rule might become a tax).

efficiency considerations, likely directed efforts toward the more heterodox CSR spending formulation.

An interesting tidbit related to the optics explanation is that, as the CSR provisions were being debated in the Companies Bill, other provisions in the Bill seemed to be making further attempts at liberalization that would be attractive to India Inc. The Bill was allowing firms to customize their corporate governance more than had been allowed in the 1956 Act as well as reducing constraints on the level of executive compensation.[93] It thus appeared that, as the Companies Bill was pushing further liberalization reforms, it was also pushing firms to engage in more CSR.[94] This is consistent with the optics account.

In light of this, it appears that the CSR reforms reflected a blend of political optics and state capacity and efficiency concerns against the background of a skeptical citizenry when it came to market-oriented policies which had a checkered history since the British Raj. Although the forces shaping the 2013 CSR reforms are fascinating, the regulatory and legislative activities in the CSR space did not end in 2013 – they had just begun.

9.5 POST-2013 CSR DEVELOPMENTS

Over time, various organizations and groups pushed for further reforms and greater involvement by Indian firms in CSR. This led to the 2019 and 2021 amendments, but also has involved other efforts to encourage firms to engage in CSR. In addition, concerns have been raised about the influence of politics on CSR and the potential for CSR to become an entry barrier of sorts to newer firms and small- and medium-sized enterprises (SMSEs).

Let us begin with the 2019 and 2021 amendments. One way to read the 2019 and 2021 amendments is that they are moving CSR regulation in India closer to a CSR

[93] See S. Sharma, Corporate Social Responsibility in India 46 *Indian Journal of Industrial Relations* 637–49; Sharma, Corporate Social Responsibility in India: The Emerging Discourse & Concerns, 586. Van Zile, India's Mandatory Corporate Social Responsibility Proposal, makes a somewhat parallel argument that the CSR provisions might have been there to reduce opposition to the pro-business tilt in the 2013 Act. However, this does not explain why the CSR provisions needed to be in the form of CSR spending requirements rather than a CSR tax. The optics account and perhaps some efficiency considerations seem to provide a likely set of explanations.

[94] Another nearly contemporaneous example of such "horse-trading" can be found in Mauritius where the Government imposed a CSR requirement at the same time as granting a corporate tax rate cut from 25 to 15 percent. See D. Kinderman, Time for a Reality Check: Is Business Willing to Support a Smart Mix of Complementary Regulation in Private Governance? (2016) 35 *Policy and Society* 29–42. Moreover, Sood and Arora, The Political Economy of Corporate Responsibility in India, have argued that generally India Inc. has not in recent years supported other social policies without receiving certain benefits (e.g., lower taxes for supporting government reservation policies).

tax structure.[95] The 2019 and 2021 amendments moved away from the "comply-or-explain" rule toward a mandatory spending rule. Further, they required that unspent CSR funds had to either be spent on CSR activities or be deposited in special funds earmarked for CSR activities (e.g., the Prime Minister's Relief Fund).[96] Thus, now the CSR rule is mandatory (like a tax rule) and the funds to be spent on CSR must be spent on that or go to accounts which seem heavily oriented to government control (in some senses like a tax).

One question raised by this is why the government moved closer to a tax structure in just six years since the 2013 reforms? There are a few likely explanations. First, the Government may not have needed to rely on political optics in 2019 as much as it did for the 2013 reforms. Economic growth in India – although hardly uniform – seemed less lop-sided than in 2009 and the government had a larger majority in Parliament to push through reforms compared to the less stable 2009 coalition.

There are also, however, reasons to think that state capacity to enforce a tax-like CSR rule had improved. In particular, the government had been increasingly relying on better technology in the tax area. This was particularly so with the advent of the Goods and Service Tax in 2017 which created a greater document trail, thereby enhancing tax administration and collection.[97] Further, the rise in e-commerce in India has precipitated greater document trails enabling better tax administration and collections.[98] Of course, there are likely to be other matters that influenced the enactment of these amendments, but it is interesting to note that at least some of the changes can be viewed through the lenses of changes in state capacity, efficiency, and political optics.

Beyond the amendments, there has been a general push by civil society organizations and social elites, CSR consultants, and others to prod firms to take a more impactful role in CSR. This is in part due to the general push toward environment, social, and governance (ESG) seen at the global level, but also because increasingly there is a sense that collaborations between the public sector and private sector in providing public goods and services could be value-enhancing for almost all parties involved.[99] Although still in its early stages in India, there is increasing interest.

[95] Some commentary in India already suspects this – see S. Rangan, Tax as CSR – Not CSR As Tax!!, *Law Street*, August 14, 2019.

[96] Although there were other changes (e.g., criminalizing and then decriminalizing noncompliance with CSR rules), these changes were the ones that have persisted.

[97] See A. Kir, India's Goods and Services Tax: A Unique Experiment in Cooperative Federalism and a Constitutional Crisis in Waiting (2021) 69 *Canadian Tax Journal* 391–445; Times of India, GST Revenue Jumps 12% in February to Rs 1.49 Lakh Crore; Cess Collection Highest, *Times of India*, March 1, 2023.

[98] See S. D. Majumder, GST and E-commerce (2016) 28 *National Law School of India Review* 123–33.

[99] See Gatignon and Bode, When Few Give to Many and Many Give to Few; Mahapatra, CSR Practices among Public and Private Sector Companies.

On the more troubling side are concerns about political interference in CSR spending and effects on smaller and newer firms. On the first point, there have been rising concerns that firms are, under the guise of CSR spending, providing financial support to certain politicians or political parties. Part of this is related to what counts as CSR spending, such as the various government schemes which tend to benefit those parties who initiated the schemes or who run them now. However, there are also concerns that, because individual states have the power to approve of new CSR programs that gives them an incentive to do so in order to secure votes or create vote banks.[100] Moreover, some managers of large public sector enterprises have expressed concerns over political interference in the choice of CSR projects.[101] If these sorts of concerns grow, then one can certainly see the likely problems from a corruption standpoint.

Another somewhat intriguing notion is that the increasing CSR requirements might operate as an entry barrier of sorts to newer or smaller firms. Although the spending requirement itself is keyed to profitability and net worth, the other requirements (forming a CSR committee, disclosure) are not. That suggests the CSR requirements might be costly for newer firms and reduce competition in India. For SMSEs the concerns are perhaps greater, but it is noteworthy that in the most recent amendments in 2021 the government did begin to ease some CSR requirements applied to smaller firms.[102]

9.6 CONCLUSION

India's landmark 2013 CSR reforms have generated a great deal of attention and discussion. There have been lively discussions about their effects, how they might be improved, whether they are consistent with the Indian ethos of business, and many more matters. However, little attention has been paid to the political economy behind the reforms. This chapter examines that question in some depth. The chapter starts by describing the reforms (and the ongoing reforms in this space) and examining some of their effects, and then transitions to exploring how the 2013 provisions came about. That analysis suggests that the genesis of the reforms was a concern that India's nearly twenty-year-long liberalization efforts had led to substantial economic improvements for only a small section of society. These lopsided effects might undermine support for further reforms or perhaps even lead to increasing support for bringing the state back into the economy. Concerns surrounding this problem appeared to motivate the government in putting forward its 2009 Voluntary Guidelines and other efforts that eventually led to Section 135 of the 2013 Companies Act.

[100] See M. Kansal et al., How Political Interference is Killing Corporate Social Responsibility in India, *Quartz*, March 14, 2019.
[101] See ibid.
[102] See note 18.

Yet, this only provides part of the answer. This is because if the goal of Section 135 was to have corporations give back more to society (in order to share the gains from liberalization), then perhaps a simpler way to do it would be for the government to impose a CSR tax rather than a more heterodox CSR spending requirement. The chapter then explores why the CSR reform took the specific shape that it did and suggests that it reflects a mix of efficiency or state capacity considerations as well as political optics tinged by skepticism over so-called market-oriented reforms. Early on it appears that the political optics may have carried the day because the government likely wanted it to *look like firms* were giving back to society rather than the state taxing them to do so. This was in part motivated by a concern that using a CSR tax would signal that liberalization efforts would not provide benefits without bringing the state back into the economy and may have led businesses to question the steadiness of the state in backing reforms. This was problematic because the government had additional reforms it was going to propose and without spreading the gains from liberalization these further reforms might lose support. A CSR spending requirement met both requirements while a CSR tax only met one. This account combines concerns of political optics with state capacity as likely explanations for the shape of the 2013 reforms, but it is increasingly looking like state capacity and efficiency issues may be influencing recent CSR developments in India. The space is still evolving rapidly so that firm conclusions on future developments may be premature, but what is clear is that interested participants and observers should stay tuned and pay close attention to the political economy concerns animating this sector of business and government interaction.

BIBLIOGRAPHY

Afsharipour, A., Directors as Trustees of the Nation? India's Corporate Governance and Corporate Social Responsibility Reform Efforts (2011) 34 *Seattle University Law Review* 995–1024.

Afsharipour, A. and Rana, S., The Emergence of New Corporate Social Responsibility Regimes in China and India (2014) 14 *UC Davis Business Law Journal* 175–230.

Aggarwal, D., The Politics of Mandatory Corporate Philanthropy (2023) Northwestern Law & Econ Research Paper No. 23-14.

Ahluwalia, M. S., Economic Reforms in India since 1991: Has Gradualism Worked? (2002) 16 *Journal of Economic Perspectives* 67–88.

Ahuja, S. et al., *Economic Reform in India: Task Force Report* (Chicago: Harris School of Public Policy University of Chicago, 2006).

Arcot, S., Bruno, V., and Faure-Grimaud, A., Corporate Governance in the UK: Is the Comply or Explain Approach Working? (2010) 30 *International Review of Law and Economics* 193–201.

Arora, B. and Puranik, R., A Review of Corporate Social Responsibility in India (2004) 47 *Development* 93–00.

Balasubramanian, B. N., Governing the Socially Responsible Corporation: A Gandhian Perspective, in A. Das Gupta (ed.), *Ethics, Business and Society: Managing Responsibly* (New Delhi: Sage Publications, 2009), pp. 157–80.

Balasubramaniam, N., Black, B. S., and Khanna, V. The Relation between Firm-Level Corporate Governance and Market Value: A Study of India (2010) 11 *Emerging Markets Review* 319–40.

Broadberry, S. and Gupta, B., Cotton Textiles and the Great Divergence: Lancashire, India and Shifting Competitive Advantage, 1600–1850 (2005) Centre for Economic Policy Research Discussion Paper No. 5183.

Broadberry, S., Custodis, J., and Gupta, B., India and the Great Divergence: An Anglo-Indian Comparison of GDP per capita, 1600–1871 (2015) 55 *Explorations in Economic History* 58–75.

Clingingsmith, D. and Williamson, J. G., Deindustrialization in the 18th and 19th Century India: Mughal Decline, Climate Shocks and British Industrial Ascent (2008) 45 *Explorations in Economic History* 209–34.

Dharmapala, D. and Khanna, V., Corporate Governance, Enforcement, and Firm Value: Evidence from India (2013) 29 *Journal of Law, Economics, and Organization* 1056–84.

The Impact of Mandating Corporate Social Responsibility: Evidence from India's Companies Act 2013 (2018) 56 *International Review of Law and Economics* 92–104.

ENS Economic Bureau, CSR Spend on Cards for India Inc., *Indian Express*, February 9, 2011.

Ferguson, N., *Empire: How Britain Made the Modern World* (London: Allen Lane, 2003).

Gatignon, A. and Bode, C., When Few Give to Many and Many Give to Few: Corporate Social Responsibility Strategies under India's Legal Mandate (2023) 44 *Strategic Management Journal* 2099–127.

Gautam, R. and Singh, A., Corporate Social Responsibility Practices in India: A Study of Top 500 Companies (2010) 2 *Global Business and Management Research: An International Journal* 41–56.

Goulding, A. J., Retreating from the Commanding Heights: Privatization in an Indian Context (1997) 50 *Journal of International Affairs* 581–612.

Guarini, E. and Nidasio, C., *CSR Role in Public–Private Partnerships: Models of Governance* (2002). Available at SSRN: https://ssrn.com/abstract=2379382 or http://dx.doi.org/10.2139/ssrn.2379382.

Herdeck, M. and Piramal, G., *India's Industrialists. Vol. 1* (Washington, DC: Three Continents Press, 1985).

Jai, S. et al., Choosing beyond Compliance over Dormancy: Corporate Response to India's Mandatory CSR Expenditure Law (2023) 19 *Management and Organization Review* 594–623.

Jain, T., Aguilera, R. V., and Jamali, D., Stakeholder Orientation in an Emerging Country Context: A Longitudinal Cross Industry Analysis (2017) 143 *Journal of Business Ethics* 701–19.

Johnson, J., Inequality Fears Sting Indian Business, *Financial Times*, May 28, 2007.

Kansal, M. et al., How Political Interference Is Killing Corporate Social Responsibility in India, *Quartz*, March 14, 2019.

Karnani, A., Mandatory CSR in India: A Bad Proposal, *Stanford Social Innovation Review*, May 20, 2013.

Khanna, V., Business Organizations in India Prior to the British East India Company, in H. Wells (ed.), *Research Handbook on the History of Corporate and Company Law* (Cheltenham: Edward Elgar, 2018), pp. 33–64.

Khanna, V., Corporate Governance in India: Past, Present & Future? (2009) 1 *Jindal Global Law Review* 171–95.

Khanna, V. and Black, B. S., Can Corporate Governance Reforms Increase Firms' Market Values?: Event Study Evidence from India (2007) 4 *Journal of Empirical Legal Studies* 749–96.

Kinderman, D., Time for a Reality Check: Is Business Willing to Support a Smart Mix of Complementary Regulation in Private Governance? (2016) 35 *Policy and Society* 29–42.

Kir, A., India's Goods and Services Tax: A Unique Experiment in Cooperative Federalism and a Constitutional Crisis in Waiting (2021) 69 *Canadian Tax Journal* 391–445.

Kohli, A., *Poverty amid Plenty in the New India* (Princeton: Princeton University Press, 2012).

Koya, N. and Roper, J., Legislated CSR in Practice: The Experience of India (2022) 22 *Journal of Public Affairs* 1–10.

Krueger, A. O. (ed.) *Economic Policy Reforms and the Indian Economy* (Chicago: The University of Chicago Press, 2002).

Li, J. and Wu, D., Do Corporate Social Responsibility Engagements Lead to Real Environmental, Social and Governance Impact? (2020) 66 *Management Science* 2291–799.

Mahapatra, M., CSR Practices among Public and Private Sector Companies: A Community Development Approach in Indian Context (2019) 10 *Journal of Management and Public Policy* 33–42.

Majumder, S. D., GST and E-commerce (2016) 28 *National Law School of India Review* 123–33.

Manchiraju, H. and Rajgopal, S., Does Corporate Social Responsibility (CSR) Create Shareholder Value? Evidence from the Indian Companies Act 2013 (2017) 55 *Journal of Accounting Research* 1257–300.

Ministry of Corporate Affairs, *Compendium on Corporate Social Responsibility in India* (New Delhi: Ministry of Corporate Affairs, 2022).

Money Control, Mandatory CSR Not a Great Idea, Feels India Inc., *CNBC-TV18 News*, August 6, 2010.

Mukherjee, K., Manmohan Says Development Threatening Security, *Reuters*, December 20, 2007.

Panwar, R. et al., Did India's CSR Mandate Enhance or Diminish Firm Value? (2023) 62 *Business & Society* 401–33.

Pingola, S., (2012) Towards Strategic Corporate Social Responsibility in Cpsus': Positive Transformation Through DPE Guidelines.

Prasad, A., India's New CSR Law Sparks Debate among NGOs and Businesses, *The Guardian*, August 11, 2014.

Rangan, S., Tax as CSR: Not CSR As Tax!!', *Law Street*, August 14, 2019.

Ray, I., *Bengal Industries and the British Industrial Revolution (1757–1857)* (New York: Routledge, 2011).

Roe, M. J., Backlash (1988) 98 *Columbia Law Review* 217–41.

Rungta, R. S., *The Rise of Business Corporations in India: 1851–1900* (New Delhi: Cambridge University Press, 1970).

Sharma, S., Corporate Social Responsibility in India (2011) 46 *Indian Journal of Industrial Relations* 637–49.

Corporate Social Responsibility in India: The Emerging Discourse & Concerns (2013) 48 *Indian Journal of Industrial Relations* 582–96.

Sikarwar, D., Government Won't Go Ahead with New CSR Rules, *The Economic Times*, August 14, 2019.

Sood, A. and Arora, B., The Political Economy of Corporate Responsibility in India (2006) Technology Business and Society Program Paper No. 18, United National Research Institute for Social Development.

Standing Committee on Finance, Twenty-First Report (The Companies Bill, 2009), *Lok Sabha*, Clause 49 (2010).

Sundar, P., *Beyond Business: From Merchant Charity to Corporate Citizenship. Indian Business Philanthropy through the Ages* (New Delhi: Tata McGraw-Hill Publishing Company, 2000).

Using CSR Funds for Political Gain, *The Wire*, December 22, 2018.

Sundaram, V., Vinod Khosla to Donate Half His Fortune to Charity, *New America Media*, May 18, 2011.

Tharoor, S., *India from Midnight to Millenium* (New York: Arcade Publishing, 1997).

Inglorious Empire: What the British Did to India (London: Hurst, 2017).

Nehru: The Invention of India (New York: Arcade Publishing, 2011).

Thomas, K. S., Corporate India Irked at New CSR Rules, *The Week*, August 3, 2019.

Times of India, GST Revenue Jumps 12% in February to Rs 1.49 Lakh Crore; Cess Collection Highest, *Times of India*, March 1, 2023.

Times of India, IT CEOs back Premji against Mandatory CSR, *Times of India*, March 26, 2011.

Times of India, It's Their Business, *Times of India*, December 24, 2010.

Van Zile, C., India's Mandatory Corporate Social Responsibility Proposal: Creative Capitalism Meets Creative Regulation in the Global Market (2012) 13 *Asian-Pacific Law & Policy Journal* 269–303.

Varottil, U., Analysing the CSR Spending Requirements under Indian Company Law, in J. J. du Plessis, U. Varottil, and J. Veldman (eds.), *Globalisation of Corporate Social Responsibility and Its Impact on Corporate Governance* (Switzerland: Springer International Publishing, 2018), pp. 231–53.

Varottil, U., Viability of Mandatory CSR, *IndiaCorpLawBlog*, August 7, 2010.

Vijayaraghavan, A., Indian Industries Oppose Mandatory CSR Reporting, *Just Means*, August 16, 2010.

10

Corporate Law in the Global South

Heterodox Stakeholderism

Mariana Pargendler

10.1 INTRODUCTION

How do the corporate laws of developing countries differ from those of their developed counterparts? A common view is that the corporate laws of Global South jurisdictions – like their private laws more generally – are either (i) outdated, (ii) failed transplants of modern foreign laws, or (iii) plagued by severe challenges of enforcement.[1] An even more extreme view, building on the former, is that corporate laws in developing countries are so ineffective that they are not worth studying, given that extralegal factors dominate.[2] While these views reflect more than a kernel of

This chapter is a modified version of the article of the same name, originally as M. Pargendler, Corporate Law in the Global South: Heterodox Stakeholderism (2024) 47 *Seattle Law Review* 535–79.

[1] See, e.g., F. R. Villamizar, The Organization of American States' Model Law on Simplified Corporations (2018) 11 *Journal of Civil Law Studies* 1–74, 1, 7, and 31; D. Berkowitz, K. Pistor, and J. F. Richard, The Transplant Effect (2003) 51 *American Journal of Comparative Law* 163–204, 168. A focus on problems of enforcement, as opposed to substantive legal differences, also exists in comparative contract law. For earlier work suggesting alternative institutional arrangements to respond to difficulties in enforcement, as well as a greater focus on distributional concerns and stakeholder issues in environments of high inequality, see M. Pargendler, Corporate Governance in Emerging Markets, in J. N. Gordon and W. G. Ringe (eds.), *Oxford Handbook on Corporate Law and Governance* (Oxford: Oxford University Press, 2018), pp. 735–55.

[2] See, e.g., R. Kraakman et al., *The Anatomy of Corporate Law: A Comparative and Functional Approach*, 2nd ed. (Oxford: Oxford University Press, 2009), p. 3 ("We focus on developed, rather than developing, economies, because where foundational legal institutions, such as functioning courts and the protection of property rights, are absent or compromised, then the way in which corporate law responds to specific problems is less likely to make a difference to the real economy"). Interestingly, the third edition of the same book simply deleted the excerpt above and included Brazil as one of the core jurisdictions examined. R. Kraakman et al., *The Anatomy of Corporate Law: A Comparative and Functional Approach*, 3rd ed. (Oxford: Oxford University Press, 2017). For the methodological recommendation from the authors of the leading treatise in comparative law to focus on a handful of advanced "parent" jurisdictions and "ignore the affiliate [legal system]," including the presumably derivative legal systems of

truth in numerous contexts, they offer an incomplete and impoverished perspective of corporate laws in the developing world. Rather than being inevitably antiquated or blind copies of Global North models, emerging economies have pioneered distinct stakeholder approaches to corporate laws. I call these approaches "heterodox stakeholderism" as they are different and often bolder than the longstanding strategies of corporate law to protect non-shareholder constituencies in the Global North.[3]

Preceding the "rise of ESG"[4] and the renaissance of a stakeholder focus on corporate law in the Global North, core developing jurisdictions such as Brazil, India, and South Africa had embraced novel, and often more aggressive, legal strategies to protect stakeholder interests.[5] In the last decades, Brazil has largely eliminated shareholders' limited liability for the benefit of stakeholders, such as workers, consumers, and victims of environmental harm. Before interest in ESG exploded in the Global North, Indonesia and India mandated corporate social

the Global South, see K. Zweigert and H. Kötz, *Introduction to Comparative Law*, 3rd ed. (Oxford: Clarendon Press, 1998), p. 4. For critiques of such devaluing of legal systems in the Global South, see J. Esquirol, The Failed Law of Latin America (2008) 56 *The American Journal of Comparative Law* 75–124, 77; D. Bonilla Maldonado, *Legal Barbarians: Identity, Modern Comparative Law and the Global South* (Cambridge: Cambridge University Press, 2021), p. 10.

3 For an overview of corporate law strategies to protect stakeholders in developed economies, see L. Enriques et al., The Basic Governance Structure: Minority Shareholders and Non-Shareholder Constituencies, in R. Kraakman et al., *The Anatomy of Corporate Law: A Comparative and Functional Approach*, 3rd ed. (Oxford: Oxford University Press, 2017), pp. 89–108. Nothing here is to suggest that corporate laws in the Global North have not been shaped by stakeholder interests until recently. M. Pargendler, The Grip of Nationalism on Corporate Law (2020) 95 *Indiana Law Journal* 533–90 (documenting the longstanding impact of nationalism and protectionism on the corporate laws of Global North jurisdictions throughout history).

4 ESG is the acronym for environmental, social, and governance issues in corporate governance and investment.

5 Scholars have highlighted the ebb and flow of shareholder–stakeholder approaches in different jurisdictions, as well as the peculiar – and particularly strong – stakeholder orientation of China's corporate law regime, which falls squarely within the concept of heterodox stakeholderism in the Global South as described here. See R. J. Gilson and C. J. Milhaupt, Shifting Influence on Corporate Governance: Capital Market Completeness and Policy Channeling (2022) 12 *Harvard Business Law Review* 1–54, 49 (describing the Chinese system under the influence of the Communist Party as "possibly the world's most stakeholder-oriented system of corporate governance"); D. W. Puchniak, No Need for Asia to be Woke: Contextualizing Anglo-American "Discovery" of Corporate Purpose (2022) 4 *Revue Européenne du Droit* 14–21, 16 ("at least on paper, Chinese corporate law and governance is as purposeful as can be"); V. Harper Ho, Beyond Regulation: A Comparative Look at State-Centric Corporate Social Responsibility and the Law in China (2013) 46 *Vanderbilt Journal of Transnational Law* 375–442, 382 (describing state-centric CSR in China as "an adaptation of the institutions and accountability structures that shape law's legitimacy, enforcement, and even substance"). Given the growing literature on China as a global superpower, as well as existing claims about "Chinese exceptionalism," this chapter focuses on the laws of democratic jurisdictions in the Global South that have received comparatively less attention.

responsibility, and India and South Africa required dedicated committees in charge of social responsibility. While legal reforms seeking to advance diversity in corporate governance date back to the last two decades in the Global North, Malaysia has boldly pursued affirmative action in corporate ownership for the benefit of the Malays since the 1970s, while South Africa has pushed for greater Black ownership and empowerment in corporate governance through its laws on Broad-Based Black Economic Empowerment (B-BBEE) since 2003. South Africa has also innovated by expanding workers' ability to enforce directors' duties under the Companies Act of 2008 and has been hailed as a "global leader in sustainable corporate governance."[6]

Taken together, these developments offer a different picture of corporate governance developments around the world. Although Global South constitutional law and courts have achieved significant recognition and notoriety in the literature on comparative constitutional law for their distinct approaches to enforcing social rights,[7] developing countries' heterodoxies in corporate law – be they regarded as promising innovations or pernicious developments – have been largely neglected. The comparative literature on corporate law remains dominated by North–North comparison,[8] individual country studies of developing economies,[9] regional studies,[10] and works focusing on the common–civil law

6 C. M. Bruner, *The Corporation as Technology: Re-Calibrating Corporate Governance for a Sustainable Future* (Oxford: Oxford University Press, 2022), p. 227.

7 See, e.g., O. V. Vieira, U. Baxi, and F. Viljoen (eds.), *Transformative Constitutionalism: Comparing the Apex Courts of Brazil, India and South Africa* (Pretoria: Pretoria University Law Press, 2013) (examining how the highest courts in Brazil, Colombia, and South Africa give effect to social rights recognized in their constitutions); D. Bonilla Maldonado (ed.), *Constitutionalism of the Global South: The Activist Tribunals of India, South Africa, and Colombia* (Cambridge: Cambridge University Press, 2013); P. Dann, M. Riegner, and M. Bönnemann, The Southern Turn in Comparative Constitutional Law: An Introduction, in P. Dann, M. Riegner, and M. Bönnemann (eds.), *The Global South and Comparative Constitutional Law* (Oxford: Oxford University Press, 2020), pp. 1–38. To be sure, the dichotomy between the transformative character of Global North and Global South constitutions can easily be exaggerated. See M. Hailbronner, Transformative Constitutionalism: Not Only in the Global South (2017) 65 *The American Journal of Comparative Law* 527–65.

8 See, e.g., Kraakman et al., *The Anatomy of Corporate Law*, 3rd ed.; A. Cahn and D. C. Donald, *Comparative Company Law: Text and Cases on the Laws Governing Corporations in Germany, the UK and the USA* (Cambridge: Cambridge University Press, 2018); M. Ventoruzzo et al., *Comparative Corporate Law* (St. Paul: West Academic Publishing, 2015).

9 See, e.g., L. W. Lin and C. J. Milhaupt, We Are the (National) Champions: Understanding the Mechanisms of State Capitalism in China (2013) 65 *Stanford Law Review* 697–760; P. Mahy, The Evolution of Company Law in Indonesia: An Exploration of Legal Innovation and Stagnation (2013) 61 *The American Journal of Comparative Law* 377–432; U. Varottil, The Evolution of Corporate Law in Post-Colonial India: From Transplant to Autochthony (2016) 31 *American University International Law Review* 253–326.

10 See, e.g., D. W. Puchniak, H. Baum, and L. Nottage (eds.), *Independent Directors in Asia: A Historical, Contextual and Comparative Approach* (Cambridge: Cambridge University Press, 2017); D. W. Puchniak, H. Baum, and M. Ewin-Chow (eds.), *The Derivative Action in Asia: A Comparative and Functional Approach* (Cambridge: Cambridge University Press, 2012).

divide.[11] The growing literature on China often embraces Chinese exceptionalism and fails to place China within a continuum of heterodox stakeholderism in developing countries.[12] Studies that incorporate a broader set of developed and developing economies often do not engage in North–South comparisons.[13]

Including a broader array of Global South jurisdictions in comparative corporate governance produces distinct intellectual and policy payoffs. First, it helps overcome existing shortcomings in our understanding of global developments. One is the "World Series" syndrome in the comparative literature, understood as the pretense that insights from a select group of "usual suspects" from the developed world are representative of global developments.[14] Another problem is the "odd duck" syndrome: because Global South jurisdictions are often examined in single-country studies, this can easily produce misleading diagnoses of exceptionalism. For instance, commentators have described India's approach to enterprise liability as "unique" and "revolutionary" from a comparative perspective, without recognizing that Brazil and other emerging economies are part of a similar trend.[15]

Second, appreciating common approaches to corporate law in developing countries generates insights into how background economic and social conditions may influence corporate law strategies. Heterodox stakeholderism in corporate law can be viewed as an institutional *adaptation* to environments of high inequality and insufficient state capacity to curb externalities and promote social welfare through other areas of law. This is the flip side of the implicit "modularity approach" that has

[11] See, e.g., S. Djankov et al., The Law and Economics of Self-Dealing (2008) 88 *Journal of Financial Economics* 430–65; K. Pistor, Legal Ground Rules in Coordinated and Liberal Market Economies, in K. J. Hopt et al., *Corporate Governance in Context: Corporations, States, and Markets in Europe, Japan, and the US* (Oxford: Oxford University Press, 2005), pp. 248–80; H. Spamann, Contemporary Legal Transplants: Legal Families and the Diffusion of (Corporate) Law (2009) 2009 *BYU Law Review* 1813–78.

[12] See note 5 and accompanying text.

[13] For a notable, if discrete, exception, see L. W. Lin, Mandatory Corporate Social Responsibility Legislation around the World: Emergent Varieties and National Experience (2021) 23 *University of Pennsylvania Journal of Business Law* 429–69 (comparing legislation in France, Mauritius, India, South Africa, China, and Indonesia, among others, and finding the diffusion of mandatory philanthropy legislation only in developing countries as well as unique approaches in developing countries, such as mandatory corporate philanthropy laws). See also Djankov et al., The Law and Economics of Self-Dealing, 443 (finding that the correlation of their anti-self-dealing interest and log of GDP is statistically insignificant).

[14] For the use of this metaphor to describe a similar phenomenon in comparative constitutional law, see R. Hirschl, *Comparative Matters. The Renaissance of Comparative Constitutional Law* (Oxford: Oxford University Press, 2014), p. 192 (explaining "the 'World Series' syndrome in comparative constitutional law" as "the pretense that insights based on the constitutional experience of a small set of 'usual suspect' settings – all prosperous, stable constitutional democracies of the 'global north' – are truly representative of the wide variety of constitutional experiences worldwide, and constitute a 'gold standard' for understanding and assessing it").

[15] M. Dearborn, Enterprise Liability: Reviewing and Revitalizing Liability for Corporate Groups (2009) 97 *California Law Review* 195–261, 226–27.

traditionally dominated law-and-economics analysis.[16] Under a modular approach premised on compartmentalization and functional specialization, each area of law should contribute to social welfare by focusing on *one* economic problem: for corporate law, the standard single objective is the reduction of agency costs associated with the corporate form.[17] However, if other areas of law (such as tax, environmental, and antitrust laws) fail in accomplishing their objectives, the case for such a modular approach – which may not be optimal to begin with[18] – falters accordingly.

This heterodox or "social turn" in the Global South is not unique to corporate law.[19] Previous work has shown how certain developing jurisdictions, such as Brazil, South Africa, and Colombia, have incorporated concerns about inequality in contract law more strongly and explicitly than their counterparts in the Global North.[20] Similarly, a common claim in comparative constitutional law is that, because of larger socioeconomic gaps and lower state capacity in the Global South, "constitutional courts in these countries will be more inclined to intervene on behalf of the poor, or to support the constitutional recognition and progressive realization of social and economic rights"[21] – an argument that mirrors our account of heterodox stakeholderism in corporate law.

Problems of state capacity to curb externalities and address inequality help explain both the rise of heterodox stakeholderism in corporate laws in the Global South and the resurgence of stakeholder approaches in the Global North and on a global scale in recent years. The ESG agenda emerged from an effort of the United Nations to recruit corporations and investors at the turn of the twenty-first century to fight the

[16] For a description of the approach, see M. Pargendler, Controlling Shareholders in the 21st Century: Complicating Corporate Governance beyond Agency Costs (2020) 45 *Journal of Corporation Law* 953–75, 969–72.

[17] Ibid., 969.

[18] This is not to endorse a modular approach to law and regulation, which is why I refrain from adopting the framing of "second-best" laws or institutions in the Global South. For such a framing, see D. Rodrik, Second-Best Institutions (2008) 98 *American Economic Review* 100–4, 100 (arguing that "dealing with the institutional landscape in developing countries requires a second-best mindset"). For a discussion of the limits of modular thinking in law, see Pargendler, Controlling Shareholders in the 21st Century, 971.

[19] These developments can be understood as the Global South's resistance to elements that Katharina Pistor has termed "The Code of Capital." K. Pistor, *The Code of Capital: How the Law Creates Wealth and Inequality* (Princeton: Princeton University Press, 2021).

[20] See generally K. E. Davis and M. Pargendler, Contract Law and Inequality (2022) 107 *Iowa Law Review* 1485–542 (2022).

[21] Hirschl, *Comparative Matters*, p. 221. Hirschl himself argues that the evidence for greater social activism by courts in the Global South is mixed, mentioning instances of activism in India and Colombia, but its absence in Mexico. My claim here is that the Global South offers important and overlooked examples of heterodox stakeholderism, not the stronger – and questionable – claim that heterodox stakeholderism is present in all Global South jurisdictions. The recognition of legal heterodoxy in the Global South does not entail a claim about the pervasiveness of legal heterodoxy in all Global South jurisdictions nor in single jurisdictions. For the same argument in the context of contract law heterodoxy, see Davis and Pargendler, Contract Law and Inequality, 1487.

regulatory gaps left by globalization, which threatened the legitimacy of global capitalism by permitting human rights abuses and environmental degradation.[22] The financial crisis of 2008, for its part, cracked the US hyper-modular law-and-economics consensus that a legal regime fostering shareholder wealth maximization is always socially optimal. In the aftermath of the crisis, a new academic consensus emerged that systemic risk externalities and the difficulties in regulating financial institutions require a distinct corporate governance model designed to mitigate risk from within.[23]

While the initial anti-modular diagnosis was limited to financial institutions,[24] it did not take long for this mode of reasoning to expand in calling for the internalization of other forms of risks and externalities, such as climate change risk and social harms.[25] Interestingly, the current crisis of the modularity approach is by no means unique to corporate law in the Global North, but is also observed in other areas of law.[26] Recent challenges to the modularity approach in other areas of law include the growing incorporation of concerns about democracy, workers' welfare, and climate change in antitrust, and climate change in financial regulation.[27] From this perspective, the increasingly welfarist, nonmodular trend in the Global North can be interpreted as a surprising and unpredicted form of "reverse convergence" in corporate law as in other areas of law, with economic and social crises – and the urgency of necessary solutions – bringing the Global North closer to the Global South in various respects.

Beyond the failure of other areas of law in addressing externalities and inequality, heterodox stakeholderism in the Global South also responds to interjurisdictional externalities and distributive implications along North–South lines. By focusing on aggregate efficiency or social welfare, comparative corporate governance has

[22] See M. Pargendler, The Rise of International Corporate Law (2021) 98 *Washington University Law Review* 1765–820, 1794 et seq.

[23] See, e.g., L. A. Bebchuk and H. Spamann, Regulating Bankers' Pay (2010) 98 *Georgetown Law Journal* 247–88, 247 (identifying how executive compensation in banks created incentives for excessive risk-taking); J. Armour and J. N. Gordon, Systemic Harms and Shareholder Value (2014) 6 *Journal of Legal Analysis* 35–85, 39–40 (proposing the imposition of stricter liability rules for directors and officers of financial institutions); J. Macey and M. O'Hara, Bank Corporate Governance: A Proposal for the Post-Crisis World (2016) 22 *Economic Policy Review* 85–105, 86 (advocating for stricter standards of conduct of bank directors and bank risk committees).

[24] J. Armour et al., What Is Corporate Law, in R. Kraakman et al., *The Anatomy of Corporate Law: A Comparative and Functional Approach*, 3rd ed. (Oxford: Oxford University Press, 2017), pp. 1–28, p. 25.

[25] See, e.g., J. N. Gordon, Systematic Stewardship (2022) 47 *Journal of Corporation Law* 627–74, 631; O. Hart and L. Zingales, Companies Should Maximize Shareholder Welfare Not Market Value (2017) European Corporate Governance Institute Working Paper No. 521, 4 .

[26] Pargendler, Controlling Shareholders in the 21st Century, 969.

[27] For a discussion of the current push for the incorporation of stakeholder concerns in corporate, antitrust, and bankruptcy law in the United States, see A. Kovvali, Stakeholderism Silo Busting (2023) 90 *University of Chicago Law Review* 203–60, 235–45.

neglected the importance of geopolitical boundaries and how they affect interjurisdictional externalities and distribution.[28] At least some facets of heterodox stakeholderism respond precisely to such a national calculus. Commentators observed that the infamous Bhopal industrial disaster – a major leakage of toxic gas caused by a subsidiary of a multinational company – played a key role in pushing Indian courts to hold parent companies liable for ultrahazardous activities.[29] Foreign wrongdoers and local victims are a tough sell to local polities. Similarly, Argentina's embrace of enterprise liability in the bankruptcy context in the 1970s favored local creditors at the expense of foreign parent company debtors.[30]

This phenomenon highlights the importance of nationalism and North–South distribution in explaining variations in comparative corporate law. This is a familiar concept in other areas of law. For instance, it is well established in the field of international intellectual property law that strong patent protection tends to transfer wealth from developing to developed countries,[31] which means that the optimal level patent protection for Global South jurisdictions is lower than for Global North ones. The existence of heterodox stakeholderism suggests that a similar distributional dynamic is in play with respect to at least certain features of corporate law rules, such as limited liability for environmental and human rights disasters caused by corporate groups, thus making developing countries more likely to embrace heterodox forms of resistance.

This chapter's description and analysis of heterodox stakeholderism in the Global South focuses on legal innovations in corporate law. Heterodoxy is defined as (i) distinct from the norm in the Global North in (ii) incorporating a broader set of public policy and distributional objectives in corporate law rules. I focus on six distinct manifestations of heterodox stakeholderism in corporate law and address each in a separate section: the erosion of limited liability for the benefit of stakeholders in Argentina, Colombia, India, and especially Brazil (Section 10.2); the adoption of mandatory corporate social responsibility (CSR) spending in India, Indonesia, and Mauritius (Section 10.3); the imposition of mandatory corporate social responsibility committees in India and South Africa (Section 10.4); workers' right to enforce directors' duties and to intervene in bankruptcy proceedings in South Africa (Section 10.5); and the pioneering efforts to deracialize economic

[28] On these issues, see generally Pargendler, The Grip of Nationalism on Corporate Law (on the significance of political boundaries and disparate distribution effects across jurisdictions); Pargendler, The Rise of International Corporate Law (on interjurisdictional externalities of corporate law).

[29] See Section 10.2.

[30] Ibid.

[31] See, e.g., D. Rodrik, What Do Trade Agreements Really Do? (2018) 32 *Journal of Economic Perspectives* 73–90, 76–77 (arguing that, because of the TRIPS agreement, "[c]onsumers in the developing nations pay higher prices for pharmaceuticals and other research-intensive products and the advanced countries' firms reap higher monopoly rents," so that "the advanced countries' gains are largely the developing countries' losses").

power by increasing ethnic diversity in corporate governance in Malaysia and South Africa (Section 10.6). The chapter then concludes by reflecting on how including Global South jurisdictions in comparative corporate governance expands our institutional imagination and enriches our understanding of the driving forces behind the evolution of corporate law around the world.

10.2 THE EROSION OF LIMITED LIABILITY TO PROTECT STAKEHOLDERS IN BRAZIL AND BEYOND

The mitigation of limited liability offers another manifestation of heterodox stakeholderism in the Global South.[32] Limited liability is the most distinctive and celebrated attribute of the corporate form,[33] having been famously hailed as "the greatest single discovery of modern times."[34] At the same time, shareholders' limited liability gets in the way of the prevailing modularity approach to law and economics, according to which concerns about stakeholder protection should be addressed not by corporate law, but by other areas of law.[35] Limited liability clearly undermines the protection of stakeholders through tort law and regulations, making the corporation "the perfect externalizing machine."[36]

Mindful of these problems, law-and-economics scholars have long questioned the efficiency of shareholder limited liability vis-à-vis involuntary creditors, such as tort victims.[37] Even the fiercest opponents of veil piercing find that the case for limited liability is weaker in the context of tort liability in corporate groups.[38] Nevertheless,

[32] This section draws heavily from M. Pargendler, How Universal Is the Corporate Form? Reflections on the Dwindling of Corporate Attributes in Brazil (2019) 58 *Columbia Journal of Transnational Law* 1–57.

[33] F. H. Easterbrook and D. R. Fischel, *The Economic Structure of Corporate Law* (Cambridge, MA: Harvard University Press, 1991), p. 40, "Limited liability is a distinguishing feature of corporate law – perhaps *the* distinguishing feature"; D. Leebron, Limited Liability, Tort Victims, and Creditors (1991) 91 *Columbia Law Review* 1565–650, 1566 ("No principle seems more established in capitalist law or more essential to the functioning of the modern corporate economy [than the principle of limited liability]") (footnote omitted).

[34] N. M. Butler, *Politics and Economics* (New York: Press of the Chamber of Commerce, 1911), p. 47.

[35] On the modularity approach, see Pargendler, Controlling Shareholders in the 21st Century.

[36] C. Gerner-Beuerle and M. A. Schillig, *Comparative Company Law* (Oxford: Oxford University Press, 2019), p. 814.

[37] See, e.g., R. A. Posner, The Rights of Creditors of Affiliated Corporations (1976) 43 *University of Chicago Law Review* 499–526, 519–20 (arguing that the creation of separate legal entities to evade tort liability permits the externalization of costs and is socially inefficient); H. Hansmann and R. Kraakman, Toward Unlimited Shareholder Liability for Corporate Torts (1991) 100 *Yale Law Journal* 1879–934, 1879–81.

[38] S. M. Bainbridge and M. T. Henderson, *Limited Liability: A Legal and Economic Analysis* (Northampton: Edward Elgar, 2016), p. 293 ("from a policy perspective, the considerations justifying limited liability insofar as individual shareholders are concerned seem far less powerful when applied to corporate shareholders"). See also H. Hansmann and R. Squire, External and Internal Asset Partitioning: Corporations and Their Subsidiaries, in J. N. Gordon

with some important exceptions,[39] progress toward overcoming limited liability for the benefit of involuntary creditors (such as tort victims) and non-adjusting creditors (such as workers and consumers)[40] has been glacial, if not completely stalled, in the Global North.[41] Contrary to law-and-economics prescriptions, US courts are *less* likely to pierce the corporate veil in tort cases compared to contract cases and in the parent–subsidiary setting compared to other contexts.[42] Katharina Pistor has recently decried how limited liability has let shareholders off the hook for harm caused to stakeholders in case after case.[43]

Unbeknownst to most observers, the strongest challenges to limited liability as an obstacle to stakeholder protection have come from the Global South, particularly from Brazil. Brazil's attack on limited liability vis-à-vis involuntary and non-adjusting creditors provides a particularly vivid example of innovative, if potentially problematic, approaches to stakeholder protection in the developing world. Brazil has effectively eliminated limited liability for compensation of harm to consumers, workers, and victims of environmental harm, as well as for directors, officers and controlling shareholders of failed financial institutions.[44] Interestingly, stakeholder-

and W. G. Ringe (eds.), *Oxford Handbook on Corporate Law and Governance* (Oxford: Oxford University Press, 2018), pp. 251–74, p. 252, for the broader argument that the costs of asset partitioning are greater, and the benefits are smaller, within the corporate group compared to outside of it.

39 See, e.g., C. Van Dam, Breakthrough in Parent Company Liability: Three Shell Defeats, an End of an Era and New Paradigms (2021) 18 *European Company and Financial Law Review* 714–18, 747 (describing how 2021 decisions in the United Kingdom and the Netherlands "have changed the course of parent company liability," confirming that parents may owe a duty of care with respect to the operational activities of subsidiaries). Interestingly, these recent bolder approaches by UK and Dutch courts can be interpreted as a form of reverse convergence to initiatives in the Global South, even if they remain narrower in imposing fault-based, rather than strict, liability on parent companies.

40 Scholars have also argued that non-adjusting creditors – that is, voluntary creditors that are unable to adjust their contract terms to account for the risk of default, such as workers and consumers – are analogous to tort victims with respect to their vulnerability to the externalization of risk. L. A. Bebchuk and J. M. Fried, The Uneasy Case for the Priority of Secured Claims in Bankruptcy (1996) 105 *Yale Law Journal* 857–934. See also J. Armour et al., Transactions with Creditors, in R. Kraakman et al., *The Anatomy of Corporate Law: A Comparative and Functional Approach*, 3rd ed. (Oxford: Oxford University Press, 2017), pp. 115–16 (discussing the distinction between adjusting and nonadjusting creditors in the context of limited liability).

41 See, e.g., P. Akey and I. Appel, The Limits of Limited Liability: Evidence from Industrial Pollution (2021) 76 *The Journal of Finance* 5–55, 9–10 (finding that, after the US Supreme Court's restrictive interpretation of parent company liability under the Comprehensive Environmental Response, Compensation, and Liability Act (CERCLA) in its 1998 decision in *United States v. Bestfoods*, there is an increase in toxic emissions by subsidiaries).

42 See, e.g., R. B. Thompson, Piercing the Corporate Veil: An Empirical Study (1991) 76 *Cornell Law Review* 1036–74, 1038; J. H. Matheson, Why Courts Pierce: An Empirical Study of Piercing the Corporate Veil (2010) 7 *Berkeley Business Law Journal* 1–71, 20.

43 K. Pistor, Limited Liability is Causing Unlimited Harm, *Project Syndicate*, February 5, 2020.

44 Pargendler, How Universal Is the Corporate Form?, 21–22.

friendly veil piercing in Brazil is a fairly recent phenomenon dating to the last few decades, not a remnant of antiquated laws, indigenous tradition, or colonial history.

Just like in other jurisdictions, limited liability is a very traditional element of the corporate form in Brazil, recognized since its first corporations in the early nineteenth century and explicitly contemplated in all corporate statutes since the Commercial Code of 1850. If anything, Brazil historically offered stronger limited liability than other jurisdictions. US banks imposed "double liability" on shareholders between the Civil War and the Great Depression.[45] Brazilian banks, by contrast, enjoyed full limited liability during the same period.[46]

The first significant encroachment to limited liability dates to Brazil's Labor Law of 1943 (*Consolidação das Leis do Trabalho* – CLT), which imposed joint and several liability on all entities belonging to an "economic group" for debts to workers. Although exceptions to shareholder liability for the benefit of workers also exist in other jurisdictions,[47] the Brazilian regime in the Labor Law was, and still is, far-reaching from a comparative perspective in imposing strict joint and several liability on companies belonging to the same economic group. In 1987, a statute on financial institutions broke new ground by making individual controlling shareholders liable in cases of Central Bank intervention due to insolvency or wrongdoing in financial institutions.[48]

Yet arguably the most important step toward Brazil's strong challenge to limited liability in the stakeholder context was the enactment of the Consumer Protection Code of 1990 (*Código de Defesa do Consumidor* – CDC). The Consumer Protection Code grants judges the ability to pierce the corporate veil of an entity "whenever its personality is, in any way, an obstacle to the compensation of harm caused to consumers."[49] Surprisingly, this expansive rule was absent from the draft bill proposed by consumerist advocates, but was included in the legislative process by politicians of center-right parties.[50] In fact, the very promulgation of this rule was likely a result of a historical accident.[51] Scholars have argued that the rule in question was supposed to have been vetoed by Brazil's president, but the official veto message contained a typo and mentioned a different paragraph of the same article instead.[52] Nevertheless, courts ultimately ignored the scholarly denunciations

45 J. R. Macey and G. P. Miller, Double Liability of Bank Shareholders: History and Implications (1992) 27 *Wake Forest Law Review* 31–62, 31.

46 Pargendler, How Universal Is the Corporate Form?, 20.

47 See, e.g., New York Consolidated Laws, Business Corporation Law §630 (imposing joint and several liability for labor debts on the ten largest shareholders of close corporations).

48 Pargendler, How Universal Is the Corporate Form?, 23 (describing how the 1997 statute extended to controlling shareholders a regime of strict liability and freezing of personal assets that applied to directors and officers of financial institutions under intervention since 1974).

49 Lei No. 8.078, de 11 de setembro de 1990, D.O.U. de 12.09.1990 (Brazil), art. 28, § 5°.

50 Pargendler, How Universal Is the Corporate Form?, 24.

51 Ibid.

52 A. P. Grinover et al., *Código de Defesa do Consumidor: Comentado Pelos Autores do Anteprojeto*, 8th ed. (Rio de Janeiro: Forense Universitária, 2005), p. 237 (advancing the view

of the typo and enforced the rule as written. The leading case imposing strict liability on shareholders for damages to consumers concerned a tragic explosion in a shopping mall, which killed numerous bystanders.[53]

Despite its serendipitous origin, the innovative provision in the Consumer Protection Code – the first statutory rule on "disregard of legal entity" in Brazilian law – came to spread and influence stakeholder protections in other areas of law. Labor courts used it by analogy to render shareholders (including minority shareholders of close corporations) jointly and severally liable for unpaid dues to employees.[54] Moreover, Brazil's environmental protection statute of 1998 adopts the same language used in the Consumer Protection Code to authorize piercing the corporate veil of an entity "whenever its personality is an obstacle to the compensation of harm caused to the quality of the environment."[55]

The erosion of limited liability in Brazil is such that scholars have decried the "end of limited liability" in the country.[56] Importantly, however, the attack on limited liability does not apply uniformly across areas of law but is concentrated in contexts of vulnerable stakeholders and difficult regulation. Brazilian economists have argued that the imposition of liability on controlling shareholders and managers of banks may be a more effective regulatory option given the well-known shortcomings of command-and-control regulations.[57] Brazilian courts are much more reluctant to overcome limited liability for the benefit of contract counterparties in commercial transactions, which are subject to the Civil Code's restrictive provisions conditioning veil piercing on a finding of "commingling of assets" or "deviation of purpose."[58]

that the Presidential veto message contained a typo). The text accompanying the veto message lends support to the "typo theory," as it argues that other provisions of the Code "already contain all the elements necessary for the application of veil piercing, which constitutes, according to widely dominant doctrine under national and foreign law, an *exceptional technique* of repression of *abusive practices*." Ibid. (emphasis added).

[53] S. T. J., Recurso Especial No. 279.273-SP, Relator: Min. Ari Pargendler, Relatora p/ Acórdão: Min. Nancy Andrighi, 02.12.2003, Diário da Justiça [D.J.] 03.03.2004 (Brazil).

[54] B. M. Salama, *O Fim da Responsabilidade Limitada no Brasil: História, Direito e Economia* (São Paulo: Malheiros, 2014), p. 208 (explaining how the Consumer Protection Code served to justify "the most varied – and increasingly aggressive – forms of rendering third parties liable for the labor debts of the firm").

[55] Lei No. 9.605, de 12 de fevereiro de 1998, D.O.U. de 13.02.1998 (Brazil), art. 4°.

[56] Salama, *O Fim da Responsabilidade Limitada no Brasil.*

[57] G. H. B. Franco, *As Leis Secretas da Economia* (Rio de Janeiro: Zahar, 2012), p. 88; G. H. B. Franco and L. A. C. Rosman, A Responsabilidade Ilimitada em Instituições Financeiras no Brasil: Antecedentes, Experiência e Considerações, in D. D. Carneiro and M. B. de Bolle (eds.), *A Reforma do Sistema Financeiro Americano: Nova Arquitetura Internacional e o Contexto Regulatório Brasileiro* (Rio de Janeiro: LTC, 2009), pp. 60–66.

[58] Pargendler, How Universal Is the Corporate Form?, 27. Despite criticism by Brazilian scholars, the disregard of asset partitioning in bankruptcy through the doctrine of substantive consolidation has run rampant in Brazil. See S. C. N. Cerezetti, Reorganization of Corporate Groups in Brazil: Substantive Consolidation and the Limited Liability Tale (2021) 30 *International Insolvency Review* 169–90, 182 (describing as "worrying" the "flexible" approach to substantive

Since the 2010s, Brazil has witnessed several legal reforms seeking to constrain veil piercing. However, the various efforts are noteworthy for their limited scope in only restricting the most outlandish fact patterns. In 2015, a new Code of Civil Procedure created procedural safeguards for the application of veil piercing, by outlawing the then prevailing practice of attaching shareholders' assets without their prior participation in the judicial process.[59] A 2019 statute called the "Law on Economic Freedom," for its overtly libertarian bent, reformed the Civil Code's section on veil piercing to include a new provision stating that "the asset autonomy of legal persons is a lawful interest of allocation and segregation of risks, established by statute with the aim of promoting enterprises, in view of the creation of jobs, tax payments, income and innovation for the benefit of all."[60]

Beyond the new rhetoric, however, the scope of the Civil Code's reform is modest. The changes are limited to defining the meaning of "commingling of assets" and "deviation of purpose" that applies to civil and commercial transactions under the Civil Code, but do nothing with respect to the broad approaches to veil piercing in consumer, environmental, and employment law.[61] The Brazilian Congress passed a more ambitious bill aiming to impose numerous procedural constraints on veil piercing in 2022, but then President Jair Bolsonaro vetoed the proposed legislation in its entirety as unconstitutional and contrary to the public interest.[62] The President's official veto message criticized, among other things, the proposed rule that would require plaintiffs to specify in the complaint the acts of shareholders that justified the piercing of the corporate veil.[63] It reasoned that such a change ran afoul of the strict regime in Brazil's environmental and consumer protection legislation allowing for veil piercing regardless of fault, and would effectively impede the use of veil piercing in consumer disputes by shifting the burden of proof to the most vulnerable party.[64]

Although Brazil's experience is particularly broad and extreme, the country is by no means alone in embracing a more expansive approach to veil piercing to protect stakeholders in the Global South. In the last decades, India has mitigated limited liability in corporate groups by recognizing a doctrine of enterprise liability for the

consolidation in Brazil, which "treats an exceptional measure as a day-to-day event, dramatically altering the rights of creditors and the obligations of debtors without regard to the limitation of liability").

59 Lei No. 13.105, de 16 março de 2015, D.O.U. de 17.03.2015 (Brazil), arts. 133–37.

60 Lei No. 13.874, de 20 de setembro de 2019, D.O.U. de 20.09.2019 (Brazil) (introducing new art. 49-A to the Civil Code).

61 For doctrinal commentary on the reform, see M. Pargendler, Comentários ao Art. 50 do Código Civil: A Desconsideração da Personalidade Jurídica, in J. Martins-Costa and G. C. M. Nitschke (eds.), *Direito Privado na Lei da Liberdade Econômica: Comentários* (Coimbra: Almedina, 2022), pp. 341–74.

62 Mensagem de Veto No. 657, de 13 de dezembro de 2022.

63 Ibid.

64 Ibid.

benefit of tort victims of hazardous activities.[65] In the wake of the much-publicized Bhopal disaster of 1984, in which the leakage of toxic gas from a Union Carbide pesticide plant took thousands of lives, Indian courts came to embrace enterprise liability and hold parent companies liable for tort victims of hazardous activities.[66] Departing from earlier precedents, the Indian Supreme Court embraced an absolute version of enterprise liability in the 1987 *Mehta* case resulting from an oleum gas leak in Delhi two years earlier.[67] The Court held that "[i]f the enterprise is permitted to carry on the hazardous or inherently dangerous activity for its profit, the law must presume that such permission is conditional on the enterprise absorbing the cost of any accident."[68]

The decision in *Mehta* contradicted the then dominant view about legal possibilities in developing countries. That year, Marc Galanter, one of the foremost scholars of law and development, had deplored the prevailing "legal torpor" in India following the Bhopal tragedy, denouncing the "absence of tort claims," the "absence of tort doctrines," and the "arid conceptualism" that prevented consideration of "problems of implementation or underlying policies."[69] Nevertheless, "[t]he sense of violation by a foreign malefactor" raised new expectations of new kinds of claims and potential redress.[70]

Indian courts then applied the new concept of enterprise liability for hazardous activities to the Bhopal case itself, after a US court declined jurisdiction on the grounds of *forum non conveniens*.[71] In 1988, the Madhya Pradesh High Court cited *Mehta* to recognize the liability of controlling shareholder Union Carbide for the harm caused in the Bhopal disaster by its Indian subsidiary.[72] The High Court rejected the parent company's argument that it did not exercise control over its subsidiary, arguing instead that Indian law on limited liability and veil piercing had to adapt to modern economic conditions, such as "a mass disaster and in which on

65 See, e.g., F. Reyes, *Latin American Company Law, A New Policy Agenda: Reshaping the Closely Held Entity Landscape II* (Durham: Carolina Academic Press, 2013), p. 23 ("The influence of new political constitutions and constitutional courts in Latin American countries has led to the creation of various piercing-the-veil doctrines – most of which rely on grounds outside of the scope of company law. Additionally, various tax, labor and environmental regulations have established a basis to allow a plaintiff to request that a legal entity be disregarded").

66 For a detailed discussion of Indian decisions on the matter, see A. Raghunathan, The Grand Trunk Road from Salomon to Mehta: Economic Development and Enterprise Liability in India (2012) 100 *Georgetown Law Journal* 571–604.

67 Ibid., 590–91.

68 *M. C. Mehta v. Shriram Food and Fertilizer Industries*, 1 S.C.R. 819 (1987). For a discussion, see Raghunathan, The Grand Trunk Road from Salomon to Mehta, 590–91.

69 M. Galanter, Legal Torpor: Why so Little has Happened in India after the Bhopal Tragedy (1985) 20 *Texas International Law Journal* 273–94, 275, 279.

70 Ibid., 281.

71 Raghunathan, The Grand Trunk Road from Salomon to Mehta, 590–91.

72 *Union Carbide Corp. v. Union of India*, Civil Revision No. 26, (1988). For a discussion, see Raghunathan, The Grand Trunk Road from Salomon to Mehta, 591–92.

the face of it the assets of the alleged subsidiary company are utterly insufficient to meet the just claims of multitude of disaster victims."[73] The Bhopal case was ultimately settled for US $470 million based on estimates that turned out to greatly underestimate the number of fatalities and victims – an outcome that is widely regarded as undercompensatory and unfair.[74]

In 1996, the Indian Supreme Court once again reaffirmed its commitment to overcome limited liability within the corporate group for the benefit of stakeholders in dangerous industries.[75] In a case involving the release of toxic chemicals that devastated local agriculture, the Court held that "the enterprise … alone has the resource to discover and guard against hazards or dangers" and criticized what it viewed as "contempt for law and lawful authorities on the part of some among the emerging breed of entrepreneurs, taking advantage, as they do, of the country's need for industrialization and export earnings."[76] Interestingly, commentators – unaware of similar developments in other developing countries – have compared Indian law exclusively to the laws of Global North jurisdictions, and concluded that it is "unique" and "revolutionary" from a comparative perspective.[77]

But India and Brazil are not the only countries in the Global South that have committed to overcome limited liability. In Colombia, shareholders of limited liability companies can be held liable for tax and labor obligations irrespective of fault.[78] Colombia's bankruptcy law also makes parent companies presumptively liable for obligations of subsidiaries.[79] In a ground-breaking 2001 decision, the Colombian Constitutional Court held the controlling shareholders of a liquidated company temporarily liable for the company's social security and pension liability.[80] The Court justified the exceptional measure as a response to the violation of the

[73] Union Carbide Civil Revision, 378–79.

[74] See, e.g., S. Jasanoff, Bhopal's Trials of Knowledge and Ignorance (2008) 42 *New England Law Review* 679–92, 684; S. Rajagopalan, Bhopal Gas Tragedy: Paternalism and Filicide (2014) 5 *Journal of Indian Law and Society* 201–24, 209 (criticizing the Bhopal Gas Leak Disaster (Processing of Claims) Act, 1985, which gave India's central government exclusive authority to represent the victims in court).

[75] *Indian-Council for Enviro-Legal Action v. Union of India* (1996) 3 S.C.C. 212, 38 (India). For a discussion, see Raghunathan, The Grand Trunk Road from Salomon to Mehta, 593.

[76] *Indian-Council for Enviro-Legal Action v. Union of India* (1996) 3 S.C.C. 212, 38 (India), 27, 1.

[77] See note 15 and accompanying text. See also Raghunathan, The Grand Trunk Road from Salomon to Mehta, 601 (claiming that India's "relatively isolated" stance in its "broad application of enterprise liability" may compromise foreign investment in the country).

[78] J. Ruggie, Report of the Special Representative of the Secretary-General, Guiding Principles on Business and Human Rights: Implementing the United Nations "Protect, Respect and Remedy" Framework, United Nations Doc. A/HRC/17/31/Add. 2 (2011).

[79] L. 1116, diciembre 27, 2006, Diario Oficial (Colombia); L. 222, diciembre 20, 1995, Diario Oficial (Colombia), art. 148.

[80] Decision SU-1023 of 2001, Jaime Córdoba Triviño, J. (Jaime Araujo Rentería, J., concurring), Librada de Dios Viuda de Fajardo y Otros, contra la Compañía de Inversiones de la Flota Mercante S.A. y Otros (Librada de Dios Viuda de Fajardo v. The Merchant Fleet Investment Company).

"fundamental right of protection of the vital minimum, of life in dignified conditions and of the protection of old age" concerning the liquidated company's pensioners.[81] On that occasion, the Court for the first time boldly extended the effects of its decision to third parties, so as to guarantee the equal treatment of the company's retired workers who did not take part in the lawsuit.[82]

There are also prominent, though isolated, examples of attacks on limited liability in other Global South jurisdictions in cases that pitch the interests of foreign companies against local stakeholders. In the Deltec case of 1973, the Supreme Court of Argentina shocked the international community by finding a "unified socio-economic unit" and imposing liability on the Canadian parent company and other foreign affiliates for the debts of a bankrupt Argentine company.[83] Although the case concerned voluntary creditors, the legal challenge in question had been initiated by a small, likely non-adjusting, trade creditor.[84] The Court considered the "paramount interests of [Argentine] society" in relation to multinational enterprises,[85] and criticized the "excessive attachment to legal traditionalism" as one of the "most serious obstacles to the success of the promotion of economic expansion and social justice."[86]

10.3 MANDATORY CSR SPENDING IN INDIA, INDONESIA, AND MAURITIUS

Since Adolf Berle and Merrick Dodd's famous exchange in the 1930s, much of the debate on stakeholder protection has focused on the scope of directors' fiduciary duties.[87] Both developed and developing jurisdictions have opted for corporate

[81] Ibid. For an analysis of the decision, see F. Reyes, *Latin American Company Law, A New Policy Agenda*; Á. R. Oquendo, *Latin American Law* (Santa Barbara: Foundation Press, 2006), p. 793 et seq.

[82] M. J. Cepeda-Espinosa, Judicial Activism in a Violent Context: The Origin, Role, and Impact of the Colombian Constitutional Court (2004) 3 *Washington University Global Studies Law Review* 529–700, 573.

[83] P. Blumberg, *The Multinational Challenge to Corporation Law: The Search for a New Corporate Personality* (Oxford: Oxford University Press, 1993), p. 187 (describing the *Deltec* case as "[t]he outstanding example of the exercise of host country extraterritoriality reflecting enterprise principles").

[84] R. S. Avi-Yonah, National Regulation of Multinational Enterprises: An Essay on Comity, Extraterritoriality, and Harmonization (2003) 42 *Columbia Journal of Transnational Law* 5–34, 16 (while the Argentine creditors were largely voluntary, some of the creditors, including the US $4,000 creditor raising the legal challenge in *Deltec*, were "trade creditors and therefore closer to involuntary creditors").

[85] Blumberg, *The Multinational Challenge to Corporation Law*, p. 188 (alteration in original).

[86] M. W. Gordon, Argentine Jurisprudence: The Parke Davis and Deltec Cases (1974) 6 *University of Miami Inter-American Law Review* 320–45, 326.

[87] A. A. Berle Jr., Corporate Powers as Powers in Trust (1931) 44 *Harvard Law Review* 1049–74, 1049; E. M. Dodd Jr., For Whom Are Corporate Managers Trustees? (1932) 45 *Harvard Law Review* 1145–63, 1145.

purpose provisions that mention broader interests beyond shareholders. While Brazil's Corporations Law of 1976 grants an unusual amount of power to shareholders,[88] it requires directors and officers to act in the interest of the company, "subject to the public good and to the social function of enterprise," and imposes liability on controlling shareholders for orienting a company toward a purpose "harmful to the national interest" or favoring another company to the detriment of the "national economy."[89] India's Companies Act of 1956 allowed shareholders to complain that the affairs of the company "are being conducted in a manner prejudicial to the public interest,"[90] with notions of public interest being "widely infused into company law."[91] India's more recent Companies Act of 2013 provides that directors "shall act in good faith in order to promote the objects of the company for the benefit of its members as a whole, and in the best interests of the company, its employees, the shareholders, the community and for the protection of environment," while its Code of Conduct for independent directors requires them to "safeguard the interests of all stakeholders, particularly the minority shareholders," and "balance the conflicting interest of the stakeholders."[92]

There are also manifestations of stakeholder-sensitive corporate purposes in the Global North, even though a bit blander. Under the UK Companies Act of 2006, directors must seek to promote the benefit "of its members as a whole, and in doing so [to] have regard (amongst other matters) to … the interests of the company's employees, … [and] the impact of the company's operations on the community and the environment."[93] Similarly, a 2019 French law reform provides that companies must be managed in view of their corporate interest, while also considering the social and environmental issues arising from their activities.[94] Various US states contain constituency statutes permitting directors to consider the interests of employees, customers, the community, and even "the economy of the state and

[88] Pargendler, How Universal Is the Corporate Form?, 32 (describing the unusually broad competence of the shareholders' meeting and the binding effects of shareholder agreements on directors' votes).

[89] Lei No. 6.404, de 15 de dezembro de 1976, D.O.U. de 17.12.1976 (Brazil), arts. 154 and 117, § 1°.

[90] J. Cottrell, Indian Judicial Activism, the Company and the Worker: A Note on National Textile Workers' Union v. Ramakrishnan (1990) 39 *International & Comparative Law Quarterly* 433–51, 435. Since 1963 the Indian Companies Act itself has required that companies take account of the interests not only of their shareholders but also of the public (citing the amended section 398 of the Companies Act 1956).

[91] U. Varottil, The Stakeholder Approach to Corporate Law: A Historical Perspective from India, in H. Wells (ed.), *Research Handbook on the History of Corporate and Company Law* (Northampton: Edward Elgar, 2018), pp. 381–400, p. 387.

[92] Companies Act, 2013, § 166, Schedules IV, II(5)-(6) (India). For a discussion, see A. Afsharipour, Redefining Corporate Purpose: An International Perspective (2017) 40 *Seattle University Law Review* 465–96, 467.

[93] Companies Act 2006 § 172(1) (UK).

[94] Code civil, art. 1833, as amended by Loi 2019-486 du 22 mai 2019, art. 169 [Law 2019-486 of May 22, 2019], *Journal Officiel de la République Française* [J.O.] [*Official Gazette of France*], May 24, 2019.

Nation."[95] At the same time, one may interpret Delaware law's greater focus on shareholders as beneficiaries of fiduciary duties as compensating for Delaware's status as "the least shareholder-centric jurisdiction" from the perspective of the allocation of corporate powers.[96] In this sense, Delaware lies on the opposite side of the spectrum from Brazil, where stakeholder-oriented fiduciary duties coexist with exceptionally strong shareholder power. Yet, given the dearth of enforcement mechanisms, there is no evidence suggesting that broader fiduciary duties to stakeholders make much difference where they exist.[97] This section, and this chapter more generally, thus concentrates on distinct stakeholder-oriented innovations in the Global South, which, at least in theory, appear to have more teeth.

India's Companies Act of 2013 attracted significant attention by introducing a requirement that large companies have a corporate social responsibility (CSR) policy providing for spending of at least 2 percent of profits on CSR.[98] Absent from the initial drafts of the proposed legislation, the CSR provision was inserted in the aftermath of the major Satyam scandal in 2009, which created the need to rebuild trust in corporate India.[99] In the parliamentary debate preceding the adoption of the bill, economic inequality was a key consideration. The Minister of the State for Corporate Affairs justified the provision as offering a much-needed "perception correction" at a time of "big division in this country," as "the divide between the rich and the poor is getting bigger and bigger."[100] The provision was also expected to minimize protest movements and buttress the popularity of the government's pro-business policies.[101]

India's CSR spending regime initially applied on a "comply-or-explain" basis, but it became mandatory ("comply or be penalized") for large companies following an

95 Pargendler, The Grip of Nationalism on Corporate Law, 573 (citing the statutes of Kentucky, Minnesota, Nevada, Ohio, and Wyoming as examples).

96 J. Armour et al., The Basic Governance Structure: The Interests of Shareholders as a Class, in R. Kraakman et al., *The Anatomy of Corporate Law: A Comparative and Functional Approach*, 3rd ed. (Oxford: Oxford University Press, 2017), pp. 49–78, p. 58 (examining the apportionment of power between shareholders and boards from a comparative perspective).

97 Enriques, The Basic Governance Structure, p. 98 ("[C]ourts are not well-placed to determine which policies maximize aggregate private welfare. This explains why, even where it is spelt out, a duty to pursue the corporation's interest (in this broad sense) is unenforceable"). See also H. Spamann and J. Fisher, Corporate Purpose: Theoretical and Empirical Foundations/Confusions (2022) European Corporate Governance Institute Working Paper No. 664 ("[E]ven structural measures like employee co-determination hardly have detectable effects, let alone mere exhortations such as those in (unenforceable) nuances of (misunderstood) fiduciary duties").

98 Companies Act 2013, § 135(5).

99 Varottil, The Stakeholder Approach to Corporate Law, p. 392.

100 D. Krichewsky, CSR Public Policies in India's Democracy: Ambiguities in the Political Regulation of Corporate Conduct (2017) 19 *Business and Politics* 510–47, 532 (also arguing that such a correction "can only be done if the companies themselves move forward and show that they are responsible, sensitive and they want to give back to the society").

101 Ibid., 532–33.

amendment in 2021,[102] thus showing a progressive hardening of heterodox stakeholderism. The statutory definition of CSR in the Companies Act is very broad in covering a wide range of social objectives involving external stakeholders, such as eradicating extreme hunger and poverty, reducing child mortality and improving maternal health, combating the human immunodeficiency virus, acquired immune deficiency syndrome, malaria, and other diseases, ensuring environmental sustainability, and contributing to the Prime-Minister's National Relief Fund.[103] The 2021 amendment also explicitly excluded from the definition of CSR activities undertaken in the normal course of business or outside of India, sponsorships from which the company derives marketing benefits, and activities that benefit employees, among others.[104] The far-reaching welfare objectives of the CSR provisions, combined with the exclusion of benefits to employees, are indicative of a mode of heterodox stakeholderism in developing countries that overly aims to complement the state's role and compensate for government failures.[105] While philanthropic spending has greatly increased following the reforms in key areas such as health, education, and sanitation, India's CSR model under concentrated ownership has produced concerns about corruption and cronyism through contributions to government funds and has failed to solve the country's deep-rooted social and economic problems.[106]

Interestingly, India's approach to mandatory CSR is not alone in the developing world. In 2007, Indonesia became the first country to introduce mandatory corporate social responsibility requirements for corporations operating in the business of natural resources or impacting natural resources. This mechanism deviated from Global North practices and, therefore, was not captured by then existing comparative literature.[107] The mandatory provisions withstood constitutional scrutiny, with the Constitutional Court of Indonesia noting that the voluntary nature of CSR is not

[102] M. R. Littenberg, India Substantially Revamps CSR Requirements: The Impact on Compliance at Indian Subsidiaries of US-Based Multinationals, *Ropes & Gray*, July 26, 2021.

[103] Companies Act 2013, schedule VII.

[104] Companies (CSR Policy) Amendment Rules, 2021.

[105] See A. Afsharipour, Lessons from India's Struggle with Corporate Purpose, in E. Pollman and R. Thompson (eds.), *Research Handbook on Corporate Purpose and Personhood* (Northampton: Edward Elgar, 2021), pp. 363–86, p. 377 (noting how critics in India describe the model as an "outsourcing of governance" that works by "taking the failure of the state and the corporates and trying to create a model out of it").

[106] Ibid., pp. 367, 375, and 377. See also D. Dharmapala and V. Khanna, The Impact of Mandated Corporate Social Responsibility: Evidence from India's Companies Act of 2013 (2018) 56 *International Review of Law and Economics* 92–104, 104 (finding that firms with less than 2 percent on CSR increased their spending, while those spending more decreased their spending, following the introduction of the 2013 Companies Act).

[107] For a discussion, see Mahy, The Evolution of Company Law in Indonesia, 416; A. Rosser and D. Edwin, The Politics of Corporate Social Responsibility in Indonesia (2010) 23 *The Pacific Review* 1–22, 2.

universal but rather depends on the culture of each country.[108] Pushed by NGOs and resisted by domestic elites, the CSR requirement in Indonesia is plagued by a lack of enforcement mechanisms.[109]

Moreover, in 2009, Mauritius preceded India as the first jurisdiction to require the allocation of 2 percent of profits to CSR activities.[110] The move followed a "neoliberal" turn in Mauritius politics, with the government seeking to slash taxes while lowering social spending.[111] Government representatives viewed the rule as a "tax," though "an intelligent tax because government has left the management of this tax in the hands of the private sector."[112] A study on the Mauritius experiment found that, despite critiques, all respondents considered that CSR has a role to play in the development of Mauritius.[113] Similarly, in 2016 and 2020 statutes, Nepal adopted mandatory corporate social responsibility spending of 1 percent of annual profits for industrial enterprises and banks to be allotted to sectors ranging from community health services and community schools to roads and sewage.[114] Nevertheless, commentators have criticized Nepal's mandatory CSR regime as "impracticable" given local constraints and the fact that it was "hastily legislated by replicating the Indian law."[115]

10.4 CORPORATE SOCIAL RESPONSIBILITY COMMITTEES IN INDIA AND SOUTH AFRICA

In addition to mandating corporate social responsibility and imposing minimum spending, developing jurisdictions have also pioneered the creation of governance arrangements designed to protect stakeholder interests in the form of dedicated board committees.[116] For example, South Africa's Companies Act of 2008 innovated

[108] Constitutional Court Decision No. 53/PUU-VI/2008, point 3.19. See also Lin, Mandatory Corporate Social Responsibility Legislation around the World, 455.

[109] See Rosser and Edwin, The Politics of Corporate Social Responsibility in Indonesia, 8–9; Lin, Mandatory Corporate Social Responsibility Legislation around the World, 456; Mahy, The Evolution of Company Law in Indonesia, 416 (noting that "there are still no strong sanctions for resources companies who fail to carry out their CSR responsibilities," which "suggests that corporate power may have reasserted itself at the central level").

[110] R. Pillay, *The Changing Nature of Corporate Social Responsibility, CSR and Development: The Case of Mauritius* (London: Routledge, 2015), p. 2 (describing Mauritius as "the first country in the world to have actually implemented an innovative CSR legislation).

[111] Ibid., 230; Lin, Mandatory Corporate Social Responsibility Legislation around the World, 441.

[112] Pillay, *The Changing Nature of Corporate Social Responsibility, CSR and Development*, p. 252.

[113] Ibid., p. 259.

[114] A. Sthapit, Corporate Social Responsibility in Nepal: Beset with the Syndrome of "Who'll Bell the Cat?" as Philanthropic Views Dominate CSR Practices, in S. O. Idowu (ed.), *Current Global Practices of Corporate Social Responsibility* (Oxfordshire: Routledge 2021), pp. 777–800, pp. 786–88.

[115] Ibid., p. 787.

[116] Corporate responsibility or similar committees are more recently making an appearance in the United States. See B. H. McDonnell, Stakeholder Engagement (2022) 51 *Florida State University Law Review* 305–72, 351 (finding that twenty-two of the S&P 100 companies have a special committee devoted to ESG, corporate social responsibility, or sustainability issues).

by instituting a social and ethics committee, whose significance in giving legal backing to a stakeholder approach "cannot be gainsaid."[117] State-owned companies, listed companies, and companies meeting certain metrics of public interest must have a social and ethics committee with at least three members, one of whom must not be involved in the day-to-day management of the company.[118] The social and ethics committee, among other things, must monitor the company's activities in view of legislation and prevailing codes of best practices on social and economic development and good corporate citizenship, including the UN Global Compact Principles, the OECD recommendations regarding corruption, the Broad-Based Economic Empowerment Act, promotion of equality, environmental matters, consumer relationships, labor, and employment matters.[119]

The social and ethics committee must draw matters to the attention of the board as appropriate, but, unlike typical board committees, it also reports directly to shareholders.[120] South African commentators have debated whether the new committee has the nature of a board committee, a shareholders' committee, or a sui generis organ of the company.[121] Despite open questions about its functioning and impact, the social and ethics committee has been hailed as a "new and creative innovation"[122] that reflects a distinct "procedural approach" to the protection of stakeholders.[123]

Similarly, India's Companies Act of 2013 also requires a CSR Committee for companies subject to the CSR spending requirements.[124] The CSR Committee formulates and recommends the CSR policy to the board, suggests the amount of expenditures to be incurred, and monitors the CSR policy of the company from time to time.[125] The CSR committees of public companies must have at least three directors, one of whom must be an independent director.[126] Still, studies have

[117] Companies Act 2008 (South Africa), section 72; T. H. Mongalo, The Social and Ethics Committee: Innovating Corporate Governance in South Africa, in B. Sjåfjell and C. M. Bruner (eds.), *Cambridge Handbook of Corporate Law, Corporate Governance and Sustainability* (Cambridge: Cambridge University Press, 2019), pp. 360–72, p. 363.

[118] Regulations in Terms of The Companies Act No. 71 (2008) (as amended), § 43.

[119] Ibid.

[120] Ibid.

[121] I. M. Esser and P. Delport, The Protection of Stakeholders: The South African Social and Ethics Committee and the United Kingdom's Enlightened Shareholder Value Approach: Part 2 (2017) 50 *De Jure* 221–41, 223–24, 228 (describing the controversy and defending that it is a company committee in view of its right to report to shareholders; Mongalo, The Social and Ethics Committee, 363, arguing that it qualifies as a board committee).

[122] Mongalo, The Social and Ethics Committee, p. 361.

[123] I. M. Esser and P. Delport, The Protection of Stakeholders: The South African Social and Ethics Committee and the United Kingdom's Enlightened Shareholder Value Approach: Part 1 (2017) 50 *De Jure* 97–110, 100 (contrasting South Africa's "procedural approach" to the UK's "rule approach" to stakeholder protection).

[124] Companies Act 2013 (India), § 135(iii).

[125] Ibid.

[126] Ibid.

denounced the CSR committee as "largely ineffective in practice," finding a tendency to favor contributions to the Prime Minister's National Relief Fund over other more labor-intensive efforts to conceive and implement CSR activities.[127]

10.5 STAKEHOLDER EMPOWERMENT IN ENFORCING DIRECTORS' DUTIES AND BANKRUPTCY IN SOUTH AFRICA

Another strategy of stakeholder protection takes the form of stakeholder empowerment through the direct grant of governance rights to non-shareholder constituencies. The most paradigmatic manifestation of stakeholder empowerment is worker participation in company boards, a practice that is characteristic of the German model and widespread among continental European countries.[128] Allusions to worker participation in company management are more common in the constitutions of the Global South compared to Global North jurisdictions, with five and two constitutional texts of the largest economies in each group, respectively, referring to the concept.[129] Nevertheless, such exhortations are often soft and voluntary in the developing world, to the effect that significant worker participation in corporate boards remains much stronger in rich countries, particularly in Continental Europe.[130] Brazil, for instance, introduced a particularly timid version of employee board participation in 2010 which is limited to one worker representative in state-owned enterprises controlled by the federal government, and curiously such representative is not allowed to participate in discussions and voting concerning labor matters.[131]

However, the Global South has pioneered distinct strategies of worker empowerment in corporate governance beyond codetermination. South Africa's Companies Act of 2008 is "unusual" to a foreign observer in "the amount of power, including direct participation, it bestows on employee groups."[132] Not only shareholders,

[127] N. Koya and J. Roper, Legislated CSR in Practice: The Experience of India (2020) 22 *Journal of Public Affairs* 1–10, 4–5.

[128] For a survey of the modes of codetermination in Europe, see generally J. Dammann and H. Eidenmueller, Corporate Law and the Democratic State (2022) *University of Illinois Law Review* 963–1020.

[129] These are Italy, Art. 46 Constituzione [Const.] (Italy), and the Netherlands, Statuut Ned [Charter] art. 19, in the Global North, and China, Xianfa art. 16 (1982), India, India Const. art. 43A, Brazil, Constituiçao Federal [C.F.] [Constitution] art. 7, XI (Brazil), Argentina, Art. 14, Constitución Nacional [Const. Nac.] (Argentina), and Egypt, Constitution of the Arab Republic of Egypt, art. 42, January 18, 2014.

[130] The 2018 version of the UK Corporate Governance Code now also recommends some form of institutionalization of board engagement with the workforce through one of the following methods: a director appointed from the workforce, a formal workforce advisory panel, or a designated non-executive director. UK Corporate Governance Code 5 (2018) (Principle 1, Provision 5).

[131] Lei No. 12.353, de 28 de dezembro de 2010, D.O.U. 29.12.2010 (Brazil), art. 2°, § 1° and 3°.

[132] J. F. Olson, South Africa Moves to a Global Model of Corporate Governance but with Important National Variations, in T. H. Mongalo (ed.), *Modern Company Law for a Competitive South African Economy* (Cape Town: Juta, 2010), p. 225.

directors, and officers, but also trade unions representing employees may initiate proceedings to prevent the company from behaving inconsistently with the Act.[133] The Companies Act also empowers trade unions and employees to enforce directors' duties under the statute by allowing them to initiate director delinquency and disqualification procedures, which are exceptionally broad in South Africa,[134] and to commence derivative actions.[135] A suit brought by the trade union South African Airways Pilot Association and the Organisation Undoing Tax Abuse (OUTA) resulted in the disqualification of a board chair of South African Airlines, a state-owned enterprise.[136] Interestingly, the court declared the director delinquent for her lifetime, an unusually draconian outcome.[137]

Concerns about unemployment and job savings played a significant role in the formulation of the new regime for business rescue proceedings.[138] South Africa has faced extraordinarily high levels of unemployment, even among developing countries.[139] The Companies Act gives a prominent role to labor by empowering trade unions and employees to ask the court to place the company in business rescue, requiring their consultation in the development of the business plan, and permitting them to address creditors at the meeting before the vote on the plan.[140] South

[133] Companies Act, 2008, section 20(4); Ibid. (shareholders, directors, and officers also have this right).

[134] See R. Cassim, A Comparative Discussion of the Judicial Disqualification of Directors under the South African Companies Act (2021) 65 *Journal of African Law* 87–110, 90, 92 (describing how the director disqualification regime under the Companies Act is "wider, stricter, and more far-reaching" than its counterparts in the United Kingdom, Australia, and the United States, including with respect to South Africa's "unique" solution of granting *locus standi* for trade unions and employee representatives).

[135] R. Croucher and L. Miles, Corporate Governance and Employees in South Africa (2010) 10 *Journal of Corporate Law Studies* 367–89, 372. Canada and Singapore grant courts discretion to allow derivative suits by stakeholders, though they remain rare. See D. Palombo, The Future of the Corporation: The Avenues for Legal Change (2022) 10 *Journal of the British Academy* 43–86, 64.

[136] *Undoing Tax Abuse and Another v. Myeni and Others* (15996/2017) [2020] ZAGPPHC 169. For a discussion, see R. Chuene, Z. Demarthe, and S. Mokoena, Directors Beware! The Court Declares Dudu Myeni (Former SAA Chair) a Delinquent Director, *African Legal Information Institute*, July 3, 2020.

[137] R. Cassim, Declaring Directors of State-Owned Entities Delinquent: Organisation Undoing Tax Abuse v Myeni (2021) 138 *South African Law Journal* 1–20, 1 (praising the decision's "strict stance against errant directors of state-owned companies"). This decision was also the first to recognize standing for a party acting in the public interest (in this case, OUTA) to bring delinquency proceedings. Ibid., 7 (describing how the court justified OUTA's standing in its role representing taxpayers, "who partly foot the bill of SAA" and "have an interest in how a company such as SAA is run").

[138] A. Loubser and T. Joubert, The Role of Trade Unions and Employees in South Africa's Business Rescue Proceedings (2015) 36 *Industrial Law Journal (Juta)* 21–39, 22.

[139] P. Naidoo, South Africa Jobless Rate Drops to Third Highest in the World, *Bloomberg*, November 29, 2022 (describing how South Africa's unemployment rate has exceeded 20 percent for about two decades, hitting 33 percent in 2022).

[140] Loubser and Joubert, The Role of Trade Unions and Employees in South Africa's Business Rescue Proceedings, 29.

Africa's Companies Act also gives employees enhanced information rights by granting unions access to information for the purposes of initiating a business rescue proceeding and requiring that unions receive notification if the company provides financial assistance to a director.[141]

Taken together, these employee rights are both distinctive and substantial compared to the norm in other jurisdictions, where workers' rights generally take the form of codetermination, workers' councils, or information and consultation rights in the context of corporate takeovers.[142] Here again, however, commentators have questioned whether these measures are effective and "likely to suffice to meet deep socio-economic challenges."[143]

While employee participation in business rescue proceedings appeared "surprisingly reticent" in the first years after the adoption of the Companies Act,[144] the high-profile bankruptcy of South African Airlines (SAA), a state-owned enterprise, paints a different picture. A union representing mostly white, Afrikaans-speaking employees filed a request for business rescue in late 2019 to avoid liquidation.[145] Subsequently, unions also successfully halted retrenchments prior to the proposal of a business rescue plan. A decision by the Labour Court of Appeal held that the best purposeful interpretation of section 136 of the Companies Act established that the presentation of a business rescue plan constituted a condition precedent for retrenchment, given that one of the main purposes of the business rescue procedure in South Africa is "the preservation of jobs."[146] The Court stated that this interpretation was consistent with the Constitution, which "recognises the rights of employers but simultaneously protects a range of rights of employees that are central to the democratic model promoted by the Constitution read as a whole."[147] International law firms have warned that the decision may deal a death knell to successful business rescue in

[141] Companies Act, 2008, §§ 31(3), 45(5); Olson, South Africa Moves to a Global Model of Corporate Governance but with Important National Variations, 226.

[142] On worker rights in the takeover context, see Pargendler, The Grip of Nationalism on Corporate Law, 543 and 551 (noting how workers' rights in the acquisition have emerged in France and the United Kingdom as a nationalistic response to foreign takeovers).

[143] Croucher and Miles, Corporate Governance and Employees in South Africa, 369.

[144] Loubser and Joubert, The Role of Trade Unions and Employees in South Africa's Business Rescue Proceedings, 39 (noting that labor had initiated only one case of business rescue by 2015). See also W. J. C. Swart, Business Rescue: Do Employees Have Better (Reasonable) Prospects of Success? Commentary on Employees of Solar Spectrum Trading 83 (Pty) Limited v AFGI Operations Limited (North Gauteng high court, Pretoria (unreported) 2012-05-16 Case no 6418/2011; 18624/2011; 66226/2011; 66226A/11) (2014) 35 *Obiter* 406–20, 410 (describing *Solar Spectrum* as a rare case of successful application for business rescue and the first case brought by employees).

[145] Reuters, South Africa Union Files Court Case to Force SAA Rescue, *Reuters*, November 21, 2019.

[146] *South African Airways (SOC) Limited v. National Union of Metalworkers of South Africa obo Members* 2020 JOL 47663 (LAC), 13 para. 29 (South Africa).

[147] Ibid, 17 para. 39.

South Africa by issuing a moratorium against retrenchments until the adoption of a business rescue plan that expressly addresses them.[148]

10.6 RACIAL INCLUSION AND DIVERSITY IN CORPORATE GOVERNANCE IN MALAYSIA AND SOUTH AFRICA

Racial and ethnic tensions have been particularly strong in shaping democracy and capitalism in the Global South.[149] Global South jurisdictions have also pioneered efforts at affirmative action in corporate governance as a means to ease ethnic tensions and redress historical economic inequities across racial lines. As noted by Howk-Aun Lee and Lumkile Mondi, "Malaysia and South Africa conduct two of the most extensive affirmative action programmes in the world and, perhaps most distinctively, the policy encompasses the corporate sphere."[150] This section examines Malaysia's pioneering policies to advance Bumiputera (Malay) ownership of corporations since the 1970s, as well as South Africa's focus on Black economic empowerment through corporate governance since the end of the apartheid regime.

10.6.1 *Malaysia*

Following independence, Malaysia's constitution of 1957 explicitly provided for the reservation of quotas for the Bumiputera (Malays or "*sons of soil*") in public service, education, and business permits.[151] At the time, Malays accounted for over half of the population but for only 2.4 percent of the country's corporate assets, compared to the 27.2 percent owned by the Chinese, who represented only 34.4 percent of the

148 Hogan Lovells Publications, COVID-19 – NUMSA v SAA – The Death Knell to Successful Business Rescue?, *Hogan Lovells*, May 11, 2020.

149 A. Chua, Markets, Democracy, and Ethnicity: Toward a New Paradigm for Law and Development (1998) 108 *Yale Law Journal* 1–107, 5 ("Entrenched ethnic divisions permeate most developing countries, and these divisions bear a distinctive and potentially subversive relationship to the project of marketization and democratization").

150 H. A. Lee and L. Mondi, Affirmative Action and Corporate Development in Malaysia and South Africa, in A. Nölke and C. May (eds.), *Handbook of the International Political Economy of the Corporation* (Northampton: Edward Elgar, 2018), pp. 229–42, p. 229.

151 Malaysia's Constitution of 1957, Art. 153 (article 153 (2) provides that "[n]otwithstanding anything in this Constitution, but subject to the provisions of Article 40 and of this Article, the Yang di-Pertuan Agong shall exercise his functions under this Constitution and federal law in such manner as may be necessary to safeguard the special position of the Malays and natives of any of the States of Sabah and Sarawak and to ensure the reservation for Malays and natives of any of the States of Sabah and Sarawak of such proportion as he may deem reasonable of positions in the public service (other than the public service of a State) and of scholarships, exhibitions and other similar educational or training privileges or special facilities given or accorded by the Federal Government and, when any permit or licence for the operation of any trade or business is required by federal law, then, subject to the provisions of that law and this Article, of such permits and licences").

population.[152] Growing ethnic tensions led to violent anti-Chinese riots in 1969 and to Malays' fear of being "swallowed" by the Chinese.[153] In response to these tensions and the perception of endemic economic discrimination, the government adopted an ambitious New Economic Policy (NEP) in 1971, which placed a strong focus on affirmative action policies.[154]

The NEP was based on two pillars: (i) "to reduce and eliminate poverty irrespective of race" and (ii) "to restructure Malay society so as to correct economic imbalance and eliminate the identification of race with economic function."[155] Geared toward the improvement of the Malays' vulnerable economic position, the NEP set a specific target of achieving 30 percent Bumiputera corporate ownership by 1990. Starting in 1976, companies seeking a listing on the local stock exchange had to allocate 30 percent of the issued shares to the Bumiputera, a requirement that was later reduced to 12.5 percent in 2009.[156] Other legal and regulatory strategies harnessed to increase Bumiputera ownership included the use of public investment vehicles for the benefit of Bumiputera, the requirement that companies operating in the old industry have both a majority Bumiputera ownership and Bumiputera representation on the board and other key positions, as well as the allocation of at least 30 percent ownership during privatizations.[157]

Although there are significant controversies surrounding measurement, existing estimates suggest that Bumiputera ownership reached 19 percent in the 1990s and peaked at 23.4 percent in 2011 before falling to 16.2 percent in 2015, when there was a corresponding increase of foreign ownership and the expense of both Bumiputera and non-Bumiputera ownership.[158] In 2015, the Eleventh Malaysia Plan expanded the scope of the 30 percent target by including a notion of "effective control,"

[152] Government of Malaysia, Mid-Term Review of the Second Malaysia Plan: 1971–1975 (1973) 23; K. S. Jomo, The New Economic Policy and Interethnic Relations in Malaysia (2004) United Nations Research Institute for Social Development, Identities, Conflict and Cohesion Programme Paper No. 7, 11.

[153] Chua, Markets, Democracy, and Ethnicity, 43.

[154] D. R. Snodgrass, Successful Economic Development in a Multi-ethnic Society: The Malaysian Case (1995) Harvard Institute for International Development Discussion Paper No. 503, 6–7.

[155] G. Hart, The New Economic Policy and Redistribution in Malaysia: A Model for Post-Apartheid South Africa? (1994) 23 *Transformation: Critical Perspectives on Southern Africa* 44–59, 48–49.

[156] A. H. Tajuddin, Do Share Allocations to the Indigenous Investor Drive the Demand for IPOs? (2023) 11 *Economies* 1–18, 3.

[157] See N. Z. Mohamad-Yusof, D. Wickramasinghe, and M. Zaman, Corporate Governance, Critical Junctures and Ethnic Politics: Ownership and Boards in Malaysia (2018) 55 *Critical Perspectives on Accounting* 33–52, 47; K. Paudyal, B. Saadouni, and R. J. Briston, Privatisation Initial Public Offerings in Malaysia: Initial Premium and Long-Term Performance (1998) 6 *Pacific-Basin Finance Journal* 427–51.

[158] C. Y. Whah and B. T. C. Guan, Malaysia's Protracted Affirmative Action Policy and the Evolution of the Bumiputera Commercial and Industrial Community (2017) 32 *SOJOURN: Journal of Social Issues in Southeast Asia* 336–73, 346 ("Bumiputera ownership of share capital in publicly listed companies increased to 19.3 per cent in 1990 and 21.9 per cent in 2008");

without, however, specifying its contours.[159] In 2019, Malaysia's "Shared Prosperity Vision 2030" decried the "crowding out" effect of rising foreign ownership, which "impedes Bumiputera ability to compete in equity ownership."[160]

The NEP also aimed to increase Malay presence in high corporate levels, though it did not impose specific legal requirements.[161] Board representation of Bumiputera increased significantly from their virtual absence at the time of independence to 11.74 percent in 1974 and 46.52 percent in 2010.[162] Initially, Bumiputera directors were not involved in management and their role was mostly symbolic.[163] Nonetheless, their presence was politically significant in securing corporate contracts and licenses from the state, and arguably helped reduce their marginalization.[164] The NEP officially ended in 1990 but policies to promote Bumiputera inclusion continued through other programs.[165]

The original and successor policies of affirmative action for the Bumiputera in Malaysian corporate governance have been, and remain, highly controversial. Critics regard these policies as an institutionalized form of racism against the Chinese[166] and as an instrument of crony capitalism.[167] Interestingly, Malaysia

Ministry of Economic Affairs, Shared Prosperity Vision 2030: Restructuring Malaysia's Development Priorities (2019) 4–36.

159 Government of Malaysia, Executive Summary Eleventh Malaysia Plan 2016–2020: Anchoring Growth on People (2015) 24. See also H. A. Lee, Malaysia's New Economic Policy and the 30% Bumiputera Equity Target: Time for a Revisit and a Reset (2021) 36 *ISESAS Perspective* 1–10, 8 (stating that "[t]he Eleventh Malaysia Plan added an emphasis to equity ownership, by specifying 30% equity ownership with effective control. What this means, though, is unclear").

160 Ministry of Economic Affairs, Shared Prosperity Vision 2030, 4–36. For a broader discussion of the persistent influence of nationalism on corporate law and governance across jurisdictions, see Pargendler, The Grip of Nationalism on Corporate Law.

161 N. Z. Mo. Yusof, Bumiputera Institution and the Development of Corporate Governance in Malaysia, PhD thesis, University of Manchester (2012), p. 135 ("The NEP did not explicitly specify the target for Malays representation on corporate boards. However, it was one of the policy's objectives to have more Malays involvement in top level management as a way to eliminate ethnic identification through profession or economic activities").

162 Mohamad-Yusof, Wickramasinghe, and Zaman, Corporate Governance, Critical Junctures and Ethnic Politics, 40.

163 Ibid., 43.

164 Ibid.

165 R. A. Aziz, New Economic Policy and the Malaysian Multiethnic Middle Class (2012) 13 *Asian Ethnicity* 29–46, 32.

166 See, e.g., J. Chin, Racism towards the Chinese Minority in Malaysia: Political Islam and Institutional Barriers (2022) 93 *The Political Quarterly* 451–59, 455 ("[t]he institutional racism imposed by the NEP reinforced the view that all non-Malays are members of the 'out group'"). See also The World Bank, Malaysia Economic Monitor: Brain Drain (2011) 13 (explaining that Bumiputera affirmative action may be one of the factors behind brain drain in the country: "Discontent with Malaysia's inclusiveness policies is a key factor too – particularly among the non-Bumiputeras who make up the bulk of the diaspora").

167 See, e.g., Z. A. Yusof and D. Bhattasali, Economic Growth and Development in Malaysia: Policy Making and Leadership (2008) Commission on Growth and Development Working Paper No. 27, 29 (describing charges that implementation of the NEP is responsible for cronyism and corruption in Malaysia today, and therefore it should be abandoned"). See also

achieved its "economic miracle" in the decades from 1970 to 1990 while simultaneously attaining most of its affirmative action goals.[168] One interpretation is that "the NEP may actually have boosted the growth rate when sociopolitical factors are taken into account."[169] In warning South Africa against the risks of state intervention of the economy, the World Bank came to describe Bumiputera policies in Malaysia as "a case of redistribution via market mechanisms," a view that unduly downplays the degree of state involvement in the program.[170] While Malaysia's efforts at ethnic inclusion in corporate governance failed to eradicate poverty and to eliminate Chinese economic dominance, they helped create a significant Malay middle class and negotiate racial tensions that thwarted the development of a market-based democracy.[171]

10.6.2 *South Africa*

South Africa has also played a leading role in promoting racial diversity in corporate governance. Despite sharing a common background of past slavery and longstanding racial inequities with South Africa, the United States has only recently and timidly begun to discuss policies for racial inclusion in corporate governance.[172] By contrast, since the end of apartheid in South Africa and the beginning of the new

L. Miles and M. R. Salim, Corporate Governance Reform in Malaysia: An Institutional Theoretical Approach (2010) 5 *Journal of Comparative Law* 314–30, 324 ("[i]t is not surprising that it has been remarked that 'Malaysia's unique policy of affirmative action launched to pull Bumiputeras out of widespread poverty has become cronyism by another name'").

168 See Snodgrass, Successful Economic Development in a Multi-ethnic Society.

169 Ibid. (abstract). See also J. K. Sundaram, K. B. Teik, and C. Y. Tan, Vision, Policy and Governance in Malaysia (1995) World Bank PSD Occasional Paper No. 10, 20 ("[s]ome critics maintained that NEP's restructuring retarded the country's growth, although it is virtually impossible to prove whether the high-growth 1970s would have seen even higher growth without NEP's interethnic distribution").

170 Hart, The New Economic Policy and Redistribution in Malaysia, 44 (noting that "[t]his neo-liberal interpretation neglects the heavy involvement of the Malaysian state in the economy, and the way in which relations between different capitalists and the state have shaped the outcomes of the New Economic Policy").

171 A. Chua, The Paradox of Free Market Democracy: Rethinking Development Policy (2000) 41 *Harvard International Law Journal* 287–380, 356.

172 For recent works on racial diversity and policies in US corporate governance, see, e.g., L. M. Fairfax, Racial Rhetoric or Reality? Cautious Optimism on the Link Between Corporate #BLM Speech and Behavior (2022) 118 *Columbia Business Law Review* 118–205 (finding that corporations' actions often followed antiracist rhetoric in the aftermath of the killing of George Floyd in 2020); C. Brummer and L. E. Strine Jr., Duty and Diversity (2022) 75 *Vanderbilt Law Review* 1–92 (arguing that corporate fiduciaries must comply with antidiscrimination laws and that the business judgment rule encourages them to go beyond the legal minimum to increase diversity, equity, and inclusion); S. Mishra, Russell 3000 Boards Becoming More Diverse, The Harvard Law School Forum on Corporate Governance, March 14, 2023 (finding that minority directors for the first time occupy more than 20 percent of board seats, with the presence of Black directors increasing more than 90 percent since 2023 to 8.3 percent, though only around 1 percent of CEOs are Black).

constitutional order, corporate ownership and governance have been at the forefront of the country's ambitions for social transformation.

In a 1990 speech after his release from prison, Nelson Mandela denounced the concentration and racialization of economic power in post apartheid South Africa, as illustrated by his statement that "less than ten conglomerates control almost 90 percent of the shares listed on the Johannesburg Stock Exchange," and that their directors would "almost exclusively be white males."[173] "If we are genuinely interested in ending the old social order and bringing in a new one, characterised by the notions of justice and equity," he contended, "it is quite obvious that the economic power relations represented by the reality of the excessive concentration of power in a few white hands have to change."[174] While conceding that international experience may counsel against tampering with the corporate power structure, Mandela pointed to the reality of South Africa, "with its own history, its own reality and its own imperatives" – one of which "is to end white domination in all its forms, to deracialize the exercise of economic power."[175] He also cautioned that "growth by itself will not ensure equity," noting "that any democratic government will have to respond to the justified popular concern about the grossly unequal distribution of economic power."[176]

In the 1994 Reconstruction and Development Programme of the African National Congress (ANC), a "central objective" was to "de-racialise business ownership completely through focused policies of black economic empowerment."[177] The incoming government perceived that continuing white economic power and racial inequality could create "social and racial tension" in the new regime at the risk of social and economic stability.[178] The first wave of Black Economic Empowerment (BEE) initiatives came from the private sector through sales of unissued stock to a Black person or Black-run company.[179] There were 231 such BEE deals by 1998, leading to Black businesses owning an estimated 10 percent of Johannesburg Stock Exchange companies.[180]

Beyond transformational objectives, some commentators have posited that BEE served as a "populist" policy of appeasement that allowed the government to rely on existing white businesses to generate growth while "maintaining legitimacy in the

[173] N. Mandela, Address by Nelson Mandela at Options for Building an Economic Future Conference convened by the Consultative Business Movement attended by South African business executives, May 23, 1990.

[174] Ibid.

[175] Ibid.

[176] Ibid.

[177] R. Tangri and R. Southall, The Politics of Black Economic Empowerment in South Africa (2008) 34 *Journal of Southern African Studies* 699–716, 699.

[178] Ibid., at 699–700.

[179] D. Acemoglu, S. Gelb, and J. A. Robinson, Black Economic Empowerment and Economic Performance in South Africa 5 (2007), unpublished working paper.

[180] Ibid., at 6.

eyes of trade unions and the impoverished masses."[181] Transfers from BEE initiatives were usually made to politically-connected Black individuals with strong ties to the ANC government but with little business experience.[182] Seeking to deflate pressure for unknown Black partners, companies sought politically influential Black partners who could push for policies to the benefit of capital and who had networking capabilities to support the business.[183]

Although government financing also played a role, this first generation of BEE transactions was mostly financed by vendor loans and secured by future earnings of the company, often at a significant discount over the market price.[184] This strategy led to the indebtedness of Black investors and was compromised by the Asian stock market crash in 1998, which contributed to a decline in the number of empowerment transactions.[185] In view of concerns that the first wave of BEE only led to a "small wealthy black elite," the government proposed a more expansive initiative of "broad-Based Black Economic Empowerment" (B-BBEE) in 2003.[186] B-BBEE's foundational policy document justified the program as promoting social stability in a society characterized by entrenched inequalities. It noted that, in the context of South Africa, redressing racial discrimination was not only a "socio-political and moral imperative," but also "an imperative dictated by the need for sustainable growth."[187]

Under the Broad-Based Black Economic Empowerment Act of 2003, the Minister of Trade and Industry would issue a code of good practice, creating indicators and qualification criteria for the purposes of procurement and other economic activities.[188] Unlike its predecessor, which focused on transfers of stock ownership, B-BBEE promoted a "balanced scorecard" combining different metrics relating to Black equity ownership, Black people in senior management, procurement from Black firms, skills development, and socio-economic development.[189] The final score relies on a point-system for compliance with measures of Black empowerment, such as 25.1 percent stock ownership, 60 percent participation in senior management, and 50 percent procurement, among various others. Thus, this system allows

[181] Tangri and Southall, The Politics of Black Economic Empowerment in South Africa, 700.
[182] Ibid., 701.
[183] Ibid., 710.
[184] Acemoglu et al., Black Economic Empowerment and Economic Performance in South Africa, 6.
[185] Department of Trade and Industry, South Africa's Economic Transformation: A Strategy for Broad-Based Black Economic Empowerment (2003) 10–11.
[186] Ibid., 18.
[187] Ibid., 4 ("Societies characterised by entrenched gender inequality or racially or ethnically defined wealth disparities are not likely to be socially and politically stable").
[188] Broad-Based Economic Empowerment Act of 2003 § 9(1)(b) (South Africa). The Act defines "black people" as "a generic term that means Africans, Coloureds and Indians." Section 1(a).
[189] Department of Trade and Industy, South Africa's Economic Transformation, 5, 25.

different dimensions of inclusion to be traded off against each other.[190] Compliance with the B-BBEE scorecard is not mandatory, but encouraged by various benefits in public procurement and licenses that trickle down the supply chain.[191] A 2013 amendment to the Act criminalized misrepresentations of a company's compliance status (known as "fronting") and established the B-BBEE Commission as a monitoring body.[192]

Racial inclusion in corporate governance in South Africa has come a long way since the Apartheid era, when legislation such as the Labour Relations Act (1956) prohibited Blacks from holding directorships and management positions.[193] By 2011, 27.6 percent of board members were Black non-executive directors, and 9.5 percent of executive directors were Black.[194] According to the 2020 report by the B-BBEE Commission based on data from reporting entities, 43.6 percent of directorships were occupied by Black persons (23.08 percent male and 20.55 percent female) and 53.67 percent were occupied by white persons and foreign nationals.[195] Black ownership of reporting companies was 29 percent in 2019.[196] Although this percentage disappointingly reflects "a low level of economic transformation at the board level,"[197] racial inclusion in South Africa is highly favorable when compared to Brazil, where a recent survey found no Black board members and only 1.05 percent Brown members despite majority representation in the population.[198]

190 Tangri and Southall, The Politics of Black Economic Empowerment in South Africa, 707 ("[t]o the chagrin of black business, there was the possibility of tradeoffs of one objective for another").

191 Ibid., 706 (despite pressures from Black businesses, "officials stressed that there would be no penalties for companies failing to achieve compliance with the scorecard other than when vying for government and parastatal contracts and licences, when they would be at a disadvantage"); A. Butler, Black Economic Empowerment since 1994: Diverse Hopes and Differentially Fulfilled Aspirations, in I. Shapiro and K. Tebeau (eds.), *After Apartheid: Reinventing South Africa?* (2011) pp. 52–70, p. 60 (noting that the codes "are binding on all state and public entities and are applied in all decisions involving procurement, licensing, concessions, public-private partnerships," to the effect that "[n]o private company can escape the codes ... because the requirements of the procurement component cascade down public sector supply chains").

192 See A. du Plessis, The Legal Combatting of B-BBEE Fronting Practices in South Africa: Past and Present (2022) 33 *Stellenbosch Law Review* 396–418, 396, 417 (finding that alternative measures of complaint resolution are more common and productive than criminal prosecution, which has been exceedingly rare).

193 N. Mans-Kemp and S. Viviers, Investigating Board Diversity in South Africa (2015) 8 *Journal of Economic and Financial Sciences* 392–414, 393.

194 Ibid., 396.

195 B-BBEE Commission, National Status and Trends on Broad-Based Black Economic Empowerment 56–57 (2020). However, the report notes that "only 42% of the listed entities complied with the mandatory reporting requirement." Ibid., 48.

196 D. Thomas, Is South African Transformation Dead?, *African Business*, September 1, 2020, 12.

197 B-BBEE Commission, National Status and Trends on Broad-Based Black Economic Empowerment, 56.

198 C. Portugal Gouvêa, Corporate Governance and Racial Diversity in Brazilian Public Companies, ECGI Blog, June 7, 2022.

The B-BBEE Act of 2003 also paid attention to intersectionality by listing as one of its key objectives "increasing the extent to which black *women* own and manage existing and new enterprises, and increasing their access to economic activities, infrastructure and skills training."[199] Moreover, the statute also specifically allowed the code of good practice to "distinguish between black men and black women."[200] The B-BBEE scorecard came to measure Black women empowerment separately, with five out of twenty-five points in the ownership section and five out of nineteen points in the management control section concerning the inclusion of Black women.[201] Interestingly, the B-BBEE Act of 2003 was enacted in the same year that Norway promulgated its pioneering legislation mandating gender quotas for corporate boards. Nevertheless, while Norway's model for increased diversity in corporate governance has been widely celebrated and influential, South Africa's groundbreaking effort to promote racial and gender diversity has been largely neglected by the international literature.

While B-BBEE policies remain controversial and contested,[202] there is a consensus that they have fallen short of expectations of deep social transformation, at least for the time being.[203] In 2007, a study by Daron Acemoglu, Stephen Gelb, and James Robinson concluded that B-BBEE policies benefited a small African elite and had no noticeable impact on inequality, though they increased the national income share accruing to Black people.[204] The authors contend that among the potential social benefits of such empowerment policies is the avoidance of destructive forms of populism that could otherwise gain ground in South Africa due to high inequality.[205]

There is little question that South Africa's empowerment measures are heterodox and avant-garde manifestations of policies for the democratization of capital more recently proposed in the Global North. In discussing Piketty's book *Capital and Ideology*, scholars have cited B-BBEE as evidence that "the well-intentioned, even radical policies that have been proposed by Piketty have been already proposed and implemented in South Africa."[206] While B-BBEE illustrates a sort of

[199] Broad-Based Economic Empowerment Act of 2003 § 2(d) (S. Afr.) (emphasis added).

[200] Ibid. at § 9(4).

[201] F. Marimbe, A Compulsory 100% Black Women Score on the B-BBEE Scorecard Is the Panacea to Women Empowerment Challenges, *Independent Online*, February 22, 2023.

[202] Butler, Black Economic Empowerment since 1994, 52.

[203] A. Cawe, M. Sachs, and I. Valodia, Dancing in Concert? – Aligning Broad-Based Black Economic Empowerment to (B-BBEE) Sector Strategies, Structural Transformation and Growth (2022) 109 *Transformation: Critical Perspectives on Southern Africa* 139–64, 140 ("much of the public's opinion of B-BBEE is a mix of derision, despondency and the 'too-little-too-late' argument").

[204] Acemoglu et al., Black Economic Empowerment and Economic Performance in South Africa, 17. The authors failed to find significant effects of BEE on firm investment, labor productivity or profitability, finding, if anything, "some weak evidence that BEE has a negative effect on investment and labor productivity." Ibid., 34.

[205] Ibid., 22.

[206] F. A. D. Pabón, et al., Piketty Comes to South Africa (2021) 72 *The British Journal of Sociology* 106–24, 114.

implementation *avant la lettre* of Piketty's proposal for "participatory" socialism initiatives, South Africa's experience shows "how difficult it has been for policies to have substantial impact in this inequality regime."[207]

Finally, South Africa's experience with Black economic empowerment illustrates how the international legal order can restrict heterodox stakeholderism in the Global South. Italian investors initiated investment arbitration against South Africa under a bilateral investment treaty in the *Foresti* case in 2010, claiming that the Mining Charter's requirement of a transfer of 26 percent of mining assets to historically disadvantaged South Africans constituted indirect expropriation and violated the obligation of fair and equitable treatment.[208] Although the case was settled before a final decision on the merits, the investor's challenge played a key role in South Africa's decision to terminate various bilateral investment treaties and adopt the Protection of Investment Act of 2015. The act provides for dispute resolution in domestic courts and aims to grant the government policy space to address "historical, social and economic inequalities" and "achieve the progressive realization of socio-economic rights."[209] Even in the absence of international investment remedies, the need to attract foreign investment also moderates the impulse for radical forms of heterodoxy. A far more extreme version of Black economic empowerment in Zimbabwe under Mugabe aimed to transfer 51 percent shareholdings of foreign-owned companies to Black Zimbabweans. However, the initiative faced challenges of enforcement and was ultimately toned down to attract investment.[210]

10.7 CONCLUSION

The study of corporate governance, including comparative corporate governance, has been plagued by a too narrow substantive focus on agency costs and a too narrow geographical focus on a handful of "usual suspects," mostly from the Global North. By expanding the scope of analysis to incorporate concerns about externalities and inequality in corporate law and experiences from Global South jurisdictions, a different picture emerges. Rather than merely providing blind or imperfect copies

207 Ibid.

208 Foresti v. Republic of South Africa ICSID Case No. ARB(AF)/07/01. For discussions, see M. A. Forere, The New South African Protection of Investment Act: Striking a Balance between Attraction of FDI and Redressing the Apartheid Legacies, in F. Morosini and M. R. S. Badin (eds.), *Reconceptualizing International Investment Law from the Global South* (Cambridge: Cambridge University Press, 2017), pp. 218–250; and M. F. Qumba, South Africa's Move away from International Investor–State Dispute: A Breakthrough or Bad Omen for Investment in the Developing World? (2019) 52 *De Jure Law Journal* 358–79, 360.

209 Forere, The New South African Protection of Investment Act, 252.

210 Tangri and Southall, The Politics of Black Economic Empowerment in South Africa, 701; BBC, Zimbabwe Deadline for Firms to be Black-Owned Passes, *BBC*, April 1, 2016; Reuters, Zimbabwe to Change Black Empowerment Law to Reassure Investors, *Reuters*, October 6, 2016.

of developed countries' institutions, Global South jurisdictions have pioneered various institutional innovations to protect stakeholders and curb inequality. Yet, because developing countries are understudied and mostly analyzed in isolation, if at all, these important patterns have been largely ignored.

Appreciating the different manifestations of heterodox stakeholderism in the Global South not only expands our institutional imagination, but also sheds light on the driving forces behind the evolution of corporate law. I suggest that problems of state capacity in fighting inequality and mitigating externalities through other areas of law create both political and functional pressure on corporate law to address broader welfare objectives. In environments of rampant inequality and significant social and environmental degradation, the view that corporate law should focus exclusively on shareholder wealth maximization tends to lose legitimacy, if not economic justification. These pressures, which have long been felt in the Global South, are now reaching the Global North, bringing about the surprising prospect of "reverse convergence" in comparative corporate governance – with institutions of the developed world coming to resemble their developing country counterparts.

Heterodox stakeholderism in the Global South also responds to the distributional consequences of corporate law rules beyond jurisdictional boundaries, which are significant but have been thus far neglected. Upholding the limited liability of parent companies for environmental harm caused in developing countries is not only questionable on efficiency grounds but also has perverse distributive implications in enriching wealthy Global North companies and their investors at the expense of poor Global South victims. The erosion of limited liability of parent companies in developing countries likely responds not only to failures of their regulatory state in preventing harm but also to the South–North distribution dynamics that limited liability entails.

The experience of developing countries reveals a broader array of institutional arrangements aimed at protecting stakeholders and reducing inequality. It shows that institutional change is possible, but that corporate law reform is no panacea for deep economic and social problems. While well-intentioned reforms are less transformational than hoped for, they are likely not as catastrophic as one might have feared. For good or for bad, heterodox stakeholderism also faces problems of enforcement. The jury is still out on which heterodoxies, if any, may be worth embracing in developing and developed country contexts. Yet the time has come to incorporate the Global South's experiences and innovations into the conversation.

BIBLIOGRAPHY

Acemoglu, D., Gelb, S., and Robinson, J. A., *Black Economic Empowerment and Economic Performance in South Africa* (2007), unpublished working paper.

Afsharipour, A., Lessons from India's Struggle with Corporate Purpose, in E. Pollman and R. Thompson (eds.), *Research Handbook on Corporate Purpose and Personhood* (Northampton: Edward Elgar, 2021), pp. 363–86.

Afsharipour, A., Redefining Corporate Purpose: An International Perspective (2017) 40 *Seattle University Law Review* 465–96.

Akey, P. and Appel, I., The Limits of Limited Liability: Evidence from Industrial Pollution (2021) 76 *The Journal of Finance* 5–55.

Armour, J. and Gordon, J. N.Systemic Harms and Shareholder Value (2014) 6 *Journal of Legal Analysis* 35–85.

Armour, J. et al., The Basic Governance Structure: The Interests of Shareholders as a Class, in R. Kraakman et al., *The Anatomy of Corporate Law: A Comparative and Functional Approach*, 3rd ed. (Oxford: Oxford University Press, 2017), pp. 49–78.

et al., Transactions with Creditors, in R. Kraakman et al., *The Anatomy of Corporate Law: A Comparative and Functional Approach*, 3rd ed. (Oxford: Oxford University Press, 2017), pp. 115–16

et al., What Is Corporate Law, in R. Kraakman et al., *The Anatomy of Corporate Law: A Comparative and Functional Approach*, 3rd ed. (Oxford: Oxford University Press, 2017), pp. 1–28.

Avi-Yonah, R. S., National Regulation of Multinational Enterprises: An Essay on Comity, Extraterritoriality, and Harmonization (2003) 42 *Columbia Journal of Transnational Law* 5–34.

Aziz, R. A., New Economic Policy and the Malaysian Multiethnic Middle Class (2012) 13 *Asian Ethnicity* 29–46.

Bainbridge, S. M. and Henderson, M. T., *Limited Liability: A Legal and Economic Analysis* (Northampton: Edward Elgar, 2016).

B-BBEE Commission, *National Status and Trends on Broad-Based Black Economic Empowerment* (South Africa: B-BBEE Commission, 2020).

BBC, Zimbabwe Deadline for Firms to be Black-Owned Passes, *BBC*, April 1, 2016.

Bebchuk, L. A. and Fried, J. M., The Uneasy Case for the Priority of Secured Claims in Bankruptcy (1996) 105 *Yale Law Journal* 857–934.

Bebchuk, L. A. and Spamann, H., Regulating Bankers' Pay (2010) 98 *Georgetown Law Journal* 247–88.

Berkowitz, D., Pistor, K., and Richard, J. F., The Transplant Effect (2003) 51 *American Journal of Comparative Law* 163–204.

Berle Jr., A. A., Corporate Powers as Powers in Trust (1931) 44 *Harvard Law Review* 1049–74.

Blumberg, P., *The Multinational Challenge to Corporation Law: The Search for a New Corporate Personality* (Oxford: Oxford University Press, 1993).

Bonilla Maldonado, D. (ed.), *Constitutionalism of the Global South: The Activist Tribunals of India, South Africa, and Colombia* (Cambridge: Cambridge University Press, 2013).

Legal Barbarians: Identity, Modern Comparative Law and the Global South (Cambridge: Cambridge University Press, 2021).

Brummer, C. and Strine Jr., L. E., Duty and Diversity (2022) 75 *Vanderbilt Law Review* 1–92.

Bruner, C. M., *The Corporation as Technology: Re-Calibrating Corporate Governance for a Sustainable Future* (Oxford: Oxford University Press, 2022).

Butler, A., Black Economic Empowerment since 1994: Diverse Hopes and Differentially Fulfilled Aspirations, in I. Shapiro and K. Tebeau (eds.), *After Apartheid: Reinventing South Africa?* (Charlottesville: University of Virginia Press, 2011) pp. 52–70.

Butler, N. M., *Politics and Economics* (New York: Press of the Chamber of Commerce, 1911).

Cahn, A. and Donald, D. C., *Comparative Company Law: Text and Cases on the Laws Governing Corporations in Germany, the UK and the USA* (Cambridge: Cambridge University Press, 2018).

Cassim, R. A Comparative Discussion of the Judicial Disqualification of Directors under the South African Companies Act (2021) 65 *Journal of African Law* 87–110.

Declaring Directors of State-Owned Entities Delinquent: Organisation Undoing Tax Abuse v Myeni (2021) 138 *South African Law Journal* 1–20.

Cawe, A., Sachs, M., and Valodia, I., Dancing in Concert?: Aligning Broad-Based Black Economic Empowerment to (B-BBEE) Sector Strategies, Structural Transformation and Growth (2022) 109 *Transformation: Critical Perspectives on Southern Africa* 139–64.

Cepeda-Espinosa, M. J., Judicial Activism in a Violent Context: The Origin, Role, and Impact of the Colombian Constitutional Court (2004) 3 *Washington University Global Studies Law Review* 529–700.

Cerezetti, S. C. N., Reorganization of Corporate Groups in Brazil: Substantive Consolidation and the Limited Liability Tale (2021) 30 *International Insolvency Review* 169–90.

Chin, J. Racism towards the Chinese Minority in Malaysia: Political Islam and Institutional Barriers (2022) 93 *The Political Quarterly* 451–59.

Chua, A., Markets, Democracy, and Ethnicity: Toward a New Paradigm for Law and Development (1998) 108 *Yale Law Journal* 1–107.

The Paradox of Free Market Democracy: Rethinking Development Policy (2000) 41 *Harvard International Law Journal* 287–380.

Chuene, R., Demarthe, Z., and Mokoena, S., Directors Beware! The Court Declares Dudu Myeni (Former SAA Chair) a Delinquent Director, *African Legal Information Institute*, July 3, 2020.

Cottrell, J., Indian Judicial Activism, the Company and the Worker: A Note on National Textile Workers' Union v. Ramakrishnan (1990) 39 *International & Comparative Law Quarterly* 433–51.

Croucher, R. and Miles, L., Corporate Governance and Employees in South Africa (2010) 10 *Journal of Corporate Law Studies* 367–89.

Dammann, J. and Eidenmueller, H., Corporate Law and the Democratic State (2022) 2022 *University of Illinois Law Review* 963–1020.

Dann, P., Riegner, M., and Bönnemann, M., The Southern Turn in Comparative Constitutional Law: An Introduction, in P. Dann, M. Riegner, and M. Bönnemann (eds.), *The Global South and Comparative Constitutional Law* (Oxford: Oxford University Press, 2020), pp. 1–38.

Davis, K. E. and Pargendler, M., Contract Law and Inequality (2022) 107 *Iowa Law Review* 1485–542.

Dearborn, M., Enterprise Liability: Reviewing and Revitalizing Liability for Corporate Groups (2009) 97 *California Law Review* 195–261.

Department of Trade and Industry, *South Africa's Economic Transformation: A Strategy for Broad-Based Black Economic Empowerment* (South Africa: Department of Trade and Industry, 2003).

Dharmapala, D. and Khanna, V., The Impact of Mandated Corporate Social Responsibility: Evidence from India's Companies Act of 2013 (2018) 56 *International Review of Law and Economics* 92–104.

Djankov, S., et al., The Law and Economics of Self-Dealing (2008) 88 *Journal of Financial Economics* 430–65.

Dodd Jr., E. M., For Whom Are Corporate Managers Trustees? (1932) 45 *Harvard Law Review* 1145–63.

Easterbrook, F. H. and Fischel, D. R., *The Economic Structure of Corporate Law* (Cambridge, MA: Harvard University Press, 1991).

Enriques, L. et al., The Basic Governance Structure: Minority Shareholders and Non-Shareholder Constituencies, in R. Kraakman et al., *The Anatomy of Corporate Law: A Comparative and Functional Approach*, 3rd ed. (Oxford: Oxford University Press, 2017), pp. 79–108.

Esquirol, J., The Failed Law of Latin America (2008) 56 *The American Journal of Comparative Law* 75–124

Esser, I. M. and Delport, P., The Protection of Stakeholders: The South African Social and Ethics Committee and the United Kingdom's Enlightened Shareholder Value Approach: Part 1 (2017) 50 *De Jure* 97–110.

The Protection of Stakeholders: The South African Social and Ethics Committee and the United Kingdom's Enlightened Shareholder Value Approach: Part 2 (2017) 50 *De Jure* 221–41.

Fairfax, L. M., Racial Rhetoric or Reality? Cautious Optimism on the Link between Corporate #BLM Speech and Behavior (2022) 118 *Columbia Business Law Review* 118–205.

Forere, M. A., The New South African Protection of Investment Act: Striking a Balance between Attraction of FDI and Redressing the Apartheid Legacies, in F. Morosini and M. R. S. Badin (eds.), *Reconceptualizing International Investment Law from the Global South* (Cambridge: Cambridge University Press, 2017), pp. 218–250.

Franco, G. H. B., *As Leis Secretas da Economia* (Rio de Janeiro: Zahar, 2012).

Franco, G. H. B. and Rosman, L. A. C., A Responsabilidade Ilimitada em Instituições Financeiras no Brasil: Antecedentes, Experiência e Considerações, in D. D. Carneiro and M. B. de Bolle (eds.), *A Reforma do Sistema Financeiro Americano: Nova Arquitetura Internacional e o Contexto Regulatório Brasileiro* (Rio de Janeiro: LTC, 2009), pp. 60–66.

Galanter, M., Legal Torpor: Why So Little Has Happened in India after the Bhopal Tragedy (1985) 20 *Texas International Law Journal* 273–94.

Gerner-Beuerle, C. and Schillig, M. A., *Comparative Company Law* (Oxford: Oxford University Press, 2019).

Gilson, R. J. and Milhaupt, C. J., Shifting Influence on Corporate Governance: Capital Market Completeness and Policy Channeling (2022) 12 *Harvard Business Law Review* 1–54.

Gordon, J. N., Systematic Stewardship (2022) 47 *Journal of Corporation Law* 627–74.

Gordon, M. W., Argentine Jurisprudence: The Parke Davis and Deltec Cases (1974) 6 *University of Miami Inter-American Law Review* 320–45.

Gouvêa, C. P., Corporate Governance and Racial Diversity in Brazilian Public Companies, *ECGI Blog*, June 7, 2022.

Hailbronner, M., Transformative Constitutionalism: Not Only in the Global South (2017) 65 *The American Journal of Comparative Law* 527–65.

Hansmann, H. and Kraakman, R., Toward Unlimited Shareholder Liability for Corporate Torts (1991) 100 *Yale Law Journal* 1879–934.

Hansmann, H. and Squire, R., External and Internal Asset Partitioning: Corporations and Their Subsidiaries, in J. N. Gordon and W. G. Ringe (eds.), *Oxford Handbook on Corporate Law and Governance* (Oxford: Oxford University Press, 2018), pp. 251–74.

Harper Ho, V., Beyond Regulation: A Comparative Look at State-Centric Corporate Social Responsibility and the Law in China (2013) 46 *Vanderbilt Journal of Transnational Law* 375–442.

Hart, G., The New Economic Policy and Redistribution in Malaysia: A Model for Post-Apartheid South Africa? (1994) 23 *Transformation: Critical Perspectives on Southern Africa* 44–59.

Hart, O. and Zingales, L., Companies Should Maximize Shareholder Welfare not Market Value (2017), European Corporate Governance Institute Working Paper No. 521.

Hirschl, R., *Comparative Matters. The Renaissance of Comparative Constitutional Law* (Oxford: Oxford University Press, 2014).

Hogan Lovells Publications, COVID-19 - NUMSA v SAA – The Death Knell to Successful Business Rescue?, Hogan Lovells, May 11, 2020.

Jasanoff, S., Bhopal's Trials of Knowledge and Ignorance (2008) 42 *New England Law Review* 679–92.

Jomo, K. S., The New Economic Policy and Interethnic Relations in Malaysia (2004) United Nations Research Institute for Social Development, Identities, Conflict and Cohesion Programme Paper No. 7.

Kovvali, A., Stakeholderism Silo Busting (2023) 90 *University of Chicago Law Review* 203–60.

Koya, N. and Roper, J., Legislated CSR in Practice: The Experience of India (2020) 22 *Journal of Public Affairs* 1–10.

Kraakman, R., et al., *The Anatomy of Corporate Law: A Comparative and Functional Approach*, 2nd ed. (Oxford: Oxford University Press, 2009).

et al., *The Anatomy of Corporate Law: A Comparative and Functional Approach*, 3rd ed. (Oxford: Oxford University Press, 2017).

Krichewsky, D., CSR Public Policies in India's Democracy: Ambiguities in the Political Regulation of Corporate Conduct (2017) 19 *Business and Politics* 510–47.

Lee, H. A., Malaysia's New Economic Policy and the 30% Bumiputera Equity Target: Time for a Revisit and a Reset (2021) 36 *ISESAS Perspective* 1–10.

Lee, H. A. and Mondi, L., Affirmative Action and Corporate Development in Malaysia and South Africa, in A. Nölke and C. May (eds.), *Handbook of the International Political Economy of the Corporation* (Northampton: Edward Elgar, 2018), pp. 229–42.

Leebron, D., Limited Liability, Tort Victims, and Creditors (1991) 91 *Columbia Law Review* 1565–650.

Lin, L. W., Mandatory Corporate Social Responsibility Legislation around the World: Emergent Varieties and National Experience (2021) 23 *University of Pennsylvania Journal of Business Law* 429–69.

Lin, L. W. and Milhaupt, C. J., We Are the (National) Champions: Understanding the Mechanisms of State Capitalism in China (2013) 65 *Stanford Law Review* 697–760.

Littenberg, M. R., India Substantially Revamps CSR Requirements: The Impact on Compliance at Indian Subsidiaries of US-Based Multinationals, *Ropes & Gray*, July 26, 2021.

Loubser, A. and Joubert, T., The Role of Trade Unions and Employees in South Africa's Business Rescue Proceedings (2015) 36 *Industrial Law Journal (Juta)* 21–39.

Macey, J. and O'Hara, M., Bank Corporate Governance: A Proposal for the Post-Crisis World (2016) 22 *Economic Policy Review* 85–105.

Macey, J. R. and Miller, G. P., Double Liability of Bank Shareholders: History and Implications (1992) 27 *Wake Forest Law Review* 31–62.

Mahy, P., The Evolution of Company Law in Indonesia: An Exploration of Legal Innovation and Stagnation (2013) 61 *The American Journal of Comparative Law* 377–432.

Mans-Kemp, N. and Viviers, S., Investigating Board Diversity in South Africa (2015) 8 *Journal of Economic and Financial Sciences* 392–414.

Marimbe, F., A Compulsory 100% Black Women Score on the B-BBEE Scorecard Is the Panacea to Women Empowerment Challenges, *Independent Online*, February 22, 2023.

Matheson, J. H., Why Courts Pierce: An Empirical Study of Piercing the Corporate Veil (2010) 7 *Berkeley Business Law Journal* 1–71.

McDonnell, B. H., Stakeholder Engagement (2022) 51 *Florida State University Law Review* 305–72.

Miles, L. and Salim, M. R., Corporate Governance Reform in Malaysia: An Institutional Theoretical Approach (2010) 5 *Journal of Comparative Law* 314–30.

Ministry of Economic Affairs, *Shared Prosperity Vision 2030: Restructuring Malaysia's Development Priorities* (Malaysia: Ministry of Economic Affairs, 2019).

Mishra, S., Russell 3000 Boards Becoming More Diverse, *The Harvard Law School Forum on Corporate Governance*, March 14, 2023.

Mohamad-Yusof, N. Z., Wickramasinghe, D., and Zaman, M., Corporate Governance, Critical Junctures and Ethnic Politics: Ownership and Boards in Malaysia (2018) 55 *Critical Perspectives on Accounting* 33–52.

Mongalo, T. H., The Social and Ethics Committee: Innovating Corporate Governance in South Africa, in B. Sjåfjell and C. M. Bruner (eds.), *Cambridge Handbook of Corporate Law, Corporate Governance and Sustainability* (Cambridge: Cambridge University Press, 2019), pp. 360–72.

Naidoo, P., South Africa Jobless Rate Drops to Third Highest in the World, *Bloomberg*, November 29, 2022.

Olson, J. F., South Africa Moves to a Global Model of Corporate Governance but with Important National Variations, in T. H. Mongalo (ed.), *Modern Company Law for a Competitive South African Economy* (Cape Town: Juta, 2010), pp. 219–47.

Oquendo, Á. R., *Latin American Law* (Santa Barbara: Foundation Press, 2006).

Pabón, F. A. D., et al., Piketty Comes to South Africa, (2021) 72 *The British Journal of Sociology* 106–24.

Palombo, D., The Future of the Corporation: The Avenues for Legal Change (2022) 10 *Journal of the British Academy* 43–86.

Pargendler, M., Comentários ao Art. 50 do Código Civil: A Desconsideração da Personalidade Jurídica, in J. Martins-Costa and G. C. M. Nitschke (eds.), *Direito Privado na Lei da Liberdade Econômica: Comentários* (Coimbra: Almedina, 2022), pp. 241–74.

Controlling Shareholders in the 21st Century: Complicating Corporate Governance beyond Agency Costs (2020) 45 *Journal of Corporation Law* 953–75.

Corporate Governance in Emerging Markets, in J. N. Gordon and W. G. Ringe (eds.), *Oxford Handbook on Corporate Law and Governance* (Oxford: Oxford University Press, 2018), pp. 735–55.

Corporate Law in the Global South: Heterodox Stakeholderism (2024) 47 *Seattle Law Review* 535–79.

The Grip of Nationalism on Corporate Law (2020) 95 *Indiana Law Journal* 533–90.

How Universal Is the Corporate Form? Reflections on the Dwindling of Corporate Attributes in Brazil (2019) 58 *Columbia Journal of Transnational Law* 1–57.

The Rise of International Corporate Law (2021) 98 *Washington University Law Review* 1765–820.

Paudyal, K., Saadouni, B., and Briston, R. J., Privatisation Initial Public Offerings in Malaysia: Initial Premium and Long-Term Performance (1998) 6 *Pacific-Basin Finance Journal* 427–51.

Pillay, R., *The Changing Nature of Corporate Social Responsibility, CSR and Development: The Case of Mauritius* (London: Routledge, 2015).

Pistor, K., Legal Ground Rules in Coordinated and Liberal Market Economies, in K. J. Hopt et al. (eds.), *Corporate Governance in Context: Corporations, States, and Markets in Europe, Japan, and the US* (Oxford: Oxford University Press, 2005), pp. 248–80.

Pistor, K., Limited Liability Is Causing Unlimited Harm, *Project Syndicate*, February 5, 2020.

The Code of Capital: How the Law Creates Wealth and Inequality (Princeton: Princeton University Press, 2021).

du Plessis, A., The Legal Combatting of B-BBEE Fronting Practices in South Africa: Past and Present (2022) 33 *Stellenbosch Law Review* 396–418.

Portugal Gouvêa, A. et al., *Código de Defesa do Consumidor: Comentado Pelos Autores do Anteprojeto*, 8th ed. (Rio de Janeiro: Forense Universitária, 2005).

Posner, R. A., The Rights of Creditors of Affiliated Corporations (1976) 43 *University of Chicago Law Review* 499–526.

Puchniak, D. W., No Need for Asia to be Woke: Contextualizing Anglo-American "Discovery" of Corporate Purpose (2022) 4 *Revue Européenne du Droit* 14–21.

Puchniak, D. W., Baum, H., and Ewin-Chow, M. (eds.), *The Derivative Action in Asia: A Comparative and Functional Approach* (Cambridge: Cambridge University Press, 2012).

Puchniak, D. W., Baum, H., and Nottage, L. (eds.), *Independent Directors in Asia: A Historical, Contextual and Comparative Approach* (Cambridge: Cambridge University Press, 2017).

Qumba, M. F., South Africa's Move away from International Investor–State Dispute: A Breakthrough or Bad Omen for Investment in the Developing World? (2019) 52 *De Jure Law Journal* 358–79.

Raghunathan, A., The Grand Trunk Road from Salomon to Mehta: Economic Development and Enterprise Liability in India (2012) 100 *Georgetown Law Journal* 571–604.

Rajagopalan, S., Bhopal Gas Tragedy: Paternalism and Filicide (2014) 5 *Journal of Indian Law and Society* 201–24.

Reuters, South Africa Union Files Court Case to Force SAA Rescue, *Reuters*, November 21, 2019.

Reuters, Zimbabwe to Change Black Empowerment Law to Reassure Investors, *Reuters*, October 6, 2016.

Reyes, F., *Latin American Company Law, A New Policy Agenda: Reshaping the Closely Held Entity Landscape II* (Durham: Carolina Academic Press, 2013).

Rodrik, D., Second-Best Institutions (2008) 98 *American Economic Review* 100–4.

What Do Trade Agreements Really Do? (2018) 32 *Journal of Economic Perspectives* 73–90.

Rosser, A. and Edwin, D., The Politics of Corporate Social Responsibility in Indonesia (2010) 23 *The Pacific Review* 1–22.

Salama, B. M., *O Fim da Responsabilidade Limitada no Brasil: História, Direito e Economia* (São Paulo: Malheiros, 2014).

Snodgrass, D. R., Successful Economic Development in a Multi-ethnic Society: The Malaysian Case (1995) Harvard Institute for International Development Discussion Paper No. 503.

Spamann, H. and Fisher, J., Corporate Purpose: Theoretical and Empirical Foundations/Confusions (2022) European Corporate Governance Institute Working Paper No. 664.

Spamann, H., Contemporary Legal Transplants: Legal Families and the Diffusion of (Corporate) Law (2009) 2009 *BYU Law Review* 1813–78.

Sthapit, A., Corporate Social Responsibility in Nepal: Beset with the Syndrome of "Who'll Bell the Cat?" as Philanthropic Views Dominate CSR Practices, in S. O. Idowu (ed.), *Current Global Practices of Corporate Social Responsibility* (Oxfordshire: Routledge, 2021), pp. 777–800.

Sundaram, J. K., Teik, K. B., and Tan, C. Y., Vision, Policy and Governance in Malaysia (1995) World Bank PSD Occasional Paper No. 10.

Swart, W. J. C., Business Rescue: Do Employees Have Better (Reasonable) Prospects of Success? Commentary on Employees of Solar Spectrum Trading 83 (Pty) Limited v AFGI Operations Limited (North Gauteng high court, Pretoria (unreported) 2012-05-16 Case no 6418/2011; 18624/2011; 66226/2011; 66226A/11) (2014) 35 *Obiter* 406–20.

Tajuddin, A. H., Do Share Allocations to the Indigenous Investor Drive the Demand for IPOs? (2023) 11 *Economies* 1–18.

Tangri, R. and Southall, R., The Politics of Black Economic Empowerment in South Africa (2008) 34 *Journal of Southern African Studies* 699–716.

The World Bank, Malaysia Economic Monitor: Brain Drain (2011) 13.

Thomas, D., Is South African Transformation Dead?, *African Business*, September 1, 2020.

Thompson, R. B., Piercing the Corporate Veil: An Empirical Study (1991) 76 *Cornell Law Review* 1036–74.

Van Dam, C., Breakthrough in Parent Company Liability: Three Shell Defeats, an End of an Era and New Paradigms (2021) 18 *European Company and Financial Law Review* 714–18.

Varottil, U., The Evolution of Corporate Law in Post-Colonial India: From Transplant to Autochthony (2016) 31 *American University International Law Review* 253–326.

Varottil, U., The Stakeholder Approach to Corporate Law: A Historical Perspective from India, in H. Wells (ed.), *Research Handbook on the History of Corporate and Company Law* (Northampton: Edward Elgar, 2018), pp. 381–400.

Ventoruzzo, M. et al., *Comparative Corporate Law* (St. Paul: West Academic Publishing, 2015).

Vieira, O. V., Baxi, U., and Viljoen, F. (eds.), *Transformative Constitutionalism: Comparing the Apex Courts of Brazil, India and South Africa* (Pretoria: Pretoria University Law Press, 2013).

Villamizar, F. R., The Organization of American States' Model Law on Simplified Corporations (2018) 11 *Journal of Civil Law Studies* 1–74.

Whah, C. Y. and Guan, B. T. C., Malaysia's Protracted Affirmative Action Policy and the Evolution of the Bumiputera Commercial and Industrial Community (2017) 32 *SOJOURN: Journal of Social Issues in Southeast Asia* 336–73.

Yusof, N. Z. Mo., Bumiputera Institution and the Development of Corporate Governance in Malaysia, PhD thesis, University of Manchester (2012).

Yusof, Z. A. and Bhattasali, D., Economic Growth and Development in Malaysia: Policy Making and Leadership (2008) Commission on Growth and Development Working Paper No. 27.

Zweigert, K. and Kötz, H., *Introduction to Comparative Law*, 3rd ed. (Oxford: Clarendon Press, 1998).

11

Global Legal Pluralism and the Rights of Nature

Daniel Bonilla Maldonado

11.1 INTRODUCTION

Nature is a subject of rights. The legal systems of countries as dissimilar as Ecuador, Bolivia, New Zealand, the United States, and Uganda have recognized this new legal subject and have granted nature rights such as the right to life, the functioning of its vital cycles, and the restoration of its processes.[1] Nature as a subject of rights therefore opposes the nature–object perspective that has historically been dominant in the West. The rights of nature challenge the notion of nature as an object that humans should describe, understand, and master; as an instrument that exists solely to satisfy human needs; and as property that humans can exploit without limit. The rights of nature thus challenge the objectification of nature, its absolute instrumentalization, and the anthropocentrism, and extractivism with which science, religion, economics, and law in the West have typically described, evaluated, and interacted with nature.[2] For the rights of nature, these ideas have not only had discursive consequences; they have also had practical consequences. These ideas are one of the main causes of the contemporary global environmental crisis. The rights of nature therefore emerge as a discursive and practical model that aims to rethink the

I would like to thank Ralf Michaels, Kevin Davis, and Mariana Pargendler for the many useful and insightful comments that they made to previous versions of this chapter. I would also like to thank Mihnea Tanasescu, Cletus Barié, Mari Margil, and Mara Tignino for their valuable comments. I presented earlier or longer versions of the chapter at the Max Planck Institute for Comparative and Private International Law, the Legal Heterodoxies Workshop organized by New York University and Universidad de Buenos Aires, the University of Brescia School of Law, the Max Planck Institute for Legal History and Legal Theory, and the International Academy of Comparative Law Ankara Roundtable on Environment, Climate Change and Constitutionalism. I would like to thank the students and professors that participated in these events. Their comments, questions, and critiques were very useful in strengthening the chapter.

1 M. Tanasescu, Rights of Nature, Legal Personality, and Indigenous Philosophies (2020) 9 *Transnational Environmental Law* 429–53.

2 M. Serres, *The Natural Contract* (Ann Arbor: Michigan University Press, 1995); and B. Latour, *Politics of Nature* (Cambridge, MA: Harvard University Press 2004).

concept of nature, as well as the relationship between nature and humans, so that we can effectively address the radical environmental degradation we are currently experiencing.[3]

The rights of nature are now a global discursive and practical pattern.[4] Between 2006, the year in which the rights of nature took precise legal form, and June 2021, we can find 409 initiatives related to the rights of nature around the world. Of these initiatives, 66.5 percent recognize the rights of nature as a whole, 17.8 percent of rivers or other aquatic ecosystems, and 10.5 percent of animals. Thirty-nine countries account for 90 percent of all initiatives.[5] However, the vast majority (80 percent) of the initiatives were submitted in the Americas, and 91 percent of the legal texts were written in English or Spanish. The biggest group among all initiatives (38 percent) is made up of local legal norms.[6]

We can divide this global discursive and practical pattern into three parts: on the one hand, the paradigmatic articulations of the discourse. The prototypical models of the rights of nature emerge from two countries in the Global South, Ecuador, and Bolivia, and from a peripheral country in the Global North, New Zealand. On the other hand, discursive and practical patterns that reproduce the conceptual structures of the prototypical discourses, although they may vary or complement them, such as the perspectives on the rights of nature that have been embraced by Argentina, Panama, India, Pakistan, and the international human rights system. Finally, the discourses and practices that have opposed the rights-of-nature discourse, including most European countries.[7]

3 R. Youatt, Personhood and the Rights of Nature: The New Subjects of Contemporary Earth Politics (2017) 11 *International Political Sociology* 39–54.

4 C. Kauffman and P. Martin, Constructing Rights of Nature Norms in the US, Ecuador, and New Zealand (2018) 18 *Global Environmental Politics* 43–62, 43–44.

5 A. Putzer et al., Putting the Rights of Nature on the Map. A Quantitative Analysis of Rights of Nature Initiatives across the World (2022) 18 *Journal of Maps* 89–96, 9093. Sixty-six percent of the initiatives offer a specific institutional design for the materialization of the rights of mother earth, while 33 percent of these initiatives are silent on the institutional structures that should be in charge of the realization of the rights that are recognized as belonging to nature. Ibid., 93.

6 Ibid., 91–93.

7 Most countries in Asia and Africa have been indifferent to the rights of nature. In the vast majority of the countries that make up these continents, rights of nature have not been an object of systematic and continuous public discussion and there have been no rights of nature initiatives introduced. Putzer et al. have produced the most complete quantitative analysis of rights of nature available yet. In map 2 of their article, they offer a powerful image of the regions and countries where rights of nature initiatives have been introduced. In gray are the countries and regions where no rights of nature initiatives have been introduced. Africa and Asia are almost all gray. See the map in Putzer et al., Putting the Rights of Nature on the Map, 92. Also see O. T. Wuraola, The Legal Rights of Natural Entities: African Approaches to the Recognition of Rights of Nature, in M. Addaney and A. O. Jegede (eds.), *Human Rights and the Environment under African Union Law* (London: Palgrave Macmillan, 2020), pp. 137–52. The case of South Africa is particularly notable in that some of its scholars and activists, such as Cormac Cullinan, have been very influential in articulating the foundations of the rights of nature, as well as promoting them internationally. However, South Africa has not legally recognized nature as a subject and there has been no proposal for such a thing to happen. See L. J. Kotzé, [Report on] South Africa (2022) *Asunción Conference of the International*

The discursive and practical pattern of rights of nature has been analyzed from a variety of academic perspectives. The rights of nature are an object of study that has firmly positioned itself in areas as diverse as constitutional law, environmental law, legal and political theory, and the social sciences. Constitutional law scholars have examined the contents of political charters that, like the Ecuadorian or Bolivian ones, recognize nature as a subject of rights or that recognize principles such as good living that intersect with this type of subject of rights.[8] Environmental law scholars have analyzed the tensions that exist between dominant environmental law and the rights of nature.[9] Legal or political theorists have been concerned with studying the conceptual architecture of these rights or their foundations.[10] Finally, social scientists are beginning to investigate the efficacy of the rights-of-nature discourse.[11]

This chapter aims to contribute to the understanding of the rights of nature from a different perspective: comparative law. More precisely, this chapter aims to contribute to the description, analysis, and comparison of the discursive patterns that convey and underpin the rights of nature. It also aims to analyze these discursive patterns from the perspective of global legal pluralism.[12] Rights of nature are a heterodox discourse that questions the conventional legal and political views on nature and its relationship with human beings, as well as the conventional views about key components of global legal pluralism. To meet these objectives, I divide this chapter into two parts. In the first part, I describe, analyze, and compare three types of discourse related to the rights of nature. Initially, I examine their prototypical models, that is, the models emerging in Bolivia, Ecuador, and New Zealand. Then, I study discourses on the rights of nature that reproduce the conceptual structures of the paradigmatic models, including those emerging in the international human rights system and the legal systems of Colombia and India. Finally, I explore discourses that resist the rights of nature, such as those emerging in the legal systems of much of Western Europe. Section 11.2 therefore divides discursive patterns related to the rights of nature into poietic, mimetic, and resistance patterns.

Academy of Comparative Law. Cullinan has written some well-known and discussed books on the rights of nature. See, for example, C. Cullinan, *Wild Law: A Manifesto for Earth Justice* (Chelsea: Green Books, 2011).

8 D. Bonilla Maldonado, El Constitucionalismo Radical Ambiental y la Diversidad Cultural en América Latina: Los Derechos de la Naturaleza y el Buen Vivir en Ecuador y Bolivia (2018) 42 *Revista Derecho del Estado* 3–23.

9 E. Gudynas, La Ecología Política del Giro Biocéntrico en la Nueva Constitución de Ecuador (2009) 32 *Revista de Estudios Sociales* 34–46.

10 M. Tanasescu, *Environment, Political Representation, and the Challenge of Rights: Speaking for Nature* (New York: Palgrave Macmillan, 2016).

11 M. V. Berros, Challenges for the Implementation of the Rights of Nature: Ecuador and Bolivia as the First Instances of an Expanding Movement (2021) 48 *Latin American Perspectives* 192–205; C. Kauffman and P. Martin, Can Rights of Nature Make Development More Sustainable? Why Some Ecuadorian Lawsuits Succeed and Others Fail (2017) 92 *World Development* 130–42.

12 R. Michaels, Global Legal Pluralism (2009) 5 *Annual Review of Law and Social Science* 243–62.

In Section 11.3, I analyze rights of nature from two perspectives that are central to contemporary comparative law: the political economy of legal knowledge and explanatory theories of legal change. These perspectives revolve around three questions that are of particular interest for a full understanding of rights of nature. The political economy of legal knowledge investigates the discursive and practical patterns that determine where legal knowledge is (and should be) created and who can (and should) create, use, and transfer it.[13] Explanatory theories of legal change account for the variables and processes that motivate transformations of legal orders.[14] Rights of nature offer a heterodox interpretation of these two perspectives; they question the conventional views about the production, exchange, and use of legal knowledge and about the variables that explain legal change. I therefore divide this second part of the chapter into two subsections.

In Section 11.3.1, I explore how rights of nature challenge the conventional interpretation of the political economy of legal knowledge. Rights of nature are culturally hybrid, as well as epistemologically, politically, and legally heterodox. Rights of nature, and their paradigmatic forms, have been articulated in countries that have historically been considered weak or marginal to the creation of original legal knowledge and that draw on knowledge, such as that of indigenous peoples, that has usually been marginalized from state lawmaking processes. Likewise, the contents of the rights of nature question some of the central premises of modern law's conventional interpretations, for example, who can be a subject of rights and what rights can be granted to nonhuman entities. In Section 11.3.2, I study how national legal systems have included rights of nature within their structures through a process of cross-fertilization that involves not only North–South processes of knowledge exchange, as the conventional view argues, but also heterodox processes of South–South and South–North exchange.

I base the theses offered in this chapter on twenty-two national reports and six special reports that were written for the 2022 Asunción Conference of the International Academy of Comparative Law.[15] The two types of reports are a

[13] D. Bonilla Maldonado, Economía Política del Conocimiento Jurídico (2015) 2 *Brazilian Journal of Empirical Legal Studies* 26–59; D. Bonilla Maldonado, The Political Economy of Legal Knowledge, in D. Bonilla Maldonado and C. Crawford (eds.), *Constitutionalism in the Americas* (Chatam: Elgar Publishing, 2018), pp. 29–78.

[14] A. Watson, Comparative Law and Legal Change (1978) 37 *Cambridge Law Journal* 313–36.

[15] The following are the reports written for the project by special and national reporters. Special reports: S. Grundmann, Globalisation and Legal Pluralism: Orders of Pluralism and Rights (2022) *Asunción Conference of the International Academy of Comparative Law*; M. Tignino, The Rights of Nature and the Rights to Nature: Emerging Trends in International Law (2022) *Asunción Conference of the International Academy of Comparative Law*; D. Hanschel and A. Mehlhorn, Rights of Nature: Reflections on Dialogues between Law and Anthropology (2022) *Asunción Conference of the International Academy of Comparative Law*; M. Margil, Birth of a Movement [NGOs in the United States] (2022) *Asunción Conference of the International Academy of Comparative Law*; Y. Vega Cárdenas and U. Mestokosho, Recognizing the Legal Personality of the Magpie River/Mutehekau Shipu in Canada (2022) *Asunción Conference of the International Academy of Comparative Law*; and M. Tanasescu, Theoretical Sources and Foundations of the Rights of Nature (2022) *Asunción Conference of the International Academy of Comparative Law*. National reports: Kotzé, [Report on] South

consequence of a set of questions that Ralf Michaels and I drafted in our capacity as general rapporteurs for the project. This set of questions touches on central dimensions of the discourse and practice of the rights of nature, for example, their contents, the institutions that recognized them, their foundations, their effectiveness, and their relationship with international law.[16] The national reports, as their name suggests, focus on the various aspects that make up the rights of nature in a particular legal system. The special reports, in contrast, focus on specific issues that we, as general rapporteurs for the project, consider key to a full understanding of the rights of nature, including their philosophical underpinnings and their tensions with international law. The theses that I offer in this chapter also draw on other primary and secondary sources to complement the empirical and theoretical information provided in the national and special reports. Finally, the theses I present in this

Africa; T. Sanni, Rights of Nature in Uganda (2022) *Asunción Conference of the International Academy of Comparative Law*; S. Roy, G. Gidrol-Mistral, and A. Popovici, The Rights of Nature in Quebec and Canada (2022) *Asunción Conference of the International Academy of Comparative Law*; C. G. Barié, Doce Años de Soledad de los Derechos de la Madre Tierra en Bolivia (2022) *Asunción Conference of the International Academy of Comparative Law*; A. C. Wolkmer and D. Ferrazzo, Los Derechos de la Naturaleza en Brasil (2022) *Asunción Conference of the International Academy of Comparative Law*; T. Luna Blanco and D. de la Torre Vargas, Grafiteando la Arquitectura Jurídica Colombiana: la Emergencia de Sujetos no Humanos y Derechos de la Naturaleza (2022) *Asunción Conference of the International Academy of Comparative Law*; G. Espinoza, La Naturaleza de los Derechos de la Naturaleza en el Ecuador (2022) *Asunción Conference of the International Academy of Comparative Law*; J. de Lisle, Rights of Nature, Globalization and Legal Pluralism: China (2022) *Asunción Conference of the International Academy of Comparative Law*; T. Thang Long and L. Minh Nhu, Sustainable Development and Distributive Equality: A Contribution from Vietnam (2022) *Asunción Conference of the International Academy of Comparative Law*; K. M. Abe, The Rights of Nature in Japan: Bringing the Alternative View to Fruition (2022) *Asunción Conference of the International Academy of Comparative Law*; M. S. Sunder Raj, Sowing the Seeds of Nature Rights in India (2022) *Asunción Conference of the International Academy of Comparative Law*; K. A. Rokas, [Report on] Cyprus (2022) *Asunción Conference of the International Academy of Comparative Law*; E. S. Ewering and T. Vetter, Rights of Nature in Germany: A Paradigm Change for The German Legal System (2022) *Asunción Conference of the International Academy of Comparative Law*; D. di Micco and M. Graziadei, Italian National Report (2022) *Asunción Conference of the International Academy of Comparative Law*; S. Koch, C. Vallejo Piedrahita, and E. Colombo Rights of Nature in the Norwegian Legal Culture: To Be or Not to Be (2022) *Asunción Conference of the International Academy of Comparative Law*; D. Botău, [Report on] Romania (2022) *Asunción Conference of the International Academy of Comparative Law*; L. Affolter and S. Affolter, Rights of Nature in Switzerland: Mapping the Scene (2022) *Asunción Conference of the International Academy of Comparative Law*; M. Attila, [Report on] Hungary (2022) *Asunción Conference of the International Academy of Comparative Law*; P. Paiement, Rights of Nature, Globalization and Legal Pluralism: The Netherlands Country Report (2022) *Asunción Conference of the International Academy of Comparative Law*; Y. Lind, Danish Report (2022) *Asunción Conference of the International Academy of Comparative Law*; and J. Harasta, Rights of Nature: Czech Report (2022) *Asunción Conference of the International Academy of Comparative Law*.

16 The questionnaire, more precisely, covers the following eight dimensions of rights of nature: existence and contents; legal and political operators; enforcement; theoretical sources and foundations; relationship between national legal systems; international law; efficacy; and consequences.

chapter are theoretically informed. The questions that guided the national and special reports, as well as the conceptual lenses that allowed for the interpretation of the empirical information they (and other sources) offer, fall within the following theoretical approaches: legal epistemology and epistemic justice; legal pluralism; and comparative law explanatory theories of legal change.

11.2 MAPPING THE GLOBAL LEGAL DISCOURSE ON RIGHTS OF NATURE

We can divide the global discourse on rights of nature into three types of patterns: poietic, mimetic, and resistance. Poietic patterns are those that provide the constitutive elements of the discourse, those that articulate the structural components of the global discourse on rights of nature.[17] These poietic patterns emerge in the legal systems of Ecuador, Bolivia, and New Zealand.[18] The rights of nature literature

[17] Poiesis comes from the Greek term ποιεῖν that means to create, to make.

[18] Espinoza, La Naturaleza de los Derechos de la Naturaleza en el Ecuador; Barié, Doce Años de Soledad de los Derechos de la Madre Tierra en Bolivia; and C. Iorns and J. Sylvester, New Zealand National Report (2022) *Asunción Conference of the International Academy of Comparative Law*. The Tamaqua Borough Ordinance No. 612 of 2006 (Pennsylvania, US) was the first legal norm that conceived nature as a subject of rights. This legal norm influenced the drafting of the Ecuadorian constitutional norms on the rights of nature. However, this ordinance did not become a central element of the prototypical discourses of the rights of nature. This norm has not proven as consequential as the recognition of these rights in the 2008 Ecuadorian Constitution, the 2010 and 2012 Bolivian Mother Earth laws, and the 2014 and 2017 New Zealand Te Ure Wera and Te Awa Tupua laws. The US ordinance is applicable only in the jurisdiction of this single town in the State of Pennsylvania, and as it has not been challenged before any court, its contents have not been clarified by judges; the authorities that administer the town have not refined it, either. C. M. Kauffman and P. L. Martin, *The Politics of Rights of Nature: Strategies for Building a More Sustainable Future* (Cambridge: MIT Press, 2021), chapter 3. Conceptually, as compared to the Ecuadorian, Bolivian, and New Zealand norms, this ordinance is more limited and less innovative: it only indicates that "natural communities and ecosystems" are the subjects of rights, affording these communities and ecosystems the civil rights to which all US citizens are entitled. According to its Section 7.6, "Borough residents, natural communities, and ecosystems shall be considered to be 'persons' for purposes of the enforcement of the civil rights of those residents, natural communities, and ecosystems". It does not grant nature any particular rights. The grounds on which it relies in establishing these new legal subjects, moreover, are anthropocentric arguments: the protection of the rights of the town's inhabitants and participatory democracy. Tamaqua Borough Ordinance No. 612 of 2006, Section 3: Findings and Purposes. Humans are the central concern of the ordinance: nature is protected for their welfare. The ordinance also emerges in a context where conflicts between municipalities, states, and the federal government over environmental issues are a constant. The ordinance is a manner of interpreting US federalism that empowers municipalities vis-à-vis the state and federal governments. This first rule has had multiple iterations in the United States. Currently, 155 localities have issued or discussed regulations affording rights to nature; their contents are remarkably similar since in most instances the Community Environmental Defense Fund (CELDF) advised on their drafting. Putzer et al., Putting the Rights of Nature on the Map, 91. Huneeus identifies fifty-six approved initiatives on rights of nature in the United States, see A. Huneeus, The Legal Struggle for Rights of Nature in the United States (2022) *Wisconsin Law Review* 133–62, 134. See also Tanasescu,

widely considers the models constructed in these three countries as prototypical.[19] Mimetic patterns are those that reproduce the structures of poietic patterns, although sometimes these are partially transformed or some new contingent components are added to them. Countries of the five continents have articulated mimetic patterns: in Africa, Uganda and Nigeria; in the Americas, Colombia, Panama, Argentina, and Canada, for example; in Asia, India, Bangladesh, and Pakistan; in Europe, Spain; and in Oceania, Australia.[20] Finally, patterns of resistance are those that oppose the recognition of the rights of nature. In Europe, for example, until 2022, no country had legally recognized rights of nature and some social, political, or academic sectors opposed them actively. The exceptional and recent recognition in Spain of the Mar Menor as a subject of rights confirms this rule.[21]

The poietic discourses on the rights of nature revolve around the following three components: subject, rights, and representation.[22] The prototypical discourses constructed in Ecuador, Bolivia, and New Zealand create a new legal subject, to whom

Environment, Political Representation, and the Challenge of Rights, p. 111, "What I want to point out here is that, from 2008 onward, US municipalities have passed strikingly similar ordinances, as a result of the central role of CELDF and the overarching representation of nature through rights, which carries its inherent elements through various cases."

19 See, on the one hand, the reports on these three countries: Espinoza, La Naturaleza de los Derechos de la Naturaleza en el Ecuador; Barié, Doce Años de Soledad de los Derechos de la Madre Tierra en Bolivia; and Iorns and Sylvester, New Zealand National Report. On the other hand, see the special report on globalization and legal pluralism and the reports from other parts of the world where the discourses on rights of nature articulated in Ecuador, Bolivia, or New Zealand are recognized as foundational or central in the global discourse on rights of nature; Grundmann, Globalisation and Legal Pluralism; Tignino, The Rights of Nature and the Rights to Nature; Hanschel and Mehlhorn, Rights of Nature; Margil, Birth of a Movement [NGOs in the United States]; Vega Cárdenas and Mestokosho, Recognizing the Legal Personality of the Magpie River/Mutehekau Shipu in Canada; Tanasescu, Theoretical Sources and Foundations of the Rights of Nature; di Micco and Graziadei, Italian National Report; Koch et al., Rights of Nature in the Norwegian Legal Culture; Affolter and Affolter, Rights of Nature in Switzerland; Paiement, Rights of Nature, Globalization and Legal Pluralism; Lind, Danish Report; Harasta, Rights of Nature; Roy et al., The Rights of Nature in Quebec and Canada; Luna Blanco and de la Torre Vargas, Grafiteando la Arquitectura Jurídica Colombiana. Finally, see Section 11.2.

20 See for example, Sanni, Rights of Nature in Uganda; Margil, Birth of a Movement [NGOs in the United States]; Luna Blanco and de la Torre Vargas, Grafiteando la Arquitectura Jurídica Colombiana; Congreso de la República de Panamá, Ley No. 287/2022; and on Argentina, F. Solanas, Proyecto de Ley Nacional S-2506/15-2015 (2015); F. Solanas, Proyecto de Ley Nacional S-0615/19-2019 (2019); F. Solanas, Proyecto de Ley Nacional 6118-D-2020 (2020).

21 Ley No 19/2022 para el Reconocimiento de Personalidad Jurídica a la Laguna del Mar Menor y su Cuenca.

22 In my interpretation, these three elements constitute the backbone of rights of nature's poietic patterns. It is important to note, though, that indigenous groups in Ecuador, Bolivia and New Zealand disagree on the contents of these elements. It is also important to note that some indigenous groups argue that these elements do not adequately reflect their traditional views on nature. Indigenous groups in these three countries do not have a monolithic descriptive or normative interpretation about rights of nature.

rights are recognized and whose representation is given to third parties, individuals, or institutions. Poietic patterns emerge with the following legal instruments: the Ecuadorian Constitution of 2008,[23] the Bolivian Mother Earth Laws 71 of 2010[24] and 300 of 2012,[25] and the New Zealand Te Urewera Act of 2014 and Te Awa Tupua Act of 2017.[26] In these legal norms a new subject is created: nature. In all three countries this new subject is structured around the following elements: nature is (i) a

[23] The key components of the rights of nature discourse in Ecuador appear in the Preamble and Article 71 of the 2008 Constitution, "Preamble: CELEBRATING nature, Pacha Mama, of which we are a part and which is vital to our existence ... Art. 71. – Nature or Pacha Mama, where life is reproduced and realized, has the right to full respect for its existence and the maintenance and regeneration of its vital cycles, structure, functions and evolutionary processes. Any person, community, people or nationality may demand from the public authority the fulfillment of the rights of nature. In order to apply and interpret these rights, the principles established in the Constitution shall be observed, as applicable. The State shall encourage natural and legal persons and collectives to protect nature, and shall promote respect for all the elements that make up an ecosystem." See also Articles 72, 73, and 74.

[24] According to Articles 1, 3 and 5 of Ley No 71/2010 del Estado Plurinacional de Bolivia, "Article 1. (OBJECT). The purpose of this Law is to recognize the rights of Mother Earth, as well as the obligations and duties of the Plurinational State and society to guarantee the respect of these rights ... Article 3. (MOTHER EARTH). Mother Earth is the dynamic living system formed by the indivisible community of all life systems and living beings, interrelated, interdependent and complementary, which share a common destiny. Mother Earth is considered sacred, from the cosmovisions of the indigenous native peasant nations and peoples ... Article 5. (LEGAL STATUS OF MOTHER EARTH). For the purposes of the protection and tutelage of its rights, Mother Earth adopts the character of a collective subject of public interest. Mother Earth and all its components, including human communities, are holders of all the inherent rights recognized in this Law. The application of the rights of Mother Earth shall take into account the specificities and particularities of its various components. The rights established in this Law do not limit the existence of other rights of Mother Earth."

[25] According to Articles 5, and 4, 1 (a) of the Ley No 300/2012 del Estado Plurinacional de Bolivia, "ARTICLE 5. – (DEFINITIONS). For the purposes of this Law, the following definitions shall apply: 1) MOTHER EARTH. It is the dynamic living system formed by the indivisible community of all life systems and living beings, interrelated, interdependent and complementary, which share a common destiny. Mother Earth is considered sacred; she nourishes and is the home that contains, sustains and reproduces all living beings, ecosystems, biodiversity, organic societies and individuals that compose her", and "ARTICLE 4. – (PRINCIPLES). 1) COMPATIBILITY AND COMPLEMENTARITY OF RIGHTS, OBLIGATIONS AND DUTIES. One right cannot materialize without the others or cannot be above the others, implying the interdependence and mutual support of the following rights: a) Rights of Mother Earth as a collective subject of public interest."

[26] According to the Te Awa Tupua (Whanganui River Claims Settlement) Act 2017: "Subpart 2- Te Awa Tupua. Te Awa Tupua and Tupua te Kawa. 12. Recognition. Te Awa Tupua Te Awa Tupua is an indivisible and living whole, comprising the Whanganui river from the mountains to the sea, incorporating all its physical and metaphysical aspects. 13. Tupua te Kawa Tupua te Kawa comprises the intrinsic values that represent the essence of Te Awa Tupua, namely Ko Te Kawa Tuatahi (a) Ko te Awa te mātāpuna o te ora: the River is the source of spiritual and physical sustenance: Te Awa Tupua is a spiritual and physical entity that supports and sustains both life and natural resources within the Whanganui River and the health and well-being of the iwi, hapū and other river communities. 14. Te Awa Tupua declared as a legal person (1) Te Awa Tupua is a legal person and has all the rights, powers, duties and responsibilities of a legal person."

juridically autonomous subject; (ii) culturally hybrid; (iii) sacred and eternal; and (iv) conceived as a space that is both inhabited and constituted by a set of interdependent organic and inorganic entities. In these countries, however, what is conceived as "nature" has some variations.[27] In Ecuador and Bolivia, the new subject is nature as a whole while in New Zealand the new subject is identified with what used to be a natural park, as well as with a river.[28]

The new legal subject has a life and interests of its own; it is a subject that is different from human beings, who also compose it, and a subject that acts according to its own dynamics and interests. This subject, moreover, is a rights-holder. In the case of Bolivia and Ecuador, nature is entitled to such rights as the right to life, to its vital cycles, and to have them reestablished in case they are disturbed.[29] In the case of New Zealand, parliament recognized Te Urewera and the Whanganui River as having the same rights as any other legal subject in the legal system.[30] This subject is also constructed from the intertwining of indigenous religious traditions (Andean and Māori) and modern Western legal traditions.[31] Indigenous peoples imagine nature as a mother, as the vital energy from which life emerges. Mother Nature has agency. Mother Nature has interests. Mother Nature is potentially responsible for her actions.[32] However, Pachamama and Papatūānuku intersect with the concepts "subject of rights" and "rights" that are central to Western legal modernity. Similarly, following the traditions of the Andean and Māori indigenous peoples, this new legal subject is imagined as a deity that escapes the finite time of humans.[33] The Ecuadorian constitution, the Bolivian Mother Earth laws, and the New Zealand Te Urewera and Te Awa Tupua laws recognize the religious dimension

[27] D. Bonilla Maldonado, Los Derechos de la Naturaleza: su Arquitectura Conceptual (2022) 4 *Naturaleza y Sociedad. Desafíos Medioambientales* 70–108.

[28] Constitución Política de la República de Ecuador 2008, Preamble and Articles 71, 72, 73, 74; Ley No 71/2010 del Estado Plurinacional de Bolivia, Articles 1, 3, 5; Ley No 300/2012 del Estado Plurinacional de Bolivia, Article 5; and Te Awa Tupua (Whanganui River Claims Settlement) Act 2017, Subpart 2, Articles, 12, 13, 14.

[29] Right to life: Ley No 71/2010 del Estado Plurinacional de Bolivia, Article 7; right to restore its cicles: Constitution Política de la República de Ecuador 2008, Articles 71 and 72; right not be contaminated and to equilibrium: Ley No 71/2010 del Estado Plurinacional de Bolivia, Article 7.

[30] Te Urewera Act 2014, Subpart 3, Article 11 (1) and Te Awa Tupua (Whanganui River Claims Settlement) Act 2017, Part 2, Subpart 2, numeral 14-1.

[31] This argument is explored in more detail in Section 11.3.1.1. It is important to consider the critiques offered against rights of nature on these issues, among others, they essentialize indigenous communities; they do not really represent the religious views of indigenous communities; they homogenize the very diverse cultures of indigenous peoples; and they can be used against indigenous groups' rights, for example, when rights of nature are used to restrict self-government rights. See, for example, Hanschel and Mehlhorn, Rights of Nature; and Tanasescu, *Environment, Political Representation, and the Challenge of Rights.*

[32] M. Tanasescu, *Understanding the Rights of Nature: A Critical Introduction* (Bielefeld: Transcript Verlag, 2022), pp. 62–69, 87–94.

[33] Bonilla Maldonado, Los Derechos de la Naturaleza: su Arquitectura Conceptual.

of Mother Earth for indigenous Andean and Māori peoples.[34] This sacralized subject is also understood as a space that forms an internally heterogeneous whole whose components are interdependent and interact continuously.[35] Nature is imagined as both a subject and a space that is inhabited by all the organic and inorganic entities that exist around the world. Humans, moreover, are not separate from, opposed to, or destined to dominate nature; humans are nature and do not occupy a privileged place in the ecosystemic whole. Humans, though, need the other elements that make up nature to survive and have a full life. Consequently, nature is not understood as a being that must be conserved, that cannot be exploited in any way. Humans can exploit the other elements that make up nature to satisfy their needs and desires. However, they cannot do so in a way that disrupts the ecosystemic balance or that ignores principles such as reciprocity and interdependence.

The nature-subject, however, cannot express its will by itself. It does not have a voice that humans can hear. Consequently, the poietic discursive patterns of the rights of nature create a system of representation for defending the interests and rights of nature.[36] In the case of Ecuador, any person can represent nature to defend its rights;[37] in Bolivia, the Defensoría de la Madre Tierra, in particular, and the State, in general, should represent nature and protect its rights;[38] in New Zealand, parliament created two legal persons to represent the interests and rights of Te Urewera and the Whanganui River.[39] Humans (or their institutions), thus, have a duty to interpret and protect nature. The rights of nature and their representatives, however, are in tension with other rights that are also part of the legal systems in which they are located, for example, the right to a healthy environment, the right to equality, and the right to sustainable development. These rights protect nature by appealing to an anthropocentric perspective (nature is defended to safeguard the interests of human beings) or conceive nature as a resource that should be exploited to generate wealth that can be redistributed in the political community. Hence, Bolivia and Ecuador are currently described as neo-extractivist countries or countries committed to "social extractivism."[40] Similarly, in New Zealand there are questions about how to balance rights of nature and environmental laws, such as,

[34] Constitución Política de la República de Ecuador 2008, Preamble and Articles 71, 72, 73, 74; Ley 71/2012 del Estado Plurinacional de Bolivia, Articles 1, 3, 5; Ley No 300/2012 del Estado Plurinacional de Bolivia, Article 5; and Te Awa Tupua (Whanganui River Claims Settlement) Act 2017, Subpart 2 and Articles, 12, 13, 14.

[35] Ibid.

[36] Tanasescu, Theoretical Sources and Foundations of the Rights of Nature.

[37] Constitución Política de la República de Ecuador 2008, Preamble.

[38] Ley No 71/2012 del Estado Plurinacional de Bolivia, Article 10.

[39] Te Urewera Act 2014, Part 2 and Te Awa Tupua (Whanganui River Claims Settlement) Act 2017, Subpart 3.

[40] Espinoza, La Naturaleza de los Derechos de la Naturaleza en el Ecuador; Barié, Doce Años de Soledad de los Derechos de la Madre Tierra en Bolivia.

the Resource Management Act of 1991, the statute "that establishes New Zealand's legislative framework for decision-making and planning of the use of the environment."[41]

The mimetic discourses that have emerged across the globe reproduce the poietic discourses of the rights of nature. The former iterate the structure of subject, rights, and representation that constitute the spine of the latter.[42] This is the case of the rights of nature discourses articulated in countries such as Colombia, Canada, India, Spain, and Uganda. In these mimetic discourses, nature is recognized as a rights-holder subject that must be represented by particular persons or institutions. However, some of these discursive patterns partially transform or complement the prototypical nature-subject discourses. Three of these modifications are particularly relevant for understanding the global discourse on the rights of nature. On the one hand, we can note a process of secularization of the foundations of the nature-subject or a variation in its religious foundations. In countries such as Colombia, Panama, Spain, and the United States, the legal recognition of the nature-subject does not appeal to religion, although in these countries legal and political operators accept that the prototypical discourses have as their source the religious traditions of some indigenous peoples.[43] Nature, in mimetic discourses, remains sacred. However, the sacredness of nature is reinterpreted as the exceptional respect it deserves given its inherent value and, therefore, as the duty of human beings not to harm it. Thus, for example, the Colombian Constitutional Court, in the Atrato River opinion, based the declaration that this river is a subject of rights on what it called biocultural rights, through which the Court connects nature with cultural minorities.[44] The Court does not explicitly allude to the cultures of indigenous peoples to support its decision to recognize rights to the river. In the case of India, the recognition of the Ganges River or some glaciers as subjects of rights was based on Hinduism. The High Court of Uttarkaband appealed to sacred writings of the majority religion in India to support the idea of the nature-subject.[45]

41 Iorns and Sylvester, New Zealand National Report.

42 See, for example, Vega Cárdenas and Mestokosho, Recognizing the Legal Personality of the Magpie River/Mutehekau Shipu in Canada; Roy et al., The Rights of Nature in Quebec and Canada; Sanni, Rights of Nature in Uganda; Luna Blanco and de la Torre Vargas, Grafiteando la Arquitectura Jurídica Colombiana; Sunder Raj, Sowing the Seeds of Nature Rights in India; and Ley No 19/2022 para el Reconocimiento de Personalidad Jurídica a la Laguna del Mar Menor y su Cuenca.

43 Margil, Birth of a Movement [NGOs in the United States]; Luna Blanco and de la Torre Vargas, Grafiteando la Arquitectura Jurídica Colombiana; Congreso de la República de Panamá, Ley No 287/2022; and Ley No 19/2022 para el Reconocimiento de Personalidad Jurídica a la Laguna del Mar Menor y su Cuenca.

44 Corte Constitucional de Colombia, *Sentencia T-622* de 2016; Luna Blanco and de la Torre Vargas, Grafiteando la Arquitectura Jurídica Colombiana.

45 Sunder Raj, Sowing the Seeds of Nature Rights in India; *Salim v. State of Uttarakhand*, Writ Petition (PIL) No. 126 of 2014 (December 5, 2016 and March 20, 2017); and see Section 11.3.2.

On the other hand, some mimetic discourses consider that the protection of nature can (and should) be achieved by using both rights of nature and environmental law.[46] Although conceptually these two types of discourses are incompatible, the former is based on an ecocentric perspective while the latter is based on an anthropocentric point of view, in political and legal practice, the argument goes, they can (and should) be used at the same time to address the serious environmental problems that human beings face today. The clearest example of this strategy for the protection of nature is the argumentation offered by the Colombian Constitutional Court in the Atrato River ruling.[47] In this judgment, the Court recognizes the river as a subject of rights and creates the institution of the "river guardians" to protect it, following the structures of the prototypical discursive pattern. However, at the same time, the Court uses national and international environmental law for the defense of the new subject of rights.[48] The Court considers that nature can (and should) be protected for the inherent value it holds, but also for the instrumental value it has for human beings. We can also find this same argument in some interpretations of the international human rights system.[49]

Finally, the mimetic discourse that emerges in international law is beginning to vary the transfer and reinterpretation processes of poietic discourses. In the prototypical discourses' moments of emergence and consolidation, these discourses traveled between national legal systems or moved from national legal systems to international law.[50] Today, however, the international law discourse promoting the rights of nature is beginning to develop a top-down diffusion process, from international law to national law.[51] This new process adds a new layer of legitimacy to the legal discourse on the rights of nature (benefiting from the legitimacy that international law enjoys in many countries), helps to entrench it as a global discourse, and contributes to weakening the objections that resistance discourses have raised against the idea of the nature-subject.

To end, resistance discourses are those that explicitly or implicitly oppose rights of nature in the legal systems in which they circulate. This does not mean, of course, that in the legal systems where resistance discourses emerge or move there are no rights of nature or there are no movements promoting or examining rights of nature. In Europe, for example, academia and social organizations have extensively

46 Luna Blanco and de la Torre Vargas, Grafiteando la Arquitectura Jurídica Colombiana; Tignino, The Rights of Nature and the Rights to Nature.

47 Corte Constitucional de Colombia, *Sentencia T-622*.

48 Tignino, The Rights of Nature and the Rights to Nature.

49 Ibid.

50 See, D. Bonilla Maldonado, Rights of Nature and Global Legal Pluralism, Max Planck Institute for Comparative and International Private Law Research Paper Series No. 23/15, 2023. In particular, see the section "External Legal Pluralism and Rights of Nature". This is a longer version of this chapter.

51 di Micco and Graziadei, Italian National Report; and Affolter and Affolter, Rights of Nature in Switzerland.

discussed or promoted rights of nature.[52] Resistance discourses oppose rights of nature for the following reasons. First, these discourses consider that the nature-subject is premised on the re-enchantment of the world – a retreat from the processes of rationalization, secularization, and scientization of the natural world that shape the modern project. This perspective identifies rights of nature with an animism that intersects with some religious perspectives rightly displaced by modernity. Second, the rights of nature call into question central elements of the grammar of modern law. Recognizing nature as a subject controverts the idea that, as a general rule, only those individuals who have agency, who are autonomous, rational, and therefore responsible, can be considered subjects of rights. For the discursive resistance patterns, the rights of nature do not fit into the modern legal machinery that allows its legal systems to function efficiently.[53]

Third, modern legal systems already have the necessary tools to confront the environmental problems that are currently degrading ecosystems all over the world. National and international environmental laws are powerful instruments to confront the environmental degradation that characterizes the Anthropocene. The challenge lies in the application of existing environmental legal frameworks, not in the creation of new frameworks that contradict environmental law's premises and conclusions.[54] Fourth, the rights of nature go against the dominant geopolitics of legal knowledge. The premises from which this geopolitics start indicate that European culture is the source of the central legal families in the history of law, civil law, and common law. Non-European legal systems, with a few exceptions such as the United States, are merely minor iterations of European legal systems. The implicit premise of some of the resistance discourses is then that the Global South would have nothing to teach the Global North on legal matters.[55] Fifth, and last, rights of nature are an obstacle for development and redistribution policies. They are a tool for unjustly limiting the exploitation of natural resources that are

[52] See, for example, Ewering and Vetter, Rights of Nature in Germany; di Micco and Graziadei, Italian National Reporte; Koch et al., Rights of Nature in the Norwegian Legal Culture; Affolter and Affolter, Rights of Nature in Switzerland; Attila, [Report on] Hungary; Paiement, Rights of Nature, Globalization and Legal Pluralism; Lind, Danish Report; and Harasta, Rights of Nature. Two recent cases are also useful to show how civil society in Europe is mobilizing for the recognition of rights of nature. First, the case of the Tavignano River in Corsica (É. Arrighi, The Fight for Corsica's "Living" River, *Le Monde*, July 25, 2022) and second, the case of the Rhone river in Switzerland and France (Rédaction Lyon, La Métropole et la Ville de Lyon Veulent que le Fleuve Rhône ait Une Personnalité Juridique, *Actu*, September 9, 2021); and Association Id Eau, Activités, 2023.

[53] See Section 11.2; di Micco and Graziadei, Italian National Report; and Koch et al., Rights of Nature in the Norwegian Legal Culture.

[54] Affolter and Affolter, Rights of Nature in Switzerland; Attila, [Report on] Hungary; Paiement, Rights of Nature, Globalization and Legal Pluralism; Lind, Danish Report; and Harasta, Rights of Nature.

[55] Bonilla Maldonado, The Political Economy of Legal Knowledge; D. Bonilla Maldonado, Introduction, in D. Bonilla Maldonado, *Constitutionalism of the Global South* (Cambridge: Cambridge University Press 2013), pp. 1–39.

central for economic growth, a key component of development. Rights of nature, furthermore, would eliminate or radically limit extractive activities that are the sources of needed jobs and tax revenues that are necessary for funding state's social programs.[56]

11.3 GLOBAL LEGAL PLURALISM

The global discourse on rights of nature has emerged, diffused, and transformed itself through processes connected to global legal pluralism.[57] In this section, I will examine the rights-of-nature discourse from the following two points of view: the political economy of legal knowledge and cross-fertilization.[58] The analysis presented revolves around the prototypical models of rights of nature. However, where relevant, I will also include mimetic discourses on the rights of nature in my analysis.

11.3.1 *The Political Economy of Legal Knowledge and the Rights of Nature*

Rights of nature challenge the dominant political economy of legal knowledge in that they are (i) culturally hybrid; (ii) epistemologically subversive; and (iii) politically and legally emancipatory.

11.3.1.1 The Rights of Nature and Cultural Hybridity

The paradigmatic models of the rights of nature, the Bolivian, Ecuadorian, and New Zealand models, challenge the political economy of legal knowledge in that they are culturally hybrid.[59] These models combine the vocabulary and grammar of modern law with the religions of indigenous Andean and Māori peoples. The prototypical models of the rights of nature simultaneously "are" and "are not": they are modern law and they are indigenous law. The syncretism of these models calls into question the following central ideas of the dominant political economy of legal knowledge:[60] (i) there are rich cultures that can create legal knowledge and poor cultures that

56 See, for example, Koch et al., Rights of Nature in the Norwegian Legal Culture; and Barié, Doce Años de Soledad de los Derechos de la Madre Tierra en Bolivia.

57 K. von Benda-Beckmann and B. Turner, Legal Pluralism, Social Theory, and the State (2018) 50 *The Journal of Legal Pluralism and Unofficial Law* 255–74.

58 In a longer piece, I also examine a third dimension related to the intersections between rights of nature and global legal pluralism: external legal pluralism. More precisely, I explore the interactions between national legal systems that recognize rights of nature and international law.

59 D. Bonilla Maldonado, *Legal Barbarians: Identity, Modern Comparative Law and the Global South* (Cambridge: Cambridge University Press, 2021), pp. 158–67.

60 Bonilla Maldonado, The Political Economy of Legal Knowledge; Bonilla Maldonado, Introduction.

cannot; (ii) the Global North has rich cultures that enable the production of law while the Global South has weak cultures that do not enable the production of real law, only morality or politics; (iii) within the Global North there are some cultures that are the origin of Western law (e.g., French, British, and German) and other cultures that, for historical reasons (imperialism and settlement colonization, for example), simply reproduce those cultural and legal matrices (e.g. Australia and New Zealand); (iv) Global North law is the only (or the most powerful) legal standard and can be transferred globally; (v) Global South countries must transplant this single global legal standard to their jurisdictions if they want to construct true law; and (vi) when the Global North law that is reproduced in the lesser cultures of the Global North or transplanted to the Global South mixes with local culture, it becomes contaminated. The purity of true law is tainted; it loses clarity and precision; and it becomes a culturally-illegitimate offspring that is conceptually and practically ineffective.[61]

The paradigmatic models of the rights of nature conceive of nature as an autonomous legal subject that has a set of rights.[62] This new legal subject thus draws conceptually on the grammar and vocabulary of modern law. Categories such as "rights," "subject of rights," "agency," "autonomy," and "interests" are central to the construction of the nature-subject. These categories, moreover, are put into action following the principles and rules that regulate their uses, for example, only subjects with agency or self-interest can be rights-holders. At the same time, however, the paradigmatic models of the rights of nature distance themselves from the grammar and vocabulary of modern law. These models, drawing on indigenous (Andean or Māori) religious, political, and legal traditions, anthropomorphize, sacralize, and interpret nature as a biocentric and ecosystemic conceptual space.[63]

The subject of rights that prototypical models of the rights of nature create, furthermore, must be interpreted in light of other legal principles and rules that are influenced by or recognize indigenous cultural traditions in order to be properly understood and applied. This set of rights and principles puts modern law (or its dominant interpretations) even more strongly into question. In the Ecuadorian and Bolivian cases, the principles of plurinationality, interculturality, and good living.[64] The first recognizes that each of these states is constituted not by a single culturally-

[61] Bonilla Maldonado, *Legal Barbarians: Identity, Modern Comparative Law and the Global South*, chapters 2, 3, and 4.

[62] Constitución Política de la República de Ecuador 2008, Preamble, Articles 71, 72, 73, 74; Ley No 71/2012 del Estado Plurinacional de Bolivia, Articles 1, 3, 5; Ley No 300/2012 del Estado Plurinacional de Bolivia, Article 5; and Te Awa Tupua (Whanganui River Claims Settlement) Act 2017, Subpart 2, Articles, 12, 13, 14.

[63] Bonilla Maldonado, Los Derechos de la Naturaleza: su Arquitectura Conceptual.

[64] Constitución Política de la República de Ecuador 2008, Title I, chapter 1, Article 1; Constitución Política del Estado Plurinacional de Bolivia, Title I, chapter 1, Article 1. Also, see R. L. Fernández, El Sumak Kawsay y sus Restricciones Constitucionales (2009) 12 *Revista de Derecho UASB* 113–25.

homogeneous nation, as the classical nation-state model advocates, but by several nations that have cultural and legal traditions different from those upheld by state law and the dominant white/mestizo culture. The second principle prescribes that the basic structure of the state must be built through the continuous dialogue of all its constituent cultures. The cultures that constitute each state should not be understood as closed and isolated systems that repel or only occasionally interact with each other. The third principle is filled with content through the principles of relationality, interdependence, reciprocity, and balance among human beings, and between them and the other components of nature.[65]

In the New Zealand case, the rights of the Whanganui River intersect with four values that the Crown–Māori agreement on the Whanganui River Basin and the Te Awa Tupua Act that ratifies it recognize explicitly (the values that intersect the forest upon which rights are conferred in the Te Urewera Act are analogous):[66] (i) *Ko te Awa te mātāpuna o te ora* (The river is a source of physical and spiritual sustenance). This first value prescribes that Te Awa Tupua (the Whanganui River basin) is a physical and spiritual entity that ensures the sustenance of all natural resources and peoples inhabiting its banks; (ii) *E rere kau mai te Awa nui mai te Kahui Maunga ki Tangaroa* (The great River flows from the mountains to the sea). This second value states that the Whanganui River basin is a living, indivisible whole from its source to its mouth; (iii) *Ko au te Awa, ko te Awa ko au* (I am the river and the river is me). This third value affirms that the Māori people are interconnected and at the same time responsible for the Whanganui River basin; and (iv) *Ngā manga iti, ngā manga nui e honohono kau ana, ka tupu hei Awa Tupua* (The large and small streams that intersect and form a river). The latter value provides that the Whanganui River basin is a whole made up of many elements that aim to maintain and promote its wellbeing.

The rights of nature, in short, are a hybrid legal product that breaks with central rules and principles of the dominant political economy of legal knowledge. Rights of nature, first, demonstrate the cultural diversity that exists in contemporary states. The rights of nature make explicit that cultural homogeneity within states is not a descriptive but a normative argument that generally leads to the marginalization of

[65] C. Silva Portero, ¿Qué es el Buen Vivir en la Constitución?, in R. Ávila (ed.), *La Constitución del 2008 en el contexto andino. Análisis desde la Doctrina y el Derecho Comparado* (Quito: Ministerio de Justicia y Derechos Humanos, 2008), pp. 112–19; J. Estermann, *Filosofía Andina. Estudio Intercultural de la Sabiduría Autóctona Andina* (Quito: Abya–Yala, 1989).

[66] Te Awa Tupua (Whanganui River Claims Settlement) Act 2017, Subpart 2, Article 13. Also see M. Boyes, Re-Envisioning Nature from a New Zealand Māori Perspective, in European Institute for Outdoor Adventure Education and Experiential Learning Conference (ed.), *Encountering, Experiencing and Exploring Nature in Education: Collection of Conference Papers* (Ljubljana: European Institute for Outdoor Adventure Education and Experiential Learning, 2010), pp. 94–99; and C. J. Iorns Magallanes, Māori Cultural Rights in Aotearoa New Zealand: Protecting the Cosmology that Protects the Environment (2015) 21 *Widener Law Review* 273–328.

minority cultures.[67] Second, it makes clear the richness of non-Western cultures and their capacity to create valuable legal knowledge.[68] Third, it shows that this legal knowledge can be useful to other cultural communities and, therefore, that it can be exportable or used productively within the states in which it emerges. Fourth, it illuminates precisely the ways in which cultural hybridity is not a source of pollution but of legal creation and innovation.[69] Fifth, and finally, it blurs the distinction between original law and copy law that forms the basis for much of the dominant political economy of legal knowledge.[70]

11.3.1.2 The Rights of Nature and Epistemic Justice

The rights of nature are epistemically subversive because they are articulated and grounded by appealing to two sources of knowledge that have traditionally been considered weak for the generation of legal products.[71] The rights of nature face a double historical epistemic injustice. The first epistemic injustice they face is the exclusion or marginalization of the three legal systems that create the prototypical models of the rights of nature (Bolivia, Ecuador, and New Zealand) from the global legal dialogue. These legal systems have been excluded or marginalized insofar as they have been qualified, generally a priori, as weak spaces for the creation of original legal products. The legal systems of these three countries, consequently, are not considered valuable objects of study by the transnational legal academy, their

[67] On rights of nature, cultural homogeneity, and the nation state see D. Bonilla Maldonado, Beyond the State, Can State Law Survive the Twenty-First Century?, in T. Duve and T. Herzog (eds.), *The History of Latin American Law* (Cambridge: Cambridge University Press, 2023), pp. 485–541 and Bonilla Maldonado, El Constitucionalismo Radical Ambiental y la Diversidad Cultural en América Latina, 9–11. On cultural homogeneity and the nation state see P. Hirst and G. Thompson, Globalization and the Future of the Nation State (1995) 24 *Economy and Society* 408–42; H. J. König, Discursos de Identidad, Estado-Nación y Ciudadanía en América Latina: Viejos problemas, Nuevos enfoques y Dimensiones (2005) 11 *Historia y Sociedad* 9–31, 18–19.

[68] K. Zimmerer, The Indigenous Andean Concept of "Kawsay," the Politics of Knowledge and Development, and the Borderlands of Environmental Sustainability in Latin America (2012) 127 *Publications of the Modern Language Association of America* 600–6; C. Walsh, Afro and Indigenous Life: Visions in/and Politics. (De)colonial Perspectives in Bolivia and Ecuador (2011) 18 *Revista de Estudios Bolivarianos* 49–69; V. Haidar and V. Berros, Entre el Sumak Ky la "Vida en Armonía con la Naturaleza": Disputas en la Circulación y Traducción de Perspectivas Respecto de la Regulación de la Cuestión Ecológica en el Espacio Global (2015) 32 *Revista THEOMAI: Estudios Críticos sobre Sociedad y Desarrollo* 128–50; and Bonilla Maldonado, *Legal Barbarians: Identity, Modern Comparative Law and the Global South*, chapter 5.

[69] Bonilla Maldonado, El Constitucionalismo Radical Ambiental y la Diversidad Cultural en América Latina.

[70] Bonilla Maldonado, *Legal Barbarians: Identity, Modern Comparative Law and the Global South*.

[71] M. Fricker, *Epistemic Injustice: Power and the Ethics of Knowing* (Oxford: Oxford University Press, 2009).

legal institutions are regarded as mere minor iterations of the law that is created in other legal systems, and their academic output is ignored or undervalued by the international nodes of legal research.[72] The second epistemic injustice with which the rights of nature struggle is the exclusion or marginalization of indigenous legal, moral, political, and religious knowledge from the processes of legal knowledge creation in modern states.[73]

This section thus focuses on showing how the political economy of legal knowledge has closed the doors to two peripheral legal voices. Section 11.3.1.1, instead, focused on the cultural hybridity of the rights of nature to show how the normative patterns that determine who can create, transfer, and legitimately use legal knowledge negatively evaluate non-Western cultures, deny the possibility that they can create legal knowledge, and disqualify any syncretic legal product. The two sections, however, are closely linked, complementing and nourishing each other.

Countries of the Global South or peripheral countries of the Global North have created the paradigmatic formulations of the rights of nature.[74] Ecuador is the only country in the world that has recognized rights of nature constitutionally.[75] Bolivia was the first country to recognize the rights of nature in two laws of national scope that develop aspects of the constitution that intersect with this type of rights: the recognition of Pachamama as a deity and the principle of good living.[76] New Zealand, finally, is the first country to issue two national laws related to the rights of nature that derive from the interpretation to be given to a country's founding treaty (the Treaty of Waitangi).[77] All three countries also offer an institutional design for the implementation of the rights of nature.[78] The countries of the Global North, in contrast, have not articulated a discourse on the rights of nature, have not included it in their legal systems, or have only done so in local spaces that have little political, legal, or economic relevance.[79] Australia and Spain are the only exception to this rule.[80] In Africa, only Uganda and Nigeria have conferred

[72] Ibid., chapter 1.

[73] Ibid. This does not mean, of course, that the discourse on rights of nature has been constructed solely by indigenous peoples' traditions. The works of authors like Christopher Stone, Cormac Cullinan, Thomas Berry, and Godofredo Stutzin have also been influential in this process. The Community Environmental Legal Defense Fund (CELDF) also played a role in the creation of the Ecuadorian and Bolivian poietic discourse on rights of nature. See Section 11.3.2.1.

[74] See Section 11.2.

[75] Constitución Política de la República de Ecuador 2008, Preamble, Articles 71, 72, 73, 74.

[76] Law 71 of 2012 of the Estado Plurinacional de Ley No 300/2012 del Estado Plurinacional de Bolivia, Article 5.

[77] Te Awa Tupua (Whanganui River Claims Settlement) Act 2017, Subpart 2, Articles, 12, 13, 14.

[78] See Section 11.2 (poietic discourses on rights of nature).

[79] Ibid. (mimetic discourses on rights of nature).

[80] E. L. O'Donnell and J. Talbot-Jones, Creating Legal Rights for Rivers: Lessons from Australia, New Zealand, and India (2018) 23 *Ecology and Society*.

upon rights to nature, and only India, Pakistan, and Bangladesh have done so in Asia.[81]

Dominant legal epistemology usually imagines Ecuador, Bolivia, and New Zealand, however, as weak spaces for the creation of legal knowledge, mimetic countries, and not poietic in legal matters.[82] The dominant political economy of legal knowledge has historically considered the legal systems of Ecuador, Bolivia, and New Zealand to be child systems that reproduce the premises and contents of the mother systems with varying degrees of precision.[83] Ecuador and Bolivia, which belong to the civil law tradition, reproduce the premises and fundamental contents of the French and German legal systems. New Zealand, which belongs to the common law tradition, reproduces the legal system of Great Britain. In the dominant comparative law interpretation of the twentieth century, largely focused on legal families, the Ecuadorian, Bolivian, and New Zealand legal systems are iterations of other legal systems. In this line of argumentation, to understand the structures of the two families that make up Western law, it is necessary to examine the parent legal systems, not the offspring.[84] The legal systems of these three countries, therefore, are not relevant objects of study and do not generate original legal products of quality. The legal voices of these three countries are therefore excluded or marginalized from the global legal dialogue.

In this case, however, Bolivia, Ecuador, and New Zealand construct a legal product that is interpreted as an instrument that can help address the radical environmental deterioration being experienced around the world.[85] Politicians, academics, and activists, among others, interpret this legal product as one that can (and should) travel from the peripheral legal spaces in which it was created to the rest of the world, including the Global North. The Ecuadorian Constitution, the Bolivian Mother Earth laws, and the Te Urewera and Te Awa Tupua laws in New Zealand are exportable legal products. The contents of these legal artifacts could

[81] Ibid. The decision made by the Uttarakhand High Court in India is presently stayed pending appeal to the Supreme Court.

[82] M. Pargendler, The Rise and Decline of Legal Families (2012) 60 *American Journal of Comparative Law* 1043–74.

[83] R. Kelemen and E. Sibbitt, The Globalization of American Law (2004) 58 *International Organization* 103–36; J. H. Merryman, Comparative Law and Social Change: On the Origins, Style, Decline and Revival of the Law and Development Movement (1977) 25 *American Journal of Comparative Law* 484–89, 457; K. Rittich, The Future of Law and Development: Second-Generation Reforms and the Incorporation of the Social, in David M. Trubek and Alvaro Santos (eds.), *The New Law and Economic Development: A Critical Appraisal* (Cambridge: Cambridge University Press, 2006), pp. 203–52; and Bonilla Maldonado, Introduction.

[84] D. S. Clark, The Idea of the Civil Law Tradition, in J. H. Merryman and D. S. Clark (eds.), *Comparative and Private International Law* (Berlin: Duncker and Humboldt, 1990), pp. 11–23; and J. R. Schmidhauser, Legal Imperialism: Its Enduring Impact on Colonial and Post-Colonial Judicial Systems (1992) 13 *International Political Science Review / Revue Internationale de Science Politique* 321–34.

[85] Gudynas, La Ecología Política del Giro Biocéntrico en la Nueva Constitución de Ecuador.

contribute to rethinking the relationships between humans, nature, law, and economy that have largely been the cause of the environmental crisis that the world is experiencing in the twenty-first century.[86] The Ecuadorian and Bolivian legal barbarians, or the New Zealand peripheral subjects of rights, are shown as autonomous legal subjects who have the capacity to create original juridical knowledge. Likewise, they are shown as subjects whose identities are a consequence of the internally-heterogeneous and strong cultures that construct them and that they, at the same time, help to construct.

The rights of nature are also epistemically innovative because they interweave the contents and interpretations of the state legal systems of Ecuador, Bolivia, and New Zealand with the religious traditions of the indigenous peoples that make up these three countries.[87] The knowledge of Andean, Aymara, and Quechua indigenous peoples, among others, and the knowledge of the Māori people, are included in state legal systems through the rights of nature. The state legal system hears and includes the voices of these cultural minorities. As indicated in Section 11.3.1.1, through the rights of nature, the Ecuadorian, Bolivian, and New Zealand legal systems incorporate into their structures central ideas from the religious and cultural traditions of the indigenous Andean and Māori peoples.[88]

This indigenous knowledge, it is important to note, is not incorporated into a part of the formal legal system that is only applicable to indigenous peoples. It is not a mechanism to enrich or complexify indigenous jurisdictions or indigenous peoples' self-governance rights. This knowledge is included in legal norms, the Constitution, or statutes that apply to all citizens.[89] The recognition of cultural diversity through the rights of nature, the recognition of the value of the historically-marginalized knowledge of indigenous peoples, is therefore transformative. Indigenous peoples' knowledge does not "go up" to the legal order to "come down" again to their own political and legal spaces, as norms to be applied only within the indigenous jurisdiction, for example. This knowledge "goes up" into the legal system and "comes down" as norms to be applied to all members of the political community. Furthermore, this knowledge, already intertwined with state law, as mentioned in

[86] E. Gudynas, La Dimensión Ecológica del Buen Vivir: entre el Fantasma de la Modernidad y el Desafío Biocéntrico (2009) 4 *Revista Obets* 49–53; and S. Radcliffe, Development for a Postneoliberal Era? Sumak Kawsay, Living Well and the Limits to Decolonisation in Ecuador (2012) 43 *Geoforum* 240–49, 241; S. Knauß, Conceptualizing Human Stewardship in the Anthropocene: The Rights of Nature in Ecuador, New Zealand and India (2018) 31 *Journal of Agricultural and Environmental Ethics* 703–22.

[87] C. G. Barié, Nuevas Narrativas Constitucionales en Bolivia y Ecuador: el Buen Vivir y los Derechos de la Naturaleza (2014) 59 *Latinoamérica* 9–40; G. Brierley, et al., A Geomorphic Perspective on the Rights of the River in Aotearoa New Zealand (2019) 35 *River Research and Applications* 1640–51.

[88] See Section 11.3.1.1.

[89] K. Zimmerer, Environmental Governance through "Speaking Like an Indigenous State" and Respatializing Resources: Ethical Livelihood Concepts in Bolivia as Versatility or Verisimilitude? (2015) 64 *Geoforum* 314–24.

Section 11.3.1.1, is reinterpreted as valuable knowledge that can be used to solve global, regional, or other states' problems.[90] Rights of nature, a hybrid legal product, a mixture of a child legal system and indigenous knowledge, is assessed as a relevant transnational academic object of study and as a legal product translatable to other state jurisdictions.[91]

The rights of nature are thus a materialization of epistemic justice. The voices of entire peoples that the law had disregarded and dismissed as primitive or barbaric are now heard to create legal knowledge. The voices of indigenous peoples, in the best interpretations of the rights of nature, are not exoticized or romanticized. Rather, they are understood as sources of knowledge that offer innovative ways of thinking about the relationship between humans, nature, law, and economics; they are sources of knowledge that can enrich thinking about these issues anywhere in the world.[92]

11.3.1.3 The Rights of Nature, Epistemic Justice, and Political Emancipation

The rights of nature are also epistemically innovative because (i) they challenge some of the assumptions of modern Western law and (ii) they are created through heterodox and emancipatory processes of legal knowledge generation. The rights of nature challenge the idea that only human beings can be rights-holders and, correspondingly, that subjective rights can only be assigned to human beings. Modern Western law, founded on liberalism, considers as a rule that only moral, autonomous, and rational agents can be holders of subjective rights.[93] Legal persons, minors, and some people with severe cognitive or physical disabilities constitute the exception that confirms the rule.[94] For this legal tradition, nature, a thing over

[90] See Section 11.3.1.1.

[91] Tanasescu, Rights of Nature, Legal Personality, and Indigenous Philosophies.

[92] The most recent quantitative analysis on the subject shows that 18.6 percent of initiatives related to the rights of nature refer to or are based on indigenous beliefs; only 2.4 percent come directly from indigenous peoples. Putzer et al., Putting the Rights of Nature on the Map, 92. However, this quantitative analysis obscures the fact that even if the initiatives do not explicitly mention indigenous traditions, many of them may have been influenced by them. CELDF, which has directly and explicitly influenced the drafting of most local legal norms on the rights of nature in the US, explicitly acknowledges the intersection between rights of nature and indigenous traditions. The other major quantitative analysis, which precedes this one, does not mention the issue from a numerical perspective, although it does emphasize the Ecuadorian, Bolivian, and New Zealand models in its analysis. Kauffman and Martin, Constructing Rights of Nature Norms in the US, Ecuador, and New Zealand.

[93] S. Epstein et al. Liberalism and Rights of Nature: A Comparative Legal and Historical Perspective (2022) *Law, Culture and the Humanities*, https://doi.org/10.1177/17438721211065735. Also see P. J. Williams, On Being the Object of Property, in K. T. Bartlett and R. Kennedy (eds.), *Feminist Legal Theory: Teadings in Law and Gender* (Boulder: Westview Press, 1991), pp. 165–80, p. 165 (examining the type of subject presupposed by classical liberalism).

[94] E. A. Q. Adriano, The Natural Person, Legal Entity or Juridical Person and Juridical Personality (2015) 4 *Penn State Journal of Law and International Affairs* 363–91.

which rights are vested, particularly the right to property, could never be the holder of subjective rights. However, the rights of nature recognize that *nature* is a non-human agent that can hold rights and, therefore, also obligations. This new legal subject has no voice of its own, but human beings can represent its voice, as managers do with respect to legal persons, or as parents and guardians represent minors or persons with particularly serious disabilities.[95] While there may be doubts about how the voice of nature can be heard, or how to interpret it, the attempt to do so implies an important shift away from the anthropocentric perspectives constitutive of modern Western law that prescribe that the only voice to be heard is that of human beings: the center of the universe.[96]

The rights of nature are also epistemically emancipatory because they are a consequence of constitutional or legal processes involving actors who have historically been on the margins of both the political community and state law-making processes.[97] Indigenous peoples in Ecuador, Bolivia, and New Zealand have had very few representatives in legislative bodies and their interests have not usually been taken into account by the three branches of government or dominant political parties. In the case of rights of nature, in contrast, indigenous peoples themselves present and defend their traditions about nature. In Ecuador, the national constituent assembly had indigenous assembly members who promoted the recognition of the rights of nature as part of the agenda of the political movements they represented.[98] Similarly, indigenous organizations put pressure on the constituent assembly to recognize the rights of nature and indigenous organizations were part of the political movement that brought President Rafael Correa to power, who later convened the national constituent assembly.[99] In Bolivia, the government of Evo Morales, an indigenous Aymara, as well as some indigenous movements and parties, promoted the recognition of Pachamama and the principle of *buen vivir* in the 2009 constitution. Likewise, they promoted the recognition of the rights of nature in the

95 Tanasescu, *Environment, Political Representation, and the Challenge of Rights*.

96 S. Borrás, New Transitions from Human Rights to the Environment to the Rights of Nature (2016) 5 *Transnational Environmental Law* 113–43; and E. Gudynas, Buen Vivir: Today's Tomorrow (2011) 54 *Development* 441–47.

97 C. Gregor, Nuevas Narrativas Constitucionales en Bolivia y Ecuador: el Buen Vivir y los Derechos de la Naturaleza (2014) 59 *Latinoamérica* 9–40, 10; P. Villavicencio Calzadilla and L. J. Kotzé. Living in Harmony with Nature? A Critical Appraisal of the Rights of Mother Earth in Bolivia (2018) 7 *Transnational Environmental Law* 397-424; Iorns Magallanes, Māori Cultural Rights in Aotearoa New Zealand.

98 M. Tanasescu, The Rights of Nature in Ecuador: The Making of an Idea (2013) 70 *International Journal of Environmental Studies* 846–61.

99 This is not to say, of course, that all indigenous (or non-indigenous) organizations and parties agreed with or promoted the rights of nature equally strongly. The disputes between the Correa government and the indigenous movements that supported them are well known, as are the conflicts between different sectors that made up the constituent assembly, liberal, conservative, and left, regarding the value of the rights of nature. Ibid.

laws of Mother Earth.[100] Cultural minorities in Bolivia and Ecuador managed to position themselves politically in these processes of legal creation and were able to make their voices heard effectively.[101]

In New Zealand, the recognition of the Whanganui River as a subject of rights is a consequence of a long political process that ended with the Te Awa Tupua agreement, which reinterpreted the founding treaty of New Zealand: the Treaty of Waitangi.[102] The Māori people, the people who inhabited the lands that are now New Zealand before the arrival of Europeans in Oceania, have been on the margins of the political community. However, in this case, they reached an agreement with the government to change the dominant understandings of the treaty that created the New Zealand political community. Both the process and its conclusions are challenging to the historical status quo in New Zealand for the following reasons: the negotiation that ends with the agreement is between the Māori people and the New Zealand government, two peoples who negotiate horizontally;[103] the agreement conferring upon rights to the Whanganui River is a syncretic product in which indigenous traditions and those of the dominant culture intersect;[104] the process of creating the statute that ratified the treaty in parliament was attended for the first time by Māori leaders;[105] and the legal person representing the Whanganui River is composed equally of representatives of the parties creating the treaty.[106] New Zealand, like Ecuador and Bolivia, is a culturally-diverse country that has

[100] J. Lazarte, Plurinacionalismo y Multiculturalismo en la Asamblea Constituyente de Bolivia (2009) 33 *Revista Internacional de Filosofía Política* 71–109.

[101] M. Becker, Correa, Indigenous movements, and the Writing of a New Constitution in Ecuador (2011) 38 *Latin American Perspectives* 47–62, 48. In both countries, however, the rights of nature were (and still are) in tension with the principle of material equality and the redistribution objectives it demands; they were (are) promoted by a notable part of those leftist and indigenist movements that have promoted the rights of nature, such as the MAS and Alianza PAIS. Material justice, in the interpretation of these movements, demands that the governments of economically-developing countries like Ecuador and Bolivia make intensive use of natural resources. The extractivism that these movements continue to defend politically and legally is in conflict with the rights of nature. R. Lalander, Entre el Ecocentrismo y el Pragmatismo Ambiental: Consideraciones Inductivas sobre Desarrollo, Extractivismo y los Derechos de la Naturaleza en Bolivia y Ecuador (2015) 6 *Revista Chilena de Derecho y Ciencia Política* 109–52, 118–19; R. Lalander, Rights of Nature and the Indigenous Peoples in Bolivia and Ecuador: A Straitjacket for Progressive Development Politics? (2014) 3 *Revista Iberoamericana de Estudios de Desarrollo* 148–73.

[102] C. M. Kauffman, Managing People for the Benefit of the Land: Practicing Earth Jurisprudence in Te Urewera, New Zealand (2020) 27 *Interdisciplinary Studies in Literature and Environment* 578–95.

[103] Ibid.

[104] K. Sanders, Beyond Human Ownership? Property, Power and Legal Personality for Nature in Aotearoa New Zealand (2017) 30 *Journal of Environmental Law* 3–28.

[105] New Zealand Parliament, Innovative Bill Protects Whanganui River with Legal Personhood, New Zealand Parliament, March 28, 2017.

[106] C. J. Iorns Magallanes, Nature as an Ancestor: Two Examples of Legal Personality for Nature in New Zealand (2015) 22 *VertigO – la Revue Électronique en Sciences de l'Environnement*.

historically discriminated against their cultural minorities. The rights of nature show that this inequality of power and these injustices are not inevitable or necessary.

11.3.2 *Cross-Fertilization and the Rights of Nature*

The emergence and transnationalization of rights of nature call explanatory theories of legal change in comparative law into question.[107] The emergence and denationalization of rights of nature are not a consequence of changes in the monolithic and homogenous cultural or economic structures of which they are supposedly their epiphenomenon, they are not a consequence of one-way transfers between two countries, usually from the Global North to the Global South, and they are not an effect of legal transfers that go from the local to the global and then travel to new local spaces that adapt and transform them. Rather, the following internal and external processes can explain the emergence and transnationalization of the rights of nature.

The paradigmatic models of the rights of nature, the Ecuadorian, Bolivian, and New Zealand models, emerged as a consequence of political processes that recognize the multicultural character that these three States have had since their inception.[108] This recognition is mainly a consequence of the agency of indigenous political movements and social organizations that, in alliance with progressive social movements, have managed to position their agendas at the center of the political community.[109] It is also the consequence of the formal or informal recognition of the principles of plurinationality and interculturality.[110] The Ecuadorian Constitution, the Bolivian Mother Earth laws, and the New Zealand Te Urewera and Te Awa Tupua laws emerged as a consequence of the recognition that these three countries are not monocultural; that the cultures that compose them must be valued; and that dialogue between these cultures must be the way to build the state they share.[111] The paradigmatic models of the rights of nature, therefore, did not

[107] A. Watson, *Society and Legal Change* (Edinburgh: Scottish Academic Press, 1977); A. Watson, *The Evolution of Law* (Baltimore: John Hopkins University Press, 1985); A. Watson, Aspects of Reception of Law (1996) 44 *American Journal of Comparative Law* 335–51; and G. Mousourakis, Comparative Law, Legal Transplants and Legal Change, in G. Mousourakis (ed.) *Comparative Law and Legal Traditions* (Cham: Springer, 2019), pp. 169–96.

[108] C. Walsh, *Interculturalidad, Estado, Sociedad. Luchas (De)coloniales de Nuestra Época* (Quito: Universidad Andina Simón Bolívar, 2009).

[109] Lazarte, Plurinacionalismo y Multiculturalismo en la Asamblea Constituyente de Bolivia; Becker, Correa, Indigenous Movements, and the Writing of a New Constitution in Ecuador; and Iorns Magallanes, Māori Cultural Rights in Aotearoa New Zealand.

[110] C. Walsh, (De)Construir la Interculturalidad. Consideraciones Críticas desde la Política, la Colonialidad y los Movimientos Indígenas y Negros en el Ecuador, in N. Fuller (ed.) *Interculturalidad y Política* (San Miguel-Lima: Red de Apoyo de las Ciencias Sociales, 2002), pp. 115–42.

[111] R. Ávila, *El Neoconstitucionalismo transformador el Estado y el Derecho en la Constitución de 2008* (Quito: Universidad Simón Bolivar, Fundación Rosa Luxemburgo, 2011), chapters 9 and 10.

arise because of a change in the unique and homogenous cultures that supposedly constitute these three states, nor are they a consequence of a change in the economic structure of these three countries.

The transnationalization of these prototypical models of the rights of nature has primarily been a process of cross-fertilization involving state and non-state actors, as well as peripheral North–South, South–South, and South–North dialogues and mutual learning. This cross-fertilization has occurred between non-governmental organizations and primary legislators; between courts; between primary or secondary legislators and courts; and between legislators. The following are globally recognized cases that support these arguments.

11.3.2.1 Cross-Fertilization between the Peripheral North and the Global South

The emergence of paradigmatic models of the rights of nature is partly a consequence of a dialogue between the peripheral North and the Global South. This dialogue is between a US non-governmental organization and the State of Ecuador.[112] The dialogue is not between the State of Ecuador and any institution of the US legal system. Ecuador invited the Community Environmental Legal Defense Fund (CELDF) to advise the Constituent Assembly on issues related to the rights of nature. CELDF had played a central role in the drafting of the Tamaqua ordinance and continued to do so in other US cities and towns that subsequently recognized rights of nature, including Toledo, Ohio; Grant Township, Pennsylvania; and Denver, Colorado.[113] However, the Montecristi Assembly intertwined CELDF's political experience and knowledge with the local political experiences and knowledge of Andean indigenous peoples. CELDF subsequently included arguments based on the knowledge of Andean indigenous peoples among those it uses to promote the rights of nature around the world.[114] In this regard, CELDF states, "CELDF recognises that the Rights of Nature are a concept deeply rooted in traditional indigenous knowledge. This timeline reflects an evolution of

[112] CELDF, Press Release: Ecuador Approves New Constitution: Voters Approve Rights of Nature, Community Environmental Legal Defense Fund, September 28, 2008; Also see CELDF, Blog: A Decade of Legality: Rights of Nature Coming of Age, Community Environmental Legal Defense Fund, September 21, 2018.

[113] CELDF, Tamaqua Borough, Pennsylvania, Community Environmental Legal Defense Fund, August 31, 2015, and CELDF, Press Release: Ecuador Approves New Constitution.

[114] CELDF also indicates that "Aboriginal nations and communities retain sovereignty and knowledge over the natural ecosystems they have evolved with. To recognize and follow the natural laws of nature necessitates the elevation particularly of the Traditional Knowledge of local indigenous communities" (CELDF, Champion the Rights of Nature, Community Environmental Legal Defense Fund, February 27, 2023).

Western law and philosophy that is influenced by indigenous cosmovisions, as well as by indigenous-led efforts around the world."[115]

The cross-fertilization between the peripheral North and the South is also evident in the dialogue that has taken place between the New Zealand legislature, the Colombian Constitutional Court, and the Uttarakhand High Court in India. In the Atrato River judgment, the Colombian Constitutional Court mentioned Te Awa Tupua as one of its sources and took the concept of river guardians from it to apply it in the Colombian context.[116] Just as the New Zealand legislator created a juridical person to represent the Whanganui River, the Colombian court created the figure of the guardians of the Atrato River to achieve this objective. Delegates from the government and the Māori people represent the Whanganui River; riparian communities and grassroots organizations that inhabit the riverbanks, as well as government officials, represent the Atrato River.[117] The Uttarakhand High Court, after recognizing the glaciers as subjects of rights, and following the New Zealand model,[118] appointed a committee of three civil servants to serve as their guardians. The Uttarakhand High Court, however, did not base its decision on Andean indigenous religions, of course, but on Hinduism.[119] The Court shows in this

[115] CELDF, Rights of Nature: Timeline, Community Environmental Legal Defense Fund, January 30, 2021.

[116] Corte Constitucional de Colombia, *Sentencia T-622*, "The most recent case of protection of the rights of nature occurred in New Zealand in 2012. It is an agreement with the force of law signed between the New Zealand government and the Māori Aboriginal community of the Whanganui River, protectors of the river – the third largest in the country – for hundreds of years. In the agreement, which is now law – Te Urewera Act 2014 – the New Zealand government recognizes the river as having the same legal status as a person or corporation, that is, it grants it the right to exist, to be maintained, and to thrive, along with the obligation to be respected. Under this design, as a legal person or rights-bearing entity, the river has two legal guardians: the New Zealand government and the Whanganui River community, which together form a stewardship and protection committee … Similarly, the government of New Zealand recently recognized the Whanganui River as a subject of rights."

[117] Ibid.

[118] *Lalit Miglani vs State of Uttarakhand & others* (Writ Petition (PIL) No.140 of 2015). The court states that, "The New Zealand Parliament has enacted 'Te 42 Urewera Act 2014' whereby the 'Urewera National Park' has been given the legal entity under Section 11 of the Act. The purpose of the Act is to preserve, as far as possible, Te Urewera in its natural state, the indigenous ecological systems, biodiversity and its historical cultural heritage."

[119] *Salim v. State of Uttarakhand*. The court states that, "Rivers Ganges and Yamuna are worshiped by Hindus. These rivers are very sacred and revered. The Hindus have a deep spiritual connection with Rivers Ganges and Yamuna. According to Hindu beliefs, a dip in River Ganga can wash away all the sins. The Ganga is also called 'Ganga Maa.' It is mentioned in ancient Hindu scriptures including 'Rigveda.' The river Ganga originates from Gaumukh Glacier and River Yamuna originates from Yamnotri Glacier … All the Hindus have deep Astha in rivers Ganga and Yamuna and they collectively connect with these rivers. Rivers Ganga and Yamuna are central to the existence of half of Indian population and their health and well-being. The rivers have provided both physical and spiritual sustenance to all of us from time immemorial. Rivers Ganga and Yamuna have spiritual and physical sustenance. They support and assist both the life and natural resources and health and well-being of the

judgment how, for Hinduism (as in an earlier judgment declaring the Ganges and Yamuna rivers to be subject to rights),[120] the Ganges and Yamuna river basins are sacred.[121] By appealing to a non-Western religion, the Indian Court grounds the personification, sacralization, hybridity, and ecosystemic character of nature, as the Ecuadorian, Bolivian, and New Zealand legal norms that recognize the rights of nature have done.

11.3.2.2 South–South Cross-Fertilization

The exchanges between the Colombian Constitutional Court, the Ecuadorian constituent, the Bolivian legislature, and the Ecuadorian Constitutional Court confirm South–South cross-fertilization. This exchange begins as a dialogue between the judicial branch and the primary constituent but later becomes a dialogue between supreme courts. In the Atrato River ruling, the Colombian Constitutional Court cites the rights of nature recognized by the Ecuadorian Constitution and the Bolivian legal system as one of the sources from which it draws.[122] This ruling is the one that starts the Colombian jurisprudential line on the rights of nature, one that has been widely discussed in the global specialized literature.[123] The Colombian Court, however, does not base its ruling on Andean indigenous religions, as the Ecuadorian constituent does, but rather on biocultural rights, which include the cultural rights held by Colombia's indigenous peoples

entire community. Rivers Ganga and Yamuna are breathing, living and sustaining the communities from mountains to sea."

120 Ibid.

121 E. L. O'Donnell, At the Intersection of the Sacred and the Legal: Rights for Nature in Uttarakhand, India (2017) 30 *Journal of Environmental Law* 135–44.

122 Corte Constitucional de Colombia, *Sentencia T-622*, "In accordance with the above, the sentence in question states that '*it is admissible for the Court to sustain that the heterogeneous approaches to environmental protection find support in the provisions of the 1991 Charter. The paradigm to which the so-called 'Ecological Constitution' leads us, because it corresponds to a dynamic and open instrument, supported by a system of evidence and collective representations, implies for contemporary society to take ecosystems and natural communities seriously, advancing towards a juridical approach that is more committed to them, as goods that are in themselves the object of guarantee and protection.*' In addition, it can be said that the Constitutions of Ecuador (2008) and Bolivia (2009) have adopted this approach to environmental protection. Similarly, the government of New Zealand recently recognized the Whanganui River as a subject of rights."

123 I. Vargas Chaves et al., Recognizing the Rights of Nature in Colombia: The Atrato River Xase (2020) 17 *Jurídicas* 13–41; P. Villiavicencio Calzadilla, A Paradigm Shift in Courts' View on Nature: The Atrato River and Amazon Basin Cases in Colombia (2019) 15 *Law, Environment and Development Journal (LEAD Journal)* 13–16; C. M. Kauffman and P. L. Martin, When Rivers Have Rights: Case Comparisons of New Zealand, Colombia, and India (2018) 4 *International Studies Association Annual Conference*; E. Macpherson and F. Clavijo Ospina, The Pluralism of River Rights in Aotearoa New Zealand and Colombia (2019) *ICON.S Conference: Public Law in Times of Change*.

according to the 1991 Constitution.[124] After 2009, the Ecuadorian Constitutional Court issued fifty rulings on the rights of nature.[125] The Colombian Constitutional law rulings on cultural diversity were one of the sources that nurtured this jurisprudence.[126]

Argentine, Peruvian, and Panamanian legislators' uses of the Ecuadorian and Bolivian experiences also confirm South–South cross-fertilization. Bill S-2506/15, presented by Argentine Congressmen Fernando E. Solanas and Rubén H. Giustiniani, proposes to recognize the rights of nature.[127] In its foundations, the bill recognizes the influence that the law of Ecuador and Bolivia had in the drafting of the proposed law. In this regard, the bill says: "This debate is circulating around the world after having been put on the political agenda by the new constitution of Ecuador in 2008 (from which – together with Bolivian legislation – we draw inspiration for this bill) which already in its preamble states ..."[128] This same bill was presented again in 2019 and 2020. The 2020 bill also explicitly acknowledges the influence of GARN in its drafting. In this regard, the bill states: "Likewise, this bill includes the contributions of the Global Alliance for the Rights of Nature (GARN), in the framework of a campaign on the rights of nature that has, among other objectives, to promote legislation that recognizes the rights of nature in the Argentine Republic."[129]

[124] Corte Constitucional de Colombia, *Sentencia T-622*; E. Macpherson, J. T. Ventura, and F. C. Ospina, Constitutional Law, Ecosystems, and Indigenous Peoples in Colombia: Biocultural Rights and Legal Subjects (2020) 9 *Transnational Environmental Law* 521–40.

[125] G. Espinoza, La Naturaleza de los Derechos de la Naturaleza en el Ecuador.

[126] Ibid.

[127] Solanas, Proyecto de Ley Nacional S-2506/15-2015, Proyecto de Ley Nacional S-0615/19-2019, and Proyecto de Ley Nacional 6118-D-2020.

[128] Solanas, Proyecto de Ley Nacional S-2506/15-2015.

[129] In Argentina, see also the proposal for the recognition of the rights of nature in the city of Santa Fe and the proposal of Rosario's Municipal Council to the Argentine Congress to recognize the Paraná River as a subject of rights. The draft ordinance of the city of Santa Fe recognizes the rights of nature in the context of the city's struggle against the use of glyphosate. In the rationale behind the draft ordinance, much of the federal bill is reproduced. In some of these paragraphs, the influence of GARN and Ecuador in the drafting of the proposal is acknowledged. It also recognizes the importance of the fact that the UN Harmony with Nature program page referenced the first proposal and its approval. This is an example of the relevance that the UN program on the rights of nature is already beginning to have in the state legal systems. In this regard, the proposed ordinance states: "This legislative milestone was the motivation, among other recognitions, for the City Council of the city of Santa Fe being referenced by Harmony With Nature, of the United Nations Organisation." C. del Frade, Proyecto de Ley Recibido No. 704 Exp No. 41320, 2020; The Municipal Council of Rosario promotes nationally a proposal made by the Cátedra del Agua of Universidad Nacional de Rosario and some Rosario's unions. The Declaration of Rosario's Municipal Council states, "That the most important of the antecedents [of the proposed recognition of rights to the Paraná River] is the Constitution of the Republic of Ecuador sanctioned in 2008, which recognized nature as a subject of rights." The Declaration also mentions the jurisprudence of the Colombian Constitutional Court and the High Court of Uttarkaband and New Zealand

Draft Law 6957 of 2020 in Peru also proposes the recognition of the rights of nature.[130] After stating in the grounds of the law section that "[d]iverse countries around the world have recognized, within their domestic regulatory framework, rights as living entities and right holders in themselves to nature, ecosystems, rivers, species, etc.,"[131] the bill includes Ecuador and Bolivia as its first two references. However, the bill also mentions other countries from the Global South (Mexico, Brazil, Argentina, Colombia, and Uganda) as well as some from the Global North (the United States, New Zealand, and Australia) as sources of its contents.[132] Finally, Panama recognized nature as a subject of rights and granted it a broad set of specific rights in Law No. 287 of February 24, 2022.[133] The law cites the Constitution and the jurisprudence of the Constitutional Court of Ecuador, the Bolivian legal system, and the jurisprudence of the Colombian Constitutional Court as sources of its contents. The bill also refers to the experiences of the United States, Brazil, Mexico, New Zealand, Australia, and Uganda with respect to the rights of nature.[134]

11.3.2.3 South–North Cross-Fertilization

The direct impacts that the peripheral legal systems that built the paradigmatic models of the rights of nature have had on the legal systems of the Global North are just beginning to be made explicit. However, there are already two cases where the South–North influence has been relevant for the creation of rights of nature: first, in the ordinances that CELDF contributed to drafting after its work in the Constituent Assembly of Ecuador. In these processes in the United States as well as in Australia,

law. See Consejo Municipal de Rosario, Declaracion de Interes Publico Expte. No. 255.740-F-2020, 2020.

[130] Congreso de la República del Perú, Proyecto de Ley 06957-CR 2020.

[131] Ibid., Exposición de Motivos, section 3.

[132] Ibid.

[133] Congreso de la República de Panamá, Ley No. 287/2022.

[134] The bill states that, "The concept of rights of nature has been developed in various jurisdictions, through laws and court decisions recognizing nature as a subject with inalienable rights at various levels ofgovernment around the world, including Ecuador, Bolivia, Colombia, India, Mexico, New Zealand, and the United States, in California. Laws are developing further in Argentina, Brazil, Cameroon, Nepal, and elsewhere."Ibid. The press release with which Leatherback Project, Earth Law Center, and Rights for Nature announced and celebrated the approval of the bill they helped construct by the Panamanian Congress also notes that "Panama now joins a number of countries that recognize the Rights of Nature at the national level. The list also includes Bolivia, which passed the Law of the Rights of Mother Earth (071) in 2010 and Law of Mother Earth and Integral Development for Living Well (300) in 2012, and Ecuador, which codified the Rights of Nature (Pachamama) into their Constitution in 2008. Uganda also has a national Rights of Nature provision that applies only to designated areas, and Chile is considering incorporating Rights of Nature into its new Constitution." See Leatherback Project, Earth Law Center, and Rights for Nature, Panama Passes National Rights of Nature Law (2022).

England, and Wales, CELDF has already incorporated components of the Ecuadorian, Bolivian, and New Zealand models.[135] CELDF, as argued in Section 11.3.2.1, has explicitly acknowledged the influence of indigenous knowledge in the way it understands and grounds the rights of nature.

Second, South–North influence has been relevant in the proposed recognition of the St. Lawrence River as a subject of rights in Quebec, Canada that was presented to the federal parliament[136] and the recognition of the Magpie River as a subject of rights by two Innui indigenous peoples.[137] These were both processes driven by the Rights of Nature Observatory, a Montreal-based non-governmental organization that promotes the rights of nature.[138] The Observatory contributed to the drafting of both the legal norm that seeks to recognize the St. Lawrence River as a subject of rights and the two mirror norms issued by the Ekuanitshit Innu Council and the Minganie MRC that serve the same purpose with respect to the Magpie River.[139] The Observatory mentions the Colombian ruling on the Atrato River, the Indian ruling recognizing the Ganges and Yamuna rivers, the Bangladeshi ruling recognizing all rivers in Bangladesh as subjects of rights, the Ecuadorian constitution, the Bolivian Mother Earth laws, and the New Zealand laws recognizing a river and a forest as subjects of rights as antecedents to the proposal to recognize the San Lorenzo River as a subject of rights.[140] It also recognizes the case of the Atrato River as one of the influences on the norms on the Magpie River. However, it also mentions the

[135] CELDF, Rights of Nature: Timeline; and CELDF, Green Party of England and Wales Adopts Rights of Nature Policy: CELDF Assisted in Drafting New Rights-Based Plank, Community Environmental Legal Defense Fund, February 29, 2016.

[136] House of Commons of Canada, Bill C-271: St. Lawrence River Capacity and Protection Act.

[137] Conseil des Innu Ekuannishit, No. Consecutif 919-082, No. de Dossier 919-01-18 (2021); and Province de Québec – Municipalité Régionale de Comté de Minganie, Résolution No 025-21, Reconnaissance de la Personnalité Juridique et des Droits de la Rivière Magpie – Mutehekau Shipu (2021).

[138] "We promote the recognition of the rights of Nature in Quebec and Canada, and contribute to their recognition worldwide."Observatoire International des Droits de la Nature, Homepage, Observatoire International des Droits de la Nature (2023).

[139] "The recognition of the Magpie River has inspired other initiatives across the country to embrace the rights of Nature movement. Some of them are the St. Lawrence River project led by the International Observatory of Nature's Rights, which seeks to recognize the personhood and rights of the river. The Observatory has started a conversation with political parties in Quebec and in Canada at federal level, also with many Indigenous territories and municipalities that the St. Lawrence flows through." Also, "The International Observatory of the Rights of Nature (IOIRN) was deeply involved in the drafting of the resolutions that were adopted in the case of the Magpie River in Canada"; and "the team of the International Observatory of the Rights of Nature, which contributed to the drafting of the two parallel resolutions [on the Magpie River], is grateful for the valuable contribution of the Observatory's research associates, experts in the rights of nature and indigenous law …" Vega Cárdenas and Mestokosho, Recognizing the Legal Personality of the Magpie River/Mutehekau Shipu in Canada, p. 20, 13.

[140] Ibid., p. 13.

New Zealand case[141] and the resolutions of some US indigenous peoples that recognize river rights.[142]

11.4 CONCLUSION

The rights of nature are a global discourse today. This global discourse constructs a new subject of rights, nature, and it recognizes a particular series of rights to nature, including the right to life and the right not to be contaminated. The discursive pattern on the rights of nature has three components: poietic discourses, mimetic discourses, and discourses of resistance. Poietic discourses articulate the central discourse patterns on rights of nature, that is, the seminal discursive structures on the rights of nature (Bolivia, Ecuador, and New Zealand). Mimetic discourses collect discursive patterns that reproduce, albeit with some variations, the prototypical models on the rights of nature. Discourses of resistance offer discursive patterns that resist or ignore rights of nature. However, we cannot fully understand the rights of nature without examining them from the perspective of comparative law. The rights of nature intersect with three central themes in contemporary comparative law: the political economy of legal knowledge, legal pluralism, and cross-fertilization.

The rights of nature challenge the dominant political economy of legal knowledge through the culturally-hybrid character of their paradigmatic models, as well as the contexts of legal knowledge production from which they originate and the political processes that led to their emergence. Similarly, the rights of nature explain legal change through heterodox political processes that question the traditional relationship between culture and law, as well as the direction taken by the dialogues and mutual learning that develop between legal systems. The rights of nature open promising doors for rethinking the way we conceive of nature and the relationship that human beings have with it. However, the rights of nature are still a young legal product. The rights of nature, their foundations, structures, and institutions are still evolving, as are the consequences they may have on the world.

141 "Innu youth were profoundly inspired by the Māori negotiations with the government of New Zealand, which spanned decades and ultimately gifted us with the fruit of legal personality for the Whanganui River. Links were created between Indigenous young leaders around the world, particularly at the second *Mni Ki Wakan*: World Indigenous Peoples Decade of Water Summit." Ibid., p. 9.

142 "The OIDN acknowledges that the rights of the River as recognized in the resolutions were inspired by the Universal Declaration of the Rights of Rivers written by the Earth Law Center, the *Te Awa Tupua* (Whanganui River Claims Settlement Act) that was adopted in New Zealand recognizing the rights of the Whanganui River, the Colombian Constitutional Court decision C-622/2016 in which the *Atrato* river was recognized as a legal entity with rights, and some Indigenous resolutions adopted in the United States to grant rights to rivers such as the Snake and Klamath River, among others." Ibid., p. 13.

BIBLIOGRAPHY

Abe, K. M., The Rights of Nature in Japan: Bringing the Alternative View to Fruition (2022) *Asunción Conference of the International Academy of Comparative Law*, Asunción, Paraguay.

Adriano, E. A. Q., The Natural Person, Legal Entity or Juridical Person and Juridical Personality (2015) 4 *Penn State Journal of Law and International Affairs* 363–91.

Affolter, L. and Affolter, S., Rights of Nature in Switzerland: Mapping the Scene (2022) *Asunción Conference of the International Academy of Comparative Law*.

Arrighi, É., The Fight for Corsica's "Living" River, *Le Monde*, July 25, 2022.

Attila, M., [Report on] Hungary (2022) *Asunción Conference of the International Academy of Comparative Law*.

Ávila, R., *El Neoconstitucionalismo transformador el Estado y el Derecho en la Constitución de 2008* (Quito: Universidad Simón Bolivar, Fundación Rosa Luxemburgo, 2011).

Barié, C. G., Doce Años de Soledad de los Derechos de la Madre Tierra en Bolivia (2022) *Asunción Conference of the International Academy of Comparative Law*.

Nuevas Narrativas Constitucionales en Bolivia y Ecuador: el Buen Vivir y los Derechos de la Naturaleza (2014) 59 *Latinoamérica* 9–40.

Becker, M., Correa, Indigenous Movements, and the Writing of a New Constitution in Ecuador (2011) 38 *Latin American Perspectives* 47–62.

von Benda-Beckmann, K. and Turner, B., Legal Pluralism, Social Theory, and the State (2018) 50 *The Journal of Legal Pluralism and Unofficial Law* 255–74.

Berros, M. V., Challenges for the Implementation of the Rights of Nature: Ecuador and Bolivia as the First Instances of an Expanding Movement (2021) 48 *Latin American Perspectives* 192–205.

Bonilla Maldonado, D., Beyond the State, Can State Law Survive the Twenty-First Century?, in T. Duve and T. Herzog (eds.), *The History of Latin American Law* (Cambridge: Cambridge University Press, 2023), pp. 485–541.

Economía Política del Conocimiento Jurídico (2015) 2 *Brazilian Journal of Empirical Legal Studies* 26–59.

El Constitucionalismo Radical Ambiental y la Diversidad Cultural en América Latina: Los Derechos de la Naturaleza y el Buen Vivir en Ecuador y Bolivia (2018) 42 *Revista Derecho del Estado* 3–23.

Introduction, in D. Bonilla Maldonado, *Constitutionalism of the Global South* (Cambridge: Cambridge University Press, 2013), pp. 1–39.

Legal Barbarians: Identity, Modern Comparative Law and the Global South (Cambridge: Cambridge University Press, 2021).

Los Derechos de la Naturaleza: su Arquitectura Conceptual (2022) 4 *Naturaleza y Sociedad. Desafíos Medioambientales* 70–108.

The Political Economy of Legal Knowledge, in D. Bonilla Maldonado and C. Crawford (eds.), *Constitutionalism in the Americas* (Chatam: Elgar Publishing, 2018), pp. 29–78.

Rights of Nature and Global Legal Pluralism, Max Planck Institute for Comparative and International Private Law Research Paper Series No. 23/15, 2023.

Borrás, S. New Transitions from Human Rights to the Environment to the Rights of Nature (2016) 5 *Transnational Environmental Law* 113–43.

Botău, D., [Report on] Romania (2022) *Asunción Conference of the International Academy of Comparative Law*.

Boyes, M., Re-Envisioning Nature from a New Zealand Māori perspective, in European Institute for Outdoor Adventure Education and Experiential Learning Conference (ed.), *Encountering, Experiencing and Exploring Nature in Education: Collection of Conference Papers* (Ljubljana: European Institute for Outdoor Adventure Education and Experiential Learning, 2010), pp. 94–99.

Brierley, G. et al., A Geomorphic Perspective on the Rights of the River in Aotearoa New Zealand (2019) 35 *River Research and Applications* 1640–51.

CELDF, Blog: A Decade of Legality: Rights of Nature Coming of Age, *Community Environmental Legal Defense Fund*, September 21, 2018.

Champion the Rights of Nature, *Community Environmental Legal Defense Fund*, February 27, 2023.

Green Party of England and Wales Adopts Rights of Nature Policy: CELDF Assisted in Drafting New Rights-Based Plank, *Community Environmental Legal Defense Fund*, February 29, 2016.

Press Release: Ecuador Approves New Constitution: Voters Approve Rights of Nature, *Community Environmental Legal Defense Fund*, September 28, 2008.

Rights of Nature: Timeline, *Community Environmental Legal Defense Fund*, January 30, 2021.

Tamaqua Borough, Pennsylvania, *Community Environmental Legal Defense Fund*, August 31, 2015.

Clark, D. S. The Idea of the Civil Law Tradition, in J. H. Merryman and D. S. Clark (eds.), *Comparative and Private International Law* (Berlin: Duncker and Humboldt, 1990).

Cullinan, C., *Wild Law: A Manifesto for Earth Justice* (Chelsea: Green Books, 2011).

Epstein, S. et al. Liberalism and Rights of Nature: A Comparative Legal and Historical Perspective (2022) *Law, Culture and the Humanities*. https://journals.sagepub.com/doi/10.1177/17438721211065735

Espinoza, G. La Naturaleza de los Derechos de la Naturaleza en el Ecuador (2022) *Asunción Conference of the International Academy of Comparative Law*.

Estermann, J., *Filosofía Andina. Estudio Intercultural de la Sabiduría Autóctona Andina* (Quito: Abya–Yala, 1989).

Ewering, E. S. and Vetter, T., Rights of Nature in Germany: A Paradigm Change for the German Legal System (2022) *Asunción Conference of the International Academy of Comparative Law*.

Fernández, R. L., El Sumak Kawsay y sus Restricciones Constitucionales (2009) 12 *Revista de Derecho UASB* 113–25.

del Frade, C. Proyecto de Ley Recibido No. 704 Exp No. 41320, 2020.

Fricker, M., *Epistemic Injustice: Power and the Ethics of Knowing* (Oxford: Oxford University Press, 2009).

Gregor, C., Nuevas Narrativas Constitucionales en Bolivia y Ecuador: el Buen Vivir y los Derechos de la Naturaleza (2014) 59 *Latinoamérica* 9–40.

Grundmann, S., Globalisation and Legal Pluralism: Orders of Pluralism and Rights (2022) *Asunción Conference of the International Academy of Comparative Law*.

Gudynas, E. Buen Vivir: Today's Tomorrow (2011) 54 *Development* 441–47.

La Dimensión Ecológica del Buen Vivir: entre el Fantasma de la Modernidad y el Desafío Bioncéntrico (2009) 4 *Revista Obets* 49–53.

La Ecología Política del Giro Biocéntrico en la Nueva Constitución de Ecuador (2009) 32 *Revista de Estudios Sociales* 34–46.

Haidar, V. and Berros, V., Entre el Sumak Ky la "Vida en Armonía con la Naturaleza": Disputas en la Circulación y Traducción de Perspectivas Respecto de la Regulación de la Cuestión Ecológica en el Espacio Global (2015) 32 *Revista THEOMAI: Estudios Críticos sobre Sociedad y Desarrollo* 128–50.

Hanschel, D. and Mehlhorn, A., Rights of Nature: Reflections on Dialogues between Law and Anthropology (2022) *Asunción Conference of the International Academy of Comparative Law*.

Harasta, J., Rights of Nature: Czech Report (2022) *Asunción Conference of the International Academy of Comparative Law*.

Hirst, P. and Thompson, G., Globalization and the Future of the Nation State (1995) 24 *Economy and Society* 408–42.

Huneeus, A., The Legal Struggle for Rights of Nature in the United States (2022) 2022 *Wisconsin Law Review* 133–62.

Iorns, C. and Sylvester, J., New Zealand National Report (2022) *Asunción Conference of the International Academy of Comparative Law*.

Iorns Magallanes, C. J., Māori Cultural Rights in Aotearoa New Zealand: Protecting the Cosmology that Protects the Environment (2015) 21 *Widener Law Review* 273–328.

Nature as an Ancestor: Two Examples of Legal Personality for Nature in New Zealand (2015) 22 *VertigO – la Revue Électronique en Sciences de l'Environnement* 1–19.

Kauffman, C., Managing People for the Benefit of the Land: Practicing Earth Jurisprudence in Te Urewera, New Zealand (2020) 27 *Interdisciplinary Studies in Literature and Environment* 578–95.

Kauffman, C. and Martin, P., Can Rights of Nature Make Development More Sustainable? Why Some Ecuadorian Lawsuits Succeed and Others Fail (2017) 92 *World Development* 130–42.

Constructing Rights of Nature Norms in the US, Ecuador, and New Zealand (2018) 18 *Global Environmental Politics* 43–62.

The Politics of Rights of Nature: Strategies for Building a More Sustainable Future (Cambridge: MIT Press, 2021).

When Rivers Have Rights: Case Comparisons of New Zealand, Colombia, and India (2018) 4 *International Studies Association Annual Conference* 1–20.

Kelemen, R. and Sibbitt, E., The Globalization of American Law (2004) 58 *International Organization* 103–36.

Knauß, S., Conceptualizing Human Stewardship in the Anthropocene: The Rights of Nature in Ecuador, New Zealand and India (2018) 31 *Journal of Agricultural and Environmental Ethics* 703–22.

Koch, S., Vallejo Piedrahita, C. and Colombo, E., Rights of Nature in the Norwegian Legal Culture: To Be or Not to Be (2022) *Asunción Conference of the International Academy of Comparative Law*.

König, H. J. Discursos de Identidad, Estado-Nación y Ciudadanía en América Latina: Viejos problemas, Nuevos enfoques y Dimensiones (2005) 11 *Historia y Sociedad* 9–31.

Kotzé, L. J., [Report on] South Africa (2022) *Asunción Conference of the International Academy of Comparative Law*.

Lalander, R., Entre el Ecocentrismo y el Pragmatismo Ambiental: Consideraciones Inductivas sobre Desarrollo, Extractivismo y los Derechos de la Naturaleza en Bolivia y Ecuador (2015) 6 *Revista Chilena de Derecho y Ciencia Política* 109–52.

Rights of Nature and the Indigenous Peoples in Bolivia and Ecuador: A Straitjacket for Progressive Development Politics? (2014) 3 *Revista Iberoamericana de Estudios de Desarrollo* 148–73.

Latour, B., *Politics of Nature* (Cambridge, MA: Harvard University Press, 2004).

Lazarte, J., Plurinacionalismo y Multiculturalismo en la Asamblea Constituyente de Bolivia (2009) 33 *Revista Internacional de Filosofía Política* 71–109.

Leatherback Project, Earth Law Center, and Rights for Nature, *Panama Passes National Rights of Nature Law* (2022). www.earthlawcenter.org/panama

Lind, Y., Danish Report (2022) *Asunción Conference of the International Academy of Comparative Law.*

de Lisle, J., Rights of Nature, Globalization and Legal Pluralism: China (2022) *Asunción Conference of the International Academy of Comparative Law.*

Luna Blanco, T. and de la Torre Vargas, D., Grafiteando la Arquitectura Jurídica Colombiana: la Emergencia de Sujetos no Humanos y Derechos de la Naturaleza (2022) *Asunción Conference of the International Academy of Comparative Law.*

Macpherson, E. and Clavijo Ospina, F., The Pluralism of River Rights in Aotearoa New Zealand and Colombia (2019) *ICON.S Conference: Public Law in Times of Change.* Santiago, Chile.

Macpherson, E., Ventura, J. T., and Ospina, F. C., Constitutional Law, Ecosystems, and Indigenous Peoples in Colombia: Biocultural Rights and Legal Subjects (2020) 9 *Transnational Environmental Law* 521–40.

Margil, M., Birth of a Movement [NGOs in the United States] (2022) *Asunción Conference of the International Academy of Comparative Law.*

Merryman, J. H., Comparative Law and Social Change: On the Origins, Style, Decline and Revival of the Law and Development Movement (1977) 25 *American Journal of Comparative Law* 484–89.

di Micco, D. and Graziadei, M., Italian National Report (2022) *Asunción Conference of the International Academy of Comparative Law.*

Michaels, R., Global Legal Pluralism (2009) 5 *Annual Review of Law and Social Science* 243–62.

Mousourakis, G., Comparative Law, Legal Transplants and Legal Change, in G. Mousourakis (ed.) *Comparative Law and Legal Traditions* (Cham: Springer, 2019), pp. 169–96.

New Zealand Parliament, Innovative Bill Protects Whanganui River with Legal Personhood, *New Zealand Parliament,* March 28, 2017.

O'Donnell, E. L., At the Intersection of the Sacred and the Legal: Rights for Nature in Uttarakhand, India (2017) 30 *Journal of Environmental Law* 135–44.

O'Donnell, E. L. and Talbot-Jones, J., Creating Legal Rights for Rivers: Lessons from Australia, New Zealand, and India (2018) 23 *Ecology and Society* 1–10.

Paiement, P., Rights of Nature, Globalization and Legal Pluralism: The Netherlands Country Report (2022) *Asunción Conference of the International Academy of Comparative Law.*

Pargendler, M., The Rise and Decline of Legal Families (2012) 60 *American Journal of Comparative Law* 1043–74.

Putzer, A. et al., Putting the Rights of Nature on the Map. A Quantitative Analysis of Rights of Nature Initiatives across the World (2022) 18 *Journal of Maps* 89–96.

Radcliffe, S., Development for a Postneoliberal Era? Sumak Kawsay, Living Well and the Limits to Decolonisation in Ecuador (2012) 43 *Geoforum* 240–49.

Rédaction Lyon, La Métropole et la Ville de Lyon Veulent que le Fleuve Rhône ait Une Personnalité Juridique, *Actu,* September 9, 2021.

Rittich, K., The Future of Law and Development: Second-Generation Reforms and the Incorporation of the Social, in D. M. Trubek and A. Santos (eds.), *The New Law and Economic Development: A Critical Appraisal* (Cambridge: Cambridge University Press, 2006), pp. 203–52.

Rokas, K. A., [Report on] Cyprus (2022) *Asunción Conference of the International Academy of Comparative Law*.

Roy, S., Gidrol-Mistral, G., and Popovici, A., The Rights of Nature in Quebec and Canada (2022) *Asunción Conference of the International Academy of Comparative Law*.

Sanders, K., Beyond Human Ownership? Property, Power and Legal Personality for Nature in Aotearoa New Zealand (2017) 30 *Journal of Environmental Law* 3–28.

Sanni, T., Rights of Nature in Uganda (2022) *Asunción Conference of the International Academy of Comparative Law*.

Schmidhauser, J. R. Legal Imperialism: Its Enduring Impact on Colonial and Post-Colonial Judicial Systems (1992) 13 *International Political Science Review / Revue Internationale de Science Politique* 321–34.

Serres, M., *The Natural Contract* (Ann Arbor: Michigan University Press, 1995).

Silva Portero, C., ¿Qué es el Buen Vivir en la Constitución?, in R. Ávila (ed.), *La Constitución del 2008 en el contexto andino. Análisis desde la Doctrina y el Derecho Comparado* (Quito: Ministerio de Justicia y Derechos Humanos, 2008), pp. 112–19.

Sunder Raj, M. S., Sowing the Seeds of Nature Rights in India (2022) *Asunción Conference of the International Academy of Comparative Law*.

Tanasescu, M., *Environment, Political Representation, and the Challenge of Rights: Speaking for Nature* (New York: Palgrave Macmillan, 2016).

Rights of Nature, Legal Personality, and Indigenous Philosophies (2020) 9 *Transnational Environmental Law* 429–53.

The Rights of Nature in Ecuador: The Making of an Idea (2013) 70 *International Journal of Environmental Studies* 846–61.

Theoretical Sources and Foundations of the Rights of Nature (2022) *Asunción Conference of the International Academy of Comparative Law*.

Understanding the Rights of Nature: A Critical Introduction (Bielefeld: Transcript Verlag, 2022).

Thang Long, T. and Minh Nhu, L., Sustainable Development and Distributive Equality: A Contribution from Vietnam (2022) *Asunción Conference of the International Academy of Comparative Law*.

Tignino, M., The Rights of Nature and the Rights to Nature: Emerging Trends in International Law (2022) *Asunción Conference of the International Academy of Comparative Law*.

Vargas Chaves, I. et al., Recognizing the Rights of Nature in Colombia: the Atrato River Case (2020) 17 *Jurídicas* 13–41.

Vega Cárdenas, Y. and Mestokosho, U., Recognizing the Legal Personality of the Magpie River/Mutehekau Shipu in Canada (2022) *Asunción Conference of the International Academy of Comparative Law*.

Villavicencio Calzadilla, P., A Paradigm Shift in Courts' View on Nature: The Atrato River and Amazon Basin Cases in Colombia (2019) 15 *Law, Environment and Development Journal (LEAD Journal)* 13–16.

Villavicencio Calzadilla, P. and Kotzé, L. J. Living in Harmony with Nature? A Critical Appraisal of the Rights of Mother Earth in Bolivia (2018) 7 *Transnational Environmental Law* 397–424.

Walsh, C., Afro and Indigenous Life: Visions in/and Politics. (De)colonial Perspectives in Bolivia and Ecuador (2011) 18 *Revista de Estudios Bolivarianos* 49–69.

(De)Construir la Interculturalidad. Consideraciones Críticas desde la Política, la Colonialidad y los Movimientos Indígenas y Negros en el Ecuador, in N. Fuller (ed.)

Interculturalidad y Política (San Miguel-Lima: Red de Apoyo de las Ciencias Sociales, 2002), pp. 115–42.

Interculturalidad, Estado, Sociedad. Luchas (De)coloniales de Nuestra Época (Quito: Universidad Andina Simón Bolívar, 2009).

Watson, A., Aspects of Reception of Law (1996) 44 *American Journal of Comparative Law* 335–51.

Comparative Law and Legal Change (1978) 37 *Cambridge Law Journal* 313–36.

The Evolution of Law (Baltimore: John Hopkins University Press, 1985).

Society and Legal Change (Edinburgh: Scottish Academic Press, 1977).

Williams, P. J., On Being the Object of Property, in K.T. Bartlett and R. Kennedy (eds.), *Feminist Legal Theory: Teadings in Law and Gender* (Boulder: Westview Press, 1991), pp. 165–80.

Wolkmer, A. C. and Ferrazzo, D. Los Derechos de la Naturaleza en Brasil (2022) *Asunción Conference of the International Academy of Comparative Law.*

Wuraola, O. T., The Legal Rights of Natural Entities: African Approaches to the Recognition of Rights of Nature, in M. Addaney and A. O. Jegede (eds.), *Human Rights and the Environment under African Union Law* (London: Palgrave Macmillan, 2020), pp. 137–52.

Youatt, R., Personhood and the Rights of Nature: The New Subjects of Contemporary Earth Politics (2017) 11 *International Political Sociology* 39–54.

Zimmerer, K., Environmental Governance through "Speaking Like an Indigenous State" and Respatializing Resources: Ethical Livelihood Concepts in Bolivia as Versatility or Verisimilitude? (2015) 64 *Geoforum* 314–24.

The Indigenous Andean Concept of "Kawsay," the Politics of Knowledge and Development, and the Borderlands of Environmental Sustainability in Latin America (2012) 127 *Publications of the Modern Language Association of America* 600–6.

For EU product safety concerns, contact us at Calle de José Abascal, 56–1°,
28003 Madrid, Spain or eugpsr@cambridge.org.

www.ingramcontent.com/pod-product-compliance
Lightning Source LLC
LaVergne TN
LVHW052028200926
848481LV00005B/1613
* 9 7 8 1 0 0 9 5 3 9 5 3 1 *